Special Education Law

Special Education Law

Third Edition

Thomas F. Guernsey
PRESIDENT AND DEAN
ALBANY LAW SCHOOL

Kathe Klare
PROFESSOR
ALBANY LAW SCHOOL

CAROLINA ACADEMIC PRESS
Durham, North Carolina

KH

ISBN: 978-1-59460-250-4
LCCN: 2008924392

Carolina Academic Press
700 Kent Street
Durham, North Carolina 27701
Telephone (919) 489-7486
Fax (919) 493-5668

Printed in the United States of America.

7/5/11

*For our parents Ruth and Richard Guernsey and
William and Anita Klare
whose wonderful support and interest encouraged us to become lawyers
in order to make a difference in other children's lives.*

For Alison and Adam who unselfishly shared their parents with other children.

For our many special education clients who have enriched our lives.

Contents

Table of Cases

Preface

More than 7.1 million children from birth through 21 years of age are receiving special education and related services from more than 46,000 teachers in the United States. That means that 7.1 million Individualized Education Programs (IEPs) are developed each year involving millions of parents, thousands of teachers, and thousands of other professionals. Most of these IEPs are developed, and the students receive the educational services, with little conflict. The Individuals with Disabilities Education Act (IDEA) in effect provides a roadmap that both the parents and the school follow toward the same destination. A fair number of parents and local educators, however, do not reach agreement about the provision of special education and related services and formal disputes result.

This book assists in reading that map as well as in resolving those disputes. The book is designed to take the lawyers, educators, and other professionals without prior experience through the process leading to an agreement. If agreement, however, is not reached between the school and the public agency responsible for educating the child, the book is designed to help the participants through the process of resolving that disagreement.

In this third edition we continue to provide a comprehensive overview of the federal statutes, regulations, and case law that affect the education of children with disabilities from birth to age 22. The book provides a solid background in special education law and is fully up-to-date with the recent recodification of IDEA, the new Department of Education regulations, and the recent case law, including the most recent Unite States Supreme Court decisions.

The text is written so that lawyers, educators and parents all can understand the intricacies of special education law. One of the overriding themes of special education is that a child's educational programming should be individualized. As such, many of the cases in this area are fact specific. For the lawyer, therefore, comprehensive citations to statutes, regulations, and case law provide the information necessary to conduct detailed legal research. In addition, numerous checklists and forms provide assistance with the practical application of the legal requirements.

The book, by its very nature, is primarily limited to federal law in general and IDEA and Section 504 of the Rehabilitation Act of 1973 (§ 504) in particular. One of the difficulties dealing with special education law is the interplay of several federal statutes, primarily IDEA and § 504, and to a lesser extent the Americans with Disabilities Act, ADA), and 42 U.S.C. § 1983, as well as supporting federal regulations. Further there are often statutes and regulations affecting general education that affect special education. For example, the Education Department General Administrative Regulations (EDGAR) and the Family Educational Rights and Privacy Act (FERPA or the Buckley Amendments) each may play a significant role. Chapter 1 provides a general overview of IDEA and its interrelationship with § 504, § 1983, EDGAR and FERPA. In each of the succeeding chapters, the primary focus is on IDEA, however, full attention is also given to the impact § 504 has on the subject, as well as any additional federal statute affecting the particular area.

State law should always be checked. Each state has its own statutes and regulations implementing the IDEA. While these state statutes and regulations usually mirror the federal statutes and regulations, this is not always the case. For example, federal statutes and regulations are silent on some points, and Congress has allowed states to develop independent standards in some areas. Further, while the state may not provide fewer rights, some states actually provide more substantive and procedural rights than required under IDEA. The addresses where copies of state regulations can be obtained, often at no cost, are listed in the Appendix.

Even the lawyer reading the footnotes may find some authorities with which he or she is not familiar. There are of course citations to court decisions, federal statutes and regulations. In addition, however, there are numerous citations to opinions written by the staff of two offices of the Department of Education: The Office of Civil Rights (OCR), the Office of Special Education and Rehabilitative Services (OSERS), and its Office of Special Education Programs (OSEP). OSEP is responsible for monitoring compliance with IDEA while OCR is responsible for monitoring compliance with § 504. Each office, therefore, has occasion to interpret the regulations of the respective statutes. OCR and OSEP opinions, being the interpretation of the agency having written the regulation, are afforded considerable deference by courts. In areas where there are no court decisions, they may be particularly significant.

For the nonlawyer, a brief explanation of the primary authorities used is contained in the Appendix.

The Individuals with Disabilities Education Act has been amended several times and its name has changed over the years. We refer to the statute as IDEA or the Act, except where quotations require reference to a previously used acronym such as EHA or EAHCA. We have also tried to inform the reader where significant changes have been made by the various amendments to the statutes and regulations over the years since their original enactment

Portions of this work have appeared, often in significantly different form, in the following law journals. The authors thank the journals for their permission to use the material in this book: Guernsey and Sweeney, The Church, The State, And the EHA: Educating the Handicapped in Light of The Establishment Clause, 73 Marquette Law Review 101 (1990); Guernsey, The Education For All Handicapped Children Act, 42 U.S.C. Section 1983 and Section 504 of the Rehabilitation Act of 1973: Statutory Interaction Following the Handicapped Children's Protection Act of 1986, 68 Nebraska Law Review 564 (1989); Guernsey, The School Pays the Piper, But How Much? Attorneys' Fees in Special Education Cases After the Handicapped Children's Protection Act of 1986, 23 Wake Forest Law Review 237 (1988); Guernsey, When the Teachers and Parents Can't Agree, Who Really Decides? Burdens of Proof and Standards of Review Under the Education for All Handicapped Children Act, 36 Cleveland State Law Review 67 (1987–1988).

We would also like to thank Albany Law School students Justin Myers, Erica Horton, and Jason Dunlap for their assistance on the third edition. The second edition saw the help of Southern Illinois University School of Law students Kathryn Giles, Rhonda Blades, Colleen Berry, Susan Frances and Scott Rice. The first edition saw the help of Scott Fell, Christopher Royer, Diane Silverman, M. Grey Sweeney, and Linda Ziegler former University of Richmond law students.

Note on Abbreviations

Special education law is replete with abbreviations beginning with the title of the Act. The abbreviations are explained throughout the text. We have, however, as a matter of convenience listed below the more common abbreviations.

AIDS	Acquired Immune Deficiency Syndrome
DOE	Department of Education
EAHCA	Education for all Handicapped Children Act
EDGAR	Education Department General Administrative Regulations
EHA	Education for the Handicapped Act
ESY	Extended School Year
FAPE	Free Appropriate Public Education
FERPA	Family Educational Rights and Privacy Act (Buckley Amendment)
HCPA	Handicapped Children's Protection Act of 1986
HIV	Human Immuno-deficiency Virus
IDEA	Individuals with Disabilities Education Act
IEE	Independent Educational Evaluation
IEP	Individualized Education Program
IFSP	Individualized Family Service Plan
ITDA	Infants and Toddlers with Disabilities Act
LEA	Local Education Authority
LRE	Least Restrictive Environment
MDR	Manifestation Determination Review
OCR	Office of Civil Rights (U.S. Department of Education)
OSEP	Office of Special Education Programs (U.S. Department of Education)
OSERS	Office of Special Education and Rehabilitative Services (U.S. Department of Education)
SEA	State Education Authority

Special Education Law

Chapter 1

An Historical Overview

1.1 Introduction

Signed into law in 1975, the Individuals with Disabilities Education Act[1] (IDEA) imposes significant responsibilities on the local and state educational authorities to insure that children with disabilities receive a free and appropriate public education (FAPE). The Act was formerly called the Education for All Handicapped Children Act. Known also as the EAHCA, EHA, or Public Law 94-142, its name was changed in December 1990.

This landmark legislation was designed to insure not only the substantive right to a FAPE, but also to insure extensive procedural protections, including the right to file a judicial action following exhaustion of administrative remedies, as a means of assuring the provision of the substantive right.

Section 504 of the Rehabilitation Act of 1973 also affects educational rights of children with disabilities.[2] Section 504 is broad and general in coverage, while IDEA is narrow and specific. Section 504 prohibits discrimination generally and covers not just educational institutions, nor simply public institutions. Section 504 covers all people with disabilities and all programs or activities receiving federal financial assistance or under any program or activity conducted by any Executive agency or by the United States Post Office.[3]

There is significant overlap between IDEA and §504.[4] There are, however, significant differences that will be discussed. The Americans with Disabilities Act of 1990 (ADA) also prohibits discrimination and affects the educational rights of children. As a general rule, however, it is interpreted similarly to §504.[5]

---

1. 20 U.S.C. §§1400–1482.
2. 29 U.S.C. §794. Section 504 provides:
   No otherwise qualified individual with a disability ... shall, solely by reason of his or her disability, be excluded from participation in, be denied the benefits of, or be subjected to discrimination under any program or activity receiving federal financial assistance.
3. *Id.*
4. New Mexico, at one time the only state to have opted out of IDEA, discovered that it would have to follow much of IDEA in order to avoid discrimination under §504. New Mexico Association for Retarded Citizens v. New Mexico, 495 F. Supp. 391 (D.N.M. 1980) *rev'd in part*, 678 F.2d 847 (10th Cir. 1982). The New Mexico legislature participated in IDEA funding after it became clear that §504 would require compliance with federal requirements without the corresponding funding of IDEA. C. Salomone, *Equal Education Under Law* 149 n.46 (1986).
5. 42 U.S.C. §§12101 *et seq.*; Letter to Rahall, 211 Individuals with Disabilities Educ. L. Rep. (LRP) 575 (OCR 1994) (responsibilities to provide FAPE are generally the same under ADA and §504).

In addition, 42 U.S.C. §1983 may play a role in insuring the protections afforded to children and their parents under IDEA. Further, in specific contexts, general educational provisions also play a role. In particular, the Family Educational Rights and Privacy Act[6] affect delivery of educational services to children with disabilities.

1.2 2004 Reauthorization of IDEA Statute and IDEA Regulations

In 1997, IDEA was reauthorized and amended.[7] There were multiple reasons for the 1997 amendments to IDEA. The statute itself, for example, identified the need to increase the effectiveness of special education services.[8] Legislative history recognized that after 22 years of identifying problems with the interpretation and implementation of the law[9] there was a need to codify judicial as well as United States Department of Education interpretations.[10] Further, there was recognition that the environment of special education, including increased litigation,[11] and increased societal expectations of children with disabilities particularly required reassessment.[12]

Among the significant amendments in 1997 were provisions for parents to have more participation into the educational decision making for their child. Parental involvement, for example, is required when reviewing evaluations and assessment data and when determining eligibility and placement.

Among the numerous codifications of judicial and regulatory interpretations in the 1997 amendments were those in the area of discipline.[13] Litigation also led to more extensive codification of the rights of children voluntarily placed by their parents in private schools.[14] The IDEA implementing regulations for the 1997 amendments became final in 1999.

The Individual with Disabilities Education Act's most recent reauthorization in 2004 was finalized in 2005 with the implementing regulations becoming effective in 2006. With this came substantive changes as well as maintaining content from the previous

---

6. 20 U.S.C. §1232(g); 34 C.F.R., Part 99.

7. *See* Pub. L. No 94-142, 89 Stat. 773 (1975) amended by 20 U.S.C. §§1400–1487.

8. 20 U.S.C. §1401(d)(4), (1997); §1400(d)(4)(2005).

9. *See* H.R. Rep. No. 105-95, at 85 ("[I]n developing these amendments the Committee distinguished between the problems of implementation and problems with the law, and responded appropriately in addressing any issue raised.").

10. Chapter 10.

11. *See* Reauthorization of the Individual With Disabilities Education Act: Hearing on S.216 Before Senate Comm. On Labor and Human Resources, 105th Cong.88 (1997) (statement of Senator Jim Jeffords, Senate bill sponsor). Senator Jeffords explained: "the writing is on the wall, if we don't make needed changes to the IDEA now, based on common sense, school districts and parents will increasingly turn to the courts to get answers. Parents will do so in hope of securing services that they believe their child needs."

12. *Id.* Statement of Jim Jeffords ("After 22 years, I think that it is appropriate to acknowledge ... that our expectations for children with disabilities have changed and the expectations we place on each other as educators and parents have changed.").

13. 34 C.F.R. §§300.519.529 (1997).

14. 34 C.F.R. §§300.450.462 (1997).

reauthorization. Many sections of the implementing regulations have been renumbered from the 1997 amendments.[15]

Among some of the significant amendments to the statute include: specifically identifying the parties who may request an initial evaluation; stating specific timeframes in which the initial evaluation must be completed;[16] establishing procedures to obtain parental consent after determining that a child is eligible for special education and related services if the parent refuses consent for provision of those services;[17] clarifying issues related to attendance at IEP meetings;[18] clarifying IEP development issues related to transferring students within school districts[19] and from out of state;[20] instituting a statute of limitations for filing in state or federal court [21]and clarifying issues related to the various procedural protections.[22] In addition, two pilot projects were created by the 2005 statute, a multi year IEP pilot project[23] and a pilot project for reduction in paperwork.[24]

1.3 Brief History

The modern legal history of education for children with disabilities began with *Brown v. Board of Education*.[25] In this famous civil rights case, the United States Supreme Court held that education, "where the state has undertaken to provide it, is a right which must be available to all on equal terms."[26] It was not, however, until 1971 that "lightning struck"[27] and significant progress was made in insuring this right for children with disabilities. In *Pennsylvania Association of Retarded Citizens (PARC) v. Pennsylvania*,[28] the state of Pennsylvania entered into a consent decree recognizing the right of children diagnosed with mental retardation to receive an education. By the terms of the consent decree, parents in Pennsylvania were provided with significant procedural and substantive rights that would "set a detailed model for future advocates"[29] and would find their national application four years later in IDEA. The rights agreed to in the *PARC* decision included the right to a free appropriate education, individualized education planning, notice of proposed changes in educational programming, and other due process procedures, including formal due process hearings.

---

15. Many cases cite to the 1997 statute and 1999 regulations.
16. 20 U.S.C. §1414 (B)(C).
17. 20 U.S.C.§1414 (a)(1)(D(ii) (I&II), if the parent fails to give consent for the initial evaluation the LEA may use the procedures under §1415 to obtain parental consent unless inconsistent with state law.
18. 20 U.S.C.§1414 (C).
19. 20 U.S.C.§1414 (3)(D–F) (4).
20. 20 U.S.C. §1414 (C)(i)(I).
21. 34 C.F.R. §§300.516(b).
22. See generally U.S.C. §1415.
23. 20 U.S.C. §.1414(5)(a).
24. 20 U.S.C.§1414 (5) (A) This is being implemented in order that more time and resources can be devoted to instruction and other activities for improving the educational and functional results for children with disabilities.
25. 347 U.S. 483 (1954).
26. *Id.* at 493.
27. Weiner and Hume, *And Education for All* 27 (2d ed. 1987).
28. 343 F. Supp. 279 (E.D. Pa. 1972) *modifying* 334 F. Supp. 1257 (E.D. Pa. 1971).
29. Goldberg, *Special Education* 3 (1982).

In a second decision of equal importance, *Mills v. Board of Education,*[30] the federal district court held that the District of Columbia's exclusion of children with disabilities from educational programming denied the children due process and equal protection of the law. Rejecting the District's argument that funds were insufficient,[31] the court ordered the District to develop a plan to provide both appropriate educational programming and due process rights to protect the substantive educational rights of the disabled children.

While litigation, as represented by *PARC* and *Mills,* was proceeding, Section 504 of the Rehabilitation Act of 1973 was enacted, providing that "No otherwise qualified individual with a handicap ... shall solely by reason of his handicap be excluded from participation in, be denied the benefits of, or be subjected to discrimination under any program or activity receiving federal assistance."[32]

In 1974, Congress took another major step, amending the Elementary and Secondary Education Act (ESEA).[33] These amendments would be the heart of the Education for All Children Act, but did not have a specific mandate or a time table requiring states to implement substantive and procedural rights. In 1975, however, Congress passed and President Ford signed into law P.L. 94-142, the Education for All Handicapped Children Act of 1975.[34] The law became fully effective in 1978, and required states accepting federal special education funding to implement explicit, detailed substantive and procedural rights. By its implementation in 1978, all states, except New Mexico, had decided to accept the funds and implement the Act. New Mexico, six years later, discovered that it was subject to many of the same requirements under §504 as it would be under IDEA, and opted to accept the federal funds and implement IDEA.[35]

Given the apparent overlap of §504 and IDEA, actions were brought to vindicate educational rights under both acts. Several advantages were readily apparent in bringing an action under §504 instead of IDEA. For example, attorneys' fees were available under §504, but prior to late 1986, they were not available under IDEA.[36] Further, §504 does not have the extensive administrative procedures that must be exhausted prior to bringing a lawsuit.[37]

---

30. 348 F. Supp. 866 (D.D.C. 1972).

31. "[I]f sufficient funds are not available to finance all of the services and programs that are needed and desirable in the system then the available funds must be expended equitably in such a manner that no child is entirely excluded from a publicly supported education consistent with his needs and ability to benefit therefrom." *Id.* at 876.

32. 29 U.S.C. §794. Amendment changed the word handicap to disability.

33. ESEA was amended again in 2002, *See generally 20 USC 7800.*

34. 20 U.S.C. §§1400 *et seq.* Renamed Individuals with Disabilities Education Act.

35. New Mexico Association for Retarded Citizens v. New Mexico (*NMARC*), 678 F.2d 847 (10th Cir. 1982).

36. Smith v. Robinson, 468 U.S. 992 (1984).

37. Polera v. Bd. of Educ., 288 F.3d 478 (2d Cir. 2002); Covington v. Knox, 205 F.3d 912 (6th Cir. 2000) (exhaustion required, except where futile); *see also* Tuck v. HCA Health Services of Tenn., 7 F.3d 465 (6th Cir. 1993); Miener v. Missouri, 673 F.2d 969 (8th Cir. 1982); Camenisch v. University of Texas, 616 F.2d 127, 135 (5th Cir. 1980) *vacated on other grounds* 451 U.S. 390 (1981); Adashunas v. Negley, 626 F.2d 600 (7th Cir. 1980); Sanders v. Marquette Pub. Schools, 561 F. Supp. 1361, 1369 (W.D. Mich. 1983); Smith, *Handicap Discrimination* 30 Ark. L. Rev. 1, 41-43 (1985); *but see* Smith v. United States Postal Service, 742 F.2d 257 (6th Cir. 1984) (requiring exhaustion under §504 where federal employee).

In addition to §504, suits were brought concurrently under 42 U.S.C. §1983[38] on claims that were covered by IDEA.[39] Section 1983 claims were brought on the assumption that failure to provide services consistent with the requirements of IDEA was a deprivation of a right guaranteed by federal statute,[40] Section 1983, unlike §504, has no separate implementing regulations. Section 1983, however, provided three important advantages: attorneys' fees,[41] damages,[42] and lack of an administrative remedy to exhaust.[43] The fact that violations of §504 or §1983 could result in the award of attorneys' fees guaranteed that suits alleging underlying violations of IDEA would also allege violations of §504 and §1983.[44]

Until 1984 and sometime afterward the lower courts split on whether IDEA was the exclusive remedy or whether actions covered by IDEA could be brought concurrently under §1983 and §504.[45] The United States Supreme Court in 1984 addressed the issue in *Smith v. Robinson.*[46] The Court held: "Congress intended the EAHCA to be the exclusive avenue through which a plaintiff may assert an equal protection claim to a publicly financed special education."[47]

In *Smith*, the Court held that IDEA and its lack of an attorneys' fee provision, as well as its detailed administrative requirements, could not be circumvented by filing suit under §504 or §1983. In the language of the Court:

> Even assuming that the reach of §504 is co-extensive with that of the EAHCA, there is no doubt that the remedies, rights, and procedures Congress set out in the EAHCA are the ones it intended to apply to a handicapped child's claim to a free appropriate education. We are satisfied that Congress did not intend a handicapped child to be able to circumvent the requirements or supplement the remedies of the EAHCA by resort to the general anti-discrimination provision of §504.[48]

Interestingly, *Smith* left open the possibility of suits under either §1983 or §504 where the respective statute provided protection in addition to that offered by IDEA.

Considering the §1983 action, the Court in *Smith* found the due process and equal protection claims raised by the plaintiffs to be virtually identical to IDEA claims that

---

38. 42 U.S.C. §1983.

39. See, *e.g.*, N.S. v. Attica Central School, 386 F.3d 107 (2d Cir. 2004) (court considers all the claims); Jose P. v. Ambach, 669 F.2d 865 (2d Cir. 1982).

40. *See, e.g.*, Weixel v. Board of Educ. of City of New York, 287 F.3d 138 (2d Cir. 2002); Quackenbush v. Johnson City School Dist., 716 F.2d 141 (2d Cir. 1983); Padilla v. School Dist. 1, 233 F3d 1268 (10th Cir. 2000) (IDEA provides comprehensive enforcement scheme that precludes §1983 suit as remedy for IDEA violations).

41. 42 U.S.C. §1988.

42. *See* §§14.3 and 14.6.

43. *See* Patsy v. Florida Bd. of Regents, 457 U.S. 496 (1982).

44. *See, e.g.*, Weixel v. Board of Educ. of City of New York, 287 F.3d 138 (2d Cir. 2002); Quackenbush v. Johnson City School Dist., 716 F.2d 141 (2d Cir. 1983); Colin K. v. Schmidt, 715 F.2d 1 (1st Cir. 1983), *affirming* 536 F. Supp. 1375 (D.R.I. 1982); Department of Educ. of Hawaii v. Katherine D., 727 F.2d 809 (9th Cir. 1983); Hymes v. Harnett County Bd. of Educ., 664 F.2d 410 (4th Cir. 1981).

45. *Compare* Georgia Association of Retarded Citizens v. McDaniel, 716 F.2d 1565, 1578–1579 (11th Cir. 1983); Quackenbush v. Johnson City School Dist., 716 F.2d 141 (2d Cir. 1983) (§1983 remedies available) *with* Department of Educ. of Hawaii v. Katherine D., 727 F.2d 809 (9th Cir. 1983) (IDEA provides exclusive remedies); Anderson v. Thompson, 658 F.2d 1205 (7th Cir. 1981).

46. 468 U.S. 992 (1984).

47. *Id.* at 1009.

48. *Id.* at 1019.

were raised. The Court, however, did not rule out relief under §1983 when the violation alleged was not the substantial equivalent to an underlying IDEA claim. In fact, the Court raised, but left undecided the issue of "whether the procedural safeguards set out in the EAHCA manifest Congress' intent to preclude resort to §1983 on a due process challenge...."[49]

Similarly, *Smith* recognized that where §504 provided greater substantive protection, suit could be brought under §504:

> We emphasize the narrowness of our holding. We do not address a situation where the EAHCA is not available or where §504 guarantees substantive rights greater than those available under the EAHCA. We hold only that where, as here, whatever remedy might be provided under §504 is, provided with more clarity and precision under the EAHCA, a plaintiff may not circumvent or en-large on the remedies available under the EAHCA by resort to §504.[50]

Congress reacted quickly to *Smith* by enacting the Handicapped Children's Protec-tion Act of 1986,[51] amending IDEA and providing for the award of attorneys' fees.[52] In addition to the award of attorneys' fees, however, Congress also provided that IDEA would not be the "exclusive avenue" and a cause of action under §1983 and §504 was again possible to vindicate educational rights of children with disabilities.[53]

The attorneys' fees provisions of the amendments were widely known and quickly acted upon by lawyers.[54] The reaffirmation of the role of §504 and §1983, however, re-ceived little attention, with courts dismissing §504 and §1983 claims well after IDEA was amended.[55] Eventually, courts began to deal with the question of whether the Con-

---

49. Smith, 468 U.S. at 1013.

50. *Id.* at 1021.

51. 20 U.S.C. §1415(i)(3)(1986),20 U.S.C.§1415(i)(3)(2005)

52. For a discussion of the attorneys' fees provisions of IDEA see Chapter 15.

53. 20 U.S.C. §1415(l). The amended Act provides:
   Nothing in this chapter shall be construed to restrict or limit the rights, procedures, and remedies available under the Constitution, the Americans with Disabilities Act of 1990, Title V of the Rehabilitation Act of 1973, or other Federal laws protecting the rights of children with disabilities, except that before the filing of a civil action under such laws seeking relief that is also available under [IDEA], the procedures ... [of this section] shall be exhausted to the same extent as would be required had the action been brought under [IDEA].

54. *E.g.,* School Bd. of Prince William County v. Malone, 662 F. Supp. 999 (E.D. Va. 1987); Burpee v. Manchester School Dist., 661 F. Supp. 731 (D.N.H. 1987). Requests for attorney's fees are now routine. *See also* Aguirre v. Los Angeles Unified School Dist., 461 F.3d 1114, (9th Cir. 2006); Neosho R-V School Dist. v. Clark, 315 F.3d 1022 (8th Cir. 2003); Yanton School Dist. v. Schramm, 93 F.3d 1369 (8th Cir. 1996); Kletzelman v. Capistrano Unified School Dist., 91 F.3d 68 (9th Cir. 1995); Combs v. School Bd. of Rockingham County, 15 F.3d 357 (4th Cir. 1994);); Abraham v. Dis-trict of Columbia, 338 F. Supp. 2d 113 (D.D.C. 2004); Curtis K. v. Sioux City Community School, 895 F. Supp. 1197 (N.D. Iowa 1995). See Chapter 15 for a discussion of attorneys' fees.

55. *See, e.g.,* Kerr Center Parents Assoc. v. Charles, 842 F.2d 1052 (9th Cir. 1988); Association for Retarded Citizens of Alabama, Inc. v. Teague, 830 F.2d 158 (11th Cir. 1987); Barwacz v. Michi-gan Dept. of Educ., 674 F. Supp. 1296 (W.D. Mich. 1987); DeFalco v. Deer Lake School Dist., 663 F. Supp. 1108 (W.D. Pa. 1987) (§1983 claims dismissed on basis of Smith v. Robinson); *see generally* Robinson v. Pinderhughes, 810 F. 2d 1270 (4th Cir. 1987).
   This lack of attention is consistent with the general lack of understanding of the relationship be-tween §504 and IDEA. In the House Report supporting the then proposed Handicapped Children's Protection Act of 1986, in reference to the ability to file complaints under §504 as well as IDEA, it was written "Several witnesses testified regarding the need to clarify the availability of these av-enues." H.R. Rep. No. 296, 99th Cong., 1st Sess. 7 (1985).

gressional action allowed an action under §1983 as well as under §504 for rights protected under IDEA. Several courts held that such actions were allowed.[56]

There are, however, court decisions that hold, often citing pre-*Smith v. Robinson* decisions, that despite Congressional action recognizing the ability to bring suit under §504 and §1983, compliance with IDEA satisfies the requirements of §504.[57] Most recently, in 2007, the United States Court of Appeals for the Third Circuit held that a §1983 action was not available to remedy violations of IDEA or for violations of the Rehabilitation Act of 1974.[58]

The courts, therefore, remain split on the issue. Assuming, however, the rights and protections in the §504 implementing regulations are valid,[59] the basic argument that §§504 and 1983 do provide educational rights in addition to any rights under IDEA is that it is unlikely Congress would have reaffirmed the ability to bring suit under both IDEA and §§504 and 1983, if it had not envisioned the ability of §504 or §1983 to provide additional rights. Truly independent claims that did not enlarge on the remedies available under IDEA were not precluded under *Smith* in any event.[60] On the other hand, in the words of one court, "The holding in *Smith,* although superseded in part by the passage of §1415(1) of the IDEA, was not overruled to the extent that the Court found that the IDEA provides a comprehensive remedial scheme."[61]

1.4 IDEA: An Overview

IDEA is a funding statute. In order to qualify to receive federal funds, commonly referred to as Part B funds,[62] a state educational authority (SEA) must assume responsibility for affecting a policy that assures a free appropriate public education (FAPE) is being provided by local agencies to all eligible children with disabilities.[63]

Funding under IDEA is determined on a state-by-state basis according to the number of children with disabilities served. The figure, determined by a formula, represents a ceiling on the amount of funds to which a state is entitled, not the actual amount a state will receive.[64]

Each state is charged with the task of devising and implementing its own program to monitor the performance of its public schools in providing special education and re-

---

56. *E.g.*, N.B. v. Alachua County School Board, 84 F.3d 1376 (11th Cir. 1996) (IDEA and §1983 claim but needed to exhaust to proceed); Urban v. Jefferson County School Dist., 89 F.3d 720 (10th Cir. 1996) (court cited Smith v. Robinson for the similarities between §504 and IDEA); Mrs. C. v. Wheaton, 916 F.2d 69 (2d Cir. 1990) (failure to provide notice violated both IDEA and §504); *see also* Brantley v. Independent School Dist. No. 625, 1996 WL 459706 (D. Minn. 1996) (court did not dismiss §1983 claim for violation of due process procedures but needed bad faith or gross misjudgment for ADA and §504 violations); Howell v. Waterford Pub. Schools, 731 F. Supp. 1314 (E.D. Mich. 1990); G.C. v. Coler, 673 F. Supp. 1093 (S.D. Fla. 1987).
57. *E.g.*, Burke County Bd. of Educ. v. Denton, 895 F.2d 973 (4th Cir. 1990).
58. A.W. v Jersey City Public Schools, 486 F3d 791 (3rd Cir. 2007). See also §§1.5 and 1.6.
59. For a discussion of the validity of the regulations, see §1.4.1.
60. *See supra* text at note 35.
61. A.W. v Jersey City Public Schools, 486 F3d 791, 803 (3rd Cir. 2007).
62. IDEA is often referred to as Part B of the Education of the Handicapped Act. Part B funds, therefore, refers to monies provided under the entitlement program added to the Act by P.L. 94-142.
63. 20 U.S.C. §1412(a).
64. *See* 20 U.S.C. §1411 (entitlements and allocations).

lated services.[65] The key provision of IDEA is that each child is entitled to a free and appropriate public education (FAPE) that prepares them for independent living.[66] A free appropriate education is defined as special education and related services provided in conformity with the requirements of IDEA.[67] The centerpiece of IDEA is the requirement that the local educational agency (LEA) review, at least annually, an individualized educational program (IEP) for each child that must be in effect at the beginning of the school year.[68] The IEP is to state the child's present level of educational achievement and behavioral performance. It must also articulate both measurable annual goals and for children taking alternate assessments benchmarks or short-term objectives.[69] Placements must be in the least restrictive environment.[70]

Beyond these general principles, Congress provided very little in the way of defining the substantive right to an education. Congress was, however, very explicit when it came to the procedural protections to which the parents and child were entitled.

The extensive procedural protections include parental consent or involvement in most decisions affecting the child's educational program.[71] Indeed, the requirement of "meaningful input into all decisions affecting their child's education...." was affirmed by the United States Supreme Court in *Honig v. Doe*.[72] The Court further stated:

> Envisioning the IEP as the centerpiece of the statute's education delivery system for disabled children, and aware that schools had all too often denied such children appropriate educations without in any way consulting their parents, Congress repeatedly emphasized throughout the Act the importance and indeed the necessity of parental participation in both the development of the IEP and any subsequent assessment of its effectiveness.[73]

Specific procedural protections require a child be identified[74] and then evaluated by a multi-disciplinary team.[75] Following evaluation, a meeting is convened to determine the child's eligibility for special education.[76] After eligibility is determined, an IEP is developed. The parents may participate in reviewing the evaluations and determining eligibility.[77]

Following development of an IEP, a placement decision, again with parental input, is made based on the goals and objectives contained in the IEP.[78] The IEP must then be reviewed at least annually. In addition, the child must be re-evaluated at least every three years.[79] Congress also required multi-disciplinary and nondiscriminatory testing.[80] To insure the parents have sufficient information available to participate in the educational

---

65. *See, e.g.,* 20 U.S.C. §1412.
66. 20 U.S.C. §1400(c); 34 C.F.R. §300.1; *see also* 20 U.S.C. §1401(9); 34 C.F.R. §300.17.
67. 34 C.F.R. §300.17; *see also* 20 U.S.C. §1401(9).
68. 20 U.S.C. §1401(14), and §1414(d). 34 C.F.R. §300.330-24.
69. 20 U.S.C. §1414(d)(1); 34 C.F.R. §300.320(a)
70. 20 U.S.C. §1412(a)(5); 34 C.F.R. §§300. 114. *See* §8.2.
71. 20 U.S.C §§1414 (d)(1)(B)(i) and(1)(B)-(d)(1)(D) and (e) and (c) (1), and 1415(b)(1 and (d)(2)(a); 34 C.F.R. §§300.501–504.
72. 484 U.S. 305, 311 (1988).
73. *Id.*
74. 20 U.S.C. §§1401(3);1412(a)(3); 34 C.F.R §300.111.
75. 20 U.S.C. §§1414(a)(1), 1414(b)(1)–(3), 1412(a)(6)(B); 34 C.F.R. §§300.122 and 300.301–306.
76. 20 U.S.C. §1414 (b)(4–5); 34 C.F.R. §300.306.
77. 20 U.S.C. §1414(d)(1)(B)(i); 34 C.F.R. §300.306.
78. 20 U.S.C. §1414(e), 1415(b)(1); 34 C.F.R. §§300.327 and 300.501(c).
79. 20 U.S.C. §1414(a)(2); 34 C.F.R. §300.303;
80. 20 U.S.C. §§1412(a)(6)(B), 1414(b)(2), and (3); *see* 34 C.F.R. §300.532.

decision-making, Congress provided the parents with the right to have an independent educational evaluation (IEE) at public expense.[81] The IEE, if at public expense, must be conduced under the same criteria the public agency uses for evaluations to the extent they are consistent with an IEE.[82]

If at any point in this process there is a disagreement between parents and the LEA, mediation[83] and/or a due process hearing may be requested.[84] Following this administrative hearing, the state may provide a state level review.[85] Following this administrative process, suit may be filed in either state or federal court.[86]

1.5 Section 504: An Overview

Regulations implementing §504 promulgated by the Department of Education (DOE)[87] provide procedural and substantive obligations that local educational agencies are required to follow. In many instances, the regulations explicitly mirror IDEA and regulations promulgated under it.[88] In fact, the relationship of §504 and IDEA was recognized by the United States Department of Education. In the comments to IDEA regulations, the Department stated:

> As the regulations being developed under section 504 ... are in the process of being finalized at the same time these proposed regulations [for IDEA] are being published, every effort will be made to have the final regulations be consistent in concept, policy, and, wherever possible, consistent with the language of the final §504 regulations.[89]

1.5.1 Historical Overview of the Validity of Section 504 Regulations and Undue Burden

Section 504 is a broad statutory prohibition. Regulations promulgated under it, however, articulate specific requirements that school systems must meet. Before a meaningful comparison of the requirements under §504 and IDEA can be made, however, a preliminary question concerning the validity of the Department of Education's regulations under §504 must be addressed: To the extent the §504 regulations require more than IDEA, do they exceed the authority Congress intended the Department of Education to exercise? This is particularly a concern in light of court decisions that hold that compliance with IDEA will always insure compliance with §504.[90]

---

81. 34 C.F.R. §300.502; *see also* 20 U.S.C. §1415(b)(1).

82. 34 C.F.R §300.502.

83. 34 C.F.R. §300.506.

84. 34 C.F.R. §300.507.

85. *20U.S.C.* §1415(g) and (h)(4),1415(i)(1)(A),1415(i)(2); 34 C.F.R. §300.514.

86. 20 U.S.C.§1415(i)(2)and (3)(A), 1415(l); 34 C.F.R. 300.516.

87. 34 C.F.R. §§104.31 *et seq.*

88. *Compare, e.g.,* 34 C.F.R. §104.33 *with* 34 C.F.R. §300.17, both of which define a free appropriate public education.

89. 41 Fed. Reg. 56967 (1976).

90. *See* Sellers by Sellers v. School Bd. of Cir. of Mannassas, 141 F.3d 524 (4th Cir. 1998); Burke County Bd. of Educ. v. Denton, 895 F.2d 973 (4th Cir. 1990). In Urban v. Jefferson County School

Any discussion of the history and the validity of §504 regulations must begin with a discussion of the Supreme Court decision in *Southeastern Community College v. Davis.*[91] *Davis* involved the efforts of a hearing impaired woman to gain enrollment in a community college nurse training program. Frances Davis filed suit in federal court alleging the community college had violated her rights under §504. Davis alleged the college failed to accept her into its nursing program and provide adjustments to its standard educational program which would allow her to benefit despite her disability. Ms. Davis' disability allowed her to understand normal speech only through lip reading.

In addressing Ms. Davis' claims of discrimination, the Court focused on §504's "otherwise qualified" language, and concluded that Ms. Davis was not otherwise qualified. Focusing on her inability to hear speech, the Court stated that such ability was "indispensable for many of the functions that a registered nurse performs."[92] Further, the Court held that the accommodations that would be required for Ms. Davis to benefit from the nursing program would require such fundamental changes in the course of study that she would not "receive even a rough equivalent of the training a nursing program normally gives."[93]

The Supreme Court placed heavy reliance on the administrative regulations in reaching its decision, holding that it "is reasonably clear that [the regulation] does not encompass the kind of curricular changes that would be necessary to accommodate respondent in the nursing program."[94] Expanding on this concern with substantive changes in the program, the Court stated:

> Moreover, an interpretation of the regulations that required extensive modifications necessary to include respondent in the nursing program would raise grave doubts about their validity. If these regulations were to require substantial adjustments in existing programs beyond those necessary to eliminate discrimination against otherwise qualified individuals, they would do more than clarify the meaning of §504. Instead, they would constitute an unauthorized extension of obligations imposed by that statute.[95]

The Court explicitly held that even if the regulation attempted to create an affirmative obligation the United States Department of Health Education and Welfare (HEW) lacked the authority to do so.[96] The Court, however, left open the door to the possibility that some affirmative action might be required. Holding that the line between "a lawful refusal to extend affirmative action and illegal discrimination" was not clear,[97] the Court

---

Dist., 89 F.3d 720, 728 (10th Cir. 1996), the court quoted *Smith v. Robinson* to support the statement that "if a disabled child is not entitled to such a neighborhood placement under IDEA, he is not entitled to such a placement under Section 504."

91. 442 U.S. 397 (1979). Numerous law review articles have been written discussing *Davis. See, e.g.,* Dupre, *Disability Defense and the Integrity of the Academic Enterprise,* 32 Ga. L. Rev. 393 (1998).

92. Davis, 442 U.S. at 407.

93. *Id.* at 410. Ms. Davis suggested that she be given individual supervision whenever attending patients directly and that certain required courses be waived. *Id.* at 407–408.

94. *Id.* at 409.

95. *Id.* at 410. The Court also pointed out Congress' specific requirement for affirmative efforts on the part of the federal government under §§501(b) and 503(a) and the absence of such a specific affirmative action requirement under §504 as an indication "that Congress understood accommodation of the needs of the handicapped individuals may require affirmative action and knew how to provide for it in those instances where it wished to do so." *Id.* at 411.

96. *Id* at 411–412.

97. *Id.* at 412.

stated that under certain circumstances continuing past practices could result in discrimination against qualified individuals. For example, technology might change such that "without imposing undue financial and administrative burdens upon a state" accommodations could be made which would allow participation by otherwise qualified individuals.[98]

What *Davis* left was a rule that §504 does not require affirmative action on the part of the recipient, unless, apparently, the requested accommodations do not impose "undue financial and administrative burdens."[99] While decisions are not consistent in determining what is an undue burden, there are decisions holding that §504 requires a great deal.

Perhaps the most important case addressing the impact of *Davis* on the special education regulations under §504 is *New Mexico Association for Retarded Citizens v. New Mexico (NMARC)*.[100] At the time of this decision, New Mexico was the only state that had not accepted funds under IDEA. Suit, therefore, was brought alleging the state's treatment of students with disabilities violated §504. In holding for plaintiffs, the district court found that the various therapies and diagnostic services offered by the state were insufficient and that the state inadequately funded special education programs.

The United States Tenth Circuit Court of Appeals held that the Supreme Court's suggestion in *Davis* that refusal to modify an existing program might become discriminatory was applicable where "the entity's practices preclude the handicapped from obtaining system benefits realized by the non-handicapped."[101] Before such a finding, however, the district court must determine whether the State's existing program precludes people with a disability from enjoying benefits realized by the non-disabled; whether the program modifications allow the person with a disability to benefit; and finally, whether the program modification would "jeopardize the overall viability of the state's educational system."[102] *NMARC* established the general validity of the regulations, conditioned most significantly on the financial impact to the school system.

But, perhaps the best argument that §504 regulations do not exceed what Congress intended, and hence are valid, is Congressional reaffirmation of §504's application to the education of children with disabilities. Although courts vary widely in relying on subsequent legislation to infer congressional intent, it is generally recognized that subsequent legislation is probative. In *Zemel v. Rusk*,[103] for example, addressing the validity of regu-

98. *Id.* at 412. The Supreme Court's use of the phrase "affirmative action" was criticized by many commentators. The Court subsequently stated, "Regardless of the aptness of our choice of words in *Davis*, it is clear from the context ... that the term 'affirmative action' referred to those 'changes,' 'adjustments,' or modifications to existing programs that would be 'substantial'... or that would constitute 'fundamental, alteration[s] in the nature of the program.... '" Alexander v. Choate, 469 U.S. 287, 301 n.20 (1985).

99. Davis, 442 U.S. at 412.

100. 678 F.2d 847 (10th Cir. 1982); *see also* S-1 v. Turlington, 635 F.2d 342 (5th Cir. 1981) (§504 requires educational services and procedural protections); Lora v. Board of Educ. of New York City, 456 F. Supp. 1211 (E.D.N.Y. 1978) (inadequate educational programming for emotionally disturbed children); Howard v. Friendswood Independent School Dist., 454 F. Supp. 634 (S.D. Tex. 1978) (failure to provide educational programming and procedural protections to brain damaged, emotionally disturbed child).

101. NMARC, 678 F.2d at 853. The court drew an analogy to two cases arising under Title VI of the Civil Rights Act of 1964, in which it was held that failure to provide educational programs for non-English speaking students discriminated against those students. *See* Lau v. Nichols, 414 U.S. 563 (1974); Serna v. Portales Municipal Schools, 499 F.2d 1147 (10th Cir. 1974).

102. NMARC, 678 F.2d at 855. This three part test, occasioned by the special circumstances involving affirmative action on the part of the recipient, would apparently be in addition to the standard analysis of a regulations validity.

103. 381 U.S. 1 (1965).

lations promulgated under passport legislation, the United States Supreme Court said that "Congress' failure to repeal or revise ... administrative interpretation has been held to be persuasive evidence that interpretation is the one intended by Congress."[104]

The history of the promulgation of the regulations was tortured.[105] The Supreme Court in *Davis* used this history to point out that the deference normally due the administrative agency was diminished.[106] It further pointed out that "isolated statements by individual Members of Congress or its committees, all made after the enactment of the statute under consideration, cannot substitute for a clear expression of legislative intent at the time of enactment."[107] The Court stated, "these comments, none of which represents the will of Congress as a whole, constitute subsequent 'legislation' such as this Court might weigh in construing the meaning of an earlier enactment."[108]

"Subsequent legislation," however, has been passed. Congressional action in reaffirming the applicability of §504 to education of children with disabilities is itself a reflection of Congress' view that §504 regulations are valid. Rather than mere isolated comments that existed at the time *Davis* was decided, this provision provides a logical inference that Congress intended to affirm the regulations promulgated under §504.

Congress was aware of existing regulations when it reinstated §504's full impact on educating children with disabilities.[109] The level of Congress' knowledge of the regulations, is the fact that rather than simply reaffirm the applicability of §504, aware that there was no obligation to exhaust administrative remedies under §504, Congress provided that if there is a cause under both IDEA and §504, then IDEA administrative proceedings must be exhausted. Congress was enacting legislation that affected both the interpretation of §504 and IDEA. It is reasonable to assume that had it disagreed with the administrative interpretation of §504, it had the perfect opportunity to express that disagreement.[110]

104. *Id.* at 11; *see also* First Gibraltar Bank v. Morales, 19 F.3d 1032 (5th Cir. 1994); *see generally* Allstate Construction Co. v. Durkin, 345 U.S. 13, 16–17 (1953) (explicit enactment that administrative interpretation would remain in effect); United States v. Bergh, 352 U.S. 40 (1956) (failure of Congress to repeal regulations is evidence of Congressional intent).

105. When originally passed, §504 was silent as to the power of federal agencies to promulgate implementing regulations. The Department of Health Education and Welfare implemented regulations in 1977 only after being ordered to by the executive as well as by court order. *See* Wegner, *The Antidiscrimination Model Reconsidered: Ensuring Equal Opportunity Without Respect To Handicap Under Section 504 of The Rehabilitation Act of 1973*, 69 Cornell L. Rev. 401, 411–413 (1984).

106. Davis, 442 U.S. at 412 n.11.

107. *Id.* at 411 n.11.

108. *Id.* at 412 n.11.

109. The House report supporting the then proposed amendment stated:
    The section 504 regulations were the result of extensive consideration in the regulatory process.... Congress had the opportunity to review these regulations during oversight hearings in 1977.... At that time, Congress explicitly approved the section 504 regulations.
H.R. Rep. No. 296, 99th Cong., 1st Sess. 8 (1985).

110. Despite the questions raised in *Davis* concerning the validity of §504 regulations. The United States Supreme Court has repeatedly relied on the regulations. In School Bd. of Nassau County, Florida v. Arline, 480 U.S. 273, 279 (1987) the Court stated:
    As we have previously recognized, these regulations were drafted with the oversight of Congress, *see* Consolidated Rail Corporation v. Darrone, 465 U.S. 624, 634–635 and nn. 14–16 (1984) (they provide 'an important source of guidance on the meaning of 504'); Alexander v. Choate, 469 U.S. 287, 304 n.24 (1985. *See also* South Carolina v. Baker, 485 U.S. 505, 517 n.10 (1988).

The counterbalancing argument, however, is that it is unlikely that Congress intended a broad brush statute like §504 would impose a greater duty on the local and state education agency than the highly specific IDEA. In *St. Louis Developmental Disabilities Treatment Center Parents Association v. Mallory*,[111] although post-*Smith v. Robinson*, the court assumed the inapplicability of *Smith* to an allegation under §504. The court held that "The Education Act sets the outer limits on what is required of a state in the area of educating the handicapped."[112]

The *Mallory* decision is the functional equivalent of the *Smith* holding. If Congress intended IDEA to provide the outer limit, why did it feel compelled to reinstate the applicability of §504 as a cause of action? Congress, it is logical to assume, saw in §504 additional protection of some type.[113] Holding that IDEA provides the outer limit, therefore, would make the Congressional reaffirmation of §504 superfluous. Congress must have intended more or it would simply have enacted the attorneys' fees provisions.

1.5.2 Section 504 Undue Burden — Case Examples

Whether a specific educational requirement would be an undue burden has been considered a factual question to be determined on a case-by-case basis. In *Sanders v. Marquette Public Schools*,[114] for example, suit was brought under §1983, IDEA, and §504 alleging the school system failed to identify and place a child in special education programming. Addressing the §504 claim the court stated that *Davis* allowed the school system to establish that the failure to provide special education services was the result of the burden such services would cause. "Such evidence might be data showing that funding was simply unavailable, or that the program requested by plaintiff could not have been provided without great expense and detriment to the system."[115] The reader should be quickly reminded that this language only concerns a §504 claim. Under IDEA, unavailability of resources has generally not been a justification for refusing to provide specific types of services, and is clearly not a justification for denying all services.[116]

---

111. 591 F. Supp. 1416 (W.D. Mo. 1984), *aff'd*, 767 F.2d 518 (8th Cir. 1985).

112. *Id.* at 1470; *see also* Darlene L. v. Illinois State Bd. of Educ., 568 F. Supp. 1340 (N.D. Ill. 1983).

113. It would be possible to argue that Congress intended §504 to retain validity in the field as a means of filling in gaps in IDEA. That §504 would provide the mechanism to insure, for example, that architectural barriers did not inhibit educational programming. The problem with this argument, however, is that even after *Smith* §504 could be relied upon for an allegation that fell beyond IDEA. The Supreme Court in *Smith* was very explicit in stating:

> We emphasize the narrowness of our holding. We do not address a situation where the EAHCA is not available or where §504 guarantees substantive rights greater than those available under the EAHCA. We hold only that where, as here, whatever remedy might be provided under §504 is provided with more clarity and precision under the EAHCA, a plaintiff may not circumvent to enlarge on the remedies available under the EAHCA by resort to §504.

Smith, 468 U.S. at 1021.

114. 561 F. Supp. 1361 (W.D. Mich. 1983).

115. *Id.* at 1371.

116. Deal v. Hamilton County Bd. of Educ., 392 F.3d 840 (6th Cir. 2004) (cost is legitimate factor only when choosing appropriate programs); *see also* Clevenger v. Oak Ridge School Bd., 744 F.2d 514 (6th Cir. 1984); *but see* 34 C.F.R. §§300. 130–300, 144 (no entitlement to all or some of special education services for children unilaterally placed in private schools). *See* §3.5.

A few courts appear to take the position that an undue burden exists *per se* if the requested educational programming requires creation of a completely new service. In *Turilio v. Tyson*,[117] for example, the district court held that although §504 might require modification of an existing program, "it never compels a school system to finance a private educational placement."[118] If modification of an existing program is requested, then apparently, an individual determination as in *Sanders* is made to decide whether the requested service will provide an undue financial or administrative burden.

Georgia Association of Retarded Citizens v. McDaniel[119] addressed the 180 day limitation in a suit brought under IDEA and §504. Although ultimately modified as a result of *Smith v. Robinson*, it held that a policy precluding educational programming for more than 180 days violated both acts. Indeed, citing one of its own earlier decisions, the Eleventh Circuit held "The Supreme Court's decision in *Southeastern Community College* says only that §504 does not require a school to provide services to a handicapped individual for a program for which the individual's handicap precludes him from ever realizing the benefit of the training."[120]

A broad reading of *Davis*, as in *McDaniel*, of course, makes increased rights under §504 much more likely. In *Yaris v. Special School District of St. Louis*,[121] for example, suit was brought under both IDEA and §504 concerning the school system's failure to provide children with disabilities with more than the standard 180 days of instruction. The court held that the plain meaning of the statute indicated a violation if children with disabilities are precluded from receiving the same benefits realized by other children. Since children without disabilities could attend summer school, §504 was violated by the failure to provide summer programming for children with disabilities.

The court in *Yaris* then went on to address the §504 regulations to determine whether they also required more than the traditional 180 days. Concluding that the regulations' requirements for individualized education required the potential for greater than 180 days of instruction, the court held that §504 regulations were violated. Addressing the validity of the regulations, the court cited *NMARC*, among other decisions, and added the interesting rationale that, since the state had already adopted virtually identical requirements under IDEA, the implementation of these regulations would not require substantial adjustments. The court specifically declined to decide whether there would be a substantial adjustment if IDEA had not been accepted by the states.

---

117. 535 F. Supp. 577 (D.R.I. 1982).

118. *Id.* at 588.; *see also* Rollison v. Biggs, 567 F. Supp. 964 (D. Del. 1983); Darlene L. v. Illinois State Bd. of Educ., 568 F. Supp. 1340 (N.D. Ill. 1983); *see generally* Kruelle v. New Castle County School Dist., 642 F.2d 687, 695–696 (3d Cir. 1981).

119. 716 F.2d 1565 (11th Cir. 1983) *modified in part* 740 F.2d 902 (11th Cir. 1984).

120. *Id.* at 1580 *quoting* Camenisch v. University of Texas, 616 F.2d 127, 133 (5th Cir. 1980); *see also* Association For Retarded Citizens In Colorado v. Frazier, 517 F. Supp. 105, 122 (D. Colo. 1981) ("*Davis* is distinguishable ... to the extent that it deals with the absence of a requirement to provide a substantial modification for a handicapped individual ... for which that person's handicap precluded her from ever realizing the benefits of that program."); *see generally* Wong v. The Regents of the University of California, 192 F.3d 807 (9th Cir. 1999); Tatro v. Texas, 625 F.2d 557, 564 (5th Cir. 1980), *aff'd on other grounds sub nom.* Irving Independent School Dist. v. Tatro, 468 U.S. 883 (1984).

121. 558 F. Supp. 545 (E.D. Mo. 1983), *aff'd*, 728 F.2d 1055 (8th Cir. 1984).

1.6 Section 1983 and IDEA

The 1986 amendments to IDEA were thought by many to have reinstated the ability to use §1983.[122] As stated by the court in *Hiller v. Board of Education of Brunswick Central School District*:[123]

> The school district's contention that plaintiff is not entitled to at least plead a cause of action under section 1983 is patently absurd in light of the Second Circuit's recent decision in *Mrs. W. v. Tirozzi*, 832 F.2d 748 (2d Cir. 1987). In *Tirozzi* the Court held that section 1415(f) was enacted to overrule the Supreme court's decision in *Smith v. Robinson*, 468 U.S. 992, 104 S. Ct. 3457, 82 L.Ed.2d 746 (1984), holding that the EACHA is the exclusive remedy and section 1983 is not available except in very limited circumstances.
>
> After a thorough discussion of the legislative history, the Second Circuit concluded that after the enactment of section 1415(f), plaintiffs are entitled to assert a cause of action under section 1983 for alleged EACHA violations.... [124]

More recently, the Third Circuit held that a §1983 action was not available for a special education student to remedy alleged violations of IDEA created rights. The court stated:

> We agree with the reasoning of the Courts of Appeals for the Fourth and Tenth Circuits, to say nothing of that of the Supreme Court in *Smith*, regarding the comprehensive nature of the IDEA's remedial scheme. The holding in *Smith*, although superseded in part by the passage of §1415(l) of the IDEA, was not overruled to the extent that the Court found that the IDEA provides a comprehensive remedial scheme. Indeed, since *Smith*, the Court has continued to refer to the IDEA as an example of a statutory enforcement scheme that precludes a §1983 remedy.... The IDEA includes a judicial remedy for violations of any right "relating to the identification, evaluation, or educational placement of [a] child, or the provision of a free appropriate public education to such child." §1415(b)(6). Given this comprehensive scheme, Congress did not intend §1983 to be available to remedy violations of the IDEA such as those alleged by A.W.[125]

If only independent §1983 claims can be brought concurrently with IDEA, nothing affecting the relationship between §1983 and IDEA was changed by the 1986 amendment other than the attorney's fee provision. As indicated above, these actions could be brought under *Smith*.[126]

---

122. 20 U.S.C. §1415(f).
123. 687 F. Supp. 735, 743–744 (N.D.N.Y. 1988).
124. *Id.* at 743–744. The court in Mrs. W. v. Tirozzi, 832 F.2d 748, 754–55 (2d Cir. 1987) stated: Congress stated that section 1415(f) was designed to "re-establish statutory rights as repealed by *Smith v. Robinson*," and to "reaffirm, in light of this decision, the viability of..., 42 U.S.C. §1983, and other statutes as separate vehicles for ensuring the rights of handicapped children."
See also Phil v. Massachusetts Dept. of Educ., 9 F.3d 184 (1st Cir. 1993) (1986 amendments superseded *Smith v. Robinson*); Susan v. Wilson School Dist., 70 F.3d 751 (3d Cir. 1995) (IDEA did not preempt other statutory claims); *but see* Jersey City Public Schools
125. A.W. v Jersey City Public Schools, 486 F3d 791, 803 (3d Cir. 2007) (citations omitted).
126. *See* §1.2.

A failure to provide any of the rights, either procedural or substantive under IDEA should allow suit to be brought under §1983. Courts have indicated a willingness to hear claims based in substantive violations of IDEA.[127] There are, however, cases holding to the contrary. For example, *Fee v. Herndon,*[128] involved an allegation that a student with a disability received excessive corporal punishment. The court, held that the §1983 claim was improper because the state had reasonable restrictions on corporal punishment and provided appropriate legal remedies for violation of these restrictions.[129]

Even the United States Supreme Court's decision in *Smith v. Robinson,* recognized that completely independent claims can be brought.[130] The Court, by way of example, stated:

> And, while Congress apparently has determined local and state agencies should not be burdened with attorney's fees to litigants who succeed, through resort to procedures outlined in the EAHCA ... there is no indication that agencies should be exempt from a fee award where plaintiffs have had to resort to judicial relief to force the agencies to provide them the process they were constitutionally due.[131]

Following *Smith,* lower courts adopted the Supreme Court's *dicta* and held that various actions by local and state agencies constituted independent violations of §1983. Not surprisingly, one of the first cases involved facts nearly identical to the example used by the Supreme Court. In *Manecke v. School Board of Pinellas County, Florida,*[132] the Eleventh Circuit Court of Appeals addressed a claim brought under §1983 and §504. In *Manecke,* plaintiffs filed suit alleging the school board failed to provide them with a due process hearing on the issue of an educational placement for their daughter. Plaintiffs further alleged that this failure required them unilaterally to place their daughter in a residential facility. The district court dismissed both the §1983 and the §504 claims. The Eleventh Circuit panel, however, after discussing *Smith,* stated:

---

127. M.J. v. De Kalb County School Dist., 446 F 3d 1153 (11th Cir. 2006); Robb v. Bethel School Dist., 308 F.3d 1047 (9th Cir. 2002); N.B. v. Alachua County School Bd., 84 F.3d 1376 (11th Cir. 1996) (IDEA and §1983 claim can be brought, but needed to exhaust IDEA procedures to proceed); Urban v. Jefferson County School Dist., 89 F.3d 720 (10th Cir. 1996) (court cited *Smith v. Robinson* for the similarities between Section 504 and IDEA); Mrs. C. v. Wheaton, 916 F.2d 69 (2d Cir. 1990) (failure to provide notice violated both IDEA and §504); Mrs. W. v. Tirozzi, 832 F.2d 748, 754–755 (2d Cir. 1987) (§1983 available for violations of IDEA); Board of Educ. v. Diamond, 808 F.2d 987, 994–95 (3d Cir. 1986) (reversing lower court dismissal of counterclaim seeking monetary damages); Fontenot v. Louisiana Bd. of Elementary and Secondary Educ., 805 F.2d 1222, 1223 (5th Cir. 1986) (approving award of attorneys' fees for success on substantive merits); Cudjoe v. Independent School Dist., 297 F.3d 1055 (10th Cir. 2002) (required to exhaust administrative remedies before seeking claims in damages under §1983 in civil suit); Frith v. Galeton Area School Dist., 900 F. Supp. 706 (M.D. Pa. 1995) (still must exhaust administrative before bringing §1983 action); Doe v. Alfred, 906 F. Supp. 1092 (S.D. W. Va. 1995); Howell v. Waterford Pub. Schools, 731 F. Supp. 1314 (E.D. Mich. 1990); G.C. v. Coler, 673 F. Supp. 1093 (S.D. Fla. 1987).

128. 900 F.2d 804 (5th Cir. 1990); *see also* Moore v, Willis, 283 F3d 871,(5th Cir. 2000); Cunningham v. Beavers, 858 F.2d 269 (5th Cir. 1988); Brown v. Johnson, 710 F. Supp. 183 (E.D. Ky. 1989).

129. The court relied upon the United States Supreme Court decision in Ingraham v. Wright, 430 U.S. 651, 673 (1977).

130. Smith, 468 U.S. at 1014 n.17 ("maintenance of an independent due process challenge to state procedures would not be inconsistent with the EAHCA's comprehensive scheme"). *See* Beth v. Carroll, 876 F. Supp. 1415 (E.D. Pa. 1995) (plaintiff was without a private right of action to enforce EDGAR compliant and could not use §1983 to enforce Edgar complaint procedures).

131. *Id.*

132. 762 F.2d 912 (11th Cir. 1985).

where the local educational agency deprives a handicapped child of due process by effectively denying that child access to the heart of the EAHCA administrative machinery, the impartial due process hearing, an action may be brought under §1983.[133]

Procedural violations other than failure of authorities to hold a due process hearing are also recognized as grounds for relief under §1983. In *Rose v. Nebraska*,[134] plaintiff brought suit under §1983 and §504. Plaintiff claimed that, in violation of the Due Process Clause of the Fourteenth Amendment, the hearing procedures used by the state did not provide for an impartial hearing.

The district court in *Rose* granted an injunction and eventually awarded attorneys' fees for work done in securing the injunction. The Eighth Circuit held *Smith* should be read as recognizing that independent procedural claims are subject to §1983. Citing the Supreme Court's references in *Smith* that due process claims might appropriately be brought under §1983, the court held "that a §1983 suit and a fee award are appropriate when a plaintiff claims that he is being denied due process...."[135]

In *Teresa Diane P. v. Alief Independent School District*,[136] the parents alleged procedural violations "in notice, evaluation, consent, development of individualized educational plans, timing of meetings, and expulsion from services."[137] Relying on *Smith*, the Court held that "attorney's fees [premised on a violation of §1983] may be appropriate where procedural due process claims were effectively raised and maintained."[138]

Another important protection provided by §1983, that is independent of IDEA, is in the enforcement of due process hearing officer decisions. In *Reid v. Lincolnshire-Prairie View School District 103*,[139] the court held that IDEA did not provide a cause of action where the school system failed to implement an educational program ordered by the administrative hearing officer. The court held, however, that §1983 did provide for such a cause of action[140] as well as using §1983 for seeking enforcement of the orders in a settlement agreement.[141] The protection afforded by the ability to bring actions to enforce due process hearing decisions is, of course, critical to the ability of IDEA to function. The administrative proceedings mandated by IDEA would be ineffective protection since the LEA has precluded use of the administrative process.

1.7 Education Department General Administrative Regulations

The federal regulations originally promulgated under IDEA were explicit in requiring adoption of procedures for reviewing, investigating and acting on allegations of vio-

---

133. *Id.* at 919.
134. 748 F.2d 1258 (8th Cir. 1984); *see also* Stark v. Walter, 592 F. Supp. 785 (S.D. Ohio 1984).
135. 748 F.2d at 1263.
136. 744 F.2d 484 (5th Cir. 1984).
137. *Id.* at 491.
138. *Id.*
139. 765 F. Supp. 965 (N.D. Ill. 1991); *see also* Jeremy H. v. Mt. Lebanon School Dist., 95 F.3d 272, 279 (3d Cir. 1996); Olson v. Robbinsdale Area Schools, 2004 WL 121081 (D. Minn. 2004).
140. *See also* Robinson v. Pinderhughes, 810 F.2d 1270, 1273–74 (4th Cir. 1987).
141. B.H.Y. b/n/f/ Young v. La Pryor Ind. Sch., 2004 WL 2735193, (W.D. Tex. 2004).

lations of IDEA.[142] These regulations were superseded by the Education Division General Administration Regulations (EDGAR). These were general regulations applying to most grants and applicants of the United States Department of Education (DOE).[143] Coming full circle, the EDGAR regulations were in turn superseded in most respects by amendments to IDEA regulations.[144] EDGAR regulations continue to impose responsibilities for special education and related service delivery to children placed in private programs.[145]

1.8 Family Educational Rights and Privacy Act

The Family Educational Rights and Privacy Act (FERPA or the Buckley Amendments) provides general regulations on maintaining and disclosing educational records. IDEA requirements are generally more stringent than FERPA.[146]

142. 34 C.F.R. §300.602 (repealed).
143. 34 C.F.R. §76.780–.783 (repealed).
144. 34 C.F.R. §300.151. *See generally,*Weber v. Cranston School Committee, 212 F.3d 41, 45 n.3 (1st Cir. 2000). See Chapter 17.
145. 34 C.F.R. §76.651–76.663. See Chapter 8, § 8.10.1.
146. *See* Chapter 16.

Chapter 2

Parties to the Process

2.1 Parents and Child as Parties

The right of the parent and child to seek relief under IDEA is, of course, the purpose of the statute. Indeed, an important element in the procedural protection afforded under the Act is the right to parental participation at most stages of the educational process. As stated by the Supreme Court in *Hendrick Hudson Board of Education v. Rowley*,[1]

> It seems to us no exaggeration to say that Congress placed every bit as much emphasis upon compliance with procedures giving parents and guardians a large measure of participation at every stage of the administrative process ... as it did upon the measurement of the resulting IEP against a substantive standard.[2]

The importance the Supreme Court attached to parental involvement in the development of the IEP was well supported in the legislative history of IDEA. As the Senate Report stated prior to the 1999 amendments, "individualized planning conferences are a way to provide parent involvement and protection to assure that appropriate services are provided to a handicapped child."[3]

---

1. 458 U.S. 176, 205–206 (1981).

2. 458 U.S. 176, 205–206 (1981); *see also* Honig v. Doe, 484 U.S. 305, 311 (1988) ("the Act establishes various procedural safeguards that guarantee parents ... an opportunity for meaningful input into all decisions affecting their child's education...."); Cerra v. Pawling Cent. Sch. Dist, 427 F.3d 186 (2d Cir. 2005); (IDEA ensures parents *meaningful participation* during identification, evaluation, and educational placement of the child); Susquenita School Dist. v. Raelee S., 96 F.3d 78 (3d Cir. 1996) (court emphasizes protection of parental rights as important element of IDEA); DeVries v. Spillane, 853 F.2d 264, 266 (4th Cir. 1988) (parents to have "meaningful participation in all aspects"); *see generally* 34 C.F.R.300.305(a)(1); §300.306(a)(1) §300.324(a)(1) and §300.320; (formally in 1999 regs. §300.533(a)(1); §300.534(a)(1); §300.433(c)(iii); §§300.346(a)(1)(i) and (b); §300.347(a)(7).

3. S. Rep. No. 68, 94th Cong., 1st Sess. at 11–12, *quoted in* Rowley, 458 U.S. at 208–209; New House Report No. 105-95 at 79 states:

> The purposes of the Individual with Disabilities Education Act Amendments of 1997 were to clarify and strengthen the Individuals with Disabilities Education Act (IDEA) by providing parent and educators with the tools to: Preserve the right of children with disabilities to a free appropriate public education; Promote improved educational results for children with disabilities through early intervention, preschool, and educational experiences that prepare them for later educational challenges and employment; Expand and promote opportunities for parent, special education, related services, regular education, and early intervention service providers, and other personnel to work in new partnerships at both the State and local level; Create incentives to enhance the capacity of schools and other community-based entities to work effectively with children with disabilities and their

Federal regulations have a broad definition of parent. Under federal regulations, a parent is defined as "a parent, a foster parent, a guardian [or] a person acting in the place of a parent of a child...."[4] Thus, the definition of a parent includes persons acting in the place of a parent, such as a grandparent or stepparent or a relative with whom a child lives, as well as individuals who are legally responsible for a child's welfare.[5]

The 1999 regulations had clarified that a foster parent could be considered a parent under IDEA, but the educational rights of the natural parent had to be extinguished and the foster parent was required to have had a long-term relationship with the child. In addition the foster parent had to be willing to make educational decisions, and not have interests that conflicted with the child's interests.[6]

In the most recent regulations, effective in 2006, the prior conditions attached to being a foster parent were limited by prohibiting a foster parent from acting as parent only if state law, regulations or contractual obligations with state or local entities prohibits it.[7] In addition new, language clarifies that the biological or adoptive parents are presumed to be authorized to make educational decisions for the child even if other individuals also meet the definition of parent, unless a judicial order states specific individuals are to make the child's educational decisions.[8]

Congress provided "a generous bill of rights for parents, guardians, and surrogates of handicapped children who might wish to contest the evaluation and placement policies of educational authorities."[9] Prior to the 1999 regulations, these parental rights were perceived to be so strong that even after the child had attained the age of majority, the parent could have brought an action under all circumstances.[10] The 2006 regulations, limited, as did the 1999 regulations, the right of parents to bring an action on behalf of their child after the child reaches the age of majority. If state law transfers a disabled child's rights to the child at the age of majority, the parent may not bring the action after such time.[11] Of course, if the student is declared incompetent or the state has a mechanism to determine the student is unable to provide informed consent, the parent may be able to bring the action in a representative capacity the same as when any person is declared incompetent.[12]

---

families, through targeted funding for personnel training, research, media, technology, and the dissemination of technical assistance and best practices.
The House Report No. 105-95 at 82 also stated: "one of the ways the authorization hopes to improve the IDEA is by 'strengthening the role of the parents.'"

4. 34 C.F.R. §§ 300.20 and 300.30; *see also* 20 U.S.C. § 1401(23).

5. 34 C.F.R. § 300.20;300.30; *see also* 20 U.S.C. § 1401(23); *Letter to Serwecki*, 44 Individuals with Disabilities Educ. L. Rep. 8 (OSEP 2005) (parent advocate could "by invitation of parent" attend IEP meeting on behalf of father despite temporary restraining order preventing father from attending meeting in person); Letter to Ford 41 Individuals with Disabilities Educ. L. Rep. 10 (LRP) (OSEP 2003) (under 34 C.F.R. § 300.515, a public agency had the obligation to assign a surrogate parent); Ysleta Indep. School Dist., 29 Individuals with Disabilities Educ. L. Rep. (LRP) 1093 (SEA Tex. 1998) (guardian ad litem is not acting as a parent; appointment of surrogate is required).

6. Formerly 34 C.F.R. § 300.515(a)(1) and § 300.20 (1999 regs); *see also* formally 20 U.S.C. § 1401(19)(1997).

7. 34 C.F.R § 300.30.

8. 34 C.F.R § 300.30.

9. Stemple v. Board of Educ., 623 F.2d 893, 898 (4th Cir. 1980).

10. Kiser v. Garret, 67 F.3d 1166 (5th Cir. 1995); Vander Malle v. Ambach, 673 F.2d 49 (2d Cir. 1982); John H. v. MacDonald, 558 Educ. Handicapped L. Rep. (CRR) 366 (D.N.H. 1987).

11. 34 C.F.R. § 300.520(a) formerly 34 C.F.R. §§ 300.517(3)(b) (1999); *see also* 20 U.S.C. § 1415(m).

12. 34 C.F.R. § 300.520(a)(1)(i)(ii) formerly 34 C.F.R. § 300.517(a)(1)(i)(ii) (1999); 20 U.S.C. § 1415(m).

If the state chooses to transfer parental rights to the child upon reaching the age of majority, the public agency retains the obligation to provide notice of the procedural safeguards to both the student and parent. All other rights transfer to the student.[13] Rights also transfer to students who are incarcerated in correctional institutions at the age of majority.[14] Where a student has not been determined to be incompetent, yet does not have the ability to provide informed consent, the state is required to have procedures to appoint the parent to represent the educational interests of the child.[15]

The IDEA allowed parents to bring suit on behalf of their children, but the Circuits were split as to whether or not to allow the parents to represent their children in court.[16] In 2007, the Supreme Court resolved the issue. In *Winkelman by Winkelman v. Parma City School District,*[17] the Court held that because parents enjoy rights under IDEA, they are entitled to prosecute IDEA claims on their own behalf. The Court wisely rejected the notion that parents' rights under IDEA were limited to specific procedural and reimbursement related issues. Now parents without an attorney can challenge in court the disagreements over substantive issues under IDEA.

Where parents are divorced, the question of which parent exercises rights under IDEA is a question of state law and the judicial order in the divorce.[18] Typically, if the parents have joint custody, both parents enjoy equal rights.[19] State law, however, governs which district is responsible for providing services when the parents have joint custody.[20]

---

13. 34 C.F.R. § 300.520(a)(2); 34 C.F.R.§ 300.517(a)(2)(1999); 20 U.S.C. § 1415(m).

14. 34 C.F.R. § 300.520(a)(2); formerly § 300.517(a)(2) (1999); 20 U.S.C. § 1415(m); *see generally,* Paul Y. v. Singletary, 979 F. Supp. 1422, 1426–27 (D. Fla. 1997) (rights of incarcerated student do not transfer until they have reached the age of majority).

15. 34 C.F.R. § 300.520(b); formerly 34 C.F.R. 34 C.F.R. § 517(3)(b); 20 U.S.C. § 1415(m).

16. Maroni v. Pemi-Baker Reg'l Sch. Dist., 346 F.3d 247 (1st Cir. 2003) (distinguishing Collinsgru v. Palmyra Bd. of Educ., 161 F.3d 225 (3d Cir. 1998), noting a distinction in "substantive" versus "procedural rights" under IDEA and holding that a parent can represent their child pro se when seeking enforcement of either substantive or procedural rights). *But see* Cavanaugh v. Cardinal Local Sch. Dist., 409 F.3d 753 (6th Cir. 2005) (parents may not represent their child's interests in federal court, but only in administrative proceedings); Tindall v. Poultney High Sch. Dist. 414 F.3d 281 (2d Cir. 2005) (rules of the Second Circuit prevent parents from representing their minor child *pro se*); Devine v. Indian River County, 121 F.3d 576 (11th Cir. 1997) (non attorney parent cannot act as counsel).

17. 127 S.Ct. 1994 (2007) (IDEA grants parents independent enforceable rights). See § 15.4 for a discussion of attorney-parents' attempts to obtain attorneys' fees.

18. In *Taylor v. Vt. Dep't of Educ.,* 313 F.3d 768, 777 (2d Cir. 2002), the court, holding that Vermont domestic law is controlling when determining whether a non-custodial parent has standing to bring claim under IDEA stated:

> It seems plain that Congress drew the procedural and substantive contours of education for disabled children, but left the shading and tinting of the details largely to the states. States are responsible for filling in the numerous interstices within the federal Act through their own statutes and regulations.

See also Navin v. Park Ridge Sch. Dist. 64, 270 F.3d 1147, 1149 (7th Cir. 2001) *additionally, on remand* Navin v. Park Ridge Sch. Dist. 64, 36 Individuals with Disabilities Educ. L. Rep. (LRP) 235 (non-custodial parent retains Due Process rights under IDEA, but parent's input as to the educational placement of the child is only relevant to the extent that it was in concert with the custodial parent).

19. Rockaway Township Bd. of Educ., 43 Individuals with Disabilities Educ. L. Rep. (LRP) 80 (SEA N.J. 2005) (mother's unilateral consent to classify student as special education eligible was invalid under the terms of divorce decree that required agreement between both parents); *see also* Arnold Inquiry, 211 Educ. Handicapped L. Rep. (CRR) 297 (EHA 1983).

20. *See* North Allegheny School Dist. v. Gregory P., 25 Individuals with Disabilities Educ. L. Rep. (LRP) 297 (Pa. Commw. Ct. 1996) (where custody placed student out of district part-time,

2.2 Effect of Termination of Parental Custody

Courts are split on the right of a parent to be involved in decision-making under IDEA after the parents have lost temporary custody of their child. For example, courts have held that the surrogate parent is to represent the interests of the child. Other courts, however, have held that parents have independent standing to challenge the educational placement even where temporary custody was awarded to the state. In *In the Interest of J.D.*,[21] for example, the Florida District Court stated:

> Finally, assuming proper adjudication of dependency and proper participation by the surrogate parent, we reiterate our strong disagreement with appellees' position that the surrogate usurps altogether the parent's role in deciding the child's educational placement. Such an argument runs counter to the "historical recognition that freedom of personal choice in matters of family life is a fundamental liberty interest protected by the Fourteenth Amendment."[22]

The Florida court's opinion is consistent with the position taken by courts that the parent and child each have separate, but related, rights under IDEA.

In *Susan R.M. v. Northeastern Independent School District*,[23] however, the father obtained appointment of the Department of Human services as the "managing conservator" of the child in order to facilitate placement in a state institution. The Fifth Circuit held that the father no longer had standing, since state law provided that only the conservator may bring suit on behalf of the child. The court also stated that when the child turned 18 and the conservatorship thereby ended, neither the father nor the state would have custody. The father, therefore, would not have independent standing to bring an action to protect the child's educational rights. After 18, the father's involvement would be limited to appointment as "next friend" under Federal Rule of Civil Procedure 17(c).[24]

The court's decision in *Susan R.M.* seems ill advised. While perhaps the result of the fact that the father was proceeding *pro se*, the opinion made reference to IDEA only to state that the underlying cause of action arose under it. No mention was made of the

---

school not obligated to provide transportation to out of district residence where transportation not required for special education); *see also* Linda W. v. Indiana Dept. of Educ., 24 Individuals with Disabilities Educ. L. Rep. (LRP) 651 (N.D. Ind. 1996); Letter to Biondi, 291 Individuals with Disabilities Educ. L. Rep. (LRP) 972 (OSEP 1997).

21. 510 So. 2d 623 (Fla. Dist. Ct. of App. 1987), *quoting* Santosky v. Kramer, 455 U.S. 745, 753 (1982).

22. *Id.* at 629; *see also* Kiser v. Garret, 67 F.3d 1166 (5th Cir. 1995) (natural parent's desire for and right to the companionship, care, custody, and management of his or her children is an interest more precious than any property right); W.T. v. Andalusia City Schools, 977 F. Supp. 1437 (M.D. Ala. 1997) (non-custodial parent can assert educational rights of her child).

23. 818 F.2d 455 (5th Cir. 1987); *but see* Collinsgru v. Palmyra Bd. of Educ., 161 F.3d 225 (3d Cir. 1998) (parent not allowed to represent child *pro se* in federal court).

24. Fed. R. Civ. P. 17(c) provides:

> Whenever an infant or incompetent person has a representative, such as a general guardian, committee, conservator, or other like fiduciary, the representative may sue or defend on behalf of the infant or incompetent person. An infant or incompetent person who does not have a duly appointed representative may sue by a next friend or by a guardian ad litem. The court shall appoint a guardian ad litem for an infant or incompetent person not otherwise represented in an action or shall make such other order as it deems proper for the protection of the infant or incompetent person.

definition of the parent or of the special role and individual rights accorded the parent under IDEA.

2.3 Surrogate Parents in General

IDEA has, as a central theme, the involvement of the parents in virtually every major decision affecting the education of their child. If the child, for one reason or another, does not have a parent or the parent cannot be located, the educational agency is responsible for appointing a surrogate parent.

Specifically, the educational agency must appoint a surrogate where either no parent can be identified, the agency after reasonable efforts cannot find the parent, or the child is, under the laws of the state, a ward of the state or the child is an unaccompanied homeless youth under the McKinney Vento Homeless Assistance Act.[25] The surrogate's responsibilities are to represent the child in all matters relating to identification, evaluation, and educational placement, as well as matters relating to the provision of a free appropriate public education.[26] The surrogate has all the rights and responsibilities of a parent under Part B of IDEA.

The agency may select the surrogate in any manner allowed by state law,[27] however, the surrogate must have no interest that conflicts with that of the child, and the surrogate must have knowledge and skills to insure the child is adequately represented.[28] Further, a surrogate may not be an employee of a public agency that is involved in the education or care of the child.[29] For homeless children employees of agencies such as emergency shelters and transitional homes may be appointed as a surrogate temporarily until a surrogate is found. In addition, the public agency must take reasonable efforts to appoint a surrogate within 30 days after such a need is determined.[30]

Section 504 and its regulations also require the appointment of surrogate parents.[31]

---

25. 34 C.F.R. §300.519 (a); *see* 20 U.S.C. §1415(b)(2); Letter to Tate, 25 Individuals with Disabilities Educ. L. Rep. (LRP) 512 (OSEP 1996) (violation of IDEA for a state department of education to direct districts to evaluate students who await appointment of surrogate parents for consent purposes); *see also* Georgia Dept. of Educ., 20 Individuals with Disabilities Educ. L. Rep. (LRP) 29 (OSEP 1993); Letter to Thompson, 23 Individuals with Disabilities Educ. L. Rep. (LRP) 890 (OSEP 1995).

26. 34 C.F.R. §300.519(g); *see* 20 U.S.C. §1415(b)(2); *see generally* Doe v. Alabama State Dept. of Educ., 915 F.2d 651 (11th Cir. 1990) (procedural violation where surrogate not notified of denial of FAPE); Abney v. District of Columbia, 849 F.2d 1491 (D.C. Cir. 1988) (procedural violation where surrogate parent was not provided notice of change in programming).

27. 34 C.F.R. §300.519(d)(1); *see* 20 U.S.C. §1415(b)(2).

28. 34 C.F.R. §300.519(d)(2)(iii); *see* 20 U.S.C. §1415(b)(2); *see also* Letter to Copenhaver, 29 Individuals with Disabilities Educ. L. Rep. (LRP) 1091 (OSEP 1997) (may remove surrogate when there is a conflict of interest or where necessary knowledge and skills are lacking, not because surrogate disagrees with the public agency over a FAPE); *but see* Scott M. v. Governor Wentworth Regional School Dist., 26 Individuals with Disabilities Educ. L. Rep. (LRP) 1012 (D.N.H. 1997) (parent could not serve as next friend due to financial conflict of interest).

29. 34 C.F.R. §§300.519(d)(3) and (e). Receiving money for acting as a surrogate does not make the surrogate an employee of the agency.

30. 34 C.F.R. §300.519(h).

31. United States Department of Education Administrative Policy Manual for the Program for Exceptional Children and Youth, Bulletin No. 26, *quoted in* Alabama Dept. of Educ. Complaint Let-

2.3.1 The State and Its Employees as Surrogate Parents

IDEA regulations provide that a surrogate may not be an employee of a public agency that is involved in the education or care of the child.[32] When the child is in the custody of the state, the public agency responsible for the care of the child, such as the department of human services or the department of corrections, may not, therefore, appoint one of its employees as surrogate. The 1997 and 1999 IDEA regulations had a provision that the public agency could, however, select a person who was an employee of a non-public agency that did not provide educational care for the child. This language does not appear in the 2006 regulations.[33]

2.4 Foster Parents in General

Under the federal 2005 regulations, a state may continue to allow a foster parent to act as a parent, unless specifically prohibited by state law, regulations or contractual obligations.[34] Foster parents are no longer required to meet the criteria established in the 1999 regulations that included the provision that the natural parents' rights had to be terminated and the foster parent had to have an ongoing long-term relationship with the child,[35] that the foster parent could not have had interests that interfered with the child, and that the foster parent had to be willing to make educational decisions on behalf of the child.[36] Thus, there is no need to appoint a surrogate for all children in foster care, and, indeed, appointment of a surrogate would be improper.[37]

2.4.1 Foster Parents as Surrogate Parents

The LEA must appoint a surrogate where no parent can be identified, the agency after reasonable efforts cannot find the parent, the child is a ward of the state, or the child is homeless.[38]

---

ter of Finding (January 24, 1990), *reprinted in* 16 Educ. Handicapped L. Rep. (LRP) 475 (January 20, 1990).

32. 34 C.F.R. §§ 300.519(d)(2)(i). Receiving money for acting as a surrogate does not make the surrogate an employee of the agency. *Id.* Letter to Yudien, 38 Individuals with Disabilities Law Rep. 245 (LRP) (OSEP 2003).

33. 34 CFR 300. 519; formerly 34 C.F.R. § 300.515(c)(3) (1999 regulations).

34. 23 C.F.R. 300.30(a)(2).

35. 34 C.F.R. § 300.20(b)(1)(2).300.30.

36. Language contained in former 34 C.F.R. §§ 300.20(b)(2)(ii) and 300.30.

37. *See* Converse County School Dist. No. Two v. Pratt, 993 F. Supp. 848 (D. Wy. 1997) (foster parents were persons acting as parent under federal regulations). Prior to the 1997 and 1999 amendments, whether foster parents were parents for the purposes of IDEA depended in large part on the relative permanency of the foster care placement. In Criswell v. State Dept. of Educ., 558 Educ. Handicapped L. Rep. (CRR) 156 (M.D. Tenn. 1986), the court held that "permanent foster parents" who had been caring for a child for eight years clearly fell within the definition of parents, and therefore it was improper to appoint a surrogate parent to make educational decisions.

38. 34 C.F.R. § 300.519(a)(1–4); *see* 20 U.S.C. § 1415(b)(2).

Although a foster parent can clearly serve as a parent, a separate question remains whether they may be appointed as a surrogate parent. Foster parents particularly short term parents may find themselves in conflict between the demand of the state agency appointing them, typically a social or human services department, and their advocacy of their child's rights.

The social or human services department itself may not act as surrogate.[39] Placing someone dependent on such an agency for continued support in their role as foster parent may, therefore, defeat the intended isolation of the surrogate from the state agency contemplated under IDEA. Further, to the extent the foster care parent receives any compensation from the social or human services department, the state agency must conduct a determination of whether there is a conflict of interest.[40] OSEP has indicated that foster parents who are paid may serve as surrogates, if they are otherwise qualified.[41]

The countervailing argument, of course, is that 1) foster care parents with long term relationships may find themselves in the same position concerning pressure from the social or human services department, 2) the conflict that does exist, if any, is no greater than the inherent conflict of a LEA appointing the surrogate who then may feel pressure when it comes to deciding, for example, whether to request a due process hearing for the child.

To the extent that a surrogate fails to represent the interests of the child adequately, Federal Rule of Civil Procedure 17 would allow an interested person to seek to protect the child's interest.[42]

2.5 The LEA as a Party

As a general principle, the parents proceed against the local educational agency (LEA) responsible for the direct provision of educational services if they have any complaint or disagreement.[43] The LEA also has the right to seek administrative and judicial review of educational decision-making.[44] The LEA does not, however, have a right to sue the state for failure to implement its statutory duties.[45]

---

39. *See* § 2.3.1.

40. Letter to Thompson, 23 Individuals with Disabilities Educ. L. Rep. (LRP) 890 (OSEP 1995).

41. Letter to Thompson, 23 Individuals with Disabilities Educ. L. Rep. (LRP) 890 (OSEP 1995) (foster parent may be surrogate parent); *see also* Converse County School Dist. No. Two v. Pratt, 993 F. Supp. 848 (1997) (appointment of a foster parent is fact specific, but where federal and state regulations conflict, federal regulations control; no surrogate appointment necessary because foster parent was acting as parent).

42. *See* § 2.2; Letter to Copenhaver, 29 Individuals with Disabilities Educ. L. Rep. (LRP) 1091 (OSEP 1997) (cannot remove surrogate over disagreement with a FAPE).

43. *But see* Tschanneral v. District of Columbia Bd. of Educ., 594 F. Supp. 407 (D.D.C. 1984) (in the District of Columbia, the proper entity is *not* the Board of Education but any suit to recover money must be against the District of Columbia, based on a D.C. statute,).

44. 34 C.F.R. § 300.507(a)(1); 20 U.S.C. § 1415(b)(6).

45. Lawrence Twp. Bd. of Educ. v. New Jersey, 417 F.3d 368 (3d Cir. 2003); County of Westchester v. New York, 286 F.3d 150, 152 (2d Cir. 2002).

2.5.1 Determining the Appropriate LEA Against Whom to Proceed (Residency)

Under both IDEA and § 504, the residency of the child determines which agency has responsibility for providing a FAPE.[46] The IDEA 2004 does not define residency. Therefore it is generally defined under state law. Residence requires physical presence and an intent to remain.[47] For most children, this test is easily applied and a child will be considered a resident of the district in which the child and parent are physically present. Further, it is clear that where a child is placed outside the district for educational reasons, either by the LEA or unilaterally by the parents, the residency remains that of the parents and does not shift to the locality of the placement.[48]

The difficulty arises when the parent and child live in different districts for some non-educational reason. Many states have statutes that provide that the child's residence is that of the parent's. It has been held, therefore, that when a child is placed in a district other than where the parents reside, the district in which the child is placed does not have an obligation to provide educational programming.[49]

Statutes that mandate that a child's residence is always that of the parent are constitutionally suspect. In *Steven M. v. Gilhool,*[50] a class action was brought on constitutional grounds challenging the Pennsylvania state law that provided "[a] child shall be considered a resident of the school district in which his parents ... reside...." The action was

46. 20 U.S.C. § 1401(3)(a); 34 C.F.R. § 300.111; 34 C.F.R. § 104.33(a); *See* Manchester School Dist. v. Crisman, 306 F.3d 1 (1st Cir. 2002) (residency is a question of state law and the facts holding the state where the child was domiciled and not the district of her residence of her out of state parents financially responsible); *but see* Wise v. Ohio Dept. of Educ., 80 F.3d 177 (6th Cir. 1996) (state not required to pay special education costs of student whose parents were not residents); Letter to McAllister, 21 Individuals with Disabilities Educ. L. Rep. (LRP) 81 (OSEP 1994) (residence creates the duty under the statute and regulations, not the location of the child or school).

47. Martinez v. Bynum, 461 U.S. 321, 331 (1982); Caitlin v. Sobel, 93 F.3d 1112, 1119 (2d Cir. 2002); Roxbury Township Board of Educ. v. West Milford Board of Educ., 662 A.2d 976 (N.J. 1995); Trenton Pub. Schools, 47 Individuals with Disabilities Law Educ. L. Rep. (LRP) 177 (SEA MI 2006) (Michigan ED defines residency as physical presence in the district with intent to remain).

48. Manchester Sch. Dist. v. Crisman, 306 F.3d 1 (1st Cir. 2002) (school district in which the disabled child most recently lived prior to placement in residential institution remained responsible for the costs of the child's special education programming, regardless of the child's legal residency); School Dist. No. 153 Cook County v. School Dist. No. 154 1/2, 54 Ill. App. 3d 587, 370 N.E.2d 22 (1977) (LEA where mother resided had responsibility, not LEA where child resided in state institution); George H. and Irene L. Walker Home for Children, Inc. v. Town of Franklin, 621 N.E.2d 376 (Mass. 1993) (father's municipality was not held liable for any cost of residential placement when son resided with the mother and the father only visited the student).

49. 5. *See, e.g.,* Joshua W. v. Board of Educ. of Wichita Public Schools, 13 F. Supp. 2d 1199 (D. Kan. 1998), *affirmed by* Joshua W. v. USD 259 Bd. of Educ, 211 F.3d 1278 (10th Cir. 2000) (table unpublished opinion) (not required to provide services for student who was not living in district at the time parent sought to enroll him); *see also* Wise v. Ohio Dept. of Education, 80 F.3d 177 (6th Cir. 1996) (state statute that requires the state to seek reimbursement from private facilities for the cost of providing services to children who live in the facility, but whose parents reside outside the state, does not conflict with IDEA); Board of Educ. of Community Unit School Dist. No. 428 v. Board of Educ. of High School Dist. No. 214, 26 Individuals with Disabilities Educ. L. Rep. (LRP) 12 (Ill. 1997) (district where natural parents resided, not foster parents, must fund special education program and state law defines place of residence where natural parent/guardians reside). Letter to State Directors of Special Education, 44 Individuals Educa. L. Rep. (LRP) 46 (OSEP 2005).

50. 700 F. Supp. 261 (E.D. Pa. 1988).

brought on behalf of school-age children in "children's institutions" who were being charged tuition by local school systems if their parents lived out of state. The court held that the Pennsylvania statute created an invalid, irrebuttable presumption. The court enjoined defendants from denying residency status solely on the fact that a parent's residence was outside the district where the child lived and attended school. The court held that plaintiffs must be given an opportunity to establish that they are residents of the district in which they live.

The United States Supreme Court has upheld as a *bona fide* residency test whether the child's presence in the district is for the primary purpose of attending public schools. If the presence of the child in-district is for primarily educational purposes, the district may treat the residency as that of the out-of-district parents.[51] Where, however, a child is placed in a non-educational institution, as a general rule the locality in which the institution is situated will have responsibility for educating the child.[52] Where a child is placed in a psychiatric hospital for only a short time, however, the location of the hospital does not constitute the residence of the child.[53]

Absent a statute to the contrary, the residency of a child in the custody of a state or local agency should be based on the residence of the child's foster parents. State law should be checked. It is common for the state to assume the obligation to educate children within state facilities,[54] or specifically to identify which local agency has responsibility for educating children in the custody of social or human services departments.[55]

Where the child has been placed by the parents in the care of another, the motivation for the parents placing the child in another district should be determinative. Where the natural parents place a child with "foster" parents for primarily non-educational reasons, the district in which the child is living may be considered the child's residence.[56]

---

51. Martinez v. Bynum, 461 U.S. 321, 323 (1982); *see also* J.A. v. Board of Educ. for Dist. of South Orange and Maplewood, 723 A.2d 1270 (N.J. 1999) (student entitled to a FAPE in the school district where her aunt lived since student could not live with her mother).

52. The People v. D.D. (*In re D.D.*), 819 N.E.2d 300 (Ill. 2004) (under Illinois law, school district is not financially responsible for student's residential placement in an out-of-state facility when the school district was not involved in the placement); Mills Inquiry, 213 Educ. Handicapped L. Rep. (CRR) 139 (OCR 1988).

53. Hall v. Freeman, 700 F. Supp. 1106 (N.D. Ga. 1987).

54. *See, e.g.*, In re Children Residing at St. Aloysius Home, 556 A.2d 552 (R.I. 1989); Doe v. Sanders, 189 Ill. App. 3d 572, 545 N.E.2d 454 (1989).

55. *See, e.g.*, In Re Juvenile 2004-789-A, 2006 N.H. Lexis 34, p.17 (N.H. 2006) (under New Hampshire law, when a child is in the legal custody of a state social services department the agency responsible for educational expenses is the one that the child most recently actually lived, rather than legal residence or domicile); Brentwood Union Free School Dist. v. Ambach, 495 N.Y.S.2d 513, 115 A.D.2d 147 (N.Y. Sup. Ct. 1985) (under New York law, agency responsible for child in custody of social services is agency in which student last resided before placement in custody of social services).

56. Rabinowitz v. New Jersey State Bd. of Educ., 550 F. Supp. 481 (D.N.J. 1982) (New York natural parents placed child with New Jersey foster parents; residence of foster parent was residence of child); *but see* Caitlin v. Sobol, 93 F.3d 1112, 1119 (2d Cir. 1996) (The traditional test for residency requires both physical presence and intent to remain. Where the residency of the child is different from the parents, the court held that the residency statute did not violate the due process clause. Court also held that the IDEA and Rehabilitation Act did not require the school district in which the handicapped child was boarded, which was different from the residence of the child's parents, to provide the student with a free public education); Board of Educ. of Comm. Unit School Dist. No. 428 v. Board of Educ. of High School Dist. No. 214, 680 N.E.2d 450 (Ill. App. 1997) (state law governs).

Several OSEP opinions have clarified the issue of a student's residence when the parents have moved.[57]

If a child changes residency during the administrative or court proceedings, the action becomes moot.[58]

2.6 The State as a Party Defendant

In determining the obligation of the state to the parents, a distinction must be drawn between the ability of the parents to force the state to provide direct services and the ability of the parents to seek reimbursement or some other form of damages from the state. Prospective injunctive relief is available from the state.[59] Damages are possibly available against the state.[60] For a full discussion of the ability to bring an action against the state see Chapter 14.

2.7 The State as a Plaintiff

For a discussion of the state educational agencies' role, see Chapter 17.

2.8 Third-Party Interests

As with any law suit, the action may be commenced only by a real party in interest who has been aggrieved. For example, an insurer lacks standing to seek reimbursement under IDEA from a school system for monies it has paid.[61] A parent may also lack

---

57. Letter to State Directors of Special Education, 44 Individuals Educa. L. Rep. (LRP) 46 (OSEP 2005); Board of Education of the Town of Bozrah v. State Bd. of Educ., 19 Individuals with Disabilities Educ. L. Rep. (LRP) 1002 (Conn. App. Ct. 1993) (whether local board or state board was responsible for the special education costs of student who was placed in foster care was governed by state law pertaining to the duties of school boards to provide special education, rather than the state law governing school privilege for nonresident children); Letter to Best, 30 Individuals with Disabilities Educ. L. Rep. (LRP) 145 (OSEP 1998) (states can designate which district is responsible where a student lives in a different district with someone other than a custodial parent); Letter to Reedy, 30 Individuals with Disabilities Educ. L. Rep. (LRP) 268 (1998) (state law determines which agency must provide FAPE to student in foster care); Letter to Moody, 23 Individuals with Disabilities Educ. L. Rep. (LRP) 833 (OSEP 1995) (student's residence became that of the parents once they moved, and the new state was responsible for seeing that the student received a FAPE).

58. Rowe v. Henry County School Board, 718 F.2d 115 (4th Cir. 1983); Monahan v. Nebraska, 687 F.2d 1164, 1168 (8th Cir. 1982); *but see* Grand Rapids Pub. Sch. v. P.C., 308 F. Supp. 2d 815 (W.D. Mich. 2004) (movement from school district does not render moot a request for an IDEA due process hearing when there are legitimate claims for relief that survives the move).

59. *See* § 14.2.1.

60. *See* § 14.6.

61. Gehman v. Prudential Property and Casualty Ins. Co., 702 F. Supp. 1192 (E.D. Pa. 1989); Allstate Ins. Co. v. Bethlehem Area School Dist., 678 F. Supp. 1132 (E.D. Pa. 1987) (court raised lack of standing *sua sponte*); Tennessee Protection and Advocacy, Inc. v. Board of Educ. of Putnam County, Tenn., 24 F. Supp. 2d 808 (M.D. Tenn. 1998) (a protection and advocacy system did not

standing to bring an action against an LEA to collect for insurance monies expended when there is no cost the parents.[62] Also, since IDEA is designed to provide protection and services to parents and children, local educational agencies do not have standing to sue state agencies to compel a state agency to perform its statutory obligations.[63]

have standing to sue on behalf of disabled people in general, but would have had standing to sue on behalf of specific individuals); *but see* Family and Children's Center, Inc. v. School City of Mishawaka, 13 F.3d 1052 (7th Cir. 1994) (private service provider had standing); Farmer's Insurance Exchange v. South Lyon Community Schools, 602 N.W.2d 588 (Mich. Ct. App. 1999) (insurance company had standing to seek judicial determination of district's responsibility for payments at issue based on state law, despite its lack of standing to seek administrative determination under IDEA).

62. Emery v. Roanoke City Sch. Bd., 432 F.3d 294 (4th Cir. 2005) (parent of disabled child did not have standing to sue LEA for reimbursement for monies paid entirely by Parent's insurance resulting in no cost to parent).

63. Andrews v. Ledbetter, 880 F.2d 1287 (11th Cir. 1989); *see* Lawrence Twp. Bd. of Educ. v. New Jersey, 417 F.3d 368 (3d Cir. 2003) and County of Westchester v. New York, 286 F.3d 150, 152 (2d Cir. 2002) (each holding that a LEA does not have standing or private right of action to bring a suit to compel a state agency to fulfill statutory duties); *but see* Board of Educ. of Oak Park and River Forest H.S. Dist. No. 2000 v. Kelly E., 207 F.3d 931 (7th Cir. 2000) (school district has standing to seek reimbursement).

Chapter 3

Provision of a Free Appropriate Education

3.1 Introduction

IDEA requires a state receiving funds to demonstrate that it "has in effect a policy that assures all children with disabilities the right to a free appropriate education"[1] (FAPE). IDEA requires provision of these educational services between the ages of five and eighteen in all cases, and between the ages of three and twenty-one in most cases. The requirement is a blanket one and affects, for example, children who are suspended or expelled from school,[2] children who are incarcerated,[3] children who attend charter schools[4] or children who cannot be transported to school because of medical reasons.[5]

Since 1999, IDEA regulations have specifically excluded children with disabilities from participating in state and district assessment programs if they were convicted as adults and incarcerated in adult prison.[6] In addition, transition planning and transition services do not apply to children with disabilities in prisons if, because of their age their eligibility would end before they are released from prison.[7] The meaning of the phrase "free appropriate education" was first addressed by the United States Supreme Court in *Hendrick Hudson District Board of Education v. Rowley*.[8] Any analysis of whether a school system is meeting its statutory obligation must begin with a consideration of that case. In *Rowley*, the Court identified two areas of inquiry in determining whether a state has met its requirements under IDEA:

> [A] court's inquiry in suits brought under § 1415(i)(B)(2) is twofold. First has the State complied with the procedures set forth in the Act? And second, is the

---

1. 34 C.F.R. § 300.101(a); *see also* 20 U.S.C. § 1412(A)(1)(a).
2. 34 C.F.R. § 300.101(a).
3. Handberry v. Thompson, 436 F.3d 52 (2d Cir. 2006) (IDEA requires State Department of Corrections to provide FAPE to identified children within their custody); Green v. Johnson, 513 F. Supp. 965 (D. Mass. 1981); *see also* 20 U.S.C. § 1414(d)(6).
4. 20 U.S.C. § 1413(a)(5); Idea Pub. Charter Sch. v. Belton, 2006 WL 667072 (D.D.C. 2006) (District of Columbia charter school, who elected to be its own LEA was required to provide FAPE for special education students).
5. Abney v. District of Columbia, 849 F.2d 1491 (D.C. Cir. 1988).
6. 34 C.F.R. § 300.320(a)(6); *see also* Letter to Anonymous, 30 Individuals with Disabilities Educ. L. Rep. (LRP) 607 (OSEP 1998).
7. 34 C.F.R. § 300.320(b).
8. 458 U.S. 176 (1981).

individualized educational program developed through the Act's procedures reasonably calculated to enable the child to receive educational benefits? If these requirements are met, the State has complied with the obligations imposed by Congress and the courts can require no more.[9]

It is useful, therefore to view the provision of a FAPE as both a procedural right and a substantive right. Failure to provide either right results in a violation of IDEA.

3.2 Provision of a FAPE as a Procedural Right in General

Congress was explicit in articulating specific procedural protections to be afforded by IDEA. The extensive procedural protections include parental consent or involvement in most decisions affecting the child's educational program.[10] Indeed, the requirement of "meaningful input into all decisions affecting their child's education ..." was reaffirmed by the United States Supreme Court in *Honig v. Doe*.[11] The Court also stated:

> Envisioning the IEP as the centerpiece of the statute's education delivery system for disabled children, and aware that schools had all too often denied such children appropriate educations without in any way consulting their parents, Congress repeatedly emphasized throughout the Act the importance and indeed the necessity of parental participation in both the development of the IEP and any subsequent assessment of its effectiveness.[12]

The United States Supreme Court has recognized that these procedural rights are as important as the substantive rights accorded under IDEA:

> When the elaborate and highly specific procedural safeguards embodied in §1415 are contrasted with the general and somewhat imprecise substantive admonitions contained in the Act, we think that the importance Congress attached to these procedural safeguards cannot be gainsaid. It seems to us no ex-

---

9. *Id.* at 206–207; *see also* Twp. Board of Educ. High School Dist. No. 211 v. Ross, 486 F.3d 267 (7th Cir. 2007); Cerra v. Pawling Central School Dist. 427 F.3d 186 (2d Cir. 2005); Lt. T.B. v. Warwick School Committee, 36 F.3d 80 (1st Cir. 2004); D.F. v. Ramapo Cent. Sch. Dist., 430 F.3d 595 (2d Cir. 2005) (valid IEP should provide for the opportunity for more than "trivial" advancement and must be evaluated as of the time the CSE devised the IEP to determine if it was reasonably calculated to confer educational benefits); Cavanagh v. Grasmick, 75 F. Supp. 2d 446 (D. Md. 1999) (IEP reasonably calculated to confer educational benefit); *see generally* Wagner v. Short, 63 F. Supp. 2d 672 (D. Md. 1999) (reasonably calculated to provide "developmental" benefit is proper analysis for IFSP).

10. 34 C.F.R. §300.300; *see also* 20 U.S.C §§1415(b)(3), 1414(a)(1)(D) and (c). IDEA 1997 and 1999 regulations strengthened this participation by permitting the parent to be part of the eligibility and placement process. *See generally* 34 C.F.R. §§300.304, .322, .324.

11. 484 U.S. 305 (1988); *see also* 34 C.F.R. §300.504.

12. Honig, 484 U.S. at 311; *see also* Deal v. Hamilton County Bd. of Educ. 392 F.3d 840 (6th Cir. 2004) (predetermination of placement effectively deprived student's parents of meaningful participation in individualized education program process, causing substantive harm and depriving student of free appropriate public education); *but see* Bradley v. Arkansas Dep't. of Educ., 443 F.3d 965 (8th Cir. 2006) ("IDEA does not require that parental preferences be implemented, so long as the IEP is reasonably calculated to provide some educational benefit"); Christen G. v. Lower Merion School Dist., 919 F. Supp. 793 (E.D. Pa. 1996) (IEP was appropriate even though it contained emotional support elements which the mother did not believe was necessary).

aggeration to say that Congress placed every bit as much emphasis upon compliance with procedures giving parents and guardians a large measure of participation at every stage of the administrative process … as it did upon the measurement of the resulting IEP against a substantive standard.[13]

3.3 Provision of a FAPE as a Substantive Right in General

Congress was much less specific in defining a FAPE on a substantive level than it was in defining it on a procedural level. IDEA provides that a FAPE:

> means "special education and related services that (a) are provided at public expense, under public supervision and direction, and without charge; (b) meet the standards of the SEA … ; (c) include preschool, elementary school, or secondary school education in the State; and (d) are provided in conformity with the individualized education program…."[14]

The statutory definition of "special education" is:

> specially designed instruction, at no cost to parents, to meet the unique needs of a child with a disability, including instruction conducted in the classroom, in the home, in hospitals and institutions, and … in physical education.[15]

"Specially designed instruction" includes adapting content, methodology, and delivery of instruction that address the unique areas of the child and ensuring access to the general curriculum.[16]

"Related Services" are defined as "transportation, and such developmental, corrective, and other supportive services … as may be required to assist a child with a disability to benefit from special education…."[17] Examples of related services are given in IDEA as well.[18] Transition services can be considered either special education or related services.[19]

---

13. Rowley, 458 U.S. at 207; *see also* Smith v. Robinson, 468 U.S. 992, 1011 (1984) (the procedures "effect Congress' intent that each child's individual educational needs be worked out through a process that … includes … detailed procedural safeguards").

14. 20 U.S.C. §1401(9)); *see also* 34 C.F.R. §300.17.

15. 20 U.S.C. §1401(29); 34 C.F.R. §300.39. Regulations also indicate that "special education" includes speech-language pathology, vocational education, and travel training if specially designed to meet the needs of a disabled child. 34 C.F.R. §300.39. Further, if "related services" have independent educational value they may constitute special education. 34 C.F.R. §300.39.

16. 34 C.F.R. §300.39(a)(3).

17. 34 C.F.R. §300.34; 20 U.S.C. §1401(26); *see also* Park v. Anaheim Union High School Dist., 464 F.3d 1025 (9th Cir. 2006) (school district did not commit substantive violation of IDEA by not providing related or support services for child).

18. *See* §3.9.

19. 34 C.F.R. §300.43; *see also* Urban v. Jefferson County School Dist., 89 F.3d 720 (10th Cir. 1996) (IEP lacked an explicit statement of transition services, however, this defect did not deny the student a FAPE); Letter to Moore, 39 Individuals with Disabilities Educ. L. Rep. (LRP) 189 (OSEP 2002) (explaining the requirements for transition planning that should occur as a student progresses through high school); Letter to Hamilton, 23 Individuals with Disabilities Educ. L. Rep. (CRR) 721 (OSEP 1995).

3.3.1 Level of Education Required to Constitute FAPE Under IDEA

The United States Supreme Court stated in *Rowley* that: "Noticeably absent from the language of the statute is any substantive standard prescribing the level of education to be accorded handicapped children."[20] In *Rowley*, the Court rejected an argument that IDEA required the provision of educational services that would "maximize each child's potential 'commensurate with the opportunity provided other children.'"[21]

Reviewing the language of IDEA and legislative history, the Court concluded that "the 'basic floor of opportunity' provided by the EAHCA consists of access to specialized instruction and related services which are individually designed to provide educational benefit to the handicapped child."[22] While specifically disclaiming any attempt to develop "any one test for determining the adequacy of educational benefits conferred upon all children,"[23] the Court did hold that the school system satisfies this requirement by "providing personalized instruction with sufficient support services to permit the child to benefit educationally from that instruction."[24]

Lower courts and school systems were quick to recognize that, absent a contrary state provision requiring a higher standard, *Rowley* did not require provision of the "best" education, but merely one that would provide some educational benefit.[25]
Lower courts have provided little additional guidance on what meets the required level of educational programming. While it appears clear that more than some minimal, or trivial,[26] educational benefit is necessary, no more precise definition has developed. Rather than identifying a prospective test of what constitutes a FAPE, lower courts have

---

20. Rowley, 458 U.S. at 189.

21. *Id.* at 198; *see also* Burke County Bd. of Educ. v. Denton, 895 F.2d 973 (4th Cir. 1990) (issue is "whether services beyond the regular school day are essential for the child to receive any educational benefit").

22. Rowley, 458 U.S. at 201; *see also* Rettig v. Kent City School Dist., 788 F.2d 328 (6th Cir. 1986) (equal opportunity with nondisabled is not the standard).

23. Rowley, 458 U.S. at 202.

24. Rowley, 458 U.S. at 203.

25. *See, e.g.,* M.M. v. Sch. Bd. of Miami-Dade County of Florida, 437 F.3d 1085 (11th Cir. 2006) (IDEA does not permit challenge to an IEP on the grounds that a placement is not the best or most desirable); L.E. v. Ramsey Bd. of Educ., 435 F.3d 384 (3d Cir. 2006) (state is not required to maximize the potential of handicapped children); T.B. v Warwicke School Committee, 361 F.3d 80, 83 (1st Cir. 2004) (best not required, only what is reasonably calculated for appropriate education is required); Gallagher v. Pontiac Pub. School Dist., 807 F.2d 75 (6th Cir. 1986) (most appropriate not required); Hessler v. State Bd. of Educ. of Md., 700 F.2d 134, 139 (4th Cir. 1983).

26. Bradley v. Arkansas Dept. of Educ., 443 F.3d 965 (8th Cir. 2006) ("The IDEA does not require that schools attempt to maximize a child's potential, or guarantee that the student actually make any progress at all." *citing* CJN v. Minneapolis Pub. Sch., 323 F.3d 630, 642 (8th Cir. 2003); County Sch. Bd. v. Z.P., 399 F.3d 298 (4th Cir. 2005) (IDEA does not require the best possible, however, Congress did not intend LEA duty satisfied by some minimal academic advancement); A.B. v. Lawson, 354 F.3d 315 (4th Cir. 2004) (need "some" educational benefit to provide a FAPE); Ridgewood Bd. of Educ. v. N.E., 172 F.3d 238 (3d Cir. 1999) (meaningful not trivial benefit required); M.C. v. Central Regional School Dist., 81 F.3d 389 (3d Cir. 1996); Oberti v. Board of Educ. of Borough of Clementin, 995 F.2d 1204 (3d Cir. 1993) (educational benefit must be more than de minimus); Polk v. Central Susquehanna Intermediate Unit 16, 853 F.2d 171 (3d Cir. 1988) (more than trivial benefit); Board of Educ. v. Diamond, 808 F.2d 987 (3d Cir. 1986) (*Rowley* requires plan that will allow progress, not regression or trivial educational benefit); Hall v. Vance County Bd. of Educ., 774 F.2d 629 (4th Cir. 1985) (more than trivial).

focused on a case-by-case determination of whether the program proposed by the LEA will provide educational benefit.

One objective factor that has been urged by school systems as an indication that a child's program does provide educational benefit is that the child has been promoted from grade to grade. In fact, in *Rowley* the Court found the child's academic progress "to be dispositive."[27] The Court, however, specifically stated it was not holding that every child who progresses from grade to grade is receiving a FAPE.[28]

The United States Fourth Circuit Court of Appeals specifically addressed grade progression as an objective indicator in *Hall v. Vance County Board of Education*:[29]

> Although the *Rowley* Court considered Amy Rowley's promotions in determining that she had been afforded a FAPE, the Court limited its analysis to that one case and recognized that promotions were a fallible measure of educational benefit.... The district court [in the instant case] did not err in discounting James' promotions in light of the school's policy of social promotion and James' test scores and independent evaluations. Nor is the district court compelled by a showing of minimal improvement on some test results to rule that the school had given James a FAPE.

Indeed, progression from grade-to-grade is an impossible measure of educational benefit where the child has a disability so severe that grade levels are irrelevant.[30]

Perhaps the clearest evidence that the educational program is not providing educational benefit is that the child is not progressing educationally, or is even actually regressing in the present educational placement.[31] The 1999 regulations for the first time defined a FAPE as including services necessary to enable the child to make progress in the general curriculum as well as advance toward achievement of the IEP goals.[32] If the

---

27. Rowley, 458 U.S. at 302 n.25; *see also* Bradley v. Arkansas Dept. of Educ., 443 F.3d 965 (8th Cir. 2006) (upholding district court's finding that student's standardized test scores were sufficient to show progress when the student maintained a pace of learning consistent with national averages); Mavis v. Sobol, 839 F. Supp. 98 (N.D.N.Y. 1993) (whether student's progress was satisfactory is measured in terms of her abilities as a disabled child); St. Johnsbury Academy v. D.H., 20 F. Supp. 2d 675 (D. Vt. 1998); Bertolucci v. San Carlos Elementary School Dist., 721 F. Supp. 1150 (N.D. Cal. 1989) (progress from grade to grade and test scores showed benefit); *but see* Mather v. Hartford School Dist., 928 F. Supp. 437(D. Vt. 1996) (gap between achievement and grade level does not necessarily reflect the fact that no educational benefit was being received).

28. 34 C.F.R. § 300.101 (first appeared in amended 1999 regulations to require that each state shall assure that a FAPE is available to any child with a disability who needs special education and related services, even though the child is advancing from grade to grade).

29. 774 F.2d 629, 635–6 (4th Cir. 1985).

30. Beth B. v. Mark Van Clay, 282 F.3d 493 (7th Cir. 2002) ("A modicum of developmental achievement does not constitute a satisfactory education," when a student's academic progress was virtually nonexistent and her developmental progress was limited); Polk v. Central Susquehanna Intermediate Unit 16, 853 F.2d 171 (3d Cir. 1988) (disability may be so severe that progress cannot be measured by grade promotion); Makentozos v. DeBuono, 923 F. Supp. 505 (S.D.N.Y. 1996) (early intervention programs not reasonably calculated to enable child to receive educational benefits).

31. Mrs. B. v. Milford Bd. of Educ. 103 F.3d 1114 (2d Cir. 1997) (over 3 years with not advancing more than one grade is not meaningful progress); Board of Educ. v. Diamond, 808 F.2d 987 (3d Cir. 1986) (regression); Garland Independent School Dist. v. Wilks, 657 F. Supp. 1163 (N.D. Tex. 1987) (failure to provide FAPE where student moved from residential to day program and regressed educationally); *but see,* Kings Local Sch. Dist. Bd. of Educ. v. Zelazny, 325 F.3d 724 (6th Cir. 2003) (school district provides FAPE where child makes minimal educational advancements, despite behavioral regressions at home).

32. 34 C.F.R. § 300.101; *see also* 20 U.S.C. § 1412(a)(1)(A).

child is unable to benefit from educational programming, however, the school system may be relieved from providing educational services.[33]

3.3.2 Higher State Standard for Level of Services

Individual state statutes and regulations must be checked to determine whether a higher level of educational benefit is required. IDEA provides the minimum level of educational services, but it does not prohibit states from providing more services. Several states establish a higher standard than articulated in *Rowley*.[34] Federal courts are not precluded under the Eleventh Amendment from enforcing these higher state standards.[35]

3.3.3 Level of Education Required to Constitute FAPE Under § 504

Section 504 arguably requires a higher level of educational benefit than IDEA. While judicial gloss provided by the United States Supreme Court in *Rowley* indicates that an appropriate education need only provide some educational benefit,[36] § 504's regulations set a standard of meeting the educational needs of the disabled "as adequately as the needs of nonhandicapped persons...."[37] Unless a school system is willing to publicly as-

---

33. *See* § 5.2.3.

34. *See, e.g.,* Iowa Code Ann. § 256B.2(3) (West 1996) (aspiring to provide special education students with "education commensurate with the level provided" children who do not receive special education services); Md. Code Ann., Educ. § 8-401(a) (2000) (providing that disabled children are entitled to educational opportunities designed to help them achieve their potential); Douglas and Susan v. Greenfield Public Schools, 164 F Supp.2d 157 (D. Mass. 2001) (not legal error in developing IEP ... to assure "maximum" possible development ...); Mass. Gen. L. ch. 71B, § 2 (A Massachusetts IEP must be reasonably calculated to assure maximum possible development in LRE); Cal. Code of Regs. § 3001(b) ("provide equal opportunity ... commensurate with the opportunity provided to other pupils") *discussed in* Pink v. Mt. Diablo Unified School Dist., 738 F. Supp. 345 (N.D. Cal. 1990); Mass. Gen. L. ch. 71B, § 3 *discussed in* David D. v. Dartmouth School Committee, 615 F. Supp. 639 (D. Mass. 1984) ("maximum possible development"), *aff'd,* 775 F.2d 411 (1st Cir. 1985); Mich. Comp. Laws Ann. §§ 380.1701, 1711, and 1751 ("shall provide education programs and services designed to develop the maximum potential of each handicapped person") *discussed in* Barwacz v. Michigan Dept. of Educ., 674 F. Supp. 1296 (W.D. Mich. 1987); N.J. Admin. Code §§ 6:28-2.1, 2.2 (1978) ("best achieve") *discussed in* Lascari v. Ramapo Indian Hills Reg. H.S. Bd. of Educ., 116 N.J. 30, 560 A.2d 1180 (1989); Geis v. Board of Educ. of Parsippany-Troy Hills, 589 F. Supp. 269, 272 (D. N.J. 1984) *aff'd,* 774 F.2d 575 (3d Cir. 1985); Tenn. Code Ann. § 49-10-101(a)(1) (maximize capabilities); *but see MCLA §§ 380.1701(a),* 380.1711(1)(a) and 380.1751(1) ("The term 'maximum potential' has not been well defined in Michigan law. Further, the standard may be more precatory than mandatory; it does not necessarily require the best education possible"); Friedman v. Board of Educ. of West Bloomfield, 427 F. Supp. 2d768,781 (E.D. Mich. 2006); Renner v. Board of Education of the Public School of Ann Arbor, 185 F.3d 635, 644 (6th Cir. 1999) ("The Michigan statute may not require public schools to maximize the potential of disabled students commensurate with the opportunities provided to other children....").

35. David D. v. Dartmouth School Committee, 775 F.2d 411, 420 (1st Cir. 1985); Geis v. Board of Educ., 774 F.2d 575, 581 (3d Cir. 1985); Barwacz v. Michigan Dept. of Educ., 674 F. Supp. 1296 (W.D. Mich. 1987).

36. *See* Rowley, 458 U.S. at 203; *see also* Cedar Rapids Community School Dist. v. Garrett F., 526 U.S. 66, 77 (1999); Hall v. Vance County Bd. of Educ., 774 F.2d 629, 635 (4th Cir. 1985). *See generally* § 3.3.1.

37. 34 C.F.R § 104.33(b)(1).

sert the proposition that it is providing a minimal educational experience to its nondisabled students, it could be argued that reliance on § 504 circumvents *Rowley's* minimal
standard in those areas where IDEA and § 504 overlap.[38] To the extent a school system
professes to maximize a nondisabled child's educational benefit, or make available educational services which provide more than some minimal educational benefit, the
school should be required, under § 504, to have the same educational goal for children
with disabilities. No case has been found to support this argument.

3.4 Education to Be at No Cost to Parents

IDEA clearly requires the provision of a *free* appropriate public education.[39] Provision of the education, therefore, must be at no cost to the parents. Parents, for example,
cannot be required to use personal insurance to pay for educational programming if it
would reduce their lifetime benefits.[40] Also, the state may not delay implementation of
the IEP while payment sources are being determined.[41] Further, the state may not require the participation of the parents in the educational program as a prerequisite to the
provision of educational services.[42]

To the extent that a residential program is required in order for a child to receive a
FAPE, "the program, including non-medical care and room and board, must be at no
cost to the parents of the child."[43]

---

38. Section 504 regulations were drafted prior to *Rowley*. It is, therefore, conceivable they were
intended to have a different standard than articulated in *Rowley*.

39. 20 U.S.C. §§ 1412(a)(1), 1401(8); Rowley, 458 U.S. at 188; *see also* Arlington Cent. Sch.
Dist. Bd. of Educ. v. Murphy, 126 S. Ct. 2455 (2006); Twp. of Bloomfield Bd. of Educ. v. S.C.,
(D.N.J. 2006) (parents are entitled to attorney's fees to pay law school clinic costs of litigating
claim. "The purposes of IDEA are furthered if parents can obtain representation"); T.F. v. Special
Sch. Dist., 449 F.3d 816 (8th Cir. 2006) (under IDEA, a local educational agency does not have to
pay for the cost of education when parents unilaterally enroll their child in a private school without the approval of the public school district if that agency made a free appropriate public education available to the child); Mahoney v. Administrative School Dist. 1, 42 Ore. App. 665, 601 P.2d
826 (Ct. App. Ore. 1979).

40. Raymond S. v. Ramirez, 918 F. Supp. 1280 (N.D. Iowa 1996) (also, parents not required to
pay insurer for unreimbursed costs of educational evaluation); Seals v. Loftis, 614 F. Supp. 302 (E.D.
Tenn. 1985); *see also* Shook v. Gaston County Bd. of Educ., 882 F.2d 119 (4th Cir. 1989) (parents
were able to sue to seek reimbursement for depletion of $100,000 medical insurance policy of
$64,200 because the education must not diminish the resources of the parent); *but see* Emery v.
Roanoke City School Bd. 432 F.3d 294 (4th Cir. 2005) (held that student did not have standing to
seek reimbursement for educational expenses paid by his father's medical insurance); Letter to
Guess, 47 Individuals with Disabilities Educ. L. Rep. (CRR) 135 (OSERS 2007) (change in services
triggers LEA's duty to obtain parental consent for access to public funds).

41. 34 C.F.R. § 300.103; *see also* 20 U.S.C. §§ 1401(8) and 1412(a)(1).

42. *See, e.g.*, Teresa Diane P. v. Alief Independent School Dist., 744 F.2d 484 (5th Cir. 1984)
(conditioning on parental participation in group therapy violates equal protection and substantive
due process).

43. 34 C.F.R. § 300.104; *see* 20 U.S.C. §§ 1412(a)(1) and (a)(10)(B); *see also* Kings Local Sch.
Dist. v. Zelazny, 325 F.3d 724 (6th Cir. 2003); Mrs. B. v. Milford Bd. of Educ., 103 F.3d 1114 (2d
Cir. 1997); New Paltz Cent. Sch. Dist. v. St. Pierre, 307 F. Supp. 2d 394 (N.D.N.Y. 2004) (district
must reimburse parent for private residential school despite parental unilateral placement of the
child); Jenkins v. Florida, 556 Educ. Handicapped L. Rep. (CRR) 471 (M.D. Fla. 1985) (where residential placement is required for educational reasons, state may not charge fee for living expenses).

Incidental fees normally charged to nondisabled students may be charged to children with disabilities.[44]

3.5 Cost as Factor in Providing FAPE

IDEA requires the provision of educational services to all eligible children with disabilities, and makes no provision for refusing to provide those services because of cost. Limitations on funding, at least from the federal government, were clearly rejected in the legislative history of IDEA as justification for denying an appropriate education:

> The Committee rejects the argument that the Federal Government should only mandate services to handicapped children if, in fact, funds are appropriated in sufficient amounts to cover the full cost of this education. The Committee recognizes the State's primary responsibility to uphold the Constitution of the United States and their own State Constitutions and State laws as well as Congress' own responsibility under the 14th Amendment to assure equal protection of the law.[45]

Further, "cost considerations are only relevant when choosing between several options, all of which offer an 'appropriate' education. When only one is appropriate, then there is no choice."[46] Where, for example, both a residential facility and a community group home will provide an appropriate education, the public agency may choose the less expensive placement.[47] Cost may also be a consideration when choosing the least restrictive placement.[48]

It is possible, of course, that funds are simply unavailable to educate both disabled and nondisabled children to the extent desired by the school system. Congress did indeed recognize that funds could be limited:

> When a state or local educational agency, because of funding limitations, places limits on the services that may be provided children with disabilities, the

---

44. 34 C.F.R. § 300.39; *see also* 20 U.S.C. § 1401(29).

45. Sen. Rep. No. 168, 94th Cong., 1st Sess. at 22, *reprinted in* 1975 U.S. Code Cong. & Admin. News 1425, 1446; *see also* 121 Cong. Rec. 37025 (remarks of Rep. Mink); 121 Cong. Rec. 19503 (1975) (remarks of Sen. Cranston).

46. Deal v. Hamilton County Bd. of Educ., 392 F.3d 840 (6th Cir. 2004) (cost may be a consideration; however, the school district is required to base placement decision on the child's IEP, rather than on the mere fact of a pre-existing investment. IDEA does not allow a "one size fits all" approach); Clevenger v. Oak Ridge School Bd., 744 F.2d 514 (6th Cir. 1984); *see also* Roncker v. Walter, 700 F.2d 1058, 1063 (6th Cir. 1983); Kruelle v. New Castle County School Dist., 642 F.2d 687, 695 (3d Cir. 1981) ("comprehensive range of services ... regardless of financial and administrative burdens"); J.P. v. West Clark Community Schools, 230 F. Supp. 2d 910 (S.D. Ind. 2002) (parents failed to state claim for violation of IDEA based upon improper consideration of costs); Delaware County Intermediate Unit #25 v. Martin, 831 F. Supp. 1206 (E.D. Pa. 1993) (cost irrelevant to requirement to provide services, but can be considered in choosing between two appropriate placements).

47. Abrahamson v. Hershman, 701 F.2d 223 (1st Cir. 1983); J.B. v. Killingly Bd. of Educ., 990 F. Supp. 57 (D. Conn. 1997) (change in placement was required in part because student posed a danger to himself and the community at his current placement due to pedophilia disability and his risk of reoffending); Ciresoli v. M.S.A.D. No. 22, 901 F. Supp. 378 (D. Me. 1995) (district's IEP was reasonably calculated even though it proposed to provide child with a day program rather than a residential program).

48. *See* § 8.2.

manner in which the financial deficit is to be adjusted is indicated by legislative history.

> If sufficient funds are not available to finance all of the services and programs that are needed and desirable in the system then the available funds must be expended equitably in such manner that no child is excluded from publicly supported education consistent with his needs and abilities to benefit therefrom. The inadequacies of [the school system] whether occasioned by insufficient funding or administrative inefficiency, certainly cannot be permitted to bear more heavily on the 'exceptional' or handicapped child than on the normal child.

> Lack of funds, therefore, may not limit the availability of "appropriate" educational services to handicapped children more severely than it does to normal or nonhandicapped children.[49]

According to the United States Department of Education's Office of Civil Rights, cost is likewise insufficient as a defense under Section 504.[50]

3.6 Age Coverage

IDEA requires educational programming for all children "aged 3 through 21 including children who have been suspended or expelled from school."[51] If the state chooses to

---

49. Crawford v. Pittman, 708 F.2d 1028, 1035 (5th Cir. 1983) *quoting* S. Rep. No. 168, 94th Cong., 1st Sess. at 23, *reprinted in* 1975 U.S. Code Cong. & Admin. News at 1447. The court also pointed out: "This quotation from the legislative history first appeared in Mills v. Board of Educ., 348 F. Supp. 866, 876 (D.D.C. 1972). It has frequently been quoted when efforts were made to explain the substantive requirements of the Act; *see, Rowley,* 458 U.S. 178, 193 n.15...." Crawford, 708 F.2d at 1035 n.30; *but see* Stacey G. v. Pasadena Indep. School Dist., 547 F. Supp. 61, 78 (S.D. Tex. 1982) *vacated and remanded on other grounds,* 695 F.2d 949 (5th Cir. 1983):

It cannot be disputed that educational funding is limited. Accordingly, it necessarily follows that competing interests must be balanced to reach a reasonable and fair accommodation. On the one hand are the personal and unique needs of the individual and handicapped child; on the other hand are the realities of limited funding and the necessity of assisting in the education of all handicapped children. These competing interests must be considered by the Court in its analysis of what is a "free appropriate public education."

The court also stated:

The fact that Congress intended or at least was acutely aware of the need to strike a balance between the competing interests ... is evidenced also by the requirement contained in the Act that the State establish "priorities for providing a free appropriate education for all handicapped children

Id. at 78; *see also* Department of Educ. v. Katherine D., 727 F.2d 809, 813 (9th Cir. 1984) ("Because budgetary constraints limit resources that realistically can be committed to these special programs, the DOE is required to make only those efforts to accommodate Katherine's needs that are 'within reason.'"); Clear Creek Indep. Sch. Dist. v. J.K., 400 F. Supp. 2d 991, 995 (D. Tex. 2005) (in deciding whether a disabled child has received a FAPE, the Court should consider the balance between the requirement to provide a meaningful education to each child and the "realities of limited funding" that school districts face (internal citations omitted). Not only do school districts have limited funds overall, but "excessive expenditures made to meet the needs of one handicapped child may reduce the resources that can be spent to meet the needs of other handicapped children.").

50. *See* Bremen High School Dist. No. 228, 257 Educ. Handicapped L. Rep. (CRR) 195 (OCR 1981) (§ 504 violated when refuse residential solely based on cost).

51. 34 C.F.R. § 300.101(a); *see* 20 U.S.C. § 1412(a)(1)(A).

educate two-year-old children, it may receive federal money.[52] IDEA, however, also limits the obligation to 3–5 and 18–21 year-old students.[53] The obligation to provide FAPE, however, does not apply to children aged 3–5 and 18–21 years of age when:

- it would be inconsistent with state law or practice or a court order to provide public education to children of those ages; [54]

- under state law children aged eighteen to twenty-one are not required to receive special education and related services if in their last educational placement before being placed in a correctional facility for adults they were not identified as a child with a disability and did not have an IEP;[55]

- the child graduated from high school with a regular high school diploma and received proper notice required by a change in placment;.[56]

Provision of a FAPE, consistent with IDEA, must be made for 18–21 year olds when:

- the child has been identified as a child with a disability, received services under an IEP, but left school prior to incarceration; or

- the child did not have an IEP in the last educational setting but was identified;[57] or

- the child graduated from high school but does not have a high school diploma.[58]

State statutes and regulations should be consulted to determine whether a particular state has chosen to limit age coverage.

It should be kept in mind that age does not usually terminate educational opportunity for children without disabilities. For example, a child who fails a grade is given an opportunity to repeat it. That student may then graduate when she is nineteen. Since this service is provided to regular education students, it must be provided to students with disabilities.[59]

Regulations promulgated under § 504, define those qualified to receive a FAPE as those who are of an age that would receive education were they not disabled, those of an age where state law requires mandatory education, or those children covered under IDEA.[60] Education services under § 504 can be terminated on the twenty-second birthday, since nothing in the statute requires funding to continue until the end of the academic year.[61]

For a child who falls below the age limit for educational programming under IDEA or § 504, parents should explore the programs for Infants and Toddlers With Disabilities.[62] This "Infants and Toddlers" program provides for interagency coordination of services, including the development of Individual Family Service Plans for children from birth through two years of age, who "are experiencing developmental delays ... or ... have a diagnosed physical or mental condition which has a high probability of resulting in developmental delay."[63]

52. 20 U.S.C. § 1419.
53. 34 C.F.R. § 300.102; *see* 20 U.S.C. §§ 1412(a)(1)(B)–(C).
54. 34 C.F.R. § 300.102(a)(1); *see also* 20 U.S.C. §§ 1412(a)(1)(B)–(C).
55. *Id.* at § 300.102(a)(2)(i)(A)(B); *see also* 20 U.S.C. §§ 1412(a)(1)(B)–(C).
56. *Id.* at § 300.102(a)(3)(i); *see also* 20 U.S.C. §§ 1412(a)(1)(B)–(C).
57. *Id.* at § 300.102(a)(2)(ii)(A)(B); *see also* 20 U.S.C. §§ 1412(a)(1)(B)–(C).
58. *Id.* at § 300.102(a)(3)(ii)(A)(B); *see also* 20 U.S.C. §§ 1412(a)(1)(B)–(C).
59. *See* Helms v. Independent School Dist. No. 3 of Broken Arrow, 750 F.2d 820 (10th Cir. 1985).
60. 34 C.F.R. § 104.(l).
61. Williamson County School Dist., 352 Educ. Handicapped L. Rep. (CRR) 514 (OCR 1988).
62. 20 U.S.C. §§ 1431–1482; 34 C.F.R. Part 303. *See* Chapter 18.
63. 34 C.F.R. § 303.16; *see also* 20 U.S.C. § 1432(5).

3.7 The Effect of Graduation Under IDEA

A special education student who graduates does not have the right to educational services beyond graduation.[64] There is no duty to provide a FAPE to students with disabilities who graduate with a regular high school diploma.[65] Where a student has successfully completed the goals and objectives of an appropriate IEP, and that completion "is analogous to successful completion of graduation requirements for non-handicapped students," the school system's obligation to educate the child ends.[66] Under IDEA, the school system is only obligated to provide post graduation educational services "to the extent and in the same proportion that it does for non-handicapped students."[67]

Of course, if the graduation is "a sham designed to terminate the school system's responsibility at the earliest possible moment under circumstances where non-handicapped children are provided further schooling,"[68] the school system can be required to provide educational services from eighteen to twenty-one consistent with its provision to educational services to children who are nondisabled.

3.8 The Effect of Graduation Under § 504

Regulations promulgated under § 504 define those qualified to receive a FAPE as those who are of an age that would receive education were they not disabled, those of an age where state law requires mandatory education, or those children covered under IDEA.[69] If, therefore, a local school system provides adult educational programming to the nondisabled, comparable adult programming should be available to the disabled. For example, there are numerous children with disabilities who could continue to receive educational benefit beyond 22 years of age. Although the school system may argue that the disabled person is not otherwise qualified to benefit from the adult educational program, once the school system has undertaken the general education of the nondis-

---

64. *See generally* 34 CFR § 300.102(a)(3)(i); *see also* 20 U.S.C. §§ 1412(a)(1)(B)–(C); T.S. v. Independent School Dist. No. 54, Stroud, Oklahoma, 265 F.3d 1090 (10th Cir. 2001) (school district's obligations to student ceased upon his graduation); Moseley v. Board of Educ. of Albuquerque Public Schools, 483 F.3d 9 (10th Cir. 2007) ("Once a student has graduated, he is no longer entitled to a FAPE; thus any claim that a FAPE was deficient becomes moot upon a valid graduation.") quoting T.S., 265 F.3d at 1092; Gorski v. Lynchburg School Bd., 441 Educ. Handicapped L. Rep. (CRR) 415 (4th Cir. 1989); Wexler v. Westfield Bd. of Educ., 784 F.2d 176, 183–184 (3d Cir. 1986); *see generally* Novato United School Dist., 22 Individuals with Disabilities Educ. L. Rep. (LRP) 1056 (OCR 1995) (graduation is a change in placement which requires parental participation.

65. 34 C.F.R. § 300.102; *see also* § 1412(a)(1)(B)–(C).

66. Wexler v. Westfield Bd. of Educ., 784 F.2d 176 (3d Cir. 1986); *see also* Gorski v. Lynchburg School Bd., 441 Educ. Handicapped L. Rep. (CRR) 415 (4th Cir. 1989); Andrew B. v. Board of Educ. of Community High School Dist. 99, WL 3147719, (N.D. Ill. 2006) (20 year old benefited from vocational training which supported graduation).

67. Wexler, 784 F.2d at 183; Daugherty v. Hamilton County School, 29 Individuals with Disabilities Educ. L. Rep. 699 (E.D. Tenn. 1998) (district not required to provide psychiatric, social, or emotional services post graduation).

68. Wexler, 784 F.2d at 183 *citing* Helms v. Independent School Dist. No. 3 of Broken Arrow, 750 F.2d 820 (10th Cir. 1985).

69. 34 C.F.R. § 104.3(l).

abled, the school system must provide services to the disabled.[70] Since the school system is already providing the services "it may be logically inferred that it would not have imposed an 'undue burden' on defendants to provide a special educational program for the plaintiff."[71]

Further, if services of a particular type are already being provided to one group of people, what is being requested is a reallocation of existing resources, not an expansion of funding.[72] By the same token, these latter cases may well result in more litigation, since if there is not dual coverage with IDEA, there is no need to exhaust administrative remedies.[73]

3.9 Related Services in General

Provision of a FAPE requires "related services" as well as special education.[74] Related services are defined in IDEA as "[t]ransportation, and such developmental, corrective, and other supportive services ... as may be required to assist a disabled child to benefit from special education."[75] The regulations specifically mention speech-language pathology and audiology, interpreting services,[76] counseling services, psychological services, physical and occupational therapy, orientation and mobility services,[77] early identification and assessment, medical services for diagnostic and evaluation purposes, recreation services, rehabilitation counseling, school health services, school social work services, and parent counseling and training.[78] The list is not exhaustive and other services have been required.[79]

---

70. *See* discussion § 1.4.2. In Georgia Association of Retarded Citizens v. McDaniel, 716 F.2d 1565, 1579 (11th Cir. 1983) (a pre-*Smith v. Robinson* decision, the court relied on the fact that § 504 does not contain specific age limitations as one of the reasons for determining that IDEA did not preclude resort to § 504).

Until overridden by Congressional action, the fact that adult education programs might not receive direct federal aid could have caused a serious problem in enforcing such a right. The United States Supreme Court had ruled that "an agency's authority under Title IX ... is subject to the program-specific limitations of §§ 901 and 902." Grove City College v. Bell, 465 U.S. 555, 570 (1984). The similarity between Title IX and § 504 led courts to adopt this program-specific approach. *See, e.g.,* Gallagher v. Pontiac School Dist., 807 F.2d 75 (6th Cir. 1986). Congress overturned *Grove City* in 1988, with the adoption of 42 U.S.C. § 2000d-4a.

71. Sanders v. Marquette Pub. Schools, 561 F. Supp. 1361, 1371 (W.D. Mich. 1983).

72. It has been suggested that in cases where there is an unequal treatment of the disabled "[d]efendant will also have little success in relying upon cost-based defenses in such situations, for ... the question is primarily one of allocation of available resources in an evenhanded fashion." Wegner, *The Antidiscrimination Model Reconsidered: Ensuring Equal Opportunity Without Respect To Handicap Under Section 504 Of the Rehabilitation Act of 1973,* 69 Cornell L. Rev. 401, 499 (1984).

73. *See* § 13.3.

74. 34 C.F.R. § 300.17; 20 U.S.C. § 1401(9).

75. 34 C.F.R. § 300.34; 20 U.S.C. § 1401(26).

76. 34 C.F.R. § 300.34 (c)(4) (added to the 2005 regulations); 20 U.S.C. § 1401(26).

77. 34 C.F.R. § 300.34 (limited to students with visual impairments); *see also* 20 U.S.C. § 1401(26). Orientation and mobility services were added with the 99 amendments.

78. 34 C.F.R. § 300.34; 20 U.S.C. § 1401(26).

79. 34 C.F.R. § 300.43 (transition services may be related services required to assist a student with a disability to benefit from special education); *see also* DeKalb County Sch. Dist. v. M.T.V., 413 F. Supp. 2d 1322 (D. Ga. 2005) (vision therapy is a necessary service in order to provide FAPE.); *affirmed by unreported decision,* 164 Fed. Appx. 900 (11th Cir. 2006); Letter to Burr, 30 Individuals with Disabilities Educ. L. Rep. 146 (OSEP 1998) (assistive technology may be special education related services); *see, e.g.,* Espino v. Besteiro, 520 F. Supp. 905 (S.D. Tex. 1981) (air conditioning).

Surgically implanted medical devices, including cochlear implants, optimization of a medical device's functioning, and maintenance of or replacement of the device are not considered related services.[80] If, however, an IEP team determines that a child with a surgically implanted medical device needs any other related services, the child is entitled to receive them.[81] In addition, the public agency is not responsible for the post-surgical maintenance, programming or replacement of the device or its external components.[82] The public agency is responsible, however, for assuring that the external components of surgically implanted devices including hearing aids function properly,[83] as well as monitoring and maintaining the medical devices that relate to the child's health and safety. The monitoring and maintenance of medical devices include those devices that relate to a child's breathing, nutrition and the operation of bodily functions. This public agency responsibility occurs only during the hours the child is at school or being transported to and from school.[84]

The related service, as is clear from the definition, must be necessary to enable the child to receive educational benefit.[85] The mere fact that the child is disabled does not entitle the child to a particular related service. For example, a hearing-impaired student enrolled in a private school is not entitled to transportation as a related service if the need for transportation is unrelated to her disability.[86]

It should also be kept in mind that *Rowley* places limits on the required provision of related services. In *Rowley*, the parents were seeking a sign-language interpreter as a related service. The Court held that, since the child was already receiving an adequate education under the standard that the LEA need not maximize educational benefit, the interpreter need not be provided.[87]

Parents may be reimbursed for unilateral provision of related services, when it is determined that the school has improperly withheld the services.[88]

3.9.1 Equipment Versus Services

The United States Supreme Court had occasion to address related services under IDEA in *Irving Independent School District v. Tatro*.[89] The Court in *Tatro* placed emphasis on the fact that what was being sought by the parents was a service, not equipment. Specifically, the Court held: "Finally, we note that respondents are not asking petitioner

---

80. 34 C.F.R. § 300.34 (b)(1) (amendments to the 2005 regulations); *see also* Letter to Gregg, 48 Individuals with Disabilities Law Rep. 17 (ED 2006) (no obligation to provide mapping services to children with cochlear implants).

81. 34 C.F.R. § 300.34(b)(2)(i).

82. 34 C.F.R. § 300.113(b)(2) ; 20 U.S.C. § 1401 and (26)(B).

83. 34 C.F.R. § 300.34(b) (2)(iii) and § 300.113(a)(b).

84. 34 C.F.R. § 300.34(b) (2)(ii).

85. *See, e.g* McNair v. Oak Hills School Dist., 872 F.2d 153 (6th Cir. 1989) (transportation not required).

86. *Id.*

87. Rowley, 458 U.S. at 211–212; County Sch. Bd. of Henrico County, Virginia v. Z.P., 399 F.3d 298 (4th Cir. 2005) (every related service available to maximize child education is not necessary).

88. *See* Max. M. v. Illinois State Bd. of Educ., 629 F. Supp. 1504, 1519 (N.D. Ill. 1986); Seals v. Loftis, 614 F. Supp. 302, 305–306 (E.D. Tenn. 1985). For a complete discussion of reimbursement see § 14.4.

89. 468 U.S. 883 (1984).

to provide equipment that Amber needs for CIC [clean intermittent catheterization]. They seek only the services of a qualified person at the school."[90]

In 1995, OSEP clarified when equipment needs to be provided. The obligation of the LEA to provide equipment such as computers, and eyeglasses is required if necessary to furnish a FAPE.[91] Transportation services, including, of course, a large piece of equipment, are also required under IDEA.[92] Assistive technology devices may be a required related service and could include equipment used to increase, maintain, or improve the functional capabilities of a child with a disability.[93] The IEP determines whether an assistive technology device or service such as a computer is needed.[94]

Section 504 also requires the provision of equipment. Section 504 regulations define an appropriate education as "regular or special education and related aids and services that are ... designed to meet individual educational needs of handicapped persons as adequately as the needs of nonhandicapped persons are met."[95] The type of aids contemplated under §504 regulations is found by analogy in the postsecondary education regulations.[96]

A United States Department of Education's Office for Civil Rights (OCR) complaint that a local school system violated §504 in failing to provide a homebound disabled student with a computer and adaptive headgear also illustrates the type of equipment that might be required. The student was enrolled in a computer class which, if he had been

---

90. *Id.*

91. Letter to Bachus, 22 Individuals with Disabilities Educ. L. Rep. (LRP) 629 (OSEP 1995) (if student requires eyeglasses regardless if student attends school LEA not required to provide but if in order to receive a FAPE and the IEP specifies glasses, then the district must provide); *see also* 34 C.F.R.4 §300. 34 and 300.113.

92. 20 U.S.C. §1401(26); 34 C.F.R. §300.34(16); District of Columbia v. Ramirez, 377 F. Supp. 2d 63 (D.D.C. 2005) (district is required to provide an aide to assist student from the door of his house to the school bus); *see also* Ms. K. v. City of South Portland, 407 F. Supp. 2d 290 (D. Me. 2006) (wheelchair accessible bus, is not the only form of special education transportation. Accommodations such as exiting bus first, and sitting in the front seat are also special education transportation accommodations); In re Farmingdale Union Free School Dist., 503 Educ. Handicapped L. Rep. (CRR) 221 (SEA N.Y. 1982) (specially equipped mini-bus required); Case No. SE 85461, 507 Educ. Handicapped L. Rep. (CRR) 416 (SEA Cal. 1985) (IEP required provision of computer with voice synthesizer similar to equipment used at home); Stoher, 213 Educ. Handicapped L. Rep. (CRR) 209 (OSEP 1989) (wheelchair may be related service as in transportation). *See* §18.7.

93. 34 C.F.R. §300.5; *see also* 20 U.S.C. §1401(1).

94. Sherman and Nishanian v. Mamaroneck Union Free Sch. Dist., 340 F.3d 87 (2d Cir. 2003) (IEP approves use of a graphing calculator attached to a computer); Letter to Anonymous, 29 Individuals with Disabilities Educ. L. Rep. (LRP) 1089 (OSEP 1997) (includes computers).

95. 34 C.F.R. §104.33(b)(1). It should be pointed out that §504 is not only broader in terms of the people it covers, but also broader in terms of the services required. IDEA clearly limits application to provision of special education and related services. Section 504, however, requires provision of an appropriate education and which may simply be provision of a regular education in a regular classroom. *See, e.g.,* Elizabeth S. v. Gilhool, 558 Educ. Handicapped L. Rep. (CRR) 461 (M.D. Pa. 1987) (children with disabilities who do not require special education may require other modifications or services to obtain access to educational programming).

96. 34 C.F.R. §104.44(d). For example, Auxiliary aids may include taped texts, interpreters or other effective methods of making orally delivered materials available to students with hearing impairments, readers in libraries for students with visual impairments, classroom equipment adapted for use by students with manual impairments, and other similar services and actions. Recipients need not provide attendants, individually prescribed devices, readers for personal use or study, or other devices or services of a personal nature.

taking the course in the regular classroom would have included access to a computer. OCR determined that, since the student would have been provided with access to a computer had he not been disabled, the LEA's failure to provide a computer and adaptive headgear in order to allow him to use the computer for homebound instruction was a violation.[97] Critical, of course, was the LEA's provision of computers to nondisabled children at no cost. A public agency must permit a child to use school purchased equipment at home or in other settings if the IEP determined that the child needs access to receive a FAPE.

A school is required to provide a specially equipped van to transport a disabled child to the school, since transportation is necessary in order to allow the child to receive educational benefit.[98]

3.9.2 Transportation as a Related Service

Transportation is specifically mentioned as a related service under IDEA.[99] Transportation includes travel to and from school, as well as travel within the school and between schools.[100] Unless the child is on homebound, or in some other type of residential educational program, it is logical that transportation from home to the educational setting is necessary for any child to receive educational benefit.

The LEA's transportation plan must be reasonable.[101] Transportation must be door-to-door if the child is unable to get to the bus stop.[102] If both parents are working, transportation to an after school caretaker is also required, even if the caretaker lives outside the student's school district.[103]

The LEA's responsibility to provide transportation extends to children placed in private facilities because of the unavailability of a FAPE in the public school, though rea-

---

97. Eldon (Mo.) R-I School Dist., 352 Educ. Handicapped L. Rep. (CRR) 144 (OCR 1986).

98. *See, e.g.*, Kennedy v. Board of Educ., 175 W. Va. 668, 337 S.E.2d 905 (1985) (purchase of vehicle required to transport over nonmaintained road).

99. 34 C.F.R. § 300.34; *see* 20 U.S.C. § 1401(26); *see also* Bradley v. Ark. Dep't of Educ., 443 F.3d 965, n.6 (8th Cir. 2006); M.M. v. M.M. v. Sch. Bd. of Miami-Dade County of Florida, 437 F.3d 1085 (11th Cir. 2006); McNair v. Oak Hills Local School Dist., 872 F.2d 153 (6th Cir. 1989).

100. 34 C.F.R. § 300.34(16); *see also* 20 U.S.C. § 1401(26).

101. *See* Pinkerton v. Moye, 509 F. Supp. 107 (W.D. Va. 1981) (because of length of time required by LEA's system, parent could seek alternative transportation and receive reimbursement).

102. District of Columbia v. Ramirez 377 F. Supp.2d 63 (D.D.C. 2005) (required district to provide student, who used wheelchair, with transportation between door of his family's apartment and school bus); Hurry v. Jones, 560 F. Supp. 500 (D.R.I. 1983), *aff'd in part, rev'd in part*, 734 F.2d 879 (1st Cir. 1984) (reimbursement for school systems failure to provide door-to-door transportation for physically impaired student); *but see*, Ms. S. v. Scarborough Sch. Committee, 366 F. Supp. 2d 98 (D. Me. 2005) (district does not violate IDEA when denying provision that calls for student to be dropped off only if an adult is present to receive the child from a regular bus. However, the district did accept the provision if the student were riding a special education bus).

103. Alamo Heights Indep. School Dist. v. State Bd. of Educ., 790 F.2d 1153 (5th Cir. 1986) (absent a showing of unfair burden, substantial additional expense, disruption of efficient planning, or lengthening transportation time of other children, LEA obligated to transport child one mile out-of-district to child caretaker); *but see*, Fick v. Sioux Falls 49-5, 337 F.3d 968 (8th Cir. 2003) (district wide policy not allowing special education student to be dropped off at daycare outside geographic "cluster" does not violate IDEA because transportation request based parents' convenience).

sonable limits on the frequency of trips can be made.[104] The LEA's obligation is to transport the student to and from the residential program, not transport the parents.[105]

As discussed elsewhere, even when the LEA is able to provide a FAPE, but the parent unilaterally decides to place the child in a private program, considerable responsibility remains on the LEA to make special education and related services available.[106] Transportation from to the private school and back is not generally required.[107] Transportatio home n, however, must be provided to students in private schools so they may take advantage of special education services. Transportation must be provided, therefore, from the child's school or home to a site other than the private school and from the service site to the child's private school or home if it is necessary for a child to benefit or participate in the services.[108]

Reimbursement for expenses of transportation to a unilateral placement by the parents ultimately determined after the due process proceedings to be appropriate is required under the Supreme Court's decision in *School Committee of the Town of Burlington v. Department of Education of Massachusetts.*10[109]

3.9.3 Speech Pathology and Audiology as Related Services

Federal regulations provide that as a related service "audiology" includes identification, determining the range, nature and degree of loss, providing rehabilitative activities, creating programs to prevent hearing loss, counseling and guidance of students, parents and teachers, and providing services related to amplification.[110]

"Speech-language pathology" as a related service includes identification, diagnosis, referral, counseling and provision of speech and language services.[111]

3.9.4 Interpreting Services

Interpreting services include oral transliteration services, cued language transliteration services, sign language transliteration and interpreting services as well as transcrip-

---

104. Cohen v. School Bd., 450 So. 2d 1238 (Fla. Dist. Ct. App. 1984) (three round trips for student between home and out of state residential placement sufficient to meet IEP goals of family integration and counseling); Wappingers Central Sch. Dist., 35 Individuals with Disabilities Educ. L. Rep. (LRP) 112 (SEA NY 2001) (district must pay transportation costs for parents of child in out-of-state preparatory school to visit him on parent-child weekend). New York Law provided for a maximum of three roundtrips for a ten-month educational program, or 4 roundtrips for a twelve-month program. *Id.*

105. Bales v. Clarke, 523 F. Supp. 1366 (E.D. Va. 1981); *but see* Wappingers Central Sch. Dist., 35 Individuals with Disabilities Educ. L. Rep. (LRP) 112 (SEA NY 2001) (district required to pay for parents travel expenses because if parents didn't participate in parent-child weekend then child would have had to travel home, per residential facility policy).

106. *See* § 8.10.

107. McNair v. Cardimone, 676 F. Supp. 1361 (S.D. Ohio 1987), *aff'd sum nom.* McNair v. Oak Hills Local School Dist., 872 F.2d 153 (6th Cir. 1989); Work v. McKenzie, 661 F. Supp. 225 (D.D.C. 1987).

108. 34 C.F.R. § 300.139; *see also* 20 U.S.C. § 1412(a)(10)(A).

109. 471 U.S. 359 (1985); *see* Taylor v. Board of Educ., 649 F. Supp. 1253 (N.D.N.Y. 1986) (citing *Burlington*). *Burlington* is discussed more fully in § 14.4.

110. 03. 34 C.F.R. § 300.34; *see also* 20 U.S.C. § 1401(26).

111. 34 C.F.R. § 300.34; *see also* 20 U.S.C. § 1401(26).

tion services such as communication access real-time translation (CART), C- Print and Type Well for children who are deaf or hard of hearing. Special interpreting services are related services available for children who are deaf or blind.[112]

3.9.5 Psychological Services and Counseling as Related Services

Psychological services include administering tests, interpreting results, planning programs, assisting in developing positive behavioral intervention strategies, and consulting with other staff.[113] Psychotherapy required in order for a child to receive educational benefit comes within psychological services.[114]

An issue that has arisen is whether psychotherapy provided by a psychiatrist is a related service, or a precluded medical service. *Max. M. v. Thompson*, (*Max M. III*)[115] addressed this issue. Balancing the recognition of psychotherapy as a related service with the limitation of medical services to diagnosis and evaluation, the court held that IDEA "requires ... cost free psychotherapy that could be carried out by psychologists, social workers, or guidance counselors."[116] The court in *Max. M III* required the LEA to reimburse for the psychiatric services at a rate "normally and reasonably charged" by a non-physician professional of this type.

The position taken in *Max M. III* is consistent with the Supreme Court's recognition in *Irving Independent School District v. Tatro*[117] of Congressional concern that school systems not be overburdened. Because of this concern, IDEA requires nursing services, but not the services of a licensed physician.[118] At least one other court, however, has held that whether the reimbursement is required depends not on who provides the service, but on nature and purpose of the services.[119]

Counseling services may overlap with psychological services because they include "services provided by qualified social workers, psychologists, guidance counselors, or other qualified personnel."[120] In fact, the requirement of counseling services has been used as an alternative justification for finding psychotherapy to be a related service.[121]

---

112. 34 C.F.R. § 300.34(4) added in 2005; *see also* 20 U.S.C. § 1401(26).

113. 34 C.F.R. § 300.34; *see also* 20 U.S.C. § 1401(26).

114. 34 C.F.R. § 300.34 (psychological counseling); *see, e.g.,* Seals v. Loftis, 614 F. Supp. 302 (E.D. Tenn. 1985); M.C. v. Voluntown Bd. of Educ., 30 F. Supp. 2d 950 (D. Conn. 1999); T.G. v. Board of Educ., 576 F. Supp. 420 (D.N.J. 1983); Papacoda v. Connecticut, 528 F. Supp. 68 (D. Conn. 1981); Gary B. v. Cronin, 542 F. Supp. 102 (N.D. Ill. 1980); In re "A" Family, 184 Mont. 145, 602 P.2d 157 (1979); *see also* 20 U.S.C. § 1401(26).

115. 592 F. Supp. 1437 (N.D. Ill. 1984).

116. *See also* Darlene L. v. Illinois State Bd. of Educ., 568 F. Supp. 1340, 1345 (N.D. Ill. 1983).

117. 468 U.S. 883 (1984). The Court did not, however, have occasion to address the issue under § 504, since on the same day it had decided IDEA was the exclusive remedy and that Section 504 did not apply. *Id.* at 895 *citing* Smith v. Robinson, 468 U.S. 992 (1984).

118. Tatro, 468 U.S. 883 (1984). *See* § 3.9.6.

119. Board of Educ. v. Department of Educ., 17 Educ. Handicapped L. Rep. (LRP) 942 (Conn. Super. Ct. 1991); *see also* Field v. Haddonfield Bd. of Educ., 769 F. Supp. 1313 (D.N.J. 1991) (whether drug treatment program is related service depends on purpose and nature of service not on provider).

120. 34 C.F.R. § 300.34; *see also* 20 U.S.C. § 1401(26).

121. *See, e.g.,* Max M. (III), 592 F. Supp. at 1444; Gary B. v. Cronin, 542 F. Supp. 102 (N.D. Ill. 1980); Northside Indep. Sch. Dist. 41 Individuals with Disabilities Educ. L. Rep. (LRP) 86 (SEA TX

3.9.6 Physical Therapy, Occupational Therapy, Orientation and Mobility, Recreation, Early Identification and Assessment of Disabilities as Related Services

Physical therapy is simply defined in the regulations as "services provided by a qualified physical therapist."[122]

"Occupational therapy" includes services provided by a qualified occupational therapist "[i]mproving, developing or restoring functions," prevention and parent counseling and training.[123]

IDEA 1997 and the 1999 amendments to the federal regulations added orientation and mobility services as a related service. "Orientation and mobility services" are defined as services that enable blind and visually impaired students to move safely within the school, home, and community environment. These services include teaching students concepts and techniques such as using information received by the senses, use of the cane and use of low vision aids.[124]

"Recreation" as a related service includes assessment, provision of therapeutic services, recreation programs and leisure education.[125] It should be kept in mind that recreation is a related service. Therefore, it is not required for all children with disabilities. Recreation should be distinguished from physical education which is contained in the definition of "special education" and is, therefore, required for all children covered by IDEA.[126] Recreation should also be distinguished from extracurricular activities which, despite specific references in the regulations, may not be required by IDEA.[127]

Early identification "means implementation of a formal plan for identifying a disability as early as possible in a child's life."[128]

3.9.7 Medical Services as Related Services

Medical services required under IDEA are limited to that necessary for diagnostic and evaluation purposes.[129] The regulations provide that "'[m]edical services' means

2004) (court classified counseling as "related service" that the child required to benefit from his education).

122. 34 C.F.R. § 300.34; *see also* 20 U.S.C. § 1401(26); Letter to Geigerman, 43 Individuals with Disabilities Educ. L. Rep. (LRP) 85 (OSEP 2004) (determination of whether physical therapy and occupational therapy services are needed should be made by the IEP team on a case-by-case basis). As with all special education and related services, the public agency's failure to provide physical therapy would be denial of a free appropriate education, Polk v. Central Susquehanna Intermediate Unit 16, 853 F.2d 171 (3d Cir. 1988), and the agency must provide physical therapy during the summer if necessary in order to receive benefit. Holmes v. Sobol, 690 F. Supp. 154 (W.D.N.Y. 1988).

123. 15. 34 C.F.R. §§ 300.34 and 300.156 (includes qualified paraprofessionals and assistants); *see also* 20 U.S.C. § 1401(26).

124. 34 C.F.R. § 300.34.

125. 34 C.F.R. § 300.34; *see also* 20 U.S.C. § 1401(26).

126. 20 U.S.C. § 1401(a)(25); 34 C.F.R. § 300.307.

127. See § 3.13.

128. 34 C.F.R. § 300.34; *see also* 20 U.S.C. § 1401(26).

129. 34 C.F.R. § 300.34; *see also* 20 U.S.C. § 1401(26).

services provided by a licensed physician to determine a child's medically related disability that results in the child's need for special education and related services."[130]

The regulation, by its own terms, limits medical services to that necessary for diagnosis of disabilities. The United States Supreme Court recognized this limitation in *Irving Independent School District v. Tatro*,[131] where it held that the services of a licensed physician were not a related service.

The Court in *Tatro* pointed out that the regulations did provide for school health services, provided by someone other than a physician. The Court held that requiring medical services only for diagnosis, but requiring other health services by nonphysicians, was a reasonable distinction. The distinction was reasonable in light of Congressional intent to avoid imposing on school systems obligations that were "unduly expensive" or beyond their competence, while at the same time recognizing that "Congress plainly required schools hire various specially trained personnel to help handicapped children...."[132]

A distinction must also be made between medical services, as just discussed, and medical evaluations that are required to determine eligibility or to plan for an IEP. Medical evaluations are clearly contemplated for under IDEA.[133]

The distinction between medical services and nursing services is also critical in the area of residential programming. In these situations, usually hospitalization for a psychiatric disorder, it must be determined whether the child is primarily receiving medical services beyond diagnosis and evaluation. Where a child requires a residential program for medical as opposed to educational reasons, courts hold that the school system is not responsible for the cost of the residential portion of the placement.[134]

Placements made primarily for medical reasons, however, must be distinguished from those cases where a child has medical problems, but the placement is necessary for educational reasons. The test to be applied to determine whether the placement is for medical or educational purposes is "are the social, emotional, medical and educational problems so intertwined 'that realistically it is not possible for the court to perform the Solomon-like task of separating them'.... [T]he unseverability of such needs is the very basis for holding that the services are an essential prerequisite for learning."[135]

---

130. 34 C.F.R. § 300.34 (emphasis added); *see also* 20 U.S.C. § 1401(26).

131. 468 U.S. 883 (1984).

132. *Id.* at 892–893.

133. Doe v. Board of Educ. of Nashville-Davidson County, 441 Educ. Handicapped L. Rep. (CRR) 106 (M.D. Tenn. 1988); Seals v. Loftis, 614 F. Supp. 302 (E.D. Tenn. 1985).

134. *See* Butler v. Evans 225 F.3d 887 (7th Cir. 2000) (hospitalization costs arose from special circumstances and were not for "education or related services"); Dale M. v. Board of Educ. of Bradley-Bourbonnais High, 237 F.3d 813 (7th Cir. 2001) (district's obligation to provide student with free appropriate education did not extent to reimbursement of placement that was essentially custodial in nature); Clovis Unified School Dist. v. California Office of Admin. Hearings, 903 F.2d 635 (9th Cir. 1990); Tice v. Botetourt County School Bd., 441 Educ. Handicapped L. Rep. (CRR) 486 (W.D. Va. 1989), *aff'd in part, vacated in part, remanded*, 908 F.2d 1200 (4th Cir. 1990); Darlene L. v. Illinois State Bd. of Educ., 568 F. Supp. 1340, 1344 (N.D. Ill. 1983); McKenzie v. Jefferson, 566 F. Supp. 404 (D.D.C. 1983) *but see Independent School Dist. No. 284 v. A.C*, 258 F.3d 769 (8th Cir. 2001) where the court stated:

> If the problem prevents a disabled child from receiving educational benefit, then it should not matter that the problem is not cognitive in nature or that it causes the child even more trouble outside the classroom than within it. What should control our decision is not whether the problem itself is "educational" or "non-educational," but whether it needs to be addressed in order for the child to learn.

135. Kruelle v. New Castle County School Dist., 642 F.2d 687, 694 (3d Cir. 1981) *quoting* North v. District of Columbia Bd. of Educ., 471 F. Supp. 136, 141 (D.D.C. 1979); *see also* County of San

An issue that is of increasing concern in distinguishing between medical and other services is whether drug treatment programs can be a related service. In *Field v. Haddonfield Board of Education*,[136] the court held that whether a drug treatment program was a related service depended on the purpose and nature of the services, not on who provided the services or the mere fact that the services involved drug treatment. Holding that the program at issue was not a related service, the court found that the particular program at issue "provided intensive therapy for Daniel's underlying psychiatric disorders, which included psychiatric counseling, numerous physical evaluations as well as medication."[137]

3.9.8 School Health Services as Related Services

As discussed in the previous section, both IDEA regulations and the United States Supreme Court in *Irving Independent School District v. Tatro*[138] recognize a distinction between the provision of medical services and school health services. "School health services" and school nurse services are "health services "that are designed to enable a child with a disability to receive a FAPE as identified in the IEP. School nurse services are provided by a qualified school nurse. School health services are provided by a school nurse or other qualified person."[139]

Tatro dealt with an 8-year-old girl, Amber, born with spina bifida:

> [S]he must be catheterized every three or four hours to avoid injury to her kidneys. In accordance with accepted medical practice, clean intermittent catheterization (CIC), a procedure involving the insertion of a catheter into the urethra to drain the bladder, has been prescribed. The procedure is a simple one that may be performed in a few minutes by a layperson with less than an hour's training.[140]

The school system refused to place in Amber's IEP a requirement that school personnel perform CIC. Since CIC did not require a licensed physician to perform, and in fact it could be performed by a nurse or trained layperson, the Court held it constituted a required school health service.

The Court concluded with what amounts to a checklist of requirements that must be met for something to be considered a related service:

1. The child must be disabled and eligible for special education;

2. The service must be "necessary to aid a handicapped child to benefit from special education …";

3. Nursing services may be required, but not if the service must be performed by a licensed physician;

Diego v. California Special Educ. Hearing Office, 93 F.3d 1458 (9th Cir. 1996) (three-part test for determining when to impose responsibility for residential placement on the special education system); Department of Educ., State of Hawaii v. Cari Rae S. 158 F. Supp. 2d 1190 (D. Haw. 2001) (costs of hospitalization of student were for "diagnostic and evaluation purposes," and thus recoverable). *See* § 5.2.2.
   136. 769 F. Supp. 1313 (D.N.J. 1991).
   137. *Id.* at 1327.
   138. 468 U.S. 883 (1984).
   139. 34 C.F.R. § 300.3(13) (additional language of school nurse services added in 2005 regulations); *see also* 20 U.S.C. § 1401(26).
   140. Tatro, 468 U.S. at 885.

4. Services are required to be provided, not equipment.[141]

In 1999, the Supreme Court in *Cedar Rapids Community School District v. Garrett F.*,[142] adopted the *Tatro* bright line test regarding the provision of health services. The Court held that continuous nursing services were "related services" the district was required to provide under IDEA. In *Cedar Rapids* the student was ventilator dependent, wheelchair bound, and quadriplegic with normal cognitive abilities. He required a responsible individual to attend to his day-to-day needs. The aide assisted the student with urinary catherization and suctioning the tracheotomy tube. The student was also assisted with eating, positioning and bagging the ventilator to help him breathe.[143]

In adapting the two-step analysis of *Tatro*, the Court found that the definition of "related services" was satisfied. The services were "supportive" because the student could not attend school without them. The services were not "medical services" because medical services refer to services that must be performed by a physician.[144] Since the services could be performed by a nurse or layperson, they were not "medical services."[145]

The Court specifically declined to accept the cost-based, multi-factor test that had been used by some lower courts. The Court stated that the test was not supported by the statute or regulations and declined to accept it as the sole test for deciding the scope of services because it believed that it would be "engaged in judicial rule making without Congressional guidance."[146]

3.9.9 Social Work Services, Parent Counseling and Training as Related Services

"Parent counseling and training" as a related service "means assisting parents in understanding the special needs of their children and providing parents with information about child development and helping parents acquire skills that will assist them to support the IEP or IFSP."[147] For example, in *Chris D. v. Montgomery County Board of Edu-*

141. *Id.* at 894–5.
142. 526 U.S. 66 (1999).
143. Cedar Rapids, 526 U.S. at 69–70.
144. *Id.* at 73–74.
145. *Id.; see also* Morton Community Unit School Dist. v. J.M., 152 F.3d 583 (7th Cir. 1998) (adopted *Tatro* bright line test); Department of Educ. v. Katherine D., 727 F.2d 809 (9th Cir. 1983) (repositioning a suction tube in a child's throat was a related service where it could be done by school personnel); Hymes v. Harnett County Bd. of Educ., 664 F.2d 410 (4th Cir. 1981) (tracheostomy care assumed to be related service).
146. Cedar Rapids, 526 U.S. at 77–78. *See* Department of Educ. v. Katherine D., 727 F.2d 809, 813 (9th Cir. 1983) (requiring tracheostomy care as related service); Tokarcik v. Forest Hills School Dist., 665 F.2d 443, 455 (3d Cir. 1981) (pre-*Tatro* requiring CIC); Fulginti v. Roxbury Township Public Schools, 921 F. Supp. 1320 (D.NJ. 1996) (constant monitoring of tracheotomy tube was medical service and district was not required to pay). After *Tatro* and before the Supreme Court decided *Cedar Rapids Community School District v. Garrett F.*, courts held that a required health service that could be performed by a nurse, did not always constitute a related service. Courts consistently had held that health services must be "within reason." Detsel v. Board of Education, 637 F. Supp. 1022 (N.D.N.Y. 1986), *aff'd*, 820 F.2d 587 (2d Cir. 1987), *abrogated by* Cedar Rapids, 526 U.S. 66 (1999).
147. 34 C.F.R. § 300.34; *see also* 20 U.S.C. § 1401(22).

cation,[148] the court ordered the public school to provide training and counseling to a child's parents because the services were necessary in order to implement the IEP.

Social work services in schools include preparing histories, group and individual counseling, working with problems in school, home and community, mobilizing resources, and assisting in developing positive behavioral intervention strategies.[149]

3.10 Related Services Without Special Education

Statutory language indicates that eligibility for special education is a prerequisite for mandated related services. The statute requires "supportive services ... as may be required to assist a child with a disability to benefit from special education."[150] There is, therefore, a specific requirement that related services be directed to those receiving special education. The United States Supreme Court recognized this in *Tatro* when it held that the related service must be "necessary to aid a handicapped child to benefit from special education...."[151]

It is possible, however, that what is generally considered a related service may have educational content. The definition of special education under the regulations indicates that:

> [t]he term includes speech-language pathology, or any other related service, if the service is considered special education rather than a "related service" under State standards.[152]

Individual state regulations should be checked to determine what "related services" are considered to have educational content.[153]

3.11 Physical Education

Congress clearly intended,[154] and IDEA clearly requires, the provision of physical education to all children with disabilities.[155] The definition of "special education" found within IDEA specifically includes physical education.[156]

---

148. 753 F. Supp. 922 (M.D. Ala. 1990); *see also*, Gonzalez v. Puerto Rico Dep't of Educ., 254 F.3d 350, 353 (1st Cir. 2001) (the court found that the child's behavioral problems at home were so severe that the IEP must provide "further services and training for Gabriel's parents designed to help them manage Gabriel's behavior at home."); Evans v. Board of Educ. of the Rhinebeck Central School Dist., 930 F. Supp. 83 (S.D.N.Y. 1996) (act requires a plan of instruction under which educational progress is likely).

149. 34 C.F.R. §300.34 *see also* 20 U.S.C. §1401(26).

150. 20 U.S.C. §1401(26).

151. Tatro, 468 U.S. at 894. *See* Dubois v. Connecticut State Bd. of Educ., 727 F.2d 44 (2d Cir. 1984) (eligibility for transportation costs to out-of-state placement paid for by LEA is dependent on whether placement is necessary for special education); A.A. v. Cooperman, 218 N.J. Super 32, 526 A.2d 1103 (1987) (orthopedically impaired student not in need of special education, therefore related service of transportation not required under IDEA).

152. 34 C.F.R. §300.39; *see also* 20 U.S.C. §1401(29).

153. OSEP Memorandum 87-21 to State Directors of Special Education, *reprinted* 202 Educ. Handicapped L. Rep. (CRR) 372 (OSEP 1987).

154. H.R. Rep. No. 332, 94th Cong., 1st Sess. 9 (1975).

155. 20 U.S.C. §1412(26); 34 C.F.R. §300.39.

156. 20 U.S.C. §1401(29).

Physical education is defined in the regulations as including physical and motor fitness and "[s]kills in aquatics, dance, and individual and group games, sports (including intramural and life sports), and adapted physical education."[157]

Consistent with the overriding requirement that the child be educated in the least restrictive environment, children with disabilities are to participate in regular physical education classes unless the child is enrolled in a separate facility or the child's IEP requires a specialized physical education program.[158]

3.12 Travel Training

IDEA 1997 and the 1999 amendments added the definition of travel training to special education. "Travel training" means providing instruction to children with significant cognitive disabilities, as well as others, who need to develop an awareness of the environment in which they live and learn the skills necessary to move safely from school, home, work and community.[159] It is a service designed to prepare the child for post-school activities.

3.13 Vocational Education

The definition of special education under IDEA includes vocational education.[160] School systems providing vocational education are also subject to the United States Department of Education's anti-discrimination regulation under §504, as well as the Guidelines for Eliminating Discrimination and Denial of Services on the Basis of Race, Color, National Origin, Sex and Handicap in Vocational Education Programs.[161]

3.14 Extracurricular Activities

Regulations promulgated under IDEA require an equal opportunity for children with disabilities to participate in nonacademic and extracurricular activities.[162] These activities "may include counseling services, athletics, transportation, health services, recreational activities, special interest groups or clubs ... referrals ... and employment...."[163]

In one of the few judicial opinions addressing extracurricular activities, the court in *Rettig v. Kent City School District*,[164] held that since the regulation requiring nonacade-

157. 34 C.F.R. §300.39; *see also* 20 U.S.C. §1401(29).
158. 34 C.F.R. §300.39; *see also* 20 U.S.C. §§1401(29).
159. 34 C.F.R. §300.39 *see also* 20 U.S.C. §1401(29).
160. 34 C.F.R. §300.39; *see also* 20 U.S.C. §1401(29).
161. 34 C.F.R. Part 100 App. B.
162. 34 C.F.R. §300.107; *see also* 20 U.S.C. §1412(a)(1).
163. 34 C.F.R. §300.107; *see also* 20 U.S.C. §1412(a)(1).
164. 788 F.2d 328 (6th Cir. 1986).

mic and extracurricular activities required strict equality of opportunity it was contrary
to the interpretation of IDEA as announced by the Supreme Court in *Hendrick Hudson
District Board of Education v. Rowley*.[165] In *Rowley*, the United States Supreme Court rejected a reading of IDEA which measured level of educational services based on equal
opportunity.[166] The court in *Rettig*, relying on the language in *Rowley*, stated "the applicable test under *Rowley* is whether the handicapped child's IEP, when taken in its entirety, is reasonably calculated to enable the child to receive educational benefits."[167]
Since the child in *Rettig* was determined by the district court to not be able to "significantly benefit,"[168] the court held "the school district was not obligated to provide extracurricular activities from which [the child] would receive no significant educational
benefit."[169]

Given the ability to bring a suit under §504 of the Rehabilitation Act of 1973 concurrently with IDEA, (something that could not have been done when *Rettig* was decided),
there is an argument that the functional equivalent of the regulation is now available by
seeking relief under §504, since §504 does establish at least a general equal opportunity
requirement.[170]

---

165. 458 U.S. 176 (1981).
166. *Id.* at 198–199.
167. Rettig, 788 F.2d at 332.
168. *Id.*
169. *Id.* For a discussion of inability to benefit generally, see §5.2.3.
170. *Compare* Grube v. Bethlehem Area School Dist., 550 F. Supp. 418 (E.D. Pa. 1982) (exclusion from athletics based on having only one kidney improper under §504 where medical testimony
indicated slight risk of harm); Arlington County (Va.) Pub. Schools, 16 Educ. Handicapped L. Rep.
(LRP) 1188 (OCR 1990) (violation of §504 where general day camp provided, but no therapeutic
day camp); Clayton (Mo.) School Dist., 16 Educ. Handicapped L. Rep. (LRP) 766 (OCR 1990)
(§504 requires equal and meaningful participation in recreation) *with* Cavallaro v. Ambach, 575 F.
Supp. 171 (W.D.N.Y. 1983) (exclusion of learning disabled student from athletics did not violate
§504 where exclusion based on age, not handicapping condition); Baisden v. West Virginia Secondary Schs. Activities Comm'n, 211 W. Va. 725 (2002) (exclusion from high school athletics based
solely on age, does not violate section 504 of the Rehabilitation Act even when the student is still in
school because of his learning disability).

Chapter 4

Identification and Evaluation

4.1 In General

Each local education agency must establish procedures by which children in need of special education and related services are identified, located, and evaluated. The states are left to develop their own identification procedures, but the law requires an active effort to identify children in need of services, including children in private schools, and migrant and homeless children.[1]

Both § 504 and IDEA provide for the evaluation of children in their regulations.[2] Section 504 mentions that reevaluations and compliance with procedural safeguards consistent with IDEA regulations will also meet standards for compliance under § 504.[3] Compliance with either IDEA or § 504 regulations, however, does not insure compliance with the other.[4]

4.2 Identification

Typically, local school systems screen kindergarten children on an annual basis. Such efforts, however, are not alone sufficient, since disabilities may not appear until later

---

1. 34 C.F.R. § 300.15, § 300.111 and § 300.131; 20 U.S.C. §§ 1401(3), §§ 1412 (a)(3), §§ 1415(a) and, 1412(a)(10)(A)(ii) (migrant and homeless children were added in the 1999 amendments).

2. *Compare* 34 C.F.R. §§ 104.35–.36 (2000) *with* 34 C.F.R. §§ 300.301–.306; *see* P.N. v. Greco, 282 F. Supp. 2d 221 (D.N.J. 2003) *citing* W.B. v. Matula, 67 F.3d at 492–93 (3d Cir. 1995) (overruled on other grounds by A.W. v. Jersey City Public Schools, 486 F.3d 791 (3rd Cir. 2007) ("The [evaluation] requirements imposed under § 504 substantially duplicate those provided under the IDEA"); Reynolds (Ore.) School Dist. 7, 28 Individuals with Disabilities Educ. L. Rep. (LRP) (OCR 1997) (district conducted evaluations where necessary); Letter to Wilson, 21 Individuals with Disabilities Educ. L. Rep. (LRP) 70 (OSEP 1994) (evaluations require specific considerations); Letter to Mentink, 19 Individuals with Disabilities Educ. L. Rep. (LRP) 1127 (OCR 1993) (no right to an evaluation on demand under § 504).

3. 34 C.F.R. §§ 104.35(d)–.36; *see* Belleville (Wash.) School Dist. No. 405, 31 Individuals with Disabilities Educ. L. Rep. (LRP) 61 (OCR 1999) (OCR considers IDEA and OSEP policy in determining whether an evaluation was timely).

4. *See* Kennedy Inquiry, 16 Educ. Handicapped L. Rep. (LRP) 226 (EHA 1989). This is particularly true in the area of the need for reevaluations based on change in placement. *See* § 4.5.

and, of course, IDEA requires services prior to school age.[5] Further, early intervention can be critical to success.[6] In addition to kindergarten screening, therefore, schools use a variety of procedures including public education programs, public meetings, contact with day-care providers, as well as other service providers, media advertising, and referrals from other sources, such as physicians, who suspect a disability. The specific activities for identification, location and evaluation of children in private religious schools is done in consultation with personnel at the private school.[7]

Once an LEA is aware or has a suspicion that a child may need special education, an evaluation is required.[8] Even when a parent fails to disclose a medical condition, if the LEA has knowledge of the condition it must evaluate the child.[9] Actions by the LEA such as excluding a child from activities or secluding him is evidence that a problem requiring evaluation exists.[10] The LEA's obligation to evaluate a child, however, can be extinguished if the parent of the child refuses to allow the evaluations to be performed. It is important to note that when parents refuse services they waive all benefits under IDEA.[11]

Absenteeism may be sufficient to warrant evaluation if an LEA's guidelines indicate that absenteeism is regarded as a condition over which counseling should be initiated. If, however, the child's absences were not believed to have resulted from any psychological disorder, disability, or disruptive behavior, and no requests for evaluation are received, absenteeism may not be sufficient to indicate an evaluation is in order.[12]

There are conflicting rulings regarding whether there is a need to evaluate based on the psychiatric hospitalization of the student. In 1990, the United States Department of Education's Office for Civil Rights (OCR) found that a student previously in a regular education program did not require an evaluation solely because she was hospitalized,

---

5. *See* § 3.6. The regulations contain procedures for child-find for children from birth-age when the SEA and lead agency for the Infant and Toddlers program are different. 34 C.F.R. § 300.111.

6. The need for early intervention led to the Infants and Toddlers with Disabilities Act. 20 U.S.C. §§ 1431–1444; 34 C.F.R. Part 303. This "Infants and Toddlers" program provides for interagency coordination of services, including the development of Individual Family Service Plans for children under three-years of age, for children who "are experiencing developmental delays ... or ... have a diagnosed physical or mental condition which has a high probability of resulting in developmental delay." 20 U.S.C. § 1432(5). See Chapter 18.

7. 34 C.F.R. § 300.131.

8. Reid v. District of Columbia, 401 F.3d 516 (D.C. Cir. 2005) ("School districts may not ignore disabled students' needs, nor may they await parental demands before providing special instruction."); New Paltz Cent. Sch. Dist. v. St. Pierre, 307 F. Supp. 2d 394 (D.N.Y. 2004) (district failed to evaluate student after parent notified the district of emotional problems, and school psychologist recommended student for counseling); Letter to Williams, 20 Individuals with Disabilities Educ. L. Rep. (LRP) 1210 (OSEP 1993); OCR Memorandum, 19 Individuals with Disabilities Educ. L. Rep. (LRP) 876 (1993) (children suspected of having ADD and believed by the LEA to need special education or related services would have to be evaluated by the LEA); Auburn, Ala. School Dist., 16 Educ. Handicapped L. Rep. (LRP) 177 (OCR 1989). *See also* Letter to Sisisky, 21 Individuals with Disabilities Educ. L. Rep. (LRP) 995 (OSEP 1994) (prior medical diagnosis of ADD/ADHD does not alleviate the need for an evaluation).

9. Letter to Sisisky, 21 Individuals with Disabilities Educ. L. Rep. (LRP) 995 (OSEP 1994); *see also* New Paltz Cent. Sch. Dist. v. St. Pierre, 307 F. Supp. 2d 394 (N.D.N.Y. 2004); Great Valley, Pa. School Dist., 16 Educ. Handicapped L. Rep. (LRP) 101 (OCR 1989).

10. New York City Bd. of Educ., 16 Educ. Handicapped L. Rep. (CCR) 455 (OCR 1989).

11. Fitzgerald v. Camdenton R-III Sch. Dist., 439 F.3d 773 (8th Cir. 2006).

12. Bloomfield Township Schs., 42 Individuals with Disabilities Educ. L. Rep. (LRP) 285 (SEA N.J. 2004) (excessive absences and failing grades warrant a reevaluation of student); Oak Harbor (WA) Sch. Dist. No. 201, 45 Individual with Disabilities Educ. L. Rep. (LRP) 228 (OCRX 2005) (OCR determined that district should have evaluated student for special education because of student's long history of absenteeism, failing grades, and behavior problems).

since her academic status showed no change.[13] In 1989, however, the OCR stated that any child who was hospitalized for psychiatric diagnoses of depression, dysthymic disorder, or emotional problems should be evaluated.[14] A third ruling, made in 1990, may indicate that when a change in academic performance is coupled with a history of psychiatric hospitalization an evaluation should then be triggered.[15] If a psychologist refers a child for evaluation after a psychiatric hospitalization, one must be performed.[16]

Substance abuse may be sufficient under § 504 to qualify the child as a proper candidate for evaluation.[17] Failing to identify the child's substance abuse problem, however, is not a violation of § 504, if his problem was never displayed in any perceivable manner (for example, a change in behavior or academic performance) and there was no pattern of refusing evaluations, or ignoring the needs of substance abusers by the LEA.[18]

4.3 Preplacement Evaluations

Having identified a child who may be in need of special education and related services, an evaluation must be performed. Evaluation procedures determine "whether the child has a disability and the nature and extent of the special education and related services that the child needs."[19] The procedure for assessing evaluation data was first expanded by IDEA 97 and the 1999 amendments.[20]

Not surprisingly, the first evaluation must be performed before any action is taken with regard to the initial special education placement.[21] It is the state's responsibility to insure that all children with disabilities are identified and evaluated.[22] Once a child has

---

13. Mehlville, Mo. R-IX School Dist., 16 Educ. Handicapped L. Rep. (LRP) 465 (OCR 1989).

14. Vancouver Sch. Dist., 42 Individuals with Disabilities Educ. L. Rep. (LRP) 160 (SEA WA 2004) (district's failure to initiate a referral after student's known psychiatric hospitalization is a "clear indicator" of a possibly disabling condition); Community Unit School Dist. No. 300, 353 Educ. Handicapped L. Rep. (CRR) 296 (OCR 1989).

15. School Admin. Unit No. 19, N.H., 16 Educ. Handicapped L. Rep. (LRP) 86 (OCR 1989).

16. Edinboro, Pa. Intermediate Unit No. Five, 352 Educ. Handicapped L. Rep. (CRR) 511 (OCR 1987).

17. *See* Highline, Wash. School Dist. No. 401, 24 Individuals with Disabilities Educ. L. Rep. (LRP) 776 (OCR 1996) (under § 504, a district shall conduct an evaluation prior to a subsequent change in placement); Lake Washington, Wash. School Dist. No. 414, 257 Educ. Handicapped L. Rep. (CRR) 611 (OCR 1985).

18. York, Ill. Community High School, 352 Educ. Handicapped L. Rep. (CRR) 116 (OCR 1985).

19. 34 C.F.R. § 300.300.

20. 34 C.F.R § 300.533 now 34 C.F.R § 300.305.

21. 34 C.F.R. § 300.301; 20 U.S.C. § 1414(a); Dubois v. Connecticut State Dept. of Educ. 727 F.2d 44 (2d Cir. 1984).

22. 34 C.F.R. §§ 104.35–.36; 34 C.F.R. § 300.111; Fitzgerald v. Camdenton R-III Sch. Dist., 439 F.3d 773 (8th Cir. 2006) ("Child find ... is an ongoing activity that [school districts] should be engaged in throughout the year for all children in order to meet the statutory obligations to ensure that all children in the State are located, identified and evaluated and that all children have the right to FAPE.") (citations omitted) *Fitzgerald* also stated that public school districts have the obligation to find and identify all private school students with disabilities in their district.); *see also* Handberry v. Thompson, 446 F.3d 335 (2d Cir. 2006) (district has an affirmative obligation to identify any inmates that are eligible for special education services); LaHonda-Pescadero (Cal.) Unified School Dist., 20 Individuals with Disabilities Educ. L. Rep. (LRP) 833 (OCR 1993) (district's failure to evaluate a child for special education services violated its obligations pursuant to 34 C.F.R. § 104.35(a)

been identified through prescreening or referral, a timely evaluation must be instituted.[23]

Prior to the 2004 IDEA reauthorization the statute and regulations did not establish a limit to the time between identification and evaluation, although the individual states were able to establish such guidelines.[24] The initial evaluation must now be conducted within 60 days of receiving a parental request or within an individual state's established timeframe.[25] The timeframe does not apply, however, if the child's parent repeatedly fails or refuses to have the public agency evaluate the child.[26] Timely completion of the evaluation is in both the student's and the LEA's interest. For example, where there is an unreasonable delay in considering a child for an evaluation, or in completing an evaluation, the LEA may be liable for the private placement costs incurred by the parents during the delay. Prior to the 2004 reauthorization, timetables were set by the court for implementation of evaluation procedures where a violation of the reasonable standard had been found.[27]

Section 504 also requires preplacement evaluations to be made on any child identified to an LEA as having a disability.[28] Under Section 504, an evaluation is required to be complete prior to placement.[29] Evaluations must be made in a "timely" manner, once

---

and Title II of the ADA); Salley v. St. Tammany Parish School Bd., 57 F.3d 458 (5th Cir. 1995) (district not at fault for not evaluating student because student had moved into the state 14 days before the end of the year and did not return to the district the following year, but did return to school later).

34 C.F.R. § 300.111 includes children in private schools, highly mobile children, and children who are suspected of having a disability and in need of special education even though they are advancing from grade to grade.

23. Kelley Inquiry, 211 Educ. Handicapped L. Rep. (CRR) 240 (EHA 1981); *see* Letter to Anonymous, 30 Individuals with Disabilities Educ. L. Rep. (LRP) 602 (OSEP 1997) (time period for evaluations not regulated by federal law, but may be by state guidelines); Letter to Anonymous, 21 Individuals with Disabilities Educ. L. Rep. (LRP) 998 (OSEP 1994) (parental request for evaluation does not automatically trigger the right to an evaluation).

24. *Id.*

25. 34 C.F.R. § 300.301(c)(i)(ii).

26. 34 C.F.R. § 300.301(d)(i). The exception also applies when a child enrolls in another public agency's school after the relevant time frame has begun and before the determination of whether the child has a disability. The subsequent pubic agency must be making sufficient progress to ensure prompt completion of the evaluation and the parent and this agency agree to a completion date.

27. *See* O.F. v. Chester Upland Sch. Dist., 246 F. Supp. 2d 409 (E.D. Pa. 2002) (district violates child find evaluation obligation by waiting twelve months to evaluate student); *see also* Jose P. v. Ambach, 553 Educ. Handicapped L. Rep. (CRR) 298 (E.D.N.Y.), *aff'd*, 669 F.2d 865 (2d Cir. 1982). Courts have not established specific events by which to calculate the time a district has waited before evaluating. For instance, in *Chester Upland Sch. Dist.*, the court measured the time between the behavior that should have indicated a disability and the completion of the evaluation to come to their twelve month delay. Other courts, however, have calculated the delay by measuring the time between the indicative behavior and the referral for the evaluation.

28. 34 C.F.R. § 104.35(a); Martin County (Fla.) School Dist., 23 Individuals with Disabilities Educ. L. Rep. (LRP) 841 (OCR 1995); *see also* Davis (Cal.) Joint Unified School Dist., 31 Individuals with Disabilities Educ. L. Rep. (LRP) 186 (OCR 1999) (temporary disability should have triggered evaluation obligations); Tift County (Ga.) School Dist., 31 Individuals with Disabilities Educ. L. Rep. (LRP) 59 (OCR 1998) (district failed to evaluate student).

29. Polera v. Bd. of Educ., 288 F.3d 478 (2d Cir. 2002); P.N. v. Greco, 282 F. Supp. 2d 221 (D.N.J. 2003); Seattle (WA) School District No.1, 44 Individuals with Disabilities Educ. L. Rep. (LRP) 9 (OCRX 2005); St. Claire, Mo. R-XIII School Dist., 352 Educ. Handicapped L. Rep. (CRR) 201 (OCR 1986).

the LEA is aware of a child's need.[30] "Timeliness" may be what is reasonable under the circumstances, or it may be measured by the maximum time allowable under LEA rules.[31] "Gross disregard" for a child's welfare may result in the LEA's liability for the cost of private placement where evaluation was not made in a timely manner.[32] Referrals for evaluation under §504 must be in writing, and evaluations must culminate in final decisions regarding the child's need for service as well as a definite placement plan.[33]

The 2005 regulations include language regarding student screenings. Specifically when a teacher or specialist screens students to determine appropriate instructional strategies for implementing the curriculum it is not considered an evaluation for determining eligibility for special education and related services.[34]

4.4 Reevaluations Under IDEA

After the initial preplacement evaluation, an evaluation must take place at least every three years under IDEA and not more then once a year, unless the parent and the public agency agree otherwise.[35] A parent or school teacher, however, may request a reevaluation sooner, and a reevaluation should be conducted sooner than three years if the public agency determines that the child's special education and related services needs, which include improved academic achievement and functional performance, warrant such a reevaluation."[36] For example, if the parties disagree concerning placement

30. 34 C.F.R. §104.35(a)(b)(c); Shelby County Bd. of Educ., 24 Individuals with Disabilities Educ. L. Rep. (LRP) 730 (OCR 1996) (hearing officer found for district when the parents challenged the timeliness of the evaluation because there was no reason to suspect the student had a disability); Steilacoom (Wash.) Historical School Dist., 23 Individuals with Disabilities Educ. L. Rep. (LRP) 362 (OCR 1995) (district did not complete the assessment of a student until 7 months after the need for the evaluation was documented); Livingston Parish (La.) School Bd., 20 Individuals with Disabilities Educ. L. Rep. (LRP) 1470 (OCR 1993) (board had to reimburse the parents for the IEE and private placement because it did not evaluate the student).

31. North Smithfield, R.I. School Dist., 16 Educ. Handicapped L. Rep. (LRP) 245 (OCR 1990); *see also* Shelby County Bd. of Educ., 24 Individuals with Disabilities Educ. L. Rep. (LRP) 730 (OCR 1996) (an evaluation team meeting within two months of the request for evaluation was not undue delay); LaHonda-Pescadero (Cal.) Unified School Dist., 20 Individuals with Disabilities Educ. L. Rep. (LRP) 833 (OCR 1993) (period of 18 months between the time the child was referred to the district as a student with a record of disability and the development of an assessment plan was not timely).

32. Foster v. District of Columbia Bd. of Educ., 553 Educ. Handicapped L. Rep. (CRR) 520 (D.D.C. 1982).

33. Allegheny, N.Y. Central School Dist., 257 Educ. Handicapped L. Rep. (CRR) 494 (OCR 1984).

34. 34 C.F.R. §300.302(2)(2); 20 U.S.C. §1414(a)(1)(E).

35. 34 C.F.R. §300.303(a)(1) and (2)(1); 20 U.S.C. §1414(a)(2) (2005 regs).

36. 34 C.F.R. §300.303(a)(1); 20 U.S.C. §1414(a)(2); *see also* Herbin v. District of Columbia, 362 F. Supp. 2d 254 (D.D.C. 2005) (district's four month delay in providing reevaluation was not a violation of IDEA where evaluation had been completed earlier that year, and there was no apparent reason to reevaluate). *See generally,* Letter to Anonymous, 35 Individuals with Disabilities Educ. L. Rep. (LRP) 218 (OSEP 2001); Des Moines Indep. Community School Dist. and Johnston Community School Dist., 22 Individuals with Disabilities Educ. L. Rep. (LRP) 172 (OCR 1994) (district directed to refrain from the three-year reevaluation because parents opposed it and student's education record and trial placement could substitute for reevaluation); *see* Letter to Anonymous, 21 Individuals with Disabilities Educ. L. Rep. (LRP) 998 (OSEP 1994) (parents' request for evaluation

changes, or there are perceived discrepancies in the individualized educational program, a reevaluation request would be proper.[37]

Also, where only two years have elapsed, but substantive changes in standards used for the evaluation are made, a reevaluation has been held to be in order.[38]

Unlike Section 504, there is no requirement under IDEA that students are reevaluated before a significant placement change is made.[39] A decision to change placement, however, must be made by persons knowledgeable about the child, and with evaluation data in their possession.[40] No reevaluation is specifically required under IDEA regulations if services are suspended.

4.5 Reevaluations Under § 504

Section 504 regulations have a requirement that a reevaluation be made "periodically." A reevaluation policy consistent with IDEA regulations is one means of meeting this requirement.[41] IDEA requires reevaluation every three years and not more then once a year, unless the parent and agency agree otherwise, and when the educational needs warrant, or if requested by parents or teachers.[42] Section 504, however, unlike IDEA also requires that each identified child be evaluated prior to any significant change in placement.[43] The United States Department of Education Office of Civil

at any time does not automatically trigger obligation to conduct evaluation, but school must provide written notice of its refusal).

37. Shelby S. v. Conroe Independent School Dist 454 F.3d 450 (5th Cir. 2006) *cert denied* 127 S. Ct. 936 (2007) (despite a lack of parental consent, school district could compel a medical examination of a special education student where it was necessary for Individuals with Disabilities Education Act (IDEA) mandated reevaluation purposes); 20 U.S.C. § 1414 (a)(2) (the LEA may pursue procedures to obtain parental consent for initial evaluations and this court held the same requirements apply for reevaluations).

38. Grkman v. Scanlon, 563 F. Supp. 793 (W.D. Pa. 1983).

39. Houseman, 305 Educ. Handicapped L. Rep. (CRR) 34 (OCR 1986).

40. Casey K. v. St. Anne Cmty. High Sch. Dist. No. 302, 400 F.3d 508 (7th Cir. 2005); White v. Ascension Parish Sch. Bd., 343 F.3d 373 (5th Cir. 2003); McKenzie v. Smith, 771 F.2d 1527 (D.C. Cir. 1985).

41. 34 C.F.R. § 104.35(b); Kansas City (MO) #33 School District, 44 Individuals with Disabilities Educ. Law Rep. (LRP) 48 (OCR 2005).

42. 34 C.F.R. § 300.303. In *Herbin v. District of Columbia,* 362 F. Supp.2d 254(D.D.C. 2005) the court held that a four-month delay in responding to a request for reevaluation was not violation of IDEA and requirement that request for reevaluation be accompanied by showing that conditions warranted reevaluation did not apply to grandmother's request. The court was interpreted 34 C.F.R. 300.536(b)(2000) (amended 2005, 34 C.F.R. 300.303) to require that a party requesting a reevaluation show that "conditions warrant" one, the hearing officer noted that there were "no time limitations provided by [the] IDEA by which a school system must complete evaluations," and that the circumstances before him did not render a four-month delay in responding unreasonable.

43. 34 C.F.R. § 104.35(a); *see also* Highline (Wash.) School Dist., No. 401, 24 Individuals with Disabilities Educ. L. Rep. (LRP) 776 (OCR 1996); Renton (Wash.) School Dist., 21 Individuals with Disabilities Educ. L. Rep. (LRP) 859 (OCR 1994) (removal of a student from a service necessary for an appropriate education is a significant change in placement); Thompson Bd. of Educ., 20 Individuals with Disabilities Educ. L. Rep. (LRP) 1307 (OCR 1994) (enrollment in a day program after residential placement and hospitalization was a significant change in placement); Kelso (Wash.) School Dist., 20 Individuals with Disabilities Educ. L. Rep. (LRP) 1003 (OCR 1993) (student's placement

Rights has identified the following as among the circumstances that constitute a "significant" placement change:

- A change from a private to a public school[44]

- Transfer to a more restrictive environment[45]

- Returning a student to special education after a brief placement in regular education[46]

- Initiation of homebound education[47]

- Termination of homebound education[48]

- A change in the number of hours per week spent in regular versus special education classes[49]

- A change in status from special education to regular education[50]

- Transfers from one type of special education program to another (e.g., learning disabled to educable mentally retarded)[51]

- A transfer of a special education student to state prison[52]

- Suspension from school in excess of ten days per year[53]

---

from a self-contained special education classroom to a regular education program was a significant change).

44. Humbodlt, Tenn. City School Dist., 352 Educ. Handicapped L. Rep. (CRR) 557 (OCR 1987).

45. Hillsborough County (FL) Sch. Dist., 45 Individuals with Disabilities Educ. L. Rep. (LRP) 102 (OCR 2005); Special School Dist. of St. Louis County, Mo., 352 Educ. Handicapped L. Rep. (CRR) 156 (OCR 1986).

46. Wright City, Mo. School Dist., 352 Educ. Handicapped L. Rep. (CRR) 161 (OCR 1986).

47. Southeastern Greene, Pa. School Dist. No. One, 353 Educ. Handicapped L. Rep. (CRR) 105 (OCR 1988); Russell County, Ky. School Dist., 352 Educ. Handicapped L. Rep. (CRR) 253 (OCR 1986).

48. Clermont, Ohio Northeastern Schools, 257 Educ. Handicapped L. Rep. (CRR) 577 (OCR 1984).

49. Eastmont (WA) Sch. Dist. No. 206, 42 Individuals with Disabilities Educ. L. Rep. (LRP) 44 (OCR 2004) (district significantly changed student's program when they did not provide a daily sixty minute special education and behavioral services session—district attempted to assert that it was detrimental to the student's education to remove him from a core class each day); Omaha, Neb. Pub. Schools, 257 Educ. Handicapped L. Rep. (CRR) 71 (OCR 1979).

50. Hillsborough County (Fla.) School Dist., 27 Individuals with Disabilities Educ. L. Rep. (LRP) 730 (OCR 1997); Dyersburg, Tenn. City School Dist., 353 Educ. Handicapped L. Rep. (CRR) 164 (OCR 1988); *but see*, Stafford (TX) Municipal Sch. Dist., 37 Individuals with Disabilities Educ. L. Rep. (LRP) 132 (OCR 2002) (discontinuing student in a dyslexia program, and placing student in a regular education program is not a significant change in placement).

51. Orcas Island (Wash.) School Dist. No. 137, 31 Individuals with Disabilities Educ. L. Rep. (LRP) 12 (OCR 1999); Powhatan, Kan. Unified School Dist. No. 150, 257 Educ. Handicapped L. Rep. (CRR) 32 (OCR 1979).

52. Brandywine, Del. School Dist., 16 Educ. Handicapped L. Rep. (LRP) 327 (OCR 1989).

53. Pennsylvania Dept. of Educ., 353 Educ. Handicapped L. Rep. (CRR) 115 (OCR 1988). *Compare* Rutland (VT) City Pub. Schs., 42 Individuals with Disabilities Educ. L. Rep. (LRP) 180 (OCR 2004) (expulsion of student with ADHD and Asperger's syndrome without manifestation determination is significant change in placement, deserving of due process) *with* Jefferson Parish (LA) Pub. Sch. System, 40 Individuals with Disabilities Educ. L. Rep. (LRP) 219 (OCR 2003) (no significant change in placement when District suspends student multiple times for a total of forty-five days when the suspensions did not amount to a pattern of exclusions); Buncombe (N.C.) County School Dist., 23 Individuals with Disabilities Educ. L. Rep. (LRP) 364 (OCR 1995) (expulsion or suspension of a student with a disability for more than 10 consecutive school days is a significant change in

- Termination of services[54] including graduation[55]
- Adding or eliminating a program or service, or substantially increasing or decreasing the amount of time a program or service is provided.[56]

4.6 Evaluation Standards Under IDEA

Minimum standards for evaluation procedures are set forth under 34 C.F.R. § 300.304.[57] A fundamental principle of these standards is that no single procedure or test may constitute an evaluation.[58] For example, where a hearing-impaired child was evaluated and placed solely on the basis of observation, his evaluation was invalid.[59]

The extent of the evaluation performed is dependent on the suspected disability of the child. All areas related to a suspected disability must be assessed, "including if appropriate, health, vision, hearing, social and emotional status, general intelligence, academic performance, communicative status, and motor abilities."[60] A child, for example, with a mild disability, such as speech impairment, may not need a full battery of assess-

---

placement); Chester County (Tenn.) School Dist., 17 Educ. Handicapped L. Rep. (LRP) 301 (OCR 1990) (10 days in-school suspension not a significant change in placement).

54. Renton (Wash.) School Dist., 21 Individuals with Disabilities Educ. L. Rep. (LRP) 859 (OCR 1994) (evaluation necessary prior to discontinuing articulation services); *see also* Brentwood, N.Y. Union Free School Dist., 257 Educ. Handicapped L. Rep. (CRR) 653 (OCR 1985).

55. Rolla (Mo.) #3 School Dist., 31 Individuals with Disabilities Educ. L. Rep. (LRP) 189 (OCR 1999) (requires evaluation before graduation because graduation is a change in placement).

56. *See* Eastmont (WA) Sch. Dist. No. 206, 42 Individuals with Disabilities Educ. L. Rep. (LRP) 44 (OCR 2004); Mansfield (Wash.) School Dist., 207 Individuals with Disabilities Educ. L. Rep. (LRP) 1050 (OCR 1995); *see also* Harlowton (Mont.) Public Schools, 26 Individuals with Disabilities Educ. L. Rep. (LRP) 1156 (OCR 1997) (requiring student to have a full-time escort not a substantial change in placement).

57. Prior to the 2005 regulations the section Procedures for Evaluation and Determination of Eligibility were 34 C.F.R § 300.530–543, now entitled Evaluations and Revaluations and contained in 34 CFR § 300.301–311

58. 34 C.F.R. § 300.304(b)(2); *see also* 20 U.S.C. §§ 1412(a)(6)(B), 1414(b)(1)–(3); A.B. v. Lawson, 354 F.3d 315 (4th Cir. 2004) (parents' argument that student should have been found to be a student with a disability based on one evaluation "squarely conflicted" with the IDEA statutory requirements); Eric H. v. Judson Indep. Sch. Dist., 2002 U.S. Dist. LEXIS 20646 (W.D. Tex. 2002) (district clearly fulfill statutory requirements when they used a variety of assessment tools and strategies to gather relevant and current functional and developmental information); Brookhart v. Illinois State Bd. of Educ., 697 F.2d 179 (7th Cir. 1982) (where a test is one of three, requirements have been held to have been fulfilled).

59. Bonadonna v. Cooperman, 619 F. Supp. 401 (D.N.J. 1985); Santa Ana Unified School Dist., 21 Individuals with Disabilities Educ. L. Rep. (LRP) 1189 (OCR 1994) (it is unnecessary to identify a processing disorder so long as such a disorder manifests itself through observable symptoms resulting in a severe discrepancy between ability and achievement).

60. 34 C.F.R. § 300.304(c)(4); *see also* 20 U.S.C. §§ 1412(a)(6)(B), 1414(b)(2),(3); Krista P. v. Manhattan Sch. Dist., 255 F. Supp. 2d 873 (D. Ill. 2003); J. S. v. Shoreline Sch. Dist., 220 F. Supp. 2d 1175 (W.D. Wash. 2002) ("The IDEA does not prescribe substantive goals for an evaluation, but provides only that it be "reasonably calculated to enable the child to receive educational benefits," citing Rowley, 458 U.S. at 205–07.); *see also,* Letter to Anonymous, 40 Individuals with Disabilities Educ. L. Rep. (LRP) 98 (OSEP 2003) (IDEA does not specifically require district to assess hearing impaired student in American Sign Language unless the IEP team specifically recommends doing so); Mary P. v. Illinois State Bd. Educ., 23 Individuals with Disabilities Educ. L. Rep. (LRP) 1064 (N.D. Ill. 1996) (variety of sources and evaluations should not just include academic performance).

ments, although additional assessments must be available if referral is later found to be needed. In fact, an assessment that is overly broad and includes tests unrelated to a suspected disability is improper.[61]

The assessment must be sufficiently comprehensive and use a variety of tools and strategies to gather relevant functional and developmental information.[62] This information is gathered from the parents as well, and assists in developing the content of the IEP.[63] The assessment must include information about the child's ability to be involved in or make progress in the general curriculum.[64] The 2005 regulations have eliminated the requirement that when an assessment was not conducted under standard conditions, the evaluation report had to contain a description of the extent to which the evaluation had varied.[65] The evaluation data needs to be sufficient to determine whether a disability exists.[66] Additional data may be needed to determine the present levels of performance and educational needs of the child, whether special education or related services are needed, and whether modifications are needed in the IEP.[67]

Any tests or other evaluation materials must be in the native language of the child (or, where appropriate, some other means of communication). The materials must be valid and reliable for the specific purpose for which they are being used and administered by trained personnel, according to instructions prepared by the producers.[68]

Any tests used to evaluate a child must also be nondiscriminatory.[69] The test must also be administered "so as best to ensure that if a test is administered to a child with impaired sensory, manual, or speaking skills, the test results accurately reflect the child's aptitude or achievement level or whatever other factors the test purports to measure...."[70]

Classroom assessments and observations by teachers and related service providers are also included to document the child's academic performance and behavior in order to determine whether a learning disability exists.[71] The observation of the child must be

---

61. 34 C.F.R. §300.304(c)(4); *see* Washington, Vt. Central Supervisory Union No. 32, 257 Educ. Handicapped L. Rep. (CRR) 509 (OCR 1984) (socio-cultural inventories performed on all parents of learning disabled children were ruled to be such a violation); Feeley Inquiry, 211 Educ. Handicapped L. Rep. (CRR) 415 (EHA 1986) (psychological assessments in mentally retarded and learning disabled children have been interpreted as proper, since both conditions have social and emotional consequences); *but see,* Springfield Sch. Dist. 44 Individuals with Disabilities Educ. L. Rep. (LRP) 202 (SEA VT 2005) (after a three-year evaluation, school district finds child not eligible for special education services).

62. 34 C.F.R. §300.304(b)(1) and (6); *see* Letter to Marion, 30 Individuals with Disabilities Educ. L. Rep. (LRP) 605 (OSEP 1998) (educational agency may choose assessment methods, but methods must meet IDEA requirements).

63. 34 C.F.R. §300.304(1)(and (7).

64. 34 C.F.R. §300.304(b)(1)(ii) and (7).

65. 34 C.F.R. §300.532(b)(1)(ii);(this requirement is not contained in the 2005 regulations); *see generally* 34 C.F.R. §300.304.

66. Letter to Gallagher, 24 Individuals with Disabilities Educ. L. Rep. (LRP) 177 (OSEP 1996) (physician's diagnosis of ADD alone cannot establish IDEA eligibility).

67. 34 C.F.R. §300.533(a)(2)(i–iv).

68. 34 C.F.R. §300.304(c)(1)(ii–v).

69. 34 C.F.R. §300.304(c)(1)(i); *see also* 20 U.S.C. §§1412(a)(6)(b), 1414(b)(2),(3). The leading case in this area held that standardized I.Q. tests were racially biased against African-Americans, and that by their use, African Americans were being erroneously evaluated, so the court ordered alternative testing. Larry P. v. Riles, 793 F.2d 969 (9th Cir. 1986). *See also* Mattie T. v. Holladay, 522 F. Supp. 72 (N.D. Miss. 1978) (consent agreement entered pursuant to discriminatory violations of children under IDEA).

70. 34 C.F.R. §300.304(c)(3); *see also* 20 U.S.C. §§1412(a)(6)(B), 1414(b)(1)–(3).

71. 34 C.F.R 34 §300.310.

performed by the child's regular education teacher or, if none, a regular classroom teacher qualified to teach the child or a teacher qualified by the SEA if the child is less then school age.[72] The observation must take place in the child's classroom setting or if the child is not in school, then in the child's usual environment and occur after a referral for evaluation is made and parental consent is obtained.[73]

Medical treatment is not the responsibility of the LEA, but it must pay for any medical diagnostic exams appropriate to insure a valid evaluation.[74]

"Substantial compliance" to standards has been held sufficient to avoid court ordered declaratory judgments.[75]

The standards for evaluation were expanded under the 97 IDEA statute and 99 regulations to include increased parental input. An example of increased parental input is the regulation that provides for a determination as to whether additional evaluation data is needed for an initial evaluation or reevaluation.[76] The review of the evaluation data specifically requires a review of evaluations and information provided by the parent.[77]

Although review of the assessment can occur without a meeting, if the data is insufficient, the public agency must obtain it. If the evaluation data indicate that the child does not have a disability, the public agency must provide the parents notice as to the reasons and as to their right to request an assessment.[78]

4.7 Evaluation Standards Under § 504

Evaluation procedures outlined in § 504 provide that validated tests, administered by trained personnel, must be used to assess specific disabilities on an individualized basis, so as not to cause the disability to defeat the test results.[79] The testing method must also result in more than a single general intelligence quotient as a result.[80]

---

72. 34 C.F.R 34 § 300.310 (2); 34 C.F.R 34 § 300.308(a)(1). This is a change from the prior regulation 34 C.F.R. § 300.542(a) that required the observation of the child must be performed by someone other than the child's teacher. *See* Ford v. Long Beach Unified Sch. Dist., 291 F.3d 1086 (9th Cir. 2002) (regulations implementing IDEA require the observation of someone other than the regular classroom teacher; however, such a procedural flaw does not violate IDEA if it does not affect the validity of the assessment); Letter to Anonymous, 21 Individuals with Disabilities Educ. L. Rep. (LRP) 64 (OSEP 1994).

73. 34 C.F.R. § 300.310(c).

74. Doe v. Board of Pub. Educ., 441 Educ. Handicapped L. Rep. (CRR) 106 (M.D. Tenn. 1988); 20 U.S.C. § 1401(22); Northeast Indep. School Dist., 22 Individuals with Disabilities Educ. L. Rep. (LRP) 523 (OCR 1995) (a neurological exam was a necessary part of the evaluation because student showed signs of depression, anxiety, irritability, and educational frustration). See § 3.9.6.

75. Powell v. Defore, 553 Educ. Handicapped L. Rep. (CRR) 293 (M.D. Ga. 1982), *aff'd on other grounds*, 699 F.2d 1078 (11th Cir. 1983).

76. 34 C.F.R. § 300.305.

77. 34 C.F.R. § 300.305(a)(1)(i–iii).

78. 34 C.F.R. § 300.305(c) and (d).

79. 34 C.F.R. § 104.35(b).

80. *Id.*; Arlington (Tex.) Indep. School Dist., 31 Individuals with Disabilities Educ. L. Rep. (LRP) 87 (OCR 1999) (evaluation was not timely or sufficiently comprehensive).

Tests used in the evaluation process must be validated for the specific purpose for which they are used and must be administered by trained personnel to conform to the producers' instructions.[81]

The tests selected for use in a §504 evaluation must be of a nondiscriminatory nature so that the results accurately reflect the child's aptitude, not his physical disability.[82] An evaluation must not be based on a single procedure.[83] A "variety of sources" must be used, and not merely I.Q. tests.[84] Indeed, I.Q. itself may not preclude a student from eligibility for special education.[85] Undue reliance on any one testing device is improper.[86]

A student's adaptive behavior must also be considered in the evaluation process.[87]

4.8 Notice and Consent for Evaluation Under IDEA

The LEA must provide the parents with notice of intent to evaluate the child.[88] Consent is required for selective procedures only. Evaluation does not include tests administered to all children in a grade or class.[89]

The notice must allow a reasonable time prior to initiation of the preplacement evaluation.[90] The notice of intent to evaluate the child must include a listing of tests that are expected to be used in the evaluation,[91] as well as the general provisions governing notice and consent.[92]

Parental consent for the preplacement evaluation under IDEA is required.[93] OSEP has stated that there is no difference between a refusal to consent for initial services and a failure to respond to a consent request.[94] Parental consent is defined as a written agreement that acknowledges the understanding of all activities sought to be performed in the evaluation process and the voluntary acquiescence to these activities, subject to

---

81. 34 C.F.R. §104.35(b)(1).

82. 34 C.F.R. §104.35(b)(3); California School for the Deaf, 257 Educ. Handicapped L. Rep. (CRR) 583 (OCR 1984).

83. 34 C.F.R. §104.35(b)(2).

84. Larry P. v. Riles, 793 F.2d 969 (9th Cir. 1984).

85. *See generally*, A.B. v. Lawson, 354 F.3d 315 (4th Cir. 2004) (student with "above average I.Q. is eligible for special education benefits); Letter to Lillie Felton, 23 Individuals with Disabilities Educ. L. Rep. (LRP) 714 (OSEP 1995); Santa Ana Unified School Dist., 21 Individuals with Disabilities Educ. L. Rep. (LRP) 1189 (SEA Cal. 1994); Ulissi Inquiry, 18 Individuals with Disabilities Educ. L. Rep. (LRP) 683 (OSEP 1992).

86. 34 C.F.R. §104.35(b)(2).

87. 34 C.F.R. §104.35(c).

88. 34 C.F.R. §300.503; *see also* 20 U.S.C. §§1415(b)(3),(4),(c), 1414(b)(1).

89. Black Inquiry, 16 Educ. Handicapped L. Rep. (LRP) 1400 (OSEP 1990).

90. 34 C.F.R. §300.503(a); *see* §§1415(b)(3), 1414(a)(1)(C) and (c)(3); 20 U.S.C. §§1415(b)(3), (4),(c), 1414(b)(1).

91. 34 C.F.R. §300.503(b)(3); Letter to Manasevit, 42 Individuals with Disabilities Educ. L. Rep. (LRP) 233 (OSEP 2004) (notice must "fully inform the parent of all information relevant to the activity for which consent is sought, which for the initial provision of special education and related services ..."); Gorski v. Lynchburg School Bd., 441 Educ. Handicapped L. Rep. (CRR) 415 (4th Cir. 1989).

92. See Chapter 9.

93. 34 C.F.R. §300.303(a); *see* 20 U.S.C. §1414(a)(1)(D) and (c).

94. Letter to Gantwerk, 39 Individuals with Disabilities Educ. L. Rep. (LRP) 215 (OSEP 2003).

unilateral revocation.[95] Parental consent is not required to review existing data as part of an evaluation or reevaluation.[96] Oral consent may never substitute for written consent.[97]

Parental consent is required for reevaluation also.[98] However, it is not needed if the local educational agency can demonstrate that it has taken reasonable measures to obtain the consent and the child's parent failed to respond.[99] Consent is a vital part of IDEA and states may amend consent requirements in only limited ways. They may, however, devise procedural steps for obtaining consent.[100]

If the parents refuse to consent to the initial evaluation the LEA may, but is not required to, either file for a due process hearing, seek mediation, or initiate any state permitted procedure, such as a request for a court order.[101] The Eighth Circuit Court of Appeals has ruled that a school district seeking permission to conduct an evaluation may not bypass parental consent when the child is being privately educated, and the parents have expressly waived all benefits under the IDEA.[102] If the parent fails to respond or refuses to consent to provision of services the public agency may not use procedures such as mediation and due process to obtain consent.[103] The public agency, however, will not be in violation for failure to provide the special education and related services.[104] If parents home school or place the child in private school at their own expense and fail to provide consent for the initial evaluation or reevaluation, the public agency may not use the consent override procedures such as mediation and due process proceedings.[105]

---

95. 34 C.F.R. § 300.309; *see also* 20 U.S.C. § 1414(a)(1)(d).

96. 34 C.F.R. § 300.300(c)(2)(1)(i).

97. Montanye v. Wissahickon Sch. Dist., 399 F. Supp. 2d 615, 624–25 (E.D. Pa. 2005) (special education teacher violated IDEA when she obtained parent's oral permission to take student to psychological evaluations but did not receive permission in writing); *see also* Cogley, 211 Educ. Handicapped L. Rep. (CRR) 212 (EHA 1980).

98. 34 C.F.R. § 300.300(c); *see* 20 U.S.C. § 1414(a)(1)(D) and (c).; Carroll v. Capalbo, 563 F. Supp. 1053 (D.R.I. 1983).

99. 34 C.F.R. § 300.300(c)(2)(i); *see* 20 U.S.C. § 1414(a)(1)(D) and (c)(3); Letter to Manasevit, 42 Individuals with Disabilities Educ. L. Rep. (LRP) 233 (OSEP 2004) (OSEP advises districts to thoroughly document attempts to obtain consent for reevaluations); Graham, 213 Educ. Handicapped L. Rep. (CRR) 250 (OSEP 1989).

100. 34 C.F.R. § 300.300(c)(2); Letter to Manasevit, 42 Individuals with Disabilities Educ. L. Rep. (LRP) 233 (OSEP 2004); *see also* Glendale Unified School Dist. 41 IDELR 88 (SEA CA 2003) (California law broadens Federal consent requirements to require local educational agencies to obtain written parental consent before any special education placement, and not just for initial placements); Lindsay, 211 Educ. Handicapped L. Rep. (CRR) 251 (EHA 1981).

101. C.F.R. § 300.300(a)(30(i); *see* 20 U.S.C. § 1414(a)(D)(1) and (c).(3); Letter to Ackerhalt, 22 Individuals with Disabilities Educ. L. Rep. (LRP) 252 (OCR 1994) (district has option, but is not required, to challenge parents refusal to consent to evaluation under both IDEA and § 504); *see also*, Los Angeles Unified Sch. Dist., 45 Individuals with Disabilities Educ. L. Rep. (LRP) 264 (SEA CA 2006) (despite parental objection, district successfully sought court order to evaluate student, who district reasonably believed had undiagnosed disabilities and who was overdue for a triennial evaluation); Hueneme Elem. School Dist., 23 Individuals with Disabilities Educ. L. Rep. (LRP) 753 (Cal. 1995); Cayuga Indep. School Dist., 22 Individuals with Disabilities Educ. L. Rep. (LRP) 815 (SEA Tex. 1995); Altoona Area School Dist., 22 Individuals with Disabilities Educ. L. Rep. (LRP) 1069 (SEA Pa. 1995).

102. Fitzgerald v. Camdenton R-III Sch. Dist., 439 F.3d 773 (8th Cir. 2006).

103. 34 C.F.R. § 300.300(b)(3).

104. 34 C.F.R. § 300.300(b)(4)(i).

105. 34 C.F.R. § 300.300(b)(4)(i); *see also* Durkee v. Livonia Cent. School Dist. 487 F. Supp.2d 313 (W.D.N.Y. 2007) (the IDEA does not permit a school district to compel the evaluation of a student for determination of that student's eligibility for publicly-funded special education services

4.9 Notice and Consent for Evaluation Under § 504

Section 504's general procedural safeguards apply to the evaluation process. Although less specific than IDEA, the regulations specifically use adherence to IDEA as an example of how to meet the requirement.[106] Further, notice is specifically required for evaluations under § 504.[107] Notice has been ruled to require a description of general types of tests to be used, even if the actual procedures are not known in advance.[108] Under IDEA, however, the notice need not list every test or outline qualifications of the examiners.[109]

Reevaluation must also be preceded by notice.[110]

4.10 Evaluators Under IDEA

The evaluation under IDEA is conducted by a multidisciplinary team.[111] This team includes the parents, at least one regular education teacher of the child, one special education teacher, a representative of the public agency, and an individual who can interpret the instructional implications of the evaluation.[112] When a specific learning disability is suspected, additional team members are required to be on the team.[113] These

---

where the student's parent has objected to such an evaluation and has refused to accept publicly-funded special-education services).

106. 34 C.F.R. § 104.36. *See, e.g.*, Eric H. v. Methacton Sch. Dist., 265 F. Supp. 2d 513 (E.D. Pa. 2003); Weber v. Cranston Pub. Sch. Comm., 245 F. Supp. 2d 401 (D.R.I. 2003) ("While Section 504 itself does not guarantee FAPE, its implementing regulations, promulgated by the Department of Health, Education and Welfare ("HEW") contemporaneously with the IDEA's regulations, substantively track the text of the IDEA itself."); Forest Park, Mich. School Dist., 352 Educ. Handicapped L. Rep. (CRR) 182 (OCR 1986); Tucson, Ariz. Unified School Dist., 257 Educ. Handicapped L. Rep. (CRR) 312 (OCR 1981). In 1987, OCR ruled that a failure to obtain parental consent prior to conducting speech and language evaluation of a child was a violation of 34 C.F.R. § 104.36. Sachem, N.Y. Central School Dist., 352 Educ. Handicapped L. Rep. (CRR) 462 (OCR 1987); *see also* Letter to Durheim, 27 Individuals with Disabilities Educ. L. Rep. (LRP) 380 (OCR 1997) (initial evaluations require parental consent; subsequent evaluations do not).

107. 34 C.F.R. § 104.36; Orcas Island (Wash.) School Dist. No. 137, 31 Individuals with Disabilities Educ. L. Rep. (LRP) 12 (OCR 1999) (§ 504 and ADA do not require prior parental notice of each test given as part of evaluations).

108. Wisconsin Dept. of Pub. Instruction, 352 Educ. Handicapped L. Rep. (CRR) 177 (OCR 1985).

109. Sutler and McCoy Inquiry, 18 Individuals with Disabilities Educ. L. Rep. (LRP) 307 (OSEP 1991).

110. East Stroudsburg, Pa. Area School Dist., 353 Educ. Handicapped L. Rep. (CRR) 108 (OCR 1988); *see also* Letter to Zirkel, 22 Individuals with Disabilities Educ. L. Rep. (LRP) 667 (OCR 1993) (§ 504 reevaluation requires due process to override parents' lack of consent, but does not require for initial evaluation).

111. 34 C.F.R. § 300(a)(4); *see* Letter to Clarkson, 28 Individuals with Disabilities Educ. L. Rep. (LRP) 482 (OSEP 1997) (special education teachers can be trained and supervised in the administration of standardized tests).

112. 34 C.F.R. § 300.321; *see also* 20 U.S.C. § 1414(d)(1)(B)–(d)(1)(D).

113. 34 C.F.R. § 300.308; *see* 34 C.F.R. § 300.309(a)(1) (must not require a state to use a severe discrepancy formula). Diagnosis of a learning disability must be made by a team judgment, and not on a prepared formula or profile, and if there is a conflict between any formula and the team's judg-

additional team members are the child's regular teachers, or if there is no regular teacher, a teacher qualified to teach such a child, including preschool children, and "at least one person qualified to conduct individual diagnostic examination of children, such as a school psychologist, speech-language pathologist, or remedial reading teacher."[114]

4.11 Evaluators Under § 504

Section 504 requires that evaluations be made by a knowledgeable and specialized group of persons, but unlike IDEA there is nothing to indicate what kind of person must be on the evaluation team.[115]

4.12 Reporting Evaluation Results Under Both IDEA and § 504

Under IDEA, the results of an evaluation must be reported in a written form for a child suspected of a specific learning disability.[116] Each team member must certify that the report reflects his or her conclusions.[117] The report must be one document, however, any team member's dissent may be presented separately.[118] Section 504 regulations require that all information obtained be documented.[119] Failure to provide a written report, however, may be found to be "minor" and not prejudicial when the parents have been actively involved in the process.[120]

---

ment, further explanation and possible further exploration may be required. O'Grady Inquiry, 211 Educ. Handicapped L. Rep. (CRR) 158 (EHA 1980).

114. 34 C.F.R. § 300.308; *see also* M.L. v. Fed. Way Sch. Dist., 394 F.3d 634 (9th Cir. 2005) ("The failure to include at least one regular education teacher ... is a structural defect that prejudices the right of a disabled student to receive a FAPE").

Where a child has multiple diagnoses, but a specific learning disability is suspected, 34 C.F.R. § 300.540 does apply. Ehrlich Inquiry, 211 Educ. Handicapped L. Rep. (CRR) 289 (OCR 1982).

115. Manteca (Cal.) Unified School Dist., 30 Individuals with Disabilities Educ. L. Rep. (LRP) 544 (OCR 1998) (district neglected duty to assess because it did not convene a group of assessors to evaluate and relied only on resource specialist's determination that student was ineligible); Lake Shore (Mich.) Pub. Schools, 25 Individuals with Disabilities Educ. L. Rep. (LRP) 324 (OCR 1996) (evaluator member of augmentative team licensed to assess communication disabilities was qualified evaluator); *see generally* S-1 v. Turlington, 635 F.2d 342 (5th Cir. 1981).

116. 34 C.F.R. § 300.311.

117. 34 C.F.R. § 300.311(b).

118. 34 C.F.R. § 300.311(b); Baer v. Klagholz, 34 Individuals with Disabilities Educ. L. Rep. (LRP) 141 (N.J. Super. Ct. App. Div. 2001) ("By requiring dissenting members of a team to write separate statements, or certify whether the joint report reflects his or her conclusions, parents who also disagree would become aware of the dissent. Without that requirement, the views of a dissenting team member may remain unknown, and the IEP report reduced to a majority decision"); McCarthy Inquiry, 211 Educ. Handicapped L. Rep. (CRR) 359 (EHA 1985).

119. 34 C.F.R. § 104.35(c)(2).

120. Hiller v. Board of Educ., 743 F. Supp. 958, 969–970 (N.D.N.Y. 1990).

4.13 Parental Participation

Under IDEA there has always been the general requirement of parental consent, notice and reasonable opportunity to attend meetings. Prior to the 1999 amendments, however, there was no participatory role required in the evaluation process. Since 1999, however, parents have a participatory role in the evaluation process.[121] The parents are part of the team that reviews existing evaluation data for both the initial and subsequent reevaluations of the child. This includes reviewing existing data as well as identifying additional data if needed.

If the parent disagrees with the evaluation, there is the right to initiate due process procedures and seek reevaluation.[122] The Supreme Court, as well as lower courts, have consistently recognized that IDEA requires parental participation at all meaningful stages during the process.[123] The arbitrary refusal of an LEA to allow the parents, for example, to observe the evaluation process might well be a violation of this requirement. But at a minimum, the parents have the explicit right to view the observations conducted by the evaluators.[124]

Under § 504 regulations, parental participation is limited to the right of consent, notice, and initiation of due process procedures.[125]

4.14 Disputes Over Evaluation

An evaluation of any child identified as having a disability may be used to either prove or disprove the need for a special education placement. Until recently, after the evaluation, the burden of proving the child is ineligible for services had been on the LEA. The United States Supreme Court decision in *Schaffer v. Weast,*[126] however, dramatically changed the distribution of burdens of proof during due process hearings. Noting that the text of IDEA is silent on the allocation of the burden of persuasion,[127] the Court in held that in the absence of state legislation to the contrary, "the burden of

---

121. 34 C.F.R. §§ 300.304; *see also* 20 U.S.C. §§ 1414(b)(1)–(2).

122. 34 C.F.R. § 300.305(d)(ii); *see* Pasatiempo v. Aizawa, 103 F.3d 796 (9th Cir. 1996) (parents request for an evaluation entitles parents to certain procedural safeguards);

123. *See, e.g.* Board of Educ. of the Hendrick Hudson Cent. School Dist. v. Rowley, 458 U.S. 176, 205–206 (1982) (IDEA gives "a large measure of participation at every stage of the administrative process"); Honig v. Doe, 484 U.S. 305, 311 (1988) ("the Act establishes various procedural safeguards that guarantee parents ... an opportunity for meaningful input into all decisions affecting their child's education ..."); N.L. v. Knox County Schs., 315 F.3d 688 (6th Cir. 2003) (citing *Rowley*); Amanda J. v. Clark County Sch. Dist., 267 F.3d 877 (9th Cir. 2001) (procedural inadequacies that seriously infringe the parents' opportunity to participate in the IEP formulation process deny FAPE); DeVries v. Spillane, 853 F.2d 264, 266 (4th Cir. 1988) ("meaningful participation in all aspects"); *see also* T.R. v. Kingwood Township Bd. of Educ., 32 F. Supp. 2d 720 (D.N.J. 1998) (board did not violate IDEA by forwarding a final draft IEP to parents before IEP meeting because "there were many copious exchanges of information"); Fuhrmann v. East Hanover Bd. of Educ., 993 F.2d 1031, 1035 (3d Cir. 1993) (school board did not violate IDEA by presenting parents with an IEP at child's classification meeting, two months before first meeting to formulate IEP).

124. 34 C.F.R. § 300.310 and 34 C.F.R. § 300.306(a)(1).

125. *See* 34 C.F. R. § 104.36.

126. Schaffer v. Weast, 126 S. Ct. 528 (2005).

127. *Id.* at 534.

proof in an administrative hearing challenging an IEP is properly placed upon the party seeking relief."[128] By leaving open the question of whether states may assign school districts the burden of proof during due process hearings, several courts have used the omission to uphold challenges to state laws.[129]

Due process procedures may be initiated at any time during the evaluation by either the LEA, the parents or a member of the evaluation team if disagreements arise.[130] If the parents do not believe the evaluation is appropriate for their child, they may seek an Independent Educational Evaluation at the LEA's expense.[131]

If the parents refuse to make the child available for an evaluation, they may be denied reimbursement for an appropriate private school placement.[132] The school district has the right to reevaluate student by an expert of its choice.[133]

4.15 Identification/Evaluation Checklist-Summary

____LEA must establish "child find" system

____Initial preplacement evaluation required

____Initial evaluation within sixty days of parental request

____Reevaluation required every three years (IDEA), unless parent and public agency agree otherwise

____Reevaluation required "periodically" (504)

____Reevaluation required earlier if:

    ____Academic achievement and functional performance warrant (IDEA)

    ____If requested by parents (IDEA & 504)[134]

    ____If requested by teachers (IDEA & 504)

    ____Evaluation may not occur more than once a year, unless parent and public agency agree otherwise

128. *Id.* at 537.

129. *See* Indep. Sch. Dist. No. 701 v. J.T., 2006 U.S. Dist. LEXIS 8474 (D. Minn. 2006); Gellert v. D.C. Pub. Schs, 2006 U.S. Dist. LEXIS 30212 (D.D.C. 2006); See also, Chapter 13 § 8 for a more complete discussion on burdens).

130. Pachl v. Seagren, 453 F.3d 1064 (8th Cir. 2006) (district requests due process hearing after disagreement with parents over student IEP.); R. R. v. Fairfax County Sch. Bd., 338 F.3d 325 (4th Cir. 2003) (student's parents can initiate due process procedures when his parents and district disagree as to IEP appropriateness); Oak Ridge City (Tenn.) School Dist., 29 Individuals with Disabilities Educ. L. Rep. (LRP) 390 (OCR 1998) (disputes over evaluations properly resolved through due process procedure); *see also* McKeever, 211 Educ. Handicapped L. Rep. (CRR) 45 (EHA 1978).

131. M.S. v. Mullica Tp. Bd. of Educ. 485 F. Supp. 2d 555 (D.N.J. 2007) (parents were not entitled to reimbursement, after they moved out of the district, for costs of independent educational evaluations unilaterally obtained outside the collaborative IEP development process); *See* also Chapter 6.

132. Patricia P. v. Board of Educ. of Oak Park, 203 F.3d 462 (7th Cir. 2000).

133. M.T.V. v. DeKalb County School Dist. 446 F.3d 1153 (11th Cir. 2006) (district court properly affirmed ALJ's order requiring student to submit to district's reevaluation in order to remain eligible for OHI services).

134. Under § 504 an agency can have a reevaluation policy or other policies that are consistent with the IDEA regulations.

____If there is a significant placement change (504)

____Evaluation Standards

    ____No single procedure or test (IDEA & 504)

    ____Must result in more than a single intelligence quotient (IDEA& § 504)

    ____All areas of suspected disability must be assessed (IDEA)

    ____Sufficiently comprehensive

    ____Native language (IDEA)

    ____Validated evaluation materials (IDEA & 504)

    ____Trained personnel following instructions of producers (IDEA &504)

    ____Administered in an individualized manner such that disability does not defeat purpose of test (IDEA & 504)

    ____Nondiscriminatory (IDEA & § 504)

    ____Observation can be by child's teacher for specific learning disability (IDEA)

    ____Observation in the classroom or usual environment for specific learning disability (IDEA)

    ____Information provided by parent (IDEA)

____Notice

    ____Required for initial preplacement evaluation (IDEA & 504)

    ____Information provided regarding general curriculum

    ____Reasonable time prior to evaluation

    ____Includes list of tests (IDEA & 504)

    ____Includes general provisions under IDEA governing notice and consent

    ____Required for reevaluations

____Consent

    ____Must be in writing

    ____Must acknowledge understanding of evaluation process

    ____Required for the evaluations unless parent failed to respond after reasonable measures to obtain consent

    ____Subject to unilateral revocation by parent

    ____Not required for reviewing existing data as part of an evaluation or reevaluation

____Evaluators

    ____Parents of the child (IDEA)

    ____Regular education teacher if child is participating in regular education

    ____At least one special education teacher or special education provider

    ____Representative of public agency who:

        ____is qualified to provide or supervise provision of specially designed instruction _____is knowledgeable about the general curriculum

_____is knowledgeable about resources of the public agency

_____An individual who can interpret instructional implications of the evaluators

_____Other qualified professionals, knowledgeable individuals, or individuals with special expertise regarding the child (at the discretion of parent or public agency)

_____When specific disability is suspected also:

_____child's regular teacher

_____person qualified to conduct individual diagnostic examination

_____Report of evaluation must be in writing

_____Disputes over evaluation

_____Parents may seek due process hearing and are required to attend resolution meeting if file due process.

_____Parents seek mediation

_____Parents may seek Independent Educational Evaluation

_____Hearing officer may seek Independent Educational Evaluation

Chapter 5

Eligibility

5.1 In General

Being an individual with a physical or mental disability does not guarantee eligibility for services under IDEA. To be eligible, the student must meet two floor requirements. The student must have a disability and be in need of special education as a result of the disability.[1] It is important to keep in mind that, unless a particular state has chosen to provide additional protections, the existence of either of these standards alone is insufficient. Indeed, the definition of the term of a child with a disability explicitly provides that you are eligible under the terms of the statute if "[the child] needs special education and related services."[2]

Special education is defined as "specially designed instruction, at no cost to the parents, to meet the unique needs of a child with a disability, including instruction conducted in the classroom, in the home, in hospitals, institutions, in other settings and instruction in physical education."[3] Special education includes speech pathology[4], travel training[5] and vocational training.[6]

Also, included under the umbrella of special education services are "transition services" and "assistive technology services." Transition services should have a results oriented design that focuses on improving the academic and functional achievement of the child and must be included as part of the individualized education program (IEP) for students no later than the age of 16, or younger if the IEP team makes that determination.[7] Transition services are those services that will promote the student's transition to life after education under IDEA. These post school activities may include vocational training, higher education, supported employment, adult education, adult services, independent living, or community participation. The various activities that are part of the transition services are based on the students' needs, preferences and interests.[8]

The IEP must include measurable goals based upon age appropriate transition assessments and services including courses of study needed to reach those goals.[9]

---

1. 34 C.F.R. § 300.8; *see* 20 U.S.C. §§ 1401(3) and 1401(30).
2. 34 C.F.R. § 300.8; *see* 20 U.S.C. §§ 1401(3) and 1401(30).
3. 34 C.F.R. § 300.39; *see* 20 U.S.C. § 1401(29).
4. 34 C.F.R. § 300.39.
5. 34 C.F.R. § 300.39.
6. 34 C.F.R. § 300.39.
7. 34 C.F.R. § 300.43 and § 300.320(b).
8. 34 C.F.R. § 300.42; *see also* 20 U.S.C. § 1401(30).
9. 34 C.F.R. § 300.320(b)(1)(2).

Assistive technology services are those services that directly assist a child with a disability in the selection, acquisition, or use of an assistive technology device, but does not include surgically implanted medical devices.[10]

As discussed elsewhere,[11] a child eligible for special education is also entitled to related services[12] required to assist the child to receive benefit from special education. A child is not eligible for a related service if the child is not also receiving special education.[13]

5.2 Specially Designed Instruction

Specially designed instruction is defined as "adapting, as appropriate to the needs of an eligible child under this part, the content, methodology, or delivery of instruction to address the unique needs of the child that result from the child's disability and to ensure access of the child to the general curriculum, so that he or she can meet the educational standard within the jurisdiction of the public agency that apply to all children."[14] Specially designed instruction would include speech-language pathology, vocational education, physical education, and travel training.

Transition services may also be considered specially designed instruction.[15] Issues often arise, therefore, concerning whether a child's particular needs are educational in nature. The three areas in which questions arise as to whether a service is educational or something else are: nonacademic instruction; disputes over whether the services are needed for educational or medical reasons; and questions of whether the child can benefit from the educational services.

5.2.1 Nonacademic Instruction

IDEA and its regulations clearly indicate that physical education is included within the definition of special education.[16] Very early in the history of IDEA it was determined that education also included a wide range of subjects not commonly considered traditional education. As stated by the United States Third Circuit Court of Appeals, "the concept of education is necessarily broad with respect to persons [severely disabled] where basic self-help and social skills such as toilet training, dressing, feeding and communication are lacking, formal education begins at that point."[17] Courts have consistently made it clear that education for those with severe disabilities is broadly defined under IDEA.[18]

---

10. 34 C.F.R. § 300.5; 20 U.S.C. § 1401.
11. *See* § 3.9.
12. 34 C.F.R. § 300.34; *see* 20 U.S.C. § 1401(26).
13. 34 C.F.R. § 300.39.
14. 34 C.F.R. § 300.39(a)(3); *see* 20 U.S.C. § 1401(26).
15. 34 C.F.R. § 300.43.
16. 34 C.F.R. § 300.39 *see also* 20 U.S.C. § 1401(29).
17. Battle v. Pennsylvania, 629 F.2d 269, 275 (3d Cir. 1981); *see also* Kruelle v. New Castle County School District, 642 F.2d 687, 693 (3d Cir. 1981).
18. *See, e.g.,* Shore Regional High School Bd. of Educ. v. P.S., 381 F.3d 194 (3d Cir. 2004) (held that district court's finding that school district provided a FAPE as required by the IDEA was clearly erroneous where could not prevent student from being bullied); Polk v. Central Susquehanna Intermediate Unit 16, 853 F.2d 171, 176 (3d Cir. 1988) ("the physical therapy itself may form the core of a severely disabled child's special education"); DeLeon v. Susquehanna Community School Dist.,

5.2.2 Medical v. Educational Needs

Many students with physical and mental disabilities have medical as well as educational problems. It is clear that if services are required for purely medical reasons, the school system is not responsible under IDEA. An emotionally disturbed child who is hospitalized solely for the purpose of psychiatric treatment is not entitled to have the psychiatric treatment paid for by the LEA.[19] The LEA may be obligated to provide hospital-based educational programming, but the treatment portion will not be the LEA's responsibility.

Quite often, however, it is impossible to separate the educational and medical problems of the student. If indeed, an emotionally disturbed child is unable to learn because the psychiatric condition interferes with the learning process, it may be impossible to separate the educational problems from the psychiatric problems. One educational goal for an emotionally disturbed child may be to develop appropriate peer relationships, but the fact that the child presently does not have those relationships may be a function of the child's psychiatric problem. Psychological or psychiatric services, therefore, may be required. In some case the "unseverability of such needs is the very basis for holding that the services are an essential prerequisite for learning."[20]

The severability of the services arises quite commonly in disputes involving residential educational programs where the LEA seeks to pay only that portion of the placement which is related to educational needs. The situation can arise in several contexts including the parents placing the child in a private program or hospital, or the state placing the child in a correctional facility. The critical question is whether the placement was for educational or noneducational reasons. If the placement is for purely a noneducational reason, the clearest example being a placement in a correctional facility, the LEA need only provide a FAPE where the child is placed, it need not pay for noneducational parts of the placement.[21]

---

747 F.2d 149, 153 (3d Cir. 1984) ("[t]he program may consist largely of 'related services' such as physical, occupational, or speech therapy"); Abrahamson v. Hershman, 701 F.2d 223, 228 (1st Cir. 1983) ("Where what is being taught is how to pay attention, talk, respond to words of warning, and dress and feed oneself, it is reasonable to find that a suitably staffed and structured residential environment providing continual training and reinforcement in those skills serves an educational service...."); Campbell v. Talladega County Bd. of Educ., 518 F. Supp. 47, 50 (N.D. Ala. 1981) (educational program consisted of "functional" skills); *see generally* M.C. v. Central Regional School Dist., 81 F.3d 389 (3d Cir. 1996) (court granted compensatory education to a student who was not placed in a residential placement); Jeffreys v. New Jersey Depart. of Educ., 23 Individuals with Disabilities Educ. L. Rep. (LRP) 945 (D.N.J. 1996) (deals with a preliminary injunction to prevent the removal of the student from a residential facility until a decision is reached); Baser v. Corpus Christi Independent School Dist., 20 Individuals with Disabilities Educ. L. Rep. (LRP) 981 (S.D. Tex. 1994) (student's IEP was appropriate and did not deny him a FAPE since part of the IEP was learning basic self-help skills).

19. Department of Educ., State of Hawaii v. Cari Rae S., 158 F. Supp. 2d 1190 (D. Haw. 2001) (costs of hospitalization of student were for "diagnostic and evaluation purposes," and thus recoverable given the "child find" and costs were necessary for a proper evaluation and diagnosis and are "related services").

20. Kruelle v. New Castle County School Dist., 642 F.2d 687, 694 (3d Cir. 1981); *see also* McKenzie v. Smith, 771 F.2d 1527, 1534 (D.C. Cir. 1985) (are the child's emotional needs "segregable from the learning process").

21. Alice M. v. Board of Educ. of Bradley-Bourbonnais High, 237 F.3d 813 (7th Cir. 2001) (district's obligation to provide student with free appropriate education did not extend to reimbursement of placement in boarding school which was essentially custodial in nature); OSEP Memorandum 87-21, 202 Educ. Handicapped L. Rep. (CRR) 372, 373–374 (June 29, 1987).

In other words, if the LEA could have provided an appropriate program in the public school, there is no obligation to pay for the hospital or correctional facility. If the parents place a child in a hospital for purely medical reasons, the LEA is not responsible for noneducational parts of the program.[22] As stated in *Kruelle v. New Castle County School*,[23] the question is "whether full-time placement may be considered necessary for educational purposes, or whether the residential placement is a response to medical, social or emotional problems that are segregable from the learning process."[24]

Where, however, placement in a hospital or other residential program is for educational reasons, the LEA is responsible for both the educational components of the placement as well as the associated costs such as room and board. Specifically, if the service is required in order for the child to benefit from educational services, it is a related service and therefore must be provided by the LEA.[25] While this requirement may ne-

---

22. *See* Butler v. Evans, 225 F. 3d 887 (7th Cir. 2000) (although school district provided educational services on site, district not responsible for student's hospitalization costs); Clovis Unified School Dist. v. California Office of Administrative Hearings, 903 F.2d 635 (9th Cir. 1990) (placement in psychiatric hospital was for medical, not educational reasons); *see also* Sanger v. Montgomery County Bd. of Educ., 916 F. Supp. 518 (D. Md. 1996) (district not required to pay for a residential placement because it was not needed for the learning process); Metropolitan Government of Nashville and Davidson County v. Tennessee Dept. of Educ., 771 S.W.2d 427 (Tenn. Ct. App. 1989).

23. 642 F.2d 687 (3d Cir. 1981).

24. *Id.* at 693; *see also* County of San Diego v. California Special Educ. Hearing Office, 93 F.3d 1458 (9th Cir. 1996) (three tests under *Clovis* for determining whether residential placement is necessary for a FAPE are where the placement is "supportive" of the pupil's education; where medical, social or emotional problems that require residential placement are intertwined with educational problems; and when the placement is primarily to aid the student to benefit from special education); Mrs. B. v. Milford Bd. Of Educ., 103 F.3d 1114 (2d Cir. 1997) (state had to fund residential program because it was necessary for the student to make educational progress, even though student had emotional and home life problems); Naugatuck Bd. of Educ. v. Mrs. D., 10 F. Supp. 2d 170 (D. Conn. 1998) (student's social and emotional problems qualified as educational needs warranting residential placement); J.B. v. Killingly Bd. of Educ., 990 F. Supp. 57 (D. Conn. 1997) (state agency and school board were ordered to provide a 21-year old language and learning disabled student, who had been diagnosed with pedophilia and multiple personality disorder, with an appropriate community-based residential special education placement); *but see* San Rafael Elementary School Dist. v. California Special Educ. Hearing, 482 F. Supp. 2d 1152 (N.D Cal. 2007) (school district was not responsible for ensuring that disabled student translated behavior skills learned in classroom to home or community settings, and district's offer to place student with autistic behaviors at private school specializing in the education of students with behavioral needs instead of residential program met requirements of the IDEA); Independent School Dist. No. 284 v. A.C., 258 F.3d 769 (8th Cir. 2001) (student whose truancy and defiance resulted from emotional disability which affected her learning and prevented her from receiving educational benefit qualified for special education services and residential placement); E.B. v. Independent School Dist. No. 720, WL 1544611 (D. Minn. 2007) (residential placement not necessary for education where student made progress in academics and behavior management); Schreiber v. Ridgewood Bd. of Educ., 952 F. Supp. 205 (D.N.J. 1997) (residential placement not needed because placement was "least restrictive which provides an educational benefit"); Hall v. Shawnee Mission School Dist., 856 F. Supp. 1521 (D. Kan. 1994) (school did not have to pay for placement since IEP included placement at a different school and had educational benefit).

25. *See, e.g.*, Drew P. v. Clarke County School Dist., 877 F.2d 927 (11th Cir. 1989); Geis v. Board of Educ., 774 F.2d 575 (3d Cir. 1985); McKenzie v. Smith, 771 F.2d 1527 (D.C. Cir. 1985); Colin K. v. Schmidt, 715 F.2d 1 (1st Cir. 1983); Abrahamson v. Hershman, 701 F.2d 223 (1st Cir. 1983); Kruelle v. New Castle County School, 642 F.2d 687 (3d Cir. 1981); Diamond v. McKenzie, 602 F. Supp. 632 (D.D.C. 1985); Lamoine School Committee v. N.S., 353 F. Supp. 2d 18 (D. Me. 2005); Papacoda v. Connecticut, 528 F. Supp. 68 (D. Conn. 1981); Gladys J. v. Pearland Indep. School Dist., 520 F. Supp. 869 (S.D. Tex. 1981).

cessitate the provision of medical services, in no event does it appear that the school is responsible for the services of a physician.[26]

5.2.3 Ability to Benefit From Educational Services

The issue of the appropriateness of a cost-benefit analysis in determining whether a child is entitled to receive educational services is an emotional question which has received inconsistent treatment by the courts. How much benefit must a child be able to receive to be entitled to receive educational services? If we take the extreme case, what of the child in a coma? Is the child entitled to receive educational programming even if it is unclear the child will receive any educational benefit?

In *Timothy W. v. Rochester, New Hampshire School District*,[27] an eight-year-old was denied any educational program or services by the LEA, relying on the LEA's "capable of benefitting" eligibility criterion. After lengthy evaluations and hearings, the United States District Court held that because the child was not capable of benefitting from special education, the LEA was not obligated to provide special education under either state or federal law. In a thorough analysis of the statutory language, legislative history, and case law, the First Circuit reversed the district court and stated:

> The language of the Act in its entirety makes clear that a "zero-reject" policy is at the core of the Act, and that no child, regardless of the severity of his or her handicap, is to ever again be subjected to the deplorable state of affairs which existed at the time of the Act's passage, in which millions of handicapped children received inadequate education or none at all. In summary, the Act mandates an appropriate public education for all handicapped children, regardless of the level of achievement that such children might attain.[28]

Other decisions have not been as broadly written as *Timothy W.* Some opinions, for example, state that a child in a coma would be completely uneducable and therefore not eligible within the meaning of IDEA.[29] Other opinions have reached what is essentially a middle ground. In *Mathews v. Davis*,[30] for example, the district court had originally ordered a residential placement. Approximately four and one-half years later, the district court "was persuaded that, although substantial educational progress had been achieved with the program, maintenance of the advances [the child] had made and acquisition of the few additional skills of which he was considered capable could be accomplished without a residential program...."[31] In affirming the district court's decision, the Fourth Circuit pointed to three factors: the fact that the child had "reached the point of diminishing marginal returns and would not be able to learn much more";[32] the residential program had become largely custodial; and experts agreed that continued educational programming "would at best yield only marginal returns and probably none at all."[33]

---

26. Irving Indep. School Dist. v. Tatro, 468 U.S. 883 (1984). *See* §§ 3.9.6, 3.9.7.
27. 875 F.2d 954 (1st Cir. 1989).
28. *Id.* at 960–61.
29. Parks v. Pavkovic, 753 F.2d 1397 (7th Cir. 1985).
30. 742 F.2d 825 (4th Cir. 1984).
31. *Id.* at 828.
32. *Id.*
33. *Id.* at 830.

Even given this language, however, the district court did not deny all educational services, holding only that the services did not have to take place in a residential setting.

5.3 Qualifying Conditions in General

Federal Regulations delineate the conditions which qualify a child for an individualized education program under IDEA.[34] The definitions contained in the regulations attempt to encompass any mental, physical or emotional condition which could have an adverse effect on a child's educational performance. While a complete discussion of the various disabilities is beyond the scope of this work, a brief summary of the disabilities from the medical perspective and its educational impact is helpful. In addition, the categories and definitions of educational disabilities are included.

The thirteen classifications which define the eligibility criteria under IDEA's regulations are most helpfully analyzed in three broad groups: physical impairments; mental, emotional and cognitive impairments; and the "catch-all" categories. The physical impairments group includes visual, auditory, speech and orthopedic impairments. The mental, emotional and cognitive impairments group includes mental retardation, specific learning disabilities, emotional disturbances, autism, and traumatic brain injury.[35] Finally, the regulations contain two "catch-all" categories: multiple disabilities and other health impaired.

5.3.1 Hearing Impairments

"Hearing impairments" encompass three related terms each defined separately: "'Deafness'[36] means a hearing impairment which is so severe that the child is impaired in processing linguistic information through hearing, with or without amplification, which adversely affects educational performance." "'Deaf-blindness' means concomitant hearing and visual impairments, the combination of which causes such severe communication and other developmental and educational problems that they cannot be accommodated in special education programs solely for deaf or blind children."[37] "'Hearing impairment' means an impairment in hearing, whether permanent or fluctuating, which adversely affects a child's educational performance but which is not included under the definition of 'deaf' in this section."[38] The distinction drawn between deaf and hard of hearing in the regulation is artificial and somewhat meaningless in terms of causation, determination, and educational impact; thus, these terms will be analyzed generally as hearing defects.[39]

---

34. 34 C.F.R. § 300.8 *see* 20 U.S.C. §§ 1401(3), and 1401(30).

35. It is recognized that many emotional disturbances have nothing to do with a child's actual intelligence. Mental and emotional deficits are grouped together in this instance because of their common lack of outward physical manifestations (aside from behavior) which separates them from the physical impairments.

36. 34 C.F.R. § 300.8.

37. 34 C.F.R. § 300.8.

38. 34 C.F.R. § 300.8.

39. Similarly, the deaf-blind category might seem to be an odd distinction, since it concerns a combination disability which would fit under the multihandicapped label. Although there is no legislative history on point, it may be reasonable to assume that Congress chose to single out deaf-blindness because of its uniquely devastating effect on a child's educational performance.

Education of the deaf-blind child involves highly specialized training and resources, including a

Educationally significant hearing impairments may stem from a number of causes occurring both prior to birth and during childhood.[40] Risk factors for hearing loss in neonates include inherited deafness, ear, nose, jaw and throat deformities, exposure to ototoxic drugs and chemicals,[41] prenatal infections,[42] fetal alcohol syndrome, AIDS, prenatal cocaine exposure[43], neonatal intensive care,[44] prematurity[45] and children with an Apgar score of 0–3 at 5 minutes, those who fail to initiate spontaneous respirations at 10 minutes or those with hypotonia persisting to 2 hours of age.[46] A child who is born with normal hearing may still be at risk for hearing loss from recurrent ear infections, childhood illness,[47] sound trauma,[48] and hearing "knock out."[49]

Children who are hearing impaired at birth may literally have an invisible disability, since many hearing losses are not associated with outward physical deformities.[50] Parents may not be aware of their child's hearing loss until it is manifested by delayed speech development, and then it is often tragically mistaken for mental retardation.[51]

The presence and extent of hearing loss are usually determined by a pediatric audiologist or educational audiologist after an initial hearing screening test is failed.[52] The audiologist may employ a variety of methods to determine the presence and extent of hearing loss, ranging from informal, at-home observation to formal behavioral and auditory evaluations.[53] Specialists use the results of such evaluations to clas-

---

special language involving the touching of the hands and fingers. Although the causes of deafness and blindness are covered separately under their respective headings, the educational impact of deaf-blindness is so all-encompassing as to be beyond the scope of this work. *See* Kramer, *Audiological Evaluation and Aural Rehabilitation of the Deaf-Blind* (1979); Yoken, *Living with Deaf-Blindness* (1979); Freeman, *Understanding the Deaf-Blind Child* (1975).

40. Bordley, *Ear, Nose and Throat Disorders in Children* (1986). Another excellent, but slightly more technical source in this area is Pappas, *Diagnosis and Treatment of Hearing Impairment in Children: A Clinical Manual* (1985); *see also* Cotton & Meyer, *Practical Pediatric Otolaryngology* (1999); Gulya & Wilson, *An Atlas of Ear, Nose and Throat Diagnosis and Treatment* (1999).

41. Ototoxic drugs are certain diuretics, antibiotics and other chemicals which can cause hearing loss in infants through gestational or postnatal exposure. Bordley, *supra* note 39, at 123. *See also* Kristina M. English, *Educational Audiology the Lifespan: Serving all Learners with Hearing Impairment* (1995).

42. During the 1960's, mumps and rubella were the predominant causes of infant deafness; however, the development of effective vaccinations has virtually eliminated these viruses. Other congenital infections which continue to cause infant deafness today include syphilis, toxoplasmosis and other intrauterine infections. *Id.* at 126.

43. Bordley, *supra* note 39, at 80.

44. The placement of an infant in a neonatal intensive care unit is an indication of serious illness, and many illnesses in this stage of a child's life may cause hearing loss. Additionally, ototoxic drugs are often used in therapy, putting the infant at additional risk. *Id.* at 134.

45. Deafness is common in premature infants. Ten to twenty-three percent of deaf children were born prematurely. *Id.* at 134.

46. *Id.* at 122.

47. Meningitis is a common cause in sudden childhood hearing losses. *Id.* at 135.

48. Sound trauma deafness, or "'boilermakers' deafness," results from prolonged exposure to loud noise, or from a single incident of acoustic trauma, such as an explosion. *Id.* at 140.

49. Hearing loss from "knock out" occurs when the ear or skull endures physical trauma. Examples include a blow to the ear, foreign bodies inserted into the ear, and skull fractures. *Id.* at 143.

50. *Id.* at 99; English, *supra* note 40, at 118–119.

51. *Id.*; *see also* Mindel, *They Grow in Silence: The Deaf Child and his Family* 32 (1977).

52. After the initial testing, the pediatric audiologist may also play a valuable role in developing the child's education. *See* Bess & McConnell, *Audiology, Education, and the Hearing Impaired Child* 201 (1981) (Chapter Nine: "Audiology in the Educational Setting").

53. Mindel, *supra* note 50, at 32. For a technical explanation of the various methods of behavioral and auditory testing, see Bordley, *supra* note 39, at 151–67; *Pediatric Audiology: Current Trends*

sify auditory deficiency in increments of decibel loss, with each increment representing an increased level of communication impairment.[54] A child with a slight loss (27–40 decibels) may have difficulty with faint or distant speech or sounds.[55] A mild to moderate loss (41–55 decibels) impairs a child's ability to interpret conversational speech at a distance more than three to five feet.[56] A child with a moderately severe loss (56–70 decibels) may hear only loud sounds at close distances, and will have difficulty in conversation.[57] A severe impairment (71–90 decibels) restricts a child's hearing to voices and sounds within one foot, often even blocking out the sound of shouted conversation.[58] Finally, a profound loss (91 or more decibels) deprives a child of most auditory awareness, forcing him to rely almost exclusively on vibrations and sight.[59]

The proper classroom setting is essential to the proper development of the hearing-impaired child. When developing an IEP,[60] the severity of the hearing loss and its impact on the child's ability to communicate and interpret should be prime considerations in the choice of special facilities.[61]

Regardless of the degree of impairment the educational impact can be significant. A child's educational needs will become more specialized as his level of impairment increases.[62] A child with a slight hearing loss may have difficulty with language subjects, and could benefit from vocabulary development programs, special seating, and speech therapy.[63] A mild to moderate hearing loss could cause a child to miss up to one half of classroom discussion and thus necessitate, in addition to the aids mentioned above, lip reading instruction, speech correction, and hearing aid evaluation.[64] Children with moderately severe losses require special classes and emphasis on communication skills, and in some cases would benefit from a full-time program for the deaf.[65] Severe and profound hearing losses impede educational performance to such a great degree that afflicted children usually receive proper instruction only in special schools for the deaf.[66]

1-124 (Jerger ed. 1984) (section on diagnostic audiometry). For a less technical, broader based assessment of auditory testing, see Bess & McConnell, *supra* note 51, at 44 (Chapter 3: "Measurement of Auditory Function"); *see also Audiological Evaluation and Management and Speech Perception and Assessment* (Mendel & Danahauer, ed. 1997).

54. Bordley, *supra* note 39, at 158; Mindel, *supra* note 50, at 33.

55. *Id.*

56. *Id.*

57. *Id.*

58. *Id.*

59. *Id.*

60. Letter to Anonymous, 49 Individuals with Disabilities Education Law Rep. 98 (OSEP 2003) (not all children are required to be assessed in America Sign Language proficiency).

61. Children with slight losses may be aided by proper classroom acoustics. *See* Borrild, "Classroom Acoustics," in *Auditory Management of Hearing Impaired Children* 145 (1978); *see also* Bess & McConnell, *supra* note 51, at 188 (Chapter 8: "The Acoustic Environment"). Three variables to evaluate in the acoustic environment of a classroom are noise levels, reverberations and distance between teacher and student. *See* English, *supra* note 40, at 153–157.

62. Some experts believe that children with any level of hearing impairment will benefit from special education in addition to normal schooling. Learning difficulties increase as severity of impairment increases. *See* Bordley, *supra* note 39, at 158.

63. *Id.*

64. *Id.*

65. *Id.*

66. *Id.*

5.3.2 Visual Impairment

"'Visual impairment including blindness' means an impairment in vision that even with correction, adversely affects a child's educational performance.[67] The term includes both partial sight and blindness."[68] This broad definition of visual impairment avoids the application of labels to degrees of visual impairment.[69] Unlike hearing impairments, which despite a variety of etiologies differ only in degree, not in the type of impairment produced, there are many different types of visual impairments. For this reason, the medical community has moved away from traditional degree-based definitions of blindness and adopted functional definitions better suited to the nature of the disability.[70] The drafters of § 300.8 seem to have fallen into step with this general trend.

Visual impairments may be either congenital or acquired, and their causes are varied.[71] Causes include diseases of the eye in general, trauma, or injuries to specific parts of the eye, such as the cornea, lens, and retina, damage to or disease in the optic nerve, poisoning, tumors, retrolental fibroplasia, and general hereditary defects.[72] The majority of visually impaired children have multiple disabilities,[73] and thus the visual impairment is sometimes an offshoot of another, more serious disability.

Visual impairment is determined by a pediatric opthalmologist, neonatologist, or pediatrician who, depending on the child's age and the presence of other disabilities, will employ a battery of tests to measure distance, visual acuity, near visual acuity, and peripheral vision.[74] It is vital that eye problems be detected and correctly diagnosed at an early age in order for effective therapy to be implemented. For example, two decades ago, without early detection of visual impairments children with congenital cataracts were referred to residential schools for the blind. Today they can be served in public school settings.[75]

---

67. OSERS Q and A, 47 Individuals with Disabilities Education Law Rep. 226 (OSERS 2007) (LEAs and SEAs must keep close watch on which students receive National Instructional Materials Accessibility Standards, NIMAS file sets. LEAs have some options with regards to the methods used to convert printed materials into alternative format for students with visual impairments but less leeway in deciding who receive files).

68. 34 C.F.R. § 300.8; *see also* 20 U.S.C. §§ 1401(3)(A),(B), and 1401(26). *See generally The Management of Visual Impairment in Childhood* (Fielder, Best, & Bax eds., 1994); Vaughan, Asbury, and Riordan-Eva, *General Ophthalmology* (2003).

69. 6. This approach is in contrast to the distinction drawn between "deafness," "deaf-blindness," and "hearing impairment." 34 C.F.R. § 300.8.

70. The traditional description used in most countries until this decade defined blindness as "visual acuity, in the better eye with correction, of not more than 20/200 or a defect in the visual fields so that the widest diameter of vision subtends an angle no greater than 20 degrees." *Visual Impairment in Children and Adolescents* 18 (Jan, Freeman & Scott eds. 1977); *see also* Webster, *Children with Visual Impairments: Social Interaction, Language and Learning* (1998).

71. *See generally Pediatric Opthamology* (Nelson ed. 1984); *see also Pediatric Opthamology* (Metz ed. 1982). This collection of essays discusses the twenty-one most common causes of visual impairment in children. Although technical, it is manageable with a medical dictionary. *See also Visual Impairment in Children and Adolescents, supra* note 67, at 38–39 (chart listing common congenital and acquired visual impairments in children).

72. *Visual Impairment in Children and Adolescents, supra* note 67, at 38–39; *Pediatric Opthamology, supra* note 68.

73. *Id.*

74. *Visual Impairment in Children and Adolescents, supra* note 67, at 12; *see also* Goble, *Visual Disorders in the Handicapped Child* (1984).

75. *Rudolph's Pediatrics* 1879–1924 (Rudolph ed. 2003).

Since visual testing requires comprehension and cooperation, a correct assessment may prove difficult in a child with multiple disabilities or a child below the age of four.[76] The pediatric opthamologist uses the data amassed through testing to determine the degree and type of visual impairment and, more important, the child's level of remaining vision or "visual efficiency."[77]

Visually impaired children may be functionally classified in three groups.[78] A child with "normal or near-normal vision" is able to perform visually related tasks without aid.[79] A child with "low vision" requires special aids to perform visually detailed work.[80] A "blind" child must rely on his other senses to accomplish tasks that sighted children accomplish primarily with sight.[81]

The educational needs of the visually impaired child will depend on the child's visual efficiency and the willingness of the child to use his remaining vision.[82] Each partially sighted child will have different needs, since there are many different types of partial sight and degrees of disability within each type.[83] A child with no residual vision, of course, may have to receive instruction in Braille.[84]

5.3.3 Orthopedic Impairments in General

An orthopedic impairment is a deformity, disease or injury of the bones or joints.[85] "Orthopedic impairment" means:

> a severe orthopedic impairment which adversely affects a child's educational performance. The term includes impairments caused by congenital anomaly (e.g., clubfoot, absence of some member, etc.), impairments caused by disease (e.g., poliomyelitis, bone tuberculosis, etc.) and impairments from other causes (e.g., cerebral palsy, amputations, and fractures or burns which cause contractures).[86]

To be eligible the impairment must adversely affect educational performance. Such impairments limit a child's mobility and, depending on the severity of the impediment, may necessitate special educational facilities ranging from special access to full time special classes.

76. *Visual Impairment of Children and Adolescents, supra* note 67, at 13.

77. *Id.* at 19.

78. *Id.* at 23. There are many ways to classify visual impairment, but the functional categories seem to be the most useful in the educational arena.

79. *Id.* at 23.

80. *Id.* at 23; *see also Understanding Low Vision* (R. Jose ed. 1983).

81. *Visual Impairment in Children and Adolescents, supra* note 67, at 23.

82. Scott, Jan & Freeman, *Can't Your Child See?* 170 (1985).

83. *Id.* at 171; *see also Understanding Low Vision, supra* note 77.

84. Scott, *supra* note 79, at 171. The educational aids and teaching techniques available for the visually impaired child are so far reaching and variable that generalization in this section would not be helpful. *See* Chapman, *Visually Handicapped Children and Young People* (1978) (Chapter 4: "The school years for visually handicapped children").

85. *See generally* Staheli, *Fundamentals of Pediatric Orthopedics* (2007); *Pediatric Orthopedics in Primary Practice* (Pizzutillo, ed. 2000); Mier, Brower, *Pediatric Orthopedics, A Guide for the Primary Care Physician* (1996).

86. 34 C.F.R. § 300.8. Children with cerebral palsy who are unable to function in a mainstream classroom setting, may require a special form of education because of the prevalence of associated disorders such as deafness, seizures, speech and visual impairments; *see also* Tachdjian, Mihran O., *Clinical Pediatrics Orthopedics: The Art of Diagnosis and Management* (2002).

Being able to determine the existence of and the educational impact of an orthopedic impairment is easier than determining the existence of other conditions.[87] The types of issues under IDEA or §504 regarding orthopedically impaired children deal with program accessibility.[88]

5.3.3.1 Congenital Orthopedic Disorders

Congenital orthopedic disorders are abnormal conditions which are detectable at birth. Such conditions may be caused by inherited factors, fetal exposure to drugs ingested by the mother, uterine abnormalities, and radiation.[89]

Clubfoot, or congenital talipes equinovarus, the first example of congenital anomaly provided in the regulation's definition, is a deformity of the bones of the foot.[90] Experts remain uncertain as to the causes of clubfoot, although many theories concerning genetic links, stunted embryonic development, and environmental causes have been advanced.[91] Clubfeet vary in type and severity; "conventional clubfeet" may be corrected by nonsurgical methods such as manipulative stretching, casts, corrective shoes, braces, and therapy, while other, more severe types require corrective surgery in order for the child to walk.[92] Most, if not all cases of clubfoot are treated within the first three months of the child's life,[93] and effects extending into the school years may involve his ability to participate fully in physical education classes.

"[A]bsence of some member" is the other example of congenital anomaly referred to in the definition of orthopedically impaired. This phrase refers to an amputation or "banding" of a limb prior to a child's birth, or a genetic or formative defect which causes an absence of a limb.[94] Congenital amputation may be caused by trauma experi-

---

87. Perhaps this is why no one has bothered to write any books on the educational impact of orthopedic impairments. Most sources on pediatric orthopedics focus on how to make the child mobile after the determination of impairment. (In the majority of cases, an orthopedic impairment may be determined by simply looking at the child). *See, e.g.,* Katz, *Common Orthopedic Problems in Children* (1981). This work is written by an orthopedist for physicians in other fields, and is a useful quick reference for the layperson as well. *See also Orthopedic Knowledge Update* (Richard, ed. 1996).

88. *See, e.g.,* San Francisco (Cal.) Unified School Dist., 23 Individuals with Disabilities Educ. L. Rep. (LRP) 1200 (1995) (inaccessible playground at school); Garfield (N.J.) School Dist., 18 Individuals with Disabilities Educ. L. Rep. (LRP) 545 (OCR 1991) (wheelchair users denied access to parking spaces, restrooms, entrance ramps and drinking fountains); Garaway (Ohio) Local School Dist., 17 Educ. Handicapped L. Rep. (LRP) 237 (OCR 1990) (carrying a mobility impaired student on and off a bus is not an acceptable means of access).

89. Cowell, "Genetic Aspects of Orthopaedic Conditions," in 1 *Pediatric Orthopaedics* 149 (Lovell & Winter eds. 2005) This two volume reference is regarded as the definitive work on pediatric orthopedics, and most citations in this section are taken from this work for this reason. However, Pediatric Orthopaedics is written for the orthopedic community, and is hypertechnical in places. A better overview for the layperson is provided by Katz, *Common Orthopedic Problems in Children* (1981).

90. Lovell, Price and Meehan, "The Foot," in 2 *Pediatric Orthopaedics* 901. *See also* Tachdjian, *supra* note 83, at 12.

91. Lovell, *supra* note 87, at 901; Tachdjian, *supra* note 83, at 22.

92. Lovell, *supra* note 87, at 904.

93. *Id.* at 905.

94. Cowell, *supra* note 86, at 148. "Banding" refers to the effect produced by the twining of a limb with the amniotic cords, which cuts off blood supply to the affected part and produces an abnormal band. *Id.* The banding process, carried to the extreme, causes congenital amputation. Absence of limbs may also be caused by maternal ingestion of drugs such as thalidomide during pregnancy and by hereditary or genetic defects. *Id.*

enced by the mother, which may cause constriction of the uterine environment around the fetal extremities, cutting off blood supply to the limb and eventually severing it.[95] A child born with an orthopedic congenital deformity may usually, depending on the severity of the deformity and the number of absent limbs, be fitted with a prosthesis at an early age and acquire sufficient mobility to attend a regular classroom.

5.3.3.2 Orthopedic Impairments Caused by Disease

Orthopedic impairments caused by disease effect a child's control over muscles and limbs, either through paralysis or destruction of bone and muscle tissues. IDEA's regulations offer poliomyelitis and bone tuberculosis as examples of such diseases.[96] Other examples of common orthopedic diseases include arthritis, muscular dystrophy, and general bone or joint infections.[97]

Poliomyelitis, or polio, is a viral infection caused by the poliomyelitis virus.[98] Polio produces paralysis (mainly in the lower extremities) by attacking and destroying portions of the spinal cord and brain stem motor cells.[99] The development of a polio vaccine has greatly reduced the number of reported cases, and today polio occurs primarily in preschool age, unimmunized children. Polio attacks vary in severity, and recovery can range from almost total muscle recovery to complete paralysis.[100] A child's educational needs will depend on the extent of the remaining paralysis and motor impairment.

5.3.3.3 Other Orthopedic Impairments

The final class of orthopedic impairments offered by IDEA regulations is a catch-all group covering disabilities from "other causes."[101] Any orthopedic condition that adversely affects a child's educational performance which is not covered by the previous two categories, congenital anomalies and diseases, would fall within the parameters of this group.

Cerebral palsy, the first condition listed in the regulation as an example of an orthopedic impairment stemming from "other causes,"[102] is a serious motor affliction caused by brain lesions.[103] The brain damage which causes cerebral palsy may stem from prenatal causes such as toxic pregnancy, rubella, and maternal ingestion of drugs or alcohol; perinatal causes, such as prematurity and delayed labor; and postnatal causes, including meningitis and head injury.[104]

---

95. *Id.*

96. 34 C.F.R. § 300.8. The inclusion of bone tuberculosis as an example of orthopedic disease is unusual, since significant cases of bone tuberculosis are rare today. Children are, however, more frequent victims than adults. Robbins, Cotran, & Kumar, *Pathologic Basis of Disease* 1325 (6th ed. 2004).

97. *See generally* 1 *Pediatric Orthopaedics* 457, 263, and 437; Tachdjian, *supra* note 83, at 405–6, 476.

98. Drennan, "Neuromuscular Disorders," in *1 Pediatric Orthopaedics* 283.

99. *Id.* at 283–85.

100. *Id.* at 284.

101. 34 C.F.R. § 300.8.

102. 34 C.F.R. § 300.8.

103. Rang, Silver, & Garza, "Cerebral Palsy", in 1 *Pediatric Orthopaedics* 345; *see also The Cerebral Palsies: Causes, Consequences and Management* (Miller & Clark, ed. 1998); Levitt, *Treatment of Cerebral Palsy and Motor Delay* (2004).

104. Rang, *supra* note 100, at 346. Prematurity is currently the leading cause of cerebral palsy. *Id.*

Cerebral palsy is generally classified according to the area of the body which is most affected, whether muscle tone is present or absent, involuntary movements and distribution of paralysis.[105] Hemiplegia, the least severe type, involves one side of the body and is characterized by a limp and a tendency to favor one hand.[106] Diplegia, caused by prematurity, affects the legs and lower body more than the upper body.[107] Total involvement, the most severe type of cerebral palsy, affects the entire brain, damaging intelligence and control over all major muscle groups. The head, neck, trunk and all four limbs are involved. Children exhibiting total involvement are unable to walk, sit, or care for themselves, and are often institutionalized.[108]

Amputations, the second example in this group, involve the surgical removal of a limb. Removal may be necessitated by a number of etiologies, including trauma to the limb (power tools, auto accidents, gunshot wounds, explosions, and railroad incidents are leading causes) and disease (malignant tumors and malformations are commonly involved).[109] When possible, pediatric amputees are fitted with prostheses which enable them to move about.[110] Educational needs could include special accesses and adapted physical education classes.

Fractures or burns which cause contractures, the final example in this group, deals with the more common serious injuries. The fracture or burn must cause a contracture, which is a shortening of muscle or bone, or scar tissue which produces deformity.[111] Contractures affect a child's gait and mobility, and necessitate the same types of educational considerations as do amputations and clubfoot.

5.3.4 Mental and Emotional Impairments in General

Mental and emotional impairments involve a child's intelligence, aptitude, ability to learn and behavior. Many of these disabilities have no outward physical manifestations, and it is often not until the child reaches school age that parents become aware of a possible problem.

5.3.4.1 Mental Retardation

The definition of mental retardation used in IDEA regulations is taken directly from the definition developed by the American Association on Mental Retardation (AAMR).[112] Mental retardation means "significantly subaverage general intellectual

---

105. Tachdjian, *supra* note 83, at 386.

106. *Id.* at 346.

107. *Id.*

108. *Id.*; *see also Orthopaedic Aspects of Cerebral Palsy*, (R. Samilson ed. 1975). Children with cerebral palsy of this severity are often afflicted with deafness, seizures and other disabilities. *Id.* at 41; Tachdjian, *supra* note 83, at 379.

109. Tooms, "The Amputee," in 2 *Pediatric Orthopaedics* 979.

110. *Id.* In growing children, prostheses must be fitted and refitted frequently, and children require time to adapt to each new prosthesis. *Id.*

111. *See generally* DeGowin & DeGowin, *Diagnostic Examination* (8th ed. 2004).

112. AAMR was previously known as AAMD. The AAMR definition reads:
Mental retardation refers to substantial limitations in present functioning. It is characterized by:
- Significantly subaverage intellectual functioning, existing concurrently with;
- Related limitations in two or more of the following applicable adaptive skill areas: communication, self-care, home living, social skills, community use, self-direction,

functioning existing concurrently with deficits in adaptive behavior and manifested during the developmental period, which adversely affects a child's educational performance."[113] States may, however, remove the term mental retardation from the state regulations and replace it with terms such as "cognitive impairment" or "intellectual disability" as long as the state continues to provide services.[114] Contrary to public belief, not all individuals with mental retardation "look" retarded, and some children with mild retardation actually progress to the fourth or fifth grade before the disability is detected.[115] Thus, mental retardation is often more prevalent in regular classroom settings than most would think, especially in poor, urban areas.[116]

One of the most common misconceptions about mental retardation is that all forms of the disability are caused by chromosomal anomalies such as Down's Syndrome, perhaps because of the visibility of Down's Syndrome characteristics.[117] However, the causes of mental retardation are as diverse and varied as the causes of any other disability. According to the AAMR, mental retardation can occur pre- or postnatally, and may stem from exposure to infection or intoxicants, trauma, metabolism or nutrition disorders, postnatal brain disease, environmental conditions, psychiatric disorders, and a wide range of other prenatal and perinatal influences, as well as chromosomal anomalies.[118] Additionally, there are some children for whom no cause for mental retardation is apparent; they simply fail to attain average mental acuity.[119]

To be classified as having mental retardation under the federal regulation a child must have both subaverage intelligence and deficits in adaptive behavior. Subaverage intelligence is determined by standard IQ testing, and a child must score below 70 on a standardized intelligence test to meet the AAMR criterion.[120] Deficits in adaptive behavior, on the other hand, must be determined by observation, and the type of adaptive deficiency required will depend on the child's level of development.[121] For instance, a preschool child might be expected to progress beyond crawling, walking and babbling to talking and learning through experience, and failure to do so could indicate an adaptive deficit. This determination will usually be difficult only in those with IQ's over 55, since those in the lower IQ ranges will demonstrate clear adaptive deficits.[122]

---

        health and safety, functional academics, leisure, or work.
    • Mental retardation manifests before age 18.
    113. 34 C.F.R. § 300.8; *see* Beirn-Smith, Kim, Patton, *Mental Retardation* (7th ed., 2005); Westling & Fox, *Teaching Students with Severe Disabilities* (2003); Teaching Students with Mental Retardation: Providing Access to the General Curriculum, (Wehmeyer, ed. 2001); Westling, *Introduction to Mental Retardation* (1986). These books are clear, understandable sources covering all aspects of mental retardation, and include discussions of mental retardation issues and teaching under IDEA.
    114. Letter to Anonymous, 48 Individuals with Disabilities Education Law Rep. (CCR) 16 (OSEP 2006).
    115. Westling, *supra* note 110, at 24.
    116. *See id.*
    117. Down's Syndrome produces distinctive facial characteristics such as oval, tilted eyes, squinting, and sloped skull. *See generally* Barlow, *Mental Retardation and Related Disorders* (1978) (neurological approach to mental retardation); *Down's Syndrome: Psychological, Psychobiological and Socio-educational Prespectives* (Rondal, ed. 1996).
    118. Westling, *supra* note 110, at 29.
    119. *Id.*
    120. Westling, *supra* note 110, at 3.
    121. *Id.* at 4.
    122. *Id.* at 5.

The AAMR maintained the classification system of mental retardation by ranges of IQ scores as guidelines.[123] Children with mild mental retardation score between 55 and 70 or 75 on standardized intelligence tests with concurrent deficits in adaptive skills behavior.[124] Moderate mental retardation is shown by scores from 35–55. Scores from 20 to 35 are evidence of severe mental retardation, and children who score below 20 are classified as profoundly mentally retarded.[125]

Another classification system, popular with educators, groups mentally retarded persons as educable mentally retarded (EMR) (50–70), trainable mentally retarded (TMR) (25–50), and profoundly mentally retarded (PMR) (below 25).[126]

Children with mental retardation have widely varying educational needs, the range of which is dependent on the severity of the impairment. The mildly retarded generally are capable of normal academic and social development until the fourth or fifth grade, while the moderately retarded may not ever achieve more than a first grade level of academic skills.[127] The severely and profoundly retarded, however, have trouble with even the simplest daily living skills, and while sometimes trainable, require constant monitoring and attention.[128] There is much overlap in the different groups, and the specific needs will depend on individual ability. All school systems provide special programs for the mentally retarded, both in regular classrooms and in special schools for children with disabilities.[129] The Westling book is a clear, understandable source covering all aspects of mental retardation, and is highly recommended for laymen by specialists in this field.

5.3.4.2 Specific Learning Disabilities in General

The definition of specific learning disabilities contained in IDEA's regulations is less of a description than it is a laundry list of minor psychological disorders which prevent affected children from keeping pace with their peers despite adequate education and opportunity. "'Specific learning disability' means a disorder in one or more of the basic psychological processes involved in understanding or in using language, spoken or written, which may manifest itself in an imperfect ability to listen, think, speak, read, write, spell or to do mathematical calculations. The term includes such conditions as perceptual disabilities, brain injury, minimal brain dysfunction, dyslexia, and developmental aphasia."[130] The definition also includes an exclusionary phrase, which specifies that the term "specific learning disability" does not include impairments from other

---

123. Bairn-Smith, *supra* note 110, at 258.
124. *Id.* at 207.
125. *Id.* at 252.
126. *Id.*
127. *Id.* at 25–26.
128. *Id.* at 27.
129. The range of programs available for the mentally retarded is all-encompassing. *See* Westling, *supra* note 110, at 175 (chapter on public school programs); *Mental Handicap A Hand Book of Care* (E. Shanley ed. 1986); *Perspectives in Mental Retardation: Social, Psychological and Educational Aspects* (Berg ed. 1984); *Strategies for Teaching Students with Severe Mental Retardation* (Gable and Warren, ed. 1993).
130. 34 C.F.R. § 300.309(a)(3)(vi); *see* 20 U.S.C. §§ 1401(30), 1414(b)(6). Parts of this definition seem to be standard in both education and medicine. *See, e.g.,* Johnston, *Learning Disabilities, Medicine, and Myth: A Guide to Understanding the Child and the Physician* (1987). This book, in addition to containing parts of the above definition of specific learning disability, is a functionally oriented guide to symptoms exhibited by learning disabled children.

causes covered elsewhere in the regulation, nor does it include disabilities stemming primarily from "environmental, cultural, or economic disadvantage or limited English proficiency."[131]

The 2004 authorization significantly changed the procedures for identifying children with specific learning disabilities. The state criteria that the public agency must use can no longer require the use of the severe discrepancy model.[132] This discrepancy model based SLD eligibility on whether a child had a severe discrepancy between his/her intellectual ability and achievement. Under the current criteria, the existence of a specific learning disability must be based on the child's response to scientific and research based interventions or alternative research based procedures.[133]

In addition, a child may be eligible as a child with a SLD if the child exhibits a pattern of strengths and weaknesses in performance achievement or both relative to his/her age, the State approved standards, his/her grade level standards or intellectual development. The determination of SLD eligibility must be based on the use of appropriate assessments.[134]

Federal regulations list the five most common types of conditions that produce specific learning disabilities, each of which will be discussed separately below. Although other causes exist, they involve difficulties in the realm of neuropsychology, which is beyond the scope of this book.[135]

5.3.4.3 Perceptual Disabilities

Unlike visual or hearing disorders that limit what a child can see and hear, perceptual disorders concern a child's recognition and understanding of something after he senses it.[136] Technically, perception involves reception of a conscious impression through the senses (in this case, usually sight or sound) by which a child distinguishes objects and recognizes them by the sensations produced. The child must store in his brain an image of what he sees, so that when he is confronted with it at a later time, he can recognize it and react properly to it.[137] Children with perceptual disabilities either fail to properly store images received through sensation or, in other cases, fail to integrate memories of past sensory experiences with immediate experience.[138] Perceptual disabilities may arise from organic causes (deficiencies in specific chemical processes within the brain itself), and from environmental causes (insufficient exposure to classes of stimuli).[139]

---

131. *Id.*

132. 34 C.F.R. § 300.307; 20 U.S.C. §§ 1221e-3;1401(30); 1414(b)(6). *see* Letter to Zirkel, 47 Individuals with Disabilities Education Law Rep. (LRP) (OSEP 2007).

133. *Id;* 34 C.F.R. § 300.309(a)(2)(i).

134. 34 C.F.R. § 300.309(a)(2)(ii); *see also* 34 C.F.R. § 300.310, Letter to Baglin, 40 Individuals with Disabilities Education Law Rep 127 (OSEP 2003).

135. *See* Gaddes, *Learning Disabilities and Brain Function: A Neuropsychological Approach* (3d ed. 1994) (written for educational diagnosticians, clinical and school psychologists, and special education teachers); *Learning About Learning Disabilities* (Wong, ed. 1998); *A Neurodevelopmental Approach to Specific Learning Disorders* (Whitmore, Hart & Willems, ed. 1999).

136. Gaddes, *Learning Disabilities and Brain Function: A Neuropsychological Approach* 147 (3d ed. 1994).

137. *Id.* at 153.

138. *Id.* at 153.

139. *Id.* at 128.

5.3.4.4 *Brain Injury and Minimal Brain Dysfunction*

Minimal brain dysfunction (MBD) is a term applied to children with normal or near normal intelligence who demonstrate abnormal behavior or specific learning disabilities.[140] MBD is caused by brain damage or by neurologic dysfunction brought on by head trauma, pre- and postnatal diseases, delivery complications, fetal alcohol syndrome, genetic factors, and a host of other etiologies.[141] In preschool children, the syndrome is manifested by signs of hyperactivity or lability, poor coordination and speech disorders. In school age children, the most common signs are failure in one specific academic area, language difficulties, awkwardness and emotional behavior.[142] There are no laboratory tests which can confirm a diagnosis of MBD, and thus detailed family history may become important when a disabled child is evaluated.[143] Brain injury, which is mentioned separately in the definition, can stem from innumerable causes and produce a wide spectrum of effects, depending on severity, location, and age. Brain damage is often cited as a cause of MBD, but may also be the cause of any of the neurological disabilities defined in IDEA regulations.

5.3.4.5 *Dyslexia*

Dyslexia is a "disorder in children who, despite conventional classroom experience, fail to attain the language skills of reading, writing and spelling commensurate with their intellectual abilities",[144] which involves reading comprehension, decoding, or both.[145] Dyslexia may be developmental (arising from congenital or acquired problems prior to the acquisition of reading skills) or traumatic (resulting from brain damage after the child has learned how to read).[146]

Traumatic dyslexia, which occurs primarily in adults, can be broken into several subgroups divided by the specific type of disability produced, such as alexia without agraphia (person can write, but cannot read), alexia with agraphia (person cannot read or write) and aphasic alexia (person cannot understand spoken or printed words).[147]

Developmental dyslexia is the reading disorder with which the public is most familiar. Most people with developmental dyslexia have no history of brain damage or cere-

---

140. *Meritt's Textbook of Neurology* 357 (8th ed. 1995).

141. *Id.*

142. *Id.* at 358.

143. *Id.* For a more detailed assessment of minimal brain dysfunctions and their causes and determination, see Pace, *The Comparison of the Academic and Behavioral Characteristics of Children with Mild Traumatic Brain Injury and Children with Learning Disabilities* (1997); *Handbook of Minimal Brain Dysfunctions: A Critical View* (Rie & Rie, eds. 1980) (very technical); Golden & Anderson, *Learning Disabilities and Brain Dysfunction: An Introduction for Educators and Parents* (1979).

144. Gaddes, *Learning Disabilities and Brain Function: A Neuropsychological Approach* 274 (3d ed. 1994). This definition was developed by the World Federation of Neurology, which also posed a second definition of Specific Developmental Dyslexia: "A disorder manifested by difficulty in learning to read despite conventional instruction, adequate intelligence, and socio-cultural opportunity. It is dependent on fundamental cognitive disabilities which are frequently of constitutional origin." *Id.* at 336; *see also* Dave Sargent & Laura Tirella, *What Every Teacher and Parent Should Know about Dyslexia* (1996); Joy Pollock and Elisabeth Waller, *Day to Day Dyslexia in the Classrroom* (1994); Maragne, *Dyslexia* (1997).

145. Johnston, *Learning Disabilities, Medicine, and Myth: A Guide to Understanding the Child and the Physician* 8 (1987).

146. Gaddes, *supra* note 138, at 336.

147. *Id.* at 340–343.

bral atrophy, and although theories abound as to the causes of the disorder, no definitive answer exists.[148] Generally, people with developmental dyslexia possess average to superior intelligence and are often gifted in other areas such as art, math, science, and athletics.[149] Such children simply have a processing disorder, and require intensive therapy to develop the most basic reading skills. Signs of developmental dyslexia include an inability to identify individual letters, syllables, and words.[150]

5.3.4.6 Developmental Aphasia

Aphasia is the congenital or acquired "loss or impairment of the use and/or understanding of language resulting from some type of brain injury or dysfunction."[151] Developmental aphasia[152] results from injury to or maldevelopment of the portions of the central nervous system that control language. The damage that causes developmental aphasia occurs sometime during the period between conception and the end of the first year of life.[153] Developmental aphasia may manifest itself in several different forms, including the inability to repeat spoken words, a lack of inner language functioning, and an inability to articulate words that are otherwise understood.[154] These disabilities produce a lack of cognitive and spontaneous speech and overall language retardation.[155]

5.3.4.7 Emotional Disturbances

Instead of listing types of emotional disturbances, IDEA regulations create an internal definition by listing five criteria, at least one of which a child must meet to fit under this classification.[156] "Emotional disturbance" is defined as follows:

(i) The term means a condition exhibiting one or more of the following characteristics over a long period of time and to a marked degree that adversely affects a child's educational performance:

(A) An inability to learn that cannot be explained by intellectual, sensory, or health factors.

(B) An inability to build or maintain satisfactory interpersonal relationships with peers and teachers.

---

148. *See id.* at 301. Since scientists do not completely understand the reading process itself, difficulties in defining a glitch in the process are to be expected.
149. *Id.* at 307–311. Darwin is perhaps the most famous developmental dyslexic. *Id.*
150. *Id.* at 366.
151. Gaddes, *Learning Disabilities and Brain Function: A Neuropsychological Approach* 261 (3d ed. 1994).
152. 34 C.F.R. § 300.8 specifically lists developmental aphasia. It should be noted, however, that children may also acquire aphasia between age two and puberty which will interfere with acquired language. Gaddes, *supra* note 138, at 321–322. Acquired aphasia may result from any of the various head traumas previously discussed.
153. *Id.* at 322.
154. *See id.* at 314–324.
155. *Id.* at 324. Although there are many functional classifications of aphasia, each specialist has a label for each type, and there is no standardized identification system. For this reason, classifications are avoided in this section. *See generally* Lees, *Children with Acquired Aphasias* (2005).
156. 34 C.F.R. § 300.8. For behavioral teaching methodologies for SED students see also Chris Ninness et al., *Assessment and Treatment of Emotional or Behavioral Disorders*(1993); *Behavioral Approach to Assessment of Youth with Emotional/ Behavioral Disorders: A Handbook for School Based Practitioners* (Breen & Fiedler, ed. 2003).

(C) Inappropriate types of behavior or feelings under normal circumstances.

(D) A general pervasive mood of unhappiness or depression.

(E) A tendency to develop physical symptoms or fears associated with personal or school problems.

(ii) The term includes children who are schizophrenic. The term does not apply to children who are socially maladjusted, unless it is determined that they have an emotional disturbance.

Four of the criteria are broad descriptions of abnormal social and associative behavior.[157] The first criterion, however, contains the broadest language in the entire regulation, allowing children with "[a]n inability to learn which cannot be explained by intellectual, sensory, or health factors" to come within the parameters of the act as "emotionally disturbed". This language could provide a shelter for parents and lawyers who find themselves at a loss to formulate a description of a child's disability for an IEP.

The only specific mental disability mentioned in the definition of "seriously emotionally disturbed" is schizophrenia. Schizophrenia is described in layperson's terms as a group of mental illnesses characterized by the disorganization and splitting of an individual's personality. There is no universally accepted medical definition of schizophrenia which covers every possible type; however, of the many definitions that exist, the easiest to comprehend was developed by the Washington University in St. Louis.[158] To confirm a diagnosis of schizophrenia under the St. Louis definition, a child must have had a chronic illness of at least six months in duration, an absence of mood disorders, suffer from hallucinations, delusions, or nonsense language, have an absence of drug or alcohol use, and a history of poor social interaction.[159]

Schizophrenia may be caused by physical and organic diseases of the brain, senility, brain tumors, diabetes, head injury, epilepsy, and use of hallucinogenic drugs.[160] Schizophrenia is a very serious, debilitating mental illness which must be diagnosed by a psychiatrist and treated by an experienced child psychiatrist or psychologist.[161] There are other mental disabilities of childhood and adolescence which cause symptoms which are either similar to the SED criteria or produce the behaviors which qualify under the

---

157. *See* 34 C.F.R. §300.8. There are literally hundreds of types of emotional disturbances and methods of treatment, and a sociological debate on causation rages about each one. *See generally* Gupta, *Manual of Developmental and Behavioral Problems in Children* (1999); Parker & Zuckerman, *Behavioral and Developmental Pediatrics: A Handbook for Primary Care* (1995); *Developmental-Behavioral Pediatrics* (Levine, Carey & Crocher, ed. 1999); *Systematic Intervention with Disturbed Children* (Fine ed. 1984); *Emotional Disorders in Children and Adolescents: Medical and Psychological Approaches to Treatment* (Sholevar ed. 1980).

158. *See* Tsuang, *Schizophrenia: The Facts* 17 (1997). This is a highly readable, interesting source on schizophrenia, containing many short case studies and examples to help the reader understand the many ways which schizophrenia may manifest itself. *See also* Richard Warner, *Schizophrenia* (1995) (for psycho-social problems).

159. Tsuang, *supra* note 152, at 17. *See also Diagnostic and Statistical Manual of Mental Disorders* (Fourth Edition-Revised) DSM-IV American Psychiatric Association 1994, at 286–287; Friedman, *Everything You Need to Know About Schizophrenia* (2000).

160. Tsuang, *supra* note 152, at 15. *See also* American Psychiatric Association, *supra* note 153, at 286–287.

161. It appears to be little written on the education of schizophrenic children. Most schizophrenics are hospitalized during the chronic phase of their illness, and due to the severe symptomology may not be able to learn or attend classes.

criteria.[162] Therefore, if the disability is impacting adversely on the education the child will be eligible.

5.3.4.8 Autism

Autism is defined in the regulations as a developmental disability significantly affecting verbal and nonverbal communication and social interaction, generally evident before age three, that adversely affects a child's educational performance.[163] Autism is a psychological disorder characterized by perceptual and language abnormalities, an inability to relate to others, and obsessive, ritualistic behavior.[164] Autistic children tend to exhibit delayed speech, flat expressions, and signs of sensory dysfunction, and engage in self-stimulatory behaviors (for example, rocking) which make education of any kind difficult.[165] The causes of autism are unknown, although some experts suspect a neurological connection.[166]

5.3.4.9 Traumatic Brain Injury

Traumatic brain injury is defined as an acquired injury to the brain caused by an external physical force, resulting in total or partial functional disability or psycho social impairment, or both, that adversely affects a child's educational performance. The term applies to open or closed head injuries resulting in impairments in one or more areas, such as cognition; language; memory; attention; reasoning; abstract thinking; judgment; problem solving; sensory, perceptual and motor abilities; psycho-social behavior; physical functions; information processing; and speech. The term does not apply to brain injuries that are congenital or degenerative, or brain injuries induced by birth trauma.[167]

5.3.5 Catch-All Categories in General

Federal regulations contain two "catch-all" categories of impairments, "multiple disabilities"[168] and "other health impaired,"[169] which are designed to provide specialized ed-

---

162. *Diagnostic and Statistical Manual of Mental Disorders* (Fourth Edition-Revised) DSM-IV American Psychiatric Association 1994, at 286–287. Some examples of additional disorders which may appear in infancy, childhood or adolescence include mood disorders, schizophreniform disorder, adjustment disorders and personality disorders.

163. 34 C.F.R. §300.8; *see generally Autism Spectrum Disorders: Identification, Education and Treatment* (Zager, ed. 2004); *Autism in Children and Adults: Etiology, Assessment, and Intervention*(Matson ed., 1994); Jordan and Powell, *Understanding and Teaching Children with Autism* (1995).

164. Koegel, Rincover, & Egel, *Educating and Understanding Autistic Children* (1982).

165. *Id.* at 2. For an overview of the education of autistic children, see Hinerman, *Teaching Autistic Children to Communicate* (1983); Siegel, *The World of the Autistic Child: Understanding and Treating Autistic Spectrum Disorders* (1998).

166. Koegel, *supra* note 158, at 3. One of the definitive sources in this area is *Handbook of Autism and Developmental Disorders* (Cohen & Volkmar, 3d ed. 2005). This massive volume, however, is technical enough to make it an impractical source for the layperson.

167. 34 C.F.R. §300.8.

168. 34 C.F.R. §300.8 states: "'Multiple disabilities' means concomitant impairments (such as mental retardation-blindness, mental retardation-orthopedic impairment) the combination of which causes such severe educational problems that they cannot be accommodated in special education programs solely for one of the impairments. The term does not include deaf-blindness."

169. 34 C.F.R. §300.8.

ucation for those children with combined disabilities and for those with chronic health problems not addressed elsewhere in the regulation.

5.3.5.1 Multihandicapped

The multiple disabilities category provides a special classification for those children with concomitant impairments, the combination of which so severely affects their ability to learn that such children cannot be properly educated in regular programs designed to accommodate a single disability. The definition contains two examples, mental retardation-blindness and mental retardation-orthopedic impairment, the singular components of which have been explored elsewhere in this Chapter.

5.3.5.2 Other Health Impaired

The "other health impairment" category of IDEA lists attention deficit disorder or attention deficit hyperactivity disorder and ten other examples of chronic health conditions which affect a child's strength, vitality or alertness. "Other health impairment" means

> having limited strength, vitality or alertness including a heightened alertness to environmental stimuli that results in limited alertness with respect to the educational environment that is due to chronic or acute health problems such as asthma, attention deficit disorder or attention deficit hyperactivity disorder, diabetes, epilepsy, a heart condition, hemophilia, lead poisoning, leukemia,[170] nephritis, rheumatic fever, sickle cell anemia, and Tourette syndrome and adversely affects a child's educational performance.[171]

These conditions are briefly defined below:

- Tuberculosis: a respiratory infection which develops into a self-limited pneumonia that heals by depositing nodules of abnormal cells in the lung tissue which may calcify and reactivate at a later time. In the active stage, the disease may cause tissue destruction, shortness of breath and pneumonia.[172]

- Rheumatic fever: a condition which is believed to be caused by the body's immune response to a bacterial organism (Group A Beta hemolytic streptococcal pharyngitis). Rheumatic fever causes nodules of abnormal cells to form in the cardiac valves, which can result in valve scarring, heart dysfunction and heart failure.[173]

- Nephritis: a term referring to a group of conditions which cause an inflammatory or similar reaction in the kidneys that leads to decreased kidney function. In the chronic state, this condition can lead to kidney failure, high blood pressure, and death.[174]

---

170. Elida Local School Dist. Bd. of Educ. v. Erickson, 252 F. Supp. (N.D. Ohio 2003) (student met "other health impaired" definition under Individuals with Disabilities Education Act (IDEA).

171. 34 C.F.R. § 300.8. The language "due to chronic or acute health problems" would allow virtually any health condition which affects a child's strength and vitality to fall within this definition. In combination with the broad language in § 300.8(9)(i), it is hard to imagine a condition affecting a child's educational performance which would not be included in one of the definitions in the regulation. *See* Davila Inquiry, 15 Educ. Handicapped L. Rep. (LRP) 552 (OSERS 1990) (another condition which could be categorized under OHI is "traumatic brain injury").

172. Cecil, *Textbook of Medicine* (23rd ed. 2007).

173. *Id.* at 60.

174. *See id.* at 230.

- Asthma: a disease process characterized by an increased responsiveness of the airways to various stimuli, causing widespread narrowing of the airways which varies over time. Asthmatics exhibit shortness of breath associated with wheezing and an intermittent cough.[175]

- Sickle cell anemia: results from a mutation in the DNA molecule which causes red blood cells to form sickle shapes when not carrying oxygen. These cells cause congestion in the capillaries, which may lead to pain in the extremities, anemia, kidney failure, and multi-organ destruction.[176]

- Hemophilia: an inherited bleeding disorder which is manifested by abnormal bleeding into muscles and joints with physical activity. In addition, spontaneous hemorrhage can occur as a result of physical trauma or illness.[177]

- Epilepsy: the result of disordered electrical activity within the brain which can cause generalized convulsions and loss of consciousness.[178]

- Lead poisoning: chronic poisoning resulting from absorption of small amounts of lead (such as children eating paint chips made with lead alloys). Lead poisoning may cause anemia and generalized loss of appetite.[179]

- Leukemia: a blood disease in which an abnormality within the bone marrow causes the production of abnormal types and numbers of white blood cells. The manifestations of the disease include anemia, increased susceptibility to infection and abnormal bleeding.[180]

- Diabetes: a condition characterized by elevated levels of blood glucose due to a diminished effectiveness of insulin, a chemical which aids in the transport of glucose into cells from the bloodstream. Diabetics often experience renal failure, blindness, weight loss, fatigue, increased susceptibility to infection, amputations of the lower extremities, and diabetic comas.[181]

- Tourette syndrome: a neurological disorder which is characterized by repetitive, stereotyped, involuntary movements and vocalizations called tics. The tics can involve only a few or several muscle groups. Some examples of tics include facial grimacing, eye blinking, grunting sounds or throat clearing. The average ages of onset of the syndrome is between 7 and 10 years.[182]

5.3.5.3 Attention Deficit Hyperactivity Disorder (ADHD) or Attention Deficit Disorder (ADD)

Attention Deficit Hyperactivity Disorder (ADHD) or Attention Deficit Disorder (ADD) is a common disorder which depending on your source affects approximately 3

---

175. *Id.* at 141–42.
176. *Id.* at 363.
177. *Id.* at 401.
178. *See generally Meritt's Textbook of Neurology* 640–42 (7th ed. 1984).
179. *See* Stanley L. Robbins, *Pathologic Basis of Disease* (6th ed. 1999).
180. *See generally* Cecil, *supra* note 165, at 378–83.
181. *Id.* at 487–89.
182. National Institute of Neurological Disorders and Strokes, http://www.ninds.nih.gov/disorders/tourette/detail_tourette.htm

to 30 percent of the school-age population.[183] The definition of this disorder is a diagnostic category of the American Psychiatric Association.[184] This disorder affects many aspects of the child's life, at home, in school and in social situations. Inattention, impulsiveness, and hyperactivity or restlessness are the common characteristics. The definition of other health impaired include ADD and ADHD.[185]

There are many examples of behaviors which are manifested by the disorder. Typically at least eight of the following behaviors must be present over the last six months, with the onset before age seven: fidgeting with hands or feet, (adolescents may feel restless); difficulty remaining in a seat; easily distracted; blurts out answers to questions; difficulty with following instructions; difficulty with sustained attention; shifts from one uncompleted activity to another frequently; talks excessively; interrupts others; poor listening skills; frequently loses things; and engages in physically dangerous activities.[186] The child with ADHD may exhibit academic difficulties, conduct problems, social and peer difficulties, and problems with self-esteem.[187]

ADHD is believed to have three causes. The first theory and the most popular explanation is the biological/chemical explanation. This explanation indicates that there is a problem with the neuro-chemical transmission in regulating brain functions. The preliminary research suggests that normal amounts of neurotransmitters are not being received by the areas of the brain which control attention.[188]

The second theory postulated is the individual's interaction with the environment or a bio-environmental theory.[189] For example, ADHD behaviors may be a result of allergies to foods, food additives or inhaled substances. In addition, eating lead-based paint during a developmental stage can result in some of the specified behaviors. Exposure to alcohol or other drugs by the developing fetus can result in attentional problems. Anticonvulsants or sedatives can also cause symptoms of ADHD.[190]

The last theory for explaining ADHD symptoms is an environmental theory. This theory is not well supported by research although it does support that parenting and other

183. Silver, *Attention Deficit Hyperactivity Disorder, A Clinical Guide to Diagnosis and Treatment for Health and Mental Health Professionals* (3d ed. 2003) (using a rating scale, teachers found 10–20 percent of students while parents using the same scale found 30 percent of all students ADHD or ADD); Braswell, Bloomquist & Pederson, *ADHD, A Guide To Understanding And Helping Children with Attention Deficit Hyperactivity Disorder in School Settings* (University of Minnesota, 1991) (3–5 percent of the school age population); *see also* Copeland, *Attention with Tension: A Teacher's Handbook on Attention Disorder* (1995).

184. *Diagnostic and Statistical Manual of Mental Disorders* (Fourth Edition-Revised) DSM-IV American Psychiatric Association 1996.

185. 34 C.F.R. § 300.8 (first included in the 1999 regulations); *see also* 34 C.F.R. § 300.308 (a)(1); Ashli C.v. Hawaii, Slip Copy 2007 WL 247761 (D.C. Haw. 2007) (child has ADHD but does not adversely affect so not entitled to special education); Alvin Independent School Dist. v. A.D., slip copy, 2006 WL 2880513 (S.D. Tex. 2006).

186. *Id.* (Diagnostic Criteria for 314.01 Attention Deficit Hyperactivity Disorder).

187. Silver, *supra* note 175; *see also* George J. DuPaul and Gary Stoner, *ADHD in the Schools, Assessment and Intervention Strategies*(1994); Sharon Neuwirth, *Attention Deficit Hyperactivity Disorder,* National Institute of Mental Health (1994).

188. *Id.* at 58.

189. *Id.*

190. Braswell, Bloomquist & Pederson, *ADHD, A Guide To Understanding And Helping Children with Attention Deficit Hyperactivity Disorder in School Settings,* (University of Minnesota, 1991).

environmental factors can influence the emergence of symptoms rather than cause them.[191]

Recognizing that ADHD can result in significant learning problems the United States Department of Education issued a Joint Policy Memo addressing the importance of the provision of educational services to children with ADHD.[192] There are several court decisions involving children with ADHD brought under either IDEA or § 504. In *Valerie J. v. Derry Cooperative School District*,[193] the court ruled that the IEP could not be contingent on the administration of the medication Ritalin, a drug often used as an integral part of a total treatment program for stabilizing the children's symptoms.[194]

A common source for guidance on these cases is complaints filed with the United States Department of Education's Office for Civil Rights (OCR) since 1991. For example, OCR issued a decision that local school divisions must evaluate students who exhibit characteristics associated with ADHD to determine whether regular or special education services were required under § 504.[195] The eligibility criteria under § 504 are different from that of the very specific conditions under IDEA. To be eligible an ADHD child would have to be found "disabled." This means that the child has a physical or mental impairment that substantially limits one or more major life activities, has a record of impairment, or is regarded as having an impairment.188 With ADHD child the major life activity affected is generally learning. Of course this does not mean that all ADHD children even with a record of impairment will be eligible.

---

191. Silver, *supra* note 175, at 59.

192. United States Dept. of Educ., Joint Policy Memo 18 Individuals with Disabilities L. Rep. (LRP) 118 (OSERS, OCR, Office of Elementary and Secondary Ed.) (Sept. 16, 1991) (children with ADHD can be eligible under the IDEA categories of other health impaired, learning disability (LD) or serious emotional disturbance; in addition children can be found eligible under § 504); *see also* West Union School Dist. #1, 23 Individuals with Disabilities Educ. L. Rep. (LRP) 1096 (1996); Letter to Anonymous, 22 Individuals with Disabilities Educ. L. Rep. (LRP) 636 (1995) (Part B funds may be used for ADD staff training, salary of personnel who provide training, and ADD materials); Letter to Sisisky, 21 Individuals with Disabilities Educ. L. Rep. (LRP) 995 (1994).

193. 771 F. Supp. 483 (D.N.H. 1991); *see also* Debord v. Board of Educ. of the Ferguson-Florissant School Dist., 126 F.3d 1102 (8th Cir. 1997) (administration of medicine in excessively prescribed dose not required); Ramon Valley (Cal.) Unified School District, 18 Individuals with Disabilities Educ. L. Rep. (LRP) 465 (OCR 1991) (school must ensure the administration of Ritalin as a related service if needed to assist a child in benefitting from his educational placement); *distinguished by* Somerville Public Schools, 23 Individuals with Disabilities Educ. L. Rep. (LRP) 932 (OCR 1996) (act of supplying Ritalin "implicates the services of a physician" and therefore is not a related service); Schultze, *Reading, Writing, and Ritalin: The Responsibility of Public School Districts to Administer Medication to Students*, 32 Creighton L. Rev. 793, 814 (1999).

194. *Physician's Desk Reference*, PDR, Medical Economics Company (2000).

195. Aberdeen (Mass.) School Dist., 321 Individuals with Disabilities Educ. L. Rep. (LRP) 11 (OCR 1999) (no duty to evaluate where parent failed to disclose ADHD to district); Anaheim (Cal.) Union H.S. Dist., 20 Individuals with Disabilities Educ. L. Rep. (LRP) 185 (OCR 1993) (required to evaluate under § 504 because of behavioral indicators). In Romulus Community School, 18 Individuals with Disabilities Educ. L. Rep. (LRP) 81 (OCR 1991), OCR pointed out that district's procedures need to comply with 34 C.F.R. § 104.33(a) (a school must provide a FAPE to each qualified handicapped person …) and § 104.35, (recipient must conduct a proper evaluation in order to evaluate for special education and related services); *see also* Thomason Inquiry, 18 Individuals with Disabilities Educ. L. Rep. (LRP) 536 (OSEP 1991) (LEA may not refuse to evaluate a child based solely on the medical diagnosis of ADHD).

Other examples of OCR rulings in addition to failure to evaluate, include failure to properly place, failure to provide appropriate services, failure to provide proper discipline,[196] failure to insure medication is taken,[197] and failure to provide notice of procedural safeguards.[198]

5.3.6 Disabilities Not Mentioned Under IDEA — the Role of § 504

On occasion, questions have been raised concerning a particular condition not specifically mentioned in IDEA regulations and whether it constitutes a qualifying condition under IDEA's other health impaired language. As a general principle, it must be kept in mind that eligibility always requires an adverse effect on educational performance. Therefore, no matter how severe the disability, whether it is listed under the regulations, the provisions of IDEA will not apply if there is no adverse impact on educational performance.

The definition of who qualifies for services, however, differs between IDEA and Section 504. IDEA provides a specific list of disabilities, one or more which must exist in order to be covered by the statute.[199] Section 504 regulations provide a broad definition of qualifying conditions which includes a physical or mental impairment which substantially limits one or more major life activities.[200] In practice, therefore, § 504 may provide education rights to children with, for example, epilepsy[201] and chemical dependencies,[202] while IDEA would not. There have been a number of children identified, and litigation generated, relating to Acquired Immune Deficiency Syndrome (AIDS) and Attention Deficit Hyperactivity Disorder (ADHD) or Attention Deficit Disorder (ADD). The latter two were added to the category of health impairment in the 99 regulations[203] discussed in the previous section.

5.3.6.1 Acquired Immune Deficiency Syndrome (AIDS)

A growing number of children are affected with Acquired Immune Deficiency Syndrome (AIDS). Three fourths of children acquire Human Immuno-deficiency Virus (HIV) across the placenta or perinatally. The rest acquire the virus through blood transfusions. There have been no known cases in which transmission has occurred in the school or day care setting.[204]

196. Templeton (Cal.) Unified School Dist., 17 Educ. Handicapped L. Rep. (CRR) 859 (OCR 1991).

197. San Juan (Cal.) Unified School Dist., 201 Individuals with Disabilities Educ. L. Rep. (LRP) 549 (OCR 1993).

198. Camdenton (Mo.) R-111 School Dist., 20 Individuals with Disabilities Educ. L. Rep. (LRP) 197 (OCR 1991); Prince George's County (Md.) Pub. Schools, 17 Educ. Handicapped L. Rep. (LRP) 875 (OCR 1991).

199. 34 C.F.R. § 300.8; see 20 U.S.C. §§ 1401(3)(A) and (B), 1401(26).

200. 34 C.F.R. § 104.3(j). But see J.D. v. Pawlet School District, 224 F.3d 60 (2d Cir. 2000) (academically gifted student with emotional-behavioral disability denied special education services).

201. Akers v. Bolton, 531 F. Supp. 300 (D. Kan. 1981).

202. Inquiry of Des Jardin, 213 Educ. Handicapped L. Rep. (CRR) 144 (OSEP 1988); Inquiry by Harris, 211 Educ. Handicapped L. Rep. (CRR) 431 (OSEP 1987).

203. 34 C.F.R. § 300.8.

204. Comprehensive Pediatrics 51–58 (Summit, ed. 1990).

Considerable litigation is developing concerning the education of children with AIDS. The consensus appears to be that children with AIDS are not covered *per se* by IDEA, but they are covered by § 504. In determining whether the child who is HIV positive (HIV infected) or has AIDS is eligible, courts generally focus on the connection between the disease and its impact on the educational performance of the child. If the child's ability to perform school work is affected, such as by limited strength and vitality, the child will be considered to have a qualifying disability under IDEA. Where, however, there is no showing that the disease is interfering with educational performance, the child will not be considered covered under the IDEA.[205]

In *Thomas v. Atascadero Unified School District*,[206] the United States District Court for the Central District of California held that a child infected with the AIDS virus was a protected person within the meaning of § 504. Further, the child was otherwise qualified to attend public school. Exclusion from school therefore was a violation of § 504.[207]

In *Doe v. Belleville Public School District No. 118*,[208] suit was brought under § 504 against the school system for excluding a child with AIDS. The LEA sought to dismiss the complaint on the grounds that the child's parents had failed to exhaust administrative remedies under IDEA.[209] The court held in denying a motion to dismiss that there was no requirement to exhaust the IDEA administrative remedies because the child was not covered by IDEA. The LEA argued that the child was "other health impaired"[210] and therefore covered by IDEA. The district court pointed out, however, that there are three elements to the other health impaired classification. There must be a health impairment limiting strength, vitality, or alertness. The impairment must adversely affect educational performance. Finally the impairment must require special education and related services. For a child who has AIDS, the AIDS does not necessarily cause an adverse educational impact. Further, at many stages of the disease there is no impairment of strength, vitality, or alertness.[211]

OSERS, interpreting IDEA and its regulations, has held that drug and alcohol addicted students are not "other health impaired" under IDEA.[212] OCR, interpreting the Americans with Disabilities Act has also held that these children are not protected within the meaning of § 504.[213]

---

205. Doe v. Belleville Public School Dist. No. 118, 672 F. Supp. 342 (S.D. Ill. 1987).

206. 662 F. Supp. 376 (C.D. Cal. 1987).

207. *See also* Robertson v. Granite City Community Unit School Dist. No. 9, 684 F. Supp. 1002 (S.D. Ill. 1988); Doe v. Belleville Indep. School Dist. No. 118, 672 F. Supp. 342 (S.D. Ill. 1987); District 27 Community School Bd. v. Board of Educ., 130 Misc. 2d 398, 502 N.Y.S.2d 325 (Sup. Ct. N.Y. Queens County, 1986).

208. 672 F. Supp. 342 (S.D. Ill. 1987).

209. It will be remembered that where IDEA provides concurrent rights, the IDEA administrative remedies must be exhausted before filing suit under § 504. 20 U.S.C. § 1415(f).

210. 34 C.F.R. § 300.8. *see also* 20 U.S.C. §§ 1401(3)(A),(B), and 1401 (26).

211. *See also* Barnes Inquiry, 211 Educ. Handicapped L. Rep. (CRR) 343 (1984). It is also possible, of course, to have AIDS and be covered by IDEA because of an unrelated disability. *See* Parents of Child, Code No. 870901W v. Coker, 676 F. Supp. 1072 (E.D. Okla. 1987) (defendants enjoined from prosecuting state court action seeking exclusion of emotionally disturbed child with AIDS who was placed pursuant to IDEA). Coverage by § 504 or IDEA, of course does not insure the child will be able to remain in the regular classroom. *See generally* Martinez v. School Bd., 675 F. Supp. 1574 (M.D. Fla. 1987) (preliminary injunction to keep LEA from barring student with AIDS Related Complex (ARC) denied).

212. Harris Inquiry, 211 Educ. Handicapped L. Rep. (CRR) 431 (EHA 1987).

213. OCR Staff Memorandum, 17 Individuals with Disabilities Educ. L. Rep. (LRP) 609 (OCR 1991); *see also* Stearns v. Board of Educ. for Warren Township High School Dist. 121, 31 Individuals with Disabilities Educ. L. Rep. (LRP) 134 (N.D. Ill. 1999).

Perhaps counter intuitively, in the circumstance where §504 appears to expand rights to those not covered by IDEA (for example AIDS), it seems that affirmative requirements are less likely to constitute an undue burden than in circumstances where §504 purports to provide additional benefits to those already covered by IDEA. Since the school system is already providing the services "it may be logically inferred that it would not have imposed an 'undue burden' on defendants to provide a special educational program for the plaintiff."[214] Further, if services of a particular type are already being provided to one group of people, what is being requested is a reallocation of existing resources, not an expansion of funding.[215] By the same token, these latter cases may well result in more litigation, since if there is not dual coverage with IDEA, there is no need to exhaust administrative remedies.

---

214. Sanders, 561 F. Supp. at 1371.
215. *See generally* §§1.4, 1.4.1.

Chapter 6

Independent Educational Evaluations

6.1 In General

Under certain circumstances, the local education agency is required to provide at public expense an Independent Educational Evaluation (IEE) of the child. An IEE is defined as an evaluation conducted by a qualified examiner who is not employed by the agency responsible for the child's education.[1] Under IDEA, the parents may have the right to obtain an Independent Educational Evaluation (IEE) at public expense, if the parents disagree with the evaluation performed by the public agency.[2] If the parents disagree with the agency evaluation and request an IEE, the agency must either provide the IEE or, if the public agency believes its evaluation is appropriate, it must initiate a due process hearing to show that its evaluation is appropriate.[3]

In addition to situations in which there are disagreements with an evaluation performed by the agency, parents have been permitted reimbursement for an IEE where "special circumstances" are shown.[4] "Special circumstances" occur, for example, when the LEA acts in bad faith, such as failing to comply with the procedural safeguards of IDEA in an egregious manner. Special circumstances have also been found where a parent took action to secure services that were in dispute and were ultimately found necessary to protect the physical health of the child and which should have

---

1. 34 C.F.R. § 300.502(a)(3)(i); *see also* 20 U.S.C. § 1415(b)(1) and (d)(2)(A).
2. 34 C.F.R. § 300.502(b); *see also* 20 U.S.C. § 1415(b)(1); Lauren W. v. Deflaminis, 480 F.3d 259 (3d Cir. 2007) (parents were not entitled to reimbursement of costs of educational evaluation where expressly agree with evaluation); Holmes v. Mill Creek Township School Dist., 2000 WL 215655 (3d Cir. 2000) (IEE reimbursement denied where parents did not show district evaluation was inappropriate); Seattle School Dist. No. 1 v. B.S., 82 F.3d 1493 (9th Cir. 1996) (reimbursed 1/4 of IEE where not conducted as part of disagreement but used by the school); Warren G. v. Cumberland County School District, 190 F.3d 80 (3d Cir. 1999) (parents have unqualified right to reimbursement if district's evaluation is not appropriate-failure to express disagreement does not foreclose parents' right to reimbursement); Raymond S. v. Ramirez, 918 F. Supp. 1280 (N.D. Iowa 1996) (district must reimburse portion of IEE paid by insurance since utilization of benefits would incur a financial loss to parents); Letter to Young, 39 Individuals with Disabilities Educ. L. Rep. (LRP) 98 (OSEP 2003) (a district is required to pay for an IEE if it is unable to show that it's evaluation was appropriate).
3. 34 C.F.R. § 300.502(b)(2); *see also* 20 U.S.C. § 1415(b)(1).
4. Akers v. Bolton, 531 F. Supp. 300 (D. Kan. 1981).

been provided by the school district.[5] Reimbursement has also been held proper when an LEA recommended an IEE which was subsequently used to determine the child's placement.[6]

Section 504 of the Rehabilitation Act of 1973 does not address public funding of an IEE, so parents must, therefore, seek protection and reimbursement for an IEE under IDEA regulations.[7]

6.2 Notice of Availability of IEE

IDEA regulations require that, *at the request of the parent*, public education agencies provide parents with information concerning where an IEE may be obtained, including a list of qualified examiners.[8] Although an LEA may provide parents with a list of qualified examiners, it cannot limit the parents in their choice of an examiner listed, unless all the qualified examiners in the geographic location are included. Even if all are listed, however, a parent may choose a different qualified examiner if the child's unique needs establishes that no one on the list is qualified.[9]

There are also more general procedural safeguard notice requirements that must be provided only one time a school year.[10] The content of this notice, however, includes notice of the availability of an independent evaluation.[11] Thus, notice of the availability of an IEE is required at initial referral or when parents request an evaluation, when a decision is made to change a student's placement because of a violation of the student conduct code, and upon receipt of the first request for a due process hearing or state complaint in a school year and when a parent requests a copy of the procedural safeguards, Further, the United States Department of Education has held that where an LEA only provided notice of the availability of IEE when the parents requested it, after classification had already been made, there was a violation of Section 504 regulations.[12] The better practice therefore is to provide notice of the possible right to an IEE following a referral for an agency evaluation under § 504.

---

5. *Id.; see also* Anderson v. Thompson, 658 F.2d 1205 (7th Cir. 1981).

6. Hoover Schrum, Ill. School Dist. No.157, 257 Educ. Handicapped L. Rep. (CRR) 136 (OCR 1980).

7. Baltimore County, Md. Pub. Schools, 352 Educ. Handicapped L. Rep. (CRR) 352 (OCR 1987).

8. 34 C.F.R. § 300.502(a)(2) (emphasis added); *see also* 20 U.S.C. § 1415(b)(1); Letter to Parker, 41 Individuals with Disabilities Educ. L. Rep. (LRP) 155 (OSERS 2004) (a parent has the final say in choosing an evaluator for an IEE, but a public agency may publish a list of qualified evaluators as suggestions to the parent).

9. Letter to Young, 39 Individuals with Disabilities Educ. L. Rep. (LRP) 98 (OSEP 2003).

10. 34 C.F.R. § 300.504(a).

11. 34 C.F.R. § 300.504(b).

12. Elmira City, NY School Dist., 352 Educ. Handicapped L. Rep. (CRR) 188 (OCR 1986) (violation of 34 C.F.R. § 104.36).

6.3 Parental Request for an IEE

If a parent requests an IEE, the public agency may ask the parent for the reasons he or she objects to the public evaluation. The parent is not required to give reasons for disagreement, nor may the public agency delay providing the IEE at public expense or proceeding without a due process hearing.[13]

6.4 Standards for IEE

Whenever an IEE is made at public expense, agency criteria for evaluations must be met.[14] An IEE should, therefore, include a determination of specific teaching methods and instructional materials to be used, as well as needs for assistive technology.[15] Likewise, the qualifications of the evaluators should be comparable to those required of agency evaluators.

6.5 Cost of IEE

IDEA regulations provide that the public agency either pay for the evaluation or "ensure that the evaluation is otherwise provided at no cost to the parent...."[16] For example, the public agency may be able to share this cost with another state or local agency such as a department of social services.[17]

---

13. 34 C.F.R. §300.502(a)(4); Warren G. v. Cumberland County School District, 190 F.3d 80 (3d Cir. 1999).

14. 34 C.F.R. §300.502(e); *see also* 20 U.S.C. §1415(b)(1); Letter to Parker, 41 Individuals with Disabilities Educ. L. Rep. (LRP) 155 (OSERS 2004) (a district "must set criteria under which an IEE can be obtained at public expense, including the location of the evaluation and the qualifications of the examiner, which must be the same as the criteria the public agency uses when it initiates an evaluation, to the extent those criteria are consistent with the parent's right to an IEE."); Rambo Inquiry, 16 Educ. Handicapped L. Rep. (CRR) 1078 (OSEP 1990).

15. Letter to Fisher, 23 Individuals with Disabilities Educ. L. Rep. (LRP) 565 (OSEP 1995) (right to request evaluation for assistive technology).

16. 34 C.F.R. §300.502(a)(3)(ii); *see also* 20 U.S.C. §1415(b)(1); Tatum Indep. School Dist., 21 Individuals with Disabilities Educ. L. Rep. (LRP) 206 (OSEP 1994) (school district can establish criteria to ensure that the cost of a publicly funded IEE is reasonable).

17. 34 C.F.R. §300.103; *see also* 20 U.S.C. §1401(8); Idea Public Charter School v. District of Columbia 374 F. Supp. 2d 158 (D.D.C. 2005) (charter school may not recover cost of IEE conducted on behalf of the parents where school had other procedural options to recoup costs of independent evaluation).

18. Letter to Anonymous, 30 Individuals with Disabilities Educ. L. Rep. (LRP) 821 (OSEP 1998) (state educational agency must ensure that school complies with request for an IEE).

6.6 Unilateral Action by Parent to Obtain IEE

If the parents disagree with the LEA's evaluation, they have three ways to proceed to obtain the IEE.[18] First, of course, they may seek the agreement of the agency to pay for the IEE.

Second, if the parents disagree with the agency evaluation, they may unilaterally seek an evaluation and subsequently seek reimbursement from the LEA. No approval from or notice to the LEA is required in order to permit later reimbursement for the IEE.[19] If the agency, however, believes that its evaluation is appropriate, it may request a due process hearing.[20] If the LEA's evaluation is found appropriate, reimbursement is not required.[21] There is no specific time limit for how long the school system has to request a due process hearing challenging the parents' IEE, though it may not delay its decision for so long that the delay in requesting the hearing acts as a denial of the IEE.[22]

Finally, rather than seeking an IEE and risking success in seeking reimbursement, a parent may opt to request a due process hearing. There is no specific requirement that parents wait to see if an LEA corrects the defects in its evaluation prior to taking action to seek an IEE.[23] IDEA sets no timelines as to either how long a parent can wait before obtaining an IEE or after receiving the evaluation results before seeking reimbursement for an IEE.[24] It has, however, been interpreted as unreasonable to require payment for an IEE conducted two years after the LEA's evaluation was done.[25]

---

19. Hudson v. Wilson, 828 F.2d 1059 (4th Cir. 1987); *see also* Thorne Inquiry, 16 Educ. Handicapped L. Rep. (LRP) 606 (OSEP 1990).

20. 34 C.F.R. § 300.502(2)(i).

21. *See* Hessler v. State Bd. of Educ. of Md., 553 Educ. Handicapped L. Rep. (CRR) 262 (D. Md. 1981), *aff'd*, 700 F.2d 134 (4th Cir. 1983).

22. 34 C.F.R. § 300.502(a)(4); Letter to Anonymous, 23 Individuals with Disabilities Educ. L. Rep. (LRP) 719 (OSEP 1995) (no timeline for a school to ask for a due process hearing to determine whether they must pay for an IEE); Smith Inquiry, 16 Educ. Handicapped L. Rep. (CRR) 1080 (OSERS 1990).

23. In an unusual 1981 decision, however, an LEA was not required to reimburse a parent for an IEE where prior notice to the LEA was not given. Norris v. Massachusetts Dept. of Educ., 529 F. Supp. 759 (D. Mass. 1981); *but see* 34 C.F.R. § 300.502(a)(4). There is no requirement to notify the public agency of the reason for the disagreement.

24. 34 C.F.R. § 300.502(a)(2).

25. Fields Inquiry, 213 Educ. Handicapped L. Rep. (CRR) 259 (OSEP 1989).

26. 34 C.F.R. § 300.502(a)(5)(added to the 2005 regulations); Edie F. v. River Falls School Dist. 243 F.3d 329 (7th Cir. 2001); Board of Educ. of Murphysboro Comm. Unit School Dist. No. 186 v. Illinois State Board of Educ., 41 F.3d 1162 (7th Cir. 1994); Hudson v. Wilson, 828 F.2d 1059 (4th Cir. 1987); Hiller v. Board of Educ., 687 F. Supp. 735 (N.D.N.Y. 1988); *see also* Warren G. v. Cumberland County, 190 F.3d 80 (3d Cir. 1999) (unqualified right to an IEE; failure to disclose disagreement not a bar to reimbursement); Board of Educ. of Oak Park & River Forest H.S. v. Illinois State Bd. Educ., 21 F. Supp. 2d 862 (N.D. Ill. 1998) (no reimbursement for second IEE), *vacated on other grounds sub nom.* Board of Educ. of Oak Park & River Forest H.S. v. Kelly E., 207 F.3d 931 (2000); Raymond S. v. Ramirez, 918 F. Supp. 1280 (N.D. Ind. 1996) (notice not required prior to IEE in order to be eligible for reimbursement); *see also* Holmes v. Mill Creek Township School Dist., 2000 WL 215655 (3d Cir. 2000).

27. Letter to Katzerman, 28 Individuals with Disabilities Educ. L. Rep. (LRP) 310 (OSEP 1997).

6.7 IEE At Public Expense Is Limited to One

A parent is entitled to only one publicly funded IEE for each time an LEA evaluation is conducted over which there is disagreement.[26] Since the results of the IEE are considered when designing appropriate programs, the district needs access to the reports. Thus, the results of the IEE can be disclosed without parental consent.[27]

6.8 Use of IEE

The results of any IEE that meets agency criteria must be considered by the LEA in a decision regarding the child's educational program.[28] The IEE may also be presented at any due process proceeding.[29]

6.9 IEE At Parental Expense

Parents always have the right to get an IEE at their own expense, even if a due process hearing holds the public agency's evaluation appropriate.[30] As with an IEE obtained at public expense, the IEE paid for by the parent must be considered by the agency in determining the child's educational needs and may be presented as evidence in any due process proceedings.[31]

6.10 Hearing Officer Ordered IEE

The hearing officer may order an IEE, which must be at public expense.[32] Any IEE that duplicates an IEE ordered by a hearing officer is, however, not reimbursable.[33]

---

28. 34 C.F.R. §300.502(c)(1); *see also* 20 U.S.C. §1415(b)(1); Letter to Katzerman, 28 Individuals with Disabilities Educ. L. Rep. (LRP) 310 (OSEP 1997) (results of IEE can be disclosed despite lack of consent).

29. 34 C.F.R. §300.502(c)(2); *see also* 20 U.S.C. §1415(b)(1).

30. 34 C.F.R. §300.502(c); *see also* 20 U.S.C. §1415(b)(1).

31. 34 C.F.R. §300.502(c); *see also* 20 U.S.C. §1415(b)(1).

32. 34 C.F.R. §300.502(d); *see also* 20 U.S.C. §1415(b)(1).

33. Williams v. Overturf, 580 F. Supp. 1365 (W.D. Wis. 1984).

Chapter 7

Individualized Education Program

7.1 In General

The centerpiece of IDEA is the requirement that each eligible student have an "individualized education program" (IEP).[1] Special education and related services must be provided in accordance with the IEP.[2] The IEP must be reviewed at least annually.[3] The contents of the IEP are designed to provide a road map for the child's educational programming during the course of the coming year.

While the IEP is not specifically required by § 504 regulations, its functional equivalent is.[4] Section 504 regulations indicate that one way to meet the special education requirements of § 504 is through the IEP process of IDEA.[5]

The IEP has several components.[6] First, it must contain a statement of the child's present levels of academic achievement and functional performance. This statement

---

1. 34 C.F.R. § 300.320; *see also* 20 U.S.C. § 1414(d)(1)(A) and (d)(6).

2. 34 C.F.R. § 300.320(4); *see also* 20 U.S.C. § 1414(d)(1)(A).

3. 34 C.F.R. § 300.324; *see also* 20 U.S.C. §§ 1414(d)(3); *see generally* 20 U.S.C. §§ 1414(d)(5). The 2004 statute contains language that provides an opportunity for the school and parents to participate in a pilot project where a muti-year IEP (3 year) may be developed.

4. 34 C.F.R. § 104.33(b)(1) and (2) provides:

(1) For the purpose of this subpart, the provision of an appropriate education is the provision of regular or special education and related aids and services that (i) are designed to meet individual educational needs of handicapped [*sic*] persons as adequately as the needs of nonhandicapped persons are met and (ii) are based upon adherence to procedures that satisfy the requirements of Regs. 104.34, 104.35, and 104.36.

(2) Implementation of an individualized education program developed in accordance with the Education of the Handicapped Act [*sic*] is one means of meeting the standard established in paragraph (b)(1)(i) of this section.

See also, Letter to McKethan, 25 Individuals with Disabilities Educ. L. Rep. 295 (OCR 1996) (parents cannot reject satisfactory IDEA IEP and compel district to develop new IEP pursuant to § 504).

5. 34 C.F.R. § 104.33(b)(2); *Letter to Morse,* 41 Individuals with Disabilities Educ. L. Rep. (LRP) 65 (OSEP 2003) (504 plan may not be substituted for an IDEA IEP, but an IDEA IEP will satisfy 504 requirements).

6. 34 C.F.R. § 300.320; *see also* 20 U.S.C. §§ 1414(d)(1)(A), (d)(6); Nack v. Orange City School Dist., 454 F.3d 604 (6th Cir. 2006) (IEP's failure to provide a baseline measure of student's future progress did not substantially harm student); School Bd. of Indep. Sch. Dist. No. 11 v. Renollett, 440 F.3d 1007 (8th Cir. 2006) (although the IEP was not perfectly executed when District failed to

must include how the child's disability affects the child's involvement and progress in the general education curriculum.

The IEP must also contain a statement of measurable annual academic and functional goals. These goals should be related to meeting the child's needs that result from the disability and to the extent possible enable the child to be involved in and make progress in the general curriculum.[7]

The IEP must contain a statement of the special education and related services and supplementary aids and services to be provided. The special education aids and services should be based on peer review research to the extent practicable.[8] It must also contain a statement of program modifications or supports for school personnel that will be provided so the child may: advance appropriately; achieve annual goals; be involved and progress in the general curriculum; participate in extracurricular and nonacademic activities; and be educated and participate in activities with nondisabled children, including the extent to which the child will be served in regular educational programs.

The IEP must also, if such is the case, contain an explanation for why the child will not participate with nondisabled children in the regular class and activities. There must be a statement of any procedural modifications in the administration of state or district wide assessments of student achievement. If the IEP team determines the child will not participate in the assessment, the IEP needs to contain a statement as to why the assessment is not appropriate and the reason that the selected alternate assessment is appropriate for the child. The IEP must also contain benchmarks or short term objectives for children taking alternate assessments when the assessments are aligned to alternate achievement standards.[9]

Beginning not later then when the first IEP is in effect for a child who turns 16, or younger if appropriate, the IEP must also contain a statement of needed transition services that focuses on the student's course of study. This means participation in vocational education or advanced placement courses. For each student whose IEP contains transition services, there must be a statement of measurable postsecondary goals relating to the child's future training, education, employment, and where appropriate, independent living skills. The IEP must also include necessary transition services, including course work, needed to assist the child in reaching these goals.[10] The child goals must be determined by using age appropriate transition assessments.

---

include a written behavioral intervention plan, the omission did not compromise the child's right to an appropriate education or deprive him of educational benefits); Cleveland Heights-University Heights City School Dist. v. Boss, 144 F.3d 391 (6th Cir. 1998) (IEP was inadequate as to more than just technical matters. IEP contained no objective way to measure progress and did not adequately explain services); Doe v. Defendant I., 898 F.2d 1186 (6th Cir. 1990) (failure to include present level of educational performance and objective criteria did not render IEP invalid where absent information was known by parents and agency); *but see Kirby v. Cabell County Bd. of Educ.*.Slip Copy, 2006 WL 2691435 (S.D.W. Va. 2006) (court directed the parties to reconvene an IEP meeting with a facilitator to develop an IEP which considers Robert's current levels of achievement and functional performance with a specific plan to address his deficiencies); Escambia County Bd. of Educ. v. Benton, 406 F.Supp.2d 1248 (S.D. Ala. 2005) (procedural inadequacies in autistic student's IEPs, which related to mastery dates of benchmarks and adequacy of annual goals, resulted in denial of FAPE to student).

  7. 34 C.F.R. § 300.320(a)(2)(i).
  8. 34 C.F.R. § 300.320(a)(4).
  9. 34 C.F.R. § 300.320(a)(2)(B)(ii).
  10. 34 C.F.R. § 300.320(b).

The IEP must contain the date the services and modifications will begin as well as the expected frequency, location, and modifications of the services. It must indicate how the child's progress toward the annual goals will be measured. In addition, it must provide when periodic progress reports for meeting the annual goals will be provided.

The IEP must also contain a statement one year before a student reaches the age of majority that the student has been informed of his or her rights which will transfer to the student at the age of majority.[11] Finally, there are also special rules concerning IEP content which apply to students with disabilities convicted as adults and incarcerated in adult prisons.[12]

The IEP acts as a guide for the provision of services and insures that those services are related to identifiable educational goals and objectives. The IEP, however, does not act as a guarantee of a child's success. The signature of the participants at the meeting is typically requested on the IEP document, though there is no statutory or regulatory requirement that the document actually be signed.[13] It is, however, good practice to memorialize the agreement of the parties in this manner.

7.2 Agency Responsible for IEP Development

Each public agency having responsibility to educate a child must insure development of an IEP.[14] Typically the public agency is the local school system where the child resides. Numerous other public agencies, however, may have responsibility for educating a child. For example, a child involuntarily committed to a mental institution or to a correctional facility may actually be educated by that particular state agency.[15]

---

11. 34 C.F.R. § 300.320(c). State law determines whether and at what age rights transfer.
12. 34 C.F.R. § 300.149(d); 34 C.F.R. §§ 300.324(d)(1) and (2) provide:
   (1)Requirements that do not apply. The following requirements do not apply to students with disabilities who are convicted as adults under state law and incarcerated in adult prisons: (i) the requirements ... relating to participation of children with disabilities in general assessments ... [and] (ii) relating to transition planning and transition services ...
   (2) Modifications of IEP or placements ... the IEP team of a student with a disability, who is convicted as an adult under state law and incarcerated in an adult prison, may modify the student's IEP or placement if the state has demonstrated a bona fide security or compelling penological interest that cannot otherwise be accommodated.
13. Bradley v. Ark. Dep't of Educ., 443 F.3d 965 (8th Cir. 2006) (the fact that the parents did not sign the revised IEP did not prevent its implementation); AW v. Fairfax County Sch. Bd., 372 F.3d 674, 683 (4th Cir. 2004) ("The right conferred by the IDEA on parents to participate in the formulation of their child's IEP does not constitute a veto power over the IEP team's decisions." Parents refusal to sign does not prevent implementation); Burilovich v. Bd. of Educ. of the Lincoln Consolidated Schools, 208 F.3d 560 (6th Cir. 2000) (oral IEP will not be enforced, must be in writing); Fuhrmann v. East Hanover Bd. of Educ., 993 F.2d 1031 (3d Cir. 1993) (although the parents did not ultimately sign the revised IEP, they had the opportunity to participate in the IEP formulation process in a meaningful way); T.R. v. Kingwood Township Bd. of Educ., 32 F. Supp. 2d 220 (D.N.J. 1998) (even though parent did not sign IEP, parental involvement in the IEP process satisfied procedural requirements).
14. 34 C.F.R. § 300.323 see also 20 U.S.C. § 1414(d)(1)(D)(2)(A).
15. 34 C.F.R. §§ 300.149(c) and (d).

Children placed in private schools by their parents must also be identified and evaluated. The LEA must insure that a "services plan" is implemented for such children.[16]

7.3 Time Frame for Development of IEP

An initial IEP must be developed within thirty calendar days of a determination that the child requires special education and related services.[17] The initial determination of need is discussed elsewhere.[18]

Subsequent IEPs must be reviewed on at least an annual basis to determine whether the annual goals for the child are being achieved.[19] Revisions must also occur to address the child's anticipated needs, lack of progress, results of any reevaluations, and information about the child provided by the parents.[20] After the annual IEP meeting is held, the parent and public agency may agree not to convene an IEP meeting to make revisions. They may, however, develop a written document to amend or modify the current IEP. The IEP team must be informed of the changes.[21] Amendments are permitted to the IEP without redrafting the entire IEP. The IEP must be "implemented as soon as possible following" its development.[22]

A placement must be based on an existing IEP.[23] Parents are part of the team making placement decisions.[24] It is usually the case, therefore, that a change in placement will have been preceded by an IEP meeting. In 2004, the statute added language regarding the disabled student's IEP status when transferring to schools from either within the state or from out of state. A student who transfers into a new school system within the academic year from within the same state should be placed in a program based on the IEP effective at the time and developed in the previous school system until the receiving school adopts the previous IEP or develops its own IEP consistent with the procedures for development and implementation. Comparable services must be provided. This placement should be done in consultation with the parents.[25] Both schools within the state are required to take reasonable steps to make sure the appropriate records are transferred promptly. [26] A student transferring into a new school system from outside the state in the same academic year and who has an effective IEP should be placed in a program based on the IEP developed at the previous school. The parents again are to be consulted. Comparable services must be provided until the receiving school conducts an evaluation if necessary, and develops a new IEP if appropriate.[27]

---

16. 34 C.F.R. §§ 300.130–.144 and 34 C.F.R. § 300.37. *See* § 8.10.
17. 34 C.F.R. § 300.323(c)(1); *see generally* 20 U.S.C. §§ 1414(d)(1).
18. See Chapter 4.
19. 34 C.F.R. § 300.324(b)(1); *see generally* 20 U.S.C. §§ 1414(d)(1).
20. 34 C.F.R. § 300.324(b)(1).
21. 34 C.F.R. § 300.324(a)(4).
22. 34 C.F.R. § 300.323(c)(2); *see also* 20 U.S.C. §§ 1414(d)(2)(A) and (B).
23. 34 C.F.R. § 300.116; *see also* 20 U.S.C. § 1412(a)(5).
24. 34 C.F.R. § 300.327.
25. 34 C.F.R 300.323(e); 20 U.S.C. § 1414 (d)(2)(C)(i)(I). Interestingly, OCR does not interpret § 504 as requiring the school to implement the existing IEP. OCR Memorandum, 307 Educ. Handicapped L. Rep. (CRR) 15 (OCR 1989)
26. 34 C.F.R 300.323(f); 20 U.S.C. § 1414 (d)(2)(C)(ii).
27. 20 U.S.C. § 1414 (d)(2)(C)(i)(II).

7.4 Placement Decisions and the IEP

Federal law requires all placements be based on an existing IEP.[28] The placement decision must also be made by the parents and other persons knowledgeable about the child, the evaluation data, and the placement options.[29]

The IEP is not written for a specific location.[30] The logical sequence, therefore, is to develop the IEP and then to determine placement. Deciding the placement of a child prior to development of an IEP upon which to base that decision constitutes a procedural violation sufficient to find that the school's placement would not provide a free appropriate education.[31] Likewise, a change in placement is improper if it will not allow implementation of the IEP.[32]

7.5 IEP Meetings

The IEP is developed at meetings involving interested parties. The public agency is responsible for initiating and conducting these meetings.[33] Participants in the meeting must include:[34]

- the parents of the child;[35]

---

28. 34 C.F.R. § 300.116(b)(2); *see also* 20 U.S.C. § 1412(a)(5)

29. Dong v. Board of Educ. of Rochester Comm. School, 197 F.3d 793 (6th Cir. 1999) (district did not need to include expert in particular teaching method in order to meet requirements of the IEP. The team included persons knowledgeable about "placement options"); B.R. v. San Ramon Valley Unified School Dist. Slip Copy, 2007 WL 216323 (N.D. Cal. 2007) (court was not persuaded that the IEPs that were developed for the periods of time in question were legally insufficient; district had the necessary competence and personnel, and was able to conform to the IEPs sufficiently to meet the needs of plaintiff).

30. P.N. and G.N. v. Greco, 37 Individuals with Disabilities Educ. L. Rep. (LRP) 255 (D.N.J. 2003) ("Neither IDEA nor the regulations promulgated there under require that an IEP name a specific school in which to enroll a child." However, the idiosyncratic goals of an IEP may limit the number of schools a child can attend); Leonard v. McKenzie, 869 F.2d 1558 (D.C. Cir. 1989); *but see* J.K. v. Alexandria City School Bd., 484 F.3d 672 (4th Cir. 2007) (held that school district failed to offer a FAPE when its individualized education program (IEP) did not identify a particular school).

31. Spielberg v. Henrico County Pub. Schools, 853 F.2d 256 (4th Cir. 1988); *see also* Deal v. Hamilton County Bd. of Educ., 392 F.3d 840, 857 (6th Cir. 2004) (policy refusing placement in a particular program or at any particular school is predetermination) (*citing Spielberg*); W.G. Target School Dist. No. Bd. of Trustees, 789 F. Supp. 1070 (D. Mont. 1991), *aff'd*, 960 F.2d 1479 (9th Cir. 1992); 23 Evans v. Board of Educ. of Rhinebeck Central School Dist., 930 F. Supp. 2d 83 (S.D.N.Y. 1996); *but see* Nack v. Orange City Sch. Dist., 454 F.3d 604 (6th Cir. 2006) (student's individualized education program (IEP) was not a result of predetermination); Schoenbach v. Dist. of Columbia, Slip Copy, 2006 WL 1663426 (D.D.C. 2006).

32. Letter to Caroll, 43 Individuals with Disabilities Educ. L. Rep. (LRP) 116 (OSEP 2004) (determination affecting the placement of a child must be made consistent with a child's IEP or placement).

33. 34 C.F.R. § 300.321(a); *see also* 20 U.S.C. § 1414(d)(1)(B)–(d)(1)(D).

34. Questions and Answers on Individual Education Plans, 47 Individuals Educ. Law Rept. (LRP) 166 (OSERS 2007) (written agreements and state regulations can modify composition of IEP members as long as does not diminish parents' rights).

35. 34 C.F.R. § 300.321; *see also* 20 U.S.C. § 1414(d)(1)(B)–(d)(1)(D)).

- at least one regular education teacher if the child is or may be participating in regular education;

- a representative of the public agency, other than the child's teacher, who is qualified to supervise or provide special education and who is knowledgeable about the curriculum and the availability of the general resources of the public agency;[36]

- the child's special education teacher or one person who provides special education to the child; [37]

- an individual who can interpret the instructional implications of evaluations;

- the child may be present where appropriate.[38]

The above listed members of an IEP are not required to attend the meeting if the parents and public agency agree in writing that the attendance of that team member is not necessary and when that area of the curriculum and or services is not being modified or discussed.[39] If the team member's area is going to be discussed or modified at the IEP meeting, they may be excused from attending only if there is a written agreement between the parents and the school. Prior to the meeting, the IEP team member must also submit written input for the development of the IEP to both the parents and the IEP team.[40]

Further, the IEP meeting may include "[o]ther individuals who have knowledge or special expertise regarding the child."[41] The determination of who has relevant knowledge and expertise is made by the party that invites the individual to the meeting.[42] The parents and school, therefore, have the right to have legal counsel at the IEP meeting if they believe the lawyer's knowledge and expertise would be helpful.

If the IEP meeting is to consider transition services, the public agency must also invite the student and a representative of the agency likely to be responsible for paying or providing the transition services.[43]

---

36. Letter to Collins, 30 Individuals with Disabilities Educ. L. Rep. (OSEP 1998) (school psychologist or guidance counselor can serve as LEA representative if they meet the criteria).

37. B. v. Napa Valley Unified School Dist. ___ F.3d ___, 2007 WL 2028132 (9th Cir. 2007) In *Napa Valley*, the court held: (1)school district's inclusion of teacher, who taught student in kindergarten six years prior, in IEP team, rather than student's current teacher, did not violate IDEA; (2) school district's inclusion of special education teacher who had never taught student did not satisfy IDEA's procedural requirement that an IEP team include at least one special education teacher or at least one special education provider of such child; and (3) district's violation of procedural requirements of IDEA by not including a special education teacher or provider of the child on the IEP team did not result in the loss of a free appropriate public education.

38. 34 C.F.R. § 300.321; *see also* 20 U.S.C. § 1414(d)(1)(B)–(d)(1)(D).

39. 34 C.F.R. § 300.321(e)(1).

40. 34 C.F.R. § 300.321(e)(2)(i–ii).

41. 34 C.F.R. § 300.321; *see also* 20 U.S.C. § 1414(d)(1)(B)–(d)(1)(D).

42. 34 C.F.R. § 300.321; *but see* § 15.2.1. Attorney's fees will not be awarded for attendance at IEP meetings unless the meeting is convened as a result of an administrative proceeding, judicial action, or at the discretion of the state, a mediation conducted prior to the request for a due process hearing. 34 C.F.R. § 300.517(C)(ii); *see also,* Letter to Garvin, 30 Individuals with Disabilities Educ. L. Rep. (OSEP 1998) (the practice of having attorneys potentially create an adversarial atmosphere and the 1999 IDEA regulations impact the legitimacy of this practice with the limitations to "other individuals who have knowledge or special expertise regarding the child").

43. 34 C.F.R § 300.321(b).

7.6 Parental Participation

The importance of parental participation in the development of the IEP can not be overestimated. Both the letter and spirit of the IEP require parental participation at every meaningful stage of the educational process, and development of the IEP and the attendant decisions are perhaps the most critical stages of that process.[44]

Central to the idea that there must be meaningful participation, of course, is the requirement that the IEP cannot be developed by the education agency prior to the IEP meeting. If the school system decides what should go into the IEP before consulting with the parents, there is a violation which itself may justify a hearing officer or judge to decide that there has been a failure to provide a FAPE.[45]

While the school may not decide the contents of the IEP prior to the meeting, it is permissible for the school to develop a draft of various proposals each of which can then be discussed with the parents at the IEP meeting.[46] There are, of course, always dif-

---

44. The importance the Supreme Court attached to parental involvement in the development of the IEP was well supported in the legislative history of IDEA. As the Senate Report stated, "individualized planning conferences are a way to provide parent involvement and protection to assure that appropriate services are provided to a handicapped child." S. Rep. No. 68, 94th Cong., 1st Sess. at 11–12, *quoted in* Hendrick Hudson Dist. Bd. of Educ. v. Rowley, 458 U.S. 176, 208–209 (1981); *see also* Honig v. Doe, 484 U.S. 305, 311 (1988) ("the Act establishes various procedural safeguards that guarantee parents ... an opportunity for meaningful input into all decisions affecting their child's education...."); Cerra v. Pawling Cent. Sch. Dist., 427 F.3d 186 (2d Cir. 2005); Kings Local School Dist., Bd. of Educ. v. Zelazny, 325 F.3d 724 (6th Cir. 2003) (serious infringement on a parent's opportunity to participate in the formulation of his or her child's IEP is actionable because it causes "substantive harm ... and thus constitutes a denial of the child's right to a FAPE"); Tennessee Dept. of Mental Health and Mental Retardation v. Paul B., 88 F.3d 1466 (6th Cir. 1996) (failure to notify parent of stay-put provision was a material fact which determined the outcome of the case); Beth v. Carroll, 87 F.3d 80 (3d Cir. 1996); Holland v. District of Columbia, 71 F.3d 417 (D.C. Cir. 1995); (parental refusal to consent to "clinical interviews" did not prevent reimbursement); Dell v. Board of Educ. Township High School, 32 F.3d 1053 (7th Cir. 1994); Amann v. Town of Stow, 991 F.2d 929 (1st Cir. 1993); DeVries v. Spillane, 853 F.2d 264, 266 (4th Cir. 1988) (parents to have "meaningful participation in all aspects"); Stemple v. Board of Educ., 623 F.2d 893, 898 (4th Cir. 1980) (parents provided with generous bill of rights); Mr. "M" v. Ridgefield Bd. of Educ., Slip Copy, 2007 WL 987483, (D. Conn. 2007) (board's procedural violation cannot be considered harmless error where did not give parents meaningful opportunity to participate in IEP meetings); Letter to Serwecki, 44 Individuals with Disabilities Educ. L. Rep. 8 (LRP) (OSEP 2005) (father's advocate could attend CSE meeting when father was prohibited from attending by a temporary restraining order, since protective order did not restrict the father's right to make educational decisions); *but see,* Navin, v. Park Ridge Sch. Dist. 64, 270 F.3d 1147, 1149 (7th Cir. 2001) (non-custodial parent retains due process rights under IDEA, but opinions only relevant to the extent that it made in concert with custodial parent).

45. Deal v. Hamilton County Bd. of Educ., 392 F.3d 840 (6th Cir. 2004) (District "predetermined" child's IEP when a "one-on-one ABA program" was never treated as a viable option, and parental participation at IEP meeting was "no more than after the fact involvement"); Spielberg v. Henrico County Pub. Schools, 853 F.2d 256 (4th Cir. 1988) *but see* Nack v. Orange City Sch. Dist., 454 F.3d 604 (6th Cir. 2006) (student's individualized education program (IEP) was not a result of predetermination); C.W. v. Rocklin Unified School Dist., Slip Copy, 2006 WL 2830172 (E.D. Cal. 2006) (pre meeting discussion does not mean predetermination).

46. N.L. v. Knox County Schs, 315 F.3d 688 (6th Cir. 2003) (no substantive violation when school-appointed experts and school officials confer ex parte to coordinate the drafting of an assessment report); *see* Letter to Anonymous, 25 Individuals with Disabilities Educ. L. Rep. (LRP) 1208 (OSEP 1996).

ficulties of proof when the question is whether the school's "suggestion" is really its decision or truly a proposal that can be affected by parental input.[47] Parents, however, have been successful in establishing premature decision-making on the part of school systems.[48]

To effectuate the central role of the parents in the IEP meeting, the educational agency is required to provide notice of the meeting to the parents,[49] indicating "the purpose, time, and location of the meeting, and who will be in attendance."[50] This notice must also inform the parents of persons invited to the meeting who have knowledge or special expertise.[51]

The IEP meeting must be held at a mutually convenient time.[52] If neither parent can attend a meeting, the LEA must attempt an alternate form of participation such as a teleconference and conference calls.[53] If both parents refuse to participate, the IEP meeting may be held, but the LEA must have a detailed set of records establishing its attempts to schedule a mutually convenient time and place.[54] To insure meaningful participation, the LEA must take whatever steps are necessary to "insure that the parent understands the proceedings ... including arranging for an interpreter for parents with deafness or whose native language is other than English."[55] It is important to note, however, that while parent participation is mandatory during the IEP creation process, IDEA does not require parental preferences be implemented.[56]

A copy of the IEP must be provided at no cost to the parent, even if not requested by the parent.[57]

7.7 Drafting the Document

It is important that it be kept in mind that the IEP provides an integrated approach to the child's educational programming. Each part is directed toward achieving the annual goals. IDEA requires "measurable annual goals." The goals must relate to meeting the academic and functional needs of the child's disability.[58] For children with disabilities who take alternate assessments that modify the normal achievement standards, a description of short term objectives or benchmarks must be listed.[59] To be rational, the

---

47. *See, e.g.,* Hudson v. Wilson, 828 F.2d 1059 (4th Cir. 1987).
48. *See* Spielberg v. Henrico County Pub. Schools, 853 F.2d 256 (4th Cir. 1988).
49. 34 C.F.R. § 300.322; *see also* 20 U.S.C. § 1414(d)(1)(B)(i); Letter to Anonymous, 25 Individuals with Disabilities Educ. L. Rep. (LRP) 1208 (OSEP 1996) (prior notice of IEP must be reasonable).
50. 34 C.F.R. § 300.322; *see also* 20 U.S.C. § 1414(d)(1)(B)(i).
51. 34 C.F.R. § 300.322.
52. 34 C.F.R. § 300.322; *see also* 20 U.S.C. § 1414(d)(1)(B)(i).
53. 34 C.F.R. § 300.322 and 328; *see also* 20 U.S.C. § 1414(d)(1)(B)(i).
54. 34 C.F.R. § 300.322. Examples of the appropriate records include detailed records of phone calls and visits to the parents' home or place of employment, as well as copies of correspondence. *Id.; see also* 20 U.S.C. § 1414(d)(1)(B)(i).
55. 34 C.F.R. § 300.322; *see also* 20 U.S.C. § 1414(d)(1)(B)(i).
56. Bradley v. Ark. Dep't of Educ., 443 F.3d 965 (8th Cir. 2006); White v. Ascension Parish Sch. Bd., 343 F.3d 373 (5th Cir. 2003).
57. 34 C.F.R. § 300.322; *see also* 20 U.S.C. § 1414(d)(1)(B)(i).
58. 34 C.F.R. § 300.320(a).
59. *Id.*

goals must be related to the child's present level of educational performance, and, of course, the objectives if required must be rationally connected to the goals.

A non-educator can play an important part in drafting the present level of educational performance and the goals and benchmarks or objectives when required by 1) insuring the level of performance, goals and objectives are all rationally related to one another, 2) insisting that the goals the parents believe are necessary are adequately articulated, and 3) pressing the participants to be descriptive and precise in writing the goals and objectives.

In general, any participant should be prepared to ask the following questions when developing goals and objectives:

- What skills and behaviors need to be addressed? What goals should the child strive for?

- What is the present level of performance? Is the present level of performance stated in objective measurable terms?

- Is there a direct relationship between the annual goals and the child's present level of performance? Are the goals reasonable?

- What short term objectives will allow the child to move toward the goals? Are the objectives measurable?[60]

- Under what conditions and by whom will the child receive educational programming?

The number of goals contained in the IEP depends on the student. By definition, it is an individual plan and the special education and related services needed by individual students will vary widely. The special education goals for a seriously emotionally disturbed child[61] will be quite different, and perhaps more comprehensive, than, for example, a child with a specific learning disability.

In addition to special education and related services, most students with a disability will also receive regular educational programming. The IEP must, therefore, include goals related to meeting the child's needs in the general curriculum.[62] The extent to which regular education is provided must be indicated in the IEP. It is important that the IEP identify where the mainstreaming will occur. For example, an IEP might provide that "Jane will be mainstreamed one and one-half hours per day in the library, cafeteria, and physical education." When a child receives regular education, the IEP must be accessible to each regular and special education teacher, related services providers, or any other providers. Each of these individuals must be informed about their responsibilities for providing and implementing the specific services contained in the IEP.[63]

Finally, any related services must be provided for in the IEP. If the child is to receive a related service such as occupational or speech\language therapy, this must be indicated and the level of service provided must be listed (for example, "Occupational therapy, 1 hour weekly").

---

60. 34 C.F.R. § 300.320(a)(2)(i)(B)(ii) (short term objectives or benchmarks are required for children who take alternate assessments).
61. *See, e.g.,* 34 C.F.R. § 300.324(a)(2)(i) (requires behavior intervention strategies when a child's behavior impedes the learning of the child or of others).
62. 34 C.F.R. §§ 300.39(b) and .320(a)(2). General curriculum is the same as what is typically referred to as "regular education."
63. 34 C.F.R. § 300. 323(d)(1)(20)(i–ii); Greider v. Shawnee Mission Unified School Dist. No. 512, 710 F. Supp. 296 (D. Kan. 1989).

7.7.1 Drafting Example

An example may be helpful to understand the interrelationship of the various parts of the IEP. Assume the child in question is an eligible thirteen-year-old with an emotional disturbance or behavior disorder. The present level of educational performance in each category in which she needs special education will usually be measured by standardized tests, such as the Peabody Individual Achievement Test Revised (PIATR). It might be described as follows:

Peabody Individual Achievement Test:

Math	G.E. 1.9 (Grade Equivalent less than second grade)
Reading Recognition	G.E. 1.6
Reading Comprehension	G.E. 2.1
Spelling	G.E. 2.2
General Information	G.E. 1.9
Total Test	G.E. 1.9
Expressive One World	
Picture Vocabulary Test	A.E. 6.7 (Age Equivalent)
Language Processing Test	A.E. 6.1
Receptive One Work Picture	
Vocabulary Test	A.E. 6.3

Educational performance, however, must not be measured only in traditional academic subjects. The definition of education is very broad under IDEA. For example, basic self-help and survival skills may need to be taught. These skills are sometimes referred to as activities of daily living. Assume, for example, that the child in our hypothetical situation has been identified as having "poor impulse control and trouble following directions in class." She may need instruction in social interaction skills, impulse control and self care skills. The present level of educational performance for these areas should also be stated. For example:

> *Social Interaction Skills/Impulse Control.* Jane inappropriately touches others when being introduced 80% of the time. Although Jane can play with her peer group, she often bosses them around and interacts inappropriately. Jane will not follow rules and yells out answers without raising hand.

Goals must be articulated that are based on the child's present level of academic achievement and functional performance. Taking just one area, reading skills, the goal might be:

Jane will increase reading skill to G.E. 3 by the end of the year. The objectives, however, must be more specific and *measurable*. Because the objectives must be measurable, it is only logical that the present skill level of the objective also must be identified so that the measurement can be made:

> Jane will identify and define basic vocabulary for functional living skills with 100% accuracy by June 15.
>
> Criteria for mastery of skill level: 60%

Jane will be able to give synonyms, antonyms, and multiple meanings for these words with 80% accuracy and intelligibility by June 15.

Skill level: Multiple meanings subtest 8th percentile.

Jane will read one story orally and silently by June 15.

Skill level: G.E. 2.1

While reading orally, Jane will be intelligible and use appropriate pitch and volume 80% of the time by June 15.

Skill level: 50%

Jane will read and explain 40 commonly seen signs with 80% accuracy by June 15.

Skill level: 65%

Jane will sequence 4 pictures with 100% accuracy by June 15.

Skill level: 10%

Jane will record a story she has created using correct sequence and grammar by June 15.

Skill level: New Skill

Jane will answer four questions about the story she recorded with 75% accuracy by June 15.

Skill level: New Skill

Jane will identify main idea and facts of a second-grade story with 80% accuracy by June 15.

Skill level: New Skill

Best practice would then suggest each identified goal will in turn have a list of intermediate objectives. Objectives are the steps to be taken to meet the goals. Objectives break the skills described in the goal down into discrete components. Benchmarks may also be used in place of objectives. Benchmarks are described as the amount of progress the child is expected to make within specific segments of the year. Generally benchmarks establish expected performance levels which measure progress during the year. The actual document used will vary widely among school divisions (see Appendix), but the content should be the same: measured level of educational development, rational goals, and measurable objectives or benchmarks.

7.8 Private Placements

Where a public agency, in order to meet its obligations under IDEA, places a child in a private facility, the public agency is responsible for developing the initial IEP upon which the placement decision is based.[64] This IEP must be developed with the participation of representatives from the private facility.[65] After development of the initial IEP,

---

64. 34 C.F.R. §300.325(a)(2); *see also* 20 U.S.C. 20 U.S.C. §1412(a)(10)(B).

65. 34 C.F.R. §300.325(a)(2); *see also* 20 U.S.C. §1412(a)(10)(B); Fuhrmann v. East Hanover Bd. of Educ., 993 F.2d 1031 (3d Cir. 1993) (regulation did not apply since the placement was at a public school); *see generally,* Gagliardo v. Arlington Cent. Sch. Dist., 418 F. Supp. 2d 559 (S.D.N.Y. 2006); W.G. v. Target School Dist. No. 23 Bd. of Trustees, 789 F. Supp. 1070 (D. Mont. 1991), *aff'd,*

subsequent IEP meetings may, at the discretion of the public school, be initiated and conducted by the private school.[66] If the public agency allows the private facility to initiate and conduct the subsequent IEP meetings, the public agency must still insure that the parents participate in decisions concerning the IEP and agree to any changes in the program before any changes are implemented.[67]

Under all circumstances, the public agency placing the child in the private facility retains responsibility to insure compliance with the IEP requirement.[68] As discussed in detail elsewhere,[69] if the child is unilaterally placed in a private facility by the parents, the public agency still retains significant responsibilities under IDEA for providing special education and related services. One of the continuing responsibilities is insuring the development of a service plan and insuring its implementation.[70] If a private school, however, agrees to undertake the responsibility of IDEA then a remedy may be pursued against them.[71]

As stated earlier, federal law requires development of an IEP and participation of a representative of the private placement at the development of the IEP before the child is actually placed in the private facility.[72] Educational placements, however, must be based on an existing IEP.[73] How do you reconcile the requirement not to decide a placement prior to development of the IEP with the requirement that the private school participate before placement in the private facility? At least one court has simply stated that when a child is being moved from a public facility to a private facility (but not from private to a public facility) there is simply an exception to the general rule that a placement decision cannot be made prior to development of the IEP.[74]

The fact is, however, no "exception" needs to exist. It is the usual case that at some point during discussions between the parents and school officials, it becomes apparent that a private facility is required. If both the parents and the school system agree that it is likely that a private facility will be needed, or that it is at least a real possibility, it would be permissible to invite a representative of the private facility to participate in the IEP meeting.

If the parents and school do not come to an agreement to include the private parties before final development of the IEP, the option available is to develop the IEP and then make a placement decision. If the decision is that the IEP can only be implemented in a private facility, then a second IEP meeting, involving the private facility can be called.

It should be kept in mind that the overriding concern with reconciling the two provisions is to protect against a premature, unilateral decision by either the parent or the

---

960 F.2d 1479 (9th Cir. 1992); North Shore School Dist., 20 Individuals with Disabilities Educ. L. Rep. 121 (OCR 1993).
    66. 34 C.F.R. §300.325(b)(1); *see also* 20 U.S.C. §1412(a)(10)(B).
    67. 34 C.F.R. §§300.327, and .325(b)(2); *see* St. Johnsbury Academy v. D.H., 240 F.3d 163 (2d Cir. 2001) *citing* McKenzie v. Smith, 771 F.2d 1527 (D.C. Cir. 1985); *see also* 20 U.S.C. §§1412(a)(10)(B) and, 1414(e).
    68. 34 C.F.R. §300.325(c); *see also* 20 U.S.C. §1412(a)(10)(B).
    69. See §8.10.
    70. 34 C.F.R. §§300.324, .325 and 27; *see also* 20 U.S.C. §§1412(a)(4), (a)(10)(B). See Chapter 8.
    71. P.N. v. Greco, 282 F. Supp. 2d 221 (D.N.J. 2003) (private school was liable under IDEA and Rehabilitation Act, for terminating student without giving required notice).
    72. 34 C.F.R. §300.325(a)(2); *see also* 20 U.S.C. §1412(a)(10)(B).
    73. 34 C.F.R. §300.116; *see also* 20 U.S.C. §1412(a)(5). *See* discussion §7.4.
    74. Spielberg v. Henrico County Pub. Schools, 853 F.2d 256 (4th Cir. 1988).

school personnel. To insure meaningful participation, the IEP must be developed with the parents and a placement decision must be made after that participation. To allow the placement decision to be made and then to develop an IEP to support that position would undermine the entire thrust of IDEA, allowing, for example, a school to decide to place the child in a program it already had available and then to develop an IEP to justify that placement. Instead the process must be to develop the IEP and then see if the school has the program or the capacity to develop the program to meet the IEP.

7.9 Children with Disabilities in Public Charter Schools

Children with disabilities in public charter schools, as well as their parents, have the same rights as other disabled children. Thus, students in public charter schools are entitled to the same requirements regarding the IEP team and procedures which include: the composition of the team, the development of the IEP, the content of the IEP, the placement decision, and the least restrictive environment requirements.[75]

The public charter school of an LEA has the same responsibility as the LEA for ensuring that the requirements of IDEA are met, unless this responsibility has been assigned to another entity.[76] If the public charter school is a school of the LEA, then the LEA is responsible for assuring compliance with the requirements under IDEA.[77] If the public charter school is not an LEA or part of an LEA, the SEA is responsible for ensuring that the requirements are met.[78]

7.10 Handling Disputes over the IEP

If the parents and LEA are unable to agree on the contents of the IEP, the LEA should draft the document as best it can, and then each party has the opportunity to resolve the dispute by way of the due process mechanism or one of the alternative dispute resolution procedures.[79] Because of the stay-put provision,[80] the preexisting IEP, if there is one, remains in force during the pendency of due process proceedings.[81] The party

---

75. 34 C.F.R. §300.209.

76. 34 C.F.R. §300.209(b).

77. 34 C.F.R. §300.209(c).

78. 34 C.F.R. §300.209(d).

79. Doe v. Maher, 793 F.2d 1470 (9th Cir. 1986), *aff'd on other grounds sub nom.* Honig v. Doe, 484 U.S. 305 (1988); Ciresoli v. M.S.A.D. No. 22, 901 F. Supp. 378 (D. Me. 1995) (some courts have looked at subsequent IEPs when they were not the IEP that the complaint was based on when the complaint remained the same though the IEP's change). See Chapter 11 for a discussion of the due process procedure and chapter 17 for alternatives to the due process procedure.

80. See §11.7.

81. 20 U.S.C. §1415(j); 34 C.F.R. §300.514(a). *See* Honig v. Doe, 484 U.S. 305, 323 (1988) (change in IEP required before long term suspension); Pardini v. Allegheny Intermediate Unit, 420 F.3d 181 (3d Cir. 2005) *cert. denied,* 126 S. Ct. 1646 (2006) (district must provide services contained in an Individualized Family Service Plan, pursuant to Part C, to a child while an initial IEP, pursuant to Part B, is created.); *but see,* AW v. Fairfax County Sch. Bd., 372 F.3d 674 (4th Cir. 2004) ("educational placement" refers "only to the setting in which the student is educated, rather than the

seeking to change the *status quo*, therefore, is the party likely to file for the due process hearing over the dispute. It is conceivable, however, that the other party might file for a due process hearing. For example, if the school system fails to abide by the stay-put provision and refuses to continue to educate the child under the preexisting IEP, the parent may have no choice but to seek a due process hearing.

Creation of a new IEP by the school system during the pendency of due process proceedings instituted by the parents does not moot the action. Because the problem is capable of repetition, yet avoiding review, the court may still hear the law suit even though the IEP has been superseded.[82]

7.11 IEP Checklist

_____An initial IEP must be developed.

_____The IEP must be reviewed at least annually.

_____The IEP must be in effect at the beginning of each school year.

_____Appropriate agency responsible for IEP development.

_____The IEP contains:

_____statement of the child's present level of academic achievement and functional performance;

_____how the child's disability affects his/her involvement and progress in the general curriculum;

_____statement of the measurable annual academic and functional goals;

_____goals are related to meeting the educational needs which involve the child in making progress in the general curriculum and meeting other educational needs arising from the disability;

_____a statement of the specific educational and related services, and supplementary aids to be provided, based on peer review research to extent practicable;

_____a statement of program modifications or supports for school personnel provided for the child to: advance toward the annual goals, to be involved and make progress in the general curriculum, and to participate in extra curricular and nonacademic activities;

_____the extent to which the child will not participate in the regular educational programs;

_____statement of individual modifications in the administration of state or district wide assessments of student achievement needed to participate; or

---

precise location," reasoning that "to the extent that a new setting replicates the educational program contemplated by the student's original assignment and is consistent with the principles of "mainstreaming" and affording access to a FAPE, the goal of protecting the student's "educational placement" served by the "stay-put" provision appears to be met"); Christopher W. v. Portsmouth School Committee, 877 F.2d 1089, 1097 (1st Cir. 1989) (change in IEP required before suspension).

82. DeVries v. Spillane, 853 F.2d 264 (4th Cir. 1988); *see also, M.S. v. Fairfax County School Bd.,* Slip Copy, 2007 WL 1378545 (E.D. Va. 2007); County Sch. Bd. v. R.T., 433 F. Supp. 2d 657 (E.D. Va. 2006).

_____ statement as to why assessment is not appropriate, how the child will be assessed and why the assessment selected is appropriate;

_____short term objectives/benchmarks for children who participate in alternate assessments;

_____the date the services will begin as well as the expected frequency, location, and duration of the services; and

_____statement of how child's progress toward the annual goals will be measured and how the parents will be routinely informed of the program;

_____beginning no later than age 16, identification of transition services including courses of study and interagency responsibilities,

_____appropriate measurable post secondary goals related to training, education, employment and or independent living skills based upon assessments.

_____statement that student is informed of transfer rights at age of majority one year before the student reaches age of majority.

_____Initial IEP must be developed within thirty calendar days following a determination that the child requires special education and related services.

_____Subsequent IEPs must be reviewed on at least an annual basis.

_____IEP must be "implemented as soon as possible following" its development.

_____Placement must be based on an existing IEP.

_____Usually a change in placement will have been preceded by an IEP meeting.

_____Participants in the meeting must include:

_____a representative of the public agency, other than the child's teacher, who is qualified to supervise or provide special education, knowledgeable about the general curriculum and the available resources;

_____the child's regular education teacher if child is or may be participating in regular education

_____special education teacher of the child or where appropriate special education provider to the child;

_____one or both of the parents of the child;

_____the child may be present where appropriate;

_____an individual who can interpret the instructional implications of evaluation data;

_____"[o]ther individuals at the discretion of the parent or agency [may be present]";

_____if discussing transition services, participants must include student and representative of agency responsible for paying for the transition services.

_____Parental Notice

_____purpose;

_____time;

_____location;

_____who will be in attendance.

_____Held at a mutually convenient time.

_____Alternate form of participation such as a teleconference if parents can not attend.

_____Where parents refuse, must have a detailed set of records establishing agency's attempts to schedule a mutually convenient time and place.

_____Steps to "insure that the parent understands the proceedings … including arranging for an interpreter for parents who are deaf or whose native language is other than English.

_____Copy of IEP provided to the parent.

_____Goals describe what a child is expected to accomplish by the end of the next year.

_____Goals related to the child's present level of academic and functional performance.

_____Present level of performance stated in objective terms.

_____Direct relationship between the annual goals and the child's present level of performance.

Private School IEPs

_____initial IEP must be developed with the participation of representatives from the private facility;

_____subsequent IEP meetings may, at the discretion of the public school, be initiated and conducted by the private school;

_____public agency must still insure that the parents participate in decisions concerning the IEP and agree to any changes in the program before any changes are implemented;

_____under all circumstances, the public agency placing the child in the private facility retains responsibility to insure compliance with the IEP requirement.[83]

---

83. See 34 C.F.R. § 300.130–144 for requirements for children with disabilities enrolled by their parent in private schools.

Chapter 8

Placement

8.1 Placement Criteria

Placement decisions are to be based on an existing Individual Education Program (IEP), and therefore must be made after the development of the IEP.[1] A decision to place a child prior to developing an IEP upon which to base that decision constitutes a violation of IDEA and can lead to a finding that the decision would not provide the child with a FAPE.[2]

In making the placement decision of a child with a disability, including a preschool child, the LEA must draw on a wide variety of information, including "aptitude and achievement tests, parent input, teacher recommendations, physical condition, social or cultural background, and adaptive behavior...,"[3] the sources of which must be considered and documented.[4] Removal of the child from an education with age-appropriate peers in regular classrooms, solely because of needed modifications in the general curriculum, is prohibited.[5]

Section 504 has equivalent criteria.[6]

As discussed in more detail elsewhere,[7] if the LEA fails to provide an appropriate placement, the parent may unilaterally place the child and seek reimbursement from the agency.[8] The United States Supreme Court has provided guidance on the extent of this

---

1. 34 C.F.R. §§ 300.116(b)(2); *see also* 20 U.S.C. § 1412(a)(5).

2. Nack v. Orange City School Dist., 454 F.3d 604 (6th Cir. 2006) (predetermination, as well as other procedural violations do not result in a *per se* violation of FAPE, but such violations will deny FAPE when they result in substantive harm to the child or parent); Deal v. Hamilton County Bd. of Educ., 392 F.3d 840 (6th Cir. 2004); Spielberg v. Henrico County Pub. Schools, 853 F.2d 256 (4th Cir. 1988); Evans v. Board of Educ. of the Rhinebeck Central School Dist., 930 F. Supp. 83 (S.D.N.Y. 1996) *but see Hjortness v. Neenah Joint School Dist.*, 498 F.3d 655, 660 (7th Cir. 2007) (predetermined public placement not a procedural violation that warrants reimbursement); C.W. v. Rocklin Unified School Dist. Slip Copy, 2006 WL 2830172 (E.D. Cal. 2006) (compiling reports prior to IEP meeting not considered predetermination of placement as long as a meaningful IEP meeting is subsequently conducted and various options are considered).

3. 34 C.F.R. § 300.306(c)(1)(i); *see* 20 U.S.C. §§ 1412(a)(6), 1414 (b)(4); Cory H. v. Board of Educ. of City of Chicago, 995 F. Supp. 900 (N.D. Ill. 1998) (settlement agreement that included provision that placement decisions are not to be based solely on disability category).

4. 34 C.F.R. § 300.306(c)(1)(ii); *see also* 20 U.S.C. §§ 1412(a)(6), 1414(b)(4).

5. 34 C.F.R. § 300.116(e).

6. 34 C.F.R. § 104.35(c).

7. See § 14.4.

8. *See, e.g.*, Diaz-Fonseca v. Puerto Rico, 451 F.3d 13 (1st Cir. 2006) (reimbursement is available for private tuition costs and related services); M.M. v. School Bd., 437 F.3d 1085 (11th Cir. 2006) (reimbursement is proper even when a child has never been enrolled in a public school if the LEA

obligation to reimburse. In *Florence County School District v. Carter*,[9] the Court held that where the state fails to provide an appropriate program the parents were eligible for reimbursement even when the parents had unilaterally placed the disabled child in a nonapproved school. The parents were entitled to reimbursement if the federal district court concluded the public agency violated IDEA and the private school placement was proper under the Act. The Court also indicated that total reimbursement would not be appropriate if the cost of the private education is unreasonable.

8.2 Location/Least Restrictive Environment/ Mainstreaming

IDEA contains several requirements governing the location of the educational placement. The placement must be as close to home as possible.[10] Also, unless the IEP requires otherwise, the child should be placed in the school where he or she would attend were there no disability.[11]

There is, however, no absolute right to have the child placed in the school closest to home. If the neighborhood school will not provide a FAPE, the agency may place the child at a more distant location. As stated by the court in *McLaughlin v. Holt Pub. School Bd.*,

> A child should be educated in the neighborhood school, ... except when the goals of the child's IEP plan require a special education placement not available at that school, and in a situation when placement elsewhere is required, the geographic proximity of schools that offer that placement to the child's home should be considered.[12]

---

has failed to offer a sufficient IEP); Mackey v. Bd. of Educ., 386 F.3d 158 (2d Cir. 2004) (tuition reimbursement claims may be based on multiple theories, such as pendency, and inadequacy of IEP); A.B. v. Lawson, 354 F.3d 315 (4th Cir. 2004) (parents are not entitled to tuition reimbursement where LEA provided FAPE); Independent School Dist. No. 283 v. S.D., 88 F.3d 556, 561 (8th Cir. 1996) (parents entitled to tuition reimbursement only if public school placement violated IDEA and placement at private school was proper under the Act); Bernardsville Bd. of Educ. v. J.H., 42 F.3d 149 (3d Cir. 1994) (parents entitled to reimbursement for private school tuition because the school district failed to provide the student with an appropriate education and cost of tuition was reasonable); J.P. v. County School Bd. of Hanover County, 447 F. Supp. 2d 553 (E.D. Va. 2006) (reimbursement ordered); Cochran v. District of Columbia, 660 F. Supp. 314 (D.D.C. 1987) (unilateral placement by parents was justified by LEA's failure to recommend a placement and the fact that private school was existing placement).

9. 510 U.S. 7 (1993); *see also* OSEP Memorandum 94-14 20 Individuals with Disabilities Educ. L. Rep. (LRP)1180 (1994) (in determining reimbursement, court might consider the cost of the private school selected by the parents in relation to the appropriate school on the approved list if the cost of the private education is unreasonable).

10. 34 C.F.R. § 300.116(b)(3); *see* 20 U.S.C. § 1412(a)(5); Flour Bluff Independent School Dist. v. Katherine M., 91 F.3d 689, 695 (5th Cir. 1996) (school which was 17 miles from the student's home satisfied the least restrictive environment requirement, despite the fact that there was a public school only 9 miles from home); Murray v. Montrose County School District RE-1J, 51 F.2d 921, 929 (10th Cir. 1995) (a disabled child should be educated in the school he would attend if not disabled, unless the child's IEP requires placement elsewhere), *see generally* White v. Ascension Parish School Bd., 343 F.3d 373 (5th Cir. 2003) *citing* Sherri A.D. v. Kirby, 975 F.2d 293 (5th Cir. 1992).

The same LRE requirement exists under Section 504. 34 C.F.R. § 104.34(a).

11. 34 C.F.R. § 300.116(c); 20 U.S.C. § 1412(a)(5).

12. 320 F.3d 663 (6th Cir. 2003); *see also* White v. Ascension Parish School Bd., 343 F.3d 373 (5th Cir. 2003) (student with cochlear implant and hearing impairment who needed a "cued speech

Further, courts have held that cost can be a factor in deciding to place a child in an otherwise appropriate placement further away from home. For example, in *Barnett v. Fairfax County School Board*,[13] the court held that "[t]he school system is not required to duplicate the Cued Speech program for [one student] merely because there exists a high school which is slightly closer to his house or one he would rather attend."[14]

Perhaps most important, IDEA requires that, "to the maximum extent appropriate," whether the child is in a public or private facility, the placement must educate the child with children who do not have a disability.[15] This requirement applies to nonacademic and extracurricular activities, for example, lunch and recess, as well as academic activities.[16] There has been some confusion over this placement requirement, perhaps caused by two related, though different, shorthand characterizations. Quite often, among both courts and commentators, this requirement is referred to indiscriminately as either a least restrictive environment (LRE) requirement or a mainstreaming requirement or incorrectly referred to as inclusion.

IDEA's requirement is an LRE requirement. The requirement is for the least restrictive environment in which educational progress can be made.[17] The child is to be educated in an environment that, given the child's individual educational needs, provides the fewest restrictions not encountered by the non-disabled student. One aspect of the LRE requirement, is that this placement be with non-disabled children in regular classrooms, that is, mainstreamed. Multiple circuits have adopted the view that, "the IDEA creates a preference for mainstream education, and a disabled student should be sepa-

---

transliterator" was not denied FAPE when services were provided at a centralized school rather than a neighborhood school);(the court also noted that no federal appellate circuit has recognized the right of a child to be educated at a neighborhood school under IDEA); Poolaw v. Bishop, 67 F.3d 830, 835 (9th Cir. 1995) (a school that allowed the necessary total immersion in American Sign Language was proper placement despite the fact that it was located 280 miles from his home); DeVries v. Fairfax County School Bd., 882 F.2d 876 (4th Cir. 1989); Johnston v. Ann Arbor Pub. Schools, 569 F. Supp. 1502 (E.D. Mich. 1983).

13. 927 F.2d 146 (4th Cir. 1991); *see also* A.W. v. Northwest R-1 School Dist., 813 F.2d 158, 163 (8th Cir. 1987) (child could receive only minimal benefit from local placement; in addition, cost of hiring staff was high).

14. Barnett, 927 F.2d at 151, 153; *see also*, White v. Ascension Parish School Bd., 343 F.3d 373 (5th Cir. 2003); McLaughlin v. Holt Pub. School Bd., 320 F.3d 663 (6th Cir. 2003); Kevin G. v. Cranston, 130 F.3d 481 (1st Cir. 1997) (not required to place medically fragile child in neighborhood school); Hudson v. Bloomfield Hills 108 F.3d 112 (6th Cir. 1997) (no right to be placed in neighborhood school); Schuldt v. Mankato Indep. School Dist. No. 77, 937 F.2d 1357 (8th Cir. 1991) (no absolute right to place in school nearest home); A.W. v. Northwest R-1 School Dist., 813 F.2d 158, 163 (8th Cir. 1987) (distance one factor); Pinkerton v. Moye, 509 F. Supp. 107 (W.D. Va. 1981) (6 miles away was acceptable because of small disabled student population).

15. 34 C.F.R. §300.114(a)(2)(i); *see* 20 U.S.C. §1412(a)(5); Letter to Yudien, 39 Individuals with Disabilities Educ. L. Rep. (LRP) 270 (OSEP 2003). The same requirement exists under Section 504. 34 C.F.R. §104.34(a). The requirements for LRE do not apply to students with disabilities enrolled in adult prisons. 34 C.F.R. §300.324(d)(2); *but see*, Handberry v. Thompson, 446 F.3d 335 (2d Cir. 2006) (New York State law requires eligible incarcerated children to receive special education services).

16. 34 C.F.R. §300.117; *see* 20 U.S.C. §1412(a)(5)(B). *See, e.g.,* L. E. v. Ramsey Bd. of Educ., 435 F.3d 384, 391 (3d Cir. 2006); Oberti v. Board of Educ. of the Borough of Clementon School Dist., 995 F.2d 1204, 1215–18 (3d Cir. 1993); Liscio v. Woodland Hills School Dist., 734 F. Supp. 689 (W.D. Pa. 1989), *aff'd*, 902 F.2d 1561 (3d Cir. 1990).

The same requirement exists under Section 504. 34 C.F.R. §104.34(a).

17. Board of Educ. v. Diamond, 808 F.2d 987 (3d Cir. 1986); *see also*, Cerra v. Pawling Cent. School Dist., 427 F.3d 186 (2d Cir. 2005); S.H. v. State-Operated School Dist., 336 F.3d 260 (3d Cir. 2003).

rated from her peers only if the services that make segregated placement superior cannot "be feasibly provided in a non-segregated setting."[18]

Mainstreaming was once thought to be a presumptive requirement under the IDEA, with the burden of establishing that a mainstream placement would not provide a FAPE falling on the local educational agency. [19] The Supreme Court's decision in *Schaffer v. Weast*,[20] however, holds that the burden of proof, agreed to in this case as the burden of persuasion, in an administrative hearing is placed on the party seeking relief While the facts of *Schaffer* challenged only the FAPE provisions of IDEA,[21] and the Supreme Court claimed to limit their holding to resolve the question presented,[22] the holding seems more likely to affect challenges to the IEP generally. As the Third Circuit Court of Appeals stated in *L.E. v. Ramsey Board of Education*,

> It would be unreasonable for us to limit that holding to a single aspect of an IEP, where the question framed by the Court [in *Schaffer*], and the answer it provided, do not so constrict the reach of its decision.[23]

The LRE requirement mandates that children be educated outside the regular classroom "only when the nature or severity of the disability is such that education in regular classes with the use of supplementary aids and services cannot be achieved satisfactorily."[24] In selecting the LRE, there is an affirmative obligation that consideration be given to any potential harmful effect on the child or on the quality of services he or she needs.[25] It is clear, therefore, that placement in the least restrictive environment is not an absolute right.

Merely because the placement is private, or even residential, does not mean the placement fails to meet the LRE requirement. The requirement must be viewed in light of the individual needs of the child.[26] The individual nature of these decisions cannot be

---

18. Pachl v. Seagren, 453 F.3d 1064 (8th Cir. 2006); *see also*, Roncker v. Walter, 700 F.2d 1058, 1063 (6th Cir. 1983).

19. Thornock v. Boise Indep. School Dist., 556 Educ. Handicapped L. Rep. (CRR) 477, 482–483 (Dist. Ct. Idaho 1985), *aff'd*, 115 Idaho 466, 767 P.2d 1241 (1988).

20. 546 U.S. 49 (2005).

21. 20 U.S.C. § 1400(d)(1)(A).

22. *Schaffer*, 546 U.S. at 56 (which party bears the burden of persuasion when assessing the appropriateness of the IEP?).

23. 435 F.3d 384 (3d Cir. 2006); *see also*, Van Duyn v. Baker School Dist. 5J, ___ F.3d ___, 5, 2007 WL 2493495 (9th Cir. 2007) (neither *Schaffer* nor IDEA supports imposing a different burden in IEP implementation cases than in formulation cases).

24. 34 C.F.R. § 300.114(a)(2)(ii); *see* 20 U.S.C. § 1412(a)(5)(A); 20 U.S.C. § 1414(d)(1)(A)(i)(IV); L.E. v. Ramsey Bd. of Educ., 435 F.3d 384 (3d Cir. 2006); Pachl v. Seagren, 453 F.3d 1064 (8th Cir. 2006); Casey K. v. St. Anne Cmty. High School Dist. No. 302, 400 F.3d 508 (7th Cir. 2005); L.B. v. Nebo School Dist., 379 F.3d 966 (10th Cir. 2004); Ms. S. v. Vashon Island School Dist., 337 F.3d 1115 (9th Cir. 2003); Independent School Dist. No. 283 v. S.D., 88 F3d 556 (8th Cir. 1996); Lachman v. Illinois State Bd. of Educ., 852 F.2d 290 (7th Cir. 1988), *cert. denied*, 488 U.S. 925 (1988); see also A.W. v. Northwest R-1 School Dist., 813 F.2d 158, 163 (8th Cir. 1987); Mark A. v. Grant Wood Area Educ. Agency, 795 F.2d 52, 54 (8th Cir. 1986); Doe v. Maher, 793 F.2d 1470, 1483 (9th Cir. 1986), *aff'd sub nom*. Honig v. Doe, 484 U.S. 305 (1988); Taylor v. Board of Educ., 649 F. Supp. 1253, 1258 (N.D.N.Y. 1986); Johnston v. Ann Arbor Pub. Schools, 569 F. Supp. 1502, 1508 (E.D. Mich. 1983).

25. 34 C.F.R. 300.116(d); *see* 20 U.S.C. § 1412(a)(5)(B).

26. *See. e.g.*, Beth B. v. Van Clay, 282 F.3d 493 (7th Cir. 2002) (English as a Second Language classroom is LRE); Board of Educ. of LaGrange v. Illinois Bd. of Educ., 184 F.3d 912 (7th Cir. 1999) (imposing LRE requirement would undercut parents right to private placement when SEA fails to provide FAPE); M.C. v. Central Regional School Dist., 81 F.3d 389 (3d Cir. 1996) (full-time residential placement satisfies LRE); Mark A. v. Grant Wood Area Educ. Agency, 795 F.2d 52 (8th Cir. 1986) (mainstreaming requirement does not always require placement in regular classroom); Geis v.

overemphasized. Indeed, children with very similar situations quite often receive very different determinations.[27] Also, as with the goal of placing the child close to home, cost has been considered as a factor to balance against mainstreaming.[28]

Courts, however, do approach the decision as to when segregation is appropriate from different perspectives. As stated by the Sixth Circuit in *Roncker v. Walter*,[29]

> The Act does not require mainstreaming in every case but its requirement that mainstreaming be provided to the *maximum* extent appropriate indicates a strong congressional preference. The proper inquiry is whether a proposed placement is appropriate under the Act.... In a case where the segregated facility is considered superior, the court should determine whether the services which make the placement superior could be feasibly provided in a non-segregated setting. If they can, the placement in the segregated school would be inappropriate under the Act.[30]

The Fifth Circuit specifically rejected this test, and in *Daniel R.R. v. Texas Board of Education*,[31] articulated the test as:

> First, we ask whether education in the regular classroom, with the use of supplemental aids and services can be achieved satisfactorily for a given child.... If it cannot and the school intends to provide special education or to remove the child from regular education, we ask, second, whether the school has mainstreamed the child to the maximum extent appropriate.[32]

The Fifth Circuit Court then went on to say that various factors are involved in the decision. These factors include whether the LEA has made attempts to accommodate the child with supplementary aids and services and whether the child will receive educational benefit from regular education. Other factors include, but are not limited to, the child's overall experience in the mainstreamed environment, and what impact the

---

Board of Educ., 774 F.2d 575 (3d Cir. 1985); Wilson v. Marana Unified School Dist., 735 F.2d 1178 (9th Cir. 1984); Taylor v. Board of Educ., 649 F. Supp. 1253 (N.D.N.Y. 1986).

27. *Compare* Bonadonna v. Cooperman, 619 F. Supp. 401 (D.N.J. 1985) (hearing impaired student should be mainstreamed where she was capable of functioning at above-average intellectual level, adjusted to regular classroom, and was learning. LEA could transport to resource program for supplemental instruction) *with* Visco v. School Dist., 684 F. Supp. 1310 (W.D. Pa. 1988) (private school for hearing impaired was least restrictive because move to public school would interrupt acquiring needed language skills).

28. Ms. S. v. Vashon Island School Dist., 337 F.3d 1115 (9th Cir. 2003); L.B. v. Nebo School Dist., 379 F.3d 966 (10th Cir. 2004); A.W. v. Northwest R-1 School Dist., 813 F.2d 158 (8th Cir. 1987) *citing* Roncker v. Walter, 700 F.2d 1058, 1063 (6th Cir. 1983); *see also* Pinkerton v. Moye, 509 F. Supp. 107 (W.D. Va. 1981) (close to home must be balanced against financial capacity of public agency).

29. 700 F.2d 1058 (6th Cir. 1983) (court ordered the child placed in a modified mainstream class since the exceptions of marginal benefits in mainstream class being outweighed by benefits gained from services which could not feasibly be provided in the mainstream setting and the fact that the child was not a disruptive force in a nonsegregated setting did not apply).

30. *Id.* at 1063; The Fourth and the Eighth Circuits have also adopted the test set forth in *Roncker*. Devries v. Fairfax County School Bd., 882 F.2d 876 (4th Cir. 1989); Pachl v. Seagren, 453 F.3d 1064 (8th Cir. 2006), citing to A.W. v. Northwest R-1 School Dist., 813 F.2d 158 (8th Cir. 1987). *See also* Greer v. Rome City School Dist., 950 F.2d 688 (11th Cir. 1991), *withdrawn on other grounds*, 956 F.2d 1025 (1992); Briggs v. Connecticut State Bd. of Educ., 882 F.2d 688 (2d Cir. 1989); McWhirt v. Williamson County Schools, 28 F.3d 1213 (6th Cir. 1983).

31. 874 F.2d 1036, 1049 (5th Cir. 1989).

32. *Id.* at 1048 (5th Cir. 1989); *see also* Doe v. Board of Educ. of Tullahoma City Schools, 9 F.3d 455, 460 (6th Cir. 1993) (even though there is a preference for mainstreaming, some children simply must be educated in segregated facilities).

child's presence will have on the other children in the regular classroom.[33] The *Daniel R.R.* test has also been adopted by the Third and Tenth Circuits.[34]

The Eighth Circuit Court of Appeals in *Pachl v. Seagren*[35], has stated that

> removing a child from the mainstream setting is permissible when "the handi-capped child would not benefit from mainstreaming," when "any marginal benefits received from mainstreaming are far outweighed by the benefits gained from services which could not feasibly be provided in the non-segre-gated setting," and when "the handicapped child is a disruptive force in the non-segregated setting." [36]

In *Sacramento City Unified School District v. Rachel H.*,[37] the Ninth Circuit devised their own four-factor balancing test similar to the *Daniel R.R.* test. The Ninth Circuit's balancing factors include: (1) the educational benefits of full-time placement in a regu-lar class; (2) nonacademic benefits of such a placement; (3) the effect the child had on the teacher and children in the regular class; and (4) the costs of mainstreaming. The additional factor added to the Daniel R.R. test was consideration of the cost of main-streaming the student.

Similarly, the Eleventh Circuit has chosen to adopt a test that considers the financial obligation that would be necessary to maintain the child in a regular classroom.[38] It ap-pears that the Seventh Circuit has not yet adopted a test, but would likely agree that any test should consider cost.[39]

Consideration of the impact of the disabled student's presence on the regular educa-tion students has been an emotional topic. Two basic concerns arise. The student may be either disruptive, taking so much attention from the instructor that the instructor will ignore the needs of other children, or the student may pose a risk of physical harm to other children. Therefore, regular placement would not be appropriate to his or her needs.[40]

Dealing with a child that requires an inordinate amount of the teacher's time requires an inquiry into whether sufficient supplemental aids and services have been provided. Merely because the child dominates the teacher's time is, by itself, insufficient to remove the child from the classroom. The provision of a teaching assistant or aide, for example, may solve the problem.[41] If, however, the time commitment still interferes with the edu-cational benefit others are receiving, removal from the classroom may be appropriate.[42]

---

33. Daniel R.R., 874 F.2d at 1048–50; *see also* 34 C.F.R. § 104.34(a).

34. Ramsey Bd. of Educ., 435 F.3d 384 (3d Cir. 2006); L.B. v. Nebo School Dist., 379 F.3d 966 (10th Cir. 2004).

35. 453 F.3d 1064 (8th Cir. 2006).

36. *Id.* at 1068 *quoting* Roncker v. Walter, 700 F.2d 1058, 1063 (6th Cir. 1983).

37. 14 F.3d 1298 (9th Cir. 1994); *see also*, Ms. S. v. Vashon Island School Dist., 337 F.3d 1115 (9th Cir. 2003).

38. Greer v. Rome City School Dist., 950 F.2d 688 (11th Cir. 1991).

39. Beth B. v. Van Clay, 282 F.3d 493, 499 (7th Cir. 2002) ("unnecessary at this point in time to adopt a formal test"); School Dist. of Wis. Dells v. Z.S., 295 F.3d 671 (7th Cir. 2002) (efficacy is rel-evant, but so is cost).

40. 20 U.S.C. § 1412(a)(5)(A); *see* L.B. v. Nebo School Dist., 379 F.3d 966 (10th Cir. 2004) (non-academic factors such as the improvement of social skills, and mild disruptive behaviors are prop-erly considered under the *Daniel R.R.* test); Hartman v. Loudon County, 118 F.3d 997, *cert. denied*, 522 U.S. 1046 (4th Cir. 1997) (disruptive effects of student's behavior proper LRE placement con-sideration).

41. Daniel R.R. v. Texas Bd. of Educ., 874 F.2d 1036, 1049 (5th Cir. 1989).

42. *Id.* at 1049–50.

Risk of physical harm to other children for medical reasons has arisen mostly in the area of AIDS and hepatitis. The general rule, whether dealing with AIDS[43] or hepatitis B,[44] appears to be that absent a finding that a particular child poses a specific threat, the child may not be segregated; the theoretical possibility of harm to others is insufficient.

The LRE requirement must also be considered if the parents are placed in the position of having to make a unilateral placement because of the agency's failure to provide a FAPE. The United States Supreme Court has held that parents who unilaterally place their child in a private placement are entitled to reimbursement only if "a federal court concludes both that the public placement violated IDEA and that the private school placement was proper under the Act." [45] For example, where the parents unilaterally placed a child in a private facility, a New Jersey court held the placement was appropriate and reimbursement was ordered for the academic program, but not for the residential costs because the placement was not in the least restrictive environment.[46] Additionally, the test for the parents' private placement is that it is appropriate, not that it is perfect.[47]

8.3 Annual Review of Placement Required

After the initial placement decision, the decision must be reviewed at least annually.[48]

8.4 Change in Placement

A placement decision must be based on an existing IEP, therefore, any change in placement must be supported by the existing IEP. If the IEP does not support a change in placement, an IEP meeting must be conducted before initiating any change.[49]

Having determined that a change in placement is appropriate, before an LEA can make the change, written notice must be given to the parents of the agency's intent to

---

43. Martinez v. School Bd., 861 F.2d 1502 (11th Cir. 1988); Thomas v. Atascadero Unified School Dist., 662 F. Supp. 376 (C.D. Cal. 1987); District 27 Community School Bd. of Educ. v. Board of Educ., 130 Misc. 2d 398, 502 N.Y.S.2d 325 (N.Y. Sup. Ct. 1986).

44. Community High School Dist. 155 v. Denz, 124 Ill. App. 3d 129, 463 N.E.2d 998 (1984).

45. Florence County School Dist. Four v. Carter, 510 U.S. 7 (1993).

46. Lascari v. Board of Educ., 116 N.J. 30, 560 A.2d 1180 (1989).

47. Frank G. v. Bd. of Educ. of Hyde Park, 459 F.3d 356 (2d Cir. 2006); M.S. v. Yonkers Bd. of Educ., 231 F.3d 96 (2d Cir. 2000); Warren G. v. Cumberland County School Dist., 190 F.3d 80 (3d Cir. 1999) (test for the parents' private placement is that it is appropriate, not that it is "perfect"); *see also* W.S. v. Rye City School Dist., 454 F. Supp. 2d 134 (S.D.N.Y. 2006).

For a discussion of remedies available if the parents unilaterally place their child in a private school, see § 14.4.

48. 34 C.F.R. § 300.116(b)(1); *see* 20 U.S.C. § 1412(a)(5).

49. *See* 34 C.F.R. § 300.116(b)(2); *see also* 20 U.S.C. § 1412(a)(5).

change placement.[50] The extent of the notice required is covered by the general regulatory provision on notice[51] and contains the requirement that the notice describe

(b) Content of notice. The notice required under paragraph (a) of this section must include —

(1) A description of the action proposed or refused by the agency;

(2) An explanation of why the agency proposes or refuses to take the action;

(3) A description of each evaluation procedure, assessment, record, or report the agency used as a basis for the proposed or refused action;

(4) A statement that the parents of a child with a disability have protection under the procedural safeguards of this part and, if this notice is not an initial referral for evaluation, the means by which a copy of a description of the procedural safeguards can be obtained;

(5) Sources for parents to contact to obtain assistance in understanding the provisions of this part;

(6) A description of other options that the IEP Team considered and the reasons why those options were rejected; and

(7) A description of other factors that are relevant to the agency's proposal or refusal.[52]

"Boilerplate language" on forms containing only general descriptions of the proposed placement without discussion of options considered for the individual child is inadequate notice.[53]

Although not required under IDEA, individual states may require parental consent prior to a change in placement.[54]

What constitutes a change in placement has been subject to some debate. Where the change does not significantly alter the educational experience of the child, it has been held not to constitute a change in placement.[55]

---

50. 34 C.F.R. § 300.503(a)(1); *see* 20 U.S.C. §§ 1415(b)(3), (4), 1415(c)(1), 1414(b)(1); *see generally,* Pardini v. Allegheny Intermediate Unit, 420 F.3d 181 (3d Cir. 2005); W.B. v. Matula, 67 F.3d 484 (3d Cir. 1995); *but see* Berger v. Medina City School Dist., 348 F.3d 513 (6th Cir. 2003) (technical violation of "notice requirement" is not enough, violation must cause substantive harm to the parent's ability to participate meaningfully); Brookline School Committee v. Golden, 628 F. Supp. 113 (D. Mass. 1986) (written notice not required where parents had actual notice of intent to change placement).

51. See Chapter 9.

52. 34 C.F.R. § 300.503(b)(1)–(7); *see also* 20 U.S.C. §§ 1415(b)(3), (4), 1415(c)(1) and 1414(b)(1).

53. McKenzie v. Smith, 771 F.2d 1527 (D.C. Cir. 1985).

54. See § 9.5.

55. AW v. Fairfax County Sch. Bd., 372 F.3d 674 (4th Cir. 2004) (change in placement occurs when a school places the student in a setting that is distinguishable from the educational environment to which the student was previously assigned. However, this definition does not contemplate that an educational placement must be administered at a specific location, in a specific classroom. Nor, does a change in placement occur because of minor disciplinary measures); Brookline School Committee v. Golden, 628 F. Supp. 113 (D. Mass. 1986) (change in day care from 2 to 3 days, with substitution of day care program on two other days not a change in placement); *see* Letter to Fisher, 21 Individuals with Disabilities Educ. L. Rep. (LRP) 992 (OSEP 1994) (change in placement involves substance of program not just physical location). The United States Supreme Court has held that suspension of a child for more than 10 days constitutes a change in placement. See Chapter 10.

Section 504 requires an evaluation prior to any significant change in placement.[56]

8.5 Placement Decision-Makers

The placement decision "is made by a group of persons, including the parents, and other persons knowledgeable about the child, the meaning of the evaluation data, and the placement options...."[57] Exclusion of health care personnel from a placement decision does not violate either IDEA or § 504, since the regulations only require a qualified group of people.[58]

8.6 Extended School Day and Year

Public agencies must ensure that extended school year (ESY) services are available if necessary to provide a FAPE.[59] What must be shown to justify an extended school year has been subject to some debate. In *Rettig v. Kent City School District*,[60] the court held that the parents must show that the child would suffer "significant regression of skills or knowledge."[61] In *M.M. v. School District of Greenville County*, the Fourth Circuit Court of Appeals stated,[62] "ESY services are only necessary to a FAPE when the benefits a disabled child gains during a regular school year will be significantly jeopardized if he is not provided with an educational program during the summer months ... the mere fact of likely regression is not a sufficient basis, because all students, disabled or not, may regress to some extent during lengthy breaks from school". Language such as this has been interpreted as an empirical test requiring a showing of prior regression.[63]

This "empirical approach," however, has been criticized and rejected as requiring a "Hobson's Choice" in which the parents must choose to either allow their child to regress to establish empirical data or provide the extended school year themselves

---

56. 34 C.F.R. § 104.35(a).

57. 34 C.F.R. § 300.316(a)(1); *see also* 20 U.S.C. § 1412(a)(5); *see generally* S-1 v. Turlington, 635 F.2d 342 (5th Cir. 1981). Section 504 requires the equivalent. 34 C.F.R § 104.35(a).

58. Hessler v. State Bd. of Educ. of Maryland, 553 Educ. Handicapped L. Rep. (CRR) 262 (D. Md. 1981), *aff'd*, 700 F.2d 134 (4th Cir. 1983).

59. 34 C.F.R. § 300.106; 20 U.S.C. § 1412 (a)(1); see also, Alamo Heights Indep. School Dist. v. State Bd. of Educ., 790 F.2d 1153 (5th Cir. 1986); Battle v. Pennsylvania, 629 F.2d 269 (3d Cir. 1980); Georgia Assn. of Retarded Citizens v. McDaniel, 511 F. Supp. 1263 (N.D. Ga. 1981), *aff'd*, 716 F.2d 1565 (11th Cir. 1983).

60. 539 F. Supp. 768, 778 (N.D. Ohio 1981), *aff'd in part vacated in part on other grounds*, 720 F.2d 463 (6th Cir. 1983); *see also* Manchester School Dist. v. Charles M.F., 1994 WL 485754 (D.N.H. 1994) (regression during summer entitles student to ESY).

61. Rettig v. Kent City School Dist., 539 F. Supp. 768, 778–779 (N.D. Ohio, 1981).

62. 303 F.3d 523 (4th Cir. 2002); *see also* J.H. v. Henrico County Sch. Bd., 326 F.3d 560 (4th Cir. 2003); Letter to Given, 39 Individuals with Disabilities Educ. L. Rep. (LRP) 129 (OSEP 2003) (in light of the 4th Circuit's decision in M.M. v. School District of Greenville County, lack of progress alone does not justify ESY services).

63. Kenton County School Dist. v. Hunt, 384 F.3d 269 (6th Cir. 2004); *see also*, Cordrey v. Euckert, 917 F.2d 1460 (6th Cir. 1990).

and forgo any possibility of proving regression.[64] As a result, the empirical approach has been modified by most courts to provide "where there is no such empirical data available, need may be proven by expert opinion based upon a professional individual assessment."[65]

ESY means special education and related services provided to a child with a disability according to an IEP, beyond the normal school year and at no cost to the parents.[66] The agency may not limit the services to certain categories of disabled children nor unilaterally limit the type, duration or amount of services delivered to the child under ESY.[67]

8.7 Continuum of Placements Required

The LEA is required to "ensure that a continuum of alternative placements is available to meet the needs of children with disabilities for special education and related services."[68] The continuum of placements must include "instruction in regular classes, special classes, special schools, home instruction, and instruction in hospitals and institutions...."[69] In addition, the LEA must insure that "supplementary services (such as resource room or itinerant instruction) be provided in conjunction with regular class placement."[70]

The continuum must be sufficient to allow the implementation of an IEP for each eligible child with a disability.[71] Because the school may be unable to meet the child's IEP goals and objectives in a publicly operated facility, the continuum of placements must

64. Polk v. Central Susquehanna Intermed. Unit 16, 853 F.2d 171, 184 (3d Cir. 1988); Alamo Heights Indep. School Dist. v. State Bd. of Educ., 790 F.2d 1153, 1156–58 (5th Cir. 1986).

65. J.H. v. Henrico County School Bd., 395 F.3d 185 (4th Cir. 2005) (aka J.H. II) (when no empirical data, need for ESY may be proven by expert testimony based on professional individual assessment); Kenton County School Dist. v. Hunt, 384 F.3d 269 (6th Cir. 2004) citing with approval, Cordrey v. Euckert, 917 F.2d 1460, 1472 (6th Cir. 1990); see also Johnson v. Independent School Dist. No. 4, 921 F.2d 1022 (10th Cir. 1990) (predictive date is also allowed); Alamo Heights Indep. School Dist. v. State Bd. of Educ., 790 F.2d 1153, 1156–58 (5th Cir. 1986); Letter to Anonymous, 22 Individuals with Disabilities Educ. L. Rep. (LRP) 986 (OSERS 1995) (states have discretion to set policies and procedures as to standards including predictive data, but ESY must be decided on case-by-case basis).

66. 34 C.F.R. §300.106(b); Letter to Kleczka, 30 Individuals with Disabilities Educ. L. Rep. (LRP) 270 (OSEP 1998) (ESY is not automatic for students who do not meet their IEP goals).

67. 34 C.F.R. §300.106(a)(3).

68. 34 C.F.R. §300.115(a); see also 20 U.S.C. §1412(a)(5)(B); L. E. v. Ramsey Bd. of Educ., 435 F.3d 384 (3d Cir. 2006) (ALJ accurately outlined the appropriate standards by distinguishing between the free appropriate public education (FAPE) and least restrictive environment (LRE) analyses); Board of Educ. of Murphysboro Comm. Unit School Dist. v. Illinois State Bd. of Educ, 41 F.3d 1162 (7th Cir. 1994) (school district did not provide the student with a continuum of program options, therefore, the court did not have to decide whether the placement provided the least restrictive environment, but had to determine if the education provided at the placement was appropriate).

69. 34 C.F.R. §300.115(b)(1); see also 20 U.S.C. §1412(a)(5)(B); Letter to Estvan, 25 Individuals with Disabilities Educ. L. Rep. (LRP) 1211 (OSEP 1997) (regular education must be subject of inquiry in the IEP process).

70. 34 C.F.R. §300.115(b)(2); see also 20 U.S.C. §1412(a)(5)(B); Letter to Copenhaver, 25 Individuals with Disabilities Educ. L. Rep. (LRP) 1213 (OSEP 1997) (resource and itinerant instruction can occur in or out of regular education).

71. 34 C.F.R. §300.116(b); see also 20 U.S.C. §1412(a)(5)(B).

include the possibility of private placements.[72] Further, a school must have authority to contract with out-of-state facilities if necessary to find an appropriate facility.[73] There is no obligation, however, to consider whether a particular private school is an appropriate placement if the public agency has an appropriate program.[74]

State and local educational agencies retain significant responsibility for children placed in private school settings. In fact, for a child placed or referred to a private school by the educational agency, the public agency remains ultimately responsible for insuring that the child receives special education and related services in conformity with the student's IEP.[75] Even for children unilaterally placed in a private school, the school system retains responsibility for providing special education and related services.[76]

8.8 Residential School Placements

As with all placement decisions, the decision whether a child requires the structure and consistency of a residential program depends on the educational needs as defined by the IEP. Generally, a residential program is required when the structure and consistency of a 24 hour program is necessary in order for the child to learn. As stated by the Sixth Circuit Court of Appeals in *Tennessee Department of Mental Health and Mental Retardation v. Paul B.,*[77]

> To assess whether a residential placement is appropriate, a determination must be made whether full time residential placement is necessary for educational purposes as opposed to medical, social, or emotional problems that are separable from the learning process ... Under the Act, residential placement is at no cost to the parents of the child only if it is necessary for "educational purposes."[78]

A residential placement is also appropriate where the child has the inability to generalize learning across environments.[79]

---

72. 34 C.F.R. § 300.118; *see* 20 U.S.C. § 1412(a)(5)(B). The same requirement exists under § 504. 34 C.F.R. § 104.33(b)(3); W.S. v. Rye City School Dist., 454 F. Supp. 2d 134, 147 (S.D.N.Y. 2006) (if district cannot provide a FAPE in a public school setting, then and only then must it place the child in a private placement); Letter to Gilbert, 291 Individuals with Disabilities Educ. L. Rep. 900 (OSEP 1998) (LRE does not eliminate private school placements).

73. Missouri Dep't of Elem. & Secondary Educ. v. Springfield R-12, 358 F.3d 992 (8th Cir. 2004); Dubner v. Ambach, 74 A.D.2d 949, 426 N.Y.S.2d 164 (1980).

74. Hessler v. State Bd. of Educ., 700 F.2d 134 (4th Cir. 1983); W.S. v. Rye City School Dist., 54 F. Supp. 2d 134 (S.D.N.Y. 2006); Letter to Trachan, 20 Individuals with Disabilities Educ. L. Rep. (LRP) 403 (OSEP 1998) (continuum must be made available, inclusion not same as LRE).

75. 34 C.F.R. § 300.146(a)(1); *see* 20 U.S.C. § 1412(a)(10)(B).

76. 34 C.F.R. § 300.132; *see* 20 U.S.C. § 1412(a)(10)(A)(i). See § 8.10.

77. 88 F.3d 1466 (6th Cir. 1996); *see also* Kings Local Sch. Dist. v. Zelazny, 325 F.3d 724 (6th Cir. 2003); Diamond v. McKenzie, 770 F.2d 225 (D.C. Cir. 1985); Colin K. v. Schmidt, 715 F.2d 1 (1st Cir. 1983); Abrahamson v. Hershman, 701 F.2d 223 (1st Cir. 1983); Kruelle v. New Castle County School Dist., 642 F.2d 687 (3d Cir. 1981); Schreiber v. Ridgewood Bd. of Educ, 952 F. Supp. 205 (D.N.J. 1997). Section 504 has the same requirement. 34 C.F.R. § 104.33(c)(3).

78. *Id.* at 1471.

79. Board of Educ. v. Diamond, 808 F.2d 987, 992 (3d Cir. 1986).

As discussed elsewhere, if a child requires a residential program for medical rather than educational reasons, the educational agency is responsible only for the educational portion of the program.[80] Where, however, the social, emotional, medical and educational needs of the child are so interrelated that it is not possible to separate them, the agency is responsible for the entire cost of the program.[81]

8.9 Private Placement by LEA in General

As part of the continuum of educational placements required to be available,[82] the LEA must include private educational programs,[83] when it is unable to provide a free appropriate education within the public school system.[84]

Where the educational authority has placed a child in a private educational setting as a means of providing the child with the required FAPE, the public agency retains responsibility for insuring the child receives special education and related services in conformity with the child's IEP.[85] The agency must also involve a representative of the private school in the development of an IEP.[86]

The public agency is responsible for insuring, in fact, that the IEP meets all the criteria that would be required were the child placed in the public school.[87] For example, the LEA must insure parental participation in developing the IEP, including developing ap-

---

80. *See, e.g.,* Zelezny, 325 F.3d 724 (6th Cir. 2003); Indep. School Dist. No. 284 v. A.C., 258 F.3d 769 (8th Cir. 2001); Clovis Unified School Dist. v. California Office of Admin. Hearings, 903 F.2d 635 (9th Cir. 1990) (psychiatric hospitalization for medical, not educational reasons); Alice M. v. Board of Educ. of Bradley-Bourbonnais High, 237 F.3d 813 (7th Cir. 2001) (placement custodial not educational); Butler v. Evans 225 F.3d 887 (7th Cir. 2000). See § 5.2.2.

81. Mrs. B. v. Milford Bd. of Educ., 103 F.3d 1114 (2d Cir. 1997); County of San Diego v. California Special Education Hearing Office, 93 F.3d 1458, 1465 (9th Cir. 1996); McKenzie v. Smith, 771 F.2d 1527, 1534 (D.C. Cir. 1985); Kruelle v. New Castle County School Dist., 642 F.2d 687 (3d Cir. 1981); Hall v. Shawnee Mission School Dist., 856 F. Supp. 1521 (D. Kan. 1994); Sanger v. Montgomery County Bd. of Educ., 916 F. Supp. 518 (D. Md. 1996).

82. 34 C.F.R. § 300.115; *see also* 20 U.S.C. § 1412(a)(5).

83. 34 C.F.R. § 300.118 & §§ 300.145–147; *see also* 20 U.S.C. §§ 1412(a)(5) & (a)(10(B); School Comm. of Town of Burlington v. Dep't of Educ., 471 U.S. 359, 369 (1985) ("The Act [IDEA] contemplates that such education will be provided where possible in regular public schools, with the child participating as much as possible in the same activities as non-handicapped children, but the Act also provides for placement in private schools at public expense where this is not possible"); M.M. v. School Bd., 437 F.3d 1085 (11th Cir. 2006); Abrahamson v. Hershman, 701 F.2d 223, 227 (1st Cir. 1983); Gladys J. v. Pearland Indep. School Dist., 520 F. Supp. 869, 875 (S.D. Tex. 1981).

84. *See, e.g.,* M.M. v. School Bd., 437 F.3d 1085 (11th Cir. 2006); D.F. v. Ramapo Cent. School Dist., 430 F.3d 595 (2d Cir. 2005) (a school district must provide a program that allows an opportunity for more than "trivial" advancement); Abrahamson v. Hershman, 701 F.2d 223 (1st Cir. 1983); Hall v. Vance County Bd. of Educ., 774 F.2d 629, 635–636 (4th Cir. 1985) ("no single substantive standard can describe.... Clearly, [however], Congress did not intend that a school system could discharge its duty under the EAHCA by providing a program that produces some minimal academic achievement, no matter how trivial.").

85. 34 C.F.R. § 300.146(a)(1).; *see* 20 U.S.C. § 1412(a)(10)(B); Antkowiak v. Ambach, 838 F.2d 635 (2d Cir. 1988).

86. 34 C.F.R. § 300.147(c); *see also* 20 U.S.C. § 1412(a)(10)(B).

87. 34 C.F.R. § 300.146(a)(1); *see* 20 U.S.C. § 1412(a)(10)(B).

propriate IEP goals and if required benchmarks or objectives.[88] This is true even if the child is placed outside the district, or even outside the state.[89]

The agency placing the child must also insure that the private education be provided at no cost to the parents,[90] and that the child placed has all the rights of a child who is directly served by the public agency.[91] Consistent with these obligations to privately placed students, the SEA is required to monitor LEA compliance with these requirements through such things as written reports, on-site visits, and parent questionnaires.[92]

8.9.1 Requirements for Private Facilities Where LEA Places Child

Where the LEA places a child in a private educational setting, the private placement must meet the standards that apply to state and local educational agencies.[93] The SEA must provide the private placements with these applicable standards[94] and provide the private placements with an opportunity to participate in the development and revision of state standards that also apply to them.[95] LEA record requirements apply to private schools.[96]

Since the Supreme Court ruling in *Florence County School District v. Carter*[97] in 1993, the state cannot limit private school placement to those schools that are state approved. Further, Title VI prohibits placement of a child in school which is racially segregated.[98]

The ability to place a child in a sectarian school is discussed in § 8.11.1

---

88. 34 C.F.R. § 300.146 (referring to 34 C.F.R. §§ 300.320–300.325); *see also* 20 U.S.C. § 1412(a)(10)(B).

89. Letter to State Directors of Special Educ., 44 Individuals with Disabilities Educ. L. Rep. (LRP) 46 (OSEP 2005); Letter to Liberera, 43 Individuals with Disabilities Educ. L. Rep. (LRP) 64 (OSEP 2004) (when transferring a student outside the district, the sending district has ultimate responsibility for the student's educational program).

90. 34 C.F.R. § 300.146(a)(2); *see also* 20 U.S.C. § 1412(a)(10)(B).

91. 34 C.F.R. § 300.146(c).; *see also* 20 U.S.C. § 1412(a)(10)(B). The private placement must meet the standards that apply to state and local educational agencies. *Id.*

92. 34 C.F.R. § 300.147. The SEA must also monitor compliance and provide private placements with applicable standards, and provide the private placements with an opportunity to participate in the development and revision of state standards that apply to them. *Id.; see also* 20 U.S.C. § 1412(a)(10)(B).

93. 34 C.F.R. § 300.146(b); *see also* 20 U.S.C. § 1412(a)(10)(B).

94. 34 C.F.R. § 300.147(b); *see also* 20 U.S.C. § 1412(a)(10)(B).

95. 34 C.F.R § 300.147(c); *see also* 20 U.S.C. § 1412(a)(10)(B).

96. 20 U.S.C § 1232g.

97. 510 U.S. 7 (1993); *see also* Briere v. Fair Haven Grade School Dist., 948 F. Supp. 1242 (D. Vt. 1996). The Supreme Court's decision made a significant impact. Prior to *Florence County School District*, courts had held that the state could limit private school placement to those schools that are state-approved. *See, e.g.,* Tucker v. Bay Shore Union Free School Dist., 873 F.2d 563 (2d Cir. 1989); Antkowiak v. Ambach, 838 F.2d 635 (2d Cir. 1988); Schimmel v. Spillane, 819 F.2d 477 (4th Cir. 1987).

98. 34 C.F.R. § 100.3 (b)(2); Alexander v. Sandoval, 532 U.S. 275 (2001) (private right of action exists under Title VI only in cases involving intentional discrimination and cannot be extended to disparate impact discrimination); Davis Inquiry, 211 Educ. Handicapped L. Rep. (CRR) 09 (EHA 1978).

8.10 Unilateral Private Placement by Parents Where LEA Offers FAPE

Even if the public agency is able to provide a free appropriate education in the public schools, the parents may choose to place the child in a private program. Each local educational agency must locate, identify, and evaluate these private school children with disabilities.[99] A parentally-placed private school child with a disability, however, does not have the same right to receive some or all of the special education and related services that he or she would receive if enrolled in a pubic school.[100] The State, however, does receive funds for children unilaterally placed in private educational settings and the State is required to spend money on services for privately placed children. The regulations provide:

> To the extent consistent with the number and location of children with disabilities who are enrolled by their parents in private, including religious, elementary schools and secondary schools located in the school district served by the LEA, provision is made for the participation of those children in the program assisted or carried out under Part B of the Act by providing them with special education and related services.... [101]

Most obviously, the LEA need not pay for the general education of the child at the private placement,[102] but there are other limitations. The regulations[103] have been inter-

---

99. 34 C.F.R. § 300.131(a); *see also* 20 U.S.C. §§ 1412(a)(10)(A)(ii); D.L. v. Dist. of Columbia, 237 F.R.D. 319 (D.D.C. 2006) (the Child Find duty applies regardless of the child's disability, and the injury suffered as a result of deprivation of the services guaranteed under the IDEA is the same for all); Letter to Mittnacht, 46 Individuals with Disabilities Educ. L. Rep. (LRP) 136 (OSERS 2006) (LEAs must complete child-find obligations to determine the number of parentally placed private school students within the LEA); Letter to McKethan, 29 Individuals with Disabilities Educ. L. Rep. (LRP) (OSEP 1998) (child find applies to all students).

100. 34 C.F.R. § 300.137(a); *see also* 20 U.S.C. § 1412(a)(10)(A).

101. 34 C.F.R. § 300.132(a); *see* KDM v. Reedsport School District, 196 F.3d 1046 (9th Cir. 1999) (IDEA requires school district to provide services to student; does not require district to provide services onsite at private school); Bristol Warren Regional School Committee v. Rhode Island Dept. of Educ. 253 F. Supp. 2d 236 (D.R.I. 2003) (not required, under the IDEA, to provide on-site services to student who was unilaterally enrolled in parochial school, even though it provided such services to students enrolled in other parochial schools within district).

102. 34 C.F.R. § 300.148(a); *see also* 20 U.S.C. § 1412(a)(10)(C).

103. The requirement as to the level of services required is stated in terms of the funding that the LEA must spend. The regulations provide:
Formula. To meet the requirement of § 300.132(a), each LEA must spend the following on providing special education and related services to parentally placed private school children with disabilities—
(1) For children aged 3 through 21, an amount that is the same proportion of the LEA's total subgrant under section 611(f) of the Act as the number of private school children with disabilities aged 3 through 21 who are enrolled by their parents in private, including religious, elementary schools and secondary schools located in the school district served by the LEA, is to the total number of children with disabilities in its jurisdiction aged 3 through 21; and
(2) For children aged 3 through 5, an amount that is the same proportion of the LEA's total subgrant under section 619(g) of the Act as the number of parentally-placed private school children with disabilities aged three to five who are enrolled by their parents in a private, including religious, elementary school located in the school district served by the LEA, is the total number of children with disabilities in its jurisdiction aged three to five.
34 C.F.R. § 300.133(a),(b); *see also* 20 U.S.C.§ 1412(A)(10)(A).

preted to provide wide discretion to the LEA as to whether to provide services to unilaterally placed private school students. Courts have held that the State's obligation is to the broader population of disabled students and it is only required to spend a proportionate share of its Part B funds on special education and related services for children in private placements.[104] This analysis led the United States Eighth Circuit Court of Appeals in *Foley v. Special School District of St. Louis*,[105] for example, to hold that a child voluntarily placed by parents in a private school had no individual right to special education services, and, even if she did, services would not have to be provided on private school grounds.

The Seventh Circuit, in *K.R. v. Anderson*,[106] held that the IDEA did not require the district to provide a unilaterally placed student with an instructional aide.[107] The court stated:

> the Amendments unambiguously show that participating states and localities have no obligation to spend their money to ensure that disabled children who have chosen to enroll in private schools will receive publicly funded special-education services generally "comparable" to those provided to public-school children.[108]

Other courts appear to require a bit more. The Tenth Circuit in *Fowler v. Unified School District No. 259*,[109] held that a child who was hearing impaired and placed voluntarily by his parents in a nonsectarian private school was entitled under Kansas law to provision of the interpreter on site at the private school, but at no greater cost of providing hearing-impaired students with interpretative services at public schools. The Second Circuit in *Russman v. Board of Education of the Enlarged City School District of the City of Watervliet*, [110] held that the obligation of the state is to pay a proportionate share of the costs of special education in the private placement. As stated by the court, "states are required to provide children voluntarily enrolled in private schools only those services that can be purchased with a proportionate amount of the federal funds received under [IDEA]."[111]

The services provided to a child placed by the parents in a private setting are contained in a "services plan."[112] The services plan must contain the same components as an IEP. It must describe the appropriate special education and related services.[113] The LEA conducts the services plan meetings in conjunction with the private school representatives.[114] The SEA has an obligation to insure compliance with this requirement.[115]

---

104. Foley v. Special School Dist. of St. Louis, 153 F.3d 863 (8th Cir. 1998).

105. 153 F.3d 863 (8th Cir. 1998) (the court also held that mandating such services on premise of private school was inconsistent with Missouri state law); *see also* Jasa v. Millard Public School District No. 17, 206 F.3d 813 (8th Cir. 2000) (student who is receiving a FAPE from the public school district and is unilaterally moved to a private school or facility has no right to continue receiving educational services from school district); Peter v. Wedl, 155 F.3d 992 (8th Cir. 1998).

106. 125 F.3d 1017 (7th Cir. 1997); *see also* Nieuwenhuis v. Delaval-Darien School Dist., 996 F. Supp. 855 (E.D. Wis. 1998) (any burden placed upon student's free exercise of religion by district's refusal to provide sign language interpreter was not so substantial so as to call into constitutional question nor was it an abuse of discretion under IDEA).

107. *Id.*

108. K.R., 125 F.3d at 1019.

109. 128 F.3d 1431 (10th Cir. 1997).

110. 150 F.3d 219 (2d Cir. 1998).

111. *Id.* at 221.

112. 34 C.F.R. §300.132(b).

113. 34 C.F.R. §300.138(b)(2).

114. 34 C.F.R. §300.137(c)(2).

115. 34 C.F.R. §300.129; *see* 20 U.S.C. §1412(a)(10).

The LEA and the private school representative must consult to determine the services that will be provided,[116] with the LEA responsible for making the final decision.[117] Decisions are made as to how the identified parentally placed private school children with disabilities can meaningfully participate in special education and related services. In addition, decisions as to how services will be apportioned if funds are insufficient to serve all parentally placed children, receive services, the types of services, how the services will be provided, the location of the services, and by whom the services will be provided.[118]

When the LEA does provide services at the private school, personnel providing the services are required to meet the same standards as the providers in the public school. Private elementary or secondary teachers, however, do not have to meet the same certification requirements that public school special education teachers must meet.[119]

Further, when Part B funds are expended, they may only be used for meeting the needs of the individual student and not for the general needs of the students or for the private school itself.[120] The funds may be also used for public school personnel to provide the necessary services that are not normally provided at the school.[121] The LEA may also pay private school employees to provide the services as long as the services are provided outside the regular school hours and are provided under public direction and supervision.[122]

The services may be provided at the school site even if the school is religious, if permitted under state law.[123]

Transportation, if necessary for a child to benefit or participate in special education programs, is required from the child's home to a service site other than the private school, from the service site to the private school, or from a service site to the child's home depending on the time of day the services are provided.[124]

Where the LEA offers a FAPE, complaints brought by unilaterally placed disabled private school children and their parents using the due process hearing procedure are limited to disputes over child find.[125] Complaints regarding the provision of services in

---

116. 34 C.F.R. § 300.134.
117. C.F.R. § 300.137(b)(2).
118. 34 C.F.R. § 300.134(d).
119. 34 C.F.R. § 300.138(a)(1).
120. 34 C.F.R. § 300.141.
121. 34 C.F.R. § 300.142(a).
122. 34 C.F.R. § 300.142(b).
123. *See* 34 C.F.R. § 300.139(a); Fowler v. Unified School Dist. No. 259, 128 F.3d 1431 (10th Cir. 1997) (permitted under state law); Gary S. v. Manchester Sch. Dist., 374 F.3d 15 (1st Cir. 2004); *but see* Foley v. Special School Dist. of St. Louis County, 153 F.3d 863 (8th Cir. 1998) (funding not allowed under state law). See § 8.11 for a more detailed discussion of the Establishment Clause's effect on funding special education services in parochial schools,
124. 34 C.F.R. § 300.139(b). *Compare* Donald B. v. Board of School Commissioners, 117 F.3d 1371 (11th Cir. 1997) (IDEA does not require the LEA to transport the student from the private school he was attending to a public school that was three blocks. Nor was the LEA required to provide therapy at the private school since disability did not create inability to walk the three blocks) *with* McNair v. Oak Hills Local School Dist., 872 F.2d 153, 156 (6th Cir. 1989) (transportation may be necessary under these or similar circumstances if in its absence a disabled child in a private school would be denied "a genuine opportunity for equitable participation in a special education program). For a fuller discussion of transportation as a related service, see § 3.9.2
125. 34 C.F.R. § 300.140.

the services plan and funding cannot be brought through the due process procedures. These complaints, however, can be brought through the state complaint procedures.[126]

As mentioned, the obligation to provide special education and related services incorporates the requirements of evaluation, eligibility, IEP and the like. Where the parents make a unilateral placement *outside* the state, the home (family) residence of the child has primary responsibility for special education and related services, but funds from the out-of-state LEA *may* be expended for that child.[127] The LEA, however, is apparently not required to send its employees out-of-state to conduct evaluations.[128]

8.10.1 Non-IDEA Services Required for Unilateral Private School Placements

Historically, the Education Department General Administrative Regulations (EDGAR) imposed responsibilities for special education and related services delivered to children placed in private programs.[129] EDGAR provided an administrative complaint mechanism designed to ensure state and local compliance with state-administered federal programs like the EAHCA, and later the IDEA.[130] Under EDGAR, public agencies were required to consult with private schools on matters including consideration of which children would receive services, how children's needs would be identified, what benefits would be provided, how the benefits would be provided, and how the provisions of services would be evaluated.[131] Today all of the benefits once provided by EDGAR have been incorporated in the reauthorization of IDEA, and its subsequent regulations.

EDGAR procedures were distinguished from the specific administrative complaint procedures detailed in the EAHCA or IDEA, and were not understood as providing concurrent avenues of relief to plaintiff's alleging violations of EDGAR procedures.[132] Instead, any administrative procedure detailed in the federal act itself would have to be exhausted prior to the use of EDGAR.[133]

Amendments made in 1992 relocated these provisions into the regulations implementing IDEA at 34 C.F.R. Part 300 and were renamed as the Complaint Resolution

---

126. 34 C.F.R. § 300.140(c) and 34 C.F.R. §§ 300.151–300.153.

127. Manchester School Dist. v. Crisman, 306 F.3d 1 (1st Cir. 2002) (school district in which the disabled child most recently lived prior to placement in residential institution remained responsible for the costs of the child's special education programming, regardless of the child's legal residency); Letter to State Directors of Special Education, 44 Individuals with Disabilities Educ. L. Rep. (LRP) 46 (OSEP 2005); Pagano, 211 Educ. Handicapped L. Rep. (CRR) 454 (EHA 1986); Wing, 211 Educ. Handicapped L. Rep. (CRR) 414 (EHA 1986); *see also* § 2.5.1.

128. Patricia P. v. Board of Educ., 203 F.3d 462 (7th Cir. 2000) (parent's unilateral placement of child in out-of-state facility denies LEA of reasonable opportunity to conduct in-state educational evaluation, thus relieving LEA of responsibility to evaluate); Lenhoff v. Farmington Pub. Schools, 680 F. Supp. 921 (E.D. Mich. 1988); Great Valley School Dist. v. Douglass, 807 A.2d 315 (Pa. Commonwealth 2002).

129. 34 C.F.R. § 76.780 (1984) (47 FR 17421, Apr. 22, 1982); *see also* 20 U.S.C. §§ 1221e-(3) and 3474.

130. Christopher W. v. Portsmouth School Comm., 877 F.2d 1089 (1st Cir. 1989).

131. 34 C.F.R. § 76.780 (1984) (47 FR 17421, Apr. 22, 1982); *see also* 20 U.S.C. §§ 1221e-(3) and 3474.

132. Christopher W., at 1099.

133. *Id.*

Procedures (CRP),[134] and can still be found there today.[135] Under the CRP, State Educational Agencies (SEA) are required to adopt written procedures for resolving complaints by individuals or local educational agencies.[136] The SEAs must also ensure that these complaint procedures are "widely" available to parents, advocates, and all others that would have an interest in their existence.[137]

The Complaint Resolution Procedures, which apply to the resolution of "*any* complaint," should not be confused with the Due Process procedures, which apply only to "the identification, evaluation or educational placement of a child with a disability, or the provision of FAPE to the child."[138] The Ninth Circuit Court of Appeals explained the interaction of these procedures as follows:

> The regulations permit a complaint to be filed with both the CRP and the IDEA due process hearing system, in which case the CRP must await the due process hearing's resolution of overlapping issues, which is then binding in the CRP. [34 C.F.R. § 300.152(c)]. The regulations state further that the CRP must resolve a complaint alleging a public agency's failure to implement a due process decision. [Id.] The regulations do not, however, state that a parent must exhaust the CRP to enforce a due process decision in court.[139]

While each SEA is charged with creating their own CRP procedures, Congress has given detailed guidelines as to how these procedures must be carried out. Within sixty days after a complaint is filed, the SEA must carry out an on-site investigation (if necessary), during which the complainant is free to submit additional information on the complaint, either orally or in writing.[140] During that same period, the public agency must be given a chance to respond to the complaint. The SEA procedure must at least allow the public agency to make a proposal to resolve the complaint, or, provided all parties consent, engage in mediation with the complainant. [141] Finally, the SEA must review all relevant information, and after making an independent determination, issue a written decision to the complainant that includes findings of facts, conclusions, and the reasons for the SEA's final decision.[142]

If an SEA receives a complaint that, any part of which, is also the subject of a due process hearing, the SEA must set aside that issue until the conclusion of the hearing.[143] Accordingly, the doctrine of collateral estoppel applies to any issue raised in a CRP complaint that was already decided at a hearing.[144]

---

134. *See* 34 C.F.R. §§ 300.660 and 300.662 (1992).

135. 34 C.F.R. §§ 300.151–300.153 (also provides for remedies in cases of denial of appropriate services). Generally, the remedies here are essentially those ones required by the SEA under its "general supervisory authority" in Part B of the Act, namely compensatory services or monetary reimbursement.

136. 34 C.F.R. §§ 300.151(a).

137. *Id.*

138. *Compare* 34 C.F.R. §§ 300.151–300.152, *with* 34 C.F.R. § 300.507.

139. Porter v. Bd. of Trustees of Manhattan Beach Unified School Dist., 307 F.3d 1064 (9th Cir. 2002); *see also,* Mrs. W. v. Tirozzi, 832 F.2d 748 (2d Cir. 1987); Jeremy H. v. Mount Lebanon School Dist. 95 F.3d 272 (3d Cir. 1996).

140. 34 C.F.R §§ 300.152(a)(1) & (2).

141. 34 C.F.R. § 300.152(a)(3).

142. 34 C.F.R. §§ 300.152(a)(4) & (5).

143. 34 C.F.R. § 300.152(c)(1).

144. 34 C.F.R. § 300.152(c)(2).

8.11 Parental Placement in Parochial School/ Separation of Church and State

Placement of a disabled child in a sectarian school raises three interrelated questions. First, when the LEA is prepared to provide a FAPE in the public school, but the parents unilaterally decide to place the child in the parochial school, is the LEA *required* to provide special education and related services for the child? Second, *may* the LEA provide services to the child unilaterally placed in the parochial school? Third, as part of the continuum of services the LEA must provide, *may* the LEA place a child in a parochial school?

Is the LEA *required* to provide special education and related services for a child placed in a parochial school when the LEA is prepared to provide a FAPE in the public school? As discussed in § 8.10, since 1997, there have been significant limitations on the obligation of the LEA to provide educational services to children unilaterally placed by parents in private schools. In light of those limitations, an LEA is not obligated to provide services at a sectarian school regardless of the Establishment Clause issues discussed below, because the LEA has little obligation to provide educational services at any private school. For example, in *Russman v. Board of Education of the Enlarged City School District of the City of Watervliet*,[145] the court, relying on the 1997 amendments, held that the LEA was not required to provide on-site special education services to a child whose parents had voluntarily chosen to enroll her in a private sectarian school.[146]

The question of whether the LEA *may* provide the services to a unilaterally placed child is a bit more confusing, since it raises constitutional questions in light of the Establishment Clause. Prior to 1993, significant questions existed about the ability of the LEA to provide any special education and related services on the site of a sectarian school.[147] In 1993, the United States Supreme Court, in *Zobrest v. Catalina Foothills School District*,[148] addressed the constitutionality of providing state aid under IDEA to children in parochial schools. The student in *Zobrest* was hearing impaired and had been provided with a sign language interpreter in public school for three years. The public school, however, refused to provide the interpreter after the student was enrolled by his parents in a parochial school. The school's denial was based on its position that providing an interpreter on school grounds would violate the Establishment Clause of the United States Constitution.

The Supreme Court held that the services could be provided. The Court held that providing services as part of a general government program that distributes benefits

---

145. 150 F.3d 219 (2d Cir. 1998).

146. 150 F.3d 219 (2d Cir. 1998); *see also* Peter v. Wedl, 155 F.3d 992 (8th Cir. 1998) (amended 1997 IDEA did not entitle student to provision of services at private parochial school); *but see,* Bay Shore Union Free Sch. Dist. v. T., 405 F. Supp. 2d 230 (E.D.N.Y. 2005) (IDEA does not require district to provide on-site services, but state law requires on-site services in some cases. State law requires districts to deliver services on the premises of a private school where a child's special academic program can only be implemented in the private school setting).

147. *See* Guernsey and Sweeney, *The Church, the State and the EHA: Educating The Handicapped in Light of the Establishment Clause,* 73 Marquette L. Rev. 259 (1989).

148. 509 U.S. 1 (1993); *see also* Witters v. Washington Dept. of Services for the Blind, 474 U.S. 481(1985) (government program which neutrally provides benefits to a broad class of citizens defined without reference to religion are not readily subject to the Establishment Clause challenge just because sectarian institutions may also receive an attenuated financial benefit).

neutrally to any eligible child qualifying under IDEA without regard to the sectarian or nonsectarian nature of the school was permissible. Since the parents chose the school, the government employee would be in the sectarian school only as a result of the private decision of the parents. Further, the Court reasoned, IDEA creates no financial incentive for parents to choose a sectarian school, thus an interpreter's presence could not be attributed to state decision making.[149] The Court held that the Establishment Clause does not lay down absolute barriers to placing public employees in sectarian schools, thus providing the student with an interpreter did not violate the Establishment Clause.[150]

The Court's approach to Establishment Clause cases had evolved over the previous 40 years moving from the neutrality rule of *Everson v. Board of Education*[151] to the trifurcated test of *Lemon v. Kurtzman.*[152] *Zobrest* was considered by some to be a departure from the Court's then current approach to state support of education in sectarian schools.[153]

Further clarification of the impact of *Zobrest*, however, came in *Agostini v. Felton.*[154] In *Agostini*, the United States Supreme Court specifically overruled its decision in *Aquilar v. Felton,*[155] citing *Zobrest* as a more correct interpretation of current law.

Agostini dealt with the provision of educational programming at a religious school under New York City's Title I program. The Court began its analysis by reaffirming the principle that "government inculcation of religious beliefs has the impermissible effect of advancing religion...."[156] The Court identified the three prongs that it uses to determine whether government aid has the effect of advancing religion: does it result in governmental indoctrination; does it define its recipients by reference to religion; or does it create an excessive entanglement?[157]

The Court, however, recognized two significant changes in the existing analysis in the context of educational services. First, the presence of public school employees on the sectarian school was not presumed to inculcate religion.[158] Second, it rejected the idea that all aid that "directly assists the educational function of the religious schools is invalid."[159]

It has been suggested that on making the decision about when direct aid would be invalid one should look to the analysis in *Zobrest*.[160] It will be remembered that in *Zo-*

---

149. Zobrest, 509 U.S. at 9.

150. *See also* Gary S. v. Manchester Sch. Dist., 374 F.3d 15 (1st Cir. 2004) (provision of lesser benefits under IDEA to private school students did not violate Free Exercise Clause, the RFRA, the Equal Protection Clause or due process); Peck v. Lansing School Dist., 148 F.3d 619 (6th Cir. 1998) (provision of occupational and physical therapy on parochial grounds does not violate establishment clause); Russman v. Board of Educ. of City of Watervliet, 150 F.3d 219, 221 (2d Cir. 1998) (school is permitted, but not required, to provide the student with the services on-site of a parochial school).

151. 330 U.S. 1 (1947).

152. 403 U.S. 602 (1971).

153. "Parochaid" has been used by some authors to refer to state aid to parochial schools. *See, e.g.*, Comment, *Shared Time Instruction in Parochial Schools: Stretching the Establishment Clause to its Outer Limits*, 89 Dick. L. Rev. 175, 175 (1984).

154. 521 U.S. 203 (1997).

155. 473 U.S. 402 (1985).

156. Agostini, 521 U.S. at 223.

157. *Id.* at 234.

158. *Id.* at 224.

159. *Id* at 225.

160. Helms v. Picard, 151 F.3d 347 (5th Cir. 1998), *cert. granted sub nom.* Mitchell v. Helms, 119 S. Ct. 2336 (1999).

brest the Court relied on the fact that benefits were distributed to any child qualifying as disabled under IDEA, the parents chose the school (and hence, the situation only arises as a result of the private decision of the parents), and there was no financial incentive for parents to choose a sectarian school.[161]

In addition to these two specific changes, the Court in *Agostini* focused on the entanglement prong traditional Establishment Clause analysis. The Court pointed out that only "excessive" entanglement is unconstitutional and that, consistent with the recognition that mere presence of public school teachers is not impermissible, "we must also discard the assumption that pervasive monitoring of ... teachers is required."[162]

Clearly under *Zobrest* and *Agostini* a wide range of services can be provided. As the Supreme Court held in *Agostini*,

> A federally funded program providing supplemental, remedial instruction to disadvantaged children on a neutral basis is not invalid under the Establishment Clause when such instruction is given on the premises of sectarian schools by government employees pursuant to a program containing safeguards such as those present here.[163]

The IDEA reflects the Supreme Court's decision in *Zobrest*. The statute provides, "services may be provided to the children on the premises of private, including religious, schools, to the extent consistent with state law."[164]

The extent of what services are permissible was again addressed by the United States Supreme Court in *Mitchell v. Helms*.[165] The Court held that a Louisiana plan that paid for full and part-time special education teachers in religious schools was not a violation of the Establishment Clause.

The *Mitchell* decision leads to the third question of whether the state may include the sectarian school as part of its continuum of services. In *Mitchell*,[166] the state of Louisiana mandated delivery of special education and related services to all eligible children and authorized the LEA to "enter into a purchase of services agreement with any other public or nonpublic school, agency or institution to provide free appropriate education to exceptional children in need of special education and related services."[167]

The LEA contracted with the Special Education Services Corporation (SESC) to provide special education services by public school teachers at schools operated by the Archdiocese of New Orleans. The sole employee of SESC was also an employee of the Archdiocese and SESC's members were all affiliated with either the Archdiocese or Louisiana Dioceses. The district court held, therefore, that SESC was a religiously affiliated corporation. In practice, the LEA was using the Church organization to meet its obligations under state law. In a plurality decision, the United States Supreme Court

---

161. Zobrest, 509 U.S. at 9.

162. Agostini, 521 U.S. at 234.

163. *Id.* at 234–235.

164. 20 U.S.C. § 1412(a)(10)(A)(I)(III); *see* Russman v. Board of Educ. of City of Watervliet, 150 F.3d 219, 221 (2d Cir. 1998). *Compare* Peter v. Wedl, 155 F.3d 992 (8th Cir. 1998) (1997 IDEA did not entitle student to provision of services at private parochial school) *with* Peck v. Lansing School Dist., 148 F.3d 619 (6th Cir. 1998) (provision of occupational and physical therapy on parochial grounds does not violate establishment clause).

165. 530 U.S. 793 (2000).

166. 151 F.3d 347 (5th Cir. 1998), *rev'd sub nom.* Mitchell v. Helms, 530 U.S. 793 (2000).

167. *Id.* at 351 *quoting* La. Rev. Stat. Ann § 17:1949–50 (1982).

upheld the validity of this arrangement.[168] It is now a short step to allow sectarian schools to become part of the continuum of educational placements the LEA may use.

---

168. Mitchell v. Helms, 530 U.S. 793 (2000).

Chapter 9

Notice and Consent

9.1 In General

Written notice and consent are required at several stages in the educational process. What follows is an overview of where notice or consent is required. Notice and consent are also discussed, as appropriate, under particular topics, such as placement and evaluation.

The significance of notice as a procedural right cannot be underestimated.[1] Failure to provide notice has been held to be sufficient to excuse exhaustion of administrative remedies.[2] Further, failure to provide notice has been held to be a sufficient procedural violation to support a finding that the agency's proposed educational program would not provide a free appropriate public education (FAPE).[3] Lack of written notice, however, has been held to be not prejudicial where oral notice was given to the parents and the parents attended the Individual Education Program (IEP) meeting.[4]

The purpose of notice is to inform parents. The proper time for notice, therefore, is after an appropriate decision has been reached by the district, but within a reasonable time before the decision is implemented.[5] Notice must also be provided within a reasonable time and contain adequate information to allow a parent to raise an objection under due process procedures if desired. For example, the United States Department of Education's Office of Special Education Programs (OSEP) interpreted the notice requirement in a way that rejected a strict 10-day notice prior to an IEP meeting. Rather, OSEP indicated that 10 days was a guideline for determining reasonableness.[6] Copies of state law and regulations are not a sufficient form of notice. Parents must be given full explanations, written in a manner that members of the general public can understand.[7]

---

1. 34 C.F.R. § 300.504.
2. *See* § 13.3.
3. *See* § 14.7.
4. Thomas F. v. Cincinnati Bd. of Educ., 918 F.2d 618 (6th Cir. 1990); *see also* Urban v. Jefferson County School Dist., 89 F.3d 720 (10th Cir. 1996) (technical deviations from the IDEA, such as failing to include a statement of transition services, do not constitute violations of IDEA).
5. Helmuth Inquiry, 16 Educ. Handicapped L. Rep. (CRR) 550 (OSEP 1990).
6. Constantian Inquiry, 17 Educ. Handicapped L. Rep. (LRP) 118 (OSEP 1990).
7. 34 C.F.R. § 300.503(c)(1)(i); Max M. v. Thompson, 592 F. Supp. 1437 (N.D. Ill. 1984).

9.2 Notice Concerning Identification, Evaluation, and Placement in General

Written notice must be given to a parent prior to an LEA proposing to change or refusing to change the identification, perform an evaluation, or make an educational placement of a child under IDEA regulations.[8] Section 504 regulations also provide for notice with respect to any actions regarding identification, evaluation, and educational placement of any child with a disability. Compliance with IDEA regulations is stated as one method by which § 504 regulations may be satisfied.[9] When notice of identification or evaluation is required under IDEA, the notice must meet several requirements. Perhaps most significantly, the notice must contain an explanation of the procedural safeguards available under IDEA. Notice of procedural safeguards includes explanations relating to: the availability of an Independent Educational Evaluation (IEE); prior written notice; parental consent; access to records; placement during pendency of due process proceedings; requirements for unilateral placement by parents in private schools; procedures, mediation; state level appeals; civil actions; attorney fees; and the ability to request a due process hearing.[10]

The notice must also describe the action taken or the reason action was not taken. It must describe the options considered by the agency and why other options were rejected.[11] In addition, the notice must describe each procedure, test, record or report relied upon by the agency in making its proposal or refusing to take action.[12] It must also contain a statement that the parents have procedural safeguards,[13] provide sources for parents to obtain special education and related services,[14] and any other factors relevant to the agency's action or inaction other than these four instances.[15]

In addition to the specific content just described, the actual notice must be written in language understood by the general public, and provided in the native language of the parent (unless it is clearly not feasible to do so).[16] If the native language of the parent is not written, the agency must insure that there is an oral translation of the notice and that the parent understands the notice. The agency must also keep written evidence that it has met these latter two requirements.[17]

Section 504 has a very general requirement that notice be a part of the procedural safeguards established by the educational agency "with respect to actions regarding the identification, evaluation, or educational placement...."[18]

---

8. 34 C.F.R. § 300.503(a); *see also* 20 U.S.C. §§ 1415(b)(3), (4), and (c), § 1414(b)(1).
9. 34 C.F.R. § 104.36.
10. 34 C.F.R. § 300.504(b); *see also* 20 U.S.C. § 1415(d).
11. 34 C.F.R. § 300.503(b)(6); *see also* 20 U.S.C. §§ 1415(b)(3) and (4); § 1414(b)(1); *see generally,* Nack v. Orange City Sch. Dist., 454 F.3d 604 (6th Cir. 2006).
12. 34 C.F.R. § 300.503(b)(3); *see generally* 20 U.S.C. §§ 1415(b)(3) and (4); § 1414(b)(1); 1415(c)(1).
13. 34 C.F.R. § 300.503(b)(4).
14. 34 C.F.R. § 300.503(b)(5).
15. 34 C.F.R. § 300.503(b)(7).
16. 34 C.F.R. § 300.503(c)(i–ii).
17. 34 C.F.R. § 300.503(c)(2)(i–iii).
18. 34 C.F.R. § 104.36.

9.2.1 Notice of Preplacement Evaluation

A notice of preplacement evaluation should list the specific tests and records on which the LEA bases its decision to conduct an evaluation.[19] OSEP, in 1989, refined its 1980 interpretation of notice requirements to require a list of tests expected to be used in the evaluation process.[20] The notice is not required to identify specific evaluators. This is not the case, however, with independent educational evaluations (IEEs) requested by the child's parent. Upon the parent's request, the parent must be provided with information about where an IEE may be obtained. To satisfy this requirement, Districts may publish a list of evaluators that meet the district's criteria, but may not limit the parents' choice to an evaluator on such a list.[21]

In the case of reevaluation, the LEA must list specific tests to be used if the reevaluation was requested by one other than the parent.[22] If the reevaluation is requested by the parent or is the mandatory triennial evaluation, a specific listing of tests is not required,[23] though it should contain a list of tests expected to be used in the reevaluation.[24]

The United States Department of Education Office for Civil Rights (OCR) decided in 1985 that providing a general description of the types of tests to be used was in compliance with notice requirements of § 504.[25] OCR also ruled that "pertinent information," such as right to counsel, right to examine records, and the right to a due process hearing must also be part of any notice for the notice to be in compliance with regulations implementing § 504 during the initial identification and evaluation proceedings.[26] The identity of the § 504 coordinator must also be publicized and provided as part of notice at the initial identification and evaluation stages.[27]

---

19. 34 C.F.R. § 300.503(3); Schaffer v. Weast, 546 U.S. 49 (2005) (districts must provide a description of all evaluations, reports, and other factors that the school used in coming to its decision).

20. Reynolds Inquiry, 213 Educ. Handicapped L. Rep. (CRR) 238 (OSEP 1989); *see also* 34 C.F.R. § 300.503(b)(3) (a description of each evaluation procedure, assessment, record or report agency uses for proposed or refused action required).

21. Sutler and McCoy Inquiry, 18 Individuals with Disabilities Educ. L. Rep. (LRP) 307 (OSEP 1991); *but see* Letter to Parker, 41 Individuals with Disabilities Educ. L. Rep. (LRP) 155 (OSERS 2004); 34 C.F.R. § 300.502(a)(2).

22. *See also,* Letter to Anonymous, 35 Individuals with Disabilities Educ. L. Rep. (LRP) 218 (OSEP 2001) (parents must give *informed* consent before their child is reevaluated, including if additional assessments or other evaluation procedures are necessary); 20 U.S.C. § 1414(b)(1); Grimes Inquiry, 211 Educ. Handicapped L. Rep. (CRR) 187 (EHA 1980).

23. Inquiry, 211 Educ. Handicapped L. Rep. (CRR) 187 (EHA 1980).

24. *See generally,* Letter to Anonymous, 35 Individuals with Disabilities Educ. L. Rep. (LRP) 218 (OSEP 2001); Reynolds Inquiry, 213 Educ. Handicapped L. Rep. (CRR) 238 (OSEP 1990).

25. Wisconsin Depart. Of Public Instruction, 352 Educ. Handicapped L. Rep. (CRR) 177 (OCR 1985) (interpreting 34 C.F.R. § 104.36).

26. Sikeston, Mo. R-VI School Dist., 16 Educ. Handicapped L. Rep. (CRR) 351 (OCR 1990); *see* 34 C.F.R. § 104.36; *see also* Yorktown, N.Y. Cent. School District, 16 Educ. Handicapped L. Rep. (CRR) 182 (OCR 1989).

27. Hyde Park, N.Y. Cent. School District, 16 Educ. Handicapped L. Rep. (CRR) 182 (OCR 1989).

9.2.2 Notice of Initial Placement

For notice of initial placement to be proper, an agency must list all the specific tests upon which it based its placement decision.[28] The LEA must also explain in the notice why the specific placement was chosen, as well as why other placements were rejected.[29]

9.2.3 Notice of Change in Placement

Notice of the intent to change placement is required.[30] "Boilerplate language" on forms containing only general descriptions of the proposed placement, without a discussion of options considered for the individual child, is inadequate notice.[31] Parents have a right to notice independent of the child's right. For example, where a student over the age of eighteen consented to a change in placement, the parents were still entitled to prior notice.[32]

What constitutes a change in placement sufficient to require notice to the parent has been the subject of considerable litigation. In general, a change in location does not constitute a change in placement if the educational program remains the same.[33] Also, a change that is superficial in nature and does not significantly affect a child's learning experience does not constitute a change in placement.[34] Where, however, a substantial change in programming will take place, a change in placement has occurred and prior notice is required.[35]

---

28. Grimes Inquiry, 211 Educ. Handicapped L. Rep. (CRR) 187 (EHA 1980).

29. 34 C.F.R. § 300.503(b); New Inquiry, 211 Educ. Handicapped L. Rep. (CRR) 383 (EHA 1986).

30. 34 C.F.R. § 300.503(a)(1); *see generally,* Pardini v. Allegheny Intermediate Unit, 420 F.3d 181 (3d Cir. 2005); *but see,* Berger v. Medina City Sch. Dist., 348 F.3d 513 (6th Cir. 2003) (technical violation of "notice requirement" is not enough, violation must cause substantive harm to the parent's ability to participate meaningfully); Brookline School v. Golden, 628 F. Supp. 113 (D. Mass. 1986) (written notice not required where parents had actual notice of intent to change placement); For a discussion of other aspects of a change in placement see § 8.4.

31. McKenzie v. Smith, 771 F.2d 1527 (D.C. Cir. 1985).

32. 34 C.F.R. § 300.520 (if a state law permits transfer of parental rights to the student at the age of majority, the parents are entitled to notice only, unless the student does not have the ability to provide informed consent or is incompetent); Mrs. C. v. Wheaton, 916 F.2d 69 (2d Cir. 1990).

33. *See* AW v. Fairfax County Sch. Bd., 372 F.3d 674 (4th Cir. 2004) (change in placement occurs when a school places the student in a setting that is distinguishable from the educational environment to which the student was previously assigned); Weil v. Board of Elementary & Secondary Educ., 931 F.2d 1069 (5th Cir. 1991); Concerned Parents & Citizens for the Continuing Educ. at Malcolm X v. New York City Bd. of Educ., 629 F.2d 751 (2d Cir. 1981); Hill v. School Board of Pinellas County, 954 F. Supp. 251 (M.D. Fla. 1997); Dima v. Macchiarola, 513 F. Supp. 565 (E.D.N.Y. 1981).

34. AW v. Fairfax County Sch. Bd., 372 F.3d 674 (4th Cir. 2004) (change in placement occurs when a school places the student in a setting that is distinguishable from the educational environment to which the student was previously assigned); Board of Education of Community High School Dist. 118 v. Ill. State Bd. of Educ., 103 F.3d 545 (7th Cir. 1996) (the natural progression in the level of the program was not a change in placement); Cavanagh v. Grasmick, 75 F. Supp. 2d 446 (D. Md. 1999) (modification to schedule was not a change in placement); Brookline School Comm. v. Golden, 628 F. Supp. 113 (D. Mass. 1986) (change in day care from 2 to 3 days, with substitution of day care program on two other days not a change in placement).

35. *See, e.g.,* Tilton v. Jefferson County Bd. of Educ., 705 F.2d 800 (6th Cir. 1983) (change in location and no longer providing year long education constituted change in placement), Alston v. District of Columbia, 439 F. Supp. 2d 86 (D.D.C. 2006) (district decision to send student home after residential placement closed was change in placement).

Termination of educational services also constitutes a change in placement requiring advance notice.[36] Suspension or expulsion of a student for more than ten days in duration constitutes a change in placement, and requires parental notice.38 Notice must be given concerning who is subject to placement in an interim alternative educational setting.[37]

9.3 Notices after Hearing Request

When a due process hearing is initiated either by the educational agency or the parents, the parents must be provided with information concerning "any free or low-cost legal and other relevant services available in the area...."[38] The parents must also be told that they may recover attorneys' fees if they are successful in the due process hearing.[39] In addition, the notice must provide an explanation of mediation rights.[40] The public agency may post the current procedural safeguards notice on its Internet Web site.[41] The parent can also receive the notices by electronic mail.[42]

9.4 When Parental Consent Required

Parental consent is required under IDEA prior to conducting an initial evaluation, a reevaluation, and an initial preplacement evaluation.[43] If the child is a ward of the state, the public agency is not required to obtain parental consent for initial evaluations under three circumstances. They include when the public agency has used reasonable efforts and cannot locate the parent, the rights of the parents have been terminated or a court order has transferred the right to make educational decisions to another individual.[44] Other than in these three instances, consent may not be required as a condition of any benefit to the child.[45] The public agency is not required to obtain consent when a

---

36. *See, e.g.*, T.S. v. Indep. Sch. Dist. No. 54, 265 F.3d 1090 (10th Cir. 2001) (district failed obligation to give student written notice prior to graduation; however, the mere technical defect did not deprive student of any substantial right); New York State Assn. of Retarded Children v. Carey, 466 F. Supp. 479 (E.D.N.Y. 1978), *aff'd*, 612 F.2d 644 (2d Cir. 1978) (exclusion of hepatitis B carrier); Mason City Community School Dist., 21 Individuals with Disabilities Educ. L. Rep. 248 (1994) (school district must notify student's parents of anticipated graduation date); Richards Inquiry, 17 Educ. Handicapped L. Rep. (LRP) 288 (OSERS 1990) (graduation constitutes change in placement).

37. 34 C.F.R. § 300.504(b)(8).

38. 34 C.F.R. § 300.507(b)(1)(2); *but see* R. v. Fairfax County School Bd., 338 F.3d 325 (4th Cir. 2003) (school district was not required by either the IDEA or its regulations to inform parent of state's two-year limitations period applicable to request for a due process hearing).

39. *See* Chapter 15; *see also* 34 C.F.R. § 300.504(c)(13).

40. 34 C.F.R. § 300.504(b)(6).

41. 34 C.F.R. § 300.504(b).

42. 34 C.F.R. § 300.505.

43. 34 C.F.R. § 300.300.

44. 34 C.F.R. § 300.300(a)(2)(i–iii).

45. 34 C.F.R. § 300.300(c)(2); Letter to Elder, 41 Individuals with Disabilities Educ. L. Rep. (LRP) 270 (OSERS 2004) (under FERPA, no parental consent is needed for disclosure of personally identifiable information of children transitioning from Part C to Part B services to allow LEA's to fulfill their child-find obligations); Letter to Katzerman, 28 Individuals with Disabilities Educ. L. Rep. 310 (OSEP 1997) (results of IEE can be disclosed to LEA without consent).

teacher or specialist conducts a screening to determine instructional strategies for implementing the curriculum.[46] States, however, may adopt more stringent standards of
notification and consent than those outlined in IDEA regulations. An agency's more
stringent standards, however, may never serve to exclude a child from receiving a
FAPE.[47]

Prior to the 1997 statute and 1999 regulations, both IDEA and § 504 regulations required only notice, and not consent for reevaluations.[48] Consent is required for reevaluations under IDEA, unless the agency can show that it has taken reasonable steps to obtain parental consent and the parents have failed to respond. Consent is not required
when existing data is reviewed as part of an evaluation or reevaluation.[49]

9.4.1 Content of Consent

The parent must be fully informed of all information relevant to the activity for
which consent is sought.[50] Where consent is required, the parent must understand and
agree to the activity in writing, and the consent must be obtained in the native language
of the parent.[51] The writing must describe the activity for which consent is sought and
list any records that will be released and to whom.[52] Further, the parent must understand that the consent is voluntary and may be unilaterally revoked by the parent.[53] Revocation of consent is not considered retroactive.[54]

The fully informed consent must include a listing of tests expected to be used if the
consent is for evaluation.[55] If the consent is for initial placement, specific tests and
records, upon which the placement decision was made, must be included to make the
consent a fully informed one.[56]

Section 504 is much less specific concerning consent requirements than IDEA,
merely calling for procedural safeguards during the evaluation and placement process.
As a model of adherence, however, § 504 regulations cite IDEA.[57] For example, in 1987,
OCR ruled that a failure to obtain parental consent prior to conducting a speech and

46. 34 C.F.R. § 300.302.
47. 34 C.F.R. § 300.300(c)(2); Letter to Anonymous, 35 Individuals with Disabilities Educ. L.
Rep. (LRP) 35 (OSEP 2000) (state has flexibility to shape its retention/promotion policies. Due
process rights are triggered only if retention/promotion policy affects FAPE issues); Hall v. Freeman,
700 F. Supp. 1106 (N.D. Ga. 1987); Baliles Inquiry, 213 Educ. Handicapped L. Rep. (CRR) 207
(EHA 1988).
48. Dunlap Inquiry, 211 Educ. Handicapped L. Rep. (CRR) 462 (EHA 1987); Dennelly Inquiry,
211 Educ. Handicapped L. Rep. (CRR) 349 (EHA 1984).
49. 34 C.F.R. § 300.300(c)(1)(i).
50. 34 C.F.R. § 300.9; see also 20 U.S.C. § 1414(a)(1)(D) (authority for the meaning of consent).
51. 34 C.F.R. § 300.9(a).
52. 34 C.F.R. § 300.9(b).
53. 34 C.F.R. § 300.9(c)(1).
54. 34 C.F.R. § 300.9(c)(2).
55. Gorski v. Lynchburg School Bd., 441 Educ. Handicapped L. Rep. (CRR) 415 (4th Cir. 1989).
56. Id.
57. 34 C.F.R. § 104.36. See, e.g., Eric H. v. Methacton Sch. Dist., 265 F. Supp. 2d 513 (E.D. Pa.
2003) (§ 504 rights can be addressed through the same hearing process as claims under IDEA);
Weber v. Cranston Pub. Sch. Comm., 245 F. Supp. 2d 401 (D.R.I. 2003) (compliance with IDEA's
procedural safeguards is one means of satisfying § 504 regulations); Forest Park, Mich. School Dist.,
352 Educ. Handicapped L. Rep. (CRR) 182 (OCR 1986).

language evaluation of a child violated § 504 regulations.[58] Placement without consent was also found to be a violation of § 504 regulations.[59]

9.4.2 Refusal to Provide Consent

Refusal to consent or revocation of consent does not lessen the obligation of the LEA to provide services to a child.[60] A school district, however, is not entitled to "unfettered discretion" to evaluate a student in the absence of parental consent.[61] The agency may not terminate attempts to evaluate or place a child based on a lack of consent.[62] If parental consent cannot be obtained for the initial evaluation and the revaluation the agency may, but is not required to, either seek a due process hearing, mediation, or follow any state permitted procedure, such as seeking a court order to allow the proposed action.[63] When requesting consent for initial evaluations and reevaluations for children who are placed by their parents in private school or children who are home schooled, the public agency may not use the consent override provisions.[64] If the parent refuses to consent to services the public agency may not override the parental failure to consent and it will not have violated its requirement to provide a FAPE.[65] Section 504 regulations indicate that the same procedures as under IDEA may be used to comply with § 504's own general requirement to provide due process.[66]

---

58. Sachem, N.Y. Cent. School District, 352 Educ. Handicapped L. Rep. (CRR) 462 (OCR 1987) (interpreting 34 C.F.R. § 104.36).

59. Weber v. Cranston Pub. Sch. Comm., 245 F. Supp. 2d 401 (D.R.I. 2003); Powhattan, Kan. Unified School Dist. No. 150, 257 Educ. Handicapped L. Rep. (CRR) 32 (OCR 1979) (interpreting 34 C.F.R. § 104.36).

60. J.J. Garcia v. Board of Educ., 558 Educ. Handicapped L. Rep. (CRR) 152 (D. Conn. 1986).

61. Fitzgerald v. Camdenton R-III Sch. Dist., 439 F.3d 773 (8th Cir. 2006) (District not entitled to conduct evaluation where a home-schooled child's parents refuse consent, privately educate the child, and expressly waive all benefits under the IDEA); Letter to Manasevit, 41 Individuals with Disabilities Educ. L. Rep. (LRP) 36 (OSEP 2003); see also, Letter to Gagliardi, 36 Individuals with Disabilities Educ. L. Rep. (LRP) 267 (OSERS 2001) (IDEA regulations only allow districts to override lack of parental consent only for evaluations and reevaluations, not the initial provision of services).

62. Dyersburg, Tenn. City School Dist., 353 Educ. Handicapped L. Rep. (CRR) 164 (OCR 1988); Letter to Manasevit, 41 Individuals with Disabilities Educ. L. Rep. (LRP) 36 (OSEP 2003).

63. 34 C.F.R. § 300.300(a)(3)(i) and (c)(2); Honig v. Doe, 484 U.S. 305 (1988); Handberry v. Thompson, 446 F.3d 335, n.5 (2d Cir. 2006) (district may seek initial evaluation through due process, mediation or other state permitted procedures, but no evaluation without any form of parental or legal authorization); Letter to Fulfrost, 42 Individuals with Disabilities Educ. L. Rep. (LRP) 271 (OSEP 2004) (district may not use due process hearing to override parent's refusal to consent to the initial services); Letter to Yudien, 38 Individuals with Disabilities Educ. L. Rep. (LRP) 267 (OSEP 2003) (if parents do not consent to initial services, they have refused FAPE and if parents refuse consent to all services, except for a related services, district is not required to provide related services); Letter to Lewis, 24 Individuals with Disabilities Educ. L. Rep. (LRP) 964 (OSEP 1996) (If portion of IEP is suspended under state rule because of parent's revocation of consent, it is not a conflict with the stay-put provision of the law; if a portion of the suspended IEP is required for FAPE, school should seek due process or other procedures).

64. 34 C.F.R. § 300.300(c)(4); Durkee v. Livonia Cent. School Dist., 487 F. Supp. 2d 313 (W.D.N.Y. 2007) (IDEA does allow district to compel the evaluation of a home schooled student where student's parent objected to evaluation and refused to accept special-education services).

65. 34 C.F.R. § 300.300(b)(3(4)(i).

66. Eric H. v. Methacton Sch. Dist., 265 F. Supp. 2d 513 (E.D. Pa. 2003); Weber v. Cranston Pub. Sch. Comm., 245 F. Supp. 2d 401 (D.R.I. 2003).

9.5 Notice Checklist

_____Notice is required:

_____Change in identification

_____Perform an evaluation

_____Make an educational placement

_____Transfer of parental rights at age of majority

_____Graduation from high school with regular diploma

_____Reasonable time before institution of any change

_____Adequate information to allow a parent to raise an objection under due process procedures if desired

_____In writing

_____Explains procedural safeguards

_____Describes action or inaction to be taken

_____Describes options considered

_____Describes why other options were rejected

_____Describes each procedure, test, record or report relied upon

_____Describes other relevant factors

_____Sources for parents to contact to understand notice provisions

_____Written in language understood by the general public

_____Written in native language of the parent

9.6 Consent Checklist

_____Parental consent required:

_____Initiation of a preplacement evaluation

_____Prior to the initial placement of a child

_____Reevaluation

_____Fully informed of all information relevant to the activity

_____Native language of the parent

_____Parent must understand and agree to the activity

_____In writing

_____Describes the activity for which consent is sought

_____Lists any records that will be released and to whom

_____Parent understands consent is voluntary

_____Listing of tests expected to be used if the consent is for evaluation

_____If the consent is for initial placement, specific tests and records upon which the placement decision was made must be included to make the consent a fully informed one

_____Due process, mediation, or other state procedure filed if consent refused or revoked

_____Consent not required for reviewing existing data for evaluation or reevaluation

_____Consent not required for reevaluation if the parent has failed to respond and agency can demonstrate reasonable efforts to obtain consent

_____Consent not required for administering a test or evaluation that is given to all children unless consent is required of all children

_____Consent not required when a teacher or specialist conducts a screening to determine instructional strategies for implementing the curriculum

Chapter 10

Discipline

10.1 In General

In general, as long as the child's educational placement does not change, the disciplinary measures available to the school are the same for students with disabilities as for other students.[1] In addition, there is often a close relationship between discipline and the educational needs of a particular student, and the Individual Education Program (IEP) may state particular modes of discipline.[2]

While students with disabilities may be disciplined, appropriate procedures need to be followed.[3] In an attempt to minimize conflict, the IDEA and its regulations require a behavioral intervention plan be included in the IEP under specific circumstances.[4] The law also identifies other factors that the IEP team must consider when a child's behavior impedes his or her or other students' learning.[5] These factors include appropriate behavioral interventions, strategies, and support services that address the behaviors that impede a child's learning.[6]

A significant limitation on the agency's ability to discipline the student exists, however, if the discipline constitutes a change in placement. In 1988, the Supreme Court in Honig v. Doe,[7] relied on the stay-put provision[8] of IDEA, and held that suspensions

---

1. 20 U.S.C. § 1415(k); 34 C.F.R. §§ 300.530(b)(1) and .101(a); *see also* Honig v. Doe, 484 U.S. 305, 325 (1988).

2. *E.g.*, Hayes v. Unified School Dist. No. 377, 877 F.2d 809 (10th Cir. 1989) ("This case is illustrative of the close relationship between the use of discipline and in-class instruction in providing a child with a 'free appropriate education.'"); *but see* Farrin v. Me. Sch. Admin. Dist. No. 59, 165 F. Supp. 2d 37 (D. Me. 2001) (student's IEP did not provide for special disciplinary measures, only that the student would be held accountable to regular procedures); Armstrong v. Alicante School, 44 F. Supp. 2d 1087 (E.D. Cal. 1999) (drug use is not inextricably intertwined in discipline, drug prevention not supportive intervention service required under IDEA); *see also* 34 C.F.R. § 300.530(g).

3. Letter to James, 44 Individuals with Disabilities Educ. L. Rep. (LRP) 256 (OSEP 2005); Letter to Anonymous, 30 Individuals with Disabilities Educ. L. Rep. (LRP) 978 (OSEP 1997).

4. Beth R. v. Forrestville Valley Community Unit School, 375 F.3d 603 (7th Cir. 2004) (district's behavioral intervention plan satisfied IDEA's substantive and procedural requirements); Lessard v. Wilton-Lyndeborough Co-op. School Dist., Slip Copy, 2007 WL 1221103 (D.N.H. 2007).

5. *Id* (disruptive impact that student had on other students is relevant consideration in deciding whether he received an appropriate education).

6. 34 C.F.R. § 300.324(a)(2)(i); *see also* 20 U.S.C. § 1414(d)(3)(B)(i).

7. Honig v. Doe, 484 U.S. 305 (1988).

8. 20 U.S.C. § 1415(k)(4)(A).

from school for longer than 10 days constitute a change in placement. Absent agreement of the parents, the Court held, this change in placement is subject to all the protections associated with other placement changes. This principle has been codified.[9]

In *Honig*, the Supreme Court found the stay-put provision unequivocal: during pendency of proceedings initiated under IDEA, "the child *shall* remain in the then-current educational placement."[10] Congress intended to strip schools of unilateral authority to exclude disabled children from school. No "dangerousness exception" was to be added to the statute. A school, however, may use normal procedures for dealing with children who endanger themselves and others. The Court listed the following alternative procedures:

- Study carrels
- Time outs[11]
- Detention
- Restriction of privileges
- Suspension up to 10 days

In exceptional cases, the school system's hands are not completely tied. As the Court stated in *Honig*:

> And in those cases in which the parents of a truly dangerous child adamantly refuse to permit any change in placement, the 10-day respite gives school officials an opportunity to invoke the aid of courts under § 1415(e)(2)[now (j)] which empowers courts to grant any appropriate relief.... The burden of proof in such cases, of course, rests with the school to demonstrate the futility or inadequacy of administrative review.... Nor do we think that § 1415(e)(3) [now (j)] operates to limit the equitable powers of district courts such that they cannot, in appropriate cases, temporarily enjoin a dangerous disabled child from attending school.[12]

Subsequent to *Honig*, school systems have been successful in seeking preliminary injunctions excluding children from school pending the administrative determination of the change in placement questions.[13] It should be kept in mind, however, that the Court

---

9. 34 C.F.R. §§ 300.530–.537; previously 34 C.F.R. §§ 300.519–.529.

10. 20 U.S.C. § 1415(k)(4)(A); *see generally*, CP v. Leon County Sch. Bd., 466 F.3d 1318 (11th Cir. 2006) (stay-put requires district to maintain then current educational placement without updating the IEP); Johnson v. Special Educ. Hearing Office, State of Cal.287 F.3d 1176 (9th Cir. 2002) (stay put" provision, the current educational placement is typically the placement described in the child's most recently implemented IEP); Spilsbury v. District of Columbia, 307 F. Supp. 2d 22 (D.D.C. 2004); placement for purposes of stay-put provision, is students' placement immediately before proposed change and includes all services needed, not mere physical location).

11. *See also* Hayes v. Unified School Dist. No. 377, 877 F.2d 809 (10th Cir. 1989) (time out and in-school suspension not a change in placement); Chicago (IL) Pub. Schs., 45 Individuals with Disabilities Educ. L. Rep. (LRP) 227 (OCRV, Chicago 2005) (14 days in ISS with all services not a change in placement).

12. Honig, 484 U.S. at 327.

13. *E.g.*, Texas City Indep. School Dist. v. Jorstad, 752 F. Supp. 231 (S.D. Tex. 1990) (psychotic behavior endangered other students); Board of Educ. of Township High School Dist. No. 211 v. Kirtz-Imig, 16 Educ. Handicapped L. Rep. (LRP) 17 (N.D. Ill. 1989) (court applied five factors identified in determining that preliminary injunction should issue excluding student from school pending administrative process: irreparable injury to plaintiff; lack of adequate remedy at law; likelihood of success on merits; balancing harms; public interest. Student was violent, threatening to kill students and faculty); *see also* Light v. Parkway c-2 School District, 41 F.3d 1223 (8th Cir. 1994) (child with multiple mental disabilities substantially likely to injure others); Webster Groves School Dist. v. Pulitzer Pub. Co., 898 F.2d 1371 (8th Cir. 1990) (court may exclude press from hearing seeking preliminary injunction suspending student); Alex G. v. Bd. of Trs., 387 F. Supp. 2d 1119 (D.

in *Honig* spoke of a "temporary" injunction. Following the temporary injunction, the administrative proceedings must still be used to determine the underlying merits of the school's change in placement.[14]

The schools also have options other than injunctive relief to manage disruptive students. A student who brings a weapon to school or a school function, or who sells or uses illegal drugs, may be placed in an interim alternative educational placement for up to 45 days. A school may also request an expedited hearing and seek placement in an alternative program for up to 45 days if the student is substantially likely to injure himself or others.[15]

Honig dealt with a case where there was an accepted connection between the disruptive behavior and the child's disability.[16] In the absence of that connection, may the school indefinitely suspend the child receiving special education services? Courts uniformly held that absent the causal connection there is no basis for treating the disabled child any differently than the nondisabled child.[17] Subsequent amendments codify this interpretation.

The LEA must conduct a manifestation determination review (MDR) to decide whether there is a causal connection. The review must be conducted within 10 days of any decision to change the placement based on the violation of the student conduct code.[18] If it is determined that the behavior is not a "manifestation of the disability," the relevant disciplinary procedures applicable to children without disabilities may be applied to the child in the same manner they are applied to children without disabilities.[19]

While in the absence of a causal connection or direct and substantial relationship between the child's disability and the behavior, the child can be suspended or expelled, and educational programming must still be provided. Historically, the courts were split on whether any obligation existed. The Fifth Circuit, for example, held that complete suspension of instruction was not permitted, even if there was no causal connection and the student was properly suspended.[20] The Ninth Circuit, however, held that, at least with regard to students whose disability was not causally connected to the reason for the suspension, the school was permitted to terminate all services for a properly expelled student.[21] The regulations make it clear that even if

Cal. 2005) *citing Light v. Parkway c-2 School District* with approval); Walton Central School District v. Kirk, 28 Individuals with Disabilities Educ. L. Rep. (LRP) 597 (N.D.N.Y. 1998) (*Honig* injunction granted).

14. Honig, 484 U.S. at 327; *see* Letter to Eldridge, 30 Individuals with Disabilities Educ. L. Rep. (LRP) 543 (1998).

15. 34 C.F.R. §§ 300.530 and .532(c); *see also* § 10.4.

16. As Justice Brennan framed the issue, "[W]e must decide whether, in the face of this statutory proscription, state or local school authorities may nevertheless unilaterally exclude disabled children from the classroom for dangerous or disruptive conduct growing out of their disabilities." Honig, 484 U.S. at 308.

17. Doe v. Maher, 793 F.2d 1470 (9th Cir. 1986), *aff'd and modified on other grounds sub nom.* Honig v. Doe, 484 U.S. 305 (1988); School Bd. of Prince William County v. Malone, 762 F.2d 1210 (4th Cir. 1985); S-1 v. Turlington, 635 F.2d 342 (5th Cir. 1981); Doe v. Koger, 480 F. Supp. 225 (N.D. Ind. 1979).

18. 34 C.F.R. § 300.530(e); *see also* 20 U.S.C. § 1415(k)(1)(E). Keep in mind that the manifestation review is only required when the suspension exceeds 10 days.

19. Wilson v. Fairfax County School Bd., 372 F.3d 674 (4th Cir. 2004) (student's Attention Deficit Hyperactivity Disorder (ADHD) did not cause misconduct, permitting school to discipline him as it would have any other student).

20. S-1 V. Turlington, 635 F.2d 342, 348 (5th Cir. 1981); *see also* Lamont X. v. Quisenberry, 606 F. Supp. 809, 815 (S.D. Ohio. 1984).

21. Doe v. Maher, 793 F.2d 1470, 1482 (9th Cir. 1986), *aff'd on other grounds sub nom.* Honig v. Doe, 484 U.S. 686 (1988).

there is no causal connection or direct and substantial relationship between the child's disability and the behavior, a FAPE must be provided to all eligible children with disabilities between three and 21 inclusive, including those who have been suspended or expelled.[22]

For purposes of a FAPE, children with disabilities who have been suspended or expelled from school are children who have been removed from their current educational placement for more than 10 school days in a given school year.[23] An issue that existed after *Honig* involved the situation where the child is subjected to repeated suspensions, each of which is shorter than ten days, but which over the school year accumulated to more than 10 days.[24]

Federal regulations now make it clear that a change in placement occurs for disciplinary reasons if the child is moved for more than 10 consecutive days[25] or if the child is subjected to a series of removals that constitute a pattern that accumulates to more than 10 days. The factors to consider determining whether such a pattern exists include the whether the child's behavior is substantially similar to the child's behavior in previous incidents resulting in a series of removals and the length of removal, total amount of time the child was removed, and the proximity of the removals to one another.[26]

10.2 Changes in Placement

A change in placement is defined as the child's removal from the current educational placement for more than 10 consecutive school days.[27] A change in placement may also occur when a child is subjected to a series of removals constituting more than 10 school days. To determine whether a series of removals constitutes a change in placement, consideration is given to the similarity of the child's previous behavior resulting in removals, the length of each removal, the total amount of time the child is removed, and the proximity of the removals to one another.[28]

The parents must be provided with notice and a copy of procedural safeguards on the date a decision is made to change the child's placement.[29]

---

22. 34 C.F.R. § 300.101; *see also* 20 U.S.C. § 1412(a)(1).
23. 34 C.F.R. § 300.530; *see also* 20 U.S.C. § 1412(a)(1); OSEP Memorandum 97-7, 26 Individuals with Disabilities Educ. L. Rep. (LRP) 981 (1997) (before imposing a short term suspension on a student with a disability, districts are not required to conduct manifestation determinations or functional behavioral assessments).
24. *See, e.g.*, In Christopher W. v. Portsmouth School Committee, 877 F.2d 1089 (1st Cir. 1989) (student was frequently suspended and sought injunction against future suspensions; court denied in part on the theory that *Honig* did not apply because the injunction sought was a permanent injunction, not a preliminary injunction pending resolution of administrative proceedings).
25. 34 C.F.R. § 300.519(a); *see also* 20 U.S.C. § 1415(k)(1)(E).
26. 34 C.F.R. § 300.536(2); Letter to Eldridge, 30 Individuals with Disabilities Educ. L. Rep. (LRP) 543 (1998) (IDEA does not impose a limitation on number of suspensions which are less than 10 days and which can be imposed in the same school year for separate incidents of misconduct, provided there is not a series of removals that constitutes a change of placement).
27. 34 C.F.R. § 300.536(a); *see also* 20 U.S.C. § 1415(k).
28. 34 C.F.R. § 300.536.
29. 34 C.F.R. § 300.536(h).

10.3 Provision of a FAPE for Suspended or Expelled Student

Schools may remove an eligible child with a disability from the current educational placement for 10 school days or less in a single school year and are not required to provide educational services, as long as such removals are applied equally to students without disabilities.[30]

If the child with disabilities is removed multiple times for more than 10 days in a school year, even if the individual removals do not constitute a change in placement, the school has an obligation to provide services. The services must enable the child to progress in the general curriculum and advance to meet the IEP goals.[31] The decision regarding which services are to be provided can be made by school personnel in consultation with one of the child's teachers.[32]

If the school is considering removing a child for disciplinary reasons for more than 10 days, a manifestation determination review (MDR) is required.[33] Even if the determination is that the behavior is not a manifestation of the disability, the child must continue to receive a FAPE. Again, the child is required to receive services which will enable the child to progress in the general curriculum and advance toward the IEP goals. The IEP team, however, decides the appropriate services that will be provided at a formal meeting.[34] The services required to enable the child to progress in the general curriculum and to advance towards achieving the IEP goals are not identified in the regulations.

10.4 Functional Assessment

Regardless of whether the IEP team has determined that the behavior was a manifestation of the child's disability, a functional assessment to address behavioral intervention services may be required, when the child is removed to an interim educational placement for 45 days for either possessing weapons, illegal drugs or inflicting serious bodily harm.[35] This behavioral assessment and its interventions are developed to ad-

---

30. 34 C.F.R. § 300.101; 20 U.S.C. § 1412(a)(1); *see also* §§ 300.519–.529; Letter to Zirkel, 31 Individuals with Disabilities Educ. L. Rep. (LRP) 138 (OSEP 1999) (clarifies timelines regarding suspension/expulsions under 1997 IDEA). Generally, a district may suspend *any* student, disability or not, for less than 10 days while providing only minimal procedural safeguards. To suspend a child for less than 10 days, a child is only entitled to oral or written notice of the charges against him, and if he denies them, an explanation of the evidence the authorities have, and an opportunity to present his side of the story. Martin v. Shawano-Gresham Sch. Dist., 295 F.3d 701 (7th Cir. 2002) *citing* Goss v. Lopez, 419 U.S. 565 (1975). Some states offer more procedural protections to students facing short-term suspensions. For instance, New York law provides parents with the opportunity for an informal conference with school personnel and if the contemplated suspension is to be for more than 5 days then the child is entitled to a fair hearing. N.Y. Educ. Law 3214 (3)(b)&(c); 8 NYCRR 100.2(l)(4).
31. 34 C.F.R. § 300.530.
32. 34 C.F.R. § 300.530
33. 34 C.F.R. § 300.530(e); *see also* 20 U.S.C. § 1415(k)(1)(E).
34. 34 C.F.R. § 300.530
35. 20 U.S.C. § 1415(k)(D)(G).

dress the behavior and prevent its recurrence.[36] If the disciplinary action constitutes a change in placement and the IEP team makes a decision that the child's behavior was a manifestation of the disability, and a functional behavior assessment plan does not already exist, one must be developed. The IEP team must convene within 10 school days to develop a functional behavioral assessment.[37] The IEP team must also meet to develop a behavior intervention plan and to implement the appropriate interventions.[38]

If a child's functional assessment has already been conducted and the IEP already contains a behavior intervention plan, the IEP team must meet to review the behavior plan and modify it as necessary.[39]

10.5 Interim Alternative Placement — Weapons, Drugs and Bodily Harm

If the child carries a weapon, knowingly possesses or uses illegal drugs, or sells or solicits the sale of illegal drugs at school or at a school function, or inflicts serious bodily harm on another person while at school or at a school function, an interim alternative placement may be appropriate.[40] The district may place the student in an alternative setting for the same amount of time that a child without a disability would be subject to discipline for the same infraction but not to exceed 45 days.[41]

---

36. 34 C.F.R. § 300.530(d)(ii).

37. 34 C.F.R. § 300.530).

38. 34 C.F.R. § 300.530; *see* Letter to Osterhout, 35 Individuals with Disabilities Educ. L. Rep. (LRP) 9 (OSEP 2000) ("The obligation to conduct a functional behavioral assessment or to review an existing behavioral intervention plan is not linked only to situations that constitute a change of placement ... It is essential for LEAs to take appropriate steps to address behavior that interferes with learning ... regardless of whether the behavior could result in a change in placement."); Letter to Anonymous, 30 Individuals with Disabilities Educ. L. Rep. (LRP) 707 (OSEP 1998) (positive behavioral intervention plans are key for children whose disability has behavioral components); *See also* H. Rutherford Turnbull, III, Brennan L. Wilcox, Ann P. Turnbull, Wayne Sailor, Donna Wickham, IDEA, Positive Behavioral Supports, And School Safety, 30 J.L. & Educ. 445 (July 2001) (contains a good discussion of behavioral supports).

39. 34 C.F.R. § 300.530(f).

40. 34 C.F.R. § 300.530(g)(i–iii). In *Farrin v. Maine Sch. Admin. Dist. No. 59*, 165 F. Supp. 2d 37 (D. Me. 2001) the court held:

> A child with a disability caught bringing drugs to school may be subject to the following disciplinary measures. First, he may be immediately suspended from school, without alternative educational services, for up to ten days. Second, he may serve an additional forty-five day suspension, during which time the school must provide him with alternative educational services. Third, in addition to or in place of the forty-five day suspension under the IDEA, he may be suspended or expelled from school under generally applicable school disciplinary rules, provided his behavior was not a manifestation of his disability. Note that there is the possibility of overlap between the IDEA's forty-five day suspension provisions and generally applicable school rules. The functional difference between the two disciplinary measures (aside from their duration) is largely semantic, however, due to the procedural protections in place for children with disabilities who are removed from school for more than ten days. (internal citations omitted).

See generally, Letter to James, 44 Individuals with Disabilities Educ. L. Rep. (LRP) 256 (OSEP 2005) (IDEA 2004 provides districts more flexibility when disciplining students with disabilities).

41. 34 C.F.R. § 300.530(g).

The same requirements for conducting a functional assessment and behavioral intervention plan apply to the 45 calendar day interim alternative placement as for the regular disciplinary removal lasting more than 10 days.[42]

The appropriate interim alternative educational placement is determined by the IEP team and must enable the child to continue to participate in the general curriculum, although in another setting.[43] The placement must also enable the child to continue to receive those services and modifications, including those on the IEP, that will enable the child to meet the goals in the IEP. There must also be modifications to the IEP addressing the behavior that triggered the action so that it does not recur.[44]

The school district may also petition a due process hearing officer to order placement into an appropriate interim alternative education setting for 45 days or less.[45] The hearing officer may order this 45-day placement if the hearing officer determines that the district has shown that maintaining the current placement is substantially likely to result in injury to the child or others.[46] The interim removal may be less than the entire 45 days.

10.6 Manifestation Determination Review

A "manifestation determination review" (MDR) is held to determine if the conduct is caused by or had a direct or substantial relationship to the student's disability or if the conduct is a direct result of the LEA's failure to implement the IEP.[47] An MDR must be held where a child's behavior is a violation of the conduct code and involves a change in placement for more than 10 school days, where injury is likely to occur to the child or others, or where disciplinary action is contemplated for a drug or weapons offense.[48] Furthermore, the Office of Special Education Programs has stated, "Part B does not require that a manifestation determination review occur when a disciplinary removal is being considered; rather, the requirement to conduct the manifestation review determination is triggered on the date that the decision is made to implement a removal that constitutes a change of placement.[49]

The parents of the child must be notified of their rights prior to the action being taken. The IEP team and other qualified personnel shall convene to conduct and review the relationship between the child's disability and the behavior subject to the discipli-

---

42. 34 C.F.R. §§ 300.530(d)(1)(i)(ii) and (f)(i).

43. 20 U.S.C. § 1415(k)(1)(D)(i); 300.530(d)(1)(i); Farrin v. Me. Sch. Admin. Dist. No. 59, 165 F. Supp. 2d 37 (D. Me. 2001) (no hard-and-fast rule as to what specific educational services need to be provided in an alternative setting); Letter to Anonymous, 30 Individuals with Disabilities Educ. L. Rep. (LRP) 604 (OSEP 1998).

44. 20 U.S.C. § 1415(k)(1)(D)(ii); 300.530(d)(1)(ii).

45. 34 C.F.R. § 300.532(b)(ii); *see generally,* Letter to James, 44 Individuals with Disabilities Educ. L. Rep. (LRP) 256 (OSEP 2005).

46. 34 C.F.R. § 300.532(b)(2)(i); Letter to Suratt, 30 Individuals with Disabilities Educ. L. Rep. (LRP) 614 (OSEP 1998).

47. 34 C.F.R. § 300.530(e); *see also* 20 U.S.C. § 1415(k)(1)(H).

48. 34 C.F.R. § 300.530(e); *see also* 20 U.S.C. § 1415(k)(1)(H).

49. Letter re: Oregon Dep't of Educ., 43 Individuals with Disabilities Educ. L. Rep. (LRP) 249 (OSEP 2005).

nary action.[50] An MDR meeting is also required for a child placed in a 45-day interim alternative setting for drug or weapons violations.[51]

The MDR team must meet within 10 school days of the decision to change the placement to the interim placement.[52] The team, in conducting the manifestation reviews, must consider all information from the school and the parent relevant to the child's behavior, including teachers' observations of the child, and the child's IEP.[53] The team must find that the behavior is a manifestation of the child's disability if it is determined that the IEP was not implemented or the conduct was caused by or had a direct or substantial relationship to the student's disability.[54] If the finding is that the IEP was not implemented, the parent and the IEP team must take immediate steps to correct the deficiencies.[55]

If the child is in a 45-day interim alternative educational placement for drugs or weapons, the school can continue to maintain the child in the placement even if there is a finding that the behavior was not a manifestation of the child's disability.[56] The MDR team may determine that the behavior was not a manifestation of the disability if the team determines that the IEP was implemented or the conduct was not caused by or did not have a direct or substantial relationship to the student's disability. [57]

If the team determines that the behavior was not a manifestation of the disability, then the relevant disciplinary procedures applicable to children without disabilities may be applied to the child. There are, however, a few exceptions. The child must receive educational services to enable him or her to continue to participate in the general education curriculum although in a different setting and to progress in meeting those goals when the disciplinary action results in a change in their placements exceeding 10 days. The child must also continue to receive services when the child is removed for guns or weapon possession or if the child inflicts substantial bodily injury. The child will also receive a functional behavioral assessment with interventions if appropriate.[58]

The statute and regulations, however, clearly require a FAPE to be provided to all children with disabilities between three and 21, including those who have been suspended or expelled.[59] The right to a FAPE for children with disabilities who have been suspended or expelled begins on the eleventh day in the school year that they are removed from their current educational placement.[60] Of course, the parent has the right to challenge the determination that there is no causal or direct and substantial connection between the child's behavior and disability through the due process hearing.

---

50. 34 C.F.R. § 300.530(e); Letter to Yudien, 39 Individuals with Disabilities Educ. L. Rep. (LRP) 242 (OSEP 2003) (IDEA scheme does not limit a manifestation determination review only to the disability that served as the basis for the child's eligibility).

51. 34 C.F.R. §§ 300.530(e) .

52. 34 C.F.R. § 300.530(e); Letter to Brune, 40 Individuals with Disabilities Educ. L. Rep. (LRP) 46 (OSEP 2004) (only one manifestation determination review should be held per incident within the required 10 day period.; if new information should arise best practice would be to use it to reexamine student's placement or program).

53. 34 C.F.R. § 300.530(e).

54. 34 C.F.R. § 300.530(g).

55. 34 C.F.R. § 300.530(e)(3).

56. 34 C.F.R. § 300.530(c); *see also* 20 U.S.C. § 1415(k)(4).

57. 34 C.F.R. § 300.530(e).

58. 34 C.F.R. § 300.530(c)(d).

59. 34 C.F.R. § 300.101; *see also* 20 U.S.C. § 1412(a)(1)(A).

60. 34 C.F.R. § 300.530(c).

If the parent requests a hearing to challenge the manifestation determination the child will remain in the current educational placement, unless drug or weapon offenses are involved or a hearing officer determines that the placement will likely result in injury to the child.[61] If the MDR determines that the behavior is related to the disability, the student is not subject to the district's expulsion procedures.[62]

10.7 Parental Appeal — Expedited Due Process Hearing

The parent has a right to an expedited hearing to challenge any decision regarding disciplinary placement changes. The parent, therefore, may challenge a decision that the child's behavior is not a manifestation of the disability or a decision to provide a 45-day interim drug or weapon placement.[63] The hearing officer, in reviewing a manifestation decision, determines whether the school met the substantive requirements of the manifestation determination review.[64]

Injunctive relief under *Honig* is also still available to the schools.[65]

Generally, the procedures for expedited hearings are the same as for regular due process hearings. There are, however, some exceptions. The SEA or LEA must arrange the expedited hearing. The hearing must occur within 20 school days. A hearing officer must make a decision within 10 days after the hearing is held.[66] Hearings which are not expedited must be preceded by a resolution meeting. In an expedited hearing, however, this requirement may be waived by both parties. If the resolution meeting is not waived then it must convene within seven days of the notice of the due process complaint. The expedited resolution meeting will also not be convened if the parents agree to mediation. The due process hearing proceeds if the dispute has not been resolved by the parties within 15 days of the receipt of the complaint.[67] Although the state may develop different procedural rules for expedited hearings, the right to appeal the decision of the hearing officer to state or federal court remains the same.[68]

10.8 Hearing Officer Authority

When it is dangerous to maintain a child in the current educational placement, the hearing officer may order a change to an appropriate interim alternative placement.[69] If the hearing officer determines that the burden is met, the child can be removed to an interim alternative setting for up to 45 days.

---

61. 34 C.F.R. §§ 300.530(g).
62. 34 C.F.R. § 300.530(f)(2); *see also* 20 U.S.C. § 1415(k)(F)(iii).
63. 34 C.F.R. § 300.532(a)(1).
64. 34 C.F.R. § 300.530(e).
65. See § 10.1.
66. § 300.532(c)(2).
67. 300.532(c)(3).
68. 34 C.F.R. § 300.532(c)(5).
69. 34 C.F.R. § 300.532(2)(ii).

10.9 Placements during Appeals

If the child has been placed in a 45-day interim setting because of a drug or weapon offense or because the hearing officer determined the child was dangerous, the child must remain in the interim placement until the 45 days are up, or the hearing officer rules that a removal from the 45-day interim placement is warranted.[70] If the school decides to change the child's placement after the 45 days have expired and there is a proceeding to challenge this change, the child's "stay-put" placement is the child's placement prior to the interim alternative placement (unless the parents and school agree otherwise).[71]

If the school believes that it is dangerous for the child to be returned to the "current" placement (that is, the placement prior to the interim), then the school may request an expedited due process hearing. This expedited hearing process may be repeated as necessary.[72]

10.10 Protections for Children Not Yet Eligible for Special Education and Related Services

If the school has "knowledge" that the child has a disability and the child engages in conduct which warrants disciplinary action, but has not yet been determined eligible, the child may invoke the same protections as a child with a disability.[73]

Knowledge is defined as when a parent has informed the school personnel that the child needs special education,[74] the child's teacher or other LEA personnel express specific written concerns about a pattern of the child's behavior to either the director of special education or to agency personnel who function in a supervisory capacity,[75] or when the parent has requested an evaluation.[76] Knowledge is not imputed when the child's parents have refused to permit an evaluation of the child or the parents has refused services for their child or the child has been found ineligible. [77]

If the school has no knowledge of a suspected disability, the child is subject to ordinary disciplinary measures.[78] If an evaluation is requested during the period that the

70. 34 C.F.R. § 300.532(a)(i)(ii); *see also* 20 U.S.C. §§ 1415(k)(3)(B)(ii).
71. 34 C.F.R. § 300.533; *see also* 20 U.S.C. § 1415(k)(4).
72. 34 C.F.R. § 300.532(a)(3).
73. 34 C.F.R. § 300.527(a); *see also* 20 U.S.C. § 1415(k)(5).
74. 34 C.F.R. § 300.534(b)(1) (concerns must be in writing unless parent is unable to write).
75. § 300.534(b)(3).
76. 34 C.F.R. § 300.534(b)(2); *see* Colven N. v. Lowndes, County School District, 32 Individuals with Disabilities Educ. L. Rep. (LRP) 32 (N.D. Miss. 2000).
77. 34 C.F.R. § 300.534(c)(1)(2); Plumbly v. Northeast Indep. Sch. Dist., Slip Copy, 2006 WL 2469169 (W.D. Tex. 2006) (previously identified student loses IDEA procedural protections when parents agree to end special education services.); *but see,* S.W. v. Holbrook Pub. Schs, 221 F. Supp. 2d 222 (D. Mass. 2002) (pending appeal precludes District from extinguishing student's "stay put" rights after initial determination that the student did not have a learning disability).
78. 34 C.F.R. § 300.534(d).

child is subject to disciplinary measures, the evaluation must be conducted in an expedited manner.[79] The child can be suspended or expelled while the evaluation is being completed.[80] If the child is found to have a disability, then appropriate services shall be provided according to the procedures regarding discipline.

10.11 Referral to and Action by Law Enforcement and Juvenile Courts

A school may report a crime committed by a child with a disability without concern that this will be a denial of a FAPE. When reporting a crime, the school is required, consistent with FERPA requirements, to send the child's special education and disciplinary records to the appropriate authorities.[81]

10.12 Chemical Dependency and Suspension

Children with drug and alcohol dependencies may be eligible for special education and related services under §504.[82] Section 504 imposes requirements on schools similar to those imposed by IDEA. The Americans with Disabilities Act, however, has amended §504 to give broader power to school systems to discipline students currently taking illegal drugs or alcohol.

Under the Americans with Disabilities Act, and the amendments made by it to §504, the school may discipline a student currently taking illegal drugs or alcohol in the same manner as it would discipline a student without a disability.[83] The student may be disciplined regardless of whether there is a causal connection between the disability and their behavior. Likewise, the student may be disciplined regardless of the fact that the student suffers from a disability other than current drug or alcohol abuse.[84] The due process procedures do not apply to such disciplinary actions.[85]

---

79. 34 C.F.R. §300.534(d).

80. 34 C.F.R. §300. 534(d)(2)(ii); *see* Rodiriecus L. v. Waukegan School District No. 60, 90 F.3d 249 (7th Cir. 1996) (although decided before the 1999 regulations, the case provides a useful discussion of principles involved).

81. 34 C.F.R. §§300.535(b)(1)(2), 300.571; *see also* 20 U.S.C. §1415(k)(6).

82. See §5.3.6.

83. 42 U.S.C. §12211 *amending* 29 U.S.C. §705(10); 29 U.S.C. §705(20)(c)(iv); Stearns v. Board of Educ. for Warren Township High School Dist. No. 121, 31 Individuals with Disabilities Educ. L. Rep. (LRP) 134 (OCR 1999) (athlete's eligibility revoked because of alcohol related incidents, not his disability).

84. 42 U.S.C. §12211, *amending* 29 U.S.C. §705(10).

85. 29 U.S.C. §705(20)(c)(iv); 34 C.F.R.§ 104. 36; Tracy (CA) Unified Sch. Dist., 43 Individuals with Disabilities Educ. L. Rep. (LRP) 41 (OCRIX, San Francisco 2004) (district not required to offer 504 procedural protections, including manifestation determination, to student expelled for selling drugs); Tustin (Cal.) Unified School District, 31 Individuals with Disabilities Educ. L. Rep. (LRP) 139 (OCR 1999) (student who violated district drug policy not entitled to manifestation determination review prior to significant change in placement).

10.13 Constitutional Considerations

In addition to *Honig*, the Supreme Court's decision in *Goss v. Lopez*,[86] must be considered in expulsion cases. *Goss v. Lopez* was a landmark Supreme Court decision where the United States Supreme Court held that students facing 10-day suspensions from school for disciplinary reasons have property and liberty interests under the Fourteenth Amendment's due process clause.

> Students facing temporary suspension have interests qualifying for protection of the Due Process Clause, and due process requires, in connection with a suspension of 10 days or less, that the student be given oral or written notice of the charges against him and, if he denies them, an explanation of the evidence the authorities have and an opportunity to present his side of the story.[87]

Furthermore, "[t]here need be no delay between the time 'notice' is given and the time of the hearing."[88] Generally, however, "notice and hearing should precede removal of the student from school."[89] In the context of children with disabilities, such children have a constitutional right to procedural due process independent of the due process rights provided in IDEA.

10.14 Steps to Take in Disciplinary Actions

Under IDEA, the following steps must be followed before disciplinary action that results in a change of placement or exceeds 10 days.

  • Determination by the IEP team and other qualified personnel whether behavior is a manifestation of the disability.

  • The manifestation review must occur no later than 10 days after the date the decision to take action is made.

  • If the behavior is not a manifestation of the disability, normal disciplinary actions may be taken. Alternate educational programming must be provided.

  • If the behavior is a manifestation of the disability, suspension may not exceed 10 days, without a change in placement having occurred.

  • If school seeks to suspend for longer than 10 school days, absent agreement of the parents to the change, procedures for a change in placement must be followed before the suspension for longer than 10 days can begin.

  • If the child is "truly dangerous," agency may seek expedited due process hearing or preliminary injunction excluding the child from school pending administrative determination of necessity to change placement.

---

86. Goss v. Lopez, 419 U.S. 565 (1974); *see also* Waln v. Todd County School Dist.388 F.Supp.2d 994, (D.S.D., 2005).
87. Goss v. Lopez, 419 U.S. 565, 581 (1974).
88. *Id*. at 582.
89. *Id*.

- Under § 504 there must be a reevaluation of the child, unless the child was involved in illegal drug use. Notice of this evaluation must be provided to the parent.
- An IEP meeting must be convened, notice of which must have been provided to the parents.
- If there is a change in placement an IEP team must meet to develop or revise a functional assessment and a behavior plan.
- If parent and school agree, revise IEP.
- If IEP revised, notice must be provided to parent of intent to change placement.
- Placement may then be changed.
- Hearing officer may also order an interim placement for 45 days or less. Manifestation Determination Review (MDR) must be conducted within 10 business days after removal.
- Under IDEA, alternate educational programming must be provided.
- If at any point in the process a disagreement occurs between the parents and the agency, a due process hearing may be initiated.

Chapter 11

Impartial Due Process Hearing

11.1 In General

The state education authority (SEA) is required by both IDEA[1] and § 504[2] to provide an impartial hearing to resolve disputes arising over provision of a free appropriate public education (FAPE). Due process is not available when parents fail to consent to initial services.[3] IDEA is quite detailed in describing the nature of the required hearing. Section 504 regulations, however, do not provide specific details, merely stating the person has the right to an impartial hearing, with the parents' and their counsel's participation.[4] Compliance with IDEA due process requirements meets the § 504 requirement.

Under IDEA, states have the option of providing either a one-tier or two-tier due process hearing procedure. The due process hearing may be conducted by either the SEA or the LEA.[5] If the initial due process hearing is conducted by a public agency other than the SEA, aggrieved parties may appeal to the SEA for an impartial review.[6] Following the SEA decision, the aggrieved party may bring a civil action in either state or federal court within 90 days unless state law provides otherwise.[7]

11.2 Statute of Limitations

The parent or agency must request a due process hearing within two years from the date the requesting party knew or should have known about the alleged issues

---

1. 20 U.S.C. § 1415(b)(6) and(f); 34 C.F.R. § 300.507.
2. 34 C.F.R. § 104.36.
3. Letter to Yudien 38 Individuals with Disabilities Educ. L. Rep. (LRP) 267 (OSEP 2003); (Letter to Cox 36 Individuals with Disabilities Educ. L. Rep. (LRP) 66 (OSEP 2001).
4. Williamson County (TN) School District 47 Individuals with Disabilities Educ. L. Rep. (LRP) 20 (OCRIV 2006) (administrative hearing proper forum for placement decision); Clear Creek (Tex.) Indep. School Dist., 29 Individuals with Disabilities Educ. L. Rep. (LRP) 394 (OCR 1998) (appropriate forum to challenge district's placement decision was due process).
5. 34 C.F.R. § 300.511(b); *see also* 20 U.S.C. § 1415(f)(1); Letter to Greer, 38 Individuals with Disabilities Educ. L. Rep. (LRP) 191 (OSEP 2002) (in state with one tier system, an administrative law judge may conduct the hearings as long using an ALJ does not conflict with state law).
6. 34 C.F.R. § 300.514(b); *see also* 20 U.S.C. § 1415(g).
7. 34 C.F.R. § 300.516; *see also* 20 U.S.C. § 1415(i)(2)(B).

that are the basis for the complaint. If an individual state has a specific statute of limitations for IDEA, that statute is controlling.[8] Therefore, state regulations should be checked.

11.3 Scope of Review

The scope of the impartial due process hearing covers disputes over the identification, evaluation, educational placement, and provision of a FAPE.[9] A hearing is also appropriate to resolve disputes challenging information contained in the child's educational records.[10] These topics cover most of the disputes that arise between parents and educators concerning rights under IDEA, and each will be discussed in turn.

Disputes over identification and evaluation are properly resolved by the due process procedures.[11] For example, where the school system and parents disagree over whether a child has a disability, or agree that the child has a disability but disagree over the appropriate classification of the child, a due process hearing is appropriate to resolve the dispute.[12] Failure to screen children as required,[13] and procedural violations occurring during the identification process are also subject to due process review.[14]

Prior to the initial preplacement evaluation, IDEA requires informed parental consent.[15] IDEA specifically states that, if consistent with state law, the due process or mediation procedures may be used to override parental veto of an initial evaluation or reevaluation.[16] If the parents fail to respond to a request for a reevaluation the school system does not need to get informed consent but must show it has taken reasonable measures to obtain consent. The LEA may seek either a due process determination, me-

---

8. 34 C.F.R. § 300.511(e) and 34 C.F.R. § 300.507(2). *See, e.g.,* Phillips v. Board of Educ. Hendrik Hudson School Dist., 949 F. Supp. 1108 (S.D.N.Y. 1997) (reimbursement denied for due process complaint brought 32, 31, and 17 months after disagreement, defense of latches applies); Inquiry, 17 Educ. Handicapped L. Rep. (LRP) 355 (OSERS 1990) (no specific time limit for due process hearing seeking IEE); *but see,* Couer D'Alene School Dist. No. 271, 35 Individuals with Disabilites Educ. L. Rep. (LRP) 261 (SEA ID 2001) (LEA notice to parents required LEA to request due process hearing within 10 days of IEE request).

9. 34 C.F.R. § 300.507(a)(1); *see also* 20 U.S.C. §§ 1415 (b)(6); Smith v. Special School Dist. No. 1, 184 F.3d 764 (8th Cir. 1999); Thompson v. Board of Educ. of Special School Dist. No. 1, 144 F.3d 574 (8th Cir. 1998) (request for hearing must be made while the student is enrolled in district that was providing the services or before removing the student); M.P. v. Independent School Dist. No. 721, 200 F.Supp.2d 1036 (D.Minn. 2002).

10. 34 C.F.R. § 300.619; *see also* 20 U.S.C. §§ 1412(a)(8) and 1417(c).

11. 34 C.F.R. § 300.507(a); *see also* 20 U.S.C. § 1415b)(6).

12. De Rosa v. City of New York, 557 Educ. Handicapped L. Rep. (CRR) 279 (Sup. Ct. N.Y. 1986); Palos Verdes Peninsula Unified School Dist., 45 Individuals with Disabilites Educ. L. Rep. (LRP) 49 (SEA CA 2005); Federal Way School Dist., 44 Individuals with Disabilites Educ. L. Rep. (LRP) 114 (SEA WA 2005) (no longer eligible for special education); *but see* Charles County Public Schools, 35 Individuals with Disabilites Educ. L. Rep. (LRP) 265 (SEA MD 2001) (ALJ cannot hold due process hearing unless there is a current case or controversy).

13. Case No. SE-45-85, 507 Educ. Handicapped L. Rep. (CRR) 388 (SEA Ill. 1986).

14. Case No. 85-29 and 85-33, 507 Educ. Handicapped L. Rep. (CRR) 265 (SEA Wash. 1985).

15. 34 C.F.R. § 300.300(a); *see also* 20 U.S.C. §§ 1414(a)(1)(D).

16. 34 C.F.R. § 300.300(a)(3)(i); *see also* 20 U.S.C. § 1414(a)(1)(D)(ii)(I); Shelby S v. Conroe Independent School Dist., 454 F.3d 450 (5th Cir. 2006) *cert denied* 127 S.Ct. 936 (2007) (despite a lack of parental consent, school district could compel a medical examination of a special education student where it was necessary for mandated reevaluation purposes).

diation or, if allowed by state procedures, a judicial determination.[17] If the child is schooled at home or placed in a private school by his or her parents at their expense and the parents refuse to respond to a request for or refuse to consent to an evaluation or reevaluation the public agency may not use the due process or mediation procedures to override the parent's refusal.[18] If the parents refuse to respond to a request for or refuse to consent to services the public agency may not use the due process or mediation procedures to override the parents' silence or veto.[19] The public agency does not violate its responsibility under IDEA to provide a FAPE to the student if his or her parents refuse to allow the school to provide special education services.[20]

One of the most litigated areas under IDEA is disagreements over educational placements. Whether a child requires a residential program,[21] or whether a child belongs in a self-contained classroom rather than a regular classroom[22] are appropriate issues to resolve through a due process hearing. There can, however, be a question whether a particular dispute involves a placement determination. For example, it has been held that merely changing the physical location of a child's program does not constitute a change in placement.[23] If there is, however, an allegation that the physical location change also resulted in program changes contrary to the requirements of the IEP, the dispute over the physical move is subject to a due process hearing.[24]

Provision of a FAPE is, of course, central to IDEA, and allegations that the LEA is failing to meet its burden are properly brought under the due process provisions. The many issues affecting the provision of a FAPE which can be resolved in the due process hearing procedure include appropriateness of the student's IEP,[25] whether a child's mis-

---

17. 34 C.F.R. § 300.300.

18. 34 C.F.R. § 300.300(b)(4)(i).

19. 34 C.F.R. § 300.300(b)(3).

20. 34 C.F.R. § 300.300(b)(3)(i).

21. *See, e.g.,* Gagliardo v. Arlington Central School Dist., 489 F.3d 105 (2d Cir. 2007); Independent School Dist. No. 284 v. A.C, 258 F.3d 769 (8th Cir. 2001); Mrs. B. v. Milford Bd. of Educ., 103 F.3d 1114 (2d Cir. 1999); Walczak v. Florida Union Free School Dist., 142 F.3d 119 (2d Cir. 1998); Colin K. v. Schmidt, 715 F.3d 1 (1st Cir. 1983); Abrahamson v. Hershman, 701 F.2d 223 (1st Cir. 1983); Kruelle v. New Castle County School Dist., 642 F.2d 687 (3d Cir. 1981); Lamoine School Committee v. N.S., 353 F. Supp. 2d 18 (D. Me. 2005); Diamond v. McKenzie, 602 F. Supp. 632 (D.D.C. 1985).

22. *See, e.g.,* Colin K. v. Schmidt, 536 F. Supp. 1375 (D.R.I. 1982), *aff'd,* 715 F.2d 1 (1st Cir. 1983).

23. Wilson v. Fairfax County School Bd., 372 F.3d 674 (4th Cir. 2004); *but see Hale v. Poplar Bluffs R-I School Dist.,* 280 F.3d 831 (8th Cir. 2002) (school district's unilateral decision that student, who had received homebound instruction during post-surgical recuperation period, would be provided the same services at school, effected a change in the student's then-current educational placement, in violation of IDEA's stay-put provision). See §§ 8.4, 9.2.3.

24. *Id.*

25. *E.g.,* Van Duyn v. Baker School Dist. 5J, ___ F.3d ___, 2007 WL 2493495(9th Cir. 2007) (material failures to implement IEP constituted violations of IDEA: child did not have to suffer demonstrable educational harm in order to prevail on claim under materiality standard that he was denied services called for by IEP; initial five hour per week shortfall in math instruction was material failure to implement IEP; school district's failure to implement several elements of child's behavior management plan in same way at middle school as at elementary school was not material violation of IEP; school district materially provided child with self-contained classroom); Neosho R-V School Dist. v. Clark, 315 F.3d 1022 (8th Cir. 2003); Houston Independent School Dist. v. Bobby R., 200 F.3d 341 (5th Cir. 2000); Logue v. Shawnee Mission Public School Unified School Dist., No 512, 959 F. Supp. 1338 (D. Kan. 1997); Brown v. District of Columbia Bd. of Educ., 551 Educ. Handicapped L. Rep. (CRR) 101 (D.D.C. 1978); Liberty Local School Dist., 26 Individuals with Disabilities Educ. L. Rep. (LRP) 497 (SEA Ohio 1997) (reimbursement of residential placement ordered be-

conduct is a manifestation of the disability,[26] the need for related services,[27] the need for special transportation requirements,[28] and the need for education beyond the normal school year.[29]

It should be kept in mind, however, that the United States Supreme Court has determined that questions of methodology "are for resolution by the States."[30] Where the parents and school system disagree over the appropriate methodology, and both methodologies will provide educational benefit, the hearing officer must defer to the school authorities.[31] Of course, if the hearing officer finds that the proposed educational methodology does not provide educational benefit, then deference to the school is inappropriate.[32]

---

cause the school district was not providing a FAPE); Menifee Union Elementary School Dist., 26 Individuals with Disabilities Educ. L. Rep. (LRP) 786 (SEA Cal. 1997) (IEP meeting held because district had been denying the student a FAPE by not taking into consideration the student's health problems and absences).

26. 34 C.F.R. § 300.525; see also 20 U.S.C. § 1415(k)(6).

27. Irving Indep. School Dist. v. Tatro, 468 U.S. 883 (1984); Cedar Rapids v. Garrett F., 526 U.S. 66 (1999).

28. See, e.g., District of Columbia v. Ramirez, 377 F. Supp. 2d, 63 (D.D.C. 2005); Hurry v. Jones, 560 F. Supp. 500 (D.R.I. 1983), aff'd in part rev. in part, 734 F.2d 879 (1st Cir. 1984); Kennedy v. Board of Educ., 175 W. Va. 668, 337 S.E.2d 905 (W. Va. 1985).

29. Drennan v. Pulaski County Special School Dist., 458 F.3d 755 (8th Cir. 2006); Battle v. Pennsylvania, 629 F.2d 269 (3d Cir. 1980) (EHA requires extended school year); Phipps v. New Hanover County Bd. of Educ., 551 F. Supp. 732 (E.D.N.C. 1982) (extended school year required under § 504); but see Kenton County School Dist. v. Hunt, 384 F.3d 269 (6th Cir. 2004) (parents failed to establish necessity of ESY; ESY must be necessary to permit the child to benefit from his instruction).

30. Board of Educ. v. Rowley, 458 U.S. 176, 208 (1982).

31. See Blackmon v. Springfield R-XII School Dist., 198 F.3d 648 (8th Cir. 1999); see also Fort Zumwalt School Dist. v. Clynes, 119 F.3d 607 (8th Cir. 1997) ("it is up to the educators to determine the appropriate educational methodology."); Lachman v. Illinois State Bd. of Educ., 852 F.2d 290 (7th Cir. 1988); Abrahamson v. Hershman, 701 F.2d 223, 230–231 (1st Cir. 1983) ("it might be inappropriate for a district court under the rubric of statutory construction to impose a particular methodology upon a state."); Alexander K. v. Virginia Bd. of Educ., 30 Individuals with Disabilities Educ. L. Rep. (LRP) 967 (E.D. Va. 1999) (courts denied payment for Lovaas based instruction); Heather S. v. Niles Township High School Dist. No. 219, 1999 WL 1100931 (N.D. Ill.); Miller v. Board of Educ. of Albuquerque Public Schools, 455 F. Supp. 2d 1286 (D.N.M. 2006) (district was not required to provide Alternative Language Therapy (ALT) to student; decision regarding methodology left to schools); but see T.H. v. Board of Educ. of Palatine Community Consolidated School, 55 F. Supp. 2d 830 (N.D. Ill. 1999) (distinguished Lachman because the school district was advocating a particular methodology, the regional hearing impaired program proposed by the district was considered to be one of the best in the country, and the district presented a number of experts on educating hearing impaired children who could testify to the benefits of the proposed program); County School Bd. of Henrico County, Va. v. R.T., 433 F. Supp. 2d 657 (E.D. Va. 2006) (private school specializing in education of autistic children and utilizing applied behavioral analysis (ABA) theory was an appropriate educational placement, and school board would have to reimburse student's parents for relevant costs associated with that school year).

32. See generally Lachman v. Illinois State Bd. Of Educ., 852 F.2d 290 (7th Cir. 1988); A.W. v. Northwest R-1 School Dist., 813 F.2d 158, 163 (8th Cir. 1987); Mark A. v. Grant Wood Area Educ. Agency, 795 F.2d 52, 54 (8th Cir. 1986); Doe v. Maher, 793 F.2d 1470, 1483 (9th Cir. 1986), aff'd sub nom. Honig v. Doe, 484 U.S. 305 (1988); S.M. v. Board of Educ. of Albuquerque Public Schools 455 F. Supp. 2d 1286 (D.N.M. 2006) (district was not required to provide Alternative Language Therapy (ALT) to student); Taylor v. Board of Educ., 649 F. Supp. 1253, 1258 (N.D.N.Y. 1986); Johnston v. Ann Arbor Pub. Schools, 569 F. Supp. 1502, 1508 (E.D. Mich. 1983); School Bd. of Martin Co. v. A.S., 727 So. 2d 1071 (D.C. App. Fla. 1999) (court reversed ALJ's determination to modify child's IEP because there was no issue of fact that district's program was providing educational benefit).

The parents have the right to an Independent Educational Evaluation (IEE) if they disagree with the school's evaluation *and* the school does not establish that its evaluation is appropriate.[33] The due process hearing is the appropriate forum to seek this determination.

The due process hearing is the appropriate mechanism to resolve disputes concerning allegations of procedural violations, as long as the procedural violation impacts directly on the individual student's educational program.[34] For example, it is appropriate to seek relief in a due process hearing for allegations that the LEA has decided to place a child before development of an IEP.[35]

It has been held, however, that compliance with procedural requirements such as adhering to state timelines for developing IEPs is not a proper subject matter.[36] There are also procedural issues to which the parents are not parties. One such example would be whether the LEA or the SEA is responsible for funding a residential placement ordered by a hearing officer.[37]

It should be stressed, however, that if the procedural violations impact the individual child's right to receive a FAPE, noncompliance is a proper subject matter for the due process hearing. For example, allegations that an LEA failed to abide by a hearing officer's decision are subject to a new due process hearing.[38] If preferred, however, direct judicial intervention is also appropriate, since exhaustion of administrative remedies would be futile given the LEA's refusal to abide by the administrative process.[39] Complaints about the due process system are subject to judicial review.[40]

---

33. See Chapter 6.

34. F.B. v. Napa Valley Unified School Dist., ___ F.3d ___, 2007 WL 2028132 (9th Cir. 2007) (school district's inclusion of teacher, who taught student in kindergarten six years prior, on team, rather than student's current teacher, did not violate IDEA; school district's inclusion of special education teacher who never taught student did not satisfy procedural requirement that team include at least one special education teacher or, where appropriate, at least one special education provider of child; school's violation of procedural requirements of IDEA did not result in the loss of a free appropriate public education); T.S. v. Independent School Dist. No. 54, Stroud, Oklahoma, 265 F.3d 1090 (10th Cir. 2001) (without a claim that free and appropriate public education (FAPE) was deficient, procedural defects were not actionable).

35. Deal v. Hamilton County Bd. of Educ., 392 F.3d 840 (6th Cir. 2004) (school system's predetermination not to offer student intensive applied behavioral analysis (ABA) amounted to procedural violation and deprived student's parents of meaningful participation in IEP); Spielberg v. Henrico County Pub. Schools, 853 F.2d 256 (4th Cir. 1988); *distinguished by* Board of Educ. of Montgomery County v. Brett Y., 155 F.3d 557 (4th Cir. 1998) (unpublished table decision) (interpretive guideline's statement that "no delay is permissible" is plainly inconsistent with the federal regulation's statements that the IEP must be implemented "as soon as possible")

36. Case No. H-0197-86, 508 Educ. Handicapped L. Rep. (CRR) 158 (SEA Cal. 1986).

37. *See* Idea Public Charter School v. District of Columbia, 374 F. Supp. 2d 158, (D.D.C. 2005); Loeffler, 211 Educ. Handicapped L. Rep. (CRR) 275 (EHA Undated); *see also* BSEA Case No. 3838, 502 Educ. Handicapped L. Rep. (CRR) 282 (SEA Mass. 1981).

38. Case No. 84-0149, 507 Educ. Handicapped L. Rep. (CRR) 160 (SEA Mass. 1985).

39. *See generally* Mackey v. Board of Educ. For Arlington Central School, 386 F.3d 158 (2d Cir. 2004); Reusch v. Fountain, 872 F. Supp. 1421 (D. Md. 1994). See discussion § 13.3.

40. D.L. v. Unified School Dist. No. 497, 392 F.3d 1223 (10th Cir. 2004) (district court properly denied relief on IDEA claim based on alleged denial of due process hearing stating, "a claim based on deprivation of [an IDEA] due process hearing ... must be linked with a consequent loss of substantive benefits;" *see generally* Mackey v. Board of Educ. for Arlington Central School, 386 F.3d 158 (2d Cir. 2004) (discussion of remedies for hearing officer violation of timelines); Murphy v. Arlington Cent. Sch. Dist. Bd. of Educ., 86 F. Supp. 2d 354, 367 (S.D.N.Y. 2000); *but see* J.D. v. Pawlet School Dist., 224 F.3d 60 (2d Cir. 2000) (student not entitled to relief based on violation of 45-day decision rule).

Whether a child is a resident of the particular school system can often be disputed, especially where each parent lives in a different jurisdiction. At least one SEA has held that issues of residency are not properly raised at a due process hearing, but are subject to the complaint procedure.[41] The majority view appears to reach a contrary result.[42]

Disputes concerning the contents of records are subject to a hearing held by the public agency, under FERPA rather than under IDEA due process proceedings.[43] The parents or their representatives have a right to examine all records maintained by educational agencies relating to their child.[44] Information found to be "inaccurate, misleading, or otherwise in violation of the privacy or other rights of the child" is to be amended.[45] If the information is not found to require amendment, the parents are entitled to place in the records a statement of disagreement.[46]

11.4 Requesting the Due Process Hearing

The agency to which the due process request is directed is controlled by state law or regulation. If the impartial due process hearing is conducted by the LEA, the request will normally go to the Superintendent of Schools or person of the same job description, or the Board of Education, with a copy to the Special Education Director.

Parents must provide notice to the public agency when the parents want to present complaints regarding any matter relating to the identification, evaluation, placement or provision of a FAPE to their child.[47] This confidential notice request must include the name, address, and residence of the child. It must also contain the school the child attends, a description of the nature of the problem, and, to the extent the parents know, a proposed resolution to the problem.[48] Model forms are required to assist parents in filing a complaint.[49]

In order to move forward with a hearing the notice requirement must be met. The complaint is deemed sufficient unless the party who receives it notifies the hearing officer and the sending party, in writing, that the required information is missing. The no-

---

41. Case No. H-0197-86, 508 Educ. Handicapped L. Rep. (CRR) 154 (SEA Mich. 1986); Brockton Public Schools, 26 Individuals with Disabilities Educ. L. Rep. (LRP) 238 (SEA Mass. 1997).

42. Lewis Cass Intermediate School Dist. v. M.K., 290 F. Supp. 2d 832 (W.D. Mich. 2003) (parent had right to raise "complaint issues" in a due process hearing, and dispute relating to alleged IDEA violations ocurring while students were residents of school district was not rendered moot by students' move outside the district); Case No. SE 84249, 506 Educ. Handicapped L. Rep. (CRR) 371 (SEA Cal. 1984) (parent may either file a complaint or seek due process); *see generally* Pires v. Commonwealth, 78 Pa. Cmwlth. 127, 467 A.2d 79 (1983); Case No. 84-0992, 506 Educ. Handicapped L. Rep. (CRR) 344 (SEA Mass. 1984).

43. 34 C.F.R. §§ 99.22, 300.619; *see also* 20 U.S.C. §§ 1412(a)(8), 1417(c).

44. 34 C.F.R. §§ 99.21, 300.613.

45. 34 C.F.R. § 300.618(a); *see also* 20 U.S.C. §§ 1412(a)(8), 1417(c).

46. 34 C.F.R. § 300.620(B); *see also* 20 U.S.C. §§ 1412(a)(8), 1417(c).

47. 34 C.F.R. § 300.508(a)(1); 20 U.S.C. § 1415(7)(A).

48. 20 U.S.C. § 1415(b)(7)(A); 34 C.F.R. § 300.508(b) and (c).

49. 34 C.F.R. § 300.509; *see also* 20 U.S.C. § 1415(b)(8).

tice must be sent to the hearing officer and opposing party within 15 days of receiving the complaint.[50] Within five days after the hearing officer receives the complaint he or she must decide and notify the parties as to whether the complaint contains the required information.[51] If the complaint is deficient the party may amend the complaint only if the opposing party gives written consent and is also given the opportunity to resolve the due process complaint through a resolution meeting.[52] A party may also amend the complaint when the hearing officer grants permission no later then five days before the dues process hearing begins.[53] If an amended complaint is filed the time lines required under the resolution process start with the amended complaint.[54] Within ten days after the LEA receives the due process complaint, the LEA must send the parents a response.[55] This LEA response must contain an explanation of why the agency proposed or refused to take action, "a description of other options the IEP team considered and the reasons why they were rejected, a description of each evaluation procedure, assessment, record or report the agency used as a basis for the proposed or refused action," and a description of other factors related to the agency's action.[56] The LEA's response does not preclude it from claiming the parent's due process complaint is deficient.[57] A party other then the LEA when responding to the complaint must address the issues raised in the complaint within ten days of its receipt.[58]

The fact that the child is not in a public school does not prohibit requesting a due process hearing. As long as the reason the child is not in the public school is related to an allegation that the LEA is failing to provide a FAPE[59] or failing to provide required services, a due process hearing is appropriate.[60]

For a discussion of whom may request the due process hearing see Chapter 2.[61]

---

50. 34 C.F.R. §300.508(c) and (d).
51. 34 C.F.R. §300.508(d)(2).
52. 34 C.F.R. §300.508(d)(3(i).
53. 34 C.F.R. §300.508(d)(3)(ii).
54. 34 C.F.R. §300.508(d)(4).
55. 34 C.F.R. §300.508(e).This response is required only if the LEA has not sent a prior written notice to the parents.
56. 34 C.F.R. §300.508(e)(i–iv).
57. 34 C.F.R. §300.508(e)(2).
58. 34 C.F.R. §300.508(f).
59. S-1 v. Turlington, 635 F.2d 342 (5th Cir. 1981); *see also* Smith v. Special School Dist. No. 1, 184 F.3d 764 (8th Cir. 1999) (no right after student left district); Thompson v. Board of Educ. of the Special School Dist. No. 1, 144 F.3d 574 (8th Cir. 1998) (request for hearing properly denied when hearing requested after student left district); T.F. v. Special School Dist. of St. Louis County, 449 F.3d 816, 818 (8th Cir. 2006); Fort Zumwalt School Dist. v. Clynes, 119 F.3d 607 (8th Cir. 1997) (court held for school district because student was unilaterally placed in a private school before a due process hearing was held to challenge the IEP); Benjamin v. Greater Clark County Schools 458 F. Supp. 2d 845 (S.D. Ind. 2006) (parents unilaterally moved student from public school after initiating administrative review proceedings and therefore not entitled to reimbursement for period between student's removal and date of Independent Hearing Officer's (IHO's) decision in their favor); Bernard v. School Bd. of City of Norfolk, 58 F. Supp. 2d 669 (E.D. Va. 1999) (parents can bring action of deceased child to challenge IEP).
60. K. v. Independent School Dist. No. 721, 326 F.3d 975 (8th Cir. 2003) (parents' failure to exhaust administrative remedies precluded them from recovering compensatory educational services from school district after child began attending school in new district). See §§8.10–8.10.1
61. Yates v. Charles County Bd. of Educ. 212 F. Supp. 2d 470 (D.Md. 2002) (school board had standing to request due process hearing).

11.5 The Resolution Process

Within fifteen days of receipt of the due process complaint filed by a parent, the LEA must conduct a resolution meeting to try and resolve the disagreements.[62] The parents and relevant IEP team members, as well as an LEA representative who can make agency decisions, must be included in the resolution meeting.[63] The LEA's attorney is not permitted to attend, unless the parents bring their attorney.[64] The resolution meeting can be waived by both parties or the LEA and the parents can agree to use mediation to resolve their dispute[65]

The LEA has 30 days to resolve the parent's complaint satisfactorily before the due process hearing can be held.[66] The hearing officer has 45 days to render his or her due process decision after the initial 30 day requirement has expired.[67] If the resolution meeting is not waived, or the mediation process used, and the parent does not participate in the resolution meeting, the timeframe for both the resolution meeting and due process hearing will be delayed until the parent participates.[68] The LEA must use reasonable efforts to obtain parental participation in the resolution meeting and if the parent does not attend the LEA may ask the hearing officer to dismiss the complaint.[69] If the LEA does not hold the resolution meeting within fifteen days or refuses to participate in the meeting the parent may ask the hearing office to start the running of the due process hearing timeline.[70]

The 45 days in which a due process decision must be rendered start one day after one of the following situations. The first is if both parties agree to waive the resolution meeting. The second is after the resolution or mediation starts but during the 30 day period the parties agree that a resolution is not possible. The last situation is when both parties have a written agreement to continue to mediate at the end of the 30 day resolution meeting period but one party later decides to withdraw from the mediation.[71] If the dispute is decided in a resolution meeting the parents and a representative of the agency must sign a legally binding document. This agreement is enforceable in any state court of competent jurisdiction or in a United States District Court. The SEA may also have an enforcement mechanism for this type of agreement.[72] This agreement may be voided by either party within three business days of its execution.[73]

---

62. 34 C.F.R. § 300.510(a); *see also* 20 U.S.C. § 1415(f)(1)(B).
63. 34 C.F.R. § 300.510(a)(i); *see also* 20 U.S.C. § 1415(f)(1)(B).
64. 34 C.F.R. § 300.510(a)(i–ii); *see also* 20 U.S.C. § 1415(f)(1)(B); Melrose Public Schools, 46 Individuals with Disabilities Educ. L. Rep. (LRP) 119 (SEA MA 2006) (attorney who was special education administrator can attend meeting when not acting as an attorney even though parents have not brought an attorney).
65. 34 C.F.R. § 300.510(a)(3)(i–ii); *see also* 20 U.S.C. § 1415(f)(1)(B).
66. 34 C.F.R. § 300.510(b); *see also* 20 U.S.C. § 1415(f)(1)(B).
67. 34 C.F.R. § 300.510(b)(2); *see also* 20 U.S.C. § 1415(f)(1)(B).
68. 34 C.F.R. § 300.510(b)(3); *see also* 20 U.S.C. § 1415(f)(1)(B).
69. 34 C.F.R. § 300.510(b)(4); *see also* 20 U.S.C. § 1415(f)(1)(B).
70. 34 C.F.R. § 300.510(b)(5); *see also* 20 U.S.C. § 1415(f)(1)(B).
71. 34 C.F.R. § 300.510(c)(1–3); *see also* 20 U.S.C. § 1415(f)(1)(B).
72. 34 C.F.R. § 300.510(d)(1–2); *see also* 20 U.S.C. § 1415(f)(1)(B).
73. 34 C.F.R. § 300.510(e); *see also* 20 U.S.C. § 1415(f)(1)(B).

11.6 The Hearing Officer in General

IDEA regulations contain only general guidelines on the qualifications of hearing officers. They are designed primarily to ensure the officer's impartiality. In fact, the regulations are written in the negative, indicating who may not be a hearing officer. Specifically, a hearing officer may not be an employee of a public agency responsible for educating the child.[74] Anyone who has a personal or professional interest that would conflict with the obligation to remain impartial is also precluded from serving as a hearing officer.[75]

The regulations point out that a person is not an employee simply because he or she is paid by the public agency to conduct the impartial hearing.[76] Other provisions of the regulations require that the hearing officer have knowledge and abilities in specifically identified areas. These include knowledge of and the ability to understand both the IDEA and its regulations and state statutes as well as their respective regulations regarding IDEA. The hearing officer must also must be aware of and have the ability to understand state and federal court decisions. Lastly, the hearing officer must be able to conduct hearings and write legal opinions according to the standards of legal practice.[77] Each public agency must keep a list, including qualifications, of persons who serve as hearing officers.[78] Parents are entitled to a copy of this list, including qualifications.[79]

Under federal regulations, parents do not have the right to participate in selection of the hearing officer.[80] State law, however, may permit parents to participate in selection of the hearing officer.[81] Of course, they may challenge the selection of an improperly selected or qualified hearing officer. There is no requirement that the hearing officers be evaluated,[82] nor are there guidelines for training the hearing officers.[83]

Any challenge to a hearing officer must be made during the administrative hearing while there is an opportunity to correct the error. For example, a challenge alleging that the hearing officer is an employee of an agency responsible for educating the child, must be made during the administrative hearing.[84]

---

74. 34 C.F.R. §300.511(c)(1)(A); *see also* 20 U.S.C. §1415(f)(3)(A–D); Thomas v. District of Columbia, 2007 WL 891367 (D.D.C. 2007) (court rejects claim that hearing officer was biased and employee of district).

75. 34 C.F.R. §300.511(c)(1)(B); *see also* 20 U.S.C. §1415(f)(3)(A–D); Board of Education of Williamson Central School Dist., 46 Individuals with Disabilities Educ. L. Rep. (LRP) 294 (SEA NY 2006) (parents' evidence failed to establish hearing office bias).

76. 34 C.F.R. §300.511(c)(2); *see also* 20 U.S.C. §1415(f)(3).

77. 34 C.F.R. §300.511(c)(1)(B).

78. 34 C.F.R. §300.511(c)(3); *see also* 20 U.S.C. §1415(f)(3).

79. Matlock v. McElrath, 557 Educ. Handicapped L. Rep. (CRR) 383 (M.D. Tenn. 1986); Salisbury Township School Dist., 26 Individuals with Disabilities Educ. L. Rep. (LRP) 919 (SEA Pa. 1997).

80. Hessler v. State Bd. of Educ., 553 Educ. Handicapped L. Rep. (CRR) 262 (D. Md. 1981), *aff'd on other grounds*, 700 F.2d 134 (4th Cir. 1983).

81. Brimmer v. Traverse City Area Public Schools, 872 F. Supp. 447 (D. Mich. 1994).

82. *See generally* Friedlander Inquiry, 211 Educ. Handicapped L. Rep. (CRR) 463 (OCR 1987).

83. *See generally* Sinclair Inquiry, 211 Educ. Handicapped L. Rep. (CRR) 335 (OCR 1984). State law may have specific requirements for training and evaluation.

84. Colin K. v. Schmidt, 715 F.2d 1 (1st Cir. 1983); H.V. v. York School Dist., 434 F. Supp. 2d 5 (D. Me. 2006) (parents' claim regarding hearing office impartiality was untimely).

11.6.1 Hearing Officer Impartiality

IDEA requires an impartial due process hearing.[85] Who constitutes an impartial hearing officer has been the subject of litigation. Virtually all the reported decisions addressing impartiality deal with the ability of people with a certain status to be hearing officers. The actions of the hearing officer, however, may also be grounds for claiming lack of impartiality. For example, *ex parte* communications between the hearing officer and a witness can affect the impartiality of the hearing officer, resulting in the decision of the officer being held invalid.[86]

IDEA specifically precludes employees of "the state educational agency or the local educational agency involved in the education or care of the child"[87] as hearing officers. The regulations add that anyone having a personal or professional interest that would conflict with his or her objectivity is also disqualified.[88] Officers and employees of an LEA are improper hearing officers.[89] Local school board members are also improper hearing officers, at least for the LEA in which they serve,[90] as are attorneys who represent the LEA.[91]

The more difficult question is where employees or officers of one LEA may act as hearing officers for a different LEA. The United States Department of Education Office of Special Education Programs (OSEP) and its Office for Civil Rights (OCR) have held that it is proper for employees of one LEA to act as hearing officers for another LEA.[92] There have also been administrative determinations to this effect.[93] Where, however, the SEA exercises considerable control over the operations of the LEA such that employees of the LEA also constitute employees of the SEA, such crossover is improper.[94]

Faculties at local private universities are acceptable hearing officers,[95] as are state university employees *not* involved in formulation of state regulations and policy.[96] Where

---

85. Robert J. v. Keller Independent School Dist., 328 F.3d 804 (5th Cir. 2003) (hearing officer was not biased in favor of school district); Donlan v. Wells Ogunquit Community School Dist., 226 F. Supp. 2d 261 (D. Me. 2002) (parents failed to establish any violation of their right to fair and impartial hearing regarding program).

86. Hollenbeck v. Board of Educ., 699 F. Supp. 658 (N.D. Ill. 1988); Letter to Stadler, 24 Individuals with Disabilities Educ. L. Rep. (LRP) 973 (OSEP 1996).

87. 20 U.S.C. § 1415(f)(3)(A); 34 C.F.R. § 300.511(C)(i)(A).

88. 34 C.F.R. § 300.511(c)(i)(B); *see also* 20 U.S.C. § 1415(f)(3)(A).

89. Mayson v. Teague, 749 F.2d 652 (11th Cir. 1984); Kotowicz v. Mississippi State Bd. of Educ., 630 F. Supp. 925 (S.D. Miss. 1986); Matlock v. McElrath, 557 Educ. Handicapped L. Rep. (CRR) 383 (M.D. Tenn. 1986).

90. *See generally* Butte (Mont.) School Dist. #1, 311 Educ. Handicapped L. Rep. (CRR) 70 (OCR 1986); Heldman v. Sobol, 846 F. Supp. 285 (S.D.N.Y. 1994) (school board employees cannot serve as hearing officers until two years after leaving such employment).

91. Allegheny (N.Y.) Cent. School Dist., 257 Educ. Handicapped L. Rep. (CRR) 494 (OCR 1984); West Bend School Dist., 24 Individuals with Disabilities Educ. L. Rep. (LRP) 1125 (SEA Wis. 1996) (school district moved that hearing officer recuse himself because he had represented only parents as an attorney, request denied).

92. Illinois State Bd. of Educ., 257 Educ. Handicapped L. Rep. (CRR) 600 (OCR 1984).

93. Half Hollow Hills Central School Dist., 21 Individuals with Disabilities Educ. L. Rep. (LRP) 406 (SEA N.Y. 1994) (hearing officer could be impartial even though she was an attorney that worked for a firm who represented many school districts and she was an officer of N.Y. State School Board Attorneys Association); Case No. 247, 508 Educ. Handicapped L. Rep. (CRR) 219 (SEA Ind. 1986) (defense attorney in another school district acceptable); Case No. 10112, 501 Educ. Handicapped L. Rep. (CRR) 319 (SEA N.Y. 1979); *but see* Case No. 80-10, 502 Educ. Handicapped L. Rep. (CRR) 336 (SEA R.I. 1980) (state law holds to contrary).

94. Mayson v. Teague, 749 F.2d 652 (11th Cir. 1984).

95. Case No. 291, 508 Educ. Handicapped L. Rep. (CRR) 161 (SEA Pa. July 28, 1986).

the impartial due process hearing is first held at the state level, employees of the SEA, including the head of the SEA are at least presumptively precluded from acting as a hearing officer.[97]

An issue of some interest is whether the LEA can challenge the impartiality of a hearing officer if they are employees of the state. At least one United States District Court, in a challenge to the use of employees of the SEA to conduct the administrative review, held that the impartial administrative review requirement (that the review officer not be an employee of an agency responsible for educating the child) is designed to benefit only the children and their parents, not the LEA. On appeal, the First Circuit indicated that it need not decide the issue, because the LEA had not properly raised its challenge to the hearing officer during the administrative hearings.[98]

11.6.2 Scope of Hearing Officer's Authority

In certain areas, hearing officers have powers that are coextensive with judicial powers. A hearing officer may, for example, order reimbursement of educational expenses incurred by parents who were forced to place a child in a private facility because of the LEA's failure to provide a FAPE.[99]

The party requesting the hearing is limited to the issues raised in the complaint unless the other party permits new issues to be raised at the hearing.[100] The hearing officer is therefore generally limited to approval or disapproval of the issue before him or her, rather than creatively formulating a solution on his or her own.[101] The hearing officer can, for example, decide that a child in public school should be placed in a special day class, but the hearing officer may not require the school system to institute the special class itself. While the LEA must provide the educational services, it could choose to do so with a private contract with an outside organization.[102] Likewise, the hearing officer cannot require a specific teacher to provide related services.[103]

---

96. Mississippi Dept. of Educ., 352 Educ. Handicapped L. Rep. (CRR) 279 (OCR 1986); *see also* Mayson, 749 F.2d 652; Silvio, 439 A.2d 893; Wisconsin Dept. of Pub. Instruction, 352 Educ. Handicapped L. Rep. (CRR) 357 (OCR 1986).

97. Robert M. v. Benton, 634 F.2d 1139 (8th Cir. 1980) (state superintendent may not be hearing officer); East Brunswick Bd. of Educ. v. New Jersey State Bd. of Educ., 554 Educ. Handicapped L. Rep. (CRR) 122 (D.N.J. 1982) (employee of SEA may not conduct hearing). For a discussion of impartiality of state level administrative review officers in general, and the impartiality of SEA employees specifically, see § 12.6.

98. Colin K. v. Schmidt, 715 F.2d 1 (1st Cir. 1983).

99. S-1 v. Spangler, 650 F. Supp. 1427 (M.D.N.C. 1986), *vacated on other grounds,* 832 F.2d 294 (4th Cir. 1987*); but see* Goldstrom v. District of Columbia, 319 F. Supp.2d 5 (D.D.C. 2004) (hearing officer was required to find violation of IDEA before reaching issue of whether reimbursement was warranted); *see also* 20 U.S.C. § 1415(k)(2).

100. 34 C.F.R. § 300.511(d); J.C. v. Vacaville Unified School Dist., 2006 WL 2644897 (E.D. Cal. 2006) (issues admitted and stipulated to on the record were "heard and decided" because admissions made on the record and that all the issues were "decided" because hearing officer's statements were on the record and in her written decision).

101. School Bd. of Martin County v. A.S., 727 So. 2d 1071 (Fla. 1999) (ALJ exceeded his authority by ordering the school board to provide 15 hours of one-to-one therapy).

102. Mayerson Inquiry, 211 Educ. Handicapped L. Rep. (CRR) 384 (EHA 1986).

103. Chattahoochee County Bd. of Educ. v. Tremaine S., 508 Educ. Handicapped L. Rep. (CRR) 295 (SEA Ga. 1987).

There is a split of opinion whether the hearing officer is able to order a specific placement. Some authority, for example, indicates that having determined that the school's proposed placement is inappropriate, the school is still left with the choice of a different appropriate placement. If the specific placement subsequently chosen is felt to be inappropriate, the parents must start the due process proceedings over to determine the appropriateness of this particular placement.[104] The better view appears to be that the hearing officer is not limited to accepting or rejecting the placement proposed by the LEA and may consider placements proposed by the parents.[105] The United States Department of Education's Office of Special Education Programs has taken the position that the hearing officer may consider alternate proposals sought by the parents.[106] The Department of Education's Office for Civil Rights has taken the position that under § 504 the hearing officer must simply accept or reject the school's proposal.[107]

If a child fits within the "dangerousness" exception, the hearing officer has authority to conduct an expedited due process hearing to order an interim alternative placement.[108] The hearing officer cannot order the placement for longer than 45 days,[109] and this expedited hearing process may be repeated as necessary.[110]

While attorneys' fees can be awarded for work done in administrative proceedings, the hearing officer does not have authority to grant those fees. Suit in state or federal court, however, can be brought solely to obtain the attorneys' fees earned as a result of work done at the administrative level.[111]

The only damages available under IDEA are reimbursement for educational expenses and compensatory education.[112] The hearing officer has authority to award both of these types of damages.[113] The hearing officer does not have authority to grant other related types of damages that may be available by way of § 504 or § 1983 actions.[114]

---

104. Davis v. District of Columbia Bd. of Educ., 530 F. Supp. 1209, 1212 (D.D.C. 1982); Hendry County School Bd. v. Kujawski, 498 So. 2d 566 (Fla. Dist. Ct. 1986); *see also* District of Columbia Public Schools, 257 Educ. Handicapped L. Rep. (CRR) 208, 209 (OCR 1981).

105. Diamond v. McKenzie, 602 F. Supp. 632 (D.D.C. 1985); *but see* Hendry County School Bd. v. Kujawski, 498 So. 2d 566 (Fla. Dist. Ct. 1986) (hearing officer exceeded his authority by *sua sponte* ordering a residential placement).

106. Eig Inquiry, 211 Educ. Handicapped L. Rep. (CRR) 174 (EHA 1980).

107. *See, e.g.,* District of Columbia Pub. Schools, 257 Educ. Handicapped L. Rep. (CRR) 208 (OCR 1981) (hearing officer may order residential placement, but not particular school).

108. 34 C.F.R. § 300.532(a) (agency must prove there is a substantial likelihood of injury to the child or others if the child is maintained in the current placement); *See also* Mauclaire v. State of Conn. Dept. of Educ., 397 F.3d 77 (2nd Cir. 2005) (hearing officer has jurisdiction to review safety challenges to IEPs where they related to disabled child's educational placement or provision of free appropriate public education (FAPE), and hearing officer erred in ruling to the contrary).

109. 34 C.F.R. §§ 300.530(g).

110. 34 C.F.R. § 300.532(3). For a fuller discussion of when such a placement is appropriate see Chapter 10.

111. See § 15.3.

112. See § 14.6.

113. *See, e.g.,* L.I. v. Maine School Admin. Dist. No. 55 480 F.3d 1(1st Cir. 2007); Wenger v. Canastota Central School Dist., 979 F. Supp. 147 (N.D.N.Y. 1997) (district accorded some deference to state review officer's decision because expertise in the field of education); Hyde Park Central School Dist. v. Peter C., 21 Individuals with Disabilities Educ. L. Rep. (LRP) 354 (S.D.N.Y. 1994) (SRO had authority to order the district to pay for the IEE); *but see* Sabatini v. Corning-Painted Post Area School Dist., 78 F. Supp. 2d 138 (W.D.N.Y. 1999) (hearing officer's decision to deny compensatory education not given much deference).

114. Case No. H-0157-83, 505 Educ. Handicapped L. Rep. (CRR) 181 (SEA Mass. 1983); Ellsworth Public Schools, 26 Individuals with Disabilities Educ. L. Rep. (LRP) 1084 (SEA Me. 1997)

The hearing officer has the right to order an independent educational evaluation.[115] The hearing officer, however, cannot delegate the outcome of the due process hearing to the IEE team.[116] Although a hearing officer has the authority to fashion a remedy he or she must not delegate it to an IEP team. In *Reid v. District of Columbia*,[117] a hearing officer awarded compensatory education to a disabled student, but "the officer empowered Mathew's IEP team to direct "implementation of the award." The hearing officer specifically directed the IEP team to reduce or discontinue the services when the team believed that the student no longer needed the services or was not benefiting from them. The court reasoned that since the IDEA due process hearings "may not be conducted by an employee of the State educational agency or the local educational agency involved in the education or care of the child," this delegation to the IEP team was prohibited. The court went on to state that since an IEP tem includes "a representative of the local educational agency," presumably an employee, the IEP team would in effect be exercising the hearing officer's authority.[118]

11.6.3 Procedural Rights Related to the Hearing

The parties have the right to be accompanied by counsel and individuals with expertise in the area of children with disabilities.[119] IDEA and supporting regulations provide a detailed list of procedural protections available to the parties in an impartial due process hearing.[120] When either the school or the parent requests a hearing, the school is obligated to provide the parent with information concerning the availability of low cost or free legal assistance.[121] There is no obligation to provide free counsel to the parents,[122] but attorneys' fees are available to the parents if they prevail.[123]

Some states may prohibit the use of lay advocates on unauthorized practice of law grounds. Many jurisdictions, however, allow the use of lay advocates, and IDEA's provision allowing parents to be accompanied by individuals with expertise seems to indicate that Congress contemplated the use of lay advocates. There is nothing, however, that requires a hearing officer to permit lay representation by someone without knowledge of the administrative procedure.[124]

(hearing officer did not have authority to order agencies to fund a placement for child). See Chapter 14.

115. M.T.V. v. DeKalb County School Dist., 446 F.3d 1153 (11th Cir. 2006) (school district the right to reevaluate student by expert of its choice, so district court properly affirmed ALJ's order requiring student to submit to district's reevaluation in order to remain eligible for OHI services).

116. DuBois v. Connecticut State Bd. of Educ., 727 F.2d 44 (2d Cir. 1984); Case No. SE 45-84, 507 Educ. Handicapped L. Rep. (CRR) 111 (SEA Ill. 1984).

117. 401 F3d 516 (D.C. Cir. 2005).

118. *Id* at 526; *see also Board of Educ. of Fayette County, Ky. v. L.M.*, 478 F.3d 307 (6th Cir. 2007) (after state Appeals Board's reversal of hearing officer's award of compensatory education in favor of a more fluid determination of appropriate compensatory education, such determination could not be delegated to the student's IEP team); Diatta v. District of Columbia, 319 F. Supp. 2d 57 (D.D.C. 2004).

119. 34 C.F.R. § 300.512(a)(1); *see also* 20 U.S.C. § 1415(h).

120. 34 C.F.R. § 300.504; *see also* 20 U.S.C. § 1415(d).

121. 34 C.F.R. § 300.507(b); *see also* 20 U.S.C. § 1415(b)(6).

122. Daniel B. v. Wisconsin Dept. of Pub. Instruction, 581 F. Supp. 585 (E.D. Wis. 1984).

123. See Chapter 15.

124. Victoria L. v. District School Bd. of Lee County, 741 F.2d 369 (11th Cir. 1984) (proper to prohibit nonlawyer from representing parent, but allowable to allow lay person to give advice).

Parties also have the right to present evidence, as well as confront, cross examine, and compel attendance of witnesses.[125] The right to present evidence, as with the right to counsel, does not give the parents the right to charge the school system for the costs associated with the witnesses.

Each party must disclose all evaluations and recommendations at least five business days prior to a hearing. Failure to meet this deadline may bar the party from introducing the evidence, unless the other party consents.[126] Failure to object at the time of the hearing will probably constitute a waiver of the rule.[127] The United States Department of Education has also taken the position that the hearing officer may exercise discretion and grant a continuance to allow five days to consider the evidence that was not previously disclosed.[128] It should be kept in mind that the review officer has discretion to allow additional evidence at the state level review, and the judge has the discretion to allow additional evidence if civil suit is filed.[129]

The parties also have the right to obtain a written or electronic verbatim record of the hearing.[130] A written transcript or "at the option of the parents" an electronic transcript must be provided.[131] The amendment, therefore, appears to provide that parents can require a written record of the hearing be provided. The difficulties inherent in using a tape recording for any review of the due process hearing should lead to the conclusion that parents seek a written transcription.

Under §504, the parents have no right to prevent a stenographer hired by the LEA from attending the due process hearing: "[A]ttendance of a court reporter is a reasonable and necessary means for the school district to secure its statutory right to a verbatim record."[132]

The parents are also given the right to have the child who is subject to the hearing be present and to open the hearing to the public.[133] It should be noted that these two rights are solely those of the parents. The LEA has no right to compel the attendance of the child, nor open the hearing to the public.

The parties have the right to "obtain written, or at the option of the parents, electronic findings and decisions" of the hearing officer.[134]

---

125. 34 C.F.R. §300.512(h)(2); *see also* 20 U.S.C. §1415(h)(2); Walled Lake Consolidated School v. Jones, 24 Individuals with Disabilities Educ. L. Rep. (LRP) 738 (E.D. Mich. 1996) (unless consented to by parties, telephone witnesses not permitted).

126. 34 C.F.R. §300.512(a)(3); *see also* 20 U.S.C. §§1415(f)(2)(A) and (B).

127. *See* Board of Educ. of Roosevelt Union Free School Dist., 23 Individuals with Disabilities Educ. L. Rep. (LRP) 748 (SEA N.Y. 1995) (hearing officer erred by not asking plaintiffs if they wanted to exercise their rights to bar evidence based on the five day evidence rule); Case No. 228, 506 Educ. Handicapped L. Rep. (CRR) 135 (SEA Pa. 1984).

128. Steinke Inquiry, 18 Individuals with Disabilities L. Rep. (LRP) 739 (OSEP 1992).

129. 34 C.F.R. §§300.514 and 516; *see* Fayetteville Perry Local School Dist. v. Reckers, 892 F. Supp. 193 (S.D. Ohio 1995); *See also* Nelson v. Southfield Pub. Schools, 148 Mich. App. 389, 384 N.W.2d 423 (1986). For a discussion of the ability to introduce additional testimony see §§12.7, 13.1, and 13.10.

130. 34 C.F.R. §300.512(a)(4); *see also* 20 U.S.C. §1415(h)(4);

131. 20 U.S.C. §1415(h)(4); *see also* Letter to Nelson, 34 Individuals with Disabilities Educ. L. Rep. (LRP) 149 (OSEP 2002) (parents are entitled to receive free copy of transcripts even though time to file appeal has expired).

132. Caroline T. v. Hudson School Dist., 915 F.2d 752, 755–756 (1st Cir. 1990); Houston (Tex.) Indep. School Dist., 25 Individuals with Disabilities Educ. L. Rep. (LRP) 163 (OCR 1996) (hearing was properly conducted even though the parents were not allowed to have a court reporter present).

133. 34 C.F.R. §300.512(c).

134. 34 C.F.R. §300.512(c)(5); *see also* 20 U.S.C. §1415(h).

11.7 Status of Child during Due Process — "Stay-Put" Provision

During the pendency of any administrative or judicial proceedings conducted ... the child shall remain in the then-current educational placement...."[135] The then current placement (stay put placement) generally can be changed if one of the following occurs:

- when the parties agree to a change in placement;
- if the decision of an independent hearing officer is not appealed;
- when a decision is rendered by a state review officer and he or she agrees with the parents' change of placement; or
- when a court renders a final decision.[136]

During the proceedings, stay put of an educational placement is generally interpreted to mean an educational program and not the particular school where the program is located.[137] Therefore, if the child is not receiving special education, and the dispute involves the eligibility of the child to receive those services, the child is to remain in the regular educational program until resolution of administrative and judicial proceedings. If the child's existing program is no longer available, such as if a private school ceases operation, the public agency must provide a comparable placement during the pendency of proceedings.[138]

If the complaint involves the initial enrollment of the student in the public school, the LEA, with the consent of the parents, shall place the student in the public school program until all proceedings have been completed.[139] When a student transfers from

---

135. 20 U.S.C. §1415(j); 34 C.F.R. §300.518(a); *see* Honig v. Doe, 484 U.S. 305, 323 (1988) (change in IEP required before long term suspension); CP v. Leon County School Bd. Florida, 483 F.3d 1151 (11th Cir. 2007) (school board properly complied with "stay-put" provision by maintaining student's current placement through school year, without updating student's individualized education program); Christopher W. v. Portsmouth School Committee, 877 F.2d 1089, 1097 (1st Cir. 1989) (change in IEP required before suspension); DeLeon v. Susquehanna Comm. School Dist., 747 F.2d 149, 151 n.3 (3d Cir. 1984) (presence of related service in IEP determines whether service required by stay-put provision).

136. Board of Educ. of Pawling Central School Dist. v. Schutz, 290 F.3d 476 (2d Cir. 2002); *see also* Hale v. Poplar Bluffs R-I School Dist., 280 F.3d 831 (8th Cir. 2002) (school district's unilateral decision that student, who had received homebound instruction during post-surgical recuperation period, would be provided the same services at school, effected a change in the student's then-current educational placement, in violation of IDEA's stay-put provision); *but see Cone v. Randolph County Schools Bd. of Educ.*, 2006 WL 3000445 (M.D.N.C. 2006) (because Plaintiffs unilaterally chose a private placement, refused to consent to educational services, and made no agreement with the state as to pendent placement, child had no "stay put" placement).

137. Wilson v. Fairfax County School Bd. 372 F.3d 674 (4th Cir. 2004) (transfer was not change in educational placement violating IDEA's "stay-put" provision, because the term "educational placement" as used in the stay-put provision refers to the overall educational environment rather than the precise location in which the disabled student is educated); White v. Ascension Parish School Bd. 343 F.3d 373, 379 (5th Cir. 2003).

138. Weil v. Board of Elementary & Secondary Educ., 931 F.2d 1069 (5th Cir. 1991); Alston v. District of Columbia, 439 F. Supp. 2d 86 (D.D.C. 2006) (district violated IDEA when it failed to enroll handicapped child in substitute residential placement program after closing residential program at which child had been placed pursuant to her individualized education program (IEP), entitling child's parents to a stay put injunction).

139. 34 C.F.R. §300.518(b); *see also* 20 U.S.C. §1415(j).

one school system to another, or from receiving early intervention services under part C, the issue arises as to whether this is an initial enrollment as contemplated under IDEA.[140] If it constitutes an initial enrollment, the LEA need provide only regular educational programming during the pendency of a complaint. If it is not an initial enrollment, that is, initial enrollment is interpreted as referring to initial enrollment in any public school, during the pendency of any dispute, the new LEA is required to continue implementation of the IEP developed by the previous school.[141]

An inter district transfer within the state does not constitute an initial admission, and, therefore, the new LEA is obligated to continue implementation of the preexisting IEP until the LEA adopts the IEP or develops a new one according to procedures.[142] The Department's Office for Civil Rights, however, has taken the position that §504 does not require the receiving school system to implement the IEP developed by the other school system, but that §504 does not preclude its implementation as required under IDEA.[143] Even under IDEA, the LEA is not required under the stay-put provision to continue a private placement in which the parents have unilaterally placed the child.[144]

The District of Columbia Circuit has held that this "stay-put" provision only applies during the pendency of the due process hearing, state level review, and trial court. Specifically, the stay-put requirement does not require the school system to maintain the current educational placement while the parents seek to appeal an adverse trial court determination. In *Andersen v. District of Columbia*,[145] the court held that the statute speaks only of proceedings through the trial level, not the appellate level. This interpretation, the court held, was also consistent with the Supreme Court's decision in *Honig v. Doe*[146] where the Court stated that the intent of the provision was to keep schools from unilaterally moving children, not "to limit or preempt the authority conferred on courts...."[147]   More recent decisions have reached the conclusion that the

140. E.P. v. School Bd. of Broward County, 483 F.3d 725 (11th Cir. 2007) (IDEA did not provide for continued provision of services to the students pursuant to IFSP after turned three); *but see*, Pardini v. Allegheny Intermediate Unit, 420 F.3d 181 (3rd Cir. 2005) (IDEA's stay-put provision mandated continuation of services for student with IFSP).

141. Johnson v. Special Educ. Hearing Office, State of Cal., 287 F.3d 1176 (9th Cir. 2002) (education agency was not required under the stay-put provision of IDEA to provide the child with exact same program he had received under his IFSP, but services were comparable).

142. 34 C.F.R. §300.32320 U.S.C. §1414(d)(2); Casey v. St. Anne Community High, 400 F.3d 508 (7th Cir. 2005) (no distinction existed between combined school district's stay-put obligations under IDEA and those of separate school districts); Board of Educ. of Community H.S. Dist. No. 218 v. Illinois State Bd. of Educ., 103 F.3d 545 (7th Cir. 1996) (student's current educational placement was the higher level of the original private program); Henry v. School Administrative Unit #29, 70 F. Supp. 2d 52 (D.N.H. 1999) (moving child from private middle school to public high school when he became too old for middle school fundamentally altered child's education placement, thus entitling parents to stay-put injunction); Hill v. School Bd. of Pinelles County, 954 F. Supp. 251 (M.D. Fla. 1997) (school district must continue student's existing IEP while student moved from a high school outside the district to one inside the district); Campbell Inquiry, 213 Educ. Handicapped L. Rep. (CRR) 265 (EHA 1989); Rieser Inquiry, 211 Educ. Handicapped L. Rep. (CRR) 403 (EHA 1986).

143. OCR Memorandum, 307 Educ. Handicapped L. Rep. (CRR) 15 (OCR July 7, 1989).

144. Joshua B. v. New Trier Township High School Dist. 203, 770 F. Supp. 431 (N.D. Ill. 1991).

145. 877 F.2d 1018 (D.C. Cir. 1989).

146. 484 U.S. 305 (1988).

147. Anderson, 877 F.2d at 1024; *see also* Manchester School Dist. v. Williamson, 17 Educ. Handicapped L. Rep. (LRP) 1 (D.N.H. 1990).

pendency provision continues throughout the appellate process or until the dispute is ultimately resolved.[148]

If the child is placed in an interim alternative setting for carrying a weapon, possessing drugs, or being dangerous, the current placement, or "stay-put" placement, is the interim.[149] If the public agency decides to change the 45-day placement after it expires and if the parent challenges the proposed placement, the "stay-put" reverts back to the placement where the child was prior to the interim placement.[150] If the school determines that it is dangerous for the child to be returned to the current placement, an expedited hearing may be requested.

11.8 Discovery

No provision is made under IDEA or its regulations for formal discovery, such as are found in the Federal Rules of Civil Procedure.[151] IDEA's extensive procedural protections, including the right to have access to records, however, provide considerable means for the parents to acquire information. For example, the LEA must provide the "opportunity for the parents of a child with a disability to examine all records relating to such child."[152] The agency is to respond to a request without unnecessary delay, but in no event more than 45 days after the request, or before any meeting regarding the IEP, identification, evaluation, or placement of the child.[153] This right includes the right to make copies,[154] and have a representative, such as an attorney, inspect and review the records.[155] The LEA may charge a fee for copying documents, but may not charge a fee to search and retrieve the documents.[156]

In addition to providing the records, the LEA must provide reasonable explanations and interpretations of the records. This requirement itself provides a fruitful source of information concerning the LEA's position in a dispute.

---

148. *See generally* Pardini v. Allegheny Intermediate Unit, 420 F.3d 181 (3d Cir. 2005) (held that IDEA's stay-put provision mandated continuation of services); Ringwood Bd. of Educ. v. K.F.J. 469 F. Supp. 2d 267 (D.N.J. 2006) (held that continuation of tuition and transportation payments were required under "stay put" provision of Individuals with Disabilities Act (IDEA).

149. 20 U.S.C. § 1415(k)(4).

150. 34 C.F.R. § 300.533; *see also* In re: Theodor A., 26 Individuals with Disabilities Educ. L. Rep. (LRP) 1090 (Iowa 1997) (student should not remain in school during pendency of proceedings because he was not previously identified as needing special educational services and school had no reason to believe he needed services); Rodiriecus L. v. Waukegan School Dist., No 60, 24 Individuals with Disabilities Educ. L. Rep. (LRP) 563 (7th Cir. 1996). See Chapter 10 for a discussion of discipline.

151. Encinitas Union School Dist., 31 Individuals with Disabilities Educ. L. Rep. (LRP) 198 (SEA Cal. 1999) (hearing officer allowed school to subpoena documents relevant to FAPE); Epsom School Dist., 31 Individuals with Disabilities Educ. L. Rep. (LRP) 120 (SEA N.H. 1999) (hearing dismissal as result of parent's failure to comply with discovery order).

152. 34 C.F.R. § 300.613(a); *see also* 20 U.S.C. § 1415(b)(1).

153. 34 C.F.R. § 300613(a); *see also* 20 U.S.C. §§ 1412(a)(8), 1417(c).

154. 34 C.F.R. § 300.613(b)(2); *see also* 20 U.S.C. §§ 1412(a)(8), 1417(c).

155. 34 C.F.R. § 300.613(b)(3); *see also* 20 U.S.C. §§ 1412(a)(8), 1417(c).

156. 34 C.F.R. § 300.617; *see also* 20 U.S.C. §§ 1412(a)(8), 1417(c). See Chapter 16.

Informal discovery is, of course, also available. Interviews with school employees should be conducted, consistent with good witness interviewing in general. Since the necessity to impeach the witness may arise, the results of the interview should be memorialized in some manner that can be authenticated at the due process hearing or at the court level. While a signed statement from the witness is obviously preferable, employees caught in the middle of a dispute between the parents and their employer are even more reluctant than disinterested witnesses to sign statements, especially if the interviewer is a lawyer. The presence of a nonlawyer is perhaps the easiest solution. It should be kept in mind that should a lawyer interview the witness and then have to take the stand to impeach the witness, disqualification of the lawyer is a real possibility.[157]

A common problem associated with lawyers interviewing witnesses who are employees of the school system is the position taken by the school system that all employees of the school system are opposing parties. While "all parties have a right to interview an adverse party's witness (the witness willing) in private, without the presence or consent of opposing counsel,"[158] *ex parte* communications with opposing parties, without the consent of opposing counsel is unethical.[159] In such a situation, a determination must be made as to whether or not the employee is considered an opposing party under applicable ethical interpretations.

As a general rule, when dealing with an entity with many employees, employees are considered opposing parties to the extent that they are able to "bind the corporation."[160] In the context of a dispute with the LEA, an individual school teacher, psychologist, social worker, or the like would be unable to bind the school system to a course of conduct such as settling the dispute, and therefore should not be considered a party.[161] School principals and superintendents, however, are likely to be considered parties.[162]

Local statutes and interpretations should, as always, be considered. A particular jurisdiction may have a provision that explicitly allows counsel to communicate directly with all public employees.[163]

Finally, state law may have a statute comparable to the federal Freedom of Information Act which may provide a means of acquiring relevant information.

---

157. Model Rules of Professional Conduct Rule 3.7; Model Code of Professional Responsibility, DR 5-101, 5-102.

158. IBM Corp. v. Edelstein, 526 F.2d 37, 42 (2d Cir. 1975); *see also* Wharton v. Calderon, 127 F.3d 1201 (9th Cir. 1997).

159. Model Code of Professional Responsibility DR 7-104; Model Rules of Professional Conduct Rule 4.2.

160. Frey v. Department of Health and Human Services, 106 F.R.D. 32, 37 (E.D.N.Y. 1985); *see also* Carter-Herman v. City of Philadelphia, 897 F. Supp. 899 (E.D. Pa. 1995); Wright v. Group Health Hosp., 103 Wash. 2d 192, 691 P.2d 564 (1984); *see generally* Leubsdorf, *Communicating With Another Lawyer's Client: The Lawyer's Veto and the Client's Interests*, 127 U. Pa. L. Rev. 683 (1979).

161. *See generally* New York State Assn. for Retarded Children v. Carey, 706 F.2d 956 (2d Cir. 1983) (denial of order prohibiting plaintiffs from interviewing employees of state school for the mentally retarded).

162. It is unclear whether counsel can tell the employee-witnesses the truthful statement that they need not talk to opposing counsel. *Compare* People v. Hannon, 19 Cal.3d 588, 138 Cal. Rptr. 885, 564 P.2d 1203 (1977) (defense lawyer not guilty of suppression) *with* State v. Martindale, 215 Kan. 667, 527 P.2d 703 (1974) (lawyer disciplined).

163. *See, e.g.*, Cal. Rules of Professional Conduct §2-100(c)(1) ("This rule shall not apply to communications with a public officer, board, committee or body.").

11.9 Burden of Proof under the Act

Allocation of the burden of proof under IDEA is discussed in §§ 13.8–13.8.2.

11.10 Rules of Evidence

As a general matter, rules of evidence do not apply to administrative hearings. The controlling principle is one of relevancy and reliability.[164] Objections based on technical rules of hearsay, for example, may not be sustained. Obviously once the dispute works its way into court, the rules of evidence apply. Counsel, therefore, should be particularly mindful, that the due process hearing (the record of which will be reviewed by the court) provides the opportunity to introduce evidence which otherwise would be inadmissible at trial.

11.11 Conducting the Hearing

The formality of the hearing varies from jurisdiction to jurisdiction and from case to case. It is safe to say, however, that the more lawyers are involved the more formal the proceeding. It is usually a good idea to seek a prehearing conference with the hearing officer to decide preliminary questions such as allocation of the burden of proof, order of presentation, whether opening statements and closing arguments will be presented and the like.

The due process hearing should be approached with the same level of preparation as a judicial proceeding. The hearing must be conducted according to appropriate legal standards.[165] Available evidence suggests that success at the local due process hearing is critical to the ultimate outcome of the case. The vast majority of disputes do not proceed to court. The importance of establishing your case at the local due process hearing, therefore, cannot be overestimated.

11.12 Hearing Officer's Decision

The LEA has 45 days from the date of the receipt of the request for a hearing to insure that a decision is reached and a copy of the decision has been mailed to each of the parties.[166] A hearing officer has authority to extend this deadline at the request of either

---

164. *See, e.g.,* Baker v. Babcock & Wilcox Co., 11 Va. App. 419, 425–426, 399 S.E.2d 630, 634 (1990) (common law or statutory rules of hearsay do not have to be applied in administrative hearings).

165. 34 C.F.R. § 300.511(c).

166. 34 C.F.R. § 300.515; The decision date may not be extended in an expedited hearing.

party.[167] Failure to meet the deadline is grounds for removing the hearing officer from the list of those approved to hear due process hearings.[168] Additional time lines within this 45-day requirement are often established by the various state regulations.

The hearing officer must be aware and understand the state and federal legal decisions regarding the legal issues presented and must be able to write a decision according to legal practice standards.[169] If the hearing office is deciding whether a child has received a FAPE the decision must be based on substantive grounds.[170] In order to determine whether a child has been denied a FAPE because of procedural violations, the hearing office must decide that the procedural violation:

- "impeded the child's right to a FAPE";
- significantly impeded the parent's opportunity to participate in the decision-making process regarding the provision of" the child's FAPE; or
- "caused deprivation of educational benefit."[171]

The hearing officer must provide written, or, at the option of the parents, electronic findings of fact and decisions.[172] The decision of the hearing officer is final unless the hearing is appealed to a review officer if the state provides for a two-tier system, or to state or federal court if there is only a one-tier administrative process.[173]

11.13 Due Process Hearing Checklist

General Requirements

_____Statute of limitations of state

_____Proper subject matter:

_____identification

_____evaluation

_____educational placement

_____provision of a FAPE

_____manifestation review

_____challenging information contained in the child's educational records

_____nonconsent of parents (if state law not to contrary)

_____obligation of LEA to pay for IEE

_____procedural violation impacting on educational program of child

---

167. 34 C.F.R. § 300.515(c).

168. Virginia State Dept. of Educ. and Prince William County Pub. Schools, 257 Educ. Handicapped L. Rep. (CRR) 648 (OCR 1985) (LEA must inform hearing officers that failure to meet 45-day time line will prohibit their employment as hearing officers in the future).

169. 34 C.F.R. § 300.511(c)(B).

170. 34 C.F.R. § 300.513(a).

171. 34 C.F.R. § 300.513(2).

172. 34 C.F.R. § 300.513; *see also* 20 U.S.C. § 1415(g)(1).

173. 34 C.F.R. § 300.516; *see also* 20 U.S.C. § 1415(h).

____residency

____Request to proper agency

____Request to proper person

____Standing to request:

____parent with custody or joint custody

____relative acting in capacity of parent

____other person acting in capacity of parent

____surrogate parent

____foster parent

____school agency responsible for education

Due Process Complaint

____model forms provided

____sufficiency of complaint

____name of child

____address of child

____name of school attending

____ description of problem

____ proposed resolution of problem

____ time line to notify is insufficient

____ timeline to amend

LEA Response to Due Process Complaint

____no prior written notice

____explanation of why agency proposed or refused to take action

____description of other options

____descriptions of evaluations assessments, reports

____other relevant factors

Hearing Officer

____meets impartiality requirements

____not employed by LEA

____not employed by SEA*

____not employed by state to advise on educational policy

____not director of special education for another jurisdiction*

____not government official in jurisdiction of LEA

____possesses required knowledge and abilities

____meets state qualifications

Requested Relief

____determine whether LEA action in identification, evaluation, educational placement, provision of FAPE, or contents of student's records is appropriate

____reimbursement under *Burlington*

____order specific placement*

____find procedural violations

____award compensatory education

____determine whether IEE must be paid for by LEA

____order related service

____Request subpoenas for appropriate witnesses

Hearing Rights

____notified of mediation

   ____notice or resolution meeting

   ____notified of low cost or free legal services

____right to counsel

____right to have others with expertise

____present evidence

____confront and cross examine witnesses

____compel attendance of witnesses

____prohibit the introduction of evidence not disclosed at least five days prior to hearing

____obtain a written or, at option of parent, electronic verbatim record of the hearing

____obtain written findings and decisions

____child present*

____open to public*

____held at a time and place which is reasonably convenient to the parents and child

Hearing Decisions

____FAPE based on substantive grounds

____Procedural grounds

   ____impeded right to FAPE

   ____impeded parent's opportunity to participate in decision making

   ____deprivation of educational benefit

____written decision in appropriate legal standards

____decisions mailed to parties

____appeal to SEA

____procedures consistent with due process

____seek additional evidence

____30 days after review

____oral or written argument

____written decision

____45 days to decide first level IHO

____additional state timelines

____continuance granted

____"Stay-Put" provisions met

____surrogate parent requirements met

____discovery opportunities

  ____access and copies of records

____explanation and interpretation of records

____interview employee witnesses

____allocation of burden of proof

____expedited Hearing (change in placement):

  ____dangerousness exception

  ____appropriateness of current placement

  ____interim placement meets requirement for IEP goals and reduces oc-
    currence of behavior

____determine current placement

*Split of opinion or at parents' option.

Chapter 12

Administrative Appeals

12.1 In General

If the impartial due process hearing is conducted by a public agency other than the state educational agency (SEA), the SEA is required to provide an administrative appeal.[1] The reviewing body must:

- examine the entire record;[2]

- ensure the procedures at the local hearing were in accord with due process requirements;[3]

- seek additional evidence if necessary;[4]

- at its discretion, allow oral or written argument;[5]

- make an independent decision;[6] and

- give a written (or at the request of the parents, an electronic) copy of the findings and decisions to the parties.[7]

12.2 Statute of Limitations and Notice of Appeal

IDEA is silent as to the time period in which an appeal may be made to the state level review.[8] Individual state regulations often address this issue, and thirty days is not atypical. Interestingly, at least one SEA decision rejected a specific state-mandated 30-day statute of limitations. The hearing officer held that since the appeal involved issues under the federal statute, it would follow the general rule of disfavoring short state-cre-

---

1. 34 C.F.R. § 300.514(b); *see* 20 U.S.C. § 1415(g).
2. 34 C.F.R. § 300.514(b)(2)(i); *see also* 20 U.S.C. § 1415(g).
3. 34 C.F.R. § 300.514(b)(2)(ii); *see also* 20 U.S.C. § 1415(g).
4. 34 C.F.R. § 300.514(b)(2)(iii); *see also* 20 U.S.C. § 1415(g).
5. 34 C.F.R. § 300.514(b)(2)(iv); *see also* 20 U.S.C. §§ 1415(g), (d).
6. 34 C.F.R. § 300.514(b)(2)(v); *see also* 20 U.S.C. § 1415(g).
7. 34 C.F.R. § 300.514(b)(2)(vi); *see also* 20 U.S.C. § 1415(g).
8. Board of Educ. of the County of Cabell v. Dienelt, 843 F.2d 813 (4th Cir. 1988).

ated statutes of limitations and allow an appeal filed beyond the 30-day state statute of limitations.[9]

The precise person to whom the notice of appeal is sent is controlled by state law. Each state department of education has an office dealing with special education and typically the notice of appeal goes to it and or the State Superintendent.[10]

12.3 Timelines

While IDEA is silent as to how long a party has to appeal a local due process hearing decision,[11] it does provide timelines under which a hearing and decision must be made at the administrative appeal level once the decision is appealed. The local due process decision must be made within 45 days of receipt of a request, but a state level review must be decided within 30 days of receipt of the request for review.[12] Consistent with the requirements of the local due process hearing, a review hearing officer may grant extensions at the request of either party,[13] and any hearing involving oral arguments must be held at a time and place convenient to the parents and child.[14]

State regulations will provide additional procedures and timelines as a means of insuring compliance with the 30-day requirement. For example, federal regulations are silent as to who should provide the review officer with the record.

12.4 Subject Matter/Scope of Review

Under IDEA, the review officer is to examine the record, insure that the due process requirements were met, seek additional evidence if necessary, allow oral or written argument at his or her discretion, and make an independent decision.[15] IDEA, therefore, implies a *de novo* review. This standard would be consistent with traditional administrative procedure where one level of an administrative agency is not bound by a lower decision within that agency.

A *de novo* review is also supported by the case law.[16] Given the United States Supreme Court's decision in *Hendrick Hudson District Board of Education v. Rowley*[17]

---

9. Case No. 55, 506 Educ. Handicapped L. Rep. (CRR) 387 (SEA Wis. 1985). For a discussion of statute of limitations in a civil action, and the policy disfavoring short, state-created time limitations, see § 13.2.

10. A list of these offices is contained in the Appendix.

11. *See* § 12.2.

12. 34 C.F.R. § 300.51 5(b)(1); *see also* 20 U.S.C. § 1415.

13. 34 C.F.R. § 300.515(c); *see also* 20 U.S.C. § 1415.

14. 34 C.F.R. § 300.515(d); *see also* 20 U.S.C. § 1415.

15. See §§ 13.7, 13.7.1.

16. *See, e.g.,* Adams v. Oregon, 195 F.3d 1141 (9th Cir. 1999); San Rafael Elementary School Dist. v. California Special Educ. Hearing 482 F. Supp. 2d 1152 (N.D.Cal. 2007); Moser v. Bret Harte Union High School Dist. 366 F. Supp. 2d 944, 975 (E.D.Cal. 2005); Tompkins v. Forest Grove School Dist. #115, 86 Ore. App. 436, 740 P.2d 186 (1987).

17. 458 U.S. 176 (1981). For a fuller discussion of *Rowley* see § 3.1.

that the courts are to give "due weight" to the administrative proceedings, the question has been raised whether the state level review must give "due weight" to the local hearing officer.[18] If due weight is considered deference, the answer should be no. *Rowley's* concern for giving due weight to the state administrative proceedings was premised on a concern that the judiciary not substitute its judgment on issues of educational policy because of the court's relative lack of expertise. Technically, there should not be the lack of expertise between the local level of review and the state level of review.[19]

On the other hand, serious consideration to the local due process hearing officer's factual conclusion should be given where the review officer relies upon the record rather than hearing the evidence firsthand. The local hearing officer was the one present to hear the testimony and judge the credibility of witnesses. Where credibility is a factor, some deference to the local hearing officer is probably sound. On issues not involving credibility, or with witnesses that the review officer has personally seen, the independent decision requirement of the Act would indicate that no deference is required.[20]

The scope of the review officer's authority is coextensive with the local hearing officer. The reviewing authority does not exceed the local officer's. For example, it would be improper for the review officer to remand the case to the local hearing officer for additional factual findings, since the review provides for the review officer to seek additional evidence.[21]

12.5 Who May Appeal — Parties Aggrieved

Clearly a parent or local educational agency that fails to achieve its goals at the local due process hearing is an aggrieved party and may institute an appeal. The question arises, however, whether the SEA that may ultimately be responsible for the implementation, and at least part of the costs, can be considered an aggrieved party even if it did not participate in the local due process hearing?

New York set up a system where the state was given authority to appeal from the local due process hearing, despite not being a party to the original dispute.[22] The New York law imposes the obligation on the state review officer of the Department of Education to review and modify any decision of the local school board, to the extent deemed necessary.[23] Lower courts held that to do so, however, the Commissioner must appeal the local due process decision under provisions that apply to the appeal by the original parties.[24] If the SEA chooses not to make the appeal, it may not unilaterally modify or reject the due process decision, since the law requires the local hearing decision be final,

---

18. Rowley, 458 U.S. at 206.
19. Community High School Dist. 155 v. Denz, 124 Ill. App. 3d 129, 463 N.E.2d 988 (1984).
20. For a complete discussion of standard of the judicial review and the impact of the court having to provide "due weight" see §§ 13.7 through 13.7.3.
21. Birmingham and Lamphere School Dist. v. Superintendent of Pub. Instruction for Mich., 554 Educ. Handicapped L. Rep. (CRR) 318 (6th Cir. 1982).
22. New York Educ. Law § 4404(2).
23. New York Educ. Law § 4404(2).
24. Sidney K. v. Ambach, 557 Educ. Handicapped L. Rep. (CRR) 268, 270 (Sup. Ct. N.Y. 1986).

unless appealed.[25] The propriety of this *sua sponte* appeal by the SEA, however, has been questioned by the Second Circuit.[26]

12.6 Impartiality

IDEA and supporting regulations require the state level review be impartial.[27] General issues of impartiality such as bias, prejudice or corruption are, of course, contemplated within this requirement.[28] By far the most litigated issue, however, is the question of whether employees of the SEA may be review officers. The question was complicated by language that appears contradictory to the legislative history. IDEA states that any party aggrieved by the findings and decision rendered in the local due process hearing may appeal to the State educational agency. The State educational agency shall conduct an impartial review of such decision.[29] The language seems to contemplate the hearing be conducted by the SEA itself. The legislative history, however, would seem to indicate that an employee of the SEA may not conduct the review. The Senate Conference Report specifically stated:

> No hearing may be conducted by an employee of the State or local educational agency involved in the education or care of the child. The conferees have adopted this language to clarify the minimum standard of impartiality which shall apply to individuals conducting a review of the local due process hearing.[30]

The federal regulations state that the impartial due process hearing officer may not be "a person who is an employee of the State agency or the LEA that is involved in the education or care of the child...."[31]

Case law is uniform that at least lower level employees of the state department of education may not be review officers.[32] There has, however, been a split of opinion on whether the state's Secretary of Education or equivalent officer may conduct the review. The language of the court decisions ranges from one court holding that arguments made by lawyers that the Florida Commissioner of Education could not act as the review officer were frivolous[33] to the majority of courts which have held that individuals at the secretary level are employees of the SEA and are precluded from conducting re-

---

25. Antkowiak v. Ambach, 638 F. Supp. 1564 (W.D.N.Y. 1986).

26. Antkowiak v. Ambach, 838 F.2d 635, 641 (2d Cir. 1988) (the system has also been held to be a violation of impartiality requirements because the Commissioner or his delegate was in effect acting as a review officer).

27. 34 C.F.R. § 300. 514(b)(2); *see also* 20 U.S.C. § 1415(g).

28. *See, e.g.,* Freidlander, 211 Educ. Handicapped L. Rep. (CRR) 463 EHLR (OCR 1987) (review officer should not discuss substantive issues with employees of SEA).

29. 20 U.S.C. § 1415(g).

30. Senate Conference Report, 1975 U.S. Code Cong. & Admin. News, 94th Congress, First Session, pp. 1425, 1502.

31. 34 C.F.R. § 300.511(c).

32. Colin K. v. Schmidt, 715 F.2d 1, 5 n. 3 (1st Cir. 1983); Grymes v. Madden, 672 F.2d 321, 323 (3d Cir. 1982); Helms v. McDaniel, 657 F.2d 800, 806 n.9 (5th Cir. 1981); *see also* Muth v. Central Bucks School Dist., 839 F.2d 113 (3d Cir. 1988), *reversed on other grounds sub nom.* Dellmuth v. Muth, 491 U.S. 223 (1989).

33. Victoria L. v. District School Bd. of Lee County, 741 F.2d 369, 374 (11th Cir. 1984); *see also* Brandon E. v. Wisconsin Department of Pub. Instruction, 595 F. Supp. 740, 746 (E.D. Wis. 1984) (constitutional officer, not employee, therefore not precluded from reviewing).

views.[34] It is probably more accurate to say that the SEA is obligated to arrange for the review, while some other entity does the actual review.[35] This other entity may be another state agency or private individuals. Appointment of a private attorney is an acceptable way of providing for a review officer.[36]

Where the state review officer fails to meet the impartiality requirements, the trial court should vacate the review officer's decision and provide "due weight" only to the due process hearing officer.[37]

12.7 Additional Evidence Allowed

IDEA provides for an impartial review by the state education authority with the right to present additional evidence.[38] No limitation on the additional evidence is stated. Federal IDEA regulations, however, allow the reviewing body to seek additional evidence "if necessary."[39] The hearing officer has considerable discretion within which to make this decision.[40] Given the *de novo* nature of the state level review, it appears that review officers should be reluctant to overly restrict the presentation of evidence.

If additional evidence is taken, the protections afforded at the local due process hearing must be made available at the SEA hearing, including the right to confront and cross-examine witnesses, and the right to have five days advance disclosure of evidence.[41] The state review officer also has the discretion to allow or preclude oral or written argument.[42] Courts will review whether denial of the opportunity for either written or oral argument is an abuse of discretion.[43]

Whether to seek introduction of additional evidence is, of course, a highly case-specific question. It should be kept in mind, however, that the administrative process provides an opportunity not often available in litigation. The ability to introduce additional evidence may be important. Among the reasons additional evidence might be admitted include: clearing up factual ambiguities in the record, rebutting evidence that

---

34. Burr v. Ambach, 863 F.2d 1071 (2d Cir. 1988), *vacated,* Sobol v. Burr, 492 U.S. 902 (1989); Muth v. Central Bucks School Dist., 839 F.2d 113 (3d Cir. 1988), *reversed on other grounds sub nom.* Dellmuth v. Muth, 491 U.S. 223 (1989); Grymes v. Madden, 672 F.2d 321, 323 (3d Cir. 1982); Helms v. McDaniel, 657 F.2d 800 (5th Cir. 1981); Robert M. v. Benton, 634 F.2d 1139, 1142 (8th Cir. 1980); Johnson v. Lancaster-Lebanon Intermediate Unit 13, 757 F. Supp. 606, 615 (E.D. Pa. 1991); Vogel v. School Bd. of Montrose, 491 F. Supp. 989, 995 (W.D. Mo. 1980).
35. Helms v. McDaniel, 657 F.2d 800, 805 n.8 (5th Cir. 1981).
36. Missouri Department of Elementary and Secondary Educ. Inquiry, 257 Educ. Handicapped L. Rep. (CRR) 487 (OCR 1984).
37. Johnson v. Lancaster-Lebanon Intermediate Unit 13, 757 F. Supp. 606, 615 (E.D. Pa. 1991).
38. 20 U.S.C. § 1415(h)(2).
39. 34 C.F.R. § 300.514(b)(2)(iii); *see also* 20 U.S.C. § 1415(g).
40. *See* Kruelle v. Biggs, 489 F. Supp. 169 (D. Del. 1980), *affirmed sub nom.* Kruelle v. New Castle County School Dist., 642 F.2d 687 (3d Cir. 1981); D.B. v. Ocean Township Bd. of Educ., 985 F. Supp. 457 (D.N.J. 1997).
41. 34 C.F.R. § 300.512(a)(3)(iii); *see also* 20 U.S.C. § 1415(g). For a discussion of these provisions see § 11.6.
42. 34 C.F.R. § 300.514(b)(2)(iv); *see also* 20 U.S.C. § 1415(g).
43. *See, e.g.,* Nelson v. Southfield Pub. Schools, 148 Mich. App. 389, 384 N.W.2d 423 (1986) (abuse of discretion to deny argument where opposing party has used "appeal form" to make arguments).

caused surprise in the due process hearing, or updating medical or educational records. This is also the last opportunity to introduce evidence under the less stringent evidentiary rules applicable to administrative hearings. Any relevant hearsay, for example, may have its last chance to be admitted.[44]

The value of the review officer meeting the parents and school officials can often be overlooked. Testimony from the parents or school officials will often help personalize the cold record. Too often the LEA and parents have characterized each other in less than favorable light and allowing the hearing officer to see them adds to the credibility of the respective cases.

Whether to see oral or written argument is an individual decision. The opportunity to be present and answer legal and factual questions for the review officer, however, should not be under estimated.

12.8 Finality of Decision

The SEA decision must be a final decision, unless suit is filed in either state or federal court.[45] Hence, review systems in which following a local due process hearing a review officer heard the appeal and made recommendations to the SEA, which the SEA could accept or reject, are in violation of IDEA.[46]

12.9 Child's Status During Proceedings

During any administrative or judicial proceeding, unless the state or local agency and the parents of the child agree otherwise, the child must remain in his or her current educational placement.[47] If the dispute involves the initial application for admission to school, the child, with the consent of the parents, must be placed in the public school until the completion of all the proceedings.[48]

If the dispute involves an application for initial services for a child who is moving from early childhood services under the Infants and Toddlers Act to services under IDEA Part B, because the child has turned three and is no longer eligible then the public agency is not required to provide the early childhood services previously received. If the child is found eligible under the IDEA for services and the parent consents to the provision of these services the public agency must provide them unless disputed.[49]

---

44. See evidentiary discussion § 11.10.
45. 34 C.F.R. § 300.514(d); *see also* 20 U.S.C. § 1415(g).
46. *E.g.*, Helms v. McDaniel, 657 F.2d 800 (5th Cir. 1981) (Ohio scheme invalid); Diatta 319 F. Supp. 2d 57, 65 (D.D.C. 2004); Monahan v. Nebraska, 491 F. Supp. 1074 (D. Neb. 1980); Christopher N. v. McDaniel, 569 F. Supp. 291 (N.D. Ga. 1983); *see also* Stark v. Walter, 556 Educ. Handicapped L. Rep. (CRR) 203 (S.D. Ohio. 1984); Hopkins v. Aldine Independent School Dist., 555 Educ. Handicapped L. Rep. (CRR) 412 (S.D. Tex. 1984) (improper to require appeal to local school board before appeal to SEA); *see generally* Birmingham v. Omaha School Dist., 220 F.3d 850 (8th Cir. 2000).
47. 34 C.F.R. § 300.518(a); *see also* 20 U.S.C. § 1415(j).
48. 34 C.F.R. § 300.518(b); *see also* 20 U.S.C. § 1415(j).
49. 34 C.F.R. § 300.518(c); *see also* 20 U.S.C. § 1415(j).

If the decision of a hearing officer either in a due process hearing or a State review agrees with the child's parents that a change of placement is appropriate, that changed placement must be treated as an agreement between the state or local agency and the parents for purposes of determining what is the current educational placement.[50]

12.10 Administrative Review Checklist

____Within statute of limitations

____Entire record has been forwarded to review officer

____Procedural allegations at local level

____Determine impartiality of hearing officer or selection system

____Identify additional evidence wish to introduce

____Request evidentiary hearing

____Request permission to file briefs and make oral argument

____Ensure hearing officer adheres to 30-day timeline for decision

---

50. 34 C.F.R. §300.518(d); *see also* 20 U.S.C. §1415(j).

Chapter 13

Judicial Review

13.1 In General

Any party aggrieved by the final administrative proceeding under IDEA may bring an action in either state or federal court.[1] The action in federal court may be maintained without regard to amount in controversy.[2] The parties, of course, may not litigate in state and federal court simultaneously and previous litigation on the same issues will constitute *res judicata*.[3]

IDEA provides that the trial court "shall receive the records of the administrative proceedings, shall hear additional evidence at the request of a party[4] and, basing its decision on the preponderance of the evidence, shall grant such relief as the court determines is appropriate."[5]

13.2 Statute of Limitations

The 2004 amendments to IDEA established a statute of limitations for filing suit in state or federal court. If state law does not have a specific statute of limitations covering

1. 20 U.S.C. § 1415(i)(2)(A); T. v. District of Columbia Slip Copy, 2007 WL 2111032 (D.D.C. 2007) (90 days SOL) Jaffess v. Council Rock School Dist. Slip Copy, 2006 WL 3097939 (E.D. Pa. 2006); *see, e.g.,* Chavez v. Board of Educ. of Tularosa Municipal School, Slip Copy, 2007 WL 709038 (D.N.M. 2007) (court does not have subject matter jurisdiction because not aggrieved parties); *but see* W. K. v. Sea Isle City Bd. of Educ. Slip Copy, 2007 WL 433323 (D.N.J. 2007) (42 U.S.C. § 1983 provides the basis for subject matter jurisdiction for the enforcement of the settlement).

2. 20 U.S.C. § 1415(i)(3)(A).

3. Coe v. Michigan Dept. of Educ., 693 F.2d 616 (6th Cir. 1982); Scruggs v. Campbell, 630 F.2d 237 (4th Cir. 1980); P.G. v. Southern York County School Dist., Slip Copy, 2006 WL 3042966 (M.D. Pa. 2006); Moubry v. Independent School Dist. 696, 9 F. Supp. 2d 1086 (D. Minn. 1998); Bruschini v. Board of Educ. Arlington Central School Dist., 911 F. Supp. 104 (S.D.N.Y. 1995).

4. C.G. v. Five Town Community School Dist. Slip Copy, 2007 WL 494994 (D. Me. 2007) (allows additional evidence); R.F. v. Warwick School Dist. Slip Copy, 2006 WL 3814555, 3 (E.D. Pa. 2006) (court's review of this additional information will be narrowly construed to consider whether the original IEP was reasonably calculated to afford some educational benefit and not to engage in "Monday Morning Quarterbacking ").

5. 20 U.S.C. § 1415(i)(2)(C).

actions brought under IDEA, a party has 90 days following a final administrative hearing to file suit. If the state has adopted a specific statute of limitations, the state statute of limitations controls.[6]

While the amendment certainly clarifies an important point that had led to considerable litigation, the question remains as to what is the appropriate statute of limitations when filing suit solely to obtain attorney's fees. This issue is discussed in § 15.3.

The statute of limitations may be tolled for equitable reasons.[7]

13.3 Exhaustion of Administrative Remedies

The right to appeal to federal or state court accrues when the parties receive notice of the final due process review decision.[8] As with more typical administrative schemes, Congress required the exhaustion of administrative remedies prior to filing an action in either state or federal court. Only the administrative remedies under IDEA, however, need be exhausted. Voluntary state dispute resolution mechanisms need not be exhausted.[9]

Congress felt sufficiently strong about the need to exhaust administrative remedies that when it amended IDEA to make explicitly that "[n]othing in this chapter shall be construed to restrict or limit the rights, procedures, and remedies available under the Constitution, [§ 504], or other Federal laws protecting the rights of children with disabilities," it also required that if relief under some other statute is also available under IDEA, administrative remedies must be exhausted.[10] In essence, Congress, recognizing that administrative remedies need not be exhausted for claims under § 504 or § 1983, did not want IDEA administrative procedures to be circumvented by resort to these statutory rights.[11]

---

6. 20 U.S.C. § 1415(i)(2)(B).

7. K. v. Sea Isle City Bd. of Educ. Slip Copy, 2007 WL 433323 ,3 (D.N.J. 2007) (90 days applies only to aggrieved parties and because the parties in this matter reached a settlement, no one was aggrieved by ALJ's order); M.M. v. Red Clay Consolidated School Dist., 19 Individuals with Disabilities Educ. L. Rep. (LRP) 967 (3d Cir. 1993) (notice about appeal to parent and child defective); Wayne County Regional Educ. Service Agency v. Pappas, 56 F. Supp. 2d 807 (E.D. Mich. 1999) (tolled for mental impairment).

8. Sandifer v. Lumberton Public School Dist. Slip Copy, 2007 WL 2071799 (S.D. Miss. 2007); Mavis v. Sobol, 839 F. Supp. 968 (N.D.N.Y. 1993); Gerasimou v. Ambach, 636 F. Supp. 1504 (E.D.N.Y. 1986).

9. Porter v. Board of Trustees of Manhattan Beach Unified School Dist., 307 F.3d 1064 (9th Cir. 2002) (parents and student were not required to exhaust state complaint resolution procedure); Upper Valley Association for Handicapped Citizens v. Mills, 928 F. Supp. 429 (D. Vt. 1996); Guy J. v. New Hampshire Dept. of Educ., 131 N.H. 742, 565 A.2d 397 (1989).

10. 20 U.S.C. § 1415(l); 34 C.F.R. § 300.516(e).

11. Ellenberg v. New Mexico Military Institute 478 F.3d 1262 (10th Cir. 2007 (claims under ADA and Rehabilitation Act were not barred by parents' failure to exhaust IDEA administrative remedies); Frazier v. Fairhaven School Committee, 276 F.3d 52 (1st Cir. 2002) (plaintiffs who seek to bring § 1983 action based on a claimed violation of IDEA, in which they seek only money damages, must first exhaust administrative process available under IDEA); *see also* Polera, 288 F.3d 478 (2d Cir. 2002); Robb v. Bethel School Dist. # 403, 308 F.3d 1047 (9th Cir. 2002); Cudjoe v. Ind. School. Dist. No. 12, 297 F.3d 1058 (10th Cir. 2002); Rafferty v. Cranston Public School Committee 315 F.3d 21 (1st Cir. 2002); Charlie F. v. Board of Educ. of Skokie School Dist. 68, 98 F.3d 989 (7th Cir. 1996); Marc V. v. North East Independent School Dist. 455 F. Supp. 2d 577 (W.D. Tex. 2006) (plaintiff's IDEA, Section 1983, Section 504, and ADA claims barred by the IDEA's administrative exhaustion requirement); Mr. & Mrs. D. v. Southington Board. of Educ., 119 F. Supp. 2d 105 (D.

Exhaustion is not an inflexible doctrine, however. While time-consuming procedures are not in and of themselves a basis for excusing the administrative process,[12] traditional notions that justify failing to exhaust administrative remedies also apply in the context of IDEA.[13]

In general, exhaustion of administrative remedies is excused "where exhaustion would be futile or inadequate."[14] The most common situation in which courts have held that exhaustion would be futile is where the administrative due process procedures themselves are being attacked. For example, exhaustion is excused where the adequacy of the administrative remedy goes to the merits of the claim, such as where a plaintiff brings a class action alleging failure of the state to implement required administrative procedures.[15] Exhaustion was also excused where the suit was to challenge the propriety of the administrative procedures actually implemented.[16]

A similar circumstance in which exhaustion would be futile is where the public agency fails to invoke the administrative procedures. For example, exhaustion was not required where the agency refused to appoint a due process hearing officer[17] or where the school failed to inform the parents of their due process rights[18] or where the state fails to monitor and insure compliance with systemic violations.[19] Exhaustion was also

---

Conn. 2000) (must exhaust under § 504); Frith v. Galeton Area School Dist., 900 F. Supp. 706 (M.D. Pa. 1995) (must exhaust before bringing a § 1983 claim).

12. Coleman v. Newburgh Enlarged City School Dist., ___ F.3d ___, 2007 WL 2768745 (2d Cir. 2007); Hope v. Cortines, 69 F.3d 687 (2d Cir. 1995) (where relief sought available under IDEA must exhaust under ADA); Spencer v. District of Columbia, 416 F.Supp.2d 5 (D.D.C. 2006); Mrs. M v. Bridgeport Board of Educ. 96 F. Supp. 2d 124 (D.Conn. 2000); Doe v. Arlington County School Bd., 41 F. Supp. 2d 599 (E.D. Va. 1999); Learning Disabilities Association of Maryland Inc. v. Board of Educ. of Baltimore Co., 837 F. Supp. 717 (D. Md. 1993); Cox v. Jenkins, 878 F.2d 414 (D.C. Cir. 1989); Howell v. Waterford Pub. Schools, 731 F. Supp. 1314 (E.D. Mich. 1990).

13. *See also* Rose v. Yeaw, 214 F.3d 206 (1st Cir. 2000) (good explanation of exceptions to exhaustion of administrative remedies requirement); Fitzpatrick v. Town of Falmouth, 321 F.Supp.2d 119 (D. Me. 2004) (citing factors in *Yeaw*)

14. Honig v. Doe, 484 U.S. 305 (1988); J.S. v. Attica Central Schools, 386 F.3d 107 (2d Cir, 2004) (complaint fell within futility exemption for cases of alleged systemic violations); Taylor v. Vermont Dept. of Educ., 313 F.3d 768 (2d Cir. 2002) (exempted from exhaustion requirement of IDEA on grounds of futility and inadequacy of remedy); Gadsden City Bd. of Educ. v. B.P., 3 F. Supp. 2d 1299 (N.D. Ala. 1998) (excused when seeking a *Honig* Injunction in response to violence); *see also* Kominos v. Upper Saddle River Bd. of Educ., 13 F.3d 775 (3d Cir.1994) (exception to exhaustion of remedies occurs where the school failed to notify the student of due process rights); Rogers v. Bennett, 873 F.2d 1387 (11th Cir. 1989) (parents required to exhaust administrative remedies absent a showing of irreparable harm); Spencer v. District of Columbia 416 F. Supp. 2d 5 (D.D.C. 2006).

15. Porter v. Board of Trustees of Manhattan Beach Unified School Dist., 307 F.3d 1064 (9th Cir. 2002) (further exhaustion of California's due process procedures enacted to comply with the procedures set forth in IDEA would be futile or inadequate); Blackman v. District of Columbia, 382 F. Supp. 2d 3 (D.D.C. 2005) (plaintiffs' claim was not barred by their failure to exhaust administrative remedies that did not exist); Lemon v. District of Columbia, 920 F. Supp. 8 (D.D.C. 1996); Andre H. v. Ambach, 104 F.R.D. 606 (S.D.N.Y. 1985); Diamond v. McKenzie, 602 F. Supp. 632 (D.D.C. 1985).

16. Monahan v. Nebraska, 491 F. Supp. 1074 (D. Neb. 1980), *aff'd in part and vacated in part*, 645 F.2d 592 (8th Cir. 1981).

17. Dreher v. Amphitheater, 2 F.3d 228 (9th Cir. 1994); Kerr Center Parents Assn. v. Charles, 897 F.2d 1463 (9th Cir. 1990); Menecke v. School Bd., 762 F.2d 912, 918 (11th Cir. 1985) (exhaustion excused where school refused to initiate due process hearing at parents' request).

18. Mason v. Schenectady City School Dist., 879 F. Supp 215 (N.D.N.Y. 1993).

19. A.A. v. Board of Educ., Central Islip Union Free School Dist. 196 F. Supp. 2d (259 E.D.N.Y. 2002).

not required where agencies failed to provide notice of procedural safeguards,[20] where there was a failure to provide notice of a change in educational programming,[21] where a school official allegedly forged the parent's signature on a permission form,[22] and where money damages are the sole remedy.[23] Exhaustion would also be futile where the substance of the suit is that decision makers do not have certain remedies available to them.[24] The mere fact that the administrative process is time consuming, however, does not mean it would be futile to pursue it.[25]

The most common situation where exhaustion is excused, because the administrative procedures are inadequate, involves system wide class action lawsuits.[26] Often, in

---

20. Doe v. Maher, 793 F.2d 1470 (9th Cir. 1986), *aff'd sub nom.* Honig v. Doe, 484 U.S. 305 (1988).

21. Abney v. District of Columbia, 849 F.2d 1491 (D.C. Cir. 1988).

22. Quackenbush v. Johnson City School Dist., 716 F.2d 141 (2d Cir. 1983).

23. Covington v. Knox County School System, 205 F.3d 912 (6th Cir. 2000) (exhaustion would be futile, and thus would be excused, where the injured child had already graduated from the special education school and money damages were the only remedy that could make him whole); Witte v. Clark County School Dist., 197 F.3d 1271 (9th Cir. 1999); *but see* Kutasi v. Las Virgenes Unified School Dist., 494 F.3d 1162 (9th Cir. 2007); Robb v. Bethel School Dist. #403 308 F.3d 1047 (9th Cir. 2002).

24. Blanchard v. Morton School Dist., 420 F.3d 918 (9th Cir. 2005) (no exhaustion since no IDEA remedy for mother who sues for emotional damages); McCormick v. Waukegan School, 374 F.3d 564 (7th Cir. 2004); Padilla v. School Dist. No. 1, 233 F.3d 1268 (10th Cir. 2000) (claim under ADA for physical injuries); St. Louis Developmental Disabilities Treatment Center Parents' Assn. v. Mallory, 591 F. Supp. 1416 (W.D. Mo. 1984), *aff'd*, 767 F.2d 518 (8th Cir. 1985) (exhaustion excused where IEP drafters did not have the option of placing children in a regular classroom); Straube v. Florida Union Free School Dist., 778 F. Supp. 774 (S.D.N.Y. 1991) (exhaustion excused because hearing officer had no authority to place in unapproved school); *see also* Christopher W. v. Portsmouth School Comm., 877 F.2d 1089 (1st Cir. 1989) (exhaustion required where there are allegations of procedural violations under §1415); DeVries v. Spillane, 853 F.2d 264 (4th Cir. 1988) (exhaustion excused where during pendency of action school proposed an IEP which was contrary to the IEP over which the parent filed the administrative proceeding); County School Bd. of Henrico County, Va. v. R.T., 433 F. Supp. 2d 657, 691 (E.D. Va. 2006) (when the complaint remains the same though the IEPs change," no exhaustion *citing De Vries*); *but see* M.M v. School Dist. of Greenville County, 303 F.3d 523 (4th Cir 2002) parents failed to exhaust their administrative remedies for certain academic years in which IEP was challenged); Christopher S. v. Stanislaus County Office of Educ., 384 F.3d 1205 (9th Cir. 2004) (exhaustion excused where policy of providing a shorter school day to autistic students); Armstrong v. Kline, 476 F. Supp. 583 (E.D. Pa. 1979), *remanded sub nom.* Battle v. Pennsylvania, 629 F.2d 269 (3d Cir. 1980) (exhaustion excused where blanket rule prohibited educational services in excess of 180 days) *but see* McQueen v. Colorado Springs School Dist. No. 11, 488 F.3d 868 (10th Cir. 2007) (must exhaust when challenging policies of ESY); Coleman v. Newburgh Enlarged City School Dist., ___ F.3d ___, 2007 WL 2768745 (2d Cir. 2007) (court properly could review exhaustion determination on appeal of award of attorney fees); Exhaustion would not be excused, however, merely because the administrative proceeding was unable to provide for attorney's fees; Buffolino v. Sachem Central School Dist., 729 F. Supp. 240 (E.D.N.Y. 1990).

25. Howell v. Waterford Pub. Schools, 731 F. Supp. 1314 (E.D. Mich. 1990).

26. J.S. v. Attica Central Schools, 386 F.3d 107 (2d Cir. 2004) (complaint fell within futility exemption for cases of alleged systemic violations); Mrs. W. v. Tirozzi, 832 F.2d 748 (2d Cir. 1987) (hearing officer lacks authority to order system-wide relief); Hendricks v. Gilhool, 709 F. Supp. 1362 (E.D. Pa. 1989) (exhaustion excused in suit to increase state-wide classroom space); *see also* New Mexico Association for Retarded Citizens v. New Mexico, 678 F.2d 847 (10th Cir. 1982); L.M.P. v. School Bd. of Broward County, Fla., ___ F.Supp.2d ___, 2007 WL 2807332 (S.D. Fla. 2007) (board had policy of automatically denying all requests for Applied Behavioral Analysis (ABA) treatment for children with autism spectrum disorder (ASD)); J.G. v. Board of Educ., 648 F. Supp. 1452 (W.D.N.Y. 1986), *aff'd in part and modified in part*, 830 F.2d 444 (2d Cir. 1987) (failure to use procedures mandated by EAHCA); *but see* Doe v. Arizona Department of Educ., 111 F.3d 678 (9th Cir.

class action suits, exhaustion is also not required because it is § 1983[27] or § 504[28] that provides relief not available under IDEA.

In addition to situations involving futility and inadequacy, exhaustion is not required in the limited circumstances of where the LEA violates the stay-put provision of IDEA. During the pendency of any proceedings, absent an agreement between the parents and the agency to the contrary, the child is to remain in the existing educational placement.[29] In effect, the stay-put provision provides an automatic basis for a preliminary injunction against the agency during pendency of proceedings, to require maintaining the present educational placement of the child.[30]

Finally, in a situation very similar to excusing exhaustion, where an LEA fails to appeal an adverse determination and fails to implement the hearing officer's decision, parents may seek enforcement by filing in federal court.[31] Since the due process hearing is final unless appealed, the party prevailing at the local due process hearing is in no position to appeal and therefore has exhausted administrative remedies.

1997) (disabled inmates must exhaust); Association for Community Living v. Romer, 992 F.2d 1040 (10th Cir. 1993) (class action to allege violations of ESY policies under IDEA must still exhaust); Association for Retarded Citizens v. Teague, 830 F.2d 158, 161–162 (11th Cir. 1987) (class action for 6,000 dismissed for failure to exhaust, stating "no indication that the disposition of a few representative claims would not satisfactorily resolve plaintiff's complaint"); Grieco v. New Jersey Dept. of Educ., Slip Copy, 2007 WL 1876498 (D.N.J. 2007) (alleging a systemic failure on the part of the State of New Jersey to include the plaintiffs and proposed members of the class in the regular classroom and/or least restrictive environment must exhaust); G.C. v. Coler, 673 F. Supp. 1093 (S.D. Fla. 1987) (class action for all children confined in detention center dismissed for failure to exhaust).

27. J.S. v. Attica Central Schools 386 F.3d 107 (2d Cir. 2004) (complaint fell within futility exemption for cases of alleged systemic violations); Mrs. W. v. Tirozzi, 832 F.2d 748 (2d Cir. 1987); Brantley v. Independent School Dist. No. 625, 936 F. Supp. 649 (D. Minn. 1996); Andrew S. v. School Committee of Town of Greenfield, 59 F. Supp. 2d 237 (D. Mass. 1999); *but see Frazier v. Fairhaven School Committee*, 276 F.3d 52 (1st Cir. 2002) (plaintiffs who seek only money damages, must first exhaust administrative process available under IDEA); Robb v. Bethel School Dist. # 403, 308 F.3d 1047 (9th Cir. 2002); Cudjoe v. Ind. School. Dist. No. 12, 297 F.3d 1058 (10th Cir. 2002); Polera v. Board of Educ. of Newburgh Enlarged City School Dist., 288 F.3d 478 (2d Cir. 2002); Rafferty v. Cranston Public School Committee 315 F.3d 21 (1st Cir. 2002); citing Frazier, Charlie F. v. Board of Educ. of Skokie School Dist. 68, 98 F.3d 989 (7th Cir.1996).

28. Ellenberg v. New Mexico Military Institute 478 F.3d 1262 (10th Cir. 2007) (claims under ADA and Rehabilitation Act were not barred by parents' failure to exhaust IDEA administrative remedies); Doe v. Belleville Pub. School Dist. No. 118, 672 F. Supp. 342 (S.D. Ill. 1987); *see also* Sullivan v. Vallejo City Unified School Dist., 731 F. Supp. 947 (E.D. Cal. 1990) (refusal to allow service dog of student with cerebral palsy—no remedy available under EAHCA, therefore no need to exhaust); *but see* Cave v. East Meadow Union Free School Dist., 480 F. Supp. 2d 610 (E.D.N.Y. 2007) (because family failed to exhaust their administrative remedies under IDEA they did not establish clear likelihood of success on merits of their claims for violations of the ADA and Rehabilitation Act).

29. 20 U.S.C. § 1415(j).

30. Rodiriecus L. v. Waukegan School Dist., 90 F.3d 249 (7th Cir. 1996); Board of Educ. of Montgomery County v. Brett Y., 959 F. Supp. 705 (D. Md. 1997); Cochran v. District of Columbia, 660 F. Supp. 314 (D.D.C. 1987); Saleh v. District of Columbia, 660 F. Supp. 212 (D.D.C. 1987).

31. Porter v. Board of Trustees of Manhattan Beach Unified School Dist. 307 F.3d 1064 9th Cir. 2002); Sellers v. School Bd. of City of Manassas, 141 F.3d 524 (4th Cir. 1998); Jeremy H. v. Mount Lebanon School Dist., 95 F.3d 272 (3d Cir. 1996); Robinson v. Pinderhughes, 810 F.2d 1270 (4th Cir. 1987); A.V. v. Burlington Tp. Bd. of Educ. Slip Copy, 2007 WL 1892469 (D.N.J. 2007).

13.4 Removal from State to Federal Court

Whether an action originally brought in state court may properly be removed to federal court appears to be an open question. One federal court held that where a school system sought review of an administrative decision in a state court and in its complaint alleged only the application of state law, removal was improper.[32] The court held that state and federal law provided the same rights and protections and that plaintiff could choose whether to proceed under one or both. At least one Circuit and at least four other district courts, however, have held that removal is proper.[33]

The better view is that removal should be proper. Removal is a purely statutory right, and, if the action is within the court's original jurisdiction, removal is proper.[34] Removal is particularly appropriate where the initial due process hearing alleged violations of IDEA. If we view the initiation of the action as at the administrative level rather than at the court level, it is difficult to say that only state law issues are present. This is particularly the case where, as in both these district court cases, one party brought the action, but the opposing party ultimately sought review in the federal court. To allow the party seeking review to preclude removal by artful pleading[35] would essentially deny the party initiating the administrative proceedings the opportunity to have the case heard on terms (that is, both state and federal) originally heard in the administrative proceeding.[36]

13.5 Issues Considered

The issues subject to review by the trial court are those IDEA claims raised in the administrative proceedings. The trial court may not hear any IDEA issue not raised in the

---

32. Amelia County School Bd. v. Virginia Bd. of Educ., 661 F. Supp. 889 (E.D. Va. 1988); *see also* Murdock v. Mingus Union High School District, 2005 WL 3199100 (D. Ariz. 2005) (remanded since state law claims predominate); Spaulding v. Mingo Bd. of Educ., 897 F. Supp. 284 (S.D. W. Va. 1995) (through artful pleading student purposely omitted references to the United States Constitution and federal laws, thus the court had original jurisdiction, but remanded the entire case because state claims substantially predominated over federal claims); *but see* Converse County School Dist. No. 2 v. Pratt, 993 F. Supp. 848 (D. Wyo. 1997) (removed for federal question jurisdiction, remand denied although complaint only sought determination that state regulations supported appointment of surrogate parent; IDEA preempts state law only if state law standards are below federal minimum).

33. Ullmo v. Gilmour Academy, 273 F.3d 671 (6th Cir. 2001) (removal proper); Escambia County Bd. of Educ. v. Benton 358 F. Supp.2d 111 (S.D. Ala. 2005); Konkel v. Elmbrook School Dist., 348 F. Supp. 2d 1018, 1019 (E.D. Wis. 2004); Moubry v. Kreb, 58 F. Supp. 2d 1041 (D. Minn. 1999) (district court had federal question jurisdiction); Yankton Area Adjustment Training Center, Inc. v. Oleson, 897 F. Supp. 431 (D.S.D. 1995) (provision of Act allowing party aggrieved by administrative ruling to sue in state or federal court does not preclude removal from state to federal court and student defendant was entitled to remove).

34. Grubbs v. General Elec. Corp., 405 U.S. 699 (1972); Sanchez v. Monumental Life Ins. Co., 95 F.3d 856 (9th Cir. 1996); Korea Exchange Bank v. Trackwise Sales Corp., 66 F.3d 46 (3d Cir. 1995); Schlumberger Industries, Inc. v. National Surety Corp., 36 F.3d 1274 (4th Cir. 1994).

35. The artful pleading doctrine recognizes that the characterization of a federal claim as a state claim will not prohibit removal and permits the court to examine the claim.

36. *See generally* Horton v. Liberty Mutual Ins. Co., 367 U.S. 348 (1961); *but see* City of Chicago v. International College of Surgeons, 522 U.S. 156 (1997).

administrative proceeding. Otherwise, the exhaustion of administrative remedies requirement would be avoided.[37]

To the extent that a matter is covered by IDEA, federal law supersedes state law. This has led several courts to make very broad statements such as "in the EHA context ... no pendent state claim will lie,"[38] or that it is "beyond argument" that there can be no pendent state claim to provide relief.[39] These same courts, however, do recognize that where the state provides for educational standards and procedural protections in excess of those required by IDEA, the federal court has authority to assure compliance with the higher standard.[40]

The more accurate statement concerning pendent state claims, therefore, is that pendent jurisdiction of state claims is always discretionary with the court,[41] and except for the circumstance in which the services and protections under the state law are in excess of federal law, federal courts have not chosen to exercise pendent jurisdiction.[42]

Additional federal claims may be heard by the court. The 1986 amendments clearly envisioned the joining of federal constitutional and statutory claims by their explicit recognition that such claims are not precluded because the same claim can be made under IDEA.[43]

---

37. A.K. v. Alexandria City School Bd., 484 F.3d 672, 679 (4th Cir. 2007); Verhoeven v. Brunswick School Committee, 207 F.3d 1 (1st Cir. 1999); Anthony v. District of Columbia, 463 F. Supp. 2d 37 (D.D.C. 2006); Leonard v. McKenzie, 869 F.2d 1558 (D.C. Cir. 1989).

38. David D. v Dartmouth School Comm., 775 F.2d 411, 422 (1st Cir. 1985).

39. Carl D. v. St. Louis County Special School Dist., 21 F. Supp. 2d 1042 (E.D. Mo. 1998) (district court applies federal standards to parents claim under state law); Barwacz v. Michigan Dept. of Educ., 674 F. Supp. 1296 (W.D. Mich. 1987); see also Town of Burlington v. Department of Educ. of the Commonwealth of Massachusetts, 736 F.2d 773, 788 (1st Cir. 1984), aff'd, 471 U.S. 359 (1985) ("state law cannot provide a separate basis for relief via a pendent state claim").

40. Doe v. Bd. of Educ. of Tullahoma City Schools, 9 F.3d 455 (6th Cir. 1993); David D. v Dartmouth School Committee, 775 F.2d 411 (1st Cir. 1985); Town of Burlington v. Department of Educ. of the Commonwealth of Massachusetts, 736 F.2d 773, 788 (1st Cir. 1984), aff'd, 471 U.S. 369 (1985); CM v. Board of Public Educ. of Henderson County, 184 F. Supp. 2d 466 (W.D.N.C. 2002) (program must provide the child with an equal opportunity to learn if that is reasonably possible, ensuring that the child has an opportunity to reach her full potential commensurate with the opportunity given other children); Douglas W. v. Greenfield Public Schools, 164 F. Supp. 2d 157 (D. Mass. 2001) (maximum possible educational development); Frank S. v. School of Committee of Dennis-Yarmouth Regional School Dist., 26 F. Supp. 2d 219 (D. Mass. 1998); Barwacz v. Michigan Dept. of Educ., 681 F. Supp. 427 (W.D. Mich. 1987); but see D.D. v. New York City Bd. of Educ., 480 F.3d 138 (2d Cir. 2007) (failure to comply with deadlines established by state regulations for implementing IEPs did not, by itself, violate IDEA); Executive Software North America, Inc. v. United States District Court for Central Dist. of California, 15 F.3d 1484 (9th Cir. 1994).

41. United Mine Workers of America v. Gibbs, 383 U.S. 715 (1966); Hamilton v. School Bd. of Commissioners of Mobile County, 993 F. Supp. 884 (S.D. Ala. 1996).

42. Fay v. South Colonie Central School Dist., 802 F.2d 21 (2d Cir. 1986) ("there is authority to hear pendent state claims, but [t]he presence of unresolved questions under New York family law regarding the rights of fathers with joint legal custody ... should have alerted [the judge] to the fact that he need not, and therefore should not, decide the pendent claim"); Daniel B. v. Wisconsin Dept. of Pub. Instruction, 581 F. Supp. 585 (E.D. Wis. 1984) (urgency of need to decide educational issues precludes consideration of pendent state claims such as misrepresentation, intentional infliction of emotional distress and invasion of privacy); see also Burke County Bd. of Educ. v. Denton, 895 F.2d 973 (4th Cir. 1990).

43. 20 U.S.C. § 1415(l).

13.6 Discovery

Discovery under IDEA should be available to the extent of discovery in any civil matter. Discovery under Federal Rule 26(b)(1) and under most state procedural systems is limited primarily by not only what is relevant but what may also lead to relevant evidence. At least one court, relying on IDEA language that only "additional evidence" shall be submitted, has limited discovery to the type of evidence that is contemplated to be admitted in the trial.[44]

13.7 Standard of Review in General

There are fundamental differences among various courts on the standard of review to be used by the trial court. The two views can be concisely presented as whether the trial court is conducting a *de novo* review of the matter or whether it is functioning in a narrower role, as in the traditional review of administrative agency action. Section 1415(i)(2)(C) of IDEA states in part:

> In any action brought under this paragraph, the court shall receive the records of the administrative proceedings, shall hear additional evidence at the request of a party, and, basing its decision on a preponderance of the evidence, shall grant such relief as the court determines is appropriate.[45]

This language tends to intermingle the burden of proof with judicial review in a way that at least implies a complete *de novo* review by the court. The United States Supreme Court in *Hendrick Hudson District Board of Education v. Rowley*,[46] however, gave some indication that §1415(i)(2)(C) might not be read as allowing the district court complete *de novo* powers of review when it held:

> [T]he provision that a reviewing court base its decision on the "preponderance of the evidence" is by no means an invitation to the courts to substitute their own notions of sound educational policy for those of school authorities which they review. The very importance which Congress has attached to compliance with certain procedures in the preparation of an IEP would be frustrated if a court were simply to set decisions at naught. The fact that §1415(i) requires the reviewing court "receive the records of the [state] (sic) administrative proceedings" carries with it the implied requirement that *due weight* shall be given to these proceedings.[47]

Clearly the Court contemplated that the administrative determination should be accorded some significant role in the judicial decision. Just what that role is remains un-

---

44. Roe v. Town of Westford, 110 F.R.D. 380 (D. Mass. 1986) (relying on *Burlington* analysis of additional evidence); *see also* Patricia P. v. Board of Educ. of Oak Park, 203 F.3d 462 (7th Cir. 2000) (held that a parent was not entitled to discovery on the issues of appropriateness of the child's residential placement prior to the granting of summary judgment); H.H. v. Indiana Board of Special Educ. Slip Copy, 2007 WL 2914461, 2 (N.D. Ind. 2007).
45. 20 U.S.C. §1415(i)(2)(C).
46. 458 U.S. 176 (1982).
47. *Id.* at 206 (emphasis added).

clear. There is the obvious question of what is due weight. Is due weight the same as deference in traditional administrative review? Also, to whom is due weight to be given: the LEA, the due process hearing officers, or the SEA?

On the one hand, the Court in *Rowley* said "[T]he provision that a reviewing court base its decision on the 'preponderance of the evidence' is by no means an invitation to the courts to substitute their own notions of sound educational policy for those of school authorities which they review...."[48] This language implies that due weight is to be given the LEA. On the other hand, the Supreme Court's language "that §1415(e)[now (i)] requires the reviewing court 'receive the records of the [state] (sic) administrative proceedings'" implies that due weight shall be given to the hearing officers' decision.[49]

13.7.1 Traditional Administrative Review

In traditional administrative settings, the judicial scope of review is controlled by at least three concerns. The first two concerns are related to the purpose in setting up the agency procedure. First, the scope of the judicial review is limited by the belief that deference should be given to agency experts.[50] Second, the scope of review is limited by the belief that courts should defer to the agency because otherwise the value of expediency will be lost. Without limited review, the administrative proceeding becomes merely an added layer causing delay.[51] The third concern limiting review is common to all appeals, that is, a degree of deference should be given to the fact finder who has heard the evidence firsthand.[52]

These three concerns have led to what might be called a typical or traditional standard of the appropriate review of administrative determinations. This traditional approach leans heavily on the belief that a court should show significant deference to the agency. Specifically, the predominate standard of review for administrative decisions is that the court should determine whether the agency decision is supported by "substantial evidence."[53]

Substantial evidence represents a narrow standard of review, permitting administrators greater discretion in fact-finding than, for example, that accorded to trial judges under the "clearly erroneous" standard by which trial factual determinations are reviewed.

---

48. *Id.*

49. *Id.*

50. B. Schwartz, *Administrative Law* §10.1 (3d ed. 1991).

51. *Id.*

52. *See* R. Pierce, S. Shapiro & P. Verkuil, *Administrative Law and Process* 358 (1985).

53. Schwartz, *supra* note 54, at §10.7. What is substantial evidence is a more difficult question. *Id.* It has been pointed out, however, that "it has been generally accepted that 'substantial evidence' represents a narrower standard of review, permitting administrators greater discretion in fact-finding than accorded to trial judges under the 'clearly erroneous' standard. S. Breyer & R. Stewart, *Administrative Law and Regulatory Policy* 185 (1979). The substantial evidence test applies to formal adjudication and rule-making. Informal adjudication is tested by an 'arbitrary and capricious' standard. *Id.* at 195–96; Pierce, *supra* note 56, at 360.

The quantum of evidence necessary has been variously described. It has been described as equivalent to the standard used in determining directed verdicts. Breyer, at 185. In *Greater Boston Television Corp. v. FCC*, 444 F.2d 841, 851 (D.C. Cir. 1970), Judge Leventhal stated the court must determine whether the agency has "taken a 'hard look' at the salient problems, and has not genuinely engaged in reasoned decision-making."

The evidence to be considered in determining whether substantial evidence exists includes not just evidence favorable to the agency decision, but also evidence opposing the agency decision. Further, the agency decision to which there will be deference is to the final or review decision. For example, in a National Labor Relations Board determination, when a hearing officer reinstates an employee, but the full board reverses the hearing officer, any deference the court owes is to the full board.[54]

13.7.2 *De Novo* Review and Due Weight

As pointed out, the United States Supreme Court has stated that IDEA "carries with it the implied requirement that due weight shall be given these proceedings."[55] The immediate question is whether this requirement of due weight is the same as the deference a court traditionally gives an administrative determination. Is the review in the nature of the review of an agency determination, or is it in the nature of a de novo review?

At least one circuit has come very close to holding that the trial court is conducting a traditional administrative review. In *Karl v. Board of Education*,[56] the parents disagreed with a placement decision and requested a due process hearing. The parents wanted their mentally retarded daughter to be placed in a commercial food preparation program and the school proposed to place her in a work study program. The local due process hearing officer determined the student should be placed in the food preparation program with a student-adult ratio of nine-to-one. The school system appealed the decision to the New York State Commissioner of Education, who upheld the placement decision, but reversed the student-adult ratio requirement.

The parents then filed suit in the United States district court. The district court held that it agreed with the decision of the local hearing officer on the student-adult ratio and indicated that the court's obligation to defer to the judgment of the state educational authorities was diminished by the failure of the hearing officer and the Commissioner to agree. The Second Circuit reversed stating:

> we disagree with Judge Telesca's view that the federal courts need not defer to state educational authorities whenever there is some disagreement among state officers in the course of state proceedings. We believe *Rowley* requires that federal courts defer to the final decision of the state authorities, and that deference may not be eschewed merely because a decision is not unanimous or the reviewing authority disagrees with the hearing officer. There is no principle of administrative law which, in the event of a disagreement between a hearing officer and reviewing agency over demeanor evidence, obviates the need for deference to an agency's final decision where such deference is otherwise appropriate.[57]

---

54. Pierce, *supra* note 56, at 358. Traditional judicial review of agency findings functions like appellate review of a court decision on the issue of what can be considered. The general rule is that the court is limited to the agency record. The court cannot expand or delete the evidence submitted during the agency proceedings. Schwartz, *supra* note 54, at § 10.4.

55. Rowley, 458 U.S. at 206

56. 736 F.2d 873 (2d Cir. 1984). It ought at least to be clear that the standard of review is something more than an abuse of discretion standard. In *Roncker v. Walter*, 700 F.2d 1058 (6th Cir. 1983), the court reversed a district court decision which applied an abuse of discretion standard to the LEA's placement decision.

57. Karl, 736 F.2d at 877; *see also* Quackenbush v. Johnson City School Dist., 716 F.2d 141 (2d Cir. 1983), in which the Second Circuit, in what is clearly a misinterpretation of *Rowley*, stated that in *Rowley*, "the Supreme Court rejected a standard of *de novo* review...." *Id.* at 146. If that were the

The court's opinion evidences the strong influence of the traditional judicial approach to agency determinations. For example, the court's emphasis on deference to the final administrative determination is the classic view of administrative review. Indeed, the word deference in itself is interesting, since the United States Supreme Court in *Rowley* used the words "due weight," not deference.[58] Further, *Rowley*, contrary to the decision in *Karl*, does not even specifically state that due weight is to be given to the final administrative determination. Rather the Court left it ambiguous as to the party to whom due weight was to be given, indicating due weight was to be given to the "administrative proceedings."[59] Be that as it may, *Karl* does provide strong support for the argument that the reviewing court is to apply a substantial evidence standard.

There was a strong dissent in *Karl*:

> The majority characterizes this process as "deferential substantive review." However characterized, "deference" or "due weight" to the administrative proceedings does not mean simple subservience to the last administrator to speak, particularly when, as here, the combined expertise within the administrative system produced three different IEPs. *Rowley's* "gloss" on a clearly written statute requires only that the district judge give "due weight" to the views of the administrators; when those views conflict, it does not require him to accept the conclusion of the state's commissioner of education, nor does it relieve him of the burden of making the *de novo* determination required by congress. In ratifying the commissioner's decision, the majority has, in effect, adopted the substantial evidence standard of review that congress carefully rejected. Indeed, by semantically shifting *Rowley's* substantively oriented "reasonably calculated" standard to a procedural inquiry of whether the determination was a "reasoned calculation," the majority has effectively eliminated the substantive step of the *Rowley* analysis.[60]

Other courts, consistent with *Karl,* have held that suits under IDEA are analogous to appeals from administrative agencies and are not *de novo*.[61]

---

case, there would be little function for judicial review; that conclusion would be in direct contradiction to the provision that the court base its decision on a preponderance of the evidence.

58. Rowley, 458 U.S. at 206; *see also* Amanda J. v. Clark County School Dist., 267 F.3d 877 (9th Cir. 2001) (where determination regarding whether student has received a FAPE is made by a two-tiered state administrative system, due weight should be accorded to the final state determination by SRO, unless SRO's decision deviates from the credibility determination of a witness whom only the hearing officer (HO) observed testify); Carlisle Area School Dist., 62 F.3d 520, 529 (3d Cir. 1995) (district court due weight to appeals panel decision when it reverses the Hearing Officer's conclusion of law, inferences from proven facts and factual findings based on credibility judgments where nontestimonial extrinsic evidence justified contrary decision);.Murphysboro Community Units School Dist. v. Illinois Bd. of Educ., 41 F.3d 1162 (7th Cir. 1994) (gave "deference" to hearing officers who had considered case previously and experts who had testified before it, as opposed to educators who testified on behalf of school district); A.S. v. Madison Metropolitan School Dist., 477 F. Supp. 2d 969 (W.D. Wis. 2007) (due weight implies some sort of deference).

59. *Id.*

60. Karl, 736 F.2d at 878–79. The court went on to state:

.... [the judge] properly faced up to the hopeless conflict among the administrators over Lisa's needs and carried out his statutory responsibility by making a *de novo* determination of her appropriate IEP. *Id.*

61. Dale M. v. Board of Educ. of Bradley-Bourbonnais High, 237 F.3d 813 (7th Cir. 2001); Powers v. Indiana Dept. of Educ., 61 F.3d 552, 555 (7th Cir. 1995); Capistrano Unified School Dist. v. Wartenberg, 59 F.3d 884 (9th Cir. 1995) (not required to review hearing officer determinations *de novo*); Amann v. Town of Stow, 991 F.2d 929, 931 (1st Cir. 1993); Beth B. v. Van Clay, 211 F. Supp. 2d 1020, 1026 (N.D. Ill. 2001) (IDEA does not require a full trial *de novo*); Spiegler v. District of

The majority view is probably that the trial court's role is somewhere between *de novo* review and traditional administrative review. The First Circuit has characterized the level of review as "bounded, independent decisions—bounded by the administrative record and additional evidence, and independent by virtue of being based on a preponderance of the evidence before the court."[62] Under this view, the district court may accept or reject an administrative determination after reviewing it. "The extent of deference to be given the administrative findings of fact is an issue left to the discretion of the district court."[63] Under this view, "[f]indings by the state hearing officer must be reviewed as bearing on the federal right to an appropriate education and must receive the court's specific consideration."[64] What remains unclear under this view is what body actually is entitled to due weight. The prevailing view appears to be that due weight is not merely given to the final review officer's decision. "The court has discretion to give the administrative findings proper weight, with the concomitant obligation to consider those findings carefully and respond to the administrative resolution of issues."[65]

The approach of leaving the amount of weight given to the discretion of the trial court makes good sense. If due weight were limited to strictly educational policy questions, such as choosing the best method for educating the deaf, as opposed to factual questions of whether a particular child would benefit from one methodology or another, it would be logical to provide special consideration to the LEA, since it indeed has the expertise.

Several problems, however, exist with giving due weight to the determination of the LEA on issues other than which of two or more methodologies should be used. First, IDEA is a remedial statute and there is some lack of logic to giving special consideration to the group whose actions are sought to be remedied. Second, the language of § 1415 provides that the administrative proceedings are to be considered by

Columbia, 866 F.2d 461 (D.C. Cir. 1988;); *but see* Bernardsville Bd. of Educ. v. J.H., 817 F. Supp. 14, 18 (D.N.J. 1993).

62. Town of Burlington v. Department of Educ. of the Commonwealth of Massachusetts, 736 F.2d 773, 791 (1st Cir. 1984), *aff'd*, 471 U.S. 359 (1985). *See also* Kirkpatrick v. Lenoir County Bd. of Educ., 216 F.3d 380 (4th Cir. 2000) (action filed in federal court is an original state civil action, not an appeal); Roland M. v. Concord School Commission, 910 F.2d 983, 989–90 (1st Cir. 1990); Colin K. v. Schmidt, 715 F.2d 1, 5 (1st Cir. 1983); Barwacz v. Michigan Dept. of Educ., 681 F. Supp. 427 (W.D. Mich. 1987).

63. The Tenth, Third, Fourth and Sixth Circuits use a modified de novo review that requires the district court to make findings of fact based on the preponderance of evidence contained in the complete record while giving some deference to the fact findings of the administrative proceedings. S.H. v. State-Operated School Dist. of City of Newark, 336 F.3d 260 (3d Cir. 2003) (modified de novo review, giving "due weight" to the ALJ's factual findings, was appropriate standard for district court review of state administrative proceedings under IDEA); M.M. v. School Dist. of Greenville County, 303 F.3d 523, 530–1, (4th Cir. 2002); Knable v. Bexley City School Dist. 238 F.3d 755 (6th Cir. 2001); Jefferson County Bd. of Educ. v. Breen, 853 F.2d 853 (11th Cir. 1988); *see also* Lauren W. v. Deflaminis, 480 F.3d 259, 265 (3d Cir. 2007) (record evidence supported denial of compensatory education); Susan N. v. Wilson School Dist., 70 F.3d 751, 758 (3d Cir. 1995); Oberti v. Bd. of Educ. of Borough of Clemonton School Dist., 995 F.2d 1204, 1219 (3d Cir. 1993); G.D. v. Westmoreland School Dist., 930 F.2d 942 (1st Cir. 1991); Gregory K. v. Longview School Dist., 811 F.2d 1307 (9th Cir. 1987); Antoine M. v. Chester Upland School Dist., 420 F. Supp. 2d 396 (E.D. Pa. 2006); D.B. v. Ocean Township Bd. of Educ., 985 F. Supp. 457, 500 (D.N.J. 1997).

64. Town of Burlington v. Department of Educ. of the Commonwealth of Massachusetts, 736 F.2d 773, 792 (1st Cir. 1984), *aff'd*, 471 U.S. 369 (1985).

65. Burke County Bd. of Educ. v. Denton, 895 F.2d 973, 981 (4th Cir. 1990) *citing* Burlington, 736 F.2d at 792; *see also*, Doe v. Alabama State Dept. of Educ., 915 F.2d 651 (11th Cir. 1990).

the judge, and makes specific provision for the court to hear additional testimony and to make a determination by a preponderance of the evidence.[66] The ability to consider additional evidence requires the court to have the concomitant freedom to give less deference to an agency determination, since the agency will not have considered that additional evidence.

Indeed, the Fourth Circuit Court of Appeals in *School Board of Prince William County v. Malone*,[67] after discussing the standard of review articulated by *Rowley*, made it clear that any deference in the district court's review was to be to the state administrative proceedings and not to the school board. The court in *Malone* stated: "To give deference only to the decision of the School Board would render meaningless the entire process of administrative review."[68]

Limiting due weight to the final administrative decision would also be a mistake. As noted above, the Second Circuit in *Karl* gave great deference to the *final* state administrative determination.[69] The Supreme Court's language in *Rowley*, however, required that due weight should be given to the "administrative proceedings."[70] The Fourth Circuit has indicated that due weight is not limited to the review officer, but to the administrative proceedings as a whole,[71] and that the facts found by the local hearing officer concerning credibility are *prima facie* correct.[72] The Sixth Circuit, however, has held that due weight is to be accorded the final administrative decision.[73]

---

66. Preponderance is clearly a burden of persuasion question not a standard of review question. *See generally* Jaffe, *Administrative Law: Burden of Proof and Scope of Review*, 79 Harv. L. Rev. 914 (1966); *see also* County School Board of Henrico County, Virginia v. Z.P., 399 F.3d 298, 304 (4th Cir. 2005) (after giving the administrative fact-findings such due weight, if any, the district court then is free to decide the case on the preponderance of the evidence, as required by the statute); Kirkpatrick v. Lenoir County Bd. of Educ., 216 F.3d 380 (4th Cir. 2000).

67. 762 F.2d 1210 (4th Cir. 1985).

68. *Id.* at 1217. See County School Board of Henrico County, Virginia v. Z.P., 399 F.3d 298, 307 (4th Cir. 2005); *but see* Muller v. Committee on Special Educ. of East Islip Union Free School Dist., 145 F.3d 95 (2d Cir. 1998); Briggs v. Connecticut State Bd. of Educ., 882 F.2d 688 (2d Cir. 1989) (deference is due local and state education agencies because of expertise); Mr. X v. New York State Educ. Dept., 975 F. Supp. 546 (S.D.N.Y. 1997) (read administrative record, consider new evidence, make independent judgment based on the preponderance of evidence giving due weight to the hearing officers' decisions); Wall v. Mattiluck-Cutchogue School Dist., 945 F. Supp. 501 (E.D.N.Y. 1996); Doe v. Smith, 16 Educ. Handicapped L. Rep. (CRR) 65 (M.D. Tenn. 1988) (due weight to school and hearing officer).

69. *See supra* text and accompanying note 54.

70. Hendrick Hudson Dist. Bd. of Educ. v. Rowley, 458 U.S. 176, 206 (1982) (emphasis added).

71. Burke County Bd. of Educ. v. Denton, 895 F.2d 973 (4th Cir. 1990) ("the … argument that deference was due only to the review officer's conclusions is simply incorrect").

72. County School Bd. of Henrico County, Virginia v. Z.P., 399 F.3d 298 (4th Cir. 2005) (district court failed to give appropriate deference to state administrative hearing officer's findings); A.B. v. Lawson, 354 F.3d 315 (4th Cir. 2004) (district court, in assessing whether student's IEP provided him with required FAPE, failed to appropriately defer to factual findings of ALJ, and instead wrongfully substituted its own views on education policy, and those of parent and her experts, for determinations of local education officials charged with formulating the IEP); *see also* Doyle v. Arlington County Pub. School Bd., 953 F.2d 100 (4th Cir. 1991).

73. Burilovich v. Board of Educ. of Lincoln Consol. Schools, 208 F.3d 560 (6th Cir. 2000); Thomas F. v. Cincinnati Bd. of Educ., 918 F.2d 618, 624 (6th Cir. 1990) (it makes no difference that there may have been some disagreement among the state officers); *see also* Amanda J. v. Clark County School Dist., 267 F.3d 877 (9th Cir. 2001) (where determination regarding whether student has received a FAPE is made by a two-tiered state administrative system, due weight should be accorded to the final state determination by SRO, unless SRO's decision deviates from the credibility determination of a witness whom only the hearing officer (HO) observed testify).

13.7.3 Issues Subject to Due Weight

Decisions made by hearing officers and judges can be placed in four different categories: purely historical fact decisions (for example, what is the age of the child, or what disability does the child have?); strictly policy questions (for example, will a developmental approach versus a behavioral approach be adopted to educate a child[74] or which of two competing methods to teach deaf children to speak is better?);[75] factual questions concerning the appropriateness of a program for a particular child (for example, does this child require a residential program versus a day program?);[76] and legal questions concerning the interpretation of the statute (for example, whether the statute contemplates provision of a particular service as part of the educational requirements imposed on the LEA).[77] Most courts assume, without discussion, that due weight must be provided to all issues raised in the suit. A few courts, however, appear to limit due weight to certain types of issues.

It is arguable that there should be a different level of review for those issues that are more a question of educational policy than a factual determination of, for example, whether a given program was appropriate. Limiting due weight to matters of policy in this manner is consistent with opinions in the United States First Circuit Court of Appeals. *Doe v. Anrig*,[78] perhaps the most thoughtful case to date addressing the issue of judicial deference, involved a Down Syndrome child who had been in residential settings his entire life. In February, 1975, the LEA proposed placing the child in a nonresidential school setting. The parents rejected the IEP, but entered into an agreement whereby they paid for a residential component and the school paid for placement in a day school.

In 1977, on reevaluation, a new IEP proposed placing the child in a different nonresidential school and provided for him to live at home with his parents. The parents rejected the IEP and sought administrative review. The Massachusetts Bureau of Special Education Appeals held that the proposed placement was appropriate but that there should be a one-year transition program. This decision was affirmed by the Department of Education's State Advisory Council for Special Education. The parents sought judicial review.

The district court found that the parents had shown by a preponderance of the evidence that the residential program was the appropriate placement. Both parties ap-

---

74. *See* Abrahamson v. Hershman, 701 F.2d 223, 230–231 (1st Cir. 1983), where the court stated:

> Thus it might be inappropriate for a district court under the rubric of statutory construction to impose a particular methodology upon a state. Nevertheless, for judicial review to have any meaning, beyond mere review of state procedures, the courts must be free to construe the term "educational" so as to insure, at least, that the state IEP provides the hope of educational benefit.

75. *See generally* Rowley, 458 U.S. at 207 n.29.

76. *E.g.*, Abrahamson v. Hershman, 701 F.2d 223 (1st Cir. 1983); Lamoine School Committee v. Ms. Z., 353 F. Supp. 2d 18 (D. Me. 2005).

77. *See* Irving Indep. School Dist. v. Tatro, 468 U.S. 883 (1984) (discussion of related services required under IDEA); Mohawk Trail Regional School Dist. v. Shaun D., 35 F. Supp. 2d 34 (D. Mass. 1999).

78. 692 F.2d 800 (1st Cir. 1982). The First Circuit argument came before Rowley, but its opinion came after *Rowley*.

pealed the district court decision. The LEA argued that the district court failed to "grant substantial deference to the decisions of the state administrative bodies...."[79] The parents appealed on the issue of reimbursement. Addressing the LEA's contention, the First Circuit held:

> We disagree with [the LEA] insofar as they would limit the district court to the kind of judicial review of agency action contemplated under the Administrative Procedure Act. The statute unambiguously provides that a reviewing court may take cognizance of evidence not before the state educational agency and must base its decision on the preponderance of the evidence before it. As such, the review mechanism which the Act creates stands in sharp contrast to the usual situation where a court is confined to examining the record made before the agency [citation omitted] and to determining whether the administrative decision is supported by substantial evidence.[80]

The court then went on to indicate that "due weight" was directed toward policy considerations:

> [W]e find nothing in the record before us to suggest that "due weight" was not accorded. In addition, the Supreme Court's concern was with courts "substitut[ing] their own notions of educational *policy* for those of the school authorities." [citations omitted] The difference here between Judge Zobel and the school authorities was not a choice of educational *policy*, but resolution of an individualized *factual* issue as to the effect of John's handicap on his ability to benefit from the proposed school setting.[81]

Then, as if to stress the point further, a footnote added:

> No contention was or is made here that the residential placement approved by the court was an option which the state would disapprove on general policy grounds.[82]

In *Abrahamson v. Hershman*,[83] the First Circuit again addressed the question of whether a child required a residential placement in order to receive a FAPE. The public school presented the parents with an IEP calling for a day program and the parents appealed to the Massachusetts Bureau of Special Education Appeals (BSEA). The BSEA hearing officer found that the student's residential needs were not educationally related and therefore not the responsibility of the school system. The parents then appealed

---

79. *Id.* at 805.

80. *Id.* at 805, *citing* Town of Burlington v. Department of Educ., 655 F.2d 428, 431 (1st Cir. 1981). The court also rejected the contention that review was limited to whether the state had complied with procedures. This argument had been made in *Rowley*, the court pointed out, and was rejected:

> We find petitioners' contention unpersuasive, for Congress expressly rejected provisions that would have so severely restricted the role of reviewing courts. In substituting the current language of the statute for language that would have made state administrative findings conclusive if supported by substantial evidence, the Conference Committee explained that courts were to make 'independent decision[s] based on a preponderance of the evidence.'

Supra note 83, at 805, *citing* Rowley, 458 U.S. at 205.

81. 692 F.2d at 806.

82. *Id.* at 806 n.12.

83. 701 F.2d 223 (1st Cir 1983).

this decision to the State Advisory Commission, which reaffirmed the hearing officer's decision. The parents then filed suit in federal district court.

The district court held that the child's residential needs were educationally related. On appeal, the school system argued that the district court had failed to give due weight to the BSEA. The Circuit Court disagreed:

> To be sure, the district court did not reach the same result as did the BSEA. But, as the Supreme Court noted in *Rowley*, while courts must give "due weight" to state administrative agencies and "be careful to avoid imposing their view of preferable educational models upon the States," ... courts ultimately must make "independent decision[s] based on a preponderance of the evidence.
>
> .... The court did not disagree with the state over educational policy, merely over whether the state-licensed program ... would serve Daniel's own particular needs. Such an issue fell clearly within the scope of the question that *Rowley* left to the courts.[84]

Limiting strong deference to educational policy determinations makes good sense in light of the theory underlying judicial deference to administrative determinations. The history of SEAs and LEAs and the remedial nature of the legislation,[85] along with the fact that the administrative agencies to be remedied are in control of the administrative procedures,[86] makes broad deference to other issues questionable.

13.8 Burden of Proof in General

Burden of proof refers to two distinct questions: who has the burden of producing evidence on a particular issue and who has the burden of persuasion on a particular issue? Failure to produce evidence will result in a finding against the party bearing that burden. Once evidence is produced, however, there remains the separate question of whether the evidence persuades the fact finder under the applicable standard—a preponderance of the evidence, clear and convincing, or beyond a reasonable doubt.[87] In determining which party has the burden of persuasion, one must take into account such things as who pled the fact, what is judicially convenient, what is fair, and are there any special policy considerations. The clear "default" rule, however, is that the party seeking relief bears the burden of persuasion.[88]

Although the statute is explicit that the standard of proof is to be by a preponderance of the evidence, there is no specific indication which party shall bear the burdens of

---

84. *Id.* at 230–231; *see also* Manchester-Essex Regional School Dist. School Committee v. Bureau of Special Education Appeals 490 F. Supp. 2d 49, 52 (D.Mass. 2007); Ross v. Framingham School Committee, 44 F. Supp. 2d 104 (D. Mass. 1999) (Legal rulings by the agency are subject to *de novo* review. A hearing officer's finding of facts are given due deference unless the hearing officer's finding depended on an error of law.).

85. Honig v. Doe, 484 U.S. 305 (1988).

86. 20 U.S.C. § 1412(6) requires the state to establish procedural safeguards.

87. McCormick, *Evidence* § 336 (6th ed. 2007).

88. *Id.* at § 337.

production and of persuasion. In the absence of this specificity, courts have reached different interpretations.[89]

13.8.1 Burden of Persuasion on Substantive Issues

Prior to the United States Supreme Court decision in *Schaffer v. Weast*,[90] there was a split of opinion as to which party has the burden of persuasion in disputes between parents and the school system. Some courts placed the burden of persuasion on the party seeking to change the *status quo*.[91] Other courts held that the burden is always on the LEA to prove the appropriateness of its IEP.[92] In *Schaffer v. Weast*, the United States Supreme Court adopted the first view, stating:

> The burden of [persuasion] in an administrative hearing challenging an IEP is properly placed upon the party seeking relief. In this case, that party is [the child], as represented by his parents. But the rule applies with equal effect to school districts: If they seek to challenge an IEP, they will in turn bear the burden of persuasion before an ALJ.[93]

It should be understood that the allocation of the burden of persuasion is not always on the parents. In *Schaffer*, the disputed IEP was the initial IEP for a student who was entering public school for the first time. It was the parents who were seeking a change in the *status* quo; the parents who were seeking relief. If the student had an existing IEP and the LEA was trying to get the parents to change it, given the stay-put provision, the LEA would need to seek relief by filing a due process hearing.

One issue that remains is whether individual state's can override the Court's determination that the burden is on the party seeking relief. Prior to *Schaffer* several states had adopted provisions placing the burden of persuasion on the LEA regardless of which party is seeking relief.[94] Other states had allocated the burden of persuasion in other manners such as depending on the relief that is sought.[95] At least one state, New York,

89. *See* § 13.8.1.

90. 546 U.S. 49 (2005).

91. *See, e.g.,* Tatro v. Texas (Tatro II), 703 F.2d 823 (5th Cir. 1983); Doe v. Brookline School Committee, 722 F.2d 910 (1st Cir. 1983); *see also* McLaughlin v. Holt Public Schools Bd. of Educ., 320 F.3d 663 (6th Cir. 2003); Dong v. Board of Educ. of Rochester Comm. Schools, 197 F.3d 793 (6th Cir. 1999) (party challenging terms of IEP should bear burden of proving that placement was not appropriate); Cordrey v. Eukert, 917 F.2d 1460, 1469 (6th Cir. 1990) ("the party challenging the terms of the IEP should bear the burden of proving the educational placement ... is not appropriate"); Doe v. Defendant I, 898 F.2d 1186, 1191 (6th Cir. 1990) (citing *Tatro*).

92. *See, e.g.* Oberti v. Board of Educ., 995 F.2d 1204, 1219 (3d Cir.1993) (in administrative and judicial proceedings, the LEA bears the burden of proving the appropriateness of the IEP it has proposed); Fuhrmann v. East Hanover Bd. of Educ., 993 F.2d 1031, 1035 (3d Cir.1993) ("[T]he burden of showing that the placement is 'appropriate' rests with the LEA). *See generally* Guernsey, *When the Teachers and Parents Can't Agree, Who Really Decides? Burdens of Proof and Standards of Review Under The Education for All Handicapped Children Act*, 36 Cleveland State Law Review 67 (1988).

93. Schaffer, 546 U.S. at 62.

94. *See, e.g.,* Alaska Admin. Code, tit. 4, § 52.550(e)(9) (2003); Ala. Admin. Code, Rule 290-8-9.08(8)(C)(6)(ii)(I) (Supp. 2004); Del. Code Ann., tit14, 3140; 1 D.C. Mun. Regs., tit. 5, § 3030.3 (2003); W. Va. Code Rules § 126-16-8.1.11(c) (2005).

95. *See, e.g.,* Ga. Comp. Rules & Regs., Rule 160-4-7-.18(g)(8) (2002); Minn. Stat. § 125A.091, subd. 16 (2004).

amended its statute in response to Schaffer, placing the burden on the LEA in all cases except when a parent seeks tuition reimbursement for a unilateral parental placement.[96] The Court in *Schaffer* refused to decide the validity of such state provisions, holding that "[b]ecause no such law or regulation exists in Maryland, we need not decide this issue today."[97]

13.8.2 Burden of Proof on Procedural Issues

There is a strong argument that the LEA should bear more responsibility for the burden of persuasion on procedural issues, regardless of which party is seeking to change the *status quo*. As stated by the United States Supreme Court, "Congress placed every bit as much emphasis upon compliance with procedures giving parents and guardians a large measure of participation at *every* stage of the administrative process."[98] Procedural violations, as a result, have occupied increased importance in disputes between the LEA and the parents.[99]

In fact, the Supreme Court in *Rowley* held that judicial inquiry begins with whether "the state complied with the procedures set forth in the EAHCA."[100] The Court added that such inquiry will require a court not only "to satisfy itself that the state has adopted a state plan, policies and assurances required by the EAHCA, but also determine that the state has created an IEP ... which conforms with the requirements of § 1401(19)[now (11)]."[101]

This language indicates that *Rowley* imposes an affirmative requirement that inquiry be made into procedural compliance. Since it is the LEA's responsibility to ensure the procedural rights of the parents,[102] it is arguably the LEA which must carry this burden. Allocating the burden of proof to the LEA to show compliance with pro-

---

96. The 2007 New York amendment provides:
   The board of education or trustees of the school district or the state agency responsible for providing education to students with disabilities shall have the burden of proof, including the burden of persuasion and burden of production, in any such impartial hearing, except that a parent or person in parental relation seeking tuition reimbursement for a unilateral parental placement shall have the burden of persuasion and burden of production on the appropriateness of such placement.
McKinney's Educ. Law, tit. VI, article 89, § 4404(1)(c)
   97. Shaffer, 546 U.S. at 61–62. Justice Breyer, argued in dissent that Congress "left the matter to the States for decision" *Id*. at 70–71 (Breyer dissenting).
   98. Rowley, 458 U.S. at 205 (emphasis added).
   99. *See, e.g.*, M.L. v. Federal Way School Dist.341 F.3d 1052 (9th Cir 2003); Erickson v. Albuquerque Public Schools, 199 F.3d 1116 (10th Cir. 1999) (procedural violation of IDEA does not preclude a finding that school district provided a FAPE); Spielberg v. Henrico County Pub. Schools, 853 F.2d 256 (4th Cir. 1988) (decision to change placement prior to development of an IEP violated procedural protections); Jackson v. Franklin County School Bd., 806 F.2d 623 (5th Cir. 1986) (procedural violations sufficient to support finding that LEA has failed to provide FAPE); Hall v. Vance, 774 F.2d 629 (4th Cir. 1985) (procedural violations sufficient to support finding that LEA has failed to provide FAPE).
   100. Rowley, 458 U.S. at 206.
   101. *Id.* at 206–07 n.27.
   102. 20 U.S.C. § 1415(a).

cedural requirements is consistent with the underlying purpose of IDEA, which was remedial in nature.[103]

In *S-1 v. Turlington*,[104] a case involving student expulsion, the court stated that in "light of the remedial purposes of these statutes we find that the burden is on the local and state defendants to make this determination. Our conclusion is buttressed by the fact that in most cases, the handicapped students and their parents lack the wherewithal to know or assert their rights under either EHA or Section 504."[105] Since the procedural rights of IDEA were designed to remedy a problem, it is logical that the agency sought to be remedied show that it has indeed complied.

As a further reason for allocating the burden of proof for procedural violations to the LEA, it should be kept in mind that the aids available to the parent on the substantive issues such as an IEE and access to documents, are of more limited use when it comes to procedural violations. Formal discovery procedures are not available at the administrative level, and evidence of procedural violations may not be in the student's educational records.[106] It should be pointed out, however, that the Sixth Circuit, in *Cordrey v. Euckert*,[107] held that "[a]bsent more definitive authorization or compelling justification, we decline to go beyond strict review to reverse the traditional burden of proof."

13.9 Jury Trials

IDEA claims are not subject to a jury trial because the statute specifically provides that the court will make a determination based on a preponderance of the evidence.[108] Further, the relief available under IDEA is equitable in nature.[109]

---

103. *See* Clune & VanPelt, *A Political Method of Evaluating The Education For All Handicapped Children Act Of 1975 And Several Gaps Of Gap Analysis*, 48 Law & Contemp. Prob. 7, 12–20 (1985); Neal & Kirp, *The Allure of Legalization Reconsidered: The Case of Special Education*, 48 Law & Contemp. Prob. 63, 67–72 (1985); *see generally* S-1 v. Turlington, 635 F.2d 342, 348–349 (5th Cir. 1981) ("In light of the remedial purposes of these statutes....").

104. 635 F.2d 342 (5th Cir. 1981).

105. *Id.* at 349.

106. It is conceivable, for example, that the school system, in violation of IDEA, has decided that it will not place children in residential programs. *See* Abrahamson v. Hershman, 701 F.2d 223, 227 (1st Cir. 1983). Evidence of this policy decision is most likely to exist in records other than the child's educational file.

107. 917 F.2d 1460, 1466 (6th Cir. 1990).

108. 20 U.S.C. § 1415(i)(2)(C)(iii).

109. *Compare* Guardians Assn v. Civil Service Commn., 463 U.S. 582 (1983) (no jury trial under Title VI); Great American Fed. Savings and Loan Assn. v. Novotny, 442 U.S. 366, 372–375 (1979) (no right to a jury trial under Title VII); Doe v. Region 13 Mental Health-Mental Retardation Comm'n, 704 F.2d 1402, 1407 n.3 (5th Cir. 1983) ("The inappropriateness of trial before the jury is underscored by the apparent absence of legal damages under Section 504."); Shuttleworth v. Broward County, 639 F. Supp. 654, 661 (S.D. Fla. 1986) ("Courts have generally found that there is no right to trial by jury under § 504 ... because the remedies under the Act are essentially equitable in nature.").

An additional argument that there is no right to a jury trial under IDEA would be that judicial jurisdiction under IDEA is in the nature of a review of an administrative determination, and therefore raises questions for the court as opposed to a jury. *See* B. Schwartz, *Administrative Law* § 10.11 (3d ed. 1991). The court's review under IDEA, however, is greater than the typical administrative

Suits brought under § 1983, however, are subject to trial by jury.[110] It is conceivable, therefore, that when Congress amended IDEA to allow suit also under § 1983,[111] it may have given the option to parties to request a jury trial by bringing suit concurrently under a § 1983 claim. At least one United States District Court has provided a jury trial in a suit alleging violations of § 1983 and IDEA.[112]

13.10 Evidence

There has been little discussion in cases concerning the nature of the judicial hearing itself. IDEA states that the record of the administrative proceedings "shall" be received and that "additional evidence" "shall" be received at the request of a party. The First Circuit is one of the few courts to interpret this language:

> this clause does not authorize witnesses at trial to repeat or embellish their prior administrative hearing testimony; this would be entirely inconsistent with the usual meaning of "additional."
>
> .... the Act contemplates that the source of the evidence generally will be the administrative hearing record, with some supplementation at trial. The reasons for the supplementation will vary; they may include gaps in the administrative transcript owing to mechanical failure, unavailability of a witness, an improper exclusion of evidence by the administrative agency, and evidence concerning relevant events occurring subsequent to the administrative hearing. The starting point for determining what additional evidence should be received, however, is the record of the administrative proceeding.[113]

---

review. The requirement that the court make an independent determination based on a preponderance of the evidence, 20 U.S.C. § 1415(i)(2)(C)(iii), while giving due weight to the administrative proceedings, Hendrick Hudson Cent. School Dist. v. Rowley, 458 U.S. 176, 205–206 (1982), makes the courts review close to a *de novo* hearing. *See generally* Guernsey, *When The Teachers And Parents Can't Agree, Who Really Decides? Burdens of Proof And Standards Of Review Under The Education For All Handicapped Children Act*, 36 Cleveland State L. Rev. 67, 77–86 (1988).

Although a claim may not technically be subject to trial by jury, if the parties request a jury trial and the court does not on its own initiative find it improper, there is no error. *See* Doe, 704 F.2d at 1407 n.3; *see also, e.g.*, Ross v. Beaumont Hospital, 678 F. Supp. 1115 (E.D. Mich. 1988) (§ 504 action tried by jury).

110. S. Nahmod, *Civil Rights and Civil Liberties Litigation* §§ 1.01, 1.13 (4th ed. 1997 and Supp. 1998–2007).

111. *See* § 1.5.

112. Dodds v. Simpson, 676 F. Supp. 1045 (D. Ore. 1987). The suit also involved claimed § 504 violations. To the extent the relief sought is equitable in nature, a jury trial is inappropriate. To the extent there are both legal issues (*e.g.*, compensatory damages) and equitable issues (*e.g.*, injunctive relief) the legal issues should first be tried by the jury and then the equitable issues tried by the court. Ross v. Bernhard, 396 U.S. 531, 537–38 (1970).

113. Town of Burlington v. Department of Educ. of the Commonwealth of Massachusetts, 736 F.2d 773, 790 (1st Cir. 1984), *aff'd*, 471 U.S. 369 (1985): West Platte R-II School Dist. v. Wilson, 439 F.3d 782, 785 (8th Cir. 2006) (may entirely preclude additional evidence under Burlington even if requested); Taylor v. Vermont Dept. of Educ. 313 F.3d 768,790 (2d Cir. 2002) ("relaxed approach to admitting additional evidence undercuts one of the purposes of the due process hearing—developing a complete factual record."); *see also* Walker County School Dist. v. Bennett, 203 F.3d 1293 (11th Cir. 2000); Monticello School District v. George L., 102 F.3d 895 (7th Cir. 1996); Ojai Unified School Dist. v. Jackson, 4 F.3d 1467 (9th Cir. 1993); Konkel v. Elmbrook School Dist. 348 F. Supp. 2d 1018 (E.D. Wis. 2004); Handleman v. Board of Educ. of Penfield Cent. School

Applying these standards, the court held that an administrative hearing witness is presumed to be foreclosed from testifying at trial. The presumption can be overcome, but the Court "must be careful not ... to change the character of the hearing from one of review to a trial *de novo*."[114]

In ruling on the motions for witnesses to testify, a court should weigh heavily the important concerns of not allowing a party to undercut the statutory role of administrative expertise, the unfairness of one party's reserving its best evidence for trial, the reason the witness did not testify at the administrative hearing, and the conservation of judicial resources.[115]

In practice, the trial court, at least outside the First Circuit, is much more likely to allow at least a brief reworking of the basic issues in the case.[116] Further, the Sixth Circuit has held that new evidence is admissible.[117] For example, in approving the school's attempt to introduce the appropriateness of placements not raised at the administrative hearing, the court stated, "[i]t is appropriate for a court that has determined that a hearing officer failed to consider the statutorily least restrictive alternative requirement to consider less restrictive placements."[118] It appears, however, that one additional witness who may not be called in the trial is the administrative review officer.[119] Of course, additional evidence should be inadmissible if it related to an issue that was not raised in the administrative proceeding.[120]

13.11 Appellate Review of Judicial Determinations

The appellate court will consider the case only under theories upon which it was tried.[121] There is, however, some disagreement as to the standard of review to which

Dist., Slip Copy, 2007 WL 3076970 (W.D.N.Y. 2007) ("showing should include an explanation as to why the evidence was not presented at the administrative level and why it is probative of the issues before the court."); Brandon H. v. Kennewick School Dist., 82 F. Supp. 2d 1174 (E.D. Wash. 2000); *see also* Independent School District v. S.D., 88 F.3d 556, 560 (8th Cir. 1996) (court takes restrictive approach to the issue without expressly adopting the *Burlington* rule); Susan N. v. Wilson School District, 70 F.3d 751, 759–60 (3d Cir. 1995) (court takes restrictive approach, "relevant non cumulative and useful").

114. Town of Burlington v. Department of Educ. of the Commonwealth of Massachusetts, 736 F.2d 773, 791 (1st Cir. 1984), *aff'd*, 471 U.S. 369 (1985); *see also* School Board of Collier County, Fla. v. K.C., 285 F.3d 977 (11th Cir. 2002) (board could be permitted to supplement record with expert testimony; and student was not entitled to supplement record to rebut board's expert testimony); Walker County School Dist. v. Bennett, 203 F.3d 1293 (11th Cir. 2000).

115. Town of Burlington v. Department of Educ. of the Commonwealth of Massachusetts, 736 F.2d 773, 791 (1st Cir. 1984), *aff'd*, 471 U.S. 369 (1985).

116. *But see* Barwacz v. Michigan Dept. of Educ., 681 F. Supp. 427 (W.D. Mich. 1987).

117. Deal v. Hamilton County Board of Educ. 392 F.3d 840 (6th Cir. 2004).

118. Metropolitan Govt. v. Cook, 915 F.2d 232 (6th Cir. 1990).

119. Feller v. Board of Educ., 583 F. Supp. 1526 (D. Ct. 1984) (state review officer may not be called as a witness in subsequent trial absence allegation of bad faith or improper motive on part of officer).

120. Metropolitan Bd. of Public Educ. v. Guest, 193 F.3d 457 (6th Cir. 1999) (court exceeded its jurisdiction to the extent that it used additional evidence to rule upon issues beyond those presented to ALJ).

121. St. Louis Developmental Disabilities Treatment Center Parents' Assn. v. Mallory, 767 F.2d 518 (8th Cir. 1985); Alexopulos v. Riles, 784 F.2d 1408 (9th Cir. 1986).

these issues will be subjected. Traditional analysis would lead one to conclude that appellate court review of the lower court's determination would be controlled by the law-
fact distinction. Trial court factual determinations are subject to review only under a
clearly erroneous standard[122] whereas decisions of law are decided *de novo*.[123] Under this
traditional analysis, questions such as whether IDEA requires provision of related services, whether prior to the 1986 amendment IDEA contemplated an award of attorneys'
fees,[124] and who under IDEA has the burden of proof are reviewed *de novo* by the appellate court.

Factual questions should, however, remain subject to the clearly erroneous standard
of review required under Federal Rule of Civil Procedure 52. For example, if it has been
decided that IDEA prohibits the LEA from making a placement decision prior to development of an IEP, it is a factual conclusion whether the LEA actually had reached the
decision to place the child prior to development of the IEP.[125]

Not all decisions, however, fall neatly into the fact or law categories. A third category
is one of mixed law and fact requiring application of a legal standard to a particular historical fact or set of facts relating to the legal standard. Many commentators have
pointed out that there is less unanimity on the standard to be applied to legal application decisions.[126]

Whether application of historical facts to a legal standard constitutes a factual determination governed by the clearly erroneous standard, or a legal question allowing *de
novo* review, varies not simply from jurisdiction to jurisdiction, but within jurisdictions
and even within topics. An often repeated example is in the area of negligence where the
question is application of a reasonable person standard to the facts of a particular incident. Most courts have held that such an application is a question of fact.[127] Other instances of fact application, however, are less uniform.[128]

In the context of IDEA, most courts have held that the basic issue of whether the
LEA's proposal will provide a free and appropriate education is a factual determination

---

122. *See* Jaffe, *Administrative Law: Burden of Proof and Scope of Review.*, 79 Harv. L. Rev. 914
(1966).

123. *Id.*; *see also* Erickson v. Albuquerque Public Schools, 199 F.3d 1116 (10th Cir. 1999) (*de
novo* review of district court granting of summary judgment applying same standard to the district
court, due weight to issues with which she disagrees with hearing officer unless hearing officer decision involved credibility determinations and the record supports the review officers decision); Stan-
court v. Worthington City School Dist. Bd. of Educ., 841 N.E.2d 812 (Ct App. Ohio 2005) (review
based on hybrid standard of clearly erroneous and de novo); Cremeans v. Fairland Local School
Dist. Bd. of Educ., 633 N.E.2d 570 (Ct. App. Ohio 1993) (appropriate standard of review for appellate courts of judicial determinations in IDEA actions is hybrid standard under which appellate
court must accept trial courts findings of fact if they are not clearly erroneous and accepting those
facts as true court must determine *de novo* whether proposed IEPs are legally appropriate); *see generally* White v. School Bd. of Henrico County,
36 Va. App. 137, 549 S.E.2d 16 (2001); School Bd. v. Beasley, 238 Va. 44, 380 So. 2d 884 (1989)
(Court of Appeals had authority to reverse trial court only if decision plainly wrong or without evidence to support it).

124. *See, e.g.*, Smith v. Robinson, 468 U.S. 992 (1984). Following *Smith*, IDEA was amended to
allow attorneys' fees. 20 U.S.C. § 1415(i)(3)(B).

125. *See, e.g.*, Spielberg v. Henrico County Pub. Schools, 853 F.2d 256 (4th Cir. 1988).

126. *See, e.g.*, Weiner, *The Civil Nonjury Trial and the Law-Fact Distinction*, 55 Cal. L. Rev. 1020,
1021–1024 (1967).

127. *Id.* at 1024; *but see id.* at 1026–1031.

128. *Id.* at 1022–1024.

and, therefore, subject to the clearly erroneous standard.[129] In *Mathews v. Davis*,[130] the Fourth Circuit affirmed the decision of the district court holding that a school system's continued funding of a residential placement was no longer necessary. In the words of the appellate court:

> We are of the opinion the finding of the district court was not clearly erroneous. FRCP 52(a). It saw some of the witnesses and heard them testify. It had lived with the case through a multitude of hearings, orders, etc., for a period of five years, and its sensitive, systematic and thorough treatment of the parties and issues in the case from beginning to end is a model. It was in a far better position than are we to make an adjudication as to whatever slight conflict there was in the evidence.[131]

At least one panel of a federal circuit court, however, has held that it will review *de novo* the appropriateness of a special education placement. In *Department of Education v. Katherine D.*,[132] the court stated:

> We apply a *de novo* standard of review to the questions whether the DOE's [Department of Education] IEPs constituted a "free appropriate education" within the meaning of the EAHCA.... Because those determinations require us to weigh the values underlying the statute in deciding the legal sufficiency of the DOE's offers—we must, for instance, determine the weight to be assigned

129. *See, e.g.*, West Platte R-II School Dist. v. Wilson, 439 F.3d 782 (8th Cir. 2006) (district court did not clearly err in determining that administrative panel members were impartial); Reid v. District of Columbia, 401 F.3d 516 (D.C. Cir. 2005) (de novo review applied to District Court's grant of summary judgment); Shore Regional High School Bd. of Educ. v. P.S., 381 F.3d 194 (3d Cir. 2004) (district court's finding that school district provided a FAPE as required by the IDEA was clearly erroneous); T.B. v. Warwick School Committee, 361 F.3d 80 (1st Cir.2004); McLaughlin v. Holt Public Schools Bd. of Educ., 320 F.3d 663, 669 (6th Cir. 2003) (clearly erroneous to findings of fact and de novo to conclusions of law); School Dist. of Wisconsin Dells v. Z.S., 295 F.3d 671 (7th Cir. 2002) (even if district judge erred by applying the wrong standard of "independent" review when reversing ALJ's determination, such error was harmless); T.R. v. Kingwood Township Bd. of Educ., 205 F.3d 572 (3d Cir. 2000) (appeals must accept district court's findings of fact unless they are clearly erroneous); Geis v. Board of Educ., 774 F.2d 575, 584 (3d Cir. 1985) ("The Board has referred us to no other evidence that would tend to indicate that the district court's finding [that residential placement was appropriate] was clearly erroneous or, indeed, even erroneous."); Cain v. Yukon Pub. Schools, Dist. I-27, 775 F.2d 15, 20 (11th Cir. 1985) ("We cannot find clearly erroneous the district court's determination that the response was adequate."); McKenzie v. Smith, 771 F.2d 1527, 1535 (D.C. Cir. 1985) ("Although the evidence could also support a contrary conclusion, we cannot say that the district court's factual findings were clearly erroneous."); Jackson v. Franklin County School Bd., 765 F.2d 535, 539 (5th Cir. 1985) ("Because the district court's finding is not clearly erroneous...."); Abrahamson v. Hershman, 701 F.2d 223, 227 (1st Cir. 1983) ("We cannot say that this conclusion was clearly erroneous."); Colin K. v. Schmidt, 715 F.2d 1, 6 (1st Cir. 1983) ("Our responsibility [is] to uphold the court's findings unless they are clearly erroneous."); Doe v. Anrig, 692 F.2d 800, 808 (1st Cir. 1982) ("The task of weighing the evidence, however, is for the trier of fact, which here was the district court. As a reviewing court we are limited to the question of whether the district court's finding was clearly erroneous."); Jose P. v. Ambach, 669 F.2d 865, 871 (2d Cir. 1982) (allocation of legal responsibility "was not clearly erroneous"); *see also* Adams Central School Dist. No. 090 v. Deist, 334 N.W.2d 775, 782 (Neb. 1983) ("We are only to determine if the hearing officer's decision is supported by the evidence, is proper under applicable law, and if it is arbitrary or capricious."); *but see* Strawn v. Missouri State Bd. of Educ., 210 F.3d 954, 958 (8th Cir. 2000)) (district court clearly erroneous when does not even acknowledge or reference the "due weight" standard of review).

130. 742 F.2d 825 (4th Cir. 1984).
131. *Id.* at 831; *see also* Hall v. Vance, 774 F.2d 629 (4th Cir. 1985).
132. 727 F.2d 809 (9th Cir. 1983).

the explicit congressional preference that handicapped children be educated in classrooms with their peers ... we treat them as questions of law.[133]

---

133. *Id.* at 814 n.2; *see also* Clovis Unified School Dist. v. California Office of Administrative Hearings, 903 F.2d 635 (9th Cir. 1990) (*de novo* review of whether psychiatric hospital placement was educational or medical); Gregory K. v. Longview School Dist., 811 F.2d 1307 (9th Cir. 1987) ("We review *de novo* the appropriateness of a special education placement."); *but see* Larry P. v. Riles, 793 F.2d 969, 978 (9th Cir. 1984) ("The district court made two findings that addressed this argument which appellant has not shown to be clearly erroneous."). This apparent inconsistency within the circuit on the issue of what standard to apply to a specific type of factual application is not new to the Ninth Circuit. *See* Weiner, 55 Cal. L. Rev., *supra* note 126, at 1029–30; *see also* Hood v. Encinitas Union School Dist., 486 F.3d 1099, 1104 (9th Cir. 2007) (This court reviews questions of law and mixed questions of fact and law de novo unless the mixed question is primarily factual).

Chapter 14

Remedies

14.1 In General

Typically, the parties in a special education case are seeking a determination of the relative responsibilities of the parents and school system for the delivery of services to the child. The parents, for example, believe the school's proposed IEP will not provide a free appropriate education or the school seeks a decision determining that the level of services it is prepared to provide are sufficient under IDEA. The most common remedy sought, therefore, is in the nature of injunctive or declaratory relief. Requests for damages, reimbursement and compensatory education, however, are frequent, and under limited circumstances, may be available.

14.2 State Immunity Abrogated

As a general matter, there is no immunity problem when seeking to sue a local education agency (LEA) in federal court.[1] The Eleventh Amendment to the United States Constitution, however, prevents a *state* or state agency from being sued for damages in federal court. Before suit can be brought in federal court against a state education agency (SEA), therefore, it must be determined whether this immunity has been abrogated.

In 1989, the United States Supreme Court in *Dellmuth v. Muth*,[2] held that Congress had not explicitly abrogated the state's Eleventh Amendment immunity in actions under IDEA, and, therefore, recovery from the state was precluded. In *Dellmuth*, the trial court found a procedural violation by the state in setting up its administrative re-

---

1. Woods v. Roundout Valley Central School Dist. Board of Educ., 466 F.3d 232 (2d Cir. 2006) (board of education is not arm of State of New York entitled to 11th amendment immunity); Holz v. Nenana City Public School Dist. 347 F.3d 1176 (9th Cir. 2003); Cuesta v. School Board of Miami-Dade County, 285 F.3d 962, 966 (11th Cir. 2002); *see also* Fay v. South Colonie Central School Dist., 802 F.2d 21 (2d Cir. 1986) (damages could not be obtained against state defendant, but damages are available against local school division*), overruled on other grounds* Taylor v. Vt. Dept of Educ. 313 F.3d 768 (2d Cir. 2002); Land v. Washington County Minnesota, 243 F.3d 1093, 1094 (8th Cir. 2001); Gilliam v. Omaha, 524 F.2d 1013 (8th Cir. 1975); Edelman v. Jordan, 415 U.S. 651, 667 n.12 (1974) ("a county defendant is not necessarily a state defendant for purposes of the Eleventh Amendment"); *see generally* Carey v. Piphus, 435 U.S. 247 (1978); Thro, *The Eleventh Amendment Revolution in Lower Court Cases, 25 J. College & Univ. L. 501 (1999).*
2. 491 U.S. 223 (1989).

view procedure. The violation resulted in a child not receiving an appropriate education. The trial court ordered reimbursement and attorneys' fees. The Supreme Court's decision overturned this result.

The United States Congress reacted quickly to *Dellmuth*, and, in 1990, passed the Education of Individuals with Disabilities Act Amendments. In a section entitled "Abrogation of State Sovereign Immunity," IDEA was amended to state explicitly that States "shall not be immune under the eleventh amendment to the Constitution of the United States from suit in Federal court for a violation of this chapter."[3]

Under the principle theory of abrogation, however, Congressional intent is not itself sufficient to abrogate Eleventh Amendment immunity. Not only must Congress unequivocally express its intent to abrogate immunity, Congress must be acting pursuant to a valid grant of constitutional authority.[4] Legislation is an appropriate exercise of congressional power when the legislation is preventive or remedial. Specifically, the question is whether the legislation is designed to enforce § 5 of the Fourteenth Amendment.[5]

Given this standard, it is not surprising that many courts have held that Congress' attempt in 1990 to abrogate the immunity was a valid exercise of Congressional authority.[6] Other courts, however, have held that the scope of IDEA exceeds what is required to enforce § 5 of the Fourteenth Amendment, and, therefore the abrogation attempt is invalid.[7]

Given that IDEA is a funding statute, an alternative theory of abrogation may apply. It has been argued that by accepting Part B funds, states have waived their Eleventh Amendment immunity. The United States Supreme Court has recognized that Congress, consistent with its spending power, may condition receipt of federal funds on such abrogation.[8]

---

3. 20 U.S.C. § 1403. Only violations that "occur in whole or in part after October 30, 1990" are affected by the abrogation amendment. Violations occurring wholly before this explicit attempt at abrogation are not covered. 20 U.S.C. § 1407; *see generally* Garro v. Connecticut, 23 F.3d 734 (2d Cir. 1994) (immunity not abrogated for conduct occurring before 1988); *see also* Joshua B. v. New Trier Township High School Dist. 293, 770 F. Supp. 431 (N.D. Ill. 1991).

4. Kimmel v. Florida Bd. of Regents, 528 U.S. 62 (2000); Seminole Tribe of Florida v. Florida, 517 U.S. 44 (1996). *Kimmel* was a 5-4 holding that despite the Age Discrimination in Employment Act, ADEA, clearly stating Congress' intent to abrogate state immunity, the attempted abrogation exceeded Congress' authority under the two step analysis. The ADEA was not appropriate legislation under the Fourteenth Amendment because the statute bars conduct that is not unconstitutional and legislative history evinces no Congressional finding to support prophylactic action against the states.

5. Florida Prepaid Postsecondary Educ. Expense Bd. v. College Sav. Bank, 527 U.S. 627 (1999); *see* City of Boerne v. Flores, 521 U.S. 507, 530 (1997); Bradley v. Arkansas Dept. of Educ., 189 F.3d 745, 750, *rehearing en banc granted, and opinion vacated in part on other grounds sub nom.* Jim C. v. Arkansas Dept. of Educ., 197 F.3d 958 (8th Cir. 1999).

6. *See, e.g.,* Pace v. Bogulusa City School Bd., 403 F.3d 272 (5th Cir. 2005); City M.A. v. State Operated School Dist. of City of Newark, 344 F.3d 335 (3d Cir. 2003); A.W. v. Jersey City Public Schools, 341 F.3d 234 (3d Cir. 2003); Board of Educ. of Oak Park and River Forest H.S. Dist. No. 200 v. Kelly E., 207 F.3d 931 (7th Cir. 2000) (IDEA validly abrogated state immunity under the 11th amendment); Alexopulos v. San Francisco Unified School Dist., 817 F.2d 551 (9th Cir. 1987) (although no Eleventh Amendment bar to claim against LEA, recovery denied on other grounds).

7. *See, e.g.,* Bradley v. Arkansas Dept. of Educ., 189 F.3d 745, *rehearing en banc granted, and opinion vacated in part on other grounds sub nom.* Jim C. v. Arkansas Dept. of Educ., 197 F.3d 958 (8th Cir. 1999) (IDEA's sovereign immunity and Rehabilitation Act's abrogation provision were not effective as proper exercise of Congress' Fourteenth Amendment enforcement clause powers); Emma v. Eastin, 985 F. Supp. 940, (N.D. Cal. 1997) (immunity not abrogated for clams brought under IDEA, Section 504 and ADA).

8. College Savings Bank v. Florida Postsecondary Educ, Expense Bd., 527 U.S. 627 (1999). Indeed, at least one court that found Congress had not validly abrogated immunity under the first theory held that "Congress provided clear, unambiguous warning of its intent to condition state participation in the IDEA program and its receipt of federal IDEA funds on the state's waiver."

Suits brought in federal court against the state alleging a violation under §504 must overcome similar Eleventh Amendment immunity issues. Again, courts are split as to whether Congress has validly abrogated immunity.[9]

Where Eleventh Amendment immunity does not exist, thus allowing suit in federal court, most courts have held that the state has some responsibility for the delivery of educational services to individual students. Citing the general obligation of the state agency to monitor local agencies, courts have held that state agencies can be made parties under some circumstances[10] but local school divisions do not have a private right of action against the state.[11]

The United States Ninth Circuit in *Doe v. Maher*,[12] reached the conclusion the state was responsible using a number of rationales. First, it relied on the state's general supervisory obligations under IDEA. Further, it relied on the provision of IDEA that requires children be educated at the state or regional level when a local agency "has one or more handicapped children who can best be served by a regional or state center...."[13] The Ninth Circuit however, stated that "the breach must be significant ... the child's parents or guardian must give the responsible state officials adequate notice of the local agency's noncompliance, and the state must be afforded a reasonable opportunity to compel local compliance."[14] In reviewing *Maher*, the United States Supreme Court evenly split on the question, therefore leaving standing the Ninth Circuit's decision that:

> It would seem incontrovertible that, whenever, the local agency refuses or wrongfully neglects to provide a handicapped child with a free appropriate education, the child can 'best be served' on a regional or state level. However, the

---

Bradley, 189 F.3d at 753. The court, however, later vacated this part of the *Bradley* opinion and ordered a rehearing specifically on this question. Jim C. v. Arkansas Dept. of Educ., 197 F.3d 958 (8th Cir. 1999).

9. College Savings Bank v. Florida Postsecondary Educ, Expense Bd., 527 U.S. 627 (1999); Nieves-Marquez v. Puerto Rico, 353 F.3d 108 (1st Cir. 2003); Doe v. Nebraska, 345 F.3d 593 (8th Cir. 2003) (waived immunity under §504 by accepting foster care funds); Lovell v. Chandler, 303 F.3d 1039 (9th Cir. 2002) (waived immunity under §504 and Title II of the Americans with Disabilities Act); Amos v. Maryland Dept. of Pub. Safety & Correctional Servs., 178 F.3d 212, 222–223 (4th Cir. 1999) (§504 abrogated Eleventh Amendment immunity); Coolbaugh v. Louisiana, 136 F.3d 430 (5th Cir. 1998) (§504 abrogated Eleventh Amendment immunity). *but see* Bradley, 189 F.3d at 755 holding §504 did not abrogate Eleventh Amendment immunity.

10. *See, e.g.,* John T. ex rel Robert T. v. Iowa Dept. of Educ., 258 F.3d 860 (8th Cir. 2001) *quoting* Gadsby v. Grasmink, 109 F.3d 940 (4th Cir. 1997) (SEA may be held liable for failure to comply with its duty to assure substantive requirements of IDEA are implemented; the district court may award reimbursement against the SEA the LEA or both); *see also* Doe v. Maher, 793 F.2d 1470 (9th Cir. 1986), *aff'd sub nom.* Honig v. Doe, 484 U.S. 305 (1988); Kruelle v. New Castle County School Dist., 642 F.2d 687, 696–99 (3d Cir. 1981); Georgia Association of Retarded Children v. McDaniel, 511 F. Supp. 1263 (N.D. Ga. 1981), *aff'd,* 716 F.3d 1565 (11th Cir. 1983), *vacated on other grounds,* 468 U.S. 1213 (1984); San Francisco Unified School Dist. v. California, 131 Cal. App. 3d 54, 182 Cal. Rptr. 525 (1982); Woolcott v. State Bd. of Educ., 134 Mich. App. 555, 351 N.W.2d 601 (1984). Where the action alleges a specific responsibility of the state, such as for failure to insure IDEA is carried out, commissioner of education or equivalent official is a proper party, Hendricks v. Gilhool, 709 F. Supp. 1362 (E.D. Pa. 1989*); but see* Pachl v. Seagren, 453 F.3d 1064 (8th Cir. 2006) (failed to allege specific ways in which DOE neglected its duties to monitor the LEA).

11. Lawrence Tp. v Bd. of Educ. v. N.J., 417 F.3d 368, (3d Cir. 2005).

12. Doe v. Maher, 793 F.2d 1470 (9th Cir. 1986), *aff'd sub nom.* Honig v. Doe, 484 U.S. 305 (1988).

13. 20 U.S.C. §1413(h)(2); *see* Doe v. Maher, 793 F.2d 1470 (9th Cir. 1986), *aff'd sub nom.* Honig v. Doe, 484 U.S. 305 (1988).

14. Doe v. Maher, 793 F.2d 1470 (9th Cir. 1986), *aff'd on other grounds sub nom.* Honig v. Doe, 484 U.S. 305 (1988).

"state is not obligated to intervene directly in an individual case whenever the local agency falls short of its responsibilities in some small regard."[15]

Regarding state agency responsibility, more recently, however, there has been an increase in children placed in residential placements at public expense. Therefore, OSEP issued a letter of guidance to State Directors of Special Education regarding the joint responsibilities of SEAs and LEAs for providing and paying for these residential placements. According to Part B of IDEA the state where the child resides is responsible for providing a FAPE. Since the IDEA, however, does not address which LEA is responsible for the cost of placement the SEA has the ultimate responsibility for the payment. The SEA is allowed to use whatever sources of funding are available but must not delay in providing the services. When another agency is responsible for the cost of placing the child, the SEA is required to enter into an interagency agreement providing for payment and ensuring a FAPE. If the other agency fails to provide or pay for the services the LEA or SEA must ensure for the provision and payment of those services but can seek reimbursement from the public agency.[16]

14.2.1 Avoiding Eleventh Amendment Immunity

Assuming there is Eleventh Amendment Immunity for IDEA and § 1983 violations, it may be avoided in one of two ways. Instead of suing the state, the state official may be sued in his or her "individual capacity." When sued in their individual capacity, the actions are considered not to be against the state for the purposes of seeking injunctive relief.[17] A frequently cited example involves suits against state officers seeking an injunction against maintaining segregated schools. The suit is considered a suit against individuals and not barred by the Eleventh Amendment.[18]

---

15. John T v. Iowa Dept. of Educ., 258 F.3d 860 (8th Cir. 2001); Maher, 793 F.2d at 1492, *aff'd on other grounds sub nom.* Honig v. Doe, 484 U.S. at 329 *quoting* Kruelle v. New Castle County School Dist., 642 F.2d 687, 696–99 (3d Cir. 1981); *see also* Eva N. v. Brock, 741 F. Supp. 626, 634 (E.D. Ky. 1990), *aff'd*, 943 F.2d 51 (6th Cir. 1991) ("Nonetheless, the state, having accepted the funds of the federal government and acceded to the administrative and appellate scheme of the EAHCA, has an overriding duty to provide an appropriate IEP for every handicapped child capable of benefiting from one."); *but see* Pachl v. Seagren, 373 F. Supp. 2d 969 (D. Minn. 2005) (no Missouri Department of Education (MDE) policy or conduct prevented student from receiving auditory brainstem response testing; and MDE did not have duty to provide parents with "knowledgeable" hearing officer).

16. Letter to State Directors of Special Education, 44 Individuals with Disabilities Educ. L. Rep. (LRP) 46 (OSEP 2005); *see also* Letter to Autin, 41 Individuals with Disabilites Educ. L. Rep. (LRP) 135 (OSEP 2003) (states cannot contract away Part B obligations); Letter to Librera, 42 Individuals with Disabilites Educ. L. Rep. (LRP) 84 (OSEP 2004) (despite inter-district contract SEA must still provide FAPE to resident students).

17. Ex Parte Young, 209 U.S. 123, 159–160 (1908); *see also* Will v. Michigan State Police, 491 U.S. 58, 70, n.10 (1989); Bradley v. Arkansas Dept. of Educ., 189 F.3d 745, *rehearing en banc granted, opinion vacated in part on other grounds sub nom.* Jim C. v. Arkansas Dept. of Educ., 197 F.3d 958 (8th Cir. 1999) (although state has Eleventh Amendment immunity, parents could pursue IDEA remedies against Arkansas Department of Education employees); Emma v. Eastin, 985 F. Supp. 940 (N.D. Cal. 1997) (insofar as Section 1983 claim sought retrospective relief, it could not be maintained against state officials in their official capacities, but could be maintained against state officials in their individual capacity for injunctive relief and plaintiffs could proceed against state defendants in their individual capacities); Zahran v. New York Dept. of Educ., 306 F. Supp. 2d 204 (N.D.N.Y. 2004) (department of education was not subject to monetary damages under § 1983 for violations of IDEA).

18. Wright, Miller & Cooper, *Federal Practice and Procedure* § 3524.

There are two disadvantages to suing in an individual capacity. First, in order to obtain relief, the state official must be acting in violation of state or federal law. If the officials are merely following state law and have not violated federal law, the suit will be considered one against the state and the Eleventh Amendment will apply.[19] Second, when suing in the individual capacity, there may be absolute or qualified immunity defenses. These defenses can only be raised when the person is sued in their individual capacity.[20]

A second means of avoiding the impact of the Eleventh Amendment is to bring suit in state court. The Eleventh Amendment does not apply in state courts.[21] For actions under § 1983, however, a problem still remains because the United States Supreme Court has held that the state is not a "person" for the purposes of § 1983 and therefore is not subject to suit under that statute.[22]

Finally, there is nothing inconsistent with holding that the Eleventh Amendment bars damage type claims but requires the SEA to provide direct educational services if the LEA fails to provide a free appropriate education. Prospective injunctive relief, even if it entails a considerable expenditure of money is not barred by the Eleventh Amendment.[23] Indeed, this is precisely what the Ninth Circuit held in *Doe v. Maher*.[24] Courts, subsequent to *Dellmuth* and before the reversal of *Dellmuth* by Congress, held that the Eleventh Amendment does not bar prospective relief where IDEA mandates specific state agency obligations.[25]

14.3 Damages in General

Damage issues must be addressed in light of three forms of damage: reimbursement when parents unilaterally place their child in a private placement; the provision of compensatory educational services; and general monetary awards.

14.4 Reimbursement for Unilateral Placements

A frequently litigated issue in the early years of IDEA was, given the stay-put provision and the general rule that damages are unavailable under IDEA,[26] are parents who

---

19. Pennhurst State School and Hospital v. Halderman, 465 U.S. 89 (1984).
20. *Id; see also* Goleta Union Elementary School Dist. v. Ordway, 166 F. Supp. 2d 1287 (C.D. Cal. 2001) (Eleventh Amendment barred suit against school district employee in her official capacity but school district official was not entitled to qualified immunity for change in placement made in violation of clearly established requirements of IDEA).
21. Maine v. Thiboutot, 448 U.S. 1, 9, n.7 (1980).
22. Will v. Michigan State Police, 491 U.S. 58 (1989).
23. Milliken v. Bradley, 433 U.S. 267 (1977) ("the federal court may award injunctive relief that governs state official's future conduct, but not one that awards retroactive monetary relief").
24. Maher, 793 F.2d at 1493, *aff'd sub nom.* Honig v. Doe, 484 U.S. 305 (1988).
25. Porter v. Board of Trustees of Manhattan Beach Unified School Dist., 307 F.3d 1064 (9th Cir. 2002) (district court erred in dismissing with prejudice claims against education officials based on Eleventh Amendment immunity); Kerr Center Parents Association v. Charles, 897 F.2d 1463 (9th 1990); Burr v. Sobel, 888 F.2d 258 (2d Cir. 1989), *reaffirming sub nom.* Burr v. Ambach, 863 F.2d 1071 (2d Cir. 1988), *vacated sub nom.* Sobol v. Burr, 492 U.S. 902 (1989); *see also* Valerie J. v. Derry Cooperative School Dist., 16 Educ. Handicapped L. Rep. (CRR) 1068 (D.N.H. 1990) (prospective relief available against state under IDEA).
26. See § 14.6.

unilaterally remove their children from public school programs and place them in private placements entitled to reimbursement if they ultimately establish that the public school placement was inappropriate?

Following a split among the Circuit Courts, the United States Supreme Court in *School Committee of the Town of Burlington v. Department of Education of Massachusetts*,[27] held that parents were entitled to reimbursement for unilateral private placements when those placements are found by the court to be necessary in order for the child to receive an appropriate education.[28] The 1999 amendments to the federal regulations incorporated the right to reimbursement.[29]

Reimbursement may be reduced or denied under certain circumstances. The parents have an obligation to inform the LEA of their belief that the public placement is improper prior to removal. Reimbursement may be reduced, or even denied, if the parents did not inform the LEA at the most recent IEP meeting that they were rejecting the proposed placement and state their intent to remove the child,[30] or if they failed to provide notice of this rejection of the placement at least 10 days prior to removing the child.[31] Reimbursement may also be reduced or denied if, before the child is removed, the LEA informs the parents (through proper notice) of its intent to evaluate the child and the child is not made available for that evaluation.[32] There can also be a reduction or denial of reimbursement "[u]pon a judicial finding of unreasonableness with respect to the actions taken by the parents."[33]

The ability to reduce or deny reimbursement is subject to several exceptions. It may not be reduced or denied if 1) the parents are illiterate and cannot write English, 2) compliance with the requirement to give prior notice to the LEA of the parents intent to place the child would result in physical or serious emotional harm to the child, 3) the school prevented the parents from providing the notice, or 4) the parents did not receive notice from the LEA of the requirement that the parents themselves must provide notice of their intent to privately place the child.[34]

The LEA has no right comparable to that of the parents to reimbursement.[35]

---

27. 471 U.S. 359 (1985).

28. 471 U.S. 359 (1985); *see also* Frank G. v. Board of Educ. of Hyde Park 459 F.3d 356 (2d Cir. 2006) (did not preclude reimbursement when student has not previously received special education and related services); Muller v. Committee on Special Educ. of the East Islip Union Free School Dist., 145 F.3d 95 (2d Cir. 1998); Seattle School Dist. No. 1 v. B.S., 82 F.3d 1493 (9th Cir. 1996); Murphysboro Community Unit School Dist. v. Illinois State Bd. of Educ., 41 F.3d 1162 (7th Cir. 1994).

29. 34 C.F.R. § 300.148(c).

30. 34 C.F.R. § 300.148(d)(1)(i).

31. 34 C.F.R. § 300.148(d)(1)(ii).

32. 34 C.F.R. § 300.148(d)(2).

33. 34 C.F.R. § 300.148(d)(3).

34. 34 C.F.R. § 300.148(e); *see also* Lang v. Braintree School Committee, 545 F. Supp. 1221 (D. Mass. 1982); *but see* James v. Arlington School Dist. 228 F.3d 764 (6th Cir. 2000) (not entitled to reimbursement when fail to seek IEP); Greenland School Dist. v. Amy N. 358 F.3d 150 (1st Cir. 2004); Berger v. Medina City School Dist. 348 F.3d 513 (1st Cir. 2003) (failed to give adequate notice private school tuition denied); Linda W. v. Indiana Dept. of Educ., 200 F.3d 504 (7th Cir. 1999); Warren G. v. Cumberland County School Dist., 190 F.3d 80 (3d Cir. 1999).

35. *See* Board of Educ. of Oak Park and River Forest High School Dist. No. 200 v. Kelly E., 207 F.3d 931 (7th Cir. 2000) (IDEA does not entitle a LEA to reimbursement from the state; LEA already received share of federal appropriation for services and not entitled to double dipping).

Bringing an action under § 1983 should provide not only the reimbursement costs under *Burlington*, but also costs associated with the need to find the appropriate placement.[36]

Courts have held that merely because the school is unapproved does not mean that parents cannot receive reimbursement. In *Carter v. Florence County School District Four*,[37] the United States Supreme Court held that to deny reimbursement where an unapproved school had provided an appropriate education would undermine the goals of IDEA. On the other hand, the school system itself has no obligation to place a child in an unapproved school when it can provide a FAPE.[38]

The discussion so far in this section has dealt with reimbursement when the child has received special education and related services and the parents remove the child from the public school. An increasing amount of litigation, however, also revolves around private school placement and reimbursement in situations where the child has never received services in the public school. In *M.M. ex rel. C.M. School Bd. of Miami-Dade County*,[39] the parents sought reimbursement for a private school placement. The child had never been enrolled in public school. The school board and administrative law judge relied on language in the IDEA that provides:

> If the parents of a child with a disability, *who previously received special education and related services under the authority of a public agency* enroll the child in a private school ... without consent or referral [reimbursement is available] if the court or hearing officer finds the agency had not made a free appropriate public education available to the child in a timely manner prior to the enrollment.[40]

Since the school and the parents had not arrived at a mutually agreed upon IEP and the parents had, therefore, not enrolled the child, the school argued that the IDEA did not require reimbursement even after a determination that what had been offered the parents would not provide a FAPE. Rejecting this argument the Eleventh Circuit Court of Appeals held:

> forcing the parents into accepting inadequate IEPs in order to preserve their right to reimbursement runs contrary to the rights recognized in the *Burlington* line of cases.[41]

While a contrary result would appear to produce what one court has characterized as "absurd results,"[42] there are courts that have held to the contrary and have denied reimbursement.[43] It is also important to emphasize that the cases providing reim-

---

36. *See* Jackson v. Franklin County School Bd., 806 F.2d 623 (5th Cir. 1986); *but see* Wayne County Regional Educational Service Agency v. Pappas, 56 F. Supp. 2d 807 (E.D. Mich. 1999); White v. California, 240 Cal. Rptr. 732, 195 Cal. App. 3d 452 (1987).

37. Carter v. Florence County School Dist. Four, 510 U.S. 7, 14 (1993); 34 C.F.R. § 300.403(c) (in 2006 regulations, § 300.148).

38. Schimmel v. Spillane, 819 F.2d 477 (4th Cir. 1987).

39. 437 F.3d 1085 (11th Cir. 2006).

40. 20 U.S.C. § 1412(a)(10)(C)(ii).

41. 437 F.3d at 1099; *see also* Frank G. v. Board of Education of Hyde Park, 459 F.3d 356 (2d Cir. 2006) (IDEA does not preclude reimbursement when student has not previously received special education and related services); E.W. v. School Bd. Of Miami-Dade, 307 F. Supp. 2d 1363 (S.D. Fla. 2004); Justin G. v. Bd. of Educ. Montgomery County, 148 F. Supp. 2d 576 (D. Md. 2001).

42. Frank G. v. Board of Education of Hyde Park, 459 F.3d 356, 372 (2d Cir. 2006).

43. Greenland School District v. Amy N., 358 F.3d 150 (1st Cir. 2004); Baltimore City Bd. of School Comm'rs. v. Taylorch, 395 F. Supp. 2d 246 (D. Md. 2005).

bursement involved a finding that the school's proposed educational program would not provide a FAPE. Indeed, one of the leading cases cited by the few courts denying such reimbursement, *Greenland School District v. Amy N.*,[44] is distinguishable precisely on the fact that the parents did not give the school district notice and therefore the school district did not have an opportunity to develop an IEP that would have provided a FAPE.

The United States Supreme Court had an opportunity to address the issue of reimbursement where the child has never received services in the public school in *Board of Education of the City School District of the City of New York v. Tom F.*[45] The Court, however, was evenly divided, thus letting stand a Second Circuit decision. The Second Circuit Court of Appeals had vacated the district court's decision denying reimbursement in light of the Second Circuit's decision in another case allowing reimbursement.[46] While it is difficult to discern the meaning of a 4-4 split on the Court when there is no opinion, it does raise concern that the full Court could eventually hold contrary to the logic of cases such as *M.M. ex rel. C.M. School Bd. of Miami-Dade County.*

In conclusion, a parent's decision to unilaterally place their child in a private school should be considered carefully, as it may limit the parents' ability to obtain reimbursement.[47] Reimbursement for placing the child in a private placement may be limited or denied under the many circumstances. For example, if the parents at the most recent IEP meeting attended do not inform the school that they are rejecting the proposed placement, and giving their reasons and informing the school that they plan to enroll their child in a private program at public expense, reimbursement has been denied.[48] Where the parents did not give written notice to the school at least 10 business days prior to the removal of their child reimbursement was denied.[49] Reimbursement may also be reduced or denied if the parents removed their child prior to the public agency giving notice of their intent to evaluate or upon a judicial finding that the parents were unreasonable in the actions.[50] If the public agency offers a FAPE and the parents choose to place their child in a private school then the LEA is not responsible for reimbursement.[51] Any disputes, however, over the appropriateness of a private school program and the issue of reimbursement can be the subject of a due process hearing.[52]

44. 358 F.3d 150 (1st Cir. 2004).

45. ___ S. Ct. ___, 2007 WL 2935030 (2007) (*per curiam,* without opinion).

46. Board of Education of the City School District of the City of New York v. Tom F., 193 Fed. Appx. 26 (2d Cir. 2006) (unpublished) *vacating and remanding,* 2005 WL 22866 (S.DN.Y. 2005) (unpublished) *in light* of Board of Educ. of Frank G. v. Board of Education of Hyde Park, 459 F.3d 356, 372 (2d Cir. 2006).

47. 34 C.F.R. § 300.148(d).

48. 34 C.F.R. § 300.148(d)(1)(i).

49. 34 C.F.R. § 300.148(d)(1)(ii).

50. 34 C.F.R. § 300.148(d)(2–3); *see* Berger v. Medina City School Dist., 348 F.3d 513 (6th Cir 2003) (parents failed to give adequate notice of their intention to withdraw student from public school); Schoenbach v. District of Columbia, 309 F. Supp. 2d 71 (D.D.C. 2004) (parents were precluded from obtaining private school tuition reimbursement due to failure to notify district of intent to enroll student in private school and for acting unreasonably).

51. 34 C.F.R. § 300.148(a).

52. 34 C.F.R. § 300.148(b).

14.5 Compensatory Education

Compensatory educational services are services designed to provide remedial educational programming to make up for the time when the school system was responsible for providing educational services but failed to do so.[53]

Courts have split on the availability of compensatory educational services under IDEA.[54] The basic argument against compensatory educational services was that IDEA did not allow the award of retrospective monetary damages. Compensatory education, it was argued, is retrospective in nature, requires the expenditure of money, and therefore constitutes a damage award. Such damage awards were 1) not contemplated by IDEA and 2) against state defendants, were in violation of the Eleventh Amendment.[55] In addition, it is argued that since *Rowley* did not require maximization of educational benefit, where a child has already received some educational benefit the *Rowley* standard has been met and there is no requirement for compensatory education.[56]

The early arguments in favor of compensatory educational services were 1) that what was sought was prospective relief and therefore did not constitute damages[57] and 2) since it was prospective in nature there was no Eleventh Amendment prohibition

---

53. M.C. v. Central Regional School Dist., 81 F.3d 389 (3d Cir. 1996) (knew or should know IEP inappropriate, covers time of deprivation, good faith irrelevant); *see also* G. v. Fort Bragg Dependent Schools 343 F.3d 295 (4th Cir. 2003) (district court's rejection of student's claim for compensatory education was error); Maine School Administrative Dist. No. 35 v. Mr. R. 321 F.3d 9 (1st Cir. 2003) (parents' claim for compensatory education was not substantively moot); Ridgewood Bd. of Educ. v. N.E., 172 F.3d 238, 249 (3d Cir. 1999) (compensatory education is not precluded); Brantley v. Independent School Dist. No 625, 936 F. Supp. 649 (D. Minn. 1996) (compensatory education may be a remedy for denial of FAPE); ABC Alternative Learning Center,38 Individuals with Disabilities Educ. Law Rep. (LRP) 41 (OSERS 2002) (charter school denied funds after failing to provide compensatory education).

54. *Compare* Sellers v. School Board of Manassas, 141 F.3d 524 (4th Cir. 1998); Powell v. Defore, 699 F.2d 1078 (11th Cir. 1983) (per curiam); Emma v. Eastin, 985 F. Supp. 940 (N.D. Ca. 1997); and Adams Central School Dist. No. 090 v. Deist, 214 Neb. 307, 334 N.W.2d 775 (1983) (each holding no compensatory education) *with* Mr. I v. Maine School Admin. Dist. No. 55, 480 F.3d 1 (1st Cir. 2007); G. v. Fort Bragg Dependent Schs., 343 F.3d 295, 308 (4th Cir. 2003); Mrs. C. v. Wheaton, 916 F.2d 69 (2d Cir. 1990); Burr v. Sobol, 888 F.2d 258 (2d Cir. 1989), *reaffirming sub nom.* Burr v. Ambach, 863 F.2d 1071 (1988); Jefferson County Bd. of Educ. v. Breen, 694 F. Supp. 1539 (N.D. Ala. 1987), *aff'd*, 853 F.2d 853 (11th Cir. 1988); Sabatini v. Corning-Painted Post Area School Dist., 78 F. Supp. 2d 138 (W.D.N.Y. 1999); Max M. v. Thompson, 592 F. Supp. 1450 (N.D. Ill. 1984); and Campbell v. Talladega Bd. of Educ., 518 F. Supp. 47 (N.D. Ala. 1981) (each holding compensatory education available).

55. Alexopulos v. San Francisco Unified School Dist., 817 F.2d 551 (9th Cir. 1987); Alexopulos v. Riles, 784 F.2d 1408, 1412 (9th Cir. 1986) (relying on original *Miener* opinion); Powell v. Defore, 699 F.2d 1078 (11th Cir. 1983) (per curiam); Miener v. Missouri, 673 F.2d 969, 973 (8th Cir. 1982), *rev'd*, 800 F.2d 749 (8th Cir. 1986); Wayne County Regional Educational Service Agency v. Pappas, 56 F. Supp. 2d 807 (E.D. Mich. 1999*); but see* A.A. v. Board of Educ., Central Islip Union Free School Dist., 196 F. Supp. 2d 259 (E.D. N.Y. 2002).

56. Timms v. Metropolitan School Dist., 718 F.2d 212 (7th Cir. 1983), *superseded*, 722 F.2d 1310 (7th Cir. 1983) (recognizing possible availability of compensatory education).

57. Timms v. Metropolitan School Dist. of Wabash County, 722 F.2d 1310 (7th Cir. 1983) (*dicta*); Max M. v. Thompson, 585 F. Supp. 317 (N.D. Ill. 1984) (Max M. II).

against state defendants.[58] Analogy has been made to *School Committee of the Town of Burlington v. Department of Education of Massachusetts.*[59] In *Burlington*, the United States Supreme Court held that IDEA "includes the power to reimburse parents for their expenditures on private special education for a child if the court ultimately determines that such placement, rather than a proposed IEP, is proper under the Act."[60] Rejecting the label that such payments constitute damages, the Court stated that it "merely requires the Town to belatedly pay expenses that it should have paid all along and would have borne in the first instance had it developed a proper IEP."[61]

A strong argument can be made that compensatory education is likewise not damages, that it merely requires the school system to provide educational services that it would have provided all along were it meeting its requirement to provide a FAPE.[62] Whether by analogy to *Burlington*, or by way of § 1983, in circumstances where compensatory education is appropriate relief, it is available under § 1983, if not under IDEA.[63]

The United States Department of Education's Office of Special Education and Rehabilitative Services has also issued an opinion interpreting IDEA as allowing compensatory education.[64]

Courts are also split on standards for awarding compensatory education as equitable relief. Some courts require a showing of bad faith or egregious conduct[65] on the part of the public agency before awarding compensatory education. Other courts require only that the school knew or should have known that the IEP was inappropriate or that there was a violation under IDEA.[66]

---

58. Max M. v. Thompson, 592 F. Supp. 1450, 1461 (N. D. Ill. 1984) (Max M. IV) (though suit dismissed against state defendants in the individual capacities because of immunity); Max M. v. Thompson, 585 F. Supp. 317 (N.D. Ill. 1984) (Max M. II); *see also* Campbell v. Talladega County Bd. of Educ., 518 F. Supp. 47 (N.D. Ala. 1981) (award of compensatory education with no discussion re appropriateness under IDEA); Martin v. School Bd. of Prince George County, 3 Va. App. 197, 348 S.E.2d 857 (1986) (*dicta* that compensatory education probably available).

59. 471 U.S. 359 (1985). Until the Supreme Court's decision in *Burlington*, the debate on the availability of reimbursement also was focused on whether reimbursement constituted damages. *Pre-Smith v. Robinson* cases which found IDEA to not be exclusive could avoid the problem by deciding that damages were available under § 1983 or § 504. *See, e.g.*, David H. v. Spring Branch Independent School Dist., 569 F. Supp. 1324 (S.D. Texas 1983).

60. Burlington, 471 U.S. at 369.

61. *Id.* at 370–371.

62. Ridgewood Bd. of Educ. v. N.E., 172 F.3d 238 (3d Cir. 1999) (award of compensatory education is not precluded for years of inappropriate education via other than IEP); *see also* Erickson v. Albuquerque Public Schools, 199 F.3d 1116 (10th Cir. 1999) (compensatory education appropriate remedy for a procedural violation); Jefferson County Bd. of Educ. v. Breen, 694 F. Supp. 1539 (N.D. Ala. 1987), *aff'd*, 853 F.2d 853 (11th Cir. 1988); Miener v. Missouri, 800 F.2d 749, 753 (8th Cir. 1986); White v. California, 240 Cal. Rptr. 732, 195 Cal. App. 3d 452 (1987).

63. *See* Jackson v. Franklin County School Bd., 806 F.2d 623, 631–632 (5th Cir. 1986).

64. Kohn Inquiry, 17 Educ. Handicapped L. Rep. (LRP) 522 (1991).

65. Garro v. Connecticut, 23 F.3d 734 (2d Cir.1994) (need gross violations of IDEA); Mrs. C. v. Wheaton, 916 F.2d 69 (2d Cir. 1990).

66. Lauren W. v. Deflaminis, 480 F.3d 259 (3d Cir. 2007) (evidence supported denial of compensatory education); M.C. v. Central Regional School Dist., 81 F.3d 389 (3d Cir. 1996); *see* Carlisle Area School v. Scott P., 62 F.3d 520 (3d Cir. 1995) (compensatory education could not be based on finding of deficiency in prior IEP where no evidence was presented); Kristi H. v. Tri-Valley School Dist., 107 F. Supp. 2d 628 (M.D. Pa. 2000) (right accrues from time school knows or should have known of IEP failure).

As a general matter, compensatory educational services when awarded are provided directly to the students. Recently, however, they have also been provided indirectly by training the teachers to meet the student's unique needs.[67] The method for determining the award is one of flexibility rather than a formulaic accounting of hour for hour.[68]

Courts are split over whether the IEP process is the appropriate mechanism for resolving issues concerning the compensatory services.[69]

14.5.1 Compensatory Education Beyond Graduation and or Beyond Age 21

Assuming compensatory education is an available remedy, a related question is whether the award of compensatory education can exceed the statutory age limits of IDEA. Can the child be awarded educational services extending beyond the twenty-second birthday? Courts have held that an award of services beyond the twenty-second birthday violates IDEA's age provisions.[70] The contrary position, however, has also been held.[71] Allowing the award of compensatory education provides logical protection to parents who are unable to make unilateral placements pending reimbursement under *Burlington*. Without such a right, it is conceivable that the 20-year-old child of wealthy parents could receive education in a unilateral placement which was subsequently reimbursed after the twenty-second birthday. The child of poor parents who must await resolution of the administrative and judicial process in order to receive the educational services, however, would be precluded from receiving those same two years of educational services since the child might be twenty-two by the time the process ends.[72] The Supreme Court has repeatedly discussed the time-consuming nature of the administrative and judicial process. Indeed, the possibility of delay in receiving educational benefits was one of the factors leading the Court to its decision in *Burlington*.[73]

---

67. Park v. Anaheim Union High School Dist., 464 F.3d 1025 (9th Cir. 2006) (discretion to IHO and courts under IDEA in awarding compensatory education).

68. Reid v. District of Columbia, 401 F.3d 516 (D.D.C. 2005) (district court's hour-per-day formula for determining amount of compensatory services, and student's suggested one-to-one formula inappropriate).

69. *Id.* (authority to reduce or discontinue compensatory services could not be delegated to IEP team); *but see* Mr. I. v. Maine School Admin. Dist. No. 55, 480 F.3d 1 (1st Cir. 2007) (child's need for compensatory education could be adequately addressed during development of IEP).

70. *E.g.*, Alexopulos v. Riles, 784 F.2d 1408, 1411 (9th Cir. 1986); Adams Central School Dist. v. Deist, 214 Neb. 307, 334 N.W.2d 775 (1983); Natrona County School Dist. No. 1 v. McKnight, 764 P.2d 1039 (Wyo. 1988).

71. *E.g.*, Phil v. Massachusetts Dept. of Educ., 9 F.3d 184, 188 (1st Cir. 1993); Lester H. v. Gilhool, 916 F.2d 865 (3d Cir. 1990); Burr v. Sobol, 888 F.2d 258 (2d Cir. 1989), *reaffirming sub nom.* Burr v. Ambach, 863 F.2d 1071 (1988); Miener v. Missouri, 800 F.2d 749, 754 (8th Cir. 1986); Wagner v. Short, 63 F. Supp. 2d 672 (D. Md. 1999); Wayne Co. Regional Educ. Service Agency v. Pappas, 56 F. Supp. 2d 807 (E.D. Mich. 1999) (29 year old entitled to compensatory education); Campbell v. Talladega County Bd. of Educ., 518 F. Supp. 47, 56 (N.D. Ala. 1981); White v. California, 240 Cal. Rptr. 732, 195 Cal. App. 3d 452 (1987) (but holding money damages not available).

72. *See* White v. California, 240 Cal. Rptr. 732, 195 Cal. App. 3d 452 (1987).

73. Burlington, 471 U.S. at 373.

14.6 Monetary Damages

As a general rule, absent egregious due process violations or endangerment of a child's health, general monetary damages are consistently held to be unavailable under IDEA.[74] There is continuing litigation over whether first, a separate cause of action exists under § 1983 for violation of substantive rights under IDEA. This question is discussed in Chapter 1.[75] Even assuming suit may be brought under § 1983, the question remains whether damages are available.[76]

Damages are generally available under § 1983.[77] One of the first cases decided after the 1990 amendment to IDEA allowing suit to be brought under both IDEA and § 1983 recognized the possibility of receiving monetary damages. In *Jackson v. Franklin County School Board*,[78] a student and his mother brought suit under IDEA and § 1983. In *Jackson*, the child was suspended for three days and then, as a result of delinquency charges, was sent to a state hospital for evaluation and treatment. Upon release from the hospital, the LEA indicated that the child should not return to school, since there was only one month remaining and exams would soon start. Plaintiffs challenged the denial of

---

74. *See, e.g.*, Diaz-Fonseca v. Puerto Rico, 451 F.3d 13, 28 (1st Cir. 2006) (monetary recovery limited to compensatory education and equitable remedies involving money reimbursement; no punitive or general compensatory damages regardless of which action brought under); Gean v. Hattaway, 330 F.3d 758, 774 (6th Cir. 2003); Nieves-Márquez v. Puerto Rico, 353 F.3d 108, 125 (1st Cir. 2003); Polera v. Bd. of Educ. of the Newburgh Enlarged City Sch. Dist., 288 F.3d 478, 483–86 (2d Cir. 2002) (noting that the Third Circuit has "addressed the issue without endorsing the view that damages are never available under the IDEA."); Sellers v. School Bd. of Manassas, 141 F.3d 524 (4th Cir. 1998) (compensatory and punitive damages not available under IDEA); Heiderman v. Rother, 84 F.3d 1021 (8th Cir. 1996) (general and punitive damages not available under IDEA); Anderson v. Thompson, 658 F.2d 1205, 1213-14 (7th Cir. 1981); Wayne County Regional Education Service Agency v. Pappas, 56 F. Supp. 2d 807 (E.D. Mich. 1999); Christopher N. v. McDaniel, 569 F. Supp. 291 (N.D. Ga. 1983); Johnson v. Clarke, 165 Mich. App. 366, 418 N.W.2d 466 (1987); *but see* Bucks County Dep't of Mental Health v. Pennsylvania, 379 F.3d 61, 68 n.5 (3d Cir. 2004) (reimbursement to parent for the time she personally spent working with her disabled daughter after county refused to provide the therapy constituted appropriate relief under the IDEA).
  Some courts have held that even under exceptional circumstances, damages are unavailable under IDEA. *See, e.g.*, Waterman v. Marquette—Alger Intermediate School Dist., 739 F. Supp. 361 (W.D. Mich. 1990); Smith v. Philadelphia School Dist., 679 F. Supp. 479, 484 (E.D. Pa. 1988); Sanders v. Marquette Public Schools, 561 F. Supp. 1361 (W.D. Mich. 1983); Miller v. Lord, 262 Mich. App. 640, 686 N.W.2d 800 (2002); Woolcott v. State Bd. of Educ., 134 Mich. App. 555, 351 N.W.2d 601, 606 (1984).
  75. See § 1.6.
  76. Taylor v. Vermont Dept. of Educ., 313 F.3d 768 (2d Cir. 2002) (a plaintiff may enforce the rights granted by the IDEA by way of an action seeking money damages pursuant to § 1983. Although monetary damages are not available under the IDEA itself, a plaintiff may recover monetary damages for a violation of the IDEA pursuant to § 1983.") *citing* Polera v. Board of Educ. of Newburgh Enlarged City School Dist. 288 F.3d 478, 483 n.5 (2d Cir. 2002); M. H. v. Bristol Bd. of Educ., 169 F. Supp. 2d 21, 29 (D.Conn.2001) (recognizing that nothing in the IDEA precludes a claim for money damages under Section 1983 and that the IDEA, in fact, expressly contemplates such claims; *see also* Capillano v. Hyde Park, 40 F. Supp. 2d 513 (S.D.N.Y. 1999) (IDEA does not prohibit nor does § 1983 and § 504).
  77. Padilla v. School Dist. No. 1, Denver, Colo., 34 F. Supp. 2d 1260 (D. Colo. 1999) (general damages available under § 1983). Damages awarded under § 1983 must be truly compensatory and not based on the abstract value or worth of the constitutional or statutory right violated. Memphis Community School Dist. v. Stachura, 477 U.S. 299 (1986). For a discussion of the ability to bring an action under § 1983 for issues also covered by IDEA see § 1.5.
  78. 806 F.2d 623 (5th Cir. 1986); *see also* Board of Educ. v. Diamond, 808 F.2d 987, 996 (3d Cir. 1986).

educational services for the final month of the 1984 school year and for the first two months of the next school year. They also sought monetary damages.[79]

The court held that failure of the LEA to convene a conference was a "*per se* violation of the EAHCA,"[80] and that the child's "due process rights, as contemplated by the Fourteenth Amendment and as specifically enumerated by the EAHCA, were violated by Franklin County School Officials' failure to provide notice and a hearing concerning his continued exclusion from school."[81] The court remanded the case to determine the extent to which the LEA's actions were the cause of any loss to the child and "what damages, either monetary, or in the form of remedial educational services ... would be appropriate."[82] The court, therefore, clearly recognized the right to money damages, however it did state, "although monetary relief is available, remedial educational services may be more valuable than any pecuniary damages that could be awarded."[83]

There are, however, decisions which hold that no compensatory damages are available under § 1983 for claims recognized under IDEA because § 1983 is derivative of IDEA.[84] Such a holding, however, raises the question of what the Congressional purpose was in providing the ability to bring suit under both IDEA and § 1983. IDEA specifically provides that "[n]othing in this title shall be construed to restrict or limit the rights procedures, and remedies available under the Constitution, the Americans with Disabilities Act of 1990, Title V of the Rehabilitation Act of 1973 or other Federal statutes protecting the rights of children with disabilities...."[85] The statute then specifically recognizes the fact that the relief may be covered under both, when it provides that "before filing for a civil action under such laws *seeking relief that is also available under*

---

79. The court seemed to assume that the provision making § 1983 and § 504 available is retroactive. Jackson, 806 F.2d at 627–628. As the court points out in a footnote, however, in response to the argument that *Smith v. Robinson* applied when the suit was originally filed:

even had Congress not amended the EAHCA, we believe James' § 1983 claim was proper. The Court's holding in *Smith* was limited to equal protection claims, whereas [the child here] sought relief for a deprivation of his due process rights.... [T]he Court explained:
.... [T]here is no indication that agencies should be exempt from a fee award where plaintiffs have had to resort to judicial relief to force the agencies to provide them the process they are constitutionally due.

Id. at 627–628 n.7.

80. *Id.* at 628.

81. *Id.* at 631.

82. *Id.* at 631; *see also* Fay v. South Colonie Central School Dist., 802 F.2d 21 (2d Cir. 1986) (upon appropriate proof, compensatory damages could be had for the LEA's failure to provide required notices).

83. *Id.* at 632. It should be emphasized that for many situations there will not be monetary damages. As the court pointed out in *Jackson*, compensatory educational services will be better suited to meet the needs of the plaintiff. *See generally* Comment, *Compensating the Handicapped: An Approach to Determining the Appropriateness of Damages for Violations of Section 504*, 1981 B.Y.U. L. Rev. 133. Also, the stay-put provisions of IDEA will often protect the LEA from damages in those instances where the LEA is improperly trying to change placement. In instances of bad faith on the part of the LEA, damages had already been recognized by the courts. *See, e.g.*, Anderson v. Thompson, 658 F.2d 1205 (7th Cir. 1981); *see generally* Miener v. Missouri, 673 F.2d 969, 978 (8th Cir. 1982); B.H. v. Southington Bd. of Educ. 273 F. Supp. 2d 194 (D. Conn. 2003); Reese v. Board of Educ. of Bismarck R-V School Dist. 225 F. Supp.2d 1149 (E.D. Mo. 2002).

84. *See, e.g.*, A.W. v. Jersey City Public Schools, 486 F.3d 791 (3d Cir. 2007); Padilla v. School Dist. No. 1 in City & County of Denver, Colo., 233 F.3d 1268 (10th Cir. 2000); Sellers v. School Bd. of Manassas, 141 F.3d 524 (4th Cir. 1998); Charlie F. v. Skokie Bd. of Educ., 98 F.3d 989 (7th Cir. 1997); Barnett v. Fairfax County School Bd., 721 F. Supp. 755 (E.D. Va. 1989), *aff'd*, 927 F.2d 146 (4th Cir. 1991).

85. 20 U.S.C. § 1415(l).

this subchapter" administrative remedies must be exhausted to the same extent as would be required as if brought under IDEA.[86] It seems logical that, as implicit in the court's holding in *Jackson,* some additional protection is available. Further, to the extent a public agency argues that Congress intended to preclude a specific remedy available under § 1983 (such as damages), it has the burden of persuasion that Congress has expressly withdrawn the § 1983 remedy.[87]

The availability of damages under § 504 has not always been clear. In *Smith v. Robinson,*[88] the Court stated:

> There is some confusion among the circuits as to the availability of a damages remedy under § 504 and under the EAHCA. Without expressing an opinion on the matter, we note that courts generally agree damages are available under § 504, but are available under the EAHCA only in exceptional circumstances.[89]

In *Consolidated Rail Corporation v. Darrone,*[90] a § 504 action seeking back pay for being wrongfully discharged, the Court had previously said:

> Without determining the extent to which money damages are available under § 504, we think it clear that § 504 authorizes a plaintiff who alleges intentional discrimination to bring an equitable action for backpay.[91]

The second indication that monetary damages should be available under both § 1983 and § 504 is found in *Franklin v. Gwinnett County Public Schools.*[92] In *Franklin,* the United States Supreme Court held that monetary damages were available in a sex discrimination action under Title IX of the Education Amendments of 1972.[93] What is significant about this case is not only that the language of Title IX is similar to § 504,[94] but that the Court explicitly stated:

> The general rule, therefore, is that absent clear direction to the contrary by Congress, the federal courts have the power to award any appropriate relief in a cognizable cause of action brought pursuant to a federal statute.[95]

---

86. *Id.* (emphasis added).
87. Golden Gate Transit Corp. v. City of Los Angeles, 493 U.S. 103 (1989); *see also* Wilder v. Virginia Hospital Association, 496 U.S. 498 (1990).
88. Smith v. Robinson, 468 U.S. 992 (1984).
89. Smith v. Robinson, 468 U.S. 992, 1020 n.24 (1984).
90. Consolidated Rail Corp. v. Darrone, 465 U.S. 624 (1984).
91. *Id.* at 630–631; *see also* Guardians Association v. Civil Service Commission, 463 U.S. 582, 607 n.27 (1983) (compensatory relief could be awarded in Title VI actions); Lovell v. Chandler, 303 F.3d 1039, 1056 (9th Cir. 2002) (need intentional discrimination for damages under the Rehabilitation Act); Briggs, *Safeguarding Equality for the Handicapped: Compensatory Relief Under Section 504 of the Rehabilitation Act of 1973,* 1986 Duke L. J. 197, 208 (1986) ("Because § 505(a)(2) ... provides that Title VI remedies are available to § 504 claimants, *Guardians* implies by analogy the existence of compensatory relief under § 504."); Flaccus, *Discrimination Legislation for the Handicapped: Much Ferment and Erosion of Coverage,* 55 Cin. L. Rev. 81, 90 (1986).
92. 503 U.S. 60 (1992).
93. 20 U.S.C. §§ 1681–1688.
94. The statute provides in pertinent part that:
No person in the United States shall, on the basis of sex, be excluded from participation in, be denied the benefits of, or be subjected to discrimination under any education program or activity receiving Federal financial assistance.
95. Franklin, 503 U.S. at 70.

The Court's language seems clearly to lead to the conclusion that, unless Congress has indicated to the contrary, damages should be available under IDEA as well as § 504.[96]

An inquiry into whether a "clear direction to the contrary" has been made by Congress leads to the third major indication that damages should be available. As discussed previously, in 1990 Congress overturned the Supreme Court's determination that states enjoyed Eleventh Amendment sovereign immunity.[97] As part of these 1990 amendments, IDEA was also amended to provide:

> In a suit against a State for a violation of this chapter, remedies (including remedies both at law and in equity) are available for such a violation to the same extent as such remedies are available for such a violation in the suit against any public entity other than a State.[98]

Monetary damages are a traditional legal remedy, and, therefore, Congress appears to have implicitly recognized their availability under IDEA much less to have not indicated a "clear direction to the contrary."

14.7 Procedural Violation Remedy

The meaning of the phrase "free appropriate public education" was first addressed by the United States Supreme Court in *Hendrick Hudson District Board of Education v. Rowley*.[99] In *Rowley*, the Court identified both substantive and procedural components of the state's responsibilities under the Act:

> [A] court's inquiry in suits brought under § 1415(e)(2) is twofold. First, has the State complied with the procedures set forth in the Act? And second, is the individualized educational program developed through the Act's procedures reasonably calculated to enable the child to receive educational benefits? If these requirements are met, the State has complied with the obligations imposed by Congress and the courts can require no more.[100]

The Court recognized that the procedural rights are as important as the substantive rights accorded under the Act:

> When the elaborate and highly specific procedural safeguards embodied in § 1415 are contrasted with the general and somewhat imprecise substantive admonitions contained in the Act, we think that the importance Congress attached to these procedural safeguards cannot be gainsaid. It seems to us no exaggeration to say that Congress placed every bit as much emphasis upon compliance with procedures giving parents and guardians a large measure of

---

96. Ortega v. Bibb County School Dist., 431 F. Supp. 2d 1296 (M.D. Ga. 2006); Tanberg v. Weld County Sheriff, 787 F. Supp. 970 (D. Colo. 1992) (citing *Gwinnett County Public Schools* to support finding that monetary damages available under § 504); *but see* Barnes v. Gorman, 536 U.S. 181 (2002) (punitive damages not available under Rehabilitation Act or ADA).

97. See § 14.2.

98. 20 U.S.C. § 1403(b).

99. 458 U.S. 176 (1981).

100. *Id.* at 206–207.

participation at every stage of the administrative process ... as it did upon the measurement of the resulting IEP against a substantive standard.[101]

Given the importance Congress and the Supreme Court attached to procedural compliance, and the central requirement under the Act to provide a FAPE, it is not surprising that a significant amount of litigation under the Act has focused on whether the school system has violated the procedural rights of the parents and if so, what remedy is available for that violation.

The procedural protections afforded by the Act are extensive. First, there are those protections afforded to both the school and to the parents for resolving disputes between them. The protections include the right to request mediation,[102] a due process hearing,[103] a state level review,[104] and, following the administrative review, the right to file suit in either state or federal court.[105]

Second, there are procedural requirements which insure that educational decision-making proceeds with appropriate information. These procedures include the requirement that the child be identified[106] and be evaluated by a team of qualified professionals with parental input as to the determination of data needed for assessment, as well as review of evaluation and information provided by the parent.[107] Other protections within this category include requiring qualified professionals and the parent to determine the child's eligibility for special education and the placement,[108] to develop initially and review [109] at least annually the Individual Education

---

101. Rowley, 458 U.S. at 207; see also Smith v. Robinson, 468 U.S. 992, 1011 (1984) (the procedures "effect Congress' intent that each child's individual educational needs be worked out through a process that ... includes ... detailed procedural safeguards"). On a substantive level, Congress was very general in defining a FAPE. IDEA provides that a FAPE:

> means special education and related services that (a) are provided at public expense, under public supervision and direction, and without charge; (b) meet the standards of the State educational agency ... ; (c) include preschool, elementary school, or secondary school education in the State involved; and (d) are provided in conformity with the individualized education program....

20 U.S.C. § 1401(9)(C); see also 34 C.F.R. § 300.17.

The statutory definition of 'special education" is:

> specially designed instruction, at no cost to the parents, to meet the unique needs of a child with a disability, including classroom instruction, instruction in physical education, home instruction, and instruction in hospitals and institutions.

20 U.S.C. § 1401(16); 34 C.F.R. § 300.39.

Regulations also indicate that "special education" includes vocational education if specially designed to meet the needs of a disabled child. Vocational education means organized educational programs directly related to the preparation of individuals for paid or unpaid employment, or for additional preparation for a career not requiring a baccalaureate or advanced degree. 20 U.S.C. 1401(29); 34 C.F.R. § 300.39. Further, if "related services" have independent educational value they may constitute special education. 34 C.F.R. § 300.39.

"Related Services" are defined as "[t]ransportation, and such developmental, corrective, and other supportive services ... as may be required to assist a child with a disability to benefit from special education." 20 U.S.C. § 1401(26); 34 C.F.R. § 300.34.

Examples of related services are given in the Act as well.

102. 20 U.S.C. § 1415(d) and (e); 34 C.F.R §§ 300.504 and .506.

103. 20 U.S.C. § 1415(b)(6) and (d).

104. Id. § 1415(g) and (h)(4), 1415 (i)(1)(A, 1415(i)(2).

105. Id. § 1415(j)(2)) and (3)(A), 1415(l).

106. 20 U.S.C. § 1402(3), 1412 (a)(3); 34 C.F.R § 300.111.

107. 20 U.S.C. § 1414(c)(1); 34 C.F.R. § 300.305.

108. 34 C.F.R. § 300.306; 34 C.F.R. §§ 300.308–311.

109. 34 C.F.R. § 300.324.

Program (IEP), and to re-evaluate at least every three years unless the parent and public agency agree that a reevaluation is unnecessary.[110] Congress also required multidisciplinary and nondiscriminatory testing,[111] and to insure the parents had sufficient information available to participate in the educational decision-making, Congress provided the parents with the right to have an independent educational evaluation (IEE) at public expense.[112] The IEE, like the school system's evaluation, is to use the same criteria that the public agency uses to the extent the criteria are consistent with parent's right to an IEE.[113]

Perhaps most important, there is a third type of protection designed to insure that parents are given participation at virtually every stage of the administrative process.[114] In *Honig v. Doe*,[115] the Court stated that the procedural rights "guarantee parents both an opportunity for meaningful input into all decisions affecting their child's education, and the right to seek review of any decisions they think inappropriate."

The significant role parents are to play is reinforced throughout the Act. Parents are permitted to be involved in the evaluation process, the eligibility determination, and development of the IEP.[116] Following development of an IEP, a placement decision is made again with parental input, based on the information contained in the IEP.[117] Written notice must be provided to the parent within a reasonable time before the school proposes to change the child's identification, evaluation, or educational placement, or refuses to take any of these actions.[118] Parental consent is explicitly required before obtaining a preplacement evaluation, initial placement of the child and for reevaluations.[119] The role of a parent is so important, that a surrogate parent must be appointed where there is no parent or the parents' whereabouts are unknown, or when the child is a ward of the state.[120] Finally, an often potent protection for the parent is the stay-put provision previously discussed.[121]

Early procedural violation cases provided what appeared to be a *per se* rule that violation of the procedural rights of the parent or child resulted in the granting of substantive relief. Existing analysis of procedural violations has developed toward asking first whether a procedural violation occurred, and second whether the parents or child were prejudiced by that violation. The burden of proof is on the parents to establish both the violation and the harm.

Two of the earliest procedural violation cases arose in the Fourth Circuit. In *Hall v. Vance County Board of Education*,[122] the court addressed the educational programming of a sixteen-year-old child with dyslexia. The district court ruled that the school had failed to provide a FAPE and had egregiously violated the procedural requirements of the Act.

---

110. 34 C.F.R. § 300.308; *see also* 20 U.S.C. § 1414(a)(2).
111. 20 U.S.C. §§ 1414(b)(1)–(3), 1412(a)(6)(B); *see* 34 C.F.R. § 300.304.
112. 20 U.S.C. § 1415(b)(1)and (d)(2)(a); *see* 34 C.F.R. § 300.502.
113. 20 U.S.C. § 1415(b)(1) and (d)(2)(a); *see* 34 C.F.R. § 300.502(e)(1).
114. Rowley, 458 U.S. at 207; *see also* Smith v. Robinson, 468 U.S. 992, 1011 (1984) (the procedures "effect Congress' intent that each child's individual educational needs be worked out through a process that ... includes ... detailed procedural safeguards").
115. 484 U.S. 305, 311–12 (1988).
116. 20 U.S.C. § 1414(d)(1)(B)(i); *see* 34 C.F.R. § 300.322; 34 C.F.R. § 300.533–535.
117. 34 C.F.R. § 300.327.
118. 34 C.F.R. § 300.503(a).
119. 34 C.F.R. § 300.300(a).
120. 34 C.F.R. § 300.519(a).
121. 34 C.F.R. § 300.518. See § 11.7.
122. 774 F.2d 629 (4th Cir. 1985).

In *Hall*, the child had difficulty in school until his parents placed him in a private educational program. Both the state level review officer and the district court found that throughout their dealings with the parents the school had consistently failed to provide the parents with notice of their procedural rights under the Act. *Hall* dealt primarily with the dispute resolution rights under the Act. While the parents and the school system had numerous contacts, the parents were never informed of their right to have the dispute resolved.[123] The Fourth Circuit held that, "[u]nder *Rowley*, these failures to meet the Act's procedural requirements are adequate grounds by themselves for holding that the school failed to provide James a FAPE before January 1982."[124]

While *Hall* dealt with excluding parents from the dispute resolution process, *Spielberg v. Henrico County Public Schools*[125] dealt with excluding the parents from the decision-making process. *Spielberg* involved a seventeen-year-old boy with the functional skills of an eighteen-month-old child. The School system decided to change the child's educational placement from a private 12-month residential program to a nine-month regular school day program, with an abbreviated summer school program of six weeks. The district court found that the school had made this decision prior to developing an IEP upon which the decision could be based. Both the district and appellate court recognized this decision-making as a violation of federal regulations which require placement decisions to be based on an existing IEP. The appellate court wrote:

> The decision to place Jonathan at [the public school placement] before developing an IEP on which to base that placement decision violates this regulation as interpreted by the Secretary of Education. It also violates the spirit and intent of the EHA, which emphasizes parental involvement. After the fact involvement is not enough.[126]

These two cases and others suggest that, at least with regard to dispute resolution and parental participation rights, in circumstances where there is a complete denial of procedural protection, substantive relief can result.[127] Such a reading is consistent with

---

123. While the court did not explicitly indicate the source of the authority to grant substantive relief, the court in discussing the nature of the procedural violation placed heavy reliance on the language in *Rowley* concerning the importance of procedural rights and in particular the importance of parental participation. Later courts have indicated that the power to award substantive relief for procedural violations "stems from the 'broad discretion' conferred on the courts to grant appropriate relief under Sec. 1415(C)." Evans v. District No. 17 of Douglas County, 841 F.2d 824, 828 (8th Cir. 1988); *see also* Amanda J. v. Clark County Sch. Dist., 267 F.3d 877, 892 (9th Cir. 2001) (school district violated requirements of IDEA by failing to timely disclose student's records, including records indicating that she possibly suffered from autism, to her parents).

124. Hall, 774 F.2d at 635.

125. 853 F.2d 256 (4th Cir. 1988).

126. *Id.* at 259.

127. *See* Deal v. Hamilton County Bd. of Educ., 392 F.3d 840 (6th Cir. 2004) (school system's predetermination not to offer student intensive applied behavioral analysis (ABA) amounted to procedural violation of IDEA and predetermination of placement effectively deprived student's parents of meaningful participation in individualized education program (IEP) process, causing substantive harm and depriving student of free appropriate public education (FAPE); and school system's procedural violation of IDEA through failure to have regular teachers present at meetings where IEP that was subject of lawsuit was prepared caused substantive harm to student or his parents); M.L. v. Federal Way School Dist., 394 F.3d 634 (9th Cir. 2005) (failure of school district to ensure participation of regular education teacher on IEP team, when there was possibility that disabled student would have been placed in integrated classroom, was significant violation of IDEA procedures and failure of school district to comply with requirement of IDEA fatally compromised integrity of IEP); Gonzales v. Puerto Rico Dept. of Educ., 969 F. Supp. 801 (D.P.R. 1997) (failure to hold due process

several other court decisions. In *Jackson v. Franklin County School Board*,[128] for example, James, a sixteen-year-old child with a learning disability, functioning at a third grade level, was suspended for three days for accosting several female classmates. Delinquency charges were filed and the mother agreed to send him to a state hospital for evaluation and treatment. In early April, after a little more than two months, he was discharged from the hospital. The director of special education programs conferred with James' social worker who told his mother that it would not be a good time for the child to return to school. James, did not return to school that academic year.

In the fall, James' mother asked about his status and was told by the director of special education that James would need a new IEP before re-enrollment. The director, however, refused to develop a new IEP or discuss re-enrollment until after the delinquency matter was resolved. The mother filed a complaint with the State Department of Education, spoke to the Superintendent of Schools, and finally sought legal counsel. An IEP meeting was finally scheduled for October 31. As a result of this meeting, the school system took the position that James required a residential program. His mother believed he should be placed in the public schools.

While there was some disagreement over whether the social worker had been speaking on behalf of the mother when she stated that in April it was not a good idea to have James come back, "the burden rests squarely on the school or agency to safeguard handicapped children's rights by informing their parents of those rights."[129]

There were in effect two types of violations in *Jackson*. First, there was the failure to provide notice of the relevant procedural rights and protection. This violation was similar to the violation in *Hall*. Second, there was the failure to develop an IEP both in April and August. The court found that the failure to provide notice and a hearing concerning his exclusion from school violated James' rights under IDEA. The court also held that the school's failure to convene an IEP meeting after the April release from the state hospital "was a *per se* violation" of the IDEA.[130] Citing *Hall*, the court held that the procedural violation was sufficient to establish that the school had failed to provide a FAPE.[131] The second violation in many ways is similar to the violation in *Spielberg* in the sense that the school precluded the parents from the decision-making process by refusing to conduct an IEP meeting. Again, total exclusion from two of the three sets of protection allowed substantive recovery.

The ultimate remedy for this failure to provide procedural rights was somewhat unclear in *Jackson*. Unlike cases such as *Spielberg* where the child was already in the placement the parents were seeking,[132] or *Hall* where the parents could afford to unilaterally place the child in the desired location and then seek reimbursement, here the child was actually denied education during the relevant time period. The court, therefore, remanded the case for a determination of whether damages or compensatory educational services were appropriate.[133]

---

hearing and parents private school placement appropriate; reimbursement due from time hearing should have been held).

128. 806 F.2d 623 (5th Cir. 1986).

129. *Id.* at 629.

130. *Id.* at 628.

131. *Id.* at 629.

132. *Spielberg*, 853 F.2d at 257.

133. The court recognized that given the Handicapped Children's Protection Act of 1986, suit could be brought concurrently under § 1983 and IDEA. While courts hold monetary damages are generally unavailable under the IDEA, money damages are available under § 1983.

Other cases have been more tolerant of procedural violations. In what is perhaps the most influential decision distinguishing cases such as *Hall*, *Spielberg*, and *Jackson*, the Eighth Circuit dealt with the educational needs of a ten-year-old girl with cerebral palsy, mental retardation, and a severe behavioral impairment in *Evans v. District No. 17 of Douglas County*.[134] In *Evans*, the parents alleged that there was a procedural violation because of a failure to provide required triennial evaluations. The district court, however, found that the failure to perform the evaluations did not deny the girl, Christine, a FAPE because there was no evidence of harm to her education.

Evans is different from *Hall*, *Spielberg*, and *Jackson* in that there was an affirmative finding by the court that educational programming was apparently not affected by the procedural violation. The court reasoned that a triennial evaluation was ultimately scheduled before the beginning of the next school year, and that no changes would have occurred before that time anyway. The court in *Evans* also stated that the earlier cases could be distinguished perhaps on the basis that the types of procedural violations involved were by their nature more likely to result in impact on the educational programming.

Two points about *Evans* are troubling, however. The court's statement that there was no proof of harm to the child's education appears to be the first time a court explicitly required a showing of prejudice. In a sense, *Evans* reconciles the cases by implying a showing of prejudice is always required and that it was obvious in the earlier cases that prejudice would occur. As significantly, the statement also seemed to place the burden of persuasion on the parents not only to show the existence of a procedural violation, but also to show that the violation caused damage.

Other courts have agreed with the *Evans* decision. In *Doe v. Alabama State Department of Education*,[135] the Eleventh Circuit court held that a procedural violation was not sufficient to warrant relief. In *Doe*, the parents of a nineteen-year-old child with a manic-depressive illness sought a private residential program for their son. The school district offered in-home tutoring services and 24-hour psychiatric supervision. The district court held that the school system's educational program was appropriate, and the parents appealed.

The parents alleged numerous procedural violations. Among the allegations, the parents claimed they were not provided with the detailed notice required under IDEA and as a result, there was ineffective parental participation. The court, however, upheld the district court's finding that the parents had actual notice, despite deficiencies in the notice, and that the parents' participation had been "full and effective."[136] The court rejected the parents' argument that violation of the notice requirement was a *per se* violation of IDEA which itself constituted a failure to provide a FAPE. Citing *Evans*, the court held that "[b]ecause the notice deficiencies in this case had no impact on the

---

134. 841 F.2d 824 (8th Cir. 1988).

135. 915 F.2d 651 (11th Cir. 1990); *see also* R.B. v. Napa Valley Unified School Dist., WL 2028132, 2007 (9th Cir.) (procedural defects did not violate FAPE); Adam J. v. Keller Independent School Dist., 328 F.3d 804, (5th Cir. 2003) (student and parents had not established that any procedural deficiency in IEP resulted in loss of educational opportunity to student or infringed parents' opportunity to participate in IEP process); MM v. School Dist. of Greenville County, 303 F.3d 523 (4th Cir. 2002) (although school district failed to abide by procedural requirements of IDEA because IEP was not finalized by the beginning of the school year, procedural defect did not result in any lost educational opportunity for student); Heather S. v. Wisconsin, 125 F.3d 1045 (7th Cir. 1997) (delay in rendering hearing decision beyond statutory time did not deny child FAPE).

136. *Id.* at 662.

Doe's full and effective participation in the IEP process and because the purpose of the procedural requirement was fully realized in this case … there has been no violation … which warrants relief."[137]

Even the Fourth Circuit, in a decision after *Hall* and *Spielberg*, followed *Evans*. In *Board of Education of the County of Cabell v. Dienelt*,[138] the parents of a child with a learning disability rejected the "standard" IEP suggested by his teacher and unilaterally placed him in a private school. The parents then instituted a due process proceeding. The district court found that the school did not conduct an interdisciplinary review or involve the parents in the IEP development. In a very brief opinion, citing *Rowley* and quoting *Hall*, the court held that the procedural violations constituted a failure to provide a FAPE, and upheld the reimbursement of the private placement. Exclusion of the parents in development of the IEP clearly falls within the complete denial of the decision-making rights, and therefore is consistent with the previous Fourth Circuit decisions and with *Evans* as well.[139]

There are, to be sure, a few courts that continue to hold open the question of whether a separate test of prejudice is required. In *Leonard v. McKenzie*,[140] for example, the District of Columbia Circuit Court left unanswered the question whether procedural violations were "subject to a separate test of 'prejudice,'" and held that an administrative "foul-up" of sending an erroneous Notice of Placement, which was corrected prior to the beginning of the academic school year, did not constitute a procedural violation.[141]

In *Kerkam v. McKenzie*,[142] however, the District of Columbia Circuit suggested that the trial court consider the "potentially prejudicial effect" of procedural violations.[143] In

---

137. *Id.* (footnote omitted). The parents also alleged that the child was suspended from school without the benefit of an IEP meeting. Such an expulsion is clearly a violation of the Act, Honig, 484 U.S. at 325–26 n.8, but the court held that the claim was waived in due process hearing by the parents. Doe v. Alabama, 915 F.2d at 660.

Another alleged violation of procedural requirements was the delivery of educational services without an IEP being in place. The court, however, found that this was the result of the parents' actions. *Id.* at 663.

The parents also contended that the initial classification of their son as emotionally conflicted was done without proper evaluations, and therefore the IEP was invalid because it was not based on appropriate evaluations. There was no violation, however, because the school had not evaluated the child because of his fragile emotional state. *Id.* at 664.

The final alleged procedural violation was that the school had a "generalized policy" against placing children in private programs and that this was in violation of the requirement that the school provide a continuum of educational services. Citing *Georgia Association of Retarded Citizens v. McDaniel*, 716 F.2d 1565 (11th Cir. 1983), *vacated*, 468 U.S. 1213 (1984), the court recognized that if this were an inflexible policy, there would be a violation of the Act. Here, however, the school had consulted with experts and found that the public school was appropriate.

138. 843 F.2d 813 (4th Cir. 1988).

139. Finding that a failure to conduct the multidisciplinary review, however, seems more in the nature of an *Evans* problem. Given that there were both types of violations, however, *Evans* is not inconsistent.

140. 869 F.2d 1558, 1562 n.3 (D.C. Cir. 1989).

141. *See also* Block v. District of Columbia, 748 F. Supp. 891, 897–98 (D.D.C. 1990) where the school failed to develop an IEP for a 13 year-old student with a learning disability. Citing *Andersen*, the court stated that "assuming without deciding that 'prejudice' is a prerequisite, the Court holds that the Blocks have shown that they were seriously prejudiced and that DCPS's failure to provide a complete and appropriate IEP and its delay in rectifying the problems directly affected the 1989–90 school year."

142. 862 F.2d 884 (D.C. Cir. 1988).

143. In the trial court, the defects in procedures alleged appear to have been that the hearing officer did not consider a placement proposed by the parents and defects in the proposed notice of placement. Court held that notice was defective, but that parents were aware of the reasons for the

Andersen v. District of Columbia,[144] the court went even further, citing *Evans* with approval, but, because counsel withdrew the claim, not deciding whether there was a separate requirement of prejudice.

Evans, therefore, is clearly the prevailing means by which courts will analyze procedural violations.[145] In summary, then, the courts will not apply a *per se* analysis. Some showing of prejudice is required, and the language in *Evans* seems to indicate that the parents have the burden of persuasion on both the question of whether there was a violation to begin with and whether the violation resulted in prejudice.

The analysis of procedural violations as it has developed through *Evans* is troubling in several respects. Assuming that a *per se* rule granting substantive relief would constitute an inappropriate windfall to the parent, very little guidance is provided on what type of procedural violation will rise to the level of justifying substantive relief. *Andersen* recognized the ambiguity created by the existing analysis. The court stated that the early Fourth Circuit cases "are themselves ambiguous, as the errors were ones that the court may have viewed as inherently carrying a high probability of prejudice."[146] Citing *Evans* and *Kerkam* and recognizing that *Leonard* left open the question, the court in *Andersen* stated that "we think the plaintiffs here are wise to have abandoned their arguments" that sending an erroneous Notice of Placement which was later corrected before the beginning of the school year, constituted a procedural violation sufficient to warrant a finding that the school had failed to provide a FAPE.[147] Classifying the error as an "administrative foul-up" the court stated "that the errors are certainly far less likely to have affected the placements or the administrative decisions than those involved in *Dienelt, Spielberg,* and *Hall.*"[148] The reference to a "foul-up" in *Andersen,* however, is, of course, conclusory and does not tell us which violations are mere technicalities.[149]

---

placement and were not prejudiced by the defective notice. Kerkam v. District of Columbia Bd. of Educ., 672 F. Supp. 519 (D.D.C. 1987), *rev'd on other grounds,* 862 F.2d 884 (D.C. Cir. 1988); *see also* Gradby v. Grasmick, 109 F.3d 940 (4th Cir. 1997) (SEA's failure to give notice of its denial of local agency's application for reimbursement on behalf of student did not obligate the SEA to reimburse for tuition. Violation did not interfere with the provision of a FAPE).

144. 877 F.2d 1018 (D.C. Cir. 1989).

145. Weiss v. School Bd. of County of Hillsborough, 141 F.3d 990 (11th Cir. 1998) (notice technically deficient but no prejudice, interim IEP also legally sufficient).

146. Andersen, 877 F.2d at 1021.

147. *Id.*

148. *Id.* at 1021–22.

149. Such conclusory statements are all too common. Doe v. Defendant I, 898 F.2d 1186 (6th Cir. 1990), for example, dealt with a child with a learning disability called dysgraphic disorder. The parents requested a delay in holding an IEP meeting prior to the child's entry into the seventh grade in order to observe the child's adjustment. An IEP was ultimately developed in November, and as a result, the school offered tutoring and testing services to the parents. The parents refused these services and obtained them privately. When the school refused to pay for these private services, the parents placed the child in a private program and requested a due process hearing. On a number of procedural challenges, the court first held that the failure to have an IEP in place at the beginning of the school year did not constitute a procedural violation. While the regulations do require the school to have an IEP in effect at the beginning of each school year that IEP can only be implemented after appropriate IEP meetings. The parents were the cause of the failure to have the IEP in effect because of their requests to delay intervention until the child's adjustment could be studied.

The parents also claimed procedural violations occurred because the IEP did not state the child's present level of educational functioning nor did it state objective criteria for determining whether the instructional objectives were being met.

Both of these items are explicitly required under both the Act and its implementing regulations. 20 U.S.C. §1414(d)(1)(A); 34 C.F.R. §300.347. The court, however, held that "to say that these technical deviations ... render appellant's IEP invalid is to exalt form over substance" since the par-

Anticipating a criticism that a prejudice test would minimize the procedural importance, the court in *Evans* stated that its decision did "not in any way render the force of [IDEA] nugatory," since the parents could invoke the procedures of the Act to compel the system to provide the evaluation, or seek reimbursement for expenses incurred as a result of the violation (apparently conducting the evaluation and seeking reimbursement).[150]

Despite the language in *Evans* to the contrary, that the force of the Act would not be "nugatory," focusing on prejudice may very well undermine the Act's primary purpose. Prejudice in the cases seems to focus on educational or financial harm.[151] The Act, however, is a remedial statute. The Act was designed to correct the inappropriate behavior of the educational establishment—behavior not motivated merely by a lack of money, but by a lack of will. As the United States Supreme Court said in *Honig v. Doe*, "[a]lthough these educational failings resulted in part from funding constraints, Congress recognized that the problem reflected more than a lack of financial resources at the state and local levels."[152] As already mentioned, according to *Rowley*, the main tool used in effecting this remedy are the procedural protection. Lower courts have emphasized the procedural protection as well. The court in *Jackson*, for example, stated that the procedural safeguards are coextensive with the substantive right.[153]

ents and school system were all aware of the information required, but missing. Doe v. Defendant I, 898 F.2d at 1190.

The court recognized that *Rowley* emphasized the importance of procedural safeguards, but took the position that *Rowley* was concerned with the process by which the IEP was developed, "rather than the myriad of technical items that must be included in the written document." *Id.* Because the parents fully participated in the development of the IEP, the procedural concerns expressed by the Supreme Court had been met. It appears that had the parents not been aware of the information, the court may have reached a contrary result, having stated, "[w]e underscore the fact that the information absent from the IEP was nonetheless known to the parents." *Id.* at 1191. *See also* Thomas F. v. Cincinnati Board of Education, 918 F.2d 618 (6th Cir. 1990), in which the school district appealed a district court's order to place an eleven-year-old severely mentally retarded and multihandicapped child in a school-based program. The parent also appealed on grounds that the district erred in not awarding compensatory education.

The student was legally blind, functioned at a one-month-old level, and required the use of a wheel chair and gastrostomy and tracheostomy tubes. The school district initially provided five hours per week of homebound instruction. Under a new IEP, the school district agreed to provide a school based program. The program was not implemented, however, because of a dispute over transportation.

The parent argued that the absence of written notice was a procedural violation. The court found that actual notice was received by telephone, and therefore the violation was harmless. Technical noncompliance did not result in any substantive deprivation.

150. Evans, 841 F.2d at 831.

151. Urban v. Jefferson County School Dist., 899 F.3d 720 (10th Cir. 1996) (procedural defects in IEP not denial of FAPE); Independent School Dist. No. 283 v. S.D., 88 F.3d 556 (8th Cir. 1996) (procedural and technical deficiencies in IEP does not entitle child to additional relief on judicial review).

152. Honig, 484 U.S. at 309.

153. Jackson, 806 F.2d at 629

Chapter 15

Attorney's Fees and Costs

15.1 Attorney's Fees in General

Prior to 1984, court actions brought pursuant to IDEA typically also alleged violations of 42 U.S.C. § 1983 and § 504 of the Rehabilitation Act of 1973[1] in an attempt to recover attorney's fees.[2] Jurisdictions split on the availability of § 1983 and § 504 in actions also covered by IDEA. In 1984, the United States Supreme Court in *Smith v. Robinson*,[3] held that the comprehensiveness of IDEA and the detail with which IDEA addressed special education evidenced Congress' intent to make IDEA the sole source for relief. The practical effect of *Smith* was to deny attorney's fees in virtually all special education cases.

Congress reacted quickly to *Smith*. *Smith* was decided July 5, 1984, and on February 6, 1985, the Handicapped Children's Protection Act of 1985 was introduced in Congress. On August 5, 1986, President Reagan signed into law the Handicapped Children's Protection Act of 1986 (HCPA),[4] amending § 1415 of IDEA, and granting courts authority to award attorney's fees. IDEA now provides:

> In any action or proceeding brought under this subsection, the court, in its discretion, may award attorneys' fees as part of the costs to the parents of a child with a disability who is the prevailing party.

The court may also award attorney's fees to a prevailing SEA or LEA against the parent's attorney if the attorney files a complaint or cause of action that is frivolous, unreasonable, or without foundation. If the attorney continues to litigate after the administrative proceeding or lawsuit becomes frivolous, unreasonable, or without foundation attorney's fees may again be awarded.

In addition, attorney's fees may be awarded to a prevailing SEA or LEA against the parent's attorney or the parent, if the parent requests a due process hearing or files a subsequent lawsuit if such action was taken for any improper purpose, such as to harass, to cause unnecessary delay, or to needlessly increase the cost of litigation.[5]

---

1. 29 U.S.C. § 794.
2. Civil Rights Attorney's Fees Awards Act of 1976, 42 U.S.C. § 1988 (1981); 29 U.S.C. § 794(a). There are additional reasons to seek relief under § 1983 and § 504. See §§ 1.4, 1.5.
3. 468 U.S. 2 (1984).
4. P.L. 99-372, 100 Stat. 796 (1986); 20 U.S.C. § 1415(i)(3).
5. 20 U.S.C.A § 1415(i)(3)(B)(i–iii); *see also* 34 C.F.R § 300.517. Prior to the 2004 amendments, the statute was explicit in referring to the ability of only the *parents* recovering attorney's fees and costs. The Federal Rule of Civil Procedure 54(d), however, covers demands for costs generally. School divisions had been successful, before their eligibility to recover attorney fees in invoking Rule

15.2 Availability of Attorney's Fees for Work in Administrative Proceedings

The most litigated issue following the 1986 adoption of the IDEA attorney's fees provision was whether recovery of fees was available for work done during administrative proceedings. The statutory language, at first glance, is less than clear. In fact the language provides, "the *court*, in its discretion, may award attorneys' fees...."[6] The vast majority of courts, however, have held that attorney's fees are recoverable for work performed during administrative proceedings, at least as long as a lawsuit was subsequently filed to resolve issues other than the attorney's fees.[7]

The fact that Congress intended the authority to award fees to extend to representation in administrative proceedings is evidenced from a reading of the fee amendment in its entirety. The statute clearly states, "In *any action or proceeding* brought under this section...."[8] The disjunctive language implies intent to distinguish between two types of proceedings. Further, in the context of placing limits on the fees, the 1986 HCPA amendment made specific reference to "the court or administrative hearing officer...."[9]

Legislative history also clearly evidences Congress' intent to allow awards for representation during the administrative stage. The Senate Report that accompanied the bill stated:

> Section 2 provides for the award of reasonable attorney's fees to prevailing parents in EAHCA civil actions *and administrative proceedings* in certain specified circumstances.[10]

The Senate Report was explicit when it stated:

> The Committee also intends that section 2 should be interpreted consistent with fee provisions of statutes such as title VII ... which authorizes courts to

54(d) to recover costs. *See, e.g.,* Cypress-Fairbanks Indep. School Dist. v. Michael F., 118 F.3d 245 (5th Cir. 1997).

6. 20 U.S.C. § 1415(i)(3)(B) (emphasis added).

7. *See, e.g.,* I.B. v. N.Y. City Dep't of Educ., 336 F.3d 79 (2d Cir. 2003); T.D. v. LaGrange School Dist. No. 102, 349 F.3d 469 (7th Cir. 2003); John T. v. Iowa Dep't of Educ., 258 F.3d 860 (8th Cir. 2001); Antonio v. Boston Pub. Schools, 314 F. Supp. 2d 95 (D. Mass. 2004); Combs v. School of Rockingham County, 15 F.3d 357, 360 (4th Cir. 1994); Borengasser v. Arkansas State Bd. of Educ., 996 F.2d 196, 199 (8th Cir. 1993); Angela L. v. Pasadena Indep. School Dist., 918 F.2d 1188 (5th Cir. 1990); McSomebodies v. Burlingame Elementary School Dist., 897 F.2d 974 (9th Cir. 1989); Duane M. v. Orleans Parish School Bd., 861 F.2d 115 (5th Cir. 1988); Eggers v. Bullitt County School Dist., 854 F.2d 892 (6th Cir. 1988); Counsel v. Dow, 849 F.2d 731 (2d Cir. 1988); Massachusetts Dept. of Public Health v. School Committee of Tewksbury, 841 F. Supp. 449 (D. Mass. 1993); Williams v. Boston School Committee, 709 F. Supp. 27 (D. Mass. 1989); Burr v. Ambach, 683 F. Supp. 46 (S.D.N.Y. 1988); Prescott v. Palos Verdes Penninsula Unified School Dist., 659 F. Supp. 921 (C.D. Ca. 1987); School Bd. of the County of Prince William v. Malone, 662 F. Supp. 999 (E.D. Va. 1987); Burpee v. Manchester School Dist., 661 F. Supp. 731 (D.N.H. 1987); *but see* Linda T. v. Rice Lake Area School Dist., 417 F.3d 704 (7th Cir. 2005) (de minimus success at administrative procedure does not entitle parents to fee award); Vultaggio v. Bd. of Educ., 216 F. Supp. 2d 96 (E.D.N.Y. 2002) (not available in state's complaint resolution procedure (CRP); Rollison v. Biggs, 660 F. Supp. 875 (D. Del. 1987). For a discussion of filing as suit solely to obtain attorney's fees see § 15.3.

8. 20 U.S.C. § 1415(i)(3)(B); *see also* 34 C.F.R § 300.513.

9. *Id.* § 1415(i)(3)(D)(III).

10. S. Rep. No. 112, 99th Cong., 2d Sees. 4, *reprinted in* 1986 U.S. Code Cong. & Admin. News 1799, 1800 (emphasis added).

award fees for time spent by counsel in mandatory administrative proceedings under those statutes.[11]

The legislative history in the House of Representatives likewise made it clear that administrative proceedings are covered by IDEA.[12]

Allowing recovery for attorney's fees for work done at the administrative level is consistent with the award of attorney's fees in other civil rights actions. Assuming there is ultimately a decision on the merits, attorney's fees are recoverable under §1988 for mandatory administrative hearings.[13] The legislative history of the attorney's fee amendment specifically indicates Congress' intent was to provide that awards would, in most circumstances, be based on the same factors as those used in granting attorney's fee awards under 42 U.S.C. §1988:

> [S]ubject to two modifications described below, determinations as to whether a parent is awarded fees and the amount of the award are governed by applicable decisions interpreting 42 U.S.C. §1988.[14]

Further, under Titles VI[15] and VII of the Civil Rights Act of 1964[16] attorney's fees may be recovered for work done in administrative proceedings, at least as long as there is ultimately a judicial resolution of the underlying merits. The United States Supreme Court in *New York Gaslight Club, Inc. v. Carey*,[17] held that mandatory state employment discrimination administrative proceedings are proceedings to enforce Title VII and therefore attorney's fees were recoverable under §2000e-5(k) which provides, "In any action or proceeding under this title the court ... may allow the prevailing party ... a reasonable attorney's fee as part of costs."[18]

Carey involved an allegation of race discrimination in employment. The respondent was denied a job as a cocktail waitress. While represented by counsel, she engaged in extensive attempts to resolve the dispute less formally than through litigation. These attempts included a state administrative hearing and appeal as well as efforts at conciliation. In addition, proceedings were conducted by the Equal Employment Opportunity Commission (EEOC). The state administrative proceedings were appealed to state court, and the EEOC's finding of reasonable cause resulted in respondent filing in United States District Court. After respondent's success in the state courts, the federal court action was withdrawn, except for the request for attorney's fees.

The issue before the Court, therefore, was whether attorney's fees were available under Title VII for work done in mandatory administrative proceedings. The Court, in holding that attorney's fees were available for work in administrative proceedings, placed heavy emphasis on the language of the statute which, just as IDEA, states, "In any action or proceeding...."[19] The Court held that "Congress' use of the broadly inclusive disjunctive phrase 'action or proceeding' indicates an intent to subject the losing

---

11. *Id.* at 14, *reprinted in* 1986 U.S. Code Cong. & Admin. News at 1804.
12. Conference Report on S. 415, Handicapped Children's Protection Act of 1986, Congressional Record—H 4841, July 24, 1986.
13. *See* North Carolina Dept. of Transportation v. Crest Street Community Council, 479 U.S. 6 (1986).
14. Conference Report on S. 415, Handicapped Children's Protection Act of 1986, Congressional Record—H 4841, 4842, July 24, 1986 (remarks of Mr. Williams).
15. Title VI of Civil Rights Act of 1964, 42 U.S.C. §§2000d *et seq.*
16. Title VII of Civil Rights Act of 1964, 42 U.S.C. §§2000e *et seq.*
17. 447 U.S. 54 (1980).
18. 42 U.S.C. §2000e-5(k).
19. *Id.*

party to an award of attorney's fees and costs that includes expenses incurred for administrative proceedings."[20] Further, the Court pointed out, Congress' intent was evidenced by the fact that another fee provision in the same Act used the words "any action commenced pursuant to this title." In the words of the Court, "The omission of the words 'or proceeding' from § 204(b) is understandable, since enforcement of Title II depends solely on court actions."[21]

It would be anomalous, especially in light of the strong legislative history indicating congressional intent to allow such an award, to deny recovery under IDEA while allowing recovery under Title VII.

15.2.1 What Constitutes the Administrative Proceedings?

It seems reasonably clear that attorney's fees are available for work done in the administrative proceedings once the due process request has been filed under IDEA.[22] The question becomes, however, how far back in the administrative process are fees taxable. Are fees available for work done in conjunction with only the due process hearing, or, for example, can fees be awarded for work completed in conjunction with the IEP meeting?

In 1997 the IDEA specifically addressed the issue of awarding fees for work done at IEP meetings. Attorney's fees are not to be awarded for work related to any meeting of the IEP team, unless the meeting is convened as a result of an administrative proceeding or judicial action or at the discretion of the SEA for mediation conducted prior to the filing of a request for a due process hearing.[23]

An issue that remains is whether recovery of fees is available for work done in conjunction with a state complaint procedure.[24] Courts have held both ways on the availability of fees in such situations.[25]

15.2.2 Authority of Administrative Officer to Award

It is clear that an award of attorney's fees can be made for work done at the administrative due process proceedings. It is equally clear, however, that only a state or federal judge is able to make the award. In *Lauren T. v. Crisp County Board of Education*,[26] the

---

20. 447 U.S. at 61.

21. *Id.*

22. See § 15.2.

23. 20 U.S.C. § 1415(i)(D)(ii); 34 C.F.R. § 300.517(c)(2)(ii); District of Columbia v. R.R., 390 F. Supp. 2d 38 (D.D.C. 2005).

24. See Chapter 17.

25. *Compare* Lucht v. Mollalla School Dist., 225 F.3d 1023 (9th Cir. 2000) (state complaint resolution was administrative proceeding for purposes of awarding attorney's fees incurred); Upper Valley Assn. for Handicapped Citizens v. Blue Mountain School Dist., 973 F. Supp. 429 (D. Vt. 1997) (as matter of first impression attorney's fees available for work done dealing with complaint resolution process: prior to IDEA 1997); *with* Vultaggio v. Bd. of Educ., 216 F. Supp. 2d 96 (E.D.N.Y. 2002) (attorney's fees are not available to parents prevailing in state's complaint resolution procedure); Megan C. v. Independent School Dist. No. 625, 57 F. Supp. 2d 776 (D. Minn. 1999).

26. 508 Educ. Handicapped L. Rep. (CRR) 298 (SEA Ga. 1987); *see also* Duneland School Corp., 31 Individuals with Disabilities Educ. L. Rep. (LRP) 222 (SEA Ind. 2000); San Francisco Unified School Dist., 20 Individuals with Disabilities Educ. L. Rep. (LRP) 153 (SEA Cal. 1998); Oakland Unified School Dist., 508 Educ. Handicapped L. Rep. (CRR) 246 (SEA Cal. 1986); Newport–Mesa Unified School Dist., 508 Educ. Handicapped L. Rep. (CRR) 263 (SEA Cal. 1986).

parent moved for an award of attorney's fees during an administrative due process hearing and the hearing officer denied the request. The SEA officer held that IDEA grants the authority to order attorney's fees only to the court: "In any action or proceeding … the *court*, in its discretion, may award…."[27] Subparagraphs (B) through (G), the officer pointed out "provide limitations on how fees are to be awarded and calculated. Thus, only the court has the general authority to award attorneys' fees, and then only if the conditions set forth in subparagraphs B through G are met."[28]

The officer did recognize that subparagraph D and its reference to an administrative officer's finding that a settlement offer was not justifiably rejected does create an ambiguity. He held, however, that the provision can be read consistently with the other subparagraphs by recognizing that a hearing officer could make the factual determination, but a court would have to make the award.

The officer also pointed to the legislative history that states, "[t]he committee intends that S. 415 will allow the Court but not the hearing officer, to award fees for time spent by counsel in mandatory EHA administrative proceedings."[29]

The *Lauren T.* decision makes good sense, both from a statutory interpretation perspective and from a practical perspective. Hearing officers are not in a position to award fees. Many are nonlawyers,[30] and as you look at the factors that go into determining an appropriate fee, it is clearly beyond their expertise. Even for lawyers who are hearing officers, they will not have the breadth of experience to judge the relative merits.[31]

15.3 Ability to File Suit Solely for Attorney's Fees

A determination that administrative officers do not have authority to grant attorney's fees should cause only a minor problem for parents.[32] The vast majority of courts, including each United States Circuit Court of Appeals that has addressed the question, have held that suit may be filed solely to obtain attorney's fees.[33]

---

27. 20 U.S.C. § 1415(i)(3)(A) (emphasis added); 34 C.F.R. § 300.517(a).
28. Lauren T., 508 Educ. Handicapped L. Rep. (CRR) at 299.
29. *Id. citing* 132 Cong. Rec. H 4841, 4842 (1986) (remarks of Representative Bartlett).
30. Neither IDEA nor its supporting regulations require the hearing officer be a lawyer. *See* 34 C.F.R. § 300.511; *see also* 20 U.S.C. § 1415(f)(3).
31. It is not unusual for due process hearing officers to hear no more than one special education case per year.
32. While there is certainly the added time and effort, attorney's fees and costs are available for time spent in recovering attorney's fees. See authorities collected in A. Conte, *Attorney Fee Awards* § 4.21 (3d ed. 2004).
33. *See* P.N. v. Seattle School Dist., 474 F.3d 1165 (9th Cir. 2007); Kaseman v. District of Columbia, 444 F.3d 637 (D.C. Cir. 2006); Linda T. v. Rice Lake Area School Dist., 417 F.3d 704 (7th Cir. 2005); T.D. v. LaGrange School Dist. No. 102 349 F.3d 469 (7th Cir. 2003); J.C. v. Reg'l. School Dist. 10, 278 F.3d 119 (2d Cir. 2002); Warner v. Independent School Dist. No. 625, 134 F.3d 1333, 1336 (8th Cir. 1998); Johnson v. Bismarck Pub. School Dist., 949 F.2d 1000 (8th Cir. 1991); Angela L. v. Pasadena Indep. School Dist., 918 F.2d 1188 (5th Cir. 1990); Moore v. Dist. of Columbia, 907 F.2d 165 (D.C. Cir. 1990) (*en banc*); McSombodies v. Burlingame Elementary School, 897 F.2d 974 (9th Cir. 1989) (as supplemented March 2, 1990); Mitten v. Muscogee County School Dist., 877 F.2d 932 (11th Cir. 1989); Duane M. v. Orleans Parish School Bd., 861 F.2d 115 (5th Cir. 1988); Eggers v. Bullitt County School Dist., 854 F.2d 892 (6th Cir. 1988); Doucet v. Chilton County Bd. of Educ., 65 F. Supp. 2d 1249 (M.D. Ala. 1999); P.L. v. Norwalk Bd. of Educ., 64 F. Supp. 2d 61 (D.

The major hurdle to overcome in filing an action solely to recover attorney's fees is the United States Supreme Court's decision in *North Carolina Department of Transportation v. Crest Street Community Council, Inc.*[34] In *Crest Street*, the Court, rejecting *dicta* in *New York Gaslight Club v. Carey*,[35] held that an action solely to recover attorney's fees could not be brought under §1988. The Court focused on the specific language of §1988 that speaks to recovery of attorney's fees in an action or proceeding to enforce specific rights. Since an action solely to recover attorney's fees was not to enforce those rights, attorney's fees could not be awarded. The Court also stated that this interpretation of the statute was consistent with the legislative history of §1988.

On this issue, *Crest Street* and §1988 are readily distinguishable from IDEA. The language of §1988 and §1415(i) is very similar. Both statutes refer to "action or proceeding," but §1988 goes on to state "to enforce a provision of [certain civil rights acts]." Unlike §1415, however, §1988 explicitly refers to actions to enforce specific statutes. Section 1415 is not as narrow.[36]

The United States Supreme Court in *Crest Street* also pointed out that the legislative history of §1988 "supports the plain import of the statutory language" not to allow separate action for attorney's fees.[37] Contrasting the legislative history under §1415(i) with that of §1988, shows particular emphasis in the House and Senate Reports that attorney's fees are available for prevailing parties at the administrative hearing level.[38]

If suit can be brought solely to recover attorney's fees, what is the statute of limitations on bringing that suit? The Supreme Court has stated that when Congress provides no specific statute of limitations for a cause of action based on federal law, as is the case with the IDEA,

> [courts should] not ordinarily assume that Congress intended that there be no time limit on actions at all; rather, our task is to "borrow" the most suitable statute or other rule of timelines from some other source. We have generally concluded that Congress intended that the courts apply the most closely analo-

---

Conn. 1999); Turton v. Crisp County School Dist., 688 F. Supp. 1535 (M.D. Ga. 1988); Mathern v. Cambell County Children's Center, 674 F. Supp. 816 (D. Wyo. 1987).

34. 479 U.S. 6 (1986).

35. 447 U.S. 54 (1980).

36. *See* P.N. v. Seattle School Dist., 474 F.3d 1165 (9th Cir. 2007); Kaseman v. District of Columbia, 444 F.3d 637 (D.C. Cir. 2006); Linda T. v. Rice Lake Area School Dist., 417 F.3d 704 (7th Cir. 2005); T.D. v. LaGrange School Dist. No. 102 349 F.3d 469 (7th Cir. 2003); J.C. v. Reg'l School Dist. 10, 278 F.3d 119 (2d Cir. 2002); Moore v. District of Columbia, 907 F.2d 165 (D.C. Cir. 1990) (*en banc*); McSombodies v. Burlingame Elementary School, 897 F.2d 974 (9th Cir. 1989) (as supplemented March 2, 1990); Mitten v. Muscogee County School Dist., 877 F.2d 932 (11th Cir. 1989); Duane M. v. Orleans Parish School Bd., 861 F.2d 115 (5th Cir. 1988); Eggers v. Bullitt County School Dist., 854 F.2d 892 (6th Cir. 1988).

37. Crest Street, 479 U.S. at 12; *see also* Eirschele v. Craven County Bd. of Educ., 7 F. Supp. 2d 655 (E.D.N.C. 1998) (no separate federal action may be brought solely to recover attorney's fees under §1988).

38. *See* P.N. v. Seattle Sch. Dist., 474 F.3d 1165 (9th Cir. 2007); Kaseman v. District of Columbia, 444 F.3d 637 (D.C. Cir. 2006); Linda T. v. Rice Lake Area Sch. Dist., 417 F.3d 704 (7th Cir. 2005); T.D. v. LaGrange School Dist. No. 102, 349 F.3d 469 (7th Cir. 2003); J.C. v. Reg'l Sch. Dist. 10, 278 F.3d 119 (2d Cir. 2002); Moore v. District of Columbia, 907 F.2d 165 (D.C. Cir. 1990) (*en banc*); McSombodies v. Burlingame Elementary School, 897 F.2d 974 (9th Cir. 1989) (as supplemented March 2, 1990); Mitten v. Muscogee County School Dist., 877 F.2d 932 (11th Cir. 1989); Duane M. v. Orleans Parish School Bd., 861 F.2d 115 (5th Cir. 1988); Eggers v. Bullitt County School Dist., 854 F.2d 892 (6th Cir. 1988).

gous statute of limitations under state law."[39] In a later case the Court stated that a state statute of limitations should only be borrowed if "it is not inconsistent with federal law or policy to do so.[40]

One possibility would be to have the statute of limitations be the same as that which applies to the appeal of the underlying merits. The 2004 reauthorization of IDEA added 90 days generally as the time for appeal on the underlying merits of the case.[41] Historically, however, there was no consensus on the statute of limitations for filing suit on the merits following the due process proceeding.[42]

While courts regularly "borrow" statutes of limitations from state law as suggested, the question then becomes, which one is the "most closely analogous"? The difficulty in determining this question arises from the fact that claims for attorney's fees could be considered independent claims for money damages or as extensions or appeals of the underlying administrative action.[43] Typically, if the claim is viewed as ancillary to the administrative action then it follows that the statute of limitations would be controlled by the standard period that a state has set for judicial review of an administrative decision; however, if the claim is viewed as independent from the administrative proceeding then there may be numerous possible statutes that a court could find "most closely analogous."[44]

Some courts have concluded that seeking fees in district court is not similar to an appeal of an administrative decision because "the district court, rather than the administrative agency, has jurisdiction to award fees." Essentially this view is that the claim for attorney's fees is one the administrative agency could not have heard; therefore, the claim should be regarded as independent.[45]

The First Circuit has developed a balancing test to determine which statute of limitations should be "borrowed" during an IDEA cause of action. In deciding the appropriate statute of limitations the First Circuit will look to the period that most effectively

---

39. Del Costello v. Int'l Bd. of Teamsters, 462 U.S. 151 (1983).

40. Wilson v. Garcia, 471 U.S. 261 (1985).

41. 34 C.F.R. § 300.516. Prior to 2004 the statute of limitations for bringing an action on the merits was left up to individual states. After 2004, the party who is aggrieved by the findings and decision of either the IHO or SRO if applicable, has 90 days from the date of the decision to file a civil action in court unless the state has specific time limit for bringing IDEA civil actions under state law.

42. *E.g.,* R.R. v. Fairfax County School Bd., 338 F.3d 325 (4th Cir. 2003) (2 years in Virginia); King v. Floyd County Board of Education, 228 F.3d 622, 626–27 (6th Cir. 2000) (30 days); Cory D. v. Burke County School Dist. 285 F.3d 1294 (11th Cir. 2002) (30 days time for appeal of administrative decision); C.M. v. Board of Educ. of Henderson County, 241 F.3d 374 (4th Cir. 2001) (North Carolina 60 days); Livingston School Dist. Numbers 4 and 1 v. Keenan 82 F.3d 912 (9th Cir. 1996) (30 days); Schimmel v. Spillane, 819 F.2d 477 (4th Cir. 1987) (Va. one year prior to 1995); Janzen v. Knox County Bd. of Educ., 790 F.2d 484 (6th Cir. 1986) (three years); Adler v. Education Dept., 760 F.2d 454 (2d Cir. 1985) (four months); Scokin v. Texas, 723 F.2d 432 (5th Cir. 1984) (two years); Department of Educ. v. Carl D., 695 F.2d 1154 (9th Cir. 1983) (30 days); Tokarcik v. Forest Hills School Dist., 665 F.2d 443 (3d Cir. 1981) (two years); Mackey v. Board of Educ. for Arlington Central School Dist., 373 F. Supp. 2d 292 (S.D.N.Y. 2005) (four months). For a discussion of statutes of limitation in general, see §§ 11.2, 12.2, and 13.2.

43. Powers v. Indiana Dep't of Educ., 61 F.3d 552 (7th Cir. 1995); Kaseman v. District of Columbia, 444 F.3d 637 (D.C. Cir. 2006).

44. B.K. v. Toms River Bd. of Educ., 998 F. Supp. 462 (D.N.J. 1998) (applying two year statute of limitations for "injury caused by wrongful act"); J.B. v. Essex-Caledonia Supervisory Union, 943 F. Supp. 387, 391–92 (D. Vt. 1996) (applying the six-year catchall statute of limitations).

45. Zipperer v. School Bd. of Seminole County, 111 F.3d 847 (11th Cir. 1997); *see also,* Holmes v. Dep't of Educ., 234 F. Supp. 2d 1156 (D. Haw. 2002) (adopting rationale of *Zipperer*); B.K. v. Toms River Bd. of Educ., 998 F. Supp. 462 (D.N.J. 1998).

balances three IDEA policy goals: the parental interest in participation, the school's interest in speedy resolution of disputes, and the child's interest in receiving educational entitlement. In *Nieves-Marquez v. Puerto Rico*,[46] the First Circuit, while not expressly deciding the issue of statute of limitations in fee cases, appears to follow the "independent claim" rationale when it stated that plaintiffs in such cases "are not in the same position as those merely seeking judicial review of adverse administrative orders." [47]

On the other hand, some circuits find an action for attorney's fees to be ancillary to the administrative proceedings. In a series of cases, the Seventh Circuit cited several policy reasons supporting this position: judicial economy,[48] the parties' interests in resolving the matter expeditiously,[49] presumably at this point in litigation no party is without legal counsel,[50] and the legislative preference for minimizing the detrimental affect of litigation on a child's program.[51] Coming to the same conclusion, the Sixth Circuit, in *King v. Floyd County Board of Education*,[52] interpreted the attorney fees provision of IDEA as suggesting that a claim for fees is ancillary to the underlying dispute because the provision allows the Court to "award the prevailing parent a fee 'in' the administrative proceeding.[53]

After determining that a claim is merely ancillary to the administrative proceeding, courts then usually go on to "borrow" the statute of limitations period for appeals from administrative orders, which generally carry much shorter periods than statutes that are borrowed from jurisdictions in circuits following the "independent claim" rationale.[54]

A rationale similar to the "ancillary" theory was employed in the District of Columbia, where a unique problem exists. The District of Columbia Appropriations Act of 2005 prohibits attorney's fees "in excess of $ 4,000" per "action" when a D.C. public school is involved in an IDEA claim.[55] In *Kaseman v. District of Columbia*,[56] the minor children and their parents were prevailing parties in various administrative complaints. Subsequently, they secured a judgment for attorney's fees exceeding $92,000. The district court determined these fees were reasonable in consideration of the Appropriations Act, and the circuit's policy of allowing "fees-on-fees." [57] The circuit court, however, disagreed. Acknowledging that IDEA provisions have generally been interpreted as allow-

---

46. Nieves-Marquez v. Puerto Rico, 353 F.3d 108 (1st Cir. 2003); Amann v. Stow, 991 F.2d 929 (1st Cir. 1993).

47. *Id.* at 119.

48. Dell v. Board of Educ., 32 F.3d 1053, 1063 (7th Cir. 1994).

49. *Id.*

50. Powers v. Indiana Dep't of Educ., Div. of Special Educ., 61 F.3d 552, 558 (7th Cir. 1995).

51. Id. at 556, n.3.

52. 228 F.3d 622, 625 (6th Cir. 2000).

53. The text of 20 U.S.C. § 1415(i)(3)(B) in pertinent part states, "In any action or proceeding brought under this section, the court, in its discretion, may award reasonable attorneys' fees as part of the costs to a prevailing party who is the parent of a child with a disability...."

54. *Compare,* King v. Floyd County Board of Education, 228 F.3d 622 (6th Cir. 2000) (30 days under Kentucky statute for appeal of administrative order); Powers v. Indiana Dep't of Educ., Div. of Special Educ., 61 F.3d 552 (7th Cir. 1995) (120 days under Illinois statute for judicial appeal of administrative decision) *with,* Zipperer v. School Bd., 111 F.3d 847 (11th Cir. 1997) (four year statute of limitations based on Florida statute for "actions founded upon statutory liability").

55. Pub. L. No. 108-335 §327, 188 Stat. 1322, 1344 (2004).

56. 444 F.3d 637 (D.C. Cir. 2006).

57. Kaseman v. District of Columbia, 355 F. Supp. 2d 205 (D.D.C. 2005). The "fees-on-fees" rule allows prevailing parties to be compensated for attorney fees incurred as a result of work performed on the action to recover fees from the initial administrative process. Therefore, the Appellants in *Kaseman* argued that they were entitled to attorney's fees (as capped by the Appropriations Act) for *two* actions, and not just *one.*

ing "[separate] claims for fees brought by parents who have prevailed at the administrative level," and such claims "[raise] issues 'collateral to' yet 'separate from' the merits of a case" the circuit court held that prevailing party's fee request are part of the same "action" as the underlying educational dispute, despite being brought pursuant to an independent "cause of action." [58]

While the court in *Kaseman* did not directly address the question of the statute of limitations the court hinted that the D.C. Circuit would apply the period that is regularly used for an appeal of an administrative decision. Support for such a determination can be found in the court's comment that, "[a] fee request is ... not a direct appeal of a decision made by the agency at the administrative hearing, as it does not call into question the child's evaluation or placement. Yet the parent's entitlement to fees arises out of the same controversy and depends entirely on the administrative hearing for its existence." [59]

It could be argued that a suit solely for attorney's fees is in the nature of a fee application and that any local rule such as one that requires filing within 10 days, or within 14 days as required by Federal Rule of Appellate Procedure 39(a), should apply. Courts, however, have rejected this approach, adopting more liberal time periods in light of the remedial nature of the legislation. [60]

15.4 Lay Advocates/Paralegals/Parent Advocates

It is not unusual for lay advocates or paralegals to represent parents during the administrative stage, including the due process hearing. [61] The availability of attorney's fees for that work may well depend on the relationship the advocate has with an attorney.

As a general matter, courts hold that fees for paralegals and law clerks are taxable as attorney's fees. [62] These cases, however, typically involve time spent by paralegals at the

---

58. Kaseman, 444 F.3d at 641–42; *see also,* Jester v. Gov't. of the Dist. of Columbia, 474 F.3d 820 (D.C. Cir. 2007).

59. *Id.* at 642.

60. *See, e.g., C.M. v. Board of Educ. of Henderson County,* 241 F.3d 374 (4th Cir. 2001) (60 days); King v. Floyd County Board of Education, 228 F3d 622, 626–27 (6th Cir. 2000) (30 days); Zipperer v. School Bd. of Seminole County, 111 F.3d 847 (11th Cir. 1997) (4 years); Powers v. Indiana Dept. of Educ., 61 F.3d 552 (7th Cir. 1995) (30 days); Reed v. Makena, 41 F.3d 1153 (7th Cir. 1994) (120 days); Rosemary B. v. Board of Educ. of Community H.S., 52 F.3d 156 (7th Cir. 1995); Murphy v. Timberlake, 22 F.3d 1186 (1st Cir. 1994) (3 year general injury action statute of limitations applies); Max M. v. New Trier High School Dist., 859 F.2d 1297 (7th Cir. 1988) (request one year after enactment of attorney's fees provision was within discretion of court where LEA not prejudiced); Armstrong v. Vance 328 F. Supp. 2d 50 (D.D.C. 2004) (year "catch all"); J.B. v. Essex-Caledonia Supervisory Union, 943 F. Supp. 387 (D. Vt. 1996) (6 year "catch all" statute); James v. Nashua School Dist., 720 F. Supp. 1053 (D.N.H. 1989); Robert D. v. Sobel, 688 F. Supp. 861, 864 (S.D.N.Y. 1988) (three year statute); Michael M. v. Board of Educ. of New York City School Dist., 686 F. Supp. 995, 1002 (E.D.N.Y. 1988) (three year statute); School Bd. of Prince William County v. Malone, 662 F. Supp. 999 (E.D. Va. 1987) (three months was not an unreasonable period of time to expect the defendants to learn about the amendment to IDEA and file a request).

61. Congress recognized the likelihood of nonlawyers being active in due process hearings. 20 U.S.C. §1415(h)(1); *but see* In re Arons, 756 A.2d 867 (Del. 2000) *certiorari denied* 532 U.S. 1065 (2001) (nonlawyer advocates cannot represent parents or guardians of child at due process hearing).

62. C.C. v. Granby Bd. of Educ., 453 F. Supp. 2d 569 (D. Conn. 2006) ($85/hour is reasonable paralegal fees); Gross v. Perrysburg Exempted Village School Dist., 306 F. Supp. 2d 726 (N.D. Ohio 2004); Doucet v. Chilton County Bd. of Educ., 65 F. Supp. 2d 1249 (M.D. Ala. 1999) ($65/hour paralegal fees for work traditionally done by attorney); Cline v. Rocky Mountain, Inc. 998 P.2d 946

direction of a lawyer and represent work that would otherwise have been done by the lawyer representing the client. This general rule should apply under IDEA as well for work done at the direction of an attorney.[63]

Whether an advocate not supervised by a lawyer is entitled to attorney's fees is more problematic. Section 1988 has been interpreted as not authorizing the award of attorney's fees for nonlawyer advocates.[64] Decisions addressing the issue agree that attorney's fees are unavailable for lay advocates handling administrative due process hearings. These decisions draw an analogy to § 1988, and point to the omission of any reference to lay advocates in IDEA.[65] For offices that employ nonlawyers to handle part or all of the administrative process, it would be wise to evaluate the lines of authority to ensure that the work was adequately supervised and directed by lawyers so as to create a more traditional paralegal-lawyer relationship.

Another issue is whether an attorney-parent who prevails and who represents his or her own disabled child is entitled to attorney's fees. In *Doe v. Board of Education of Baltimore County*,[66] the attorney-parent represented his son, and, after prevailing, sought an award of attorney's fees. The Board maintained that the fees were prohibited under the Supreme Court's decision in *Kay v. Ehrler*.[67] *Kay* held that a *pro se* plaintiff who is an attorney cannot be awarded attorney's fees under the fee shifting provision of the Civil Rights Attorney's Fees Award Act, 42 U.S.C. § 1888. In *Kay*, the United States Supreme Court held that the term attorney assumes an agency relationship as the predicate for an award under § 1988.[68]

Although the Fourth Circuit in *Doe* did not view the parental representation as *pro se*, the court held that the underlying rationale of the *Kay* decision was applicable. In particular, the court held that the statutory policy of furthering successful prosecution of

(Wyo. 2000) (paralegal expenses can be included in an attorney fee award in appropriate cases); *but see*, Mr. & Mrs. R. v. Maine. School Administrative. District No. 35, 295 F. Supp. 2d 120 (D. Me. 2003) (denying fees billed by paralegals and summer associates); Bill Rivers Trailers Inc. v. Miller, 489 So. 2d 1139 (Fla. Ct. App. 1986) (no recovery for time spent by nonlawyer assistant).

63. *See generally* Muth v. Smith, 646 F. Supp. 280 (E.D. Pa. 1986) (court denied law clerk fees for failure to establish time, implicit recognition that fees awardable if properly established).

64. *E.g.*, Pitts v. Vaughn, 679 F.2d 311 (3d Cir. 1982) (*pro se* nonlawyer advocate); Peniman v. Cartwright, 550 F. Supp. 1302 (S.D. Iowa 1982) (§ 1988 does not allow award for "jailhouse lawyers").

65. Shapiro v. Paradise Valley Unified School Dist. No. 69 374 F.3d 857 (9th Cir 2004) (fees for work performed by parents' attorney prior to his admission to practice *pro hac vice* in state court were properly excluded from award); Bowman v. District of Columbia 496 F. Supp. 2d 160 (D.D.C. 2007) (court-appointed educational advocates were parents for purposes of IDEA's attorney fee provision; but court-appointed educational advocates were prohibited from recovering attorney fees under IDEA); Z.A. v. San Bruno Park School Dist., 165 F.3d 1273 (9th Cir. 1999) (state law precluded attorney's fees for services at state special education proceeding of attorney not admitted to Bar); Arons v. New Jersey State Bd. of Educ., 842 F.2d 58 (3d Cir. 1988) (nonlawyer not entitled to attorney's fees); Agapito v. District of Columbia 477 F. Supp. 2d 103 (D.D.C. 2007) (attorneys not licensed to practice in District could not collect attorney fees under IDEA for successfully representing special-needs children in administrative proceedings before DCPS).

66. 165 F.3d 260 (4th Cir. 1998); Van Duyn v. Baker School Dist., 2007 WL 2493495 (9th Cir. 2007) (fees to attorney but not for attorney mother); Bowman v. District of Columbia 496 F. Supp. 2d 160 (D.D.C. 2007) (court-appointed educational advocates were parents for purposes of IDEA's attorney fee provision; but court-appointed educational advocates were prohibited from recovering attorney fees under IDEA).

67. 499 U.S. 432 (1991).

68. Kay, 499 U.S. at 435–6.

meritorious claims was better served by a rule that creates an incentive to retain independent counsel in every case. Thus, the court invoked the "special circumstances doctrine" and denied an award of fees for services performed by an attorney-parent in IDEA proceedings. Clearly the holding of *Doe* has proven strong, as every circuit addressing the issue of whether an attorney-parent may collect attorney's fees when representing his or her own child has come to the same conclusion that the attorney-parent may not.[69]

15.5 Costs As Well As Attorney's Fees

IDEA also contemplates the award of costs associated with administrative and judicial proceedings. As indicated above, IDEA granted the court authority to award attorney's fees "*as part of the costs* to the parents of a child with a disability who is a prevailing party."[70]

Awarding costs in federal court is generally governed by Federal Rule of Civil Procedure 54(d)[71] and 28 U.S.C. § 1920.[72] Federal Rule 54(d) provides that "costs shall be allowed as of course to the prevailing party unless the court otherwise directs...." Section 1920 allows the court to award 1) fees of the clerk and marshal; 2) fees for the court reporter for necessary parts of the transcript; 3) fees for witnesses and printing; 4) fees for copies of necessary papers; 5) docket fees; and 6) costs of interpretation.

15.5.1 Expert Fees and Expenses

Perhaps the single largest expense associated with litigation in special education is expert testimony. In many instances, the LEA has paid for an Independent Educational Evaluation (IEE) prior to the due process hearing,[73] but the parent still confronts the costs and travel of the expert testifying at trial as well as any additional expert testimony.

In other contexts, the United States Supreme Court has been reluctant to award expert witness fees. In *1987*, in *Crawford Fitting Co. v. J.T. Gibbons, Inc.*,[74] the Court held that when a prevailing party seeks reimbursement for expert witness fees, the party is bound by the statutory limit set by Congress for general witness fees. *Crawford Fitting*

---

69. Doe, 165 F.3d at 262; *see, e.g.,* Ford v. Long Beach Unified School Dist., 461 F.3d 1087 (9th Cir. 2006); Woodside v. School Dist. of Philadelphia Bd. of Educ., 248 F.3d 129 (3d Cir. 2001); *but see,* Matthew v. Dekalb County School System, 244 F. Supp. 2d 1331 (N.D. Ga. 2003) (disagreeing with *Doe* and *Woodside*; *Kay* does not extend to IDEA, and is contrary to IDEA policy, therefore attorney-parent could recover fees pursuant to IDEA); *see generally* Hensley v. Eckerhart, 461 U.S. 424, 429 (1983) ("special circumstances" can render "such an award unjust").
70. 20 U.S.C. § 1415(i)(3)(B) (emphasis added); 34 C.F.R. § 300.513 (a).
71. Fed. R. Civ. Proc. 54(d).
72. 28 U.S.C. § 1920.
73. 20 U.S.C. § 1415(b)(1) provides as part of the procedural protections of the parents, the right to obtain an independent educational evaluation. 34 C.F.R. § 300.502(b)(1), (b)(2)(i) provides: "A parent has the right to an independent educational evaluation at public expense if the parent disagrees with an evaluation obtained by the public agency. However, the public agency may initiate a [due process] hearing ... to show that its evaluation is appropriate...."
74. 482 U.S. 437 (1987).

involved two consolidated cases: one alleging violation of the antitrust laws; and the other alleging racial discrimination in violation of Title VII and 42 U.S.C. § 1981. The Court reasoned that if the district court had the discretion under Federal Rule of Civil Procedure 54(d) to pay more than the statutory witness fee, such discretion would be directly contrary to Congressional intent in establishing the witness fee. Therefore, absent explicit statutory authority to the contrary, a trial court is limited to the award of witness fees as provided under the general witness fee provisions.[75]

In 1991, the United States Supreme Court held that the limitations in *Crawford Fitting* were applicable to actions brought under § 1988. In *West Virginia University Hospitals, Inc. v. Casey*,[76] the Court held that:

> The record of statutory usage demonstrates convincingly that attorney's fees and expert fees are regarded as separate elements of litigation cost. While some fee-shifting provisions, like § 1988, refer only to "attorney's fees," *see, e.g.*, Civil Rights Act of 1964, 42 U.S.C. § 2000e-5(k), many others explicitly shift expert witness fees as well as attorney's fees.[77]

The Court then went on to state that:

> None of the categories of expenses listed in § 1920 can reasonably be read to include fees for services rendered by an expert employed by a party in a non-testimonial advisory capacity.[78]

The Court also reiterated that to overcome the limitations of § 1920 there must be "contract or explicit statutory authority to the contrary."[79]

Following *Casey*, Congress once again responded to a Supreme Court decision limiting the award of fees by amending both § 1988 and § 2000e-5(k). The legislative history of these amendments contains explicit language indicating Congressional intent to include expenses associated with experts:

> The conferees intend that the term 'attorneys' fees' as part of the 'costs' include reasonable expenses and fees of expert witnesses and the reasonable costs of any test or evaluation which is found to be necessary for the preparation of the parent or guardian's case in the action or proceeding, as well as traditional costs incurred in the course of litigating a case.[80]

Several courts, relying on this history, did hold that expert costs could be reimbursed,[81] others did not.[82] There is, however, authority that interprets *Casey* as apply-

---

75. *Id.* Witness fees are provided for in 28 U.S.C. § 1821.
76. 499 U.S. 83 (1991).
77. *Id.* at 88.
78. *Id.*
79. *Id.* at 86.
80. H.R. Conf. Rep. No. 687, 99th Cong., 2d Sess. 5, *reprinted in* 1986 U.S. Code Cong. & Admin. News 1808.
81. *See, e.g.,* Gross v. Perrysburg Exempted Village School Dist., 306 F. Supp. 2d 726 (N.D. Ohio 2004) (expert fees recoverable); Mr. J. v. Bd. of Educ., 98 F. Supp. 2d 226 (D. Conn. 2000); BD v. DeBuono,177 F. Supp. 2d 201 (S.D.N.Y. 2001); Mr. and Mrs. B. v. Weston Bd. of Educ., 34 F. Supp. 2d 777 (D. Conn. 1999); Bailey v. District of Columbia, 839 F. Supp. 888, 892 (D.D.C. 1993) (statute and the legislative history, however, convinced court expert witness costs not barred by *Casey*).
82. *See, e.g.,* Aranow v. District of Columbia, 780 F. Supp. 46 (D.D.C. 1992) (parents in a special education action were entitled to reimbursement for only the statutory witness fee and transportation costs of their expert; reimbursement that totaled $49); Neosho R-V School Dist. v. Clark, 315 F.3d 1022 (8th Cir. 2003) (expert fees not recoverable); T.D. v. LaGrange School Dist. No. 102, 349

ing to actions under IDEA. The United States Supreme Court settled the matter in *Arlington Central School District Board of Education v. Murphy*.[83] The Court in *Murphy* held that expert fees may not be recovered, stating: "in the face of the unambiguous text of the IDEA and the reasoning of *Crawford Fitting* and *Casey,* we cannot say that the legislative history on which respondents rely is sufficient to provide requisite fair notice."[84]

15.5.2 Transcripts

IDEA entitles the parents to a written or electronic verbatim record of the due process hearing.[85] A stenographic copy of the due process proceedings is at least helpful, if not crucial to the parent's preparation of the judicial action, as well as to the court's understanding of the due process hearing. Costs of a stenographic transcription of the due process hearing would also seem to be covered under § 1920.[86] Since the due process hearing is part of the record in the judicial action,[87] recovery of its cost seems appropriate.

15.5.3 Discovery and Miscellaneous Expenses

Discovery expenses can be significant once judicial action has been instituted. Costs related to interrogatories, requests to admit and the like are for the most part covered by the attorney's fees provisions. Generally, if depositions are introduced in evidence, the costs are taxable.[88] Depositions that "simply are investigative or preparatory in character, rather than for the presentation of the case, typically are not taxable."[89]

Many related expenses associated with the litigation, including long distance phone calls, postage and attorney's traveling expenses are generally not taxable as costs.[90] Statutory fee provisions, such as § 1988, that provide attorney's fees as part of costs, however, have usually been interpreted to allow reimbursement of reasonable expenses of litigation, including these miscellaneous items.[91] While the issue of expert fees is now settled, there is no indication from the statute or from the legislative history regarding payment of miscellaneous expenses under IDEA. Therefore, the question is again presented whether the Supreme Court under, *Crawford Fitting, Casey,* and *Arlington* would consider states to have voluntarily and knowingly accepted IDEA funds upon the condition that they be responsible for such costs if a parent should be a prevailing party.

F.3d 469 (7th Cir. 2003); Pawling Cent. School Dist. v. Munoz, 14 A.D.3d 838, 788, N.Y.S.2d 267 (N.Y.A.D. 3 Dept. 2005); Eirschele v. Craven County Bd. of Educ., 7 F. Supp. 2d 655 (E.D.N.C. 1998).

83. 126 S. Ct. 2455 (2006).
84. *Id.* at 2463.
85. 20 U.S.C. § 1415(h)(3). See § 11.6.
86. See § 15.5.
87. *See* 20. U.S.C. § 1415(i)(2).
88. Wright, Miller, Kane, *Federal Practice and Procedure* § 2676.
89. *Id.*
90. *Id.* at § 2677.
91. *See* authorities collected in A. Conte, *Attorney Fee Awards* §§ 2.19, 2.22, 4.41 (3d ed. 2004).

15.6 Is There a Dispute and are the Parents Prevailing Parties?

To be eligible for an award of attorney's fees, there must be a dispute and the parents must prevail.[92] Whether a dispute exists for attorney's fees purposes is not always clear. In *Payne v. Board of Education*,[93] for example, a parent challenged a long term IEP that would have eventually placed her child in home schooling. After the request for a due process hearing, the school modified the IEP and the hearing was dismissed. The court noted that the school "never took a position contrary to that of *Payne*" and it "acknowledged its responsibility for Payne's education." Further, the school had begun a multidisciplinary team meeting process before the due process hearing request.[94] Thus, the court concluded, there was no "dispute" between the parties that would warrant the granting of attorney's fees to the parent. The Ninth Circuit Court of Appeals used similar reasoning in denying a request for attorney's fees, holding that two IEP meetings that resulted in a school placement that satisfied the parents did not give rise to a dispute for the purposes of the IDEA.[95]

Of course, if there is a dispute, the parents must also prevail before there is an award of fees and costs. In *Farrar v. Hobby*,[96] the United States Supreme Court addressed the question of when a party is considered to have prevailed under §1983 sufficient to qualify as a prevailing party. The Court held that plaintiff must obtain at least some relief on the merits of the claim. The plaintiff must obtain an enforceable judgment against the defendant from whom the fees are sought or comparable relief through a consent decree or settlement.[97]

Most courts addressing the issue, draw an analogy to §1983 and applied the *Farrar* test in IDEA actions.[98] Occasionally other courts applied a test that predated *Farrar* called the catalyst test.[99] In *Doucet* the court held there was a "dispute" within the meaning of IDEA where Doucet waited ten months after her initial referral for special educa-

---

92. Buckhannon Bd. & Care Home v. W. Va. Dep't of Health & Human Res., 532 U.S. 598 (2001) (plaintiff's must be able to point to a *court ordered* resolution of a dispute which changes the legal relationship between the defendant and itself); Texas State Teachers Association v. Garland, 489 U.S. 782, 792 (1989) (plaintiff must be able to point to a resolution of a dispute which changes the legal relationship between itself and the defendant).

93. 88 F.3d 392 (6th Cir. 1996); *see also* W.L.G. v. Houston County Bd. of Educ., 975 F. Supp. 1317 (M.D. Ala. 1997) (no dispute at the time hearing requested where school did not oppose an IEE or the addition of a new behavior plan in the IEP).

94. *Id.* at 398.

95. 20 U.S.C.§1415(b)(6); see Park v. Anaheim Union High School Dist., 464 F.3d 1025 (9th Cir. 2006); Kletzelman v. Capistrano Unified School Dist., 91 F.3d 68 (9th Cir. 1996).

96. 506 U.S. 103 (1992).

97. *Id.* at 111.

98. *See, e.g.,* Board of Educ. Oak Park v. Nathan, 199 F.3d 377 (7th Cir. 2000) (applies *Farrar* test); Peter v. Jax, 18 F.3d 829 (8th Cir. 1999) (catalyst theory does not survive *Farrar*); S1 v. State Bd. of Educ., 21 F.3d 49 (4th Cir. 1994) (deeply divided court 7-6, held that after *Farrar* a person may not be a prevailing party under a catalyst theory for changes in the opposing party's conduct instigated after judgment or dismissal); Virginia McC v. Corrigan-Camden Indep. School Dist., 909 F. Supp. 1023 (E.D. Tex. 1995) (citing *Farrar*).

99. *See, e.g.,* Doucet v. Chilton County Board of Education, 65 F. Supp. 2d 1249 (M.D. Ala. 1999); *see also* W. T. v. Andalusia City Schools, 922 F. Supp. 1437 (M.D. Ala. 1997); *see generally* American Council of the Blind of Colorado v. Romer, 992 F.2d 249 (10th Cir. 1993); Little Rock School v. Pulaski Special School Dist., 17 F.3d 260 (8th Cir. 1994); Craig v. Gregg County, 988 F.2d 18 (5th Cir. 1993); Trotter, *The Catalyst Theory of Civil Rights Fee Shifting After Farrar v. Hobby*, 80 Va. L. Rev. 1429 (1994).

tion services before initiating a due process hearing. During this time the school completed an inadequate evaluation and offered a service plan that was insufficient. The court analyzed the prevailing party status under the catalyst test. Doucet met the prevailing party because the parents received at least some relief on the merits of the claim. Under the catalyst test, the issue is whether the plaintiff's legal action was a catalyst for the delivery of the relief granted. Even in the absence of judicial relief, a plaintiff may still be a prevailing party if the plaintiff can show that the lawsuit was a causal link prompting some remedial action, or a substantial factor, or significant catalyst in motivating the defendants to end their unlawful behavior. It is unlikely that the catalyst test still applies in an IDEA action. In 2001, the United States Supreme Court decided *Buckhannon Board and Care Home v. West Virginia Department of Health of Human Resources.*[100] Although *Buckhannon* involved actions brought under the Fair Housing Amendments Act and the Americans with Disabilities Act there appears little to distinguish those actions for attorney's fees from those brought under the IDEA. In the language of the Court:

> We have only awarded attorney's fees where plaintiff has received a judgment on the merits ... or obtained a court-ordered consent decree.... We cannot agree that the term "prevailing party" authorizes federal courts to award attorney's fees to a plaintiff who, by simply filing a nonfrivolous but nonetheless potentially meritless lawsuit (it will never be determined), has reached the "sought-after destination" without obtaining any judicial relief.[101]

The Court therefore rejected the "catalyst theory" as too broad because it allowed an award of attorney's fees "where there is no judicially sanctioned change in the legal relationship of the parties."[102] Accordingly, every United States circuit court that has addressed the definition of "prevailing party" in an IDEA action for attorney's fees has adopted the *Buckhannon* Court's definition.[103]

Additionally, the Court's discussion of 20 U.S.C. § 1415(i)(3)(B) in *Arlington*, as well as its decision in *Crawford Fitting*, makes certain that parents must also "prevail" before they are entitled to an award of fees and costs, as set out in 28 U.S.C. § 1920.[104] Where,

---

100. 532 U.S. 598 (2001) (Court defined "prevailing party" as requiring "judicial imprimatur" of the material alterations of the parties' legal relationship).

101. *Id.* at 609–610.

102. *Id.* at 605.

103. P.N. v. Seattle School Dist., 474 F.3d 1165 (9th Cir. 2007); Doe v. Boston Pub. School, 358 F.3d 20, 30 (1st Cir. 2004); Alegria v. Dist. of Columbia, 391 F.3d 262, 263 (D.C. Cir. 2004) (no judicial imprimatur, enforceable judgment or decree); John T. v. Del. County Intermediate Unit, 318 F.3d 545, 555 (3d Cir. 2003) (preliminary injunction not prevailing party); T.D. v. LaGrange School Dist. No. 102, 349 F.3d 469, 478 (7th Cir. 2003); J.C. v. Reg'l School Dist. 10, 278 F.3d 119, 125 (2d Cir. 2002).

Most circuits have applied *Buckhannon* broadly by not limiting attorney's fees to only "judgments on the merits or consent decrees." *See* Roberson v. Giuliani, 346 F.3d 75 (2d Cir. 2003) ("Judicial action other than a judgment on the merits or a consent decree can support an award of attorney's fees, so long as such action carries with it sufficient judicial imprimatur." Also citing other circuits in agreement.); *see also,* A.R. v. N.Y. City Dep't of Educ., 407 F.3d 65 (2d Cir. 2005) (attorney's fees available to prevailing party at administrative (IHO) hearing where IHO ordered adoption of settlement terms).

104. Arlington Cent. School Dist. Bd. of Educ. v. Murphy, 126 S. Ct. 2455, 2459–62. (2006); Crawford Fitting Co. v. J.T. Gibbons, Inc., 482 U.S. 437 (1987). 28 U.S.C § 1920 provides:

A judge or clerk of any court of the United States may tax as costs the following:

(1) Fees of the clerk and marshal; (2) Fees of the court reporter for all or any part of the

for example, a state agency, in a consent decree, agreed to provide services, but the local agency refused, the local agency is not obligated to pay fees.[105]

15.6.1 Prevailing on Part of the Claim

The United States Supreme Court addressed the issue of the effect of partial success in *Hensley v. Eckerhart*,[106] a case arising under 42 U.S.C. § 1988 and it said:

> Where a plaintiff has obtained excellent results, his attorney should recover a fully compensatory fee.... In these circumstances the fee award should not be reduced simply because plaintiff failed to prevail on every contention raised in the lawsuit.... Litigants in good faith may raise alternative legal grounds for a desired outcome, and the court's rejection of *or failure to reach certain grounds* is not sufficient reason for reducing a fee. *The result is what matters.*[107]

Hensley also made it clear that a "reduced fee award is appropriate if the relief, however significant, is limited in comparison to the litigation as a whole.... [W]here the plaintiff achieved only limited success, the district court should award only that amount of fees that is reasonable in relation to the results obtained."[108] Courts have fairly consistently held, in accord with *Hensley*, that partial success does not preclude an award of attorney's fees, but that an award may be reduced for unsuccessful claims.[109]

How this standard applies is very case-specific. Suppose, for example, the issue is whether an emotionally disturbed child needs a residential program and, if so, whether a specific residential program is appropriate. If we assume the child is already in a residential setting and the LEA alleges 1) the child does not need a residential program and 2) if he does, the particular program in which he is presently placed is too restrictive, we can see the difficulty of allocating attorney's fees for partial success.

If the final decision is that a residential program is necessary, but that the existing program is more restrictive than needed, what portion of the attorney's fees will be tax-

---

stenographic transcript necessarily obtained for use in the case; (3) Fees and disbursements for printing and witnesses; (4) Fees for exemplification and copies of papers necessarily obtained for use in the case; (5) Docket fees under section 1923 of this title [28 USCS § 1923]; (6) Compensation of court appointed experts, compensation of interpreters, and salaries, fees, expenses, and costs of special interpretation services under section 1828 of this title [28 USCS § 1828].

A bill of costs shall be filed in the case and, upon allowance, included in the judgment or decree.

105. Counsel v. Dow, 849 F.2d 731 (2d Cir. 1988) (settlement obligated only the state, and, therefore, local agency not required to pay fees).

106. 461 U.S. 424 (1983).

107. *Id.* at 436 (emphasis added); *see also* Angela L. v. Pasadena Indep. School Dist., 918 F.2d 1188 (5th Cir. 1990).

108. Hensley, 461 U.S. at 437.

109. Aguirre v. L.A. Unified School Dist., 461 F.3d 1114 (9th Cir. 2006); Park v. Anaheim Union High School Dist., 464 F.3d 1025 (9th Cir. 2006); Linda T. v. Rice Lake Area School Dist., 417 F.3d 704, 708 (7th Cir. 2005) (applying *Hensley,* parents success found to be de minimus); Wikol v. Birmingham Pub. Schools. Board. of Educ., 360 F.3d 604, 612 (6th Cir. 2004); Neosho R-V School Dist. v. Clark, 315 F.3d 1022, 1030–31 (8th Cir. 2003); Holmes v. Millcreek Twp. School Dist., 205 F.3d 583, 595–96 (3d Cir. 2000); *but see,* Drennan v. Pulaski County Special School Dist., 458 F.3d 755 (8th Cir. 2006) (award of ESY is only "limited relief," attorney's fees not available).

able? Focusing on the result obtained, the parents have clearly not prevailed on a major separate issue and it would seem logical to deny them complete recovery. It then becomes incumbent on the parents' attorney to establish that portion of his time which was spent on each issue.

15.6.2 Procedural and Substantive Violations

In *Hendrick Hudson District Board of Education v. Rowley*,[110] the United States Supreme Court held that a court's inquiry into an action arising under § 1415 is twofold: procedural and substantive. It is not surprising, therefore, that a large number of cases allege procedural violations of IDEA. What happens when the parents have partial success by prevailing on one of these two prongs, but loses on the other?

The problem can arise in a number of different contexts. The United States Supreme Court's language in *Hensley*, that the result is what matters, is particularly helpful in organizing the analysis.[111] There are, for example, situations where procedural violations and the substantive merits are so distinct that they are independent, requested outcomes and failure to succeed on one should preclude attorney's fees for work done seeking that particular outcome. For example, the Third Circuit held that where the parents established the state agency had set up an improper procedure for hearing appeals, but that the parents had not prevailed on the independent question of whether the IEP was appropriate, the parents were entitled to attorney's fees only on the procedural question.[112]

Likewise, a case can arise where the parties agree that a residential program is required, but the LEA contends the particular residential program in which the parents have placed the child is inappropriate.[113] Suppose further that it is also alleged that the procedural protections afforded the parents were violated by the LEA's failure to pay for the Independent Educational Evaluation (IEE). If the parents prevail on the procedural issue, but lose on the substantive issue, attorney's fees should be awarded only for work done on the issue on which they were successful. The procedural violation is clearly distinct and unrelated to the decision of the parents to place the child in the inappropriate placement and therefore recovery should be had only for prevailing on the procedural issue.

In other cases, the substantive and procedural claims may be so interrelated that success on one issue should result in full recovery. Take, for example, a dispute in which the parents allege that the LEA's proposed placement will not provide a FAPE for their child and in which they also allege that the LEA failed to provide the parents with notice of their procedural rights.[114]

In such a case, the parents are asserting one position, the inability of the LEA to provide a FAPE. They happen to assert two grounds for that position: one substantive, one procedural. But, because the apparent remedy for violation of procedural protections is the same as for an inappropriate finding on the substantive issue, that is, that the LEA is unable to provide a FAPE,[115] recovery of attorney's fees should be available for all work

---

110. 458 U.S. 176, 205 (1982).

111. Hensley, 461 U.S. at 436.

112. Muth v. Central Bucks School Dist., 839 F.2d 113 (3d Cir. 1988), *rev'd on other grounds sub nom.* Dellmuth v. Muth, 491 U.S. 223 (1989).

113. *See generally* Schimmel v. Spillane, 819 F.2d 477 (4th Cir. 1987).

114. *See, e.g.,* Hall v. Vance County Bd. of Educ., 774 F.2d 629 (4th Cir. 1985).

115. See § 14.7.

done regardless of whether the court decides that the parents have not "prevailed" on one of their contentions. If the parents win on procedural violations, but lose on the substantive position, the result is the same, a finding that the LEA was not proposing a FAPE.

A procedural violation may also force the parents to defend a substantive issue they would otherwise not have to defend. Suppose the LEA has violated the procedural protections by failing to provide an Independent Educational Evaluation (IEE) and seeks to place the child in an inappropriate setting. As a result, the parents file a request for a due process hearing. The due process hearing should address both the procedural and substantive violations. Had the LEA not violated the procedural protections, that is, had they provided the IEE, there may have been no need for the parents to incur any costs in responding to the underlying substantive allegations. Attorney's fees, therefore, should be awarded for both the procedural violation and work done in defending on the merits.[116] To encourage the court to accept this reasoning, it is incumbent on the parents' counsel to have a consistent theory of the case and consistently argue the interrelation of the issues. It must be made clear to the court that there is only one issue in the case; whether the LEA's proposed or existing action can provide a FAPE.

15.7 Setting the Fee

IDEA requires an award of attorney's fees be reasonable and based on the prevailing rates in the community for similar services.[117] This is the general standard applied by courts in most statutory fee awards.[118]

---

116. *See* Deal v. Hamilton County Bd. of Educ., 392 F.3d 840 (6th Cir. 2004) (school system's predetermination not to offer student intensive applied behavioral analysis (ABA) amounted to procedural violation of IDEA and predetermination of placement effectively deprived student's parents of meaningful participation in individualized education program (IEP) process, causing substantive harm and depriving student of free appropriate public education (FAPE); and school system's procedural violation of IDEA through failure to have regular teachers present at meetings where IEP that was subject of lawsuit was prepared caused substantive harm to student or his parents); M.L. v. Federal Way School Dist., 394 F.3d 634 (9th Cir. 2005) (failure of school district to ensure participation of regular education teacher on IEP team, when there was possibility that disabled student would have been placed in integrated classroom, was significant violation of IDEA procedures and failure of school district to comply with requirement of IDEA fatally compromised integrity of IEP); Gonzales v. Puerto Rico Dept. of Educ., 969 F. Supp. 801 (D.P.R. 1997) (failure to hold due process hearing and parents private school placement appropriate; reimbursement due from time hearing should have been held).

117. 20 U.S.C. § 1415(i)(3)(C); Farbotko v. Clinton County, 433 F.3d 204 (2d Cir. 2005) ("[A] reasonable hourly rate is not itself a matter of binding precedent. Rather, under established caselaw, a reasonable hourly rate is the 'prevailing market rate,' i.e., the rate 'prevailing in the [relevant] community for similar services by lawyers of reasonably comparable skill, experience, and reputation.'" (internal citations omitted)); Beard v. Teska, 31 F.3d 942 (10th Cir. 1994) (approval of attorney's customary rate in civil rights and other matters when *prevailing* rate is less is clearly erroneous); Murphy v. Board of Education of Rochester City School Dist., 420 F. Supp. 2d 131 (D.N.Y. 2006); Doe v. East Haven Board. of Education. 430 F. Supp. 2d 54 (D. Conn. 2006) (prevailing community rate).

118. *See, e.g.,* Blum v. Stenson, 465 U.S. 886, 895 (1984); C.C. v. Granby Bd. of Educ., 453 F. Supp. 2d 569 (D. Conn. 2006) (fee is set by appropriate rate within the community, and sufficiently documented work performed); Zayas v. Commonwealth of Puerto Rico, 451 F. Supp. 2d 310 (D.P.R. 2006) (abbreviated time sheets, limited success warrant reduction of fees); Kristi W. v. Graham Indep. School Dist., 663 F. Supp. 86 (N.D. Tex. 1987) (number of hours and information concerning the kind and quality of services).

The general principles governing the amount of statutory fee awards are well developed. Numerous cases have discussed the factors to consider in determining the prevailing rate. The court will usually follow what has been termed the lodestar approach. The basic approach is to multiply the customary hourly rate for the services rendered by the number of hours reasonably expended. The result is the so-called "lodestar" figure.[119] The lodestar is then adjusted on the basis of enumerated other factors.[120]

The enumerated other factors have been generally recognized as those identified in *Johnson v. Georgia Highway Express, Inc.*,[121] and cited with approval by the United States Supreme Court in *Hensley v. Eckerhart*.[122] They are time and labor required; amount involved and results obtained; experience, reputation and ability of the attorney; skill necessary to perform the legal service; customary fee in the community; nature and length of the professional relationship; novelty and difficulty of issues or undesirability of the case; awards on similar cases; whether the fee is fixed or contingent; time limitations imposed by the client or circumstances; and preclusion of other employment.

IDEA actually codifies some of these factors to be used to reduce attorney's fees:

Whenever the court finds that ...

(ii) the amount of the attorneys' fees otherwise authorized to be awarded unreasonably exceeds the hourly rate prevailing in the community for similar services by attorneys of reasonably comparable skill, experience, and reputation; or

(iii) the time spent and legal services furnished were excessive considering the nature of the action or proceeding; or

(iv) the attorney representing the parent did not provide to the local education agency the appropriate information in the notice of the complaint ... the court shall reduce, accordingly, the amount of the attorneys' fees awarded under this subsection.[123]

By definition, the lodestar is first determined by reference to rates prevailing in the community in which the action or proceeding arose. Simply because the parents' attorney is young or works for legal aid there is no need to reduce the fee award. In *City of Riverside v. Rivera*,[124] a case in which $125 per hour was awarded to two recent law school graduates, the United States Supreme Court cited with approval the language found in *Johnson v. Georgia Highway Express, Inc.*,[125] that "[i]f a young attorney demonstrates the

---

119. Blanchard v. Bergeron, 489 U.S. 87, 94 (1989); *see also* A.R. v. N.Y. City Dep't of Educ., 407 F.3d 65,79 (2d Cir. 2005); G.M. v. New Britain Bd. of Educ., 173 F.3d 77, 81 (2d Cir. 1999); Jason D.W. v. Houston Indep. School Dist., 158 F.3d 205, 208 (5th Cir. 1998); Beard v. Teska, 31 F.3d 942, 945 (10th Cir. 1994).

120. Blum v. Stenson, 465 U.S. 886, 903 (1984).

121. 488 F.2d 714 (5th Cir. 1974), *overruled on other grounds*, Blanchard v. Bergeron, 489 U.S. 87 (1989); *see generally* I.B. v. New York City Dept. of Educ. 336 F.3d 79 (2d Cir. 2003) (district court did not abuse its discretion by failing to reduce lodestar figure based on local administrative nature of proceedings and lodestar figure could be adjusted upward to reflect attorney's considerable experience).

122. 461 U.S. 424, 431 n.3 (1983).

123. 20 U.S.C. § 1415(i)(3)(F). *See, e.g.,* Jason D.W. v. Houston Indep. School Dist., 158 F.3d 205 (5th Cir. 1998) (fees reduced).

124. 477 U.S. 561 (1986).

125. 488 F.2d 714 (5th Cir. 1974), *overruled on other grounds*, Blanchard v. Bergeron, 489 U.S. 87, 94 (1989).

skill and ability, he should not be penalized for only recently being admitted to the bar."[126]

The parents' counsel has the burden of establishing what hours were expended and on what issues.[127] The attorney must be sure to maintain adequate records to establish hours spent. These will typically be the actual time sheets kept by the attorney.[128] Further, affidavits by attorneys familiar with special education litigation that attest to the reasonableness of the time spent may be helpful. The attorney must also be prepared to establish the prevailing rate within the community.[129] Establishing the prevailing rate may be done in a number of ways including affidavits of practicing attorneys, where permitted by the court.

One piece of evidence that has proved particularly useful to parents in establishing that rate is a survey of the fees paid to attorneys who represent local school divisions in special education cases. If the state has a freedom of information statute, the information is quite easy to obtain.

15.7.1 No Bonus or Multiplier

One explicit exception to treating the award of attorney's fees under IDEA the same as under § 1988 is in the area of the ability of the court to grant "upward enhancement." Given the imprecise nature of determining the prevailing rate, many courts award upward adjustments, or multipliers, for various factors such as efficiency, economy, delay in fee payment, or contingency of success.[130] Such multipliers were specifically approved under some circumstances by the United States Supreme Court in *Blum v. Stenson.*[131]

IDEA specifically states, that "[n]o bonus or multiplier may be used in calculating the fees under this subsection."[132] As will be discussed later, however, under some very

---

126. *Id.* at 718–719; *see also* Blum v. Stenson, 465 U.S. 886 (1984) ($95 to $105 per hour awarded to second and third year associates). *Blum* also set out the general requirement that plaintiffs must establish by "sufficient evidence" the rate in the prevailing community. *Id.* at n.11.

127. G.M. v. New Britain Bd. of Educ., 173 F.3d 77, 81 n.12 (2d Cir. 1999); Jason D.W. v. Houston Indep. School Dist., 158 F.3d 205 (5th Cir. 1998); Alfonso v. Dist. of Columbia, 464 F. Supp. 2d 1 (D.D.C. 2006); C. v. Plainfield Bd. of Educ., 382 F. Supp. 2d 347 (D. Conn. 2005).

128. *See* C.C. v. Granby Bd. of Educ., 453 F. Supp. 2d 569 (D. Conn. 2006) (fee is set by appropriate rate within the community, and sufficiently documented work performed); Zayas v. Commonwealth of Puerto Rico, 451 F. Supp. 2d 310 (D.P.R. 2006) (abbreviated time sheets, limited success warrant reduction of attorney's fees); Behavior Research Institute v. Ambach, 535 N.Y.S.2d 465, 144 A.D.2d 872 (1988) (attorney narrative insufficient, required production of time sheets).

129. *See* Gray v. Metts, 203 F. Supp. 2d 426 (D. Md. 2002) (parents precluded from collecting attorney's fees for failure to provide evidence as to the prevailing rate in the community); Williams v. Boston School Committee, 709 F. Supp. 27 (D. Mass. 1989) (where there is an absence of evidence concerning prevailing rate in the community, court had discretion to reduce fee request); Virginia McC v. Corrigan-Camden Indep. School Dist., 909 F. Supp. 1023 (E.D. Tex. 1995) (reduced because no evidence of prevailing rate); *see also* Nadeau v. Helgemoe, 581 F.2d 275, 279 (1st Cir. 1978) ("As for the future, we would not view with sympathy any claim that a district court abused its discretion in awarding unreasonably low attorney's fees in a suit in which plaintiffs were only partially successful if counsel's records do not provide a proper basis for determining how much time was spent on particular claims."); Bretford Mfg., Inc. v. Smith System Mfg. Co. 421 F. Supp. 2d 1117 (N.D. Ill. 2006) (citing Nadeau v. Helgemoe, 581 F.2d 275, 279 (1st Cir. 1978) *later abrogated on other grounds by* Richardson v. Miller, 279 F.3d 1 (1st Cir. 2002)).

130. A. Conte, *Attorney Fee Awards* §§ 4.29–4.34 (3d ed. 2004).

131. 465 U.S. 886, 896–902 (1984).

132. 20 U.S.C. § 1415(i)(III)(ii)(C); 34 C.F.R. § 300.517(c)(1).

limited circumstances, including those in which the school system has violated the procedural protections of §1415, the functional equivalent of a multiplier may well be authorized.[133]

15.8 Fees or Costs Subsequent to Time of Written Offer to Settle

IDEA precludes the award of attorney's fees and costs for services performed subsequent to a written offer of settlement made to a parent within the time requirements of Federal Rule of Civil Procedure 68, or in the case of an administrative hearing, more than 10 days before the proceeding begins, if the relief finally obtained is not more favorable to the parents than the settlement offer.[134]

The settlement offer provision in IDEA is interesting in its reference to, yet obvious difference from, Rule 68. Federal Rule 68 provides that if an offer of settlement is made more than 10 days prior to trial, and the settlement offer is rejected, "[i]f the judgment finally obtained by the offeree is not more favorable than the offer, the offeree must pay the costs incurred after the making of the offer."[135]

IDEA is different from Rule 68 in that it is negative in its impact, whereas Rule 68 is positive. IDEA denies the parent recovery of costs, while Rule 68 requires the payment of the other party's costs. As such, under IDEA, if an offer of settlement is made by the LEA more than 10 days prior to the due process hearing, and the ultimate result is not more favorable, the parent would be precluded from recovering fees and related costs. The parents, however, would not be required to pay the fees and related costs of the LEA because Rule 68 does not apply.

If suit is subsequently brought in federal court, however, the parents would become liable for the fees and costs of the LEA incurred in federal court if they did not obtain a more favorable result. The question becomes, would the parents now also be responsible for the costs and fees incurred in the administrative process? If so, the risk of incurring this additional obligation would provide a major disincentive for filing in federal court. Indeed, in many cases, the LEA would be wise to make a very modest offer of settlement early in the process. This offer, if not improved upon by the parents might preclude the parents from claiming attorney's fees and might ultimately allow shifting of LEA fees and costs from the administrative proceeding to the parents should the dispute end up in court.[136]

---

133. See §15.9.
134. 20 U.S.C. §1415(i)(3)(I); 34 C.F.R. §300.513(c)(2)(i). *See, e.g.,* J.C. v. Vacaville Unified School Dist. Slip Copy, 2007 WL 112138 (E.D. Cal. 2007); Dell v. Board of Educ. Township 115, 918 F. Supp. 212 (N.D. Ill. 1995).
135. Fed. R. Civ. Pro. 68. This language has been interpreted by the United States Supreme Court in §1988 cases as requiring the payment of attorney's fees as well, since §1988 includes attorney's fees as part of costs. Marek v. Chesney, 473 U.S. 1 (1985). In *Marek,* the Court held the term "costs" in Rule 68 included attorney's fees. The Court held that since §1988 defined attorney's fees as part of costs, Rule 68 precluded plaintiffs from recovering attorney's fees incurred after the settlement offer.
136. *But see* §15.8.1.

15.8.1 Justified Rejection of the Offer

IDEA's settlement offer provision provides an interesting exception. An award may be made after a failure to accept, if the parent "was substantially justified in rejecting the settlement offer."[137]

What would be a substantial justification for rejecting an offer? A proposed amendment to Rule 68, which was ultimately not sent to Congress, provides some useful guidance. The proposed rule identified six circumstances under which an offer could be reasonably rejected:

> In making this determination the court shall consider all of the relevant circumstances at the time of the rejection, including (1) subject of the offer, (2) the closeness of the questions of fact and law, (3) whether the offeror had unreasonably refused to furnish information necessary to evaluate the reasonableness of the offer, (4) whether the suit was in the nature of a "test case," presenting questions of far-reaching importance affecting non-parties, (5) the relief that might reasonably have been expected if the claimant should prevail, and (6) the amount of additional delay, cost, and expense the offeror reasonably could be expected to incur if the litigation should be prolonged.[138]

These six factors are useful in determining whether the rejection by the parent under IDEA was reasonable. For example, it would appear reasonable to reject an offer made so early in the process that there was insufficient time to determine the facts. An offer made prior to an IEE, for example, might justifiably be rejected, since prior to the IEE the only available expert evaluations might be those controlled by the LEA.[139]

Further, it might be reasonable to reject a settlement offer at the administrative level because, absent formal discovery mechanisms in the due process hearing, information may be severely limited.[140] Once discovery is available, rejecting the same offer might be unreasonable.

It should be noted that reliance on the above-mentioned factors would also protect against the LEA making an unreasonably low settlement offer in a nonfrivolous dispute simply in an attempt to take advantage of the potential cost shifting under Rule 68 once suit is filed.[141] As pointed out in the Committee Note to the proposed Rule 68:

---

137. 20 U.S.C. §1415(B)(I)(3); 34 C.F.R. §300.517(c)(3); Gross v. Perrysburg Exempted Village School Dist. 306 F. Supp. 2d 726 (N.D.Ohio 2004). Further, merely engaging in settlement discussions does not immunize the public agency from liability for attorney's fees even if the public agency acted in good faith. *See* Borengasser v. Arkansas State Bd. of Educ., 996 F.2d 196 (8th Cir. 1993); Laura I. v. Clausen, 676 F. Supp. 717, 720 (M.D. La. 1988).

138. Fed. R. Civ. Proc. 68 (Official Proposed Rule), 105 S. Ct. LXXIX (1985); *see generally* Comment, *Current Federal Rule of Civil Procedure 68 and Official Proposed Changes: Important Impacts on Attorney's Fee Awards*, 31 S.D. L. Rev. 209 (1985).

139. *See generally* Ms. C. v. Plainfield Bd. of Educ., 382 F. Supp. 2d 347 (D. Conn. 2005) (parents mistaken perception of statute of limitations period to appeal, justifies quick appeal and defeats District's claim of "unnecessary initiating and prolonging litigation"); Hyden v. Wilson County Bd. of Educ., 714 F. Supp. 290 (M.D. Tenn. 1989) ("counsel should have *promptly* informed the Board of any objection to the offer, so that negotiations could continue. He [counsel] might not have wished to accept this particular olive branch, but it does not follow that he was 'substantially justified' in answering with cannon fire").

140. IDEA provides no discovery provisions other than the right to access the student's educational records. 34 C.F.R. §300.501(a)(1).

141. See §15.8.

The court has sufficient authority [under the proposed rule] to prevent the rule from being used by a party who makes an offer in bad faith. The purpose is to prevent a defendant offeror from taking unfair advantage of a claimant-offeree by making a reckless offer; for example, offering to settle a non-frivolous claim for an amount so small in relation to the merits of the claim that the offeror should know the offeree certainly will decline to accept it.[142]

15.9 Procedural Violations or Undue Protraction By LEA

IDEA requires the reduction of attorney's fees under circumstances where the parents, or the parent's attorney, have unduly protracted the final resolution; the amount of fees unreasonably exceeds the hourly rate prevailing in the community; or the time spent or the legal services performed were excessive.[143] IDEA, however, also provides:

The provisions [authorizing the reduction of attorneys' fees] shall not apply in any action or proceeding if the court finds the State or local educational agency unreasonably protracted the final resolution of the action or proceeding or there was a violation of this section.[144]

This provision appears to be a response to recurring criticisms parents have had concerning the advantage to the school system of delaying the administrative process. As often as not, the dispute arises over parents' attempt to acquire special education services not currently provided. Since the child's current placement must remain pending resolution of the administrative and judicial process,[145] it is often in the LEA's interest to delay the process.

Further, reference to procedural violations is in response to the emphasis IDEA has placed on the importance of the procedural requirements. This importance as already mentioned was recognized by the Supreme Court in *Hendrick Hudson District Board of Education v. Rowley*.[146] In fact, the Court in *Rowley* stated that "[a]dequate compliance with the procedures [will] in most cases assure much if not all of what Congress wished in the way of substantive content in an IEP."[147]

---

142. Fed. R. Civ. Proc. 68 (Official Proposed Rule), 105 S. Ct. LXXXII (1985). The justified rejection language in IDEA was at least in part a reaction to the United States Supreme Court decision in Marek v. Chesney, 473 U.S. 1 (1985). The legislative history to the attorney's fee provisions provides:

The conferees intend that this provision clarify the application of the *Marek v. Chesney* decision [to this amendment]. One exception is made to the applicability of the … decision. When the parent or guardian is substantially justified in rejecting the settlement offer … the decision would not apply.

Joint Explanatory Statement of the Committee of the Conference, Rep. No. 687, 99th Cong., 2d Sess. 5, *reprinted in* 1986 U.S. Code Cong. & Admin. News 1809.
143. 20 U.S.C. §1415(i)(3)(F); 34 C.F.R. §300.517(c)(4). See §15.7.
144. 20 U.S.C. §1415(i)(3)(G); 34 C.F.R. §300.517(c)(5).
145. 20 U.S.C. §1415(j) provides that "During the pendency of any proceedings conducted pursuant to this section … the child shall remain in the then current educational placement…."
146. 458 U.S. 176 (1982).
147. Rowley, 458 U.S. at 206.

The practical import of the prohibition in IDEA against reduction of attorney's fees may well be to negate the "no bonus or multiplier" provision in certain circumstances.[148] The law appears to state that even when the parents unreasonably protract the resolution (with the likely result that billable hours have increased), and the parents ask for attorney's fees beyond those prevailing in the community or for hours that were excessive, the fees shall be awarded in full if the LEA protracted the process or violated § 1415. This prohibition against reduction looks suspiciously like a bonus for having had to cope with the inappropriate behavior of the LEA.

Even with this provision, there are limits on what can be sought. Ethical provisions prohibit a lawyer seeking inflated hours, or alleging tasks that were not actually done.[149] If, however, the tasks were actually done and the hours were actually worked, then the court would seem to be prohibited from reducing the fee requested.

This provision, however, should be read with a rule of reason in mind. Indeed, the fact that awarding attorney's fees is discretionary would allow the court to place reasonable restraints on requested fees. Thus, for example, when the prevailing rate in the community ranges between $125 and $200, the court should be justified in refusing to award fees at an hourly rate of $250. However, if the requesting attorney normally charges $125 per hour, but establishes procedural violations and requests $150, the court ought not reduce the fee, since it is within the range of what attorneys charge in that jurisdiction for work under IDEA.[150]

As indicated, the fee reduction provision does not apply if the LEA unreasonably delays final resolution or violates § 1415. There, of course, will be factual disputes over whether the LEA has "unreasonably protracted the final resolution." An interesting legal question, however, is what constitutes a violation of § 1415? Section 1415 refers specifically to a limited number of procedural safeguards. These are the parental right to examine records and obtain an IEE,[151] the requirement to protect the rights of children when the parents are unknown,[152] the requirement of written prior notice when the LEA proposes to initiate or change or refuses to initiate or change the identification, evaluation, or educational placement of the child,[153] the opportunity to present complaints, the right to request a due process hearing,[154] the right to mediation,[155] as well as specific protections accorded in that hearing,[156] and finally, the right to judicial review.[157]

---

148. See § 15.7.1.

149. ABA Model Code of Professional Responsibility DR 7-102 and ABA Model Rules of Professional Conduct 4.1 both provide that a lawyer shall not make a knowingly false statement of law or fact.

150. *See generally* Farbotko v. Clinton County, 433 F.3d 204 (2d Cir. 2005) ("[A] reasonable hourly rate is not itself a matter of binding precedent. Rather, under established caselaw, a reasonable hourly rate is the 'prevailing market rate,' i.e., the rate 'prevailing in the [relevant] community for similar services by lawyers of reasonably comparable skill, experience, and reputation.'" (citations omitted)); Beard v. Teska, 31 F.3d 942 (10th Cir. 1994) (prevailing rate, not attorney's own rate, is used to establish lodestar). See § 15.7.

151. 20 U.S.C. § 1415(b)(1).

152. *Id.* § 1415(b)(2).

153. *Id.* §§ 1415(b)(3)(A) and (B).

154. *Id.* §§ 1415(b)(6) and (7).

155. *Id.* § 1415(e).

156. *Id.* § 1415(h).

157. *Id.* § 1415(i).

What happens, however, if there is a violation of other procedural protections? For example, what happens if, contrary to regulations under IDEA, the LEA makes a placement decision prior to development of an IEP,[158] or an IEP is developed without parental participation?[159] Are these procedural violations a violation of § 1415?

Technically, it could be said that the regulations controlling IEP development, eligibility hearings, placement decisions and the like are derivative of §§ 1412-1414,[160] not of § 1415, and, therefore, violation of these protections would not be a violation that would prohibit a reduction in the fees requested. But it is also quite logical to say that these procedural protections are also derivative of the language of § 1415(b)(1) that provides: "The procedures required by this section shall include, *but not be limited to*...."[161]

Additional statutory support for this position is found in subsection (b)(6), which authorizes the due process hearings for disputes arising under procedures outside the specifically delineated protections of § 1415 with respect to matters "relating to identification, evaluation, or educational placement of the child, or the provision of a free appropriate public education to such child."[162] Since subsection (i) incorporates due process proceedings, and due process proceedings are designed to protect procedural rights more fully articulated outside § 1415, it is arguable that a violation of subsection (i) in turn includes a violation of rights "relating to identification, evaluation, or educational placement of the child, or the provision of a free appropriate public education to such child."[163]

An expansive reading of procedural violations is also consistent with the legislative intent of the original IDEA, as recognized by the United States Supreme Court in *Rowley* as well as in *Smith v. Robinson*,[164] where the Supreme Court further stressed the importance of faithful compliance with the procedural mechanism of IDEA. In *Smith*, the Court stated that the procedures, "effect Congress' intent that each child's individual educational needs be worked out through a process that ... includes ... detailed procedural safeguards."[165]

It is precisely the procedural protections inherent in the IEP and placement process that insure the individual educational needs of the child are met. Hence, the Supreme Court was equating procedural safeguards with the provisions in the entire IDEA, not simply § 1415. It would make little sense to read IDEA as providing less

---

158. 34 C.F.R. § 300.316 (placement to be based on IEP); *see also* 20 U.S.C. § 1412(a)(5).

159. 34 C.F.R. § 300.322.

160. 20 U.S.C. §§ 1412, 1414.

161. *Id.* § 1415(b)(3) (emphasis added). Section 1415(b)(3) provides that the LEA shall provide "written prior notice to the parents of the child whenever such agency ... proposes to initiate or change ... the identification, evaluation, or educational placement of the child ... or the provision of a free appropriate public education to the child...." This duty to provide notice also supports an expanded view of § 1415 violations. For example, if the placement decision was made before the IEP was developed, the parents never received notice that the decision process was *to begin*. In other words, the notice provision of § 1415 was violated because there was never any notice of the process which led to the predecision.

162. 20 U.S.C. § 1415(b)(6). These protections are more fully articulated in §§ 1412–1414.

163. 20 U.S.C. § 1415(b)(6).

164. 468 U.S. 992 (1984).

165. *Id.* at 1011.

importance to the procedural protections that Congress and the Court recognized as paramount.

15.10 Complaints Resolved By Settlement

The fact that a dispute under IDEA had been settled rather than litigated did not itself affect the availability of attorney's fees. *J.G. v. Board of Education of the Rochester City School District*,[166] was the first significant decision under IDEA's attorney's fee provisions. In *J.G.*, plaintiffs filed a class action suit against both the LEA and the SEA alleging a violation of IDEA. A consent decree was then entered resolving the merits between plaintiffs and the LEA. The plaintiffs then filed a motion to dismiss the SEA and requested attorney's fees. The motion to dismiss was granted, but the motion for attorney's fees was denied. The denial of attorney's fees was appealed. Before the appeal was heard, the attorney's fee provisions were signed into law. The parties agreed to withdraw the appeal and resubmit the question to the district court.

The court held that the fact that the plaintiffs prevailed by settlement did not preclude an award of fees. The court drew the clear analogy between actions arising under IDEA and those brought under § 1988 where the United States Supreme Court had held that "the fact that [plaintiff] prevailed through settlement rather than through litigation does not weaken her claim to fees."[167]

As mentioned previously, *Buckhannon* established criteria for deciding when a party is a prevailing party.[168] The Court held that that a party must secure either a judgment on the merits or a court-ordered consent decree in order to qualify as a "prevailing party." Thus, a prevailing party is required to have some form of "judicial imprimatur," or in other words, "a court ordered change in the legal relationship between the parties." Parties who come to favorable decisions as a result of private voluntary settlements will not be entitled to attorney's fees.[169]

The Court acknowledged, however, that a party benefiting from a settlement agreement could be a prevailing party provided the change in legal relationship was in some way "judicially sanctioned," essentially, a decree.[170] While courts are generally in dis-

---

166. 648 F. Supp. 1452 (W.D.N.Y. 1986), *modified on other grounds*, 830 F.2d 444 (2d Cir. 1988). Interestingly, the Second Circuit modified *J.G.* in part by awarding attorney's fees under the Civil Rights Act §§ 1983 and 1988, saying that this would avoid the question of whether attorney's fees were available to litigants who, under one of the recognized exceptions, filed suit directly in district court by-passing the administrative process of IDEA.

167. *Id.* at 1458, *citing* Maher v. Gagne, 448 U.S. 122, 129 (1980).

168. Buckhannon Bd. & Care Home v. W. Va. Dep't of Health & Human Res., 532 U.S. 598, 604 (2001) (a stipulated settlement is judicially sanctioned where it (1) contained mandatory language; (2) was entitled "Order;" (3) bore the signature of the District Court judge; and (4) provided for judicial enforcement. *Id.* at 558. See § 15.6, above.

169. *Id.* at 604. P.N. v. Seattle Sch. Dist., 474 F.3d 1165 (9th Cir. 2007); Doe v Boston Pub. Schools, 358 F3d 20 (1st Cir. 2004).

170. Buckhannon Bd. & Care Home, 532 U.S. at 605; Mr. L. v. Sloan, 449 F.3d 405 (2d Cir. 2006) (administrative consent decrees which sufficiently changed legal relationship of parties, and were judicially enforceable gave parents "prevailing party" status); A.R. v N.Y. City Dep't of Educ., 407 F3d 65 (2d Cir. 2005).

agreement as to what precisely constitutes a judicial sanction,[171] the fact that a stipulated settlement is not labeled, "decree" will not be fatal.[172]

15.11 Waiver of Attorney's Fees

Where the settlement agreement is silent as to attorney's fees but refers to a settlement including "costs incurred to date," the court must inquire into the fairness of awarding attorney's fees and also whether costs are to include attorney's fees. Although there is some split of authority, it is likely a court would find that such a settlement agreement waives attorney's fees.[173] For example, in *Alison H. v. Byard*,[174] the court held that a provision in the settlement agreement that there was "a release of any and all claims arising prior to the execution of the agreement," constituted a waiver of fees and costs. Where the agreement is silent on the award of attorney's fees, and the parties are aware that attorney's fees are an issue, the court should grant reasonable attorney's fees.[175]

Since attorney's fees can be waived, it is logical that LEAs will attempt to insert a waiver provision into settlement offers to parents. The ability of the district court to enforce such a waiver was addressed by the United States Supreme Court in *Evans v. Jeff D.*[176] In *Evans*, the parties had entered into an agreement in a class action suit. The agreement was then submitted for court approval. The agreement provided for a waiver of the attorney's fees. Plaintiffs' lawyer asked for approval of the agreement except for the fee waiver provision. The district court denied the request.

The issue on appeal was "whether the District Court had a duty to reject the proposed settlement because it included a waiver of statutorily authorized attorneys' fees."[177] The United States Supreme Court held that the district court had the discretion to approve a settlement that included the waiver provision.

It should be kept in mind that Evans also recognizes the discretion of the trial court to reject fee waivers. Evans seems to stress the need to look at the circumstances of the

---

171. *Compare,* Smith v. Fitchburg Pub. School., 401 F.3d 16 (1st Cir. 2005) (judicial orders postponing final resolution and promoting settlement does not amount to judicial imprimatur); Smyth v. Rivero, 282 F.3d 268 (4th Cir. 2002) (judicial imprimatur not present where order acknowledges settlement agreement, but does not incorporate terms of agreement, nor provide for continued jurisdiction over claim); *with,* P. N. v. Clementon Bd. of Educ., 442 F.3d 848 (3d Cir. 2006) (judicial imprimatur present where consent orders are actionable under § 1983); Pres. Coalition v. Fed. Transit Admin., 356 F.3d 444 (2d Cir. 2004) (judicial order placing district under threat of injunctive relief makes parents prevailing party); T.D. v. La Grange School Dist. No. 102, 349 F.3d 469 (7th Cir. 2003) (despite settlement, earlier IHO order gives parents "prevailing party" status).

172. Roberson v. Giuliani, 346 F.3d 75 (2d Cir. 2003) ("Judicial action other than a judgment on the merits or a consent decree can support an award of attorney's fees, so long as such action carries with it sufficient judicial imprimatur."); Smyth v. Rivero, 282 F.3d 268, 281 (4th Cir. 2002) ("an order containing an agreement reached by the parties may be functionally a consent decree for purposes of [Buckhannon], even if not entitled as such.").

173. *See* authorities collected in Fed. R. Civ. Proc. 68 (Official Proposed Rule), 105 S. Ct. LXXXI (1985).

174. 163 F.3d 2 (1st Cir. 1998).

175. *See generally* Barlow/Gresham Union High School Dist. No. 2 v. Mitchell, 940 F.2d 1280 (9th Cir. 1991).

176. 475 U.S. 717 (1986).

177. *Id.* at 1537.

particular case. For example, the Solicitor General, in his argument in Evans, had suggested that fee waivers should not be approved when the defendant acts vindictively or where the defendant has no reasonable defense.[178]

---

178. *Id.* at 1544. See Johnson v. District of Columbia, 190 F. Supp. 2d 34 (D.D.C. 2002) ("settlement offers conditioned on fee waivers, when part of a consistent policy by DCPS, or as part of a vindictive effort to undermine the right of parents and children to counsel, violate the IDEA's attorney's fee provision …"). Bar organizations in several jurisdictions have been successful in promulgating ethical opinions which make entering into waiver agreements unethical. *See* Note, *The Ethics of Fee Waivers: Negotiation of Statutory Fees In Civil Rights Cases*, 5 Yale Law & Policy Rev. 157–58 (1986).

Chapter 16

Records

16.1 In General

Student records are subject to at least four sets of federal government regulations: IDEA, § 504, EDGAR,[1] and the Family Educational Rights and Privacy Act (FERPA or the Buckley Amendments).[2] IDEA requirements are consistent with, and go beyond the requirements of, the other provisions. For example, § 504 regulations provide only a general requirement that the agency "shall establish and implement ... a system of procedural safeguards that includes an opportunity for the parents or guardian of the person to examine relevant records...."[3] IDEA as well as Part C, Infants and Toddlers[4] regulations, specifically reference FERPA regulations.[5]

IDEA contains broad parental rights for access to educational records of the child: "The parents of a handicapped child shall be afforded ... an opportunity to inspect and review all education records with respect to ... [t]he identification, evaluation, and educational placement of the child, and ... [t]he provision of a free appropriate public education to the child."[6] The right to access includes all records "relating to their children which are collected, maintained, or used by the agency...."[7]

The local educational agency is responsible for responding to a request to inspect documents "without unnecessary delay and before any meeting regarding an individualized education program or hearing relating to the identification, evaluation, or placement of the child, and in no case more than 45 days after the request has been made."[8]

---

1. 34 C.F.R. § 75.740; 20 U.S.C. 1221e-3, 1232g, 1232h, and 3474.
2. 20 U.S.C. § 1232(g); Gonzaga Univ. v. Doe 536 U.S. 273 (2002) (held that FERPA's nondisclosure provisions created no personal rights to enforce under § 1983); Meury v. Eagle-Union Community School Corp., 714 N.E.2d 233, 239 (Ind. Ct. App. 1999) (alleged violation of Family Educational Rights and Privacy Act (FERPA) did not give rise to private cause of action by means of § 1983).
3. 34 C.F.R. § 104.36.
4. Letter to Anonymous, 41 Individuals with Disabilities Educ. L. Rep. (LRP) 146 (OSEP 2004) (hospital is obligated to provide a lead agency with the child's name, birth date, and parent contact information in order to meet the Part C child find obligations even without parental consent. Child is not a "student" as defined in FERPA).
5. 34 C.F.R. § 300.611.
6. 34 C.F.R. § 300.501(a); *see* 20 U.S.C. §§ 1414(e), 1415(b)(1).
7. 34 C.F.R. § 300.613(a); *see also* 20 U.S.C. §§ 1412(a)(8), 1417(c).
8. 34 C.F.R. § 300.613(a); *see also* 20 U.S.C. §§ 1412(a)(8), 1417(c).

The right to inspect the records includes the right to have explanations and interpretations of the records, the right to have copies of the record if failure to have copies would prevent the parent from reviewing the records, and the right to have a representative review the records.[9]

The agency is required to maintain records of all parties obtaining access to the educational records of the child.[10] If the records contain information related to a child of another parent, the inspecting parent has the right to review only their own child's portion.[11]

The agency must, at the parent's request, list the types and locations of all educational records of the child.[12]

Fees for copying the records may be charged to the parent, if the fee does not preclude the review by the parent. In no event may a fee be charged for search or retrieval of the records.[13]

Any parent who believes the education records contain information that is "inaccurate or misleading or violates the privacy or other rights of the child" may request that the information be changed.[14] The agency must then review the information and within a reasonable time inform the parent whether the information will be changed.[15] If after a review of the information the agency refuses to change the records, the parents may seek a hearing to challenge the information.[16] The parents must be given notice of the right to this hearing when they are informed by the agency that the agency will not change the record.[17]

A finding from the hearing that the information is inaccurate, misleading, or violates the privacy or other rights of the child will result in amending the records. If, however, there is a finding that the records are inaccurate, misleading, or violate the privacy or other rights of the child the parent still has the option of placing an explanation in the child's record which will become a part of the child's educational record and must be disclosed whenever the contested information is disclosed.[18]

The hearing required to determine whether the records are inaccurate, misleading, or violate the privacy or other rights of the child is *not* held in accord with the requirements of IDEA due process hearings. Rather the hearing is held in accordance with the Family Educational Rights and Privacy Act (FERPA).[19] The hearing under FERPA must, at a minimum,

   • be held within a reasonable period of time;

---

9. 34 C.F.R. § 300.613(b); *see also* 20 U.S.C. §§ 1412(a)(8), 1417(c).

10. 34 C.F.R. § 300.614; *see also* 20 U.S.C. §§ 1412(a)(8), 1417(c).

11. 34 C.F.R. § 300.615; *see also* 20 U.S.C. §§ 1412(a)(8), 1417(c).

12. 34 C.F.R. § 300.616; *see also* 20 U.S.C. §§ 1412(a)(8), 1417(c).

13. 34 C.F.R. § 300.617; *see also* 20 U.S.C. §§ 1412(a)(8), 1417(c).

14. 34 C.F.R. § 300.618(a); *see also* 20 U.S.C. §§ 1412(a)(8), 1417(c); Letter to Anonymous, 40 Individuals with Disabilities Educ. L. Rep. (LRP) 262 (OSEP 2003) (IDEA regulations provide no mechanism for OSEP to review state complaint and due process decisions).

15. 34 C.F.R. § 300.618(b); *see also* 20 U.S.C. §§ 1412(a)(8), 1417(c).

16. 34 C.F.R. §§ 300.618(c), .619; *see also* 20 U.S.C. §§ 1412(a)(8), 1417(c).

17. 34 C.F.R. § 300.618(c); *see also* 20 U.S.C. §§ 1412(a)(8), 1417(c).

18. 34 C.F.R. § 300.620; *see also* 20 U.S.C. §§ 1412(a)(8), 1417(c).

19. 34 C.F.R. § 300.621; *see also* 20 U.S.C. §§ 1412(a)(8), 1417(c). FERPA regulations are contained in 34 C.F.R. Part 99.22.

- within a reasonable period of time, provide the parent or eligible child notice of the date, time, and place of the hearing;

- must be conducted by an individual who has no interest in the outcome of the hearing, but who may be an employee of the agency;

- there must be an opportunity to present evidence relevant to the issue of whether the records are inaccurate, misleading, or violate the privacy or other rights of the child;

- the decision of the agency must be in writing, be based only on the evidence present, and include a summary of the evidence and a reason for its decision.[20]

16.2 Safeguards

The agency is under an obligation to provide significant safeguards protecting the confidentiality of the students' records. Parental consent is required before any personally identifiable information [21] is disclosed 1) to anyone "other than officials of participating agencies"[22] or 2) used in a meeting contemplated under IDEA. IDEA, however, effectively defines officials of participating agencies as those to whom disclosure may be made without consent under FERPA.[23] An agency who reports a crime committed by a child with a disability must ensure copies of the special education and discipline records are transmitted to the authorities to whom the agency reports the crime. This transmission of records must be in accord with the provisions under FERPA.[24]

---

20. 34 C.F.R. § 99.22; *see also* 20 U.S.C. § 1232g(a)(2).

21. *See, e.g.,* Brown v. City of Oneonta, New York Police Dept., 106 F.3d 1125 (2d Cir. 1997) (state university released students' names and addresses to law enforcement); *see also* Doe v. Knox County Bd. of Educ., 918 F. Supp. 181 (E.D. Ky. 1996); *but see,* Disability Rights Wisconsin, Inc. v. State of Wisconsin Dept. of Public Instruction, 463 F.3d 719 (7th Cir. 2006) (agency was not required to obtain authorization from students' guardians before it could learn names of students placed in seclusion room, and Family Educational Rights and Privacy Act (FERPA) did not prevent department from releasing records); Conn. Office of Prot. & Advocacy for Persons with Disabilities v. Hartford Bd. of Educ., 464 F.3d 229 (2d Cir. 2006) (Protection and Advocacy group entitled to records without parents permission under Protection and Advocacy for Mentally Ill Individuals Act, (PAIMI) the federal Developmental Disabilities and Bill of Rights Act (DD Act) and Protection and Advocacy of Human Rights Act (PAIR) to carry out investigation of abuse claims); Letter to Elder, 41 Individuals with Disabilities Educ. L. Rep. (LRP) 270 (OSERS 2004) (when IDEA requires Part C agency to disclose information to Part B agency for child find purposes, parental consent is not required).

22. 34 C.F.R. § 300.622a)(1); *see also* 20 U.S.C. §§ 1412(a)(8), 1417(c).

23. Letter to DuRant, 39 Individuals with Disabilities Education Law Rept. (LRP) 130 (OSEP 2002) (SEA cannot release records to Medicaid to obtain funds prior to obtaining parental consent); Letter to Attorney for School District, 40 Individuals with Disabilities Education Law Rept. (LRP) 99 (FCPO 2003) (parents not entitled to review personally identifiable information on other students contained in education records of their child. Information must be redacted); Letter to Tommasini, 38 Individuals with Disabilites Education Law Rept. (LRP) 155 (FPCO 2002) (must obtain parental consent to share findings in IDEA complaints with individuals who are not the student's parents or guardians).

24. 34 C.F.R. § 300.535; *see also* 20 U.S.C. § 1415(k)(6).

25. Letter re: Moriah Central Sch., 38 Individuals with Disabilities Law Rept. (LRP) 43 (FCPO 2002) (exceptions under FERPA allow disclosure to person evaluating student without parental consent if the school official revealed only personal observations or opinions to the evaluator not in

Under FERPA, disclosure without the consent of the parents or child 18 or over may be made only if:

- it is to other school officials, including teachers, within the agency or institution whom the agency or institution has determined to have legitimate educational interests;[25]
- it is to officials of another school in which the child intends to enroll;
- it is to state, federal and accrediting authorities for auditing or evaluating educational programming requirements;
- it is to agencies or organizations involved in developing, validating or improving tests, instruction or programming;
- the disclosure is in connection with the students application for financial aid;
- the disclosure is by court order;
- the information is necessary because of a health or safety emergency;
- the information is "directory information."[26]

Additional safeguards available to the parents include informing the parents when personally identifiable information is no longer necessary to be maintained, and destroying this information at the request of the parent. The student's name, address, phone number, classes attended, grade, attendance record, years and grade level completed, however, may be kept indefinitely.[27]

---

records or the evaluator was considered a school official with legitimate educational interest or if the evaluator was under contract to the district).
26. 34 C.F.R. §99.31; *see also* 20 U.S.C. §1232g(b)(1)(D).
27. 34 C.F.R. §300.624; *see also* 20 U.S.C. §§1412(a)(8), 1417(c).

Chapter 17

Monitoring and Compliance

17.1 State Monitoring and Compliance

Each State Education Agency (SEA) is responsible for ensuring that all educational programs for children with disabilities are in compliance with IDEA.[1] Part of this responsibility requires the state to have a complaint procedure that:

- provides for receiving and resolving complaints against the SEA or LEA;[2]
- give the complainant the opportunity to respond to the allegations by submitting additional oral or written information [3]
- permits the public agency to respond to the complaint with a proposed resolution and an opportunity for the parent and agency voluntarily to mediate the dispute;[4]
- reviews an appeal from an LEA complaint decision;[5]
- provides for conducting an independent on-site investigation;[6]
- has a 60-day time limit to investigate and resolve the complaint;[7]
- allows for an extension of time only under exceptional circumstances;[8]
- reviews all relevant information and issues a written decision;[9] and
- has an enforcement mechanism.[10]

The complaint must allege a violation that occurred not more than one year prior to the date the complaint is received. [11] The complaint must also include the underlying facts and the signature and contact information of the complainant. If the allegation involves a specific child the following information must also be included:

---

1. 20 U.S.C. § 1412(a)(11); 34 C.F.R. § 300.149.
2. 34 C.F.R. § 300.151; Letter to Garrett, 29 Individuals with Disabilities Educ. L. Rep. (LRP) 975 (OSEP 1997) (SEA receives and investigates complaints).
3. 34 C.F.R. § 300.152(a)(2).
4. 34 C.F.R. § 300.152(a)(3)(i–ii).
3. 34 C.F.R. § 300.153(a)(4)(i–v).
5. 34 C.F.R. § 300.151(a)(1)(ii).
6. 34 C.F.R. § 300.152(a)(1).
7. 34 C.F.R. § 300.152(a).
8. 34 C.F.R. § 300.152(5)(b)(1).
9. 34 C.F.R. §§ 300.152(a)(4).
10. Illinois State Bd. of Educ., 257 Educ. Handicapped L. Rep. (CRR) 573 (OCR August 16, 1984).
11. 34 C.F.R. § 300.153(c).

- the child's name, address and name of the school;
- a factual description of the problem; and
- the proposed resolution. [12]

The regulations also specifically authorize, as part of the complaint process, that remedies

for denial of appropriate services be granted, including, as appropriate, awarding reimbursement.[13]

SEAs have, as a result of complaints, withdrawn Part B funding from LEAs.[14] Prior to withdrawing funds, however, the SEA must provide the LEA with a hearing.[15]

Given the SEA's overriding responsibility, courts have held that a school system's failure to provide educational services requires the SEA to directly provide those services.[16]

The scope of subject matter covered by the complaint procedure includes violations of state or federal laws and regulations.[17] It has been held that this coverage precludes raising in a complaint any issue that can be resolved in a due process hearing.[18] If a written complaint is received that is also the subject of a due process hearing or contains multiple issues, of which one or more are part of that hearing, the SEA must set aside any part of the complaint that is being addressed in the due process hearing, until the conclusion of the hearing. However, any issue in the complaint that is not a part of the due process action must be resolved according to the SEA complaint procedures.[19]

An issue raised in a complaint to the SEA that has previously been decided in a due process hearing involving the same parties is binding.[20]

---

12. *Id.*
13. 34 C.F.R. §300.151(b).
14. *See* Wilson v. McDonald, 558 Educ. Handicapped L. Rep. (CRR) 364 (E.D. Ky. 1987).
15. 20 U.S.C. §1416 (e)(4); 34 C.F.R. §76.783.
16. Gadsby v. Grasmick, 109 F.3d 940 (4th Cir. 1997) (state may be liable when LEA unwilling or unable to provide FAPE); *see also* Doe v. Maher, 793 F.2d 1470 (9th Cir. 1986), *aff'd sub nom.* Honig v. Doe, 484 U.S. 305 (1988); Petties v. District of Columbia, 894 F. Supp. 465 (D.D.C. 1995); K.P. v. Juzwic, 891 F. Supp. 703 (D. Conn. 1995); Wilson v. McDonald, 558 Educ. Handicapped L. Rep. (CRR) 364 (E.D. Ky. 1987) (LEA's failure to implement hearing); *but see* Carnwath v. Grasmick, 115 F.Supp.2d 577 (D. Md. 2000) (state Department of Education was not liable for alleged procedural errors of ALJ; Department was not liable for failure to comply with regulation requiring decision on IEP within 45 days of request for hearing; Department was not liable for any failure to provide free appropriate public education); Gordon v. Board of Educ. Howard County, 22 F. Supp. 2d 499 (D. Md. 1998) (not liable).
17. 34 C.F.R. §76.783(a).
18. *E.g.*, Wilson v. School Dist. No. 1, 556 Educ. Handicapped L. Rep. (CRR) 235 (Ore. Ct. of App. 1984); *see also* Johnson Inquiry, 18 Individuals with Disabilities Educ. L. Rep. (LRP) 589 (OSERS 1991) (when a complaint and a due process hearing are filed simultaneously the SEA must review complaints not covered by the hearing decision); Letter to Ash, 23 Individuals with Disabilities Educ. L. Rep. 647 (OSEP 1994) ("When reviewing a complaint, the SEA should hold in abeyance issues that are under consideration in a Due Process hearing and defer to the hearing officer's judgment to avoid conflict. However, even if there is a Due Process claim pending, the SEA must resolve any issue that is either not under consideration in the Due Process proceeding, or is not ultimately resolved. Issues addressed by the Due Process hearing are not subject to SEA complaint resolution.").
19. 34 C.F.R. §300.152(c)(1).
20. 34 C.F.R. §300.152(c)(2).

17.1.1 State Complaint Checklist

____Jurisdiction

____LEA violation of statute or regulation, or

____SEA violation of statute or regulation, or

____Appeal from LEA complaint procedure

____Mandated statute of limitations met

____Complaint states LEA or SEA has violated law or regulation

____Complaint alleges facts which indicates violation of law or regulation

____Complaint contains complainant's signature and contact information

____If allegations concern a specific child complaint contains

   ____child's name, address and name of school

   ____factual description of child's problem

   ____proposed resolution if known or available

   ____Complaint provided to LEA

____Investigation and Resolution

   ____60-day time limit

   ____May involve on-site investigation

   ____Extension of time only under exceptional circumstances

   ____Enforcement mechanism

   ____Due process hearing filed on same issue

17.2 Office of Special Education Programs

The Office of Special Education Programs of the Department of Education (OSEP) was authorized by §1402 of IDEA and "shall be the principal agency in such Department for administering and carrying out [IDEA]."[21] In addition to general administrative activities, the Department of Education (DOE) was given specific enforcement powers. Specifically, DOE has authority to withhold funds where "there has been a failure to comply substantially with any provision [section 1412 or section 1413]...."[22] The DOE also has this authority concerning violations of the state plan.[23]

In the representation of an individual parent or child, the DOE enforcement power can be significant. It provides a mechanism, other than the formal due process hear-

---

21. 20 U.S.C. §1402(a).

22. 20 U.S.C. §§1416(e)(3); Letter to Anonymous, 40 Individuals with Disabilities Educ. L. Rep. (LRP) 262 (OSEP 2003) (OSEP does not have authority to review state complaint and due process decisions).

23. 20 U.S.C. §§1416(e)(3).

ing, that may bring even greater pressure on the LEA or SEA to fulfill its obligations under IDEA. Sections 1412 and 1413 of IDEA articulate the requirements the states must meet in order to be eligible for funding under IDEA and the details to be contained in the State plan. These two sections require, for example, the provisions contained in the regulations concerning items such as identification, evaluation, FAPE, and procedural protections.

On a practical level, a complaint to OSEP concerning the actions of an LEA operates as filing a complaint with the SEA, since it is the normal practice of OSEP to refer complaints of this type to the individual state SEAs. The SEA is then required to investigate the complaint and report back to OSEP within 60 days concerning findings and resolution.[24] If the complaint is about a SEA, OSEP will investigate the SEA to determine if there is noncompliance. If there is a finding of noncompliance, OSEP will order corrective action.[25]

OSEP, upon a finding of noncompliance has several options, including withholding funds, canceling a grant, reviewing a state plan, and seeking a cease and desist order [26] or referring the matter to the Justice Department.[27]

17.3 Office for Civil Rights

The Office for Civil Rights of the Department of Education (OCR) has responsibility for monitoring state compliance with the provisions of § 504. In furtherance of this requirement, OCR publishes a number of documents useful to the lawyer representing the school, child or parent.

First, OCR publishes formal policy interpretations. Second, there are informal policy interpretations that are generally written in response to specific inquiries concerning OCR's interpretation of § 504.[28] Finally, there are two types of letters related specifically to the compliance requirements imposed on OCR. There are Compliance Letters of Finding, generally letters which summarize matters as a result of inspections conducted of institutions being monitored by the DOE. There are also Complaint Letters of Finding which are responses to complaints concerning LEAs and SEAs received from individuals or groups.

While none of these documents has the force of law, they are persuasive authority concerning the interpretation of the regulations promulgated under § 504, since an agency is given deference in the interpretation of its own regulations.

As implied by the existence of complaint letters, OCR will investigate certain complaints against an LEA or SEA that allege a violation of § 504. OCR has discretion

---

24. Trible Inquiry, 211 Educ. Handicapped L. Rep. (CRR) 395, 397 (EHA 1986). This 60 days is the 60-day time frame required of complaints under the SEA complaint procedure required by 34 C.F.R. § 300.152(a).

25. Trible Inquiry, 211 Educ. Handicapped L. Rep. (CRR) 395, 397 (1986).

26. 34 C.F.R. § 76.901(3).

27. Trible Inquiry, 211 Educ. Handicapped L. Rep. (CRR) 395, 397 (EHA July 23, 1986).

28. California Department of Education, 47 Individuals with Disabilities Educ. L. Rep. (LRP) 45 (OCR 2006) (violation of § 504, Title II of ADA and IDEA for transcripts to contain notation that students received special education. May, however, be information contained on report card); Calcasieu Parish (LA) School Board, 44 Individuals with Disabilities Educ. L. Rep. (LRP) 49 (OCRVI 2005) (violation of § 504, where district requires parents of students taking insulin to attend field trips. District agrees to develop an appropriate policy as corrective action).

whether to investigate an individual complaint. The stated policy of the Office for Civil Rights is that as long as the procedural requirements of the law are met it will not investigate individual placement[29] or other educational decisions,[30] unless there are extraordinary circumstances. In those extraordinary circumstances, the emphasis will be on cases excluding a child from services or cases evidencing a pattern and practice.[31]

In 1983, OCR was placed under a court order to comply with specified time lines to conduct its compliance review. In *Adams v. Bell*,[32] the court ordered DOE to implement the following procedures for investigating complaints:

- Notify the complainant within 15 calendar days in writing whether the complaint is complete.

- A complete complaint is one that:

    1. identifies the complainant by name and address;

    2. generally identifies or describes those injured;

    3. identifies the institution or individual who has allegedly discriminated "in sufficient detail to inform the Office of Civil Rights" what occurred, when it occurred and to permit the commencement of an investigation;

    4. to be complete the complaint does not need to allege the law or laws that were violated.

- If the complaint is complete, the DOE has 15 days in which to inform the complainant:

    1. whether the DOE has jurisdiction over the complaint;

    2. whether the complaint is frivolous;

    3. of the time frames, procedures and the laws affecting processing of the complaint;

    4. whether an on-site investigation will take place.

- If the complaint is not complete, the DOE shall inform the complainant in what manner the complaint is incomplete. The complainant will then have 60 days in which to provide the information to complete the complaint.[33] Following provi-

---

29. 34 C.F.R. Part 104, App. A, Subpart D; Yucaipa-Calimesa (Cal.) 30 897 (OCR 1998) (due process is the proper forum to resolve placement decisions).

30. 34 C.F.R. Part 104, App. A, Subpart D; Falmouth (Mass.) Pub. School 25 84 (OCR 1996) (due process proper forum for appropriateness).

31. 34 C.F.R. Part 104, App. A Subpart D; *see, e.g.,* San Francisco (Cal.) Unified School Dist., 17 Educ. Handicapped L. Rep. (LRP) 487 (OCR 1990) (OCR investigations found multiple FAPE violations including failure to ensure educational placements with nonhandicapped to the maximum extent appropriate, failure to place children in nonpublic schools in a timely manner, failure to conduct the triennial evaluations in a timely manner and failure to evaluate the data of the reevaluations, placing unqualified teachers in special education classes, and failure to ensure that children receive necessary mental health services); Shelby County (Tenn.) School District, 22 Individuals with Disabilities Educ. L. Rep. (LRP) 904 (1995) ("OCR did not review placement decisions as long as the district complied with the procedural requirement of Section 504"); *see also* Darien Bd. of Educ., 22 Individuals with Disabilities Educ. L. Rep. (LRP) 900 (OCR 1995); Richland County School District #1, 22 Individuals with Disabilities Educ. L. Rep. (LRP) 1143 (OCR 1995); Los Angeles City Unified School Dist., 257 Educ. Handicapped L. Rep. (CRR) 06 (OCR 1978).

32. 48 Fed. Reg. 15,509 (D.D.C. 1983).

33. For good cause, the Assistant Secretary for Civil Rights may reopen a complaint that is completed after this 60-day deadline.

sion of this additional information, the DOE has 15 days in which to respond as if the complaint were correctly filed originally.[34]

- Within 15 days of the completed complaint, the DOE will notify the institution against whom the complaint was made of the same information provided the complainant.

- During the investigation, DOE shall:

    1. investigate all allegations in the complaint;

    2. interview the complainant;

    3. contact the institution and gather information from it and relevant witnesses;

    4. afford all parties a full opportunity to present evidence.

- Make its determination in writing within 105 calendar days from the receipt of a complete complaint.

- At any point when the DOE anticipates even a partial adverse finding to the complainant, DOE will give notice to the complainant and an opportunity to respond to the evidence relied upon by the DOE.

- If the DOE finds no violation it will inform the complainant and the institution in writing. This notice will address allegations providing an analysis of the information upon which the conclusion was made.

- If there is a finding of noncompliance, DOE will seek voluntary compliance. If voluntary compliance is ineffective, administrative or judicial remedies are available. DOE has 195 days from the date of receipt of a complete complaint in which to seek voluntary compliance. If after 195 days voluntary compliance was not effective, DOE has no later than 225 days following the receipt of a complete complaint in which to seek administrative or other remedies.

- Time frames may be tolled if, among other things:

    1. witnesses are unavailable because of an extended absence (for example, summer vacation);

    2. court order;

    3. pending litigation on the same issues.

Although the OCR is no longer under the court order in *Adams v. Bell*, it continues to impose these requirements on itself.

If voluntary means are ineffective, OCR can seek compliance through withdrawal of funding or referral to the Justice Department with a recommendation to file suit. A § 504 violation can result in termination of all federal funds to the affected program, whereas the EHA violation would only affect Part B funds. Termination of funding has been ordered.[35] Before federal funds are withheld, however, a formal administrative

---

34. The complainant will also be notified that the institution or individual against whom the complaint was filed may not retaliate against the complainant.

35. *See, e.g.,* Freeman v. Cavazos, 939 F.2d 1527 (11th Cir. 1991) (court refused to order a stay of funding for failure to cooperate with an OCR investigation); Virginia Dept. of Educ., 22 Individuals with Disabilities Educ. L. Rep. (LRP) 474 (OCR 1995) ("it is within the Secretary's discretion to seek withholding of unobligated FY 1995 IDEA B funds and any future funding until the applicant comes into compliance with the requirements of the statute"); In re Mo. Dept. of Elementary and Secondary Educ., 311 Educ. Handicapped L. Rep. (CRR) 98 (OCR 1987).

hearing must be held.[36] The results of this hearing may then be reviewed by the Secretary of DOE in certain cases where important reasons are found for doing so.[37] The OCR and DOE decisions are subject to judicial review.[38]

OCR complaints are handled by one of its regional offices. A list of those offices is found in the Appendix. Complaints must be made within 180 days of the alleged discriminatory action.[39] Given the reluctance of OCR to review individual complaints concerning educational issues, the best use of OCR is to seek systemic changes in the manner in which a LEA is meeting its responsibilities under § 504 and its regulations. This is particularly true for violations of procedures. A reading of OCR Complaint Letters of Findings shows that by far the most common complaints investigated, as the result of third party complaints are violations of procedural issues such as failure of LEAs and SEAs to monitor time lines appropriately,[40] failure to provide impartial hearing officers,[41] substantive issues that represent a pattern and practice such as standard policies limiting educational rights,[42] or where the parties have agreed to the appropriate educational benefit and the LEA withdraws the benefit.[43]

There is no obligation to exhaust administrative remedies under § 504 in order to preserve the complaint for judicial review. To the extent that the same complaint is covered by IDEA, the administrative remedies under that act, however, must be exhausted.

17.3.1 OCR Complaint Checklist

Filing the Complaint

    ____180-day statute of limitations met

    ____Appropriate Regional Office

    ____Complaint complete

    ____Complainants name and address

    ____Identifies or describes those injured

    ____Identifies the institution or individual who has allegedly discriminated

    ____Indicates what happened and when it happened in sufficient detail to allow commencement of an investigation

---

36. 34 C.F.R. § 100.8(c).
37. 34 C.F.R. § 100.10(e).
38. 34 C.F.R. § 100.11.
39. 34 C.F.R. § 104.61, incorporating § 100.7(b).
40. Virginia Dept. of Educ. and Prince William County Pub. Schools, 257 Educ. Handicapped L. Rep. (CRR) 648 (OCR 1985).
41. Allegany (N.Y.) Central School Dist., 257 Educ. Handicapped L. Rep. (CRR) 494 (OCR 1984).
42. Antelope Valley (CA) Union High School Dist., 47 Individuals with Disabilities Educ. L. Rep. (LRP) 107 (OCR 2006) (violation of § 504 regulations and ADA by failing to provide proper notice of its textbook policy and course selection opportunities to high school special education students); Robbinsdale (Minn.) Pub. School Dist., 257 Educ. Handicapped L. Rep. (CRR) 304 (OCR 1981) (violation of § 504 regulations to offer home training only after three week absence from school).
43. San Diego Unified School Dist., 352 Educ. Handicapped L. Rep. (CRR) 257 (OCR 1986) (students denied adaptive physical education as required by IEP).

_____Allegation that § 504 and supporting regulations were violated[44]

If Complaint Was Complete

   Notice to Complainant
   _____15 days in which to inform the complainant
   _____Whether the DOE has jurisdiction over the complaint
   _____Whether the complaint is frivolous
   _____Of the time frames, procedures and the laws affecting processing of the complaint
   _____Whether an on-site investigation will take place

   Notice to the Institution
   _____Whether the DOE has jurisdiction over the complaint
   _____Whether the complaint is frivolous
   _____Of the time frames, procedures and the laws affecting processing of the complaint
   _____Whether an on-site investigation will take place

If Complaint Was Incomplete

   _____15 days notice of manner in which the complaint is incomplete
   _____60 days in which to provide the information to complete the complaint

OCR Investigation

   _____Investigate all allegations
   _____Interview the complainant
   _____Gather information from institution
   _____Gather information from relevant witnesses
   _____Afford all parties a full opportunity to present evidence
   _____105 calendar days from the receipt of a complete complaint in which to make its determination

OCR Decision

   _____Notice to complainant of anticipated finding in favor of institution
   _____Opportunity to respond to the evidence relied upon by the DOE for anticipated decision
   _____Notice of finding to complainant and the institution in writing
   _____Notice of decision addresses allegations providing an analysis of the information upon which the conclusion was made

---

44. Not required, but clearly helpful.

OCR Enforcement

_____If there is a finding of noncompliance, DOE will seek voluntary compliance within 195 days of receipt of a complete complaint.

_____If after 195 days voluntary compliance was not effective, DOE has no later than 225 days following the receipt of a complete complaint in which to seek administrative or other remedies.

Time Frame Tolled

_____Witnesses are unavailable because of an extended absence (e.g. summer vacation)

_____Court order

_____Pending litigation on the same issues

Exhaustion of this remedy is *not* required before judicial action sought.

17.4 Coordination of OCR and OSEP

The overlapping responsibilities of OCR and OSEP for monitoring and investigation of educational issues does lead to the possibility of inconsistent positions within the United States Department of Education (DOE). To limit this possibility, the two offices have developed a memorandum of understanding which outlines their effort to coordinate and communicate with each other.[45] Of particular importance is the agreement that "[w]hen policy is being formulated, by either OCR or OSERS, on any issue concerning the provision of a free appropriate education, every effort will be made to consult on the issue prior to issuance of the policy."[46] Each has also agreed to refer cases involving the other's area of coverage to each other.[47]

17.5 Mediation

The statute and regulations require that public agencies insure procedures are in place for the parties to resolve complaints under IDEA through mediation.[48] Mediation involves the use of a neutral third party to help the parents and the LEA arrive at their own solution to the disagreement. Mediation is voluntary and must not be used to deny or delay a parent's rights. The mediation must be conducted by a quali-

---

45. Revised Memorandum of Understanding, August 20, 1987, published in 202 Educ. Handicapped L. Rep. (CRR) 395 (1987).

46. *Id.* at 396.

47. *Id.*

48. 34 C.F.R. § 300.506; *see also* 20 U.S.C. § 1415(e); Board of Educ. of the Chippewa Valley School Authority, 27 Individuals with Disabilities Educ. L. Rep. (LRP) 429 (1997) ("one of the underlying purposes of IDEA is to strongly encourage the resolution of disputes through compromise and settlement is inherent in the IEP process itself and reinforced by the new provisions recently added regarding mediation").

fied impartial and trained mediator selected on a random rotational or impartial basis.[49]

The impartiality requirements for mediators are quite similar to the requirements for impartial due process hearing officers and include not being an employee of the LEA or SEA providing direct services. There must also not be a professional or personal conflict of interest.[50]

Any agreement reached through mediation is legally binding and must be reduced to writing. The discussions during mediation are confidential and may not be used as evidence in any subsequent due process or civil court hearings.[51] There is also a provision in the regulations where the public agency can establish procedures that require parents to meet with disinterested parties who can explain the benefits of and encourage the use of mediation.[52] The cost of the mediation process is paid by the state.[53] The Office for Civil Rights had also made it clear that mandatory mediation is inconsistent with the procedural requirements of the § 504 regulations. Despite this warning, on occasion LEAs have been called to task for making mediation a mandatory step.[54]

A written signed mediation agreement can be enforced in any State court of competent jurisdiction or in a district court of the United States. [55]

17.6 Choosing Dispute Resolution Process

The advantages to following any of the above complaint procedures discussed in this chapter are twofold. First, of course, for some problems, a complaint may be the only means short of litigation that is available to resolve the issue. Due process hearings provided for under IDEA cover disputes over the identification, evaluation, educational placement, and provision of a FAPE.[56] A hearing is also appropriate to resolve disputes challenging information contained in the child's educational records.[57] These topics cover most of the disputes that arise between parents and educators concerning rights under the IDEA, but not all of the disputes.[58] Not all complaints can be resolved, therefore, by way of the due process mechanism.

---

49. 34 C.F.R. § 300.506(b).

50. 34 C.F.R. § 300.506(c) (not an employee solely because paid by the agency).

51. The cost of the mediation process is paid by the state. 34 C.F.R. § 300.506(b) (the parties maybe required to sign a confidentiality pledge).

52. 34 C.F.R. § 300.506(b) (the disinterested party may be a parent training resource center or a mediation agency; as with the actual mediation process failure to participate in these meetings cannot deny the parent's right to due process).

53. 34 C.F.R. § 300.506(b)(4).

54. Missouri Dept. of Elementary and Secondary Educ., 352 Educ. Handicapped L. Rep. (CRR) 397 (OCR 1987) (mandatory informal administrative review prior to impartial hearing violates regulations); Massachusetts Dept. of Educ., 352 Educ. Handicapped L. Rep. (CRR) 313 (OCR 1986) (mediation process improperly characterized as mandatory); West Hartford Bd. of Educ., 352 Educ. Handicapped L. Rep. (CRR) 300 (OCR 1986) (violation of 34 C.F.R. § 104.36 by failure to inform parents that mediation was not mandatory).

55. 34 C.F.R. § 300.506(7).

56. 34 C.F.R. § 300.507(a)(1); *see also* 20 U.S.C. § 1415(b)(6).

57. 34 C.F.R. § 300.619.

58. See § 11.5.2.

A second advantage to these complaint procedures may be to save considerable expense. If the Office of Special Education Programs (OSEP) or the Office of Civil Rights (OCR) investigates, for example, investigation and compliance mechanisms are controlled and paid for by the office. It is possible that the complaint investigation will provide valuable information for use in the subsequent due process hearings.[59] A negative result of the complaint process is not *res judicata*, therefore the due process mechanism under the IDEA will still be an option after exhaustion of the complaint process.[60] An agreement between the parties resolving the complaint should not, however, be overturned absent a showing that "the complaint resolution process did not address and resolve the questions presented in the hearing."[61] Mediation is also generally less expensive than litigating through a due process proceeding.

The disadvantages of these processes are that neither the parents nor the LEA's lawyers exercise control over the investigation. The complaint is controlled by the respective governmental office, and any investigation or hearing such as is done by OCR will not make counsel an active participant. Further, should a negative result occur, though it is not *res judicata*, its precedential impact on a subsequent hearing officer could be damaging.

Finally, it should be kept in mind that these complaint mechanisms are not mandatory and the parents need not exhaust them, unlike the due process procedures under the EHA which must be exhausted. Further, it is unlikely that attorneys' fees will be awarded for time spent on the nonmandatory complaint mechanism.

Joint filing of due process and complaint procedures will not provide any additional immediate substantive benefit, since OCR, as well as most states will stay the investigation pending the litigation. OSEP issued a letter holding that when reviewing a complaint, the SEA should hold in abeyance issues that are under consideration in a due process hearing and defer to the hearing officer's judgment to avoid conflict. However, even if there is a due process claim pending, the SEA must resolve any issue that is either not under consideration in the due process proceeding or is not ultimately resolved. The issues addressed by the due process hearing are not subject to SEA complaint resolution.[62] However, filing of the complaint concurrently with the due process hearing may be wise in order to toll the statute of limitations for the complaint process. If it is possible that the due process hearing may not resolve all contested issues, it will be necessary to seek relief under the complaint procedures. Failure to file the complaint during the pendency of the due process litigation may, therefore, allow the statute of limitations to run.

---

59. Johnson Inquiry, 18 Individuals with Disabilities Educ. L. Rep. (LRP) 589 (OSERS 1991) (Due process and complaints are separate proceedings. Generally the hearing officer's decision prevails over the complaint investigation of the same issue. The findings of an SEA complaint can be used as subsequent evidence in a Due Process proceeding); *see also* Case No. SE-10-85, 507 Educ. Handicapped L. Rep. (CRR) 188 (SEA Ill. 1985) (records and resolution admissible in subsequent due process hearing).

60. *Id.*

61. *Id.* at 188.

62. Letter to Ash, 23 Individuals with Disabilities Educ. L. Rep. 647 (OSEP 1994); Johnson Inquiry, 18 Individuals with Disabilities Educ. L. Rep. (LRP) 589 (OSERS 1991).

Chapter 18

Infants and Toddlers

18.1 Introduction to Infants and Toddlers with Disabilities Act

The Infants and Toddlers with Disabilities Act (ITDA), a subchapter of IDEA,[1] was enacted to satisfy a need to identify and provide services to a specified population of infants and toddlers.[2] ITDA requires provision of coordinated, multiagency, multidisciplinary services necessary to "enhance" the development of infants and toddlers with disabilities. In addition to enhanced development, the law seeks to:

- minimize the potential for developmental delay of children and recognize the brain development that occurs during a child's first 3 years of life;[3]
- eventually reduce the need for special education and related services, and thereby reduce the cost of educating these children;[4]
- "maximize" their potential for independent living in society;[5]
- work with families to assist them in meeting their children's needs;[6] and
- assist the state and localities in meeting the needs of populations which are often under represented, for example, minority children, low income rural and inner city children and infants and toddlers in foster care.[7]

Early intervention services are designed to meet the developmental needs of the eligible child as well as the needs of the family so as to enhance the child's development. The services are selected in collaboration with the parent, are provided under public supervision by qualified personnel, are in conformity with an individualized family service plan (IFSP), are provided at no cost to the parent,[8] and meet any other state standards.[9]

---

1. 20 U.S.C. § 1431.
2. OSEP Policy Memorandum 90-14, (March 20, 1990) (memorandum provides a discussion of Part H, now Part C, regarding entitlement and eligibility, fiscal responsibility, monitoring requirements, and timelines).
3. 20 U.S.C. § 1431(a)(1).
4. 20 U.S.C. § 1431(a)(2).
5. 20 U.S.C. § 1431(a)(3).
6. 20 U.S.C. § 1431(a)(4).
7. 20 U.S.C. § 1431(a)(5).
8. 20 U.S.C. § 1432(4)(b) (except where federal or state law requires payments by families).
9. 20 U.S.C. §§ 1401(15–16) and 1432(4); § 34 C.F.R. 303.12.

An early intervention program means the total effort that a state engages in to meet the needs of eligible families and children.[10]

"Infant and toddlers" refers to children from birth through age two[11] who need early intervention services because of developmental delay in one or more of the following areas: cognitive development; physical development; communication development; social or emotional development; and adaptive development.[12] For example, this may include children who are deaf or blind.

The term developmental delay also includes children having a diagnosed physical or mental condition that has a high probability of resulting in developmental delay. This may include children who have chromosomal abnormalities, disorders that reflect disturbance in the nervous system, fetal alcohol syndrome, or severe attachment disorders.[13] The state may also include in its definition children who are at risk of having substantial developmental delay if early intervention services are not provided.[14] For example, children may be included who have biological and environmental risk factors such as low birth weight, respiratory distress as a newborn, infection, nutritional deprivation, or history of abuse.[15] Appropriate diagnostic instruments and procedures must be used to measure the developmental delay.

18.2 ITDA Relationship to Other Laws

Just as with IDEA, when dealing with ITDA, several other statutes and regulations need to be considered. For example, EDGAR, FERPA, and IDEA regulations pertaining to confidentiality of information need to be considered.[16] Care should be taken, however, in applying these regulations since there is often a need to transfer definitions from one set of regulations to the other. For example, when dealing with ITDA, a state educational agency means the lead agency. The lead agency will not always be the state educational agency. For example, the lead agency could be any agency designated by the Governor as long as it has responsibility for administering the ITDA.[17] Examples of lead agencies include mental health, social services, or health agencies, generally those which have already provided services to infants and toddlers.

---

10. 20 U.S.C. §§ 1431–1445, 34 C.F.R. 303.11.

11. Letter to Frymoyer, 3 Early Childhood Law & Policy Rep. (LRP) 33 (OSEP 1996) (FAPE must be available on child's third birthday).

12. 20 U.S.C. § 1432(3); 34 C.F.R. § 303.16(a)(1).

13. 34 C.F.R. § 303.16 Note 1.

14. 20 U.S.C. § 1432(5); 34 C.F.R. § 303.16(2)(b).

15. 34 C.F.R. § 303.16 Note 2; *see* Letter to Baglin, 23 Individuals with Disabilities Educ. L. Rep. (LRP) 339 (OSEP 1995) (may use Part H funds, now Part C, to provide services for children at risk but not for collateral issues such as child abuse, family preservation or juvenile delinquency).

16. 34 C.F.R. § 303.460. See §§ 1.6, 1.7, and Chapter 16.

17. 34 C.F.R. § 303.500; Letter to Anonymous, 41 Individuals with Disabilities Educ. L. Rep. (LRP) 86 (OSEP 2004) (lead agency and referral sources must cooperate in obtaining child find information).

18.3 Funds

Federal funds provided under ITDA may be used for maintaining and implementing the statewide system; for providing direct early intervention services not otherwise provided from other public or private sources; for expanding and improving existing services; for providing a free and appropriate public education to children with disabilities from their third birthday to the beginning of the following school year; and, with the parents' written consent, to continue to provide early intervention services from the child's third birthday until he or she is eligible to enter kindergarten.[18]

There are, however, some restrictions on the use of the money. The funds may not be used for services that otherwise would be paid for from some other public or private sources, except where it would be necessary to prevent a delay in receiving services.[19] The state may not reduce the benefits available to eligible children under either Title V of the Social Security Act, SSA, or title XIX under the SSA regarding Medicaid payments.[20]

18.4 Eligibility

Three groups of infants and toddlers are potentially eligible for services under the ITDA. The first group includes infants and toddlers under age three who need early intervention services because of "developmental delays" as measured in specific areas.[21] The areas of delay can be in the area of cognitive or physical development including vision and hearing, language and speech or communication development, social or emotional development, and adaptive development.[22]

The second group of infants and toddlers who are eligible includes those children who have been diagnosed with a physical or mental condition that has a "high probability" of resulting in a developmental delay.[23] Third, a state may choose to serve those infants and toddlers who would be at risk of having "substantial" developmental delays if services were not provided.[24]

---

18. 20 U.S.C. § 1438(4); *see* Letter to Howell, 4 Early Childhood Law & Policy Rep. (LRP) 95 (OSEP 1998) (state cannot impose fees on parents for services provided as early intervention services because services are required to be provided at no cost to the parents).

19. 20 U.S.C. § 1440(a); 34 C.F.R. §§ 303.527(a) and (b). In addition, payment must be pending from the appropriate source.

20. 20 U.S.C. § 1440(c); 34 C.F.R.§ 303.527(c); *see* Letter to Lucas, 3 Early Childhood Law & Policy Rep. (LRP) 32 (OSEP 1996) (private insurance can be used to cover services if no costs will be incurred; asking about Medicaid coverage is permissible); Letter to Thaler, 2 Early Childhood Law & Policy Rep. (LRP) 253 (OSEP 1996) (agency may inquire about insurance coverage as long as parents do not perceive they are required to use insurance benefits).

21. 20 U.S.C. §§ 1432(3) and 1435(a)(1).

22. 20 U.S.C. § 1432(5); 34 C.F.R. § 303.16(a)(1).

23. 20 U.S.C. § 1432(5)); 34 C.F.R. § 303.16(a)(2).

24. 34 C.F.R. § 303.16(b); 20 U.S.C.A. § 1432(5).

18.5 Identification and Assessment

Each state early intervention system must establish procedures by which children that may be in need of services are identified, located and evaluated.[25] Effective referral efforts are to be included in this child find system. This may include tracking high risk birth conditions.[26]

The identification and assessment process begins by a referral to the lead agency. After a child is referred, the state agency must complete an evaluation to determine eligibility. If the child is eligible, an individual family service plan (IFSP) meeting must be conducted within 45 days of the initial referral.[27]

ITDA has defined both evaluations and assessments, although the distinction is not clear. For example, ITDA has defined evaluations as the procedures used to determine whether a child is eligible for early intervention services.[28] Assessments are defined as the on-going procedures for identifying the unique needs of the child, the family's strengths and needs related to the child, and the nature and extent of services needed. The evaluations and assessments draw conclusions about the level of the child's developmental functioning.

These evaluations and assessments are to be conducted by trained personnel, based on informed clinical judgments and should include a review of pertinent health/medical records.[29] With the parent's consent, the family must also be assessed to determine its strengths and needs as they relate to the developmental enhancement of the child. A personal interview, conducted by trained personnel, is held to obtain this information. The results of this interview are then, with parental permission, incorporated into the IFSP as the strengths and needs which are viewed as enhancing the child's development.[30]

Evaluations and assessments must be conducted using nondiscriminatory procedures and are to be administered in the parents' native language unless it is not feasible. The evaluations and assessments may not discriminate based on race or culture.[31] In conducting the evaluation and assessment, more than one criterion must be used for determining eligibility. Further, only qualified personnel may administer them.[32]

---

25. Letter to Munday, 45 Individuals with Disabilities Educ. L Rep. (LRP) 225 (OSEP 2005) (obtain parental consent to contact previous service providers to restart early intervention services for displaced infants and toddlers; may use interim IFSP; must make services available regardless of state of residence; may offer services temporarily in other then natural environment); *see also* Letter to Kane, 45 Individuals with Disabilities Educ. L Rep. (LRP) 254 (OSEP 2005) (state must provide transportation if family must travel to access services not provided in natural environment).

26. 34 C.F.R § 303.321 Note 1.

27. 34 C.F.R. § 303.321(e)(2).

28. 34 C.F.R. § 303.322(b)(1).

29. 34 C.F.R. § 303.322(c).

30. 34 C.F.R. § 303.322(d).

31. 34. C.F.R. § 300.323(b); *see* No Name Inquiry, 18 Individuals with Disabilities Educ. L. Rep. (LRP) 741 (OSEP 1992) (tests cannot be culturally or racially biased; local norms may be used).

32. 34 C.F.R. § 303.323(d).

18.6 Individualized Family Service Plan

Just as the individual education program (IEP) is the centerpiece of IDEA, the individual family service plan (IFSP) is the centerpiece of ITDA. It serves as the road map for the provision of services, and the early intervention services must be provided in accordance with this IFSP.[33] The services must be evaluated at least annually[34] and reviewed every six months, or more frequently if requested or need warrants a review.[35] The IFSP has eight components. It must contain:[36]

- a statement of the child's present level of skills in the areas of physical development, cognitive, speech-language, and social-emotional development as well as in self-help areas (The determination of the level of skills must be based on objective criteria);

- a "statement of the family's resources, priorities, and concerns relating to enhancing the development of the family's infant or toddler with a disability";

- a statement of the "measurable results or outcomes to be achieved, including pre-literacy and language skills, as developmentally appropriate for the child" (The procedures, criteria, and timelines used to determine achievement of outcomes must also be included);

- a statement of the early intervention services based on peer-reviewed research, to the extent practicable, necessary to meet the unique needs of the child and family (The frequency, intensity, and method and location of delivery of the services, and the method of payment if required must also be included);[37]

- a statement of the natural environment in which early intervention services will be provided, including a justification of the extent to which the services will not be provided in a natural environment;[38]

- the date the services will begin, as well as the expected length, duration, and frequency of the services;

- the name of the qualified service coordinator must also be included; and

---

33. 20 U.S.C. § 1436(d); 34 C.F.R. § 303.340(b).

34. 20 U.S.C. § 1436; 34 C.F.R. § 303.342(c).

35. 20 U.S.C. § 1436(b); 34 C.F.R. § 303.342(b).

36. 20 U.S.C. § 1436(d); 34 C.F.R. § 303.344.

37. *See* Letter to Wilson, 37 Individuals with Disabilities Educ. L. Rep. (LRP) 96 (OSEP 2002) (may include methodology but decision of IFSP team and child's needs); Adams v. Oregon 195 F.3d 1141(9th Cir. 1999) (revised IFSP which reduced the number of weekly service hours during summer was inappropriate, therefore, parents entitled to reimbursement for educational therapist consultation during time revised IFSP in place).

38. *See* 34 C.F.R. §§ 303.18; *see also* Andrew M. v. Delaware County Office of Mental Health and Mental, 490 F.3d 337 (3rd Cir. 2007) (preschool was type of natural environment for infants and toddlers contemplated by IDEA and county violated IDEA by failing to provide developmentally-delayed twins with early intervention (EI) services at preschool); Letter to Morris, 44 Individuals with Disabilities Educ. L. Rep. (LRP) 97 (OSEP 2005) (provision of services in natural environment required); Letter to Elder, 4 Early Childhood Law & Policy Rep. (LRP) 94 (OSEP 1998) (IFSP services in natural environment, agency may not use C funds to provide in different location); Letter to Dicker, 2 Early Childhood Law & Policy Rep. 85 (OSEP 1995) (funding child care in natural setting may be part of early intervention services).

- the steps necessary to ensure appropriate transition to other services or programs that may be required when the child reaches the age of three.[39]

It is also important that the document delineate those actions required by the case manager and those actions which are the responsibility of the parents. The IFSP must include these required components, but in order to avoid a detailed repetition of service requirements, documents containing the various information may be attached.[40]

The IFSP acts as a guide for the provision of services but does not act as a guarantee of the child's success. Neither the public agencies nor personnel involved in the delivery of services are accountable if the child does not achieve the outcomes in the IFSP.[41]

Informed written consent must be obtained prior to the delivery of any services in the IFSP.[42] The parents and appropriate personnel jointly develop the IFSP based on the input from the multidisciplinary evaluation and assessments.[43] The parents have a right to attend the initial and subsequent IFSP meetings. Other participants who are required to attend are the case manager/service coordinator who has been working with the family since the child's initial referral for evaluation, or the case manager/service coordinator who is responsible for implementing the IFSP, a person who has conducted an evaluation or assessment, and appropriate service providers.[44] In addition, at the request of the parents, other family members and advocates may attend. For those persons required to attend and who are unable to, alternative arrangements must be made in order that they have input.[45] If it is evident that services are needed before the evaluation process is complete, they can only be provided if the parents agree and an interim IFSP is developed.[46]

18.7 Early Intervention Services

Early intervention services are defined as services to meet the developmental need of infants and toddlers with a disability. The services are designed to meet the needs of delay and are selected in collaboration with the parents and provided under public supervision, by qualified personnel. The services must be provided in conformity with an individualized family service plan (IFSP), meet state standards, and be provided at no cost to the parent, unless payment is required by law.[47]

---

39. 34 C.F.R. § 300.121 (polices required for smooth transition from EIS to preschool programs at age three and can use appropriate IEP or IFSP).
40. 34 C.F.R. § 303.344 Note 4.
41. 34 C.F.R. § 303.346.
42. 20 U.S.C. § 1436(e); 34 C.F.R. § 303.342; Letter to Gill, 2 Early Childhood Law & Policy Rep. (LRP) 125 (OSEP 1995) (agency can challenge refusal for initial evaluation but not refusal of parents to accept provision of services).
43. 20 U.S.C. § 1436; 34 C.F.R. § 303.340.
44. 34 C.F.R. § 303.343(a) (regulations use the word service coordinator); Letter to Frymoyer, 3 Early Childhood Law & Policy Rep. (LRP) 33 (OSEP 1996) (service providers cannot be totally excluded from IFSP meetings).
45. 34 C.F.R. § 303.343(a)(2).
46. 34 C.F.R § 303.345.
47. 34 C.F.R. § 303.12(a)(3); *see* 34 C.F.R. § 303.521. The following services must be provided at no cost: child find; evaluation and assessment; service coordination; and the activities related to the administration and coordination for developing the IFSP and implementation of procedural safeguards. *See also* Letter to Lucas, 3 Early Childhood Law & Policy Rep. (LRP) 32 (OSEP 1996) (private insurance can be used if no costs will be incurred by parents); Inquiry of Eaton, 18 Individuals

Early intervention services include family training, counseling, and home visits; special instruction; speech-language pathology and audiology; occupational and physical therapy; psychological services; case management services; medical diagnosis and evaluation; early identification, screening, and assessment services; necessary health services so that the infant and toddler can benefit from other early intervention services; social work services, nursing services, nutrition services, vision services and, assistive technology services; and transportation services.[48]

These services must be provided in the environments where children without disabilities normally participate.[49] In addition, the role of the service providers is included in the regulations. This includes consultation with the parents; training the parents and others; participating in the multidisciplinary assessment; and developing goals and objectives in the IFSP.[50]

The subsections that follow provide a more comprehensive list of the services required under the ITDA. This list is not exhaustive and may include other services.

18.7.1 Assistive Technology Services

ssistive technology devices are commercial or customized items and equipment that assist the child in increasing, maintaining or improving functional capabilities. An assistive technology service is a service that assists with the selection, acquisition or use of a technology device. These services may include functional evaluations, coordination with other therapies and training for the families and the professionals who work with the child.[51]

18.7.2 Audiology Services

Audiology services are required under ITDA where necessary. Federal regulations provide that audiology means identification of and determining the range, nature and degree of loss, referral for habilitation or rehabilitation, auditory training, aural rehabilitation, speech reading and listening device orientation and training, prevention of hearing loss services, and providing services for amplification including selecting fitting and dispensing and evaluating the effectiveness of appropriate listening and vibrotactile devices.[52]

---

with Disabilities Educ. L. Rep. (LRP) 183 (OSEP 1990) (discussing child find and impermissible fees).
    48. 20 U.S.C. § 1432(4); 34 C.F.R. §§ 303.12(d)(1)–(16).
    49. 20 U.S.C. § 1432(4)(G); 34 C.F.R. §§ 303.18; Andrew M. v. Delaware County Office of Mental Health and Mental, 490 F.3d 337 (3rd Cir. 2007) (preschool was type of natural environment of infants and toddlers contemplated by IDEA and county violated IDEA by failing to provide developmentally-delayed twins with early intervention (EI) services at preschool); see also Letter to Ziemnoff, 2 Early Childhood Law & Policy Rep. (LRP) 150 (OSEP 1995) (services provided in the natural environment to the maximum extent appropriate).
    50. 34 C.F.R. §§ 303.12(c)(1)–(3).
    51. s34 C.F.R. §§ 303.12(d)(ii–vi).
    52. 34 C.F.R. § 303.12(d)(2).

18.7.3 Service Coordination/Case Management Services

One of the unique concepts of ITDA is the requirement that each eligible family and child have a case manager. The responsibilities of the case manager include assisting the family in obtaining services, coordinating the delivery of the identified services,[53] facilitating the timely delivery of the services,[54] and continuously seeking the services necessary to benefit the child's development.[55] The case manager also assists in protecting the child's and parent's rights.[56]

The regulations further delineate specific case management activities. These responsibilities include performing assessments and evaluations delivering services, and coordinating with the medical and health personnel.[57]

The case manager also facilitates the individual family service plan process and the transition plan to preschool services.[58] Lastly, the case manager has the responsibility to work with the family in identifying service providers and informing the family of available advocacy services.[59]

18.7.4 Family Training, Counseling, Home Visits

Family training, counseling, and home visits are, where needed, required under ITDA. These services are to be provided by "qualified" personnel and are intended to assist the family in understanding the "special" needs of the child and to assist with the enhancement of the child's development.[60] Qualified personnel, including professionals representing various disciplines, are required to meet state approved or other recognized certification, licensing, registration or comparable requirements required by the state.[61] In addition, states must establish policies and procedures related to the personnel standards.[62]

18.7.5 Health Services

Health services, where needed, are required under ITDA. Health services are those services which help a child benefit from other services they might be receiving at the time.[63] These services include intermittent catheterization (a procedure used to drain urine from the bladder), tracheotomy care (which may include suctioning or cleaning

---

53. 34 C.F. R. § 303.23 (a)(3). These services may include medical services other then for diagnostic and evaluative purposes. *See* Letter to FryMoyer, 3 Early Childhood Law & Policy Rep. (LRP) 33 (OSEP 1996) (states can establish additional duties for Part C service coordinators).
54. 34 C.F.R. § 303.23(b).
55. 34 C.F.R. § 303.23(a)(3)(iv).
56. 34 C.F.R. § 303.23(a).
57. 34 C.F.R. §§ 303.23(b)(1), (4) and (6).
58. 34 C.F.R. §§ 303.23(b)(2) and (7).
59. 34 C.F.R. §§ 303.23(b)(3) and (5).
60. 34. C.F.R. § 303.12(3).
61. 20 U.S.C. § 1432(4)(F); 34 C.F.R. § 303.22.
62. 34 C.F.R. § 303.361.
63. 34 C.F.R. § 303.13(a).

an artificial airway), tube feeding, changing dressings, and changing colostomy bags (bags used to collect bodily wastes).[64] Health services also include consultation by physicians with other service providers.[65]

Several items are specifically excluded from the definition of health services under ITDA. These services include "medical-health" services such as surgical services and services that are purely medical in nature, for example prescribing medications. Also excluded are those devices used to treat or control a medical condition. Well baby services such as immunizations are also excluded.[66]

Although these medical-health services need not be provided, they should be included in the IFSP to the extent appropriate. The IFSP should also contain the sources available for payment of these other medical-health services.[67] Identification of these other services assists the case manager and the family to understand what other services they should be accessing.

18.7.6 Medical Services for Diagnosis or Evaluation

Medical services for diagnosis or evaluation are available under ITDA. These services must be provided by a physician to determine whether a developmental delay exists and whether the child needs early intervention services.[68]

18.7.7 Nursing Services

Nursing services must also be available under ITDA. Nursing services are those activities and services used to assess health status, to identify the child's and family's response to actual or potential health problems, to provide direct care in order to prevent, promote or restore health, and to administer medications and any other regimens prescribed by physicians.[69]

18.7.8 Nutrition Services

Nutrition services are also available services under ITDA. Nutrition services include conducting assessments regarding the child's nutrition, diet, and feeding issues and developing appropriate plans based on the assessments. These services also include making appropriate referrals to allow the nutritional goals for the child to be carried out.[70]

---

64. 34 C.F.R. §303.13(b)(1).
65. 34 C.F.R. §303.13(b)(2).
66. 34 C.F.R. §§303.13(c)(1)–(3).
67. 34 C.F.R. §§303.344(e), 303.13 and Note.
68. 34. C.F.R. §303.12(5); Letter to Gully, 42 Individuals with Disabilities Educ. L. Rep. (LRP) 38 (OSEP 2004) (no requirement to provide "surgical" or purely medical services).
69. 34 C.F.R. §303.12(6).
70. 34 C.F.R. §§303.12(7)(i)–(iii).

18.7.9 Occupational Therapy

Occupational therapy services designed to improve the functional ability of a child in the performance of various skills are included in the required available services. The required services relate to the areas of self-help, adaptive behavior, sensory, motor and postural development.[71] These skills, which are to be performed in all settings, include identification, assessment, and intervention, that includes the required adaptation of the environment to promote the acquisition of the skills.[72]

18.7.10 Physical Therapy

Physical therapy is a service available under ITDA that addresses the child's sensorimotor functions through "enhancement of musculosketal status, neurobehavioral organization, perceptual and motor development, cardiopulmonary status and effective environmental adaptation."[73] The definition of physical therapy includes screening activities to identify movement problems and services to prevent or alleviate movement dysfunction and related functional problems. The services can be provided to individuals or in groups. [74]

18.7.11 Psychological Services

ITDA requires that psychological services be available if needed. Psychological services include administering tests and assessments, interpreting results related to child and family behavior, providing psychological services including family counseling, and providing consultation and training on child development.[75]

18.7.12 Social Work Services

Required social services that must be available, if needed, include visiting the home to assess the environmental context,[76] conducting a psycho-social assessment within the family structure,[77] providing counseling and social skill building activities within the family,[78] working on the identified problems and identifying and coordinating community resources to assist the family in receiving maximum benefit from the early intervention services.[79]

---

71. 34 C.F.R. § 303.12(8).
72. 34 C.F.R. §§ 303.12(8)(i)–(iii).
73. 34 C.F.R. §§ 303.12(9)(i)–(iii).
74. *Id.*
75. 34 C.F.R. §§ 303.12(10)(i)–(iv).
76. 34 C.F.R. § 303.12(12)(i).
77. 34 C.F.R. § 303.12(12)(ii).
78. 34 C.F.R. § 303.12(12)(iii).
79. 34 C.F.R. § 303.12(12)(iv).

18.7.13 Special Instruction

Special instruction is required under ITDA and is defined as designing learning activities to assist in promoting the acquisition of skills in the various developmental areas,[80] developing curriculum that leads to achieving the outcomes in the child's IFSP,[81] and assisting the family with skill development of the child.[82]

18.7.14 Speech-Language Pathology

Speech-language services are required under ITDA and focus on the identification of children with delays and disorders in oropharyngeal and communication skills,[83] referral for medical or professional habilitation or rehabilitation services,[84] and provision of those identified services.[85]

18.7.15 Vision Services

Vision services include evaluations and assessment of a child's visual disorders, delays and abilities, referrals for medical or professional habilitation or rehabilitation services for visual disorders and communication. The child may also receive training in orientation and mobility and independent living skills as well as to activate visual motor skills.[86]

18.7.16 Transportation

ITDA requires transportation services. Transportation costs are defined as the cost of travel and the related cost necessary to enable a child to obtain early intervention services.[87]

18.7.17 Personnel

The people qualified to provide early intervention services are defined in both the statute and regulations. They include a wide variety of professional service providers,

---

80. 34 C.F.R. § 303.12(13)(i).
81. 34 C.F.R. § 303.12(13)(ii).
82. 34 C.F.R. § 303.12(13)(iii).
83. 34 C.F.R. § 303.12(14)(i).
84. 34 C.F.R. § 303.12(14)(ii).
85. 34 C.F.R. § 303.12(14)(iii).
86. 34 C.F.R. § 303.12(16)(i–iii).
87. 34 C.F.R. § 303.12(15). These costs include mileage or costs of a taxi, common carrier or other means and other expenses such as tolls and parking. Letter to Kane, 45 Individuals with Disabilities Educ. L Rep. (LRP) 254 (OSEP 2005) (state must provide transportation if family must travel to access services not provided in natural environment).

including audiologists, nutritionists, nurses, pediatricians, orientation and mobility specialists, occupational physical, speech and language and family therapists, psychologists, social workers and special educators.[88]

18.8 Procedural Safeguards

Parents are entitled to certain procedural safeguards under ITDA. The lead agency has the responsibility to develop and implement the procedural safeguards. The agency may follow those safeguards that have been developed under IDEA.[89] The safeguards, however, must include that the parents cannot be charged fees for costs associated with a due process hearing or other procedural safeguards.[90] In addition, the following safeguards are the minimum requirements to which parents or guardians are entitled:[91]

- Timely resolution of parents' complaints. A written decision must be rendered and sent to the parents not later than 30 days;

- The aggrieved party has the right to bring a civil action in the appropriate federal or state court. The court receives the administrative record, shall hear additional evidence if a party requests it and shall grant appropriate relief;[92]

- Confidentiality of personally identifiable information. The parents must receive written notice and give written consent for agencies to exchange information consistent with federal and state law;

- The right to accept or decline services without jeopardizing the receipt of other early intervention services;

- The opportunity to inspect assessment, screening, eligibility and the IFSP records.

- The right to the appointment of a surrogate parent if the parents or guardians whereabouts are unknown, if they are unavailable, or if the child is a ward of the state;

- Written prior notice whenever the service provider or state agency proposes to initiate or change or refuses to initiate or change the identification, evaluation, placement, or provision of the services;

- Notice provided in the parents' or guardian's native language;

- The right of parents to use mediation;[93]

---

88. 20 U.S.C. § 1432(4)(F); 34 C.F.R. § 303.12(e); *but see* Still v. DeBuono, 101 F.3d 888 (2d Cir. 1996) (services need not be provided by qualified personnel to receive reimbursement where there is a shortage of the providers).

89. 20 U.S.C § 1439; 34 C.F.R. § 303.400.

90. 20 U.S.C. § 1432(4); 34 C.F.R. § 303.521(b); *see* Kemmer Inquiry, 18 Individuals with Disabilities Educ. L. Rep. (LRP) 624 (OSEP 1991). The Kemmer Inquiry also indicates that the attorney's fees provisions are not applicable to Part C.

91. 20 U.S.C. § 1439(a); 34 C.F.R. §§ 303.420–423, 460(a).

92. Bucks County Dept. of Mental Health/Mental Retardation v. Pennsylvania, 379 F.3d 61 (3rd Cir. 2004) (as a matter of first impression that reimbursement to parent for the time she personally spent working with her disabled daughter after county refused to provide the therapy constituted appropriate relief under the IDEA).

93. 20 U.S.C. § 1415(e); 34 C.F.R. § 303.419. These mediation procedures are very similar to those provided for under IDEA. States, however, may establish its own system for mediation.

- The continuation of early intervention services during the pendency or the stay-put provision of a dispute unless there is another agreement. If the parents are applying for initial services then the child shall receive those services not in dispute.[94]

18.9 Comparison of IDEA and ITDA

ITDA recognizes that early intervention is not limited to education alone, but also includes a combination of services designed to meet the needs of infants and toddlers across a range of domains.[95] ITDA, therefore, reflects the need to provide services in conjunction with multiple agencies. It also serves to strengthen some of the weaker aspects of IDEA.

One main difference is the age and criteria for eligibility. ITDA serves eligible birth through age two population. IDEA serves children and youth from ages 3–21.[96]

Under IDEA, children with disabilities must be identified under one of the many categories of disabling conditions and be in need of special education and related services.[97] These impairments must "adversely" affect their educational performance as well. Under ITDA, categorization as disabled is not necessary. Rather there are three potential groups who could qualify for early intervention services.[98] ITDA, therefore, tends to avoid labeling that may later lead to problems with self-esteem and discrimination in providing services.

Another major difference between IDEA and ITDA is the role of the family. The family's role is expanded in ITDA beyond the parental input required by IDEA.[99] ITDA requires the family to become an integral part of the process. The IFSP includes the family's strengths and needs in relationship to the child's development, the outcomes expected to be achieved by the parents, and the services necessary to meet the unique needs of both the child and family.[100]

The role of agencies is also different between IDEA and ITDA. Under IDEA, one agency, the state education agency, has ultimate responsibility, although other agencies may actually provide services.[101] Under ITDA, the lead agency may be any designated

---

94. 20 U.S.C. § 1439(b); Pardini v. Allegheny Intermediate Unit, 420 F.3d 181 (3d Cir. 2005) (IDEA's stay-put provision mandated continuation of services). In *Pardini* the parents of three-year-old child with cerebral palsy, challenged education agency's transition of the child's individual family service plan (IFSP) to the individualized education plan (IEP) under IDEA and sought continued provision of certain therapeutic services to child while the parties disputed the child's proposed IEP); *see also* E.P. v. School Bd. of Broward County 483 F.3d 725 (11th Cir. 2007) (IDEA did not provide for continued provision of services to the students pursuant to their Individualized Family Service Plans (IFSP) after they turned three; *but see* 34 C.F.R. § 300.518(c) (2006 IDEA) (if the complaint, however, "involves an application for initial services under this part from a child who is transitioning from Part C of the Act to Part B and is no longer eligible for Part C services because the child has turned three, the public agency is not required to provide the Part C services that the child had been receiving.").
95. 132 Cong. Rec. 13504 (1986) (Senator Stafford).
96. Letter to Anonymous, 2 Early Childhood Law & Policy Rep. (LRP) 117 (OSERS 1995) (children who turn three during summer must receive an extended school year if needed for FAPE).
97. 20 U.S.C. § 1401(3)(A).
98. See § 18.4.
99. 1997 IDEA and 1999 regulations provide for increased parental input.
100. 20 U.S.C. §§ 1436(d)(2)–(4).
101. 20 U.S.C. § 1412(11) (other state agencies may ensure that the requirements of Part B are met for students with disabilities convicted as adults and incarcerated in adult prisons).

agency assuming major responsibility for administering the program. In addition, under ITDA, a state Interagency Coordinating Council (ICC) assists the lead agency in the development and implementation of its statewide system.[102]

Responsibilities of the ICC include defining contracting and reimbursement responsibilities between the agencies, ensuring the coordinated delivery of services to all children with disabilities and their families, assisting the lead agency in the resolution of disputes, and assisting the transition to preschool and other services.[103] Thus, while IDEA obligates the education agency, ITDA places the responsibility in multiple agencies with the lead agency having extensive input from the ICC. Practically speaking this means that the educational agency has responsibility for developing, implementing and financing the IEP.[104] Under ITDA there is a greater interdependence of both public and private agencies.

The multiagency approach has several advantages. One is the wide spectrum of services which can be provided.[105] Further, interagency coordination maximizes use of community resources,[106] reduces duplication of services,[107] balances the influence of a variety of agencies,[108] and balances funding.[109] There are several other relevant comparisons. Following is a chart.

Comparison IDEA & ITDA

	IDEA	*ITDA*
Definition of Parent	Yes	Same
Surrogates	Yes	Same
Lead Agency	Education	Governor designated & ICC
Interagency Agreements	For transition services	For all services
Cost for Services	None	None, but State Law may require it for specific services
Personnel Qualifications	Yes	Same
Funding Statute	Yes	Yes
Child Find	Yes	Same
Evaluations		
Multidisciplinary	Yes	Same
Nondiscriminatory	Yes	Same

---

102. 20 U.S.C. § 1441(e)(1)(A) and (e)(2); 34 C.F.R. § 303.650(1).
103. 20 U.S.C. § 1441(e)(1).
104. H.R. Rep. No. 860, 99th Cong., at 94 (1986).
105. *Id.* at 121 (testimony of Charlotte Jones Fraas, Specialist in Education).
106. *Id.* at 295.
107. *Id.*
108. *Id.* at 153.
109. *Id.*

Reevaluations	Yes	Same
Ages of Eligibility	3–21	0–2
Disabling Conditions	13 categories	Developmental delay
Types of Services	Fewer	More, e.g.,? Nursing, Nutrition
Educational Plan	IEP Student focus Annual review	IFSP Family focus Annual & 6 months
Notice	Yes	Same
Consent	Yes	Same
Parental Involvement	Yes	Yes, more involvement
Procedural Protections	Yes	Same
Responsible Agency	SEA, LEA	Lead
Examination of Records	Yes	Same
Confidentiality of Information	Yes	Same
Complaint to SEA/Lead Agency	Yes	Yes
Complaint	Written procedures	Same
Timelines	60 days	Same, can use IDEA's
Due Process Hearing	Yes	Yes, can use same system
Due Process Time Line	45 days	30 days
Status of Child Pending Dispute Resolution	Stay-put	Same
Judicial Action Following Hearing	Yes	Same
Attorney's Fees	Yes	No

Appendix 1
Note to Nonlawyers

The Individuals with Disabilities Education Act is a Federal statute. Each state in turn has adopted statutes implementing special education requirements. As a general matter, a state may provide more protection or insure additional rights not required by IDEA. States may not, however, offer fewer services, protections, or rights. This book is intended as an overview of the law that applies in all jurisdictions, we have, therefore, focused on the federal statute and on federal cases.

This book is not intended to act as a substitute for legal counsel. On the other hand, it is clearly intended that the book provide practical information for day-to-day use by educational professionals as well as lawyers.

Many of the footnotes will be most useful for lawyers wishing to conduct further legal research. For nonlawyers, we offer the following, brief explanation of the legal citations.

U.S.C.

United States Code. These volumes are the compilation of federal statutes.

C.F.R.

Code of Federal Regulations. These volumes contain the compilation of regulations promulgated by federal agencies pursuant to authority Congress has granted in the statutes contained in the United States Code. In this work we cite primarily regulations developed by the United States Department of Education.

F. Supp.

Federal Supplement. This is the reporter service publishing United States District Court opinions. The United States District Court is the general trial court in the federal system. Not all decisions of the District Court are printed. In fact, the percentage of decisions printed is quite low. Each state has at least one United States District Court. Most states have several, each covering a particular geographic area. Virginia, for example, has two: the Eastern District and the Western District. New Hampshire, on the other hand, has one.

F. Supp. 2d

Federal Supplement, Second. This is a continuation of the Federal Supplement. Rather than have volume numbers greater than 1000, the publisher began renumbering in a new series.

F.2d

> Federal Reporter, Second. This reporter reprints United States Circuit Court of Appeals opinions. Appeals from the United States District Courts go to a Circuit Court of Appeals covering a particular region within the country. The Fourth Circuit Court, for example, hears appeals from United States District Courts in Maryland, North Carolina, Virginia, West Virginia, and South Carolina. This structure of appellate courts means that the various appellate courts can reach directly contrary results on the same issue. It is not unusual for Circuit Courts to disagree on an interpretation of the law. When this happens, district courts will apply the law as interpreted by the Circuit Court to which appeals from that district go. The existence of a significant split among the Circuit Courts is one criterion the United States Supreme Court uses when deciding whether to hear a case.

F.3d

> Federal Reporter, Third. Same as F.2d, simply later cases.

U.S.

> United States Reporter. This reporter reprints opinions of the United States Supreme Court. The United States Supreme Court, as a general matter, does not have to hear education cases on appeal from the Circuit Courts. A party wishing to appeal beyond the Circuit Court must seek a discretionary grant of a *writ of certiorari*. The Supreme Court actually reviews very few cases. Among the reasons that the Court will grant a *writ of certiorari* is that the Circuit Courts have reached differing opinions on a particular issue.

S. Ct.

> Supreme Court Reporter. Before the United States Reporter is printed, United States Supreme Court cases appear in this reporter.

Educ. Handicapped L. Rep. (CRR)

> Education of the Handicapped Law Reporter. This reporter specializes in reporting cases dealing with special education issues. This service reports cases cited in other reporters as well as other useful information including cases not reported in the previous mentioned reporters, opinions of OSEP, OSERS, and OCR, and selected state administrative decisions.

Individuals with Disabilities Educ. L. Rep. (LRP)

> Individuals with Disabilities Law Reporter. The Education for all Handicapped Law Reporter was renamed in 1991. It also contains the complete text of IDEA and its regulations.

Early Childhood Law & Policy Rep. (LRP)

Early Childhood Law and Policy Reporter. This reporter, published by the same company that publishes the Individuals with Disabilities Law Reporter, publishes the same type of material, but focuses on the Infants and Toddlers with Disabilities Act.

Appendix 2
Education Directory of States and Territories

Alabama
Alabama Department of Education
Gordon Persons Office Building
50 North Ripley Street
P.O. Box 302101
Montgomery, AL 36104-3833
Phone: (334) 242-9700
Fax: (334) 242-9708
Email: dmurray@alsde.edu
Website:
http://www.alsde.edu/html/home.asp

Alaska
Alaska Department of Education and
Early Development
Suite 200
801 West 10th Street
P.O. Box 110500
Juneau, AK 99811-0500
Phone: (907) 465-2800
Fax: (907) 465-4156
TTY: (907) 465-2815
Email: dorothy_knuth@eed.state.ak.us or
webmaster@eed.state.ak.us
Website: http://www.eed.state.ak.us/

Arizona
Arizona Department of Education
1535 West Jefferson Street
Phoenix, AZ 85007
Phone: (602) 542-4361
Toll-Free: (800) 352-4558
Fax: (602) 542-5440
Email: ADEINBOX@ade.az.gov
Website: http://www.ade.az.gov/

Arkansas
Arkansas Department of Education
Room 304A
Four State Capitol Mall
Little Rock, AR 72201-1071
Phone: (501) 682-4204
Fax: (501) 682-1079
Email: Ken.James@arkansas.gov
Website: http://ArkansasEd.org/

California
California Department of Education
1430 N Street
Sacramento, CA 95814-5901
Phone: (916) 319-0800
Fax: (916) 319-0100
Email: joconnell@cde.ca.gov
Website: http://www.cde.ca.gov/

Colorado
State Department of Education (Colorado)
201 East Colfax Avenue
Denver, CO 80203-1704
Phone: (303) 866-6600
Fax: (303) 830-0793
Email: howerter_c@cde.state.co.us
Website: http://www.cde.state.co.us/

Connecticut
Connecticut Department of Education
State Office Building
165 Capitol Avenue
Hartford, CT 06106-1630
Phone: (860) 713-6548
Toll-Free: (800) 465-4014
Fax: (860) 713-7001
Email: mark.mcquillan@ct.gov
Website: http://www.sde.ct.gov/

Delaware
Delaware Department of Education
Suite Two
401 Federal Street
Dover, DE 19901-3639
Phone: (302) 735-4000
Fax: (302) 739-4654
Email: mcollier@doe.k12.de.us or
vwoodruff@doe.k12.de.us
Website: http://www.doe.state.de.us/

District of Columbia

District of Columbia Public Schools
Ninth Floor
825 North Capitol Street, NE
Washington, DC 20002
Phone: (202) 442-5885

Fax: (202) 442-5026
Email: ContactDCPS@k12.dc.us
Website: http://www.k12.dc.us/

Florida

Florida Department of Education
Turlington Building
Suite 1514
325 West Gaines Street
Tallahassee, FL 32399-0400
Phone: (850) 245-0505
Fax: (850) 245-9667
Email: nyla.benjamin@fldoe.org or commissioner@fldoe.org
Website: http://www.fldoe.org/

Georgia

Georgia Department of Education
2066 Twin Towers East
205 Jesse Hill Jr. Drive, SE
Atlanta, GA 30334-5001
Phone: (404) 656-2800
Toll-Free: (800) 311-3627
Toll-Free Restrictions: GA residents only
Fax: (404) 651-8737
Email: brturner@doe.k12.ga.us or kathy-cox@doe.k12.ga.us
Website:
http://public.doe.k12.ga.us/index.aspx

Hawaii

Hawaii Department of Education
Systems Accountability Office
Room 411
1390 Miller Street
Honolulu, HI 96813
Phone: (808) 586-3283
Fax: (808) 586-3440
Email:
robert_mcclelland@notes.k12.hi.us
Website: http://doe.k12.hi.us/

Idaho

Department of Education (Idaho)
Len B. Jordan Office Building
650 West State Street
P.O. Box 83720
Boise, ID 83720-0027
Phone: (208) 332-6800
Toll-Free: (800) 432-4601
Toll-Free Restrictions: ID residents only
Fax: (208) 334-2228
TTY: (800) 377-3529
Email: news@sde.state.id.us
Website: http://www.sde.state.id.us/Dept/

Illinois

Illinois State Board of Education
100 North First Street
Springfield, IL 62777
Phone: (217) 782-4321
Toll-Free: (866) 262-6663
Toll-Free Restrictions: IL residents only
Fax: (217) 524-4928
TTY: (217) 782-1900
Email: cgroves@isbe.net or
statesup@isbe.net
Website: http://www.isbe.net/

Indiana

Indiana Department of Education
State House, Room 229
Indianapolis, IN 46204-2795
Phone: (317) 232-6610
Fax: (317) 233-6326
Email: webmaster@doe.state.in.us
Website: http://www.doe.state.in.us/

Iowa

Iowa Department of Education
Grimes State Office Building
400 East 14th Street
Des Moines, IA 50319-0146
Phone: (515) 281-3436
Fax: (515) 281-4122
Email: kathy.petosa@iowa.gov
Website: http://www.state.ia.us/educate/

Kansas

Kansas Department of Education
120 South East 10th Avenue
Topeka, KS 66612-1182
Phone: (785) 296-3201
Fax: (785) 296-7933
TTY: (785) 296-6338
Email: lasnider@ksde.org or
aposny@ksde.org
Website: http://www.ksde.org/

Kentucky

Kentucky Department of Education
Capital Plaza Tower
First Floor
500 Mero Street
Frankfort, KY 40601
Phone: (502) 564-2000
Fax: (502) 564-3049
Email: webmaster@education.ky.gov
Website: http://www.education.ky.gov

Louisiana

Louisiana Department of Education
1201 North Third
P.O. Box 94064
Baton Rouge, LA 70804-9064
Phone: (225) 342-4411
Toll-Free: (877) 453-2721
Fax: (225) 342-0781
Email: customerservice@la.gov
Website:
http://www.louisianaschools.net/lde/inde
x.html

Maine

Maine Department of Education
Burton M. Cross State Office Building
111 Sewall Street
23 State House Station
Augusta, ME 04333-0023
Phone: (207) 624-6600
Fax: (207) 624-6601
TTY: (207) 624-6800
Email: tammy.morrill@maine.gov or
susan.gendron@maine.gov
Website:
http://www.maine.gov/portal/education/

Maryland

State Department of Education (Maryland)
200 West Baltimore Street
Baltimore, MD 21201
Phone: (410) 767-0100
Fax: (410) 333-6033
Email: rpeiffer@msde.state.md.us
Website: http://www.marylandpublic-schools.org/MSDE

Massachusetts

Massachusetts Department of Education
350 Main Street
Malden, MA 02148
Phone: (781) 338-3000
Fax: (781) 338-3395
TTY: (800) 439-2370
Email: www@doe.mass.edu
Website: http://www.doe.mass.edu/

Michigan

Michigan Department of Education
P.O. Box 30008
608 West Allegan Street
Lansing, MI 48909
Phone: (517) 373-3324
Fax: (517) 335-4565
Email: thelens3@michigan.gov or
schaferm@michigan.gov
Website: http://www.michigan.gov/mde/

Minnesota

Minnesota Department of Education
1500 Highway 36 West
Roseville, MN 55113-4266
Phone: (651) 582-8200
Fax: (651) 582-8727
TTY: (651) 582-8201
Email: mde.commissioner@state.mn.us
or alice.seagren@state.mn.us
Website:
http://education.state.mn.us/mde/index.
html

Mississippi
Mississippi Department of Education
Central High School
359 North West Street
P.O. Box 771
Jackson, MS 39205
Phone: (601) 359-3513
Fax: (601) 359-3242
Email: cblanton@mde.k12.ms.us
Website: http://www.mde.k12.ms.us/

Missouri
Missouri Department of Elementary and
Secondary Education
205 Jefferson Street
P.O. Box 480
Jefferson City, MO 65102-0480
Phone: (573) 751-4212
Fax: (573) 751-8613
TTY: (800) 735-2966
Email: pubinfo@dese.mo.gov
Website: http://dese.mo.gov/

Montana
Montana Office of Public Instruction
P.O. Box 202501
Helena, MT 59620-2501
Phone: (406) 444-2082
Toll-Free: (888) 231-9393
Toll-Free Restrictions: Montana residents
only
Fax: (406) 444-3924
Email: cbergeron@mt.gov
Website: http://www.opi.mt.gov/

Nebraska
Nebraska Department of Education
301 Centennial Mall South, Sixth Floor
P.O. Box 94987
Lincoln, NE 68509-4987
Phone: (402) 471-2295
Fax: (402) 471-0117
TTY: (402) 471-7295
Email: john.clark@nde.ne.gov or
doug.christensen@nde.ne.gov
Website: http://www.nde.state.ne.us/

Nevada
Nevada Department of Education
700 East Fifth Street
Carson City, NV 89701
Phone: (775) 687-9217
Fax: (775) 687-9202
Email: darnold@doe.nv.gov
Website: http://www.doe.nv.gov/

New Hampshire
New Hampshire Department of Education
Hugh J. Gallan State Office Park
101 Pleasant Street
Concord, NH 03301
Phone: (603) 271-3495
Toll-Free: (800) 339-9900
Fax: (603) 271-1953
TTY: Relay NH 711
Email: lkincaid@ed.state.nh.us
Website: http://www.ed.state.nh.us

New Jersey
New Jersey Department of Education
P.O. Box 500
100 Riverview Plaza
Trenton, NJ 08625-0500
Phone: (609) 292-4469
Fax: (609) 777-4099
Website: http://www.state.nj.us/education/

New Mexico
New Mexico Public Education Department
300 Don Gaspar
Santa Fe, NM 87501-2786
Phone: (505) 827-5800
Fax: (505) 827-6520
Email: Bev.Friedman@state.nm.us or
lori.bachman@state.nm.us
Website: http://www.ped.state.nm.us/

New York
New York State Education Department
Education Building
Room 111
89 Washington Avenue
Albany, NY 12234
Phone: (518) 474-5844
Fax: (518) 473-4909
Email: rmills@mail.nysed.gov
Website: http://www.nysed.gov/

North Carolina
Department of Public Instruction (North Carolina)
301 North Wilmington Street
Raleigh, NC 27601
Phone: (919) 807-3300
Fax: (919) 807-3445
Email: information@dpi.state.nc.us
Website:
http://www.ncpublicschools.org/

North Dakota
North Dakota Department of Public Instruction
Department 201
600 East Boulevard Avenue
Bismarck, ND 58505-0440
Phone: (701) 328-2260
Fax: (701) 328-2461
Email: lnorbeck@nd.gov or
wsanstead@nd.gov
Website: http://www.dpi.state.nd.us/

Ohio
Ohio Department of Education
25 South Front Street
Columbus, OH 43215-4183
Phone: (614) 466-4839
Toll-Free: (877) 644-6338
Fax: (614) 728-9300
TTY: (888) 886-0181
Email: patricia.grey@ode.state.oh.us or
susan.zelman@ode.state.oh.us
Website: http://www.ode.state.oh.us/

Oklahoma
Oklahoma State Department of Education
2500 North Lincoln Boulevard
Oklahoma City, OK 73105-4599
Phone: (405) 521-3301
Fax: (405) 521-6205
Email: sandy_garrett@sde.state.ok.us
Website: http://sde.state.ok.us/

Oregon
Oregon Department of Education
255 Capitol Street, NE
Salem, OR 97310-0203
Phone: (503) 947-5600
Fax: (503) 378-5156
TTY: (503) 378-2892
Email: gene.evans@state.or.us
Website: http://www.ode.state.or.us/

Pennsylvania
Pennsylvania Department of Education
333 Market Street
Harrisburg, PA 17126-0333
Phone: (717) 787-5820
Fax: (717) 787-7222
TTY: (717) 783-8445
Email: 00admin@state.pa.us
Website: http://www.pde.state.pa.us/

Rhode Island
Rhode Island Department of Elementary and Secondary Education
255 Westminster Street
Providence, RI 02903-3400
Phone: (401) 222-4600
Fax: (401) 222-6178
TTY: (800) 745-5555
Email: maureen.dandrea@ride.ri.gov
Website: http://www.ridoe.net/

South Carolina

South Carolina Department of Education
1006 Rutledge Building
1429 Senate Street
Columbia, SC 29201
Phone: (803) 734-8815
Fax: (803) 734-3389
Email: cclark@ed.sc.gov or
info@ed.sc.gov
Website: http://ed.sc.gov/

South Dakota

Department of Education (South Dakota)
700 Governors Drive
Pierre, SD 57501-2291
Phone: (605) 773-5669
Fax: (605) 773-6139
TTY: (605) 773-6302
Email: betty.leidholt@state.sd.us or
deb.barnett@state.sd.us
Website: http://doe.sd.gov/

Tennessee

Tennessee State Department of Education
Andrew Johnson Tower, Sixth Floor
710 James Robertson Parkway
Nashville, TN 37243-0375
Phone: (615) 741-2731
Fax: (615) 532-4791
Email: Education.Comments@state.tn.us
Website: http://www.state.tn.us/education/

Texas

Texas Education Agency
William B. Travis Building
1701 North Congress Avenue
Austin, TX 78701-1494
Phone: (512) 463-9734
Fax: (512) 463-9838
TTY: (512) 475-3540
Email: teainfo@tea.state.tx.us
Website: http://www.tea.state.tx.us/

Utah

Utah State Office of Education
250 East 500 South
P.O. Box 144200
Salt Lake City, UT 84114-4200
Phone: (801) 538-7500
Fax: (801) 538-7521
Email: mark.peterson@schools.utah.gov
Website: http://www.schools.utah.gov/

Vermont

Vermont Department of Education
120 State Street
Montpelier, VT 05620-2501
Phone: (802) 828-3135
Fax: (802) 828-3140
TTY: (802) 828-2755
Email: edinfo@state.vt.us or helen.oatley@state.vt.us
Website: http://www.education.vermont.gov/

Virginia

Virginia Department of Education
P.O. Box 2120
James Monroe Building
101 North 14th Street
Richmond, VA 23218-2120
Phone: (804) 225-2420
Email: charles.pyle@doe.virginia.gov
Website: http://www.doe.virginia.gov/

Washington

Office of Superintendent of Public Instruction (Washington)
Old Capitol Building
600 South Washington
P.O. Box 47200
Olympia, WA 98504-7200
Phone: (360) 725-6000
Fax: (360) 753-6712
TTY: (360) 664-3631
Email: karen.conway@k12.wa.us
Website: http://www.k12.wa.us/

West Virginia
West Virginia Department of Education
Building 6, Room 358
1900 Kanawha Boulevard East
Charleston, WV 25305-0330
Phone: (304) 558-2681
Fax: (304) 558-0048
Email: dvermill@access.k12.wv.us
Website: http://wvde.state.wv.us/

Wisconsin
Department of Public Instruction (Wisconsin)
125 South Webster Street
P.O. Box 7841
Madison, WI 53707-7841
Phone: (608) 266-3108
Toll-Free: (800) 441-4563
Fax: (608) 266-2529
TTY: (608) 267-2427
Email: kay.ihlenfeldt@dpi.state.wi.us
Website: http://dpi.wi.gov/

Wyoming
Wyoming Department of Education
Hathaway Building
Second Floor
2300 Capitol Avenue
Cheyenne, WY 82002-0050
Phone: (307) 777-7675
Fax: (307) 777-6234
TTY: (307) 777-8546
Email: supt@educ.state.wy.us
Website: http://www.k12.wy.us/index.asp

Native American Education Programs
U.S. Department of the Interior Bureau
of Indian Affairs
Office of Indian Education Programs
1849 C Street, NW/MS - 3512 MIB
Washington, DC 20240-0001
www.oiep.bia.edu
1-866-703-7100

Territories

American Samoa
Special Education
Department of Education
Pago Pago, American Samoa 96799 (684)
633-1323
www.doe.as

Department of Education: Special Education
Suzanne Lizama, Acting Coordinator
CNMI Public School System, Special Education
P.O. Box 501370
Saipan, MP 96950
(670) 237-3029
Web: www.pss.cnmi.mp

Federated States Of Micronesia National Government
FSM Adult Education Program
Department of Education
FSM National Government
PO Box PS 87
Palikir, Pohnpei, FM 96941
011-691-320-2609/2647/2302
fax 011-691-320-5500/5504
email: ccantero@literacynet.org

Commonwealth of the Northern Marina Islands (CNMI) Public School System
Special Education Programs
P.O. Box 1370
Saipan, MP 96950
Contact: Barbara T. Rudy, (670) 322-9956

Republic of Palau
P.O. Box 278
Koror, PW 96940
(680) 488-2568

Guam
Guam Public School System
P.O. Box DE
Hagatna, GU 96932
Phone: (671) 475-0462
Fax: (671) 472-5003
Email: lreyes@gdoe.net or
icsantos@gdoe.net
Website: http://www.gdoe.net/

Puerto Rico
Puerto Rico Department of Education
P.O. Box 190759
San Juan, PR 00919-0759
Phone: (787) 759-2000
Fax: (787) 250-0275
Email: webmaster@ogp.gobierno.pr
Website: http://www.gobierno.pr/GPR-
Portal/Inicio/EducacionEInvestigacion/D
E.ht ...

Virgin Islands
Virgin Islands Department of Education
1834 Kongens Gade
Charlotte Amalie, VI 00802
Phone: (340) 774-2810
Fax: (340) 779-7153
Email: ejcorneiro@excite.com
Website: http://www.doe.vi/

Appendix 3
United States Department of Education Addresses

U.S. Department of Education
Office for Civil Rights
Customer Service Team
400 Maryland Avenue, SW
Washington, D.C. 20202-1100 Telephone: 1-800-421-3481
FAX: 202-245-6840; TDD: 877-521-2172
Email: OCR@ed.gov

Office of Special Education Programs
Office of Special Education and Rehabilitative Services
U.S. Department of Education
400 Maryland Ave., S.W.
Washington, DC 20202-7100
Telephone: (202) 245-7459

Regional Offices Office for Civil Rights

EASTERN DIVISION

Serving Connecticut, Maine, Massachusetts, New Hampshire, Rhode Island, Vermont

Boston Office
Office for Civil Rights
U.S. Department of Education
33 Arch Street, Suite 900
Boston, MA 02110-1491
Telephone: 617-289-0111
FAX: 617-289-0150; TDD: 877-521-2172
Email: OCR.Boston@ed.gov

Serving New York, New Jersey, Puerto Rico, Virgin Islands

New York Office
Office for Civil Rights
U.S. Department of Education
32 Old Slip, 26th Floor
New York, NY 10005-2500
Telephone: 646-428-3900
FAX: 646-428-3843; TDD: 877-521-2172
Email: OCR.NewYork@ed.gov

Serving Delaware, District of Columbia, Maryland, Pennsylvania, West Virginia

Philadelphia Office
Office for Civil Rights
U.S. Department of Education
100 Penn Square East, Suite 515
Philadelphia, PA 19107-3323
Telephone: 215-656-8541
FAX: 215-656-8605; TDD: 877-521-2172
Email: OCR_Philadelphia@ed.gov

SOUTHERN DIVISION
Serving Alabama, Florida, Georgia, South Carolina, Tennessee

Atlanta Office
Office for Civil Rights
U.S. Department of Education
61 Forsyth St. S.W., Suite 19T70
Atlanta, GA 30303-3104
Telephone: 404-562-6350
FAX: 404-562-6455; TDD: 877-521-2172
Email: OCR.Atlanta@ed.gov

Serving Arkansas, Louisiana, Mississippi, Oklahoma, Texas

Dallas Office
Office for Civil Rights
U.S. Department of Education
1999 Bryan Street, Suite 1620
Dallas, Texas 75201-6810
Telephone: 214-661-9600
FAX: 214-661-9587; TDD: 877-521-2172
Email: OCR.Dallas@ed.gov

Serving North Carolina, Virginia, Washington, D.C.

District of Columbia Office
Office for Civil Rights
U.S. Department of Education
1100 Pennsylvania Ave., N.W., Rm. 316
P.O. Box 14620
Washington, D.C. 20044-4620
Telephone: 202-786-0500
FAX: 202-208-7797; TDD: 877-521-2172
Email: OCR.DC@ed.gov

MIDWESTERN DIVISION

Serving Iowa, Illinois, Indiana, Minnesota, North Dakota, Wisconsin

Office for Civil Rights
U.S. Department of Education
Citigroup Center
500 W. Madison Street, Suite 1475
Chicago, IL 60661
Telephone: 312-730-1560
FAX: 312-730-1576; TDD: 877-521-2172
Email: OCR.Chicago@ed.gov

Serving Michigan and Ohio

Office for Civil Rights
U.S. Department of Education
600 Superior Avenue East, Suite 750
Cleveland, OH 44114-2611
Telephone: 216-522-4970
FAX: 216-522-2573; TDD: 877-521-2172
Email: OCR.Cleveland@ed.gov

Serving, Kansas, Missouri, Nebraska, South Dakota

Kansas City Office
Office for Civil Rights
U.S. Department of Education
8930 Ward Parkway, Suite 2037
Kansas City, MO 64114-3302
Telephone: 816-268-0550
FAX: 816-823-1404; TDD: 877-521-2172
Email: OCR.KansasCity@ed.gov

WESTERN DIVISION

Serving Arizona, Colorado, Montana, New Mexico, Utah, Wyoming

Office for Civil Rights
U.S. Department of Education
Cesar E. Chavez Memorial Building
1244 Speer Boulevard, Suite 310
Denver, CO 80204-3582
Telephone: 303-844-5695
FAX: 303-844-4303; TDD: 877-521-2172
Email: OCR.Denver@ed.gov

Serving California

Office for Civil Rights
U.S. Department of Education
50 Beale Street, Suite 7200
San Francisco, CA 94105
Telephone: 415-486-5555
FAX: 415-486-5570; TDD: 877-521-2172
Email: ocr.sanfrancisco@ed.gov

Serving Alaska, Hawaii, Idaho, Nevada, Oregon, Washington, Guam, American Samoa, Trust Territory of Pacific Islands Wake Island

Seattle Office
Office for Civil Rights
U.S. Department of Education
915 Second Avenue Room 3310,
Seattle, WA 98174-1099
Telephone: 206-220-7900
FAX: 206-220-7887; TDD: 877-521-2172
Email: OCR.Seattle@ed.gov

Appendix 4
Forms

PRIOR NOTICE

The [School Division Name] offers many special programs and services. In order to better meet the educational needs of your child, [Child's Name], a formal evaluation is needed.

All components of the evaluation are available at no cost to the parent.

The purpose of the evaluation is as follows:

1. _____ (Initial evaluation) This evaluation is to determine the eligibility of your child for special education and related services. Before we can begin formal initial evaluation we must have your written permission to give the evaluation(s) checked below.

2. _____ (Triennial evaluation) This evaluation is to be conducted every three years to see if your child continues to be eligible for special education and related services. Your written permission is required to give the formal evaluation(s) checked below.

3. _____ (Other) This evaluation is being conducted because the division needs to determine whether the child has a disability or continues to have a disability; the present level of performance and educational needs; whether the child needs services; and whether modifications or additions are needed for the child to meet goals in the IEP and to participate as appropriate in the general curriculum. Your written permission is required to give the evaluation(s) checked below.[1]

Attached you will find a copy of procedural safeguards which explain your rights pertaining to the proposed action(s).

_____EDUCATIONAL: Written report describing current educational performance and identifying instructional strengths and weaknesses in academic skills and language performance.

_____MEDICAL: Written report from a licensed physician indicating general medical history and any medical/health problems which may impede learning.

_____SOCIO-CULTURAL: Written report from a qualified visiting teacher or school social worker based on information collected through social appraisal instruments which shall include background and social/adaptive behavior in home, school, and community.

---

1. These are just examples of evaluations the school may request permission to conduct.

____PSYCHOLOGICAL: Written report from a qualified psychologist based on the use of a battery of appropriate instruments, which include individual intelligence test(s) and psychoeducational tests.

____DEVELOPMENTAL: Written report of assessment of how your child functions in the major areas of development such as cognition, motor, social/adaptive behavior, perception, and communication.

____SPEECH AND LANGUAGE: Written report to evaluate your child's articulation, voice fluency, and expressive and receptive language skills.

____OTHER RECOMMENDED EVALUATIONS OR CHECKLISTS (i.e., audiological, vision, occupational therapy, physical therapy, psychiatric, hearing screening, or other assessment components as appropriate and as specified below).

These evaluations are given as examples of those that may need to be conducted. The law requires that the child be assessed in all areas of suspected disability.

_____

Signature of School Official

_____

Title

_____

Date

CONSENT

I give permission for [Public School Division] to proceed with the evaluation of my
child in order to determine whether or not [Child's Name] is eligible for special education and related services. I have received a copy of the procedural safeguards
and I understand these rights.

_____
Signature(s) of Parent, Guardian,
or Surrogate

_____
Date

* * *

I DO NOT give permission for [Public School Division] to proceed with the evaluation
of my child in order to determine whether or not [Child's Name] is eligible for special education and related services. I have received a copy of the procedural safeguards and I understand these rights.

_____
Signature(s) of Parent, Guardian,
or Surrogate

_____
Date

NOTICE OF PROCEDURAL SAFEGUARDS

As a parent(s)/guardian(s) or surrogate parent of a child with a disability or a child who is suspected of having a disability, you should know and understand the procedural safeguards that are in effect to protect your rights and those of your child.

Your child has the right to a free appropriate public education (FAPE) in the least restrictive environment (your child is to be educated with children without disabilities and who are age appropriate children to the maximum extent appropriate). Special education and related services, including all assessments needed for a comprehensive evaluation, are provided at no cost to parent(s).

RIGHTS IN ASSESSMENT

1. You must give written permission before your child is given individual tests or evaluations for the first time and for any reevaluations.

2. You must be informed of the nature of tests and evaluations utilized by the school division to assess your child.

3. You have the right to have your child assessed in a non-discriminatory manner, thus tests and evaluations must not be either culturally or racially biased and must be validated. The assessments must include information related to enabling the child to be involved in and make progress in the general curriculum.

4. You have the right to have your child evaluated in all areas of the suspected disability.

5. You have the right to be part of the team that reviews the data.

6. You have the right to an independent educational evaluation or evaluation of your child at public expense if you disagree with the evaluation conducted by the school division. The school division may also initiate a due process hearing to show that its evaluation is appropriate. If the final decision is that the evaluation is appropriate, the parent still has the right to an independent evaluation, but not at public expense.

7. If you obtain an independent evaluation at your own expense the school division must consider it in developing the IEP.

RIGHTS TO PRIOR NOTICE AND CONSENT

1. The parent of a child with a disability must be given written notice before the school division proposes (or refuses) to initiate or change the identification, evaluation, or educational placement of the child.

2. You have a right to written notice regarding transfer of parental rights when your disabled child reaches the age of majority.

3. Consent is required for the preplacement evaluation, initial placement, and reevaluations. Consent is voluntary and may be revoked at any time.

RIGHTS IN PARTICIPATION

1. The parent is assured of the opportunity for participation in all conferences including reviewing assessment data, eligibility determination, manifestation determination review, the development of an Individualized Education Program (IEP), and the determination of placement.

2. The parent has a right to receive a copy of the written IEP at no cost.

RIGHTS IN RECORDS

1. You have the right to have your child's evaluations and reports treated in a confidential manner.

2. Your written permission is needed before any confidential information is released to other agencies.

3. You have the right to inspect and review your child's educational records upon request and the school must comply without unnecessary delay and in no case more than 45 days after your request.

4. You have the right to request that information contained in these records be changed or removed if you believe that the information is incorrect, misleading, or in violation of your child's right to privacy. If a disagreement occurs when information in your child's records is challenged, you have the right to be provided an opportunity for a hearing.

RIGHTS IN IMPARTIAL DUE PROCESS HEARING [2]

1. The parent of a child determined or believed to have a disability shall have the right to initiate a hearing, as does the school division, on matters relating to identification, evaluation, or educational placement of the child or the provision of a free appropriate public education to the child. Information may be requested as to whom you should address your request for a hearing.

2. You have the right to:

a. Receive the names of any low cost legal or other relevant services and agencies available.

b. An impartial hearing officer.

c. Bring other persons, including you own attorney or other persons with knowledge or training about disabled children.

---

2. Rights in an expedited hearing may differ slightly. *See* 34 C.F.R. § 300.532.

d. Present evidence, compel attendance of witnesses, and examine or cross-examine witnesses.

e. Have the child present at the hearing.

f. Open the hearing to the public.

g. Prohibit the introduction of evidence not disclosed 5 business days before the hearing.

h. Obtain a written or electronic verbatim recording of the decision.

i. Receive a written copy of the written findings of fact and the decision.

j. Appeal the decision of the local hearing officer (allowed by either party) in dual level state proceedings to the state educational agency who shall conduct an impartial review of the hearing according to state procedures.

k. Bring a civil action in the appropriate court upon completion of all administrative procedures if you are the aggrieved party.[3]

l. Have the hearing completed in forty-five (45) calendar days and when the hearing decision is appealed, the review is to be completed in thirty (30) calendar days.

m. During any administrative or judicial proceedings regarding an appeal, unless the local school division and the parent agree otherwise, the student shall remain in his/her present educational placement.

n. Attorney's Fees - if you are the prevailing party. These fees will not be awarded if you reject a settlement offer from the school division and do not obtain better relief in a subsequent hearing or court action. Other limitations may also apply.

3. Before or during the time that parents seek relief in due process hearings or court action, they may exhaust their school division's mediation/appeal mechanisms. These procedures may not, however, delay the administrative process.

4. You must provide notice to the public agency in requesting a hearing that contains a description of the problem and the proposed resolution to the extent known.

RIGHTS IN PLACEMENT

1. Information which is documented and considered carefully must come from a variety of sources.

---

3. Statute of limitations is 90 days unless state provides other wise.

2. Placement decision must be made by a group of persons including the parents who have knowledge about the child, the evaluation data, and the placement options.

3. Placement must be made in the least restrictive environment with age appropriate peers.

4. Placement must be based on the IEP.

5. If you, on your own and without the agreement of the IEP committee, decide to place your child in an approved private nonsectarian school for children with disabilities, the school division will not be responsible for the cost of the placement, if it is proven by the due process procedure that the school division's proposed placement does provide a free appropriate public education in the least restrictive environment for your child.

FOR ADDITIONAL INFORMATION PLEASE CONTACT YOUR SCHOOL DIVISION AND REQUEST/REFER TO ANY MATERIAL RELATED TO THE RIGHTS OF DISABLED STUDENTS AND THEIR PARENTS UNDER STATE LAW, SECTION 504, ADA, AND IDEA.

ELIGIBILITY COMMITTEE SUMMARY OF DELIBERATIONS

[ ] Initial
[ ] Triennial
[ ] Transfer
[ ] Request by Individual
[ ] Other

Name of Student
          Last   First   Middle

Date of Birth _____ School _____ Grade _____

Student ID Number/Social Security Number _____

Name of Parent(s), Guardian(s) or Surrogate: _____
                                        Last   First   Middle

Address _____
          Number & Street   City/County   Zip

Home Telephone No. _____ Work Telephone No. _____

Name of Person Requesting Evaluation/Reevaluation _____

Eligibility Committee Meeting held _____
                              Month/Day/Year

Reasons for Referral:

_____
_____
_____

Interventions Attempted Prior to Referral:

_____
_____
_____

EVIDENCE OF DELIBERATIONS: The following reports (as appropriate)[1] were presented by school division personnel representing the disciplines providing the assessment components. All evidence was carefully considered. The major points of discussion were:

A. Classroom Observation: (required for suspected LD but recommended for all)

1. The following are recommended multi disciplinary assessments but not required.

Date: _____

_____
_____
_____

B.   Educational:

Date: _____

_____
_____
_____

C.   Medical/Health:

Date: _____

_____
_____
_____

D.   Psychological:

Date: _____

_____
_____
_____

E.   Social/Behavioral/Emotional:

Date: _____

_____
_____
_____

F.   Speech and Language/Communication:

Date: _____

_____
_____
_____

G.   Hearing Test:

Date: _____

_____

_____

_____

H.   Vision:

Date: _____

_____

_____

_____

I.   Other Assessment Reports:

Date: _____

_____

_____

_____

The student is eligible for special education and related services [ ] Yes [ ] No

Identified Disabling Conditions(s) (Complete addendum if LD):

Primary _____

Other Conditions _____

Essential Deliberations Supporting the Findings of the Committee

ADDENDUM TO ELIGIBILITY COMMITTEE
SUMMARY OF DELIBERATIONS FOR LEARNING DISABLED STUDENT

Name of Student: _____
                        Last   First   Middle

Student ID or Social Security Number _____

The above named student was determined to have a specific learning disability.

I.   Basis for making the determination:
     a.   Child does not make sufficient progress to meet age or grade level standards in one of more of the following areas; oral expression, listening comprehension, written expression, basic reading, reading fluency, reading comprehension, mathematical calculation or problem solving.

     b.   List assessments which identify strengths and weaknesses in performance and/or achievement related to age, grade level standards or intellectual development used in determining that a learning disability exists.

     _____
     _____
     _____
     _____

II. Describe instruction provided in regular class and assessments of achievement.

     _____
     _____
     _____
     _____

III. Relevant behavior noted during the observation and the relationship of the behavior to the student's academic functioning:

     _____
     _____
     _____
     _____

IV. Educationally relevant medical findings:

     _____
     _____
     _____
     _____

V. What are the effects of any visual, hearing or motor disability, mental retardation, emotional disturbance, environmental, cultural, economic disadvantage or limited English proficiency as determined by the team?

_____
_____
_____
_____

Support Conclusions and Recommendations

Signatures of Committee Members	Position	Date

Oppose Conclusions and Recommendations

Each dissenting member will attach a statement reflecting their conclusions.

Signatures of Committee Members,	Position	Date

Others in Attendance:

Name	Position	Date

PARENT(S), GUARDIAN(S) OR SURROGATE LETTER OF INITIAL ELIGIBILITY AND IEP

[DATE]

[ADDRESS]

Dear [PARENT(S) NAME]

On [DATE], our Eligibility Committee met to discuss results of the formal evaluation concerning [CHILD'S NAME]. We have determined that your child has the following disabling condition(s):

_____

_____

and is eligible for special education and related services.

Before we are permitted to proceed with developing a program for your child, we must have your written permission, and request your involvement in the writing of an Individualized Education Program (IEP). A meeting has been scheduled as follows:

Date _____   Time: _____

Location: _____

Participants:

        _____

        _____

        _____

        _____

        _____

If this time is not convenient for you, please contact your child's teacher, [TEACHER'S NAME] at [TELEPHONE NUMBER], or principal,[PRINCIPAL'S NAME] at [TELEPHONE NUMBER], to discuss another time.

Attached is a copy of the procedural safeguards. If you would like to discuss this matter, please call me at [TELEPHONE NUMBER].

I look forward to meeting with you.

Sincerely yours,

_____

[TITLE]

PARENT(S), GUARDIAN(S) OR SURROGATE LETTER OF INELIGIBILITY

[DATE]

[ADDRESS]

Dear [PARENT(S) NAME]:

On [DATE], our Eligibility Committee met to discuss results of the formal evaluation concerning [CHILD'S NAME]. We determined, after a careful review and discussion of all the information, that your child is not eligible for special education services at this time. We would be happy to discuss the results of the evaluation with you.

We want to inform you that you have the right to appeal our decision. You have already received a copy of the procedural safeguards. If you would like to discuss this or receive another copy of the procedural safeguards, please call me at [TELEPHONE NUMBER].

Sincerely,

_____

[TITLE]

CONFIDENTIAL

SPECIAL EDUCATION INDIVIDUALIZED EDUCATION PROGRAM

LEA _____

SCHOOL_____

GRADE_____

Name of Student _____
                Last   First   Middle

Date of Birth _____   Age _____

Student ID/Social Security Number: _____

Parent(s)/Guardian(s)/Surrogate Name: _____
                                       Last   First   Middle

Telephone (Home): _____   Work _____

Address _____
           Number & Street   City/County   Zip Code

Most Recent: Eligibility _____   IEP Meeting _____
                            Date   Date

Triennial Date: _____

Disability/Disabilities _____

Beginning Date: _____   Ending Date: _____

PRESENT LEVEL OF EDUCATIONAL PERFORMANCE

Summary of Data/Strengths and Weaknesses to include academic, social, emotional, motor, communication, cognition, and behavior. (**Explain in narrative, test scores alone are insufficient.**)

_____
_____
_____
_____
_____
_____
_____

Services Provided (Type and Intensity of Service)

Special Education /Related Services	Frequency & Duration (per week)	Date to Begin	Anticipated Completion	Location/ Environment/ Provider
_____	_____	_____	_____	_____

Transportation:

[ ] General
    Special (Describe special transportation)

_____
_____
_____

Extent of Participation with Students Without Disabilities:

Subject and/or Activity   Frequency and Duration
                                           (per week)

Physical Education:

_____   _____

_____   _____

Subject and/or Activity   Frequency and Duration
                                   (per week)
Vocational Education:

_____   _____

_____   _____

Recess/Lunch/Other:

_____   _____

_____   _____

Student will participate in _____

(Name of State and District-wide Assessments)

[ ] Yes
[ ] No

If yes, list accommodations/modifications needed:

_____

_____

Alternate Assessment

_____

_____

Reasons why cannot participate in state or district wide assessments

_____

_____

Is it appropriate?
[ ] Yes
[ ] No

List alternative assessments that will be used and benchmarks or short term objectives.

_____

_____

Transition Planning:

[ ] Yes
[ ] No

Measurable Transition Goals:

[ ] Yes
[ ] No

Special Disciplinary Concerns:

[ ] Yes
[ ] No

If yes, please list accommodations:

_____

_____

Behavior Management Plan:

[ ] Yes
[ ] No

ESY:

[ ] Yes
[ ] No

Statement of how the parent will be informed of progress:

_____

_____

INSTRUCTIONAL SECTIONS
(Use Additional Sheets, if Necessary)

Relate to Present Level of Educational Performance:

School _____   Grade _____

Area of instruction _____

Annual Goal (for each area identified *needed*)

Short Term Objectives/Benchmarks[2]	Evaluation Criteria	Evaluation Procedures	Evaluation Schedule	Date Completed
1. _____	_____	_____	_____	_____
2. _____	_____	_____	_____	_____
3. _____	_____	_____	_____	_____
4. _____	_____	_____	_____	_____

2. Required for students taking alternate assessments.

CONFIDENTIAL

JUSTIFICATION FORM

The Least Restrictive Environment has been addressed in placement decision for [NAME OF STUDENT].

Date of Birth _____   Student ID/Social Security No. _____

Check the following items YES or NO. A written explanation for items marked No must be provided.

YES	NO	
[ ]	[ ]	1. The school the student would normally attend, if without disability, is the recommended placement or is the placement. Placement is as close as possible to the student's home.
[ ]	[ ]	2. The student is educated in the regular class with the use of supplementary aids and services.
[ ]	[ ]	3. The student is educated in special education class in the regular school building.
[ ]	[ ]	4. The placement providing educational services required to meet the student's IEP goals is appropriate taking into account the potential harmful effects to the student.
[ ]	[ ]	5. The student is educated with chronologically age appropriate peers (age appropriate to school and class).
[ ]	[ ]	6. The student will participate in a regular physical education program with nondisabled, chronologically age appropriate peers.
[ ]	[ ]	7. The student is educationally integrated with nondisabled chronologically age appropriate peers.
[ ]	[ ]	8. The placement in a more restrictive environment is based on the individualized needs of the student.

After considering all the options on the continuum below, select the appropriate placement and provide a written explanation for the placement chosen, to include why the lesser restrictive placements are not appropriate.

Direct instruction and/or consultative
services within the regular class.   [ ]

Regular class with instruction in the
resource room.   [ ]

Self-contained class with full-time
academic instruction in regular public
school facility; non-academic instruction
with peers.   [ ]

Self-contained class with full-time
academic and non-academic instruction in
regular public school facility.   [ ]

Separate day school.   [ ]

Private day school for disabled.   [ ]

Public and/or private residential facility.   [ ]

Homebound.   [ ]

Hospital.   [ ]

Homebound instruction for pre-school age
students with disabilities.   [ ]

Placement Justification:

_____
_____
_____
_____

CONFIDENTIAL

Signature of Participants   Position   Date

_____   _____   _____

_____   _____   _____

_____   _____   _____

_____   _____   _____

_____   _____   _____

_____   _____   _____

I give permission for my child, _____, to be enrolled in the special education program described in this Individualized Education Program (IEP). I understand the contents of this document and I have been informed of my due process rights. I understand that I have the right to review my child's records and to request a change in the IEP at anytime. I also understand that I have the right to refuse this placement and to have my child continue in his/her present placement pending exhaustion of due process procedures. I have received a copy of the IEP.

_____   _____

Signature of Parent(s),   Date

Guardian(s) or

Surrogate

* * *

I do not give permission for my child, _____, to be enrolled in the special education program described in the Individualized Education Program (IEP). I understand that I have the right to review his/her records and to request another placement. I understand that the action described above will not take place without my permission or until due process procedures have been exhausted. I understand that if my decision is appealed, I will be notified of my due process rights in this procedure. I have received a copy of the IEP.

_____   _____

Signature of Parent(s),   Date
Guardian(s) or
Surrogate

Permission is required for initial placement, evaluations, and reevaluations.

IEP INSTRUCTIONS

1. *Triennial Date*
   Indicate month/day/year.

2. *Disability or Disabilities*
   Spell out the label for each disabling condition, such as Learning Disabled or Emotionally Disturbed. Do not use initials.

3. *Frequency and Duration*
   Frequency is defined as number of times per time period, such as two times per week or once per month. Duration is the length of each session, such as 15 minutes or 30 minutes.

4. *Environment/Location/Provider*
   Environment is defined as the type of class, such as resource or self-contained. Location is where the service is provided, such as Lakeview Middle School. Provider is the person who will provide the instruction, such as LD teacher or Instructional Aide.

5. *Extent of Participation with Students Without Disabilities*
   Indicate both academic and nonacademic activities including school sponsored activities, games, lifetime sports, band, lunch, recess…as appropriate.

6. *Extent of Participation in the Administration of State or District Wide Assessments of Student Achievement.*
   Include a statement of any modifications appropriate or if the child will not participate in the state or district wide tests indicate why the assessment is not appropriate and how the child will be assessed.

7. *Justification Form*
   The written explanation for negative responses (1–8) must describe the modifications considered or attempted and the criteria used to determine that the child's IEP goals cannot be achieved in this situation. This would include factors considered potentially harmful and the criteria used to determine that the child's IEP goals cannot be achieved. Explanation cannot be based on such criteria as: availability of educational or related services, availability of space, category of disabling condition, or administrative conveniences.

REQUEST FOR DUE PROCESS HEARING[2]

DATE

Address of Superintendent
or Other Designated Official

    Re: [Student Name]

          [Student's Address]

          [School Attending]

Dear _____:

As attorney for [Student's Name] and his/her parents, [Parents' Names], a due process hearing is requested under 20 U.S.C. § 1415, 29 U.S.C. § 794,[3] and the supporting regulations of each (34 C.F.R. Parts 104 and 300), as well as [State Special Education Law] and supporting state regulations. The due process hearing is requested to consider issues related to the failure of [Education Agency] to [list complaint with facts, e.g., provide educational services consistent with IEP] as required by law. We are requesting [proposed resolution if known, *e.g.*, a residential placement].

                                     Sincerely,

                                 _____

cc: Director of Special Education

---

2. This format can also be used by the parents who request a hearing.
3. *See* 42 U.S.C. § 1983; 20 U.S.C. § 1471; and 42 U.S.C. §§12101 *et seq.*

REQUEST FOR ADMINISTRATIVE APPEAL

DATE

Address of State Education Agency
Official Responsible for Appointing
Hearing Officers

    Re: _____ v. _____

Dear _____ :

    [Name of Appealing Party] hereby appeals the decision of the Hearing Officer in the above referenced case with respect to the determination that [Insert Complaint With Hearing Officer's Decision, e.g. the Public School's proposed placement is not appropriate to meet the educational needs of _____].

                                        Sincerely,

                                        _____

cc: [Attorney for Opposing Side]

COMPLAINT

UNITED STATES DISTRICT COURT
DISTRICT OF ——-

JONATHAN SMITH, a minor, by
his parents, Howard and Susan
Smith, as his next friend;
HOWARD SMITH; SUSAN SMITH,
 	
    Plaintiffs,
 	
    v.
 	
COLUMBIA COUNTY PUBLIC SCHOOLS,
ADAM DOE, Superintendent, in his
individual and official capacity,
 	
    Defendants.
	)
	)
	)
	)
	)
	) CA 00-0304-R
	)
	)
	)
	)
	)
	)
	)
	)

COMPLAINT

1. Jurisdiction is conferred upon this court by 28 U.S.C. § 1331 and 20 U.S.C. § 1415. The action arises as the result of violations of 20 U.S.C. § 1401 *et seq.*, 29 U.S.C. § 794, and 42 U.S.C. § 1983.

2. Defendant is organized and exists under the laws of the State of _____ and is the local educational agency responsible under 20 U.S.C. § 1411(d) for the educational program of plaintiff Jonathan.

3. Defendant receives federal financial assistance.

4. Plaintiff has exhausted all administrative procedures required to allow filing this action.

COUNT I

5. [Insert facts which set forth a claim for relief].

#. As a result of these actions, defendants have violated the plaintiff's rights under the Individuals with Disabilities Education Act, 20 U.S.C. §§ 1401 *et seq.*, state special education statutes [insert state statutory citation], and supporting state and federal regulations.

COUNT II

\#. Plaintiff realleges each allegation contained in paragraphs 1 through __.

\#. [Allege any additional facts necessary to set forth claim for relief under Count II].

\#. As a result of these actions, defendants have violated the Civil Rights of plaintiff under § 42 U.S.C. § 1983.

COUNT III

\#. Plaintiff realleges each allegation contained in paragraphs 1 through __.

\#. [Allege any additional facts necessary to set forth claim for relief under Count III].

\#. As a result of these actions, defendants have violated Section 504 of the Rehabilitation Act of 1973, 29 U.S.C. § 794, and supporting federal regulations, 34 C.F.R. Part 104.

WHEREFORE, Plaintiffs pray this Court:

1. Assume jurisdiction of this case;

2. Order transfer to this Court of the transcript, documents, memoranda, and briefs used by the administrative review officer;

3. Find that Defendant's proposed placement of Jonathan is not reasonably calculated to provide educational benefit as required by 20 U.S.C. § 1401 *et seq.*, 29 U.S.C. § 794, [State Special Education Statute], and supporting federal and state regulations.

4. Find that the actions of Defendant have violated Plaintiffs' rights under 42 U.S.C. § 1983;

5. Award plaintiff's attorneys' fees and costs under 20 U.S.C. § 1415; 29 U.S.C. § 794a(b); and 42 U.S.C. § 1988.

By Their Attorney

_____

Name

Address

MOTION FOR ALLOWANCE OF ATTORNEY'S FEES AND COSTS

UNITED STATES DISTRICT COURT
|DISTRICT OF ——-

JONATHAN SMITH, a minor, by	)
his parents, Howard and Susan	)
Smith, as his next friend;	)
HOWARD SMITH; SUSAN SMITH,	)
	)
Plaintiffs,	) CA 00-0304-R
	)
v.	)
	)
COLUMBIA COUNTY PUBLIC SCHOOLS,	)
ADAM DOE, Superintendent, in his	)
individual and official capacity,	)
	)
Defendants.	)

MOTION FOR ALLOWANCE OF ATTORNEY'S FEES AND COSTS

Comes now the plaintiffs and respectfully move this court for an order allowing attorney's fees and costs in favor of the plaintiffs.

In support of this motion, plaintiffs attach:

1. an affidavit of plaintiffs' counsel itemizing the time and services expended in the above matter as well as costs incurred by plaintiffs (Appendix 1);

2. an affidavit of Frank Jones, Esq., indicating his standard charge for representing parents in proceedings under the Individuals with Disabilities Education Act (IDEA) (Appendix 2); and

3. letters obtained under the Freedom Information Act which indicate what school systems within the geographic area of Columbia County are paying lawyers for representing the school system in proceedings under the IDEA (Appendix 3).

Based on the attachments, plaintiffs request that their attorney be awarded $_____ in attorney's fees and that they be awarded $_____ as costs of the above captioned proceeding for a total of $_____.

————————————————

Attorney for Plaintiffs

Address

CERTIFICATE

I hereby certify that a true copy of the original Motion for Allowance of Attorney's Fees and Costs, along with supporting affidavits, memorandum and attachments were mailed the _____ day of _____, 20__, to [Opposing Counsel], Esq., at [Address].

——————————————————————

UNITED STATES DISTRICT COURT
DISTRICT OF ———————

Appendix 1

UNITED STATES DISTRICT COURT
DISTRICT OF ———-

JONATHAN SMITH, a minor, by	)
his parents, Howard and Susan	)
Smith, as his next friend;	)
HOWARD SMITH; SUSAN SMITH,	)
	)
Plaintiffs,	) CA 00-0304-R
	)
v.	)
	)
COLUMBIA COUNTY PUBLIC SCHOOLS,	)
ADAM DOE, Superintendent, in his	)
individual and official capacity,	)
	)
Defendants.	)

AFFIDAVIT OF [Attorney's Name]

[Attorney's Name], being duly sworn, deposes and says:

1. I am an attorney at law duly licensed to practice in the State of _____ and in the United States District Court for the District of ———————. I am the attorney representing the plaintiffs in the above entitled action. I was first admitted to the bar in____ I was admitted to the bar of _____ in _____.

2. I began representing the plaintiffs in this matter on _____, 20__.

3. The following is an itemization of the work performed by me in the above captioned proceeding:

Itemization Of Time
Based On Contemporaneous Records

Date	Work Performed	Time/hours
May 10, 20__	Initial Client Interview	2.1

[insert remainder of date/work/time]

4. The total hours spent by me representing the Plaintiffs, based on the itemizations in paragraph 3 is 392.95

5. The costs incurred by Plaintiffs in this action are itemized as follows:

Fees & expenses
Due Process Hearing $3862.37

* * *

Total $_____

6. I routinely charge $____ per hour for client representation.

_____

Attorney for Plaintiff

This day, _____ personally appeared before me, a Notary Public, and made oath and affirmed that the matters contained in the foregoing Affidavit are true to the best of his knowledge and belief.

Given under my hand this _____ day of _____, 20__.

_____

Notary Public

My Commission expires:

_____

UNITED STATES DISTRICT COURT
DISTRICT OF ——————

Appendix 2

UNITED STATES DISTRICT COURT
DISTRICT OF ——-

JONATHAN SMITH, a minor, by	)
his parents, Howard and Susan	)
Smith, as his next friend;	)
HOWARD SMITH; SUSAN SMITH,	)
	)
Plaintiffs,	) CA 00-0304-R
	)
v.	)
	)
COLUMBIA COUNTY PUBLIC SCHOOLS,	)
ADAM DOE, Superintendent, in his	)
individual and official capacity,	)
	)
Defendants.	)

AFFIDAVIT OF FRANK M. JONES, ESQ.

Frank M. Jones, being duly sworn, deposes and says:

1. I am an attorney at law duly licensed to practice in the State of ——————— and in the United States District Court for the District of ————.

2. I am presently associated with the firm of Jones and Associates, [address].

3. Jones and Associates routinely represents parents from the in proceedings and actions arising under P.L. 94-142.

4. I presently bill parents $_____ per hour for representation in proceedings under P.L. 94-142.

———————————————
Frank M. Jones

This day, Frank M. Jones personally appeared before me, a Notary Public, and made oath and affirmed that the matters contained in the foregoing Affidavit are true to the best of his knowledge and belief.

Given under my hand this _____ day of _____, 20____.

_____

My Commission expires:

_____

SETTLEMENT AGREEMENT

THIS AGREEMENT is made this ___ day of ____, 20___, by and between the School Board of _____ ("School Board") and _____ ("Parents") individually and on behalf of _____.

A dispute has arisen between the School Board and Parents over the provision of a free appropriate public education to _____ under P.L. 94-142, the Individuals with Disabilities Education Act (IDEA); Section 504 of the Rehabilitation Act of 1973; and 42 U.S.C. § 1983. The parents requested a due process hearing. The School Board and Parents now wish to resolve all issues in dispute which gave rise to the due process hearing.

It is, therefore, agreed as follows:

    1.   [Describe the nature of the agreement]

    2.   The Parents rescind their objection to the current IEP. The Parents will sign the proposed IEP, which is attached, indicating their agreement.

    3.   The Parents will dismiss the Due Process Hearing requested to resolve the issues addressed by this Agreement.

    5.   The School Board will pay $_____ for all attorney's fees and costs incurred by virtue of this dispute. The check will be made payable to _____.

    6.   By signing this Agreement, the Parents, for good and valuable consideration, do hereby release the School Board of _____ from all claims, actions, causes of action, demands, rights, damages, costs, expenses and compensation whatsoever, on account of or in any way resulting from the provision of educational services in accordance with the Individual Education Plan for _____ for the 20__–20__ academic school year.

Agreed this_____day of_____, 20__.

/s/_____   /s/_____

/s/_____/s/

PARENTS   SCHOOL BOARD OF_____

Appendix 5 Tables

Table 1-7. Children and students served under IDEA, Part B, in the U.S. and outlying areas, by age and disability category: Fall 2006

Disability category	3 Years Old	4 Years Old	5 Years Old	6 Years Old	7 Years Old	8 Years Old	9 Years Old
Specific learning disabilities	3,070	3,261	8,518	26,764	66,509	128,958	186,312
Speech or language impairments	61,088	105,184	171,963	227,479	221,289	197,089	156,680
Mental retardation	4,997	6,462	11,920	15,249	20,019	26,010	30,832
Emotional disturbance	981	1,530	3,933	7,109	13,011	19,038	24,313
Multiple disabilities	1,993	2,416	5,061	6,900	7,075	8,240	9,188
Hearing impairments	2,174	2,579	3,455	4,269	4,877	5,485	5,663
Orthopedic impairments	2,165	2,579	3,426	4,411	4,587	5,009	5,220
Other health impairments	3,422	3,731	8,828	18,414	25,934	38,353	48,069
Visual impairments	974	1,155	1,417	1,654	1,910	2,046	2,134
Autism	7,583	10,570	16,958	21,315	21,292	22,163	21,425
Deaf-blindness	61	61	85	90	88	103	94
Traumatic brain injury	214	309	510	721	963	1,254	1,446
Developmental delays	76,954	107,143	65,654	37,542	28,547	14,762	3,080
All disabilities	165,676	246,980	301,728	371,917	416,101	468,510	494,456

Disability category	10 Years Old	11 Years Old	12 Years Old	13 Years Old	14 Years Old	15 Years Old	16 Years Old
Specific learning disabilities	227,377	253,808	275,882	282,455	287,661	291,988	285,015
Speech or language impairments	115,478	76,880	53,263	36,828	26,271	18,749	14,557
Mental retardation	34,403	37,980	41,526	45,207	48,846	50,877	51,777
Emotional disturbance	29,139	34,668	41,424	47,854	53,128	57,267	56,464
Multiple disabilities	9,420	9,835	10,324	10,771	10,900	11,268	11,122
Hearing impairments	5,913	6,039	6,269	6,110	6,089	5,998	5,782
Orthopedic impairments	5,052	5,034	5,021	4,827	4,695	4,751	4,535
Other health impairments	54,131	57,800	59,224	60,169	59,321	57,740	53,530
Visual impairments	2,105	2,132	2,071	2,048	2,235	2,119	2,192
Autism	20,034	19,715	17,744	16,759	16,063	13,887	11,769
Deaf-blindness	87	104	117	107	109	123	118
Traumatic brain injury	1,786	1,918	2,012	2,177	2,213	2,319	2,399
Developmental delays	0	0	0	0	0	0	0
All disabilities	504,925	505,913	514,877	515,312	517,531	517,086	499,260

Disability category	17 Years Old	18 Years Old	19 Years Old	20 Years Old	21 Years Old	22+ Years Old
Specific learning disabilities	250,522	118,268	22,009	5,281	1,667	179
Speech or language impairments	10,527	4,478	926	328	82	6
Mental retardation	49,054	34,836	17,925	12,310	6,389	2,196
Emotional disturbance	46,450	20,607	5,480	2,083	846	131
Multiple disabilities	10,192	7,483	5,232	4,102	2,137	506
Hearing impairments	5,405	2,911	1,096	475	178	17
Orthopedic impairments	3,954	2,394	1,107	773	496	90
Other health impairments	43,436	17,732	3,860	1,282	499	58
Visual impairments	1,858	999	455	256	138	18
Autism	9,444	5,870	3,450	2,415	1,249	377
Deaf-blindness	110	76	71	50	25	2
Traumatic brain injury	2,328	1,320	557	342	177	18
Developmental delay[a]	0	0	0	0	0	0
All disabilities	433,280	216,974	62,168	29,697	13,883	3,598

Source: U.S. Department of Education, Office of Special Education Programs, Data Analysis System (DANS)," OMB #1820-0043: "'Children with Disabilities Receiving Special Education Under Part B of the Individuals with Disabilities Education Act,'" 2006. Data updated as of July 15, 2007."

Note: Please see the Part B Child Count Data Notes in appendix B for information the state submitted to clarify its data submission.

[a] Developmental delay is applicable only to children ages 3 through 9.

Table 5-1. Children and students with disabilities served under IDEA, Part B, unilaterally removed or suspended/expelled more than 10 days, by type of removal and state: 2005–06

	Number of Children			
	Removed to an IAES[a]		Suspension/expulsion[b]	
	By school personnel for drugs/weapons	By hearing officer for likely injury	> 10 days in school year	Multiples sum to > 10 days
State				
Alabama	95	x	1,380	1,351
Alaska	15	x	306	237
Arizona	416	x	1,041	619
Arkansas	19	x	661	586
California	292	11	292	59
Colorado	48	x	657	309
Connecticut	7	17	2,019	1,927
Delaware	15	x	405	387
District of Columbia	-	-	-	-
Florida	86	x	8,369	8,369
Georgia	186	x	1,207	1,165
Hawaii	x	x	211	94
Idaho	25	x	45	18
Illinois	536	292	2,762	1,962
Indiana	663	x	2,105	1,448
Iowa	14	x	513	496
Kansas	109	18	617	554
Kentucky	7	x	353	314
Louisiana	235	x	1,031	964
Maine	80	41	121	86
Maryland	55	6	2,141	1,440
Massachusetts	55	45	1,483	1,211
Michigan	275	178	3,488	2,944
Minnesota	41	x	1,008	1,008
Mississippi	29	x	461	378
Missouri	227	x	3,283	2,735
Montana	43	x	106	70
Nebraska	28	x	557	448
Nevada	403	x	636	473
New Hampshire	x	x	217	198
New Jersey	49	9	1,542	1,491
New Mexico	912	x	529	485
New York	-	125	5,297	3,963
North Carolina	114	130	5,507	4,758
North Dakota	5	7	x	x
Ohio	1,657	258	788	653
Oklahoma	249	x	1,454	776
Oregon	21	x	581	244
Pennsylvania	1,050	x	2,317	2,136
Rhode Island	x	x	489	486
South Carolina	249	49	2,035	1,836
South Dakota	13	x	72	60
Tennessee	159	21	1,290	939
Texas	3,169	125	5,904	5,258
Utah	481	33	695	455
Vermont	x	x	61	49
Virginia	58	x	4,917	3,807
Washington	489	x	1,735	1,135
West Virginia	x	x	920	862
Wisconsin	202	x	2,034	1,693
Wyoming	x	196	31	16

BIE schools	73	5	356	114
50 states and D.C. (including BIE schools)	12,963	1,580	76,036	63,073
American Samoa	x	x	x	x
Guam	17	x	80	80
Northern Marianas	14	x	x	x
Puerto Rico	x	x	x	x
Virgin Islands	x	x	x	x
U.S. and outlying areas	12,996	1,580	76,121	63,156

Source: U.S. Department of Education, Office of Special Education Programs, Data Analysis System (DANS), OMB #1820-0621:
Children with Disabilities Unilaterally Removed or Suspended/Expelled for More Than 10 Days, 2005-06. Data updated as of July 15, 2007.

Note: Please see the Part B Discipline Data Notes in appendix B for information the state submitted to clarify its data submission.

[a] IAES is an interim alternative educational setting.

[b] Children are reported only once within each column. However, the same child may be reported in more than one column if he/she was involved in two or more incidents. In addition, the children reported in the final column (multiples sum to > 10 days) are a subset of the children reported in the third column (>10 days in school year).

- Data not available.

x Data suppressed.

Table 5-1a. Children and students with specific learning disabilities served under IDEA, Part B unilaterally removed or suspended/expelled more than 10 days, by type of removal and state: 2005–06

	Number of Children			
	Removed to an IAES[a]		Suspension/expulsion[b]	
	By school personnel for drugs/weapons	By hearing officer for likely injury	> 10 days in school year	Multiples sum to > 10 days
State				
Alabama	73	x	963	942
Alaska	9	x	168	124
Arizona	274	x	676	394
Arkansas	10	x	325	286
California	231	x	231	43
Colorado	25	x	280	111
Connecticut	x	6	842	796
Delaware	10	x	218	207
District of Columbia	-	-	-	-
Florida	49	x	3,936	3,936
Georgia	76	x	380	366
Hawaii	x	x	102	40
Idaho	13	x	25	11
Illinois	341	160	1,310	884
Indiana	326	x	813	545
Iowa	9	x	306	297
Kansas	62	12	306	267
Kentucky	x	x	65	55
Louisiana	122	x	510	471
Maine	35	19	54	28
Maryland	19	x	891	562
Massachusetts	27	27	755	606
Michigan	160	93	1,824	1,537
Minnesota	8	x	242	242
Mississippi	24	x	309	251
Missouri	117	x	1,605	1,283
Montana	29	x	71	43
Nebraska	12	x	239	174
Nevada	299	x	460	335
New Hampshire	x	x	86	79
New Jersey	35	7	831	800
New Mexico	592	x	339	317
New York	-	78	2,339	1,601
North Carolina	45	34	1,673	1,449
North Dakota	x	x	x	x
Ohio	747	67	328	256
Oklahoma	159	x	911	467
Oregon	11	x	310	118
Pennsylvania	684	x	1,407	1,282
Rhode Island	x	x	220	217
South Carolina	136	30	1,158	1,050
South Dakota	10	x	46	38
Tennessee	103	13	776	560
Texas	2,137	86	3,389	2,998
Utah	395	12	412	248
Vermont	x	x	21	14
Virginia	28	x	1,908	1,364
Washington	246	x	838	526
West Virginia	x	x	377	343
Wisconsin	76	x	706	544
Wyoming	x	93	17	6

BIE schools	50	x	258	94
50 states and D.C. (including BIE schools)	7,821	762	36,257	29,208
American Samoa	x	x	x	x
Guam	16	x	72	72
Northern Marianas	x	x	x	x
Puerto Rico	x	x	x	x
Virgin Islands	x	x	x	x
U.S. and outlying areas	7,850	762	36,333	29,282

Source: U.S. Department of Education, Office of Special Education Programs, Data Analysis System (DANS), OMB #1820-0621:
Children with Disabilities Unilaterally Removed or Suspended/Expelled for More Than 10 Days, 2005-06. Data updated as of July 15, 2007.

Note: Please see the Part B Discipline Data Notes in appendix B for information the state submitted to clarify its data submission.

[a] IAES is an interim alternative educational setting.

[b] Children are reported only once within each column. However, the same child may be reported in more than one column if he/she was involved in two or more incidents. In addition, the children reported in the final column (multiples sum to > 10 days) are a subset of the children reported in the third column (>10 days in school year).

- Data not available.

x Data suppressed.

Table 5-1b. Children and students with speech or language impairments served under IDEA, Part B, unilaterally removed or suspended/expelled more than 10 days, by type of removal and state: 2005–06

| | Number of Children | | | |
| | Removed to an IAES[a] | | Suspension/expulsion[b] | |
State	By school personnel for drugs/weapons	By hearing officer for likely injury	> 10 days in school year	Multiples sum to > 10 days
Alabama	5	x	59	58
Alaska	x	x	8	6
Arizona	5	x	5	x
Arkansas	x	x	28	25
California	13	x	13	x
Colorado	x	x	48	16
Connecticut	x	x	97	90
Delaware	x	x	x	x
District of Columbia	-	-	-	-
Florida	x	x	435	435
Georgia	8	x	23	23
Hawaii	x	x	x	x
Idaho	x	x	x	x
Illinois	x	x	62	37
Indiana	15	x	14	9
Iowa	x	x	43	42
Kansas	x	x	7	7
Kentucky	x	x	7	7
Louisiana	15	x	28	27
Maine	x	x	5	5
Maryland	x	x	91	50
Massachusetts	x	8	53	35
Michigan	x	x	46	33
Minnesota	x	x	20	20
Mississippi	x	x	24	20
Missouri	17	x	174	137
Montana	x	x	x	x
Nebraska	x	x	23	16
Nevada	5	x	8	8
New Hampshire	x	x	18	17
New Jersey	x	x	29	27
New Mexico	72	x	54	50
New York	-	x	201	95
North Carolina	x	x	141	124
North Dakota	x	x	x	x
Ohio	44	x	24	21
Oklahoma	x	x	17	12
Oregon	x	x	27	8
Pennsylvania	35	x	25	24
Rhode Island	x	x	10	10
South Carolina	x	x	31	23
South Dakota	x	x	x	x
Tennessee	12	x	68	47
Texas	19	x	71	66
Utah	13	9	12	10
Vermont	x	x	x	x
Virginia	x	x	158	136
Washington	x	x	22	13
West Virginia	x	x	11	11
Wisconsin	x	x	30	23
Wyoming	x	27	x	x

BIE schools	x	x	12	x
50 states and D.C. (including BIE schools)	313	58	2,297	1,846
American Samoa	x	x	x	x
Guam	x	x	x	x
Northern Marianas	x	x	x	x
Puerto Rico	x	x	x	x
Virgin Islands	x	x	x	x
U.S. and outlying areas	313	58	2,298	1,847

Source: U.S. Department of Education, Office of Special Education Programs, Data Analysis System (DANS), OMB #1820-0621:
Children with Disabilities Unilaterally Removed or Suspended/Expelled for More Than 10 Days, 2005-06. Data updated as of July 15, 2007.

Note: Please see the Part B Discipline Data Notes in appendix B for information the state submitted to clarify its data submission.

[a] IAES is an interim alternative educational setting.

[b] Children are reported only once within each column. However, the same child may be reported in more than one column if he/she was involved in two or more incidents. In addition, the children reported in the final column (multiples sum to > 10 days) are a subset of the children reported in the third column (>10 days in school year).

- Data not available.

x Data suppressed.

Table 5-1c. Children and students with mental retardation served under IDEA, Part B, unilaterally removed or suspended/expelled more than 10 days, by type of removal and state: 2005–06

	Number of Children			
	Removed to an IAES[a]		Suspension/expulsion[b]	
State	By school personnel for drugs/weapons	By hearing officer for likely injury	> 10 days in school year	Multiples sum to > 10 days
Alabama	8	x	143	140
Alaska	x	x	11	9
Arizona	10	x	24	19
Arkansas	x	x	141	126
California	7	x	7	x
Colorado	x	x	18	10
Connecticut	x	x	64	61
Delaware	x	x	41	38
District of Columbia	-	-	-	-
Florida	9	x	712	712
Georgia	15	x	196	190
Hawaii	x	x	9	x
Idaho	x	x	x	x
Illinois	35	16	250	178
Indiana	68	x	346	191
Iowa	x	x	91	87
Kansas	7	x	43	38
Kentucky	x	x	56	55
Louisiana	25	x	120	111
Maine	x	x	x	x
Maryland	x	x	78	52
Massachusetts	x	x	148	128
Michigan	30	12	462	398
Minnesota	x	x	40	40
Mississippi	x	x	32	27
Missouri	10	x	293	263
Montana	x	x	x	x
Nebraska	x	x	53	50
Nevada	13	x	11	9
New Hampshire	x	x	5	x
New Jersey	x	x	14	14
New Mexico	17	x	13	11
New York	-	x	166	153
North Carolina	20	29	1,039	947
North Dakota	x	x	x	x
Ohio	285	75	162	138
Oklahoma	13	x	123	75
Oregon	x	x	14	8
Pennsylvania	63	x	93	87
Rhode Island	x	x	9	9
South Carolina	34	x	247	216
South Dakota	x	x	x	x
Tennessee	10	x	107	72
Texas	51	x	160	154
Utah	12	x	20	9
Vermont	x	x	x	x
Virginia	x	x	421	375
Washington	8	x	30	26
West Virginia	x	x	166	160
Wisconsin	14	x	155	138
Wyoming	x	5	x	x

BIE schools	x	x	10	x
50 states and D.C. (including BIE schools)	785	144	6,354	5,540
American Samoa	x	x	x	x
Guam	x	x	x	x
Northern Marianas	x	x	x	x
Puerto Rico	x	x	x	x
Virgin Islands	x	x	x	x
U.S. and outlying areas	787	144	6,355	5,541

Source: U.S. Department of Education, Office of Special Education Programs, Data Analysis System (DANS), OMB #1820-0621:
Children with Disabilities Unilaterally Removed or Suspended/Expelled for More Than 10 Days, 2005-06. Data updated as of July 15, 2007.

Note: Please see the Part B Discipline Data Notes in appendix B for information the state submitted to clarify its data submission.

[a] IAES is an interim alternative educational setting.

[b] Children are reported only once within each column. However, the same child may be reported in more than one column if he/she was involved in two or more incidents. In addition, the children reported in the final column (multiples sum to > 10 days) are a subset of the children reported in the third column (>10 days in school year).

- Data not available.

x Data suppressed.

Table 5-1d. Children and students with emotional disturbance served under IDEA, Part B, unilaterally removed or suspended/expelled more than 10 days, by type of removal and state: 2005–06

| | Number of Children | | | |
| | Removed to an IAES[a] | | Suspension/expulsion[b] | |
State	By school personnel for drugs/weapons	By hearing officer for likely injury	> 10 days in school year	Multiples sum to > 10 days
Alabama	x	x	121	119
Alaska	x	x	67	59
Arizona	89	x	209	132
Arkansas	x	x	29	27
California	14	x	14	x
Colorado	13	x	219	131
Connecticut	x	x	596	577
Delaware	x	x	78	77
District of Columbia	-	-	-	-
Florida	24	x	2,803	2,803
Georgia	55	x	409	397
Hawaii	x	x	60	31
Idaho	x	x	6	x
Illinois	113	98	875	646
Indiana	185	x	731	548
Iowa	x	x	52	49
Kansas	22	x	124	117
Kentucky	x	x	140	130
Louisiana	32	x	189	181
Maine	16	x	20	18
Maryland	16	x	556	399
Massachusetts	8	6	325	274
Michigan	44	31	826	719
Minnesota	14	x	352	352
Mississippi	x	x	34	29
Missouri	31	x	743	668
Montana	x	x	22	21
Nebraska	7	x	124	109
Nevada	57	x	114	86
New Hampshire	x	x	54	48
New Jersey	7	x	276	268
New Mexico	127	x	68	62
New York	-	22	1,604	1,232
North Carolina	23	43	1,580	1,373
North Dakota	x	x	x	5
Ohio	326	111	193	167
Oklahoma	42	x	246	136
Oregon	x	x	113	58
Pennsylvania	219	x	717	673
Rhode Island	x	x	151	151
South Carolina	52	13	373	338
South Dakota	x	x	8	6
Tennessee	17	x	148	123
Texas	533	21	1,458	1,321
Utah	32	x	192	154
Vermont	x	x	27	25
Virginia	12	x	1,196	966
Washington	75	x	335	231
West Virginia	x	x	204	191
Wisconsin	71	x	760	652
Wyoming	x	32	8	7

BIE schools	16	x	53	7
50 states and D.C. (including BIE schools)	2,325	400	19,607	16,895
American Samoa	x	x	x	x
Guam	x	x	x	x
Northern Marianas	x	x	x	x
Puerto Rico	x	x	x	x
Virgin Islands	x	x	x	x
U.S. and outlying areas	2,326	400	19,611	16,899

Source: U.S. Department of Education, Office of Special Education Programs, Data Analysis System (DANS), OMB #1820-0621:
Children with Disabilities Unilaterally Removed or Suspended/Expelled for More Than 10 Days, 2005-06. Data updated as of July 15, 2007.

Note: Please see the Part B Discipline Data Notes in appendix B for information the state submitted to clarify its data submission.

[a] IAES is an interim alternative educational setting.

[b] Children are reported only once within each column. However, the same child may be reported in more than one column if he/she was involved in two or more incidents. In addition, the children reported in the final column (multiples sum to > 10 days) are a subset of the children reported in the third column (>10 days in school year).

- Data not available.

x Data suppressed.

Table 5-1e. Children and students with multiple disabilities served under IDEA, Part B, unilaterally removed or suspended/expelled more than 10 days, by type of removal and state: 2005–06

| | Number of Children | | | |
| | Removed to an IAES[a] | | Suspension/expulsion[b] | |
State	By school personnel for drugs/weapons	By hearing officer for likely injury	> 10 days in school year	Multiples sum to > 10 days
Alabama	x	x	x	x
Alaska	x	x	5	x
Arizona	x	x	10	x
Arkansas	x	x	10	10
California	x	x	x	x
Colorado	x	x	7	6
Connecticut	x	x	28	27
Delaware	x	x	x	x
District of Columbia	-	-	-	-
Florida	x	x	x	x
Georgia	x	x	x	x
Hawaii	x	x	x	x
Idaho	x	x	x	x
Illinois	x	x	20	17
Indiana	x	x	x	x
Iowa	x	x	x	x
Kansas	x	x	34	32
Kentucky	x	x	16	8
Louisiana	x	x	x	x
Maine	x	x	6	5
Maryland	x	x	79	61
Massachusetts	x	x	42	33
Michigan	x	x	x	x
Minnesota	x	x	x	x
Mississippi	x	x	x	x
Missouri	x	x	11	8
Montana	x	x	x	x
Nebraska	x	x	8	5
Nevada	x	x	x	x
New Hampshire	x	x	x	x
New Jersey	5	x	249	243
New Mexico	x	x	x	x
New York	-	6	130	123
North Carolina	x	x	22	15
North Dakota	x	x	x	x
Ohio	18	x	8	7
Oklahoma	x	x	x	x
Oregon	x	x	x	x
Pennsylvania	x	x	x	x
Rhode Island	x	x	x	x
South Carolina	x	x	9	9
South Dakota	x	x	x	x
Tennessee	x	x	x	x
Texas	6	x	7	x
Utah	x	x	36	20
Vermont	x	x	x	x
Virginia	x	x	49	44
Washington	x	x	22	21
West Virginia	x	x	x	x
Wisconsin	x	x	x	x
Wyoming	x	x	x	x

BIE schools	x	x	x	x
50 states and D.C. (including BIE schools)	65	18	840	729
American Samoa	x	x	x	x
Guam	x	x	x	x
Northern Marianas	x	x	x	x
Puerto Rico	x	x	x	x
Virgin Islands	x	x	x	x
U.S. and outlying areas	65	18	840	729

Source: U.S. Department of Education, Office of Special Education Programs, Data Analysis System (DANS), OMB #1820-0621:
Children with Disabilities Unilaterally Removed or Suspended/Expelled for More Than 10 Days, 2005-06. Data updated as of July 15, 2007.

Note: Please see the Part B Discipline Data Notes in appendix B for information the state submitted to clarify its data submission.

[a] IAES is an interim alternative educational setting.

[b] Children are reported only once within each column. However, the same child may be reported in more than one column if he/she was involved in two or more incidents. In addition, the children reported in the final column (multiples sum to > 10 days) are a subset of the children reported in the third column (>10 days in school year).

- Data not available.

x Data suppressed.

Table 5-1f. Children and students with hearing impairments served under IDEA, Part B, unilaterally removed or suspended/expelled more than 10 days, by type of removal and state: 2005–06

| | Number of Children | | | |
| | Removed to an IAES[a] | | Suspension/expulsion[b] | |
State	By school personnel for drugs/weapons	By hearing officer for likely injury	> 10 days in school year	Multiples sum to > 10 days
Alabama	x	x	5	5
Alaska	x	x	x	x
Arizona	x	x	35	9
Arkansas	x	x	x	x
California	x	x	x	x
Colorado	x	x	x	x
Connecticut	x	x	10	10
Delaware	x	x	x	x
District of Columbia	-	-	-	-
Florida	x	x	19	19
Georgia	x	x	x	x
Hawaii	x	x	x	x
Idaho	x	x	x	x
Illinois	x	x	18	9
Indiana	x	x	10	5
Iowa	x	x	x	x
Kansas	x	x	x	x
Kentucky	x	x	x	x
Louisiana	x	x	5	x
Maine	x	x	x	x
Maryland	x	x	5	5
Massachusetts	x	x	x	x
Michigan	x	x	13	10
Minnesota	x	x	x	x
Mississippi	x	x	x	x
Missouri	x	x	18	17
Montana	x	x	x	x
Nebraska	x	x	x	x
Nevada	x	x	x	x
New Hampshire	x	x	x	x
New Jersey	x	x	7	7
New Mexico	9	x	x	x
New York	-	x	13	6
North Carolina	x	x	21	17
North Dakota	x	x	x	x
Ohio	7	x	x	x
Oklahoma	x	x	7	6
Oregon	x	x	x	x
Pennsylvania	6	x	6	5
Rhode Island	x	x	x	x
South Carolina	x	x	x	x
South Dakota	x	x	x	x
Tennessee	x	x	x	x
Texas	15	x	24	19
Utah	x	x	6	x
Vermont	x	x	x	x
Virginia	x	x	8	7
Washington	7	x	14	5
West Virginia	x	x	x	x
Wisconsin	x	x	x	x
Wyoming	x	x	x	x

BIE schools	x	x	x	x
50 states and D.C. (including BIE schools)	74	11	306	216
American Samoa	x	x	x	x
Guam	x	x	x	x
Northern Marianas	x	x	x	x
Puerto Rico	x	x	x	x
Virgin Islands	x	x	x	x
U.S. and outlying areas	74	11	306	216

Source: U.S. Department of Education, Office of Special Education Programs, Data Analysis System (DANS), OMB #1820-0621:
Children with Disabilities Unilaterally Removed or Suspended/Expelled for More Than 10 Days, 2005-06. Data updated as of July 15, 2007.

Note: Please see the Part B Discipline Data Notes in appendix B for information the state submitted to clarify its data submission.

[a] IAES is an interim alternative educational setting.

[b] Children are reported only once within each column. However, the same child may be reported in more than one column if he/she was involved in two or more incidents. In addition, the children reported in the final column (multiples sum to > 10 days) are a subset of the children reported in the third column (>10 days in school year).

- Data not available.

x Data suppressed.

Table 5-1g. Children and students with orthopedic impairments served under IDEA, Part B, unilaterally removed or suspended/expelled more than 10 days, by type of removal and state: 2005–06

	Number of Children			
	Removed to an IAES[a]		Suspension/expulsion[b]	
	By school personnel for drugs/weapons	By hearing officer for likely injury	> 10 days in school year	Multiples sum to > 10 days
State				
Alabama	x	x	x	x
Alaska	x	x	x	x
Arizona	x	x	7	5
Arkansas	x	x	x	x
California	x	x	x	x
Colorado	x	x	72	27
Connecticut	x	x	x	x
Delaware	x	x	x	x
District of Columbia	-	-	-	-
Florida	x	x	14	14
Georgia	x	x	x	x
Hawaii	x	x	x	x
Idaho	x	x	x	x
Illinois	x	x	x	x
Indiana	x	x	x	x
Iowa	x	x	5	5
Kansas	x	x	x	x
Kentucky	x	x	x	x
Louisiana	x	x	x	x
Maine	x	x	x	x
Maryland	x	x	x	x
Massachusetts	x	x	x	x
Michigan	7	x	44	36
Minnesota	9	x	225	225
Mississippi	x	x	x	x
Missouri	x	x	8	x
Montana	x	x	x	x
Nebraska	x	x	x	x
Nevada	x	x	x	x
New Hampshire	x	x	x	x
New Jersey	x	x	x	x
New Mexico	x	x	x	x
New York	-	x	x	x
North Carolina	x	5	8	7
North Dakota	x	x	x	x
Ohio	x	x	x	x
Oklahoma	x	x	x	x
Oregon	x	x	x	x
Pennsylvania	x	x	x	x
Rhode Island	x	x	x	x
South Carolina	x	x	x	x
South Dakota	x	x	x	x
Tennessee	x	x	x	x
Texas	5	x	8	6
Utah	x	x	x	x
Vermont	x	x	x	x
Virginia	x	x	x	x
Washington	x	x	x	x
West Virginia	x	x	x	x
Wisconsin	x	x	x	x
Wyoming	x	x	x	x

BIE schools	x	x	x	x
50 states and D.C. (including BIE schools)	45	8	435	358
American Samoa	x	x	x	x
Guam	x	x	x	x
Northern Marianas	x	x	x	x
Puerto Rico	x	x	x	x
Virgin Islands	x	x	x	x
U.S. and outlying areas	45	8	435	358

Source: U.S. Department of Education, Office of Special Education Programs, Data Analysis System (DANS), OMB #1820-0621:
Children with Disabilities Unilaterally Removed or Suspended/Expelled for More Than 10 Days, 2005-06. Data updated as of July 15, 2007.

Note: Please see the Part B Discipline Data Notes in appendix B for information the state submitted to clarify its data submission.

[a] IAES is an interim alternative educational setting.

[b] Children are reported only once within each column. However, the same child may be reported in more than one column if he/she was involved in two or more incidents. In addition, the children reported in the final column (multiples sum to > 10 days) are a subset of the children reported in the third column (>10 days in school year).

- Data not available.

x Data suppressed.

Table 5-1h. Children and students with other health impairments served under IDEA, Part B, unilaterally removed or suspended/expelled more than 10 days, by type of removal and state: 2005–06

	Number of Children			
	Removed to an IAES[a]		Suspension/expulsion[b]	
	By school personnel for drugs/weapons	By hearing officer for likely injury	> 10 days in school year	Multiples sum to > 10 days
State				
Alabama	x	x	81	79
Alaska	x	x	39	28
Arizona	29	x	61	46
Arkansas	8	x	125	110
California	20	x	20	6
Colorado	x	x	x	x
Connecticut	x	x	365	349
Delaware	x	x	58	56
District of Columbia	-	-	-	-
Florida	x	x	413	413
Georgia	30	x	188	179
Hawaii	x	x	31	16
Idaho	7	x	9	x
Illinois	27	12	187	157
Indiana	54	x	144	115
Iowa	x	x	x	x
Kansas	12	x	89	80
Kentucky	x	x	59	51
Louisiana	33	x	161	155
Maine	23	11	34	28
Maryland	13	x	415	291
Massachusetts	8	x	130	112
Michigan	28	33	233	184
Minnesota	x	x	66	66
Mississippi	x	x	51	44
Missouri	46	x	408	336
Montana	x	x	9	x
Nebraska	8	x	102	90
Nevada	26	x	34	27
New Hampshire	x	x	51	47
New Jersey	x	x	127	124
New Mexico	82	x	39	31
New York	-	16	807	724
North Carolina	18	16	967	778
North Dakota	x	x	x	x
Ohio	207	x	60	53
Oklahoma	25	x	131	68
Oregon	5	x	104	47
Pennsylvania	33	x	52	50
Rhode Island	x	x	94	94
South Carolina	25	5	185	170
South Dakota	x	x	10	9
Tennessee	15	x	171	121
Texas	381	14	751	656
Utah	11	x	x	x
Vermont	x	x	6	5
Virginia	16	x	1,110	856
Washington	144	x	441	298
West Virginia	x	x	146	143
Wisconsin	38	x	366	324
Wyoming	x	34	x	x

BIE schools	x	x	17	8
50 states and D.C. (including BIE schools)	1,403	160	9,156	7,634
American Samoa	x	x	x	x
Guam	x	x	x	x
Northern Marianas	x	x	x	x
Puerto Rico	x	x	x	x
Virgin Islands	x	x	x	x
U.S. and outlying areas	1,404	160	9,159	7,637

Source: U.S. Department of Education, Office of Special Education Programs, Data Analysis System (DANS), OMB #1820-0621:
Children with Disabilities Unilaterally Removed or Suspended/Expelled for More Than 10 Days, 2005-06. Data updated as of July 15, 2007.

Note: Please see the Part B Discipline Data Notes in appendix B for information the state submitted to clarify its data submission.

[a] IAES is an interim alternative educational setting.

[b] Children are reported only once within each column. However, the same child may be reported in more than one column if he/she was involved in two or more incidents. In addition, the children reported in the final column (multiples sum to > 10 days) are a subset of the children reported in the third column (>10 days in school year).

- Data not available.

x Data suppressed.

Table 5-1i. Children and students with visual impairments served under IDEA, Part B, unilaterally removed or suspended/expelled more than 10 days, by type of removal and state: 2005–06

	Number of Children			
	Removed to an IAES[a]		Suspension/expulsion[b]	
State	By school personnel for drugs/weapons	By hearing officer for likely injury	> 10 days in school year	Multiples sum to > 10 days
Alabama	x	x	x	x
Alaska	x	x	x	x
Arizona	x	x	5	x
Arkansas	x	x	x	x
California	x	x	x	x
Colorado	x	x	x	x
Connecticut	x	x	7	7
Delaware	x	x	x	x
District of Columbia	-	-	-	-
Florida	x	x	8	8
Georgia	x	x	x	x
Hawaii	x	x	x	x
Idaho	x	x	x	x
Illinois	x	x	11	8
Indiana	x	x	7	x
Iowa	x	x	x	x
Kansas	x	x	x	x
Kentucky	x	x	x	x
Louisiana	x	x	x	x
Maine	x	x	x	x
Maryland	x	x	x	x
Massachusetts	x	x	x	x
Michigan	x	x	x	x
Minnesota	x	x	24	24
Mississippi	x	x	x	x
Missouri	x	x	x	x
Montana	x	x	x	x
Nebraska	x	x	x	x
Nevada	x	x	x	x
New Hampshire	x	x	x	x
New Jersey	x	x	x	x
New Mexico	x	x	x	x
New York	-	x	5	x
North Carolina	x	x	x	x
North Dakota	x	x	x	x
Ohio	x	x	x	x
Oklahoma	x	x	x	x
Oregon	x	x	x	x
Pennsylvania	x	x	x	x
Rhode Island	x	x	x	x
South Carolina	x	x	x	x
South Dakota	x	x	x	x
Tennessee	x	x	x	x
Texas	8	x	x	6
Utah	x	x	x	x
Vermont	x	x	x	x
Virginia	x	x	x	x
Washington	x	x	x	x
West Virginia	x	x	x	x
Wisconsin	x	x	x	x
Wyoming	x	x	x	x

BIE schools	x	x	x	x
50 states and D.C. (including BIE schools)	15	3	121	97
American Samoa	x	x	x	x
Guam	x	x	x	x
Northern Marianas	x	x	x	x
Puerto Rico	x	x	x	x
Virgin Islands	x	x	x	x
U.S. and outlying areas	15	3	121	97

Source: U.S. Department of Education, Office of Special Education Programs, Data Analysis System (DANS), OMB #1820-0621:
Children with Disabilities Unilaterally Removed or Suspended/Expelled for More Than 10 Days, 2005-06. Data updated as of July 15, 2007.

Note: Please see the Part B Discipline Data Notes in appendix B for information the state submitted to clarify its data submission.

[a] IAES is an interim alternative educational setting.

[b] Children are reported only once within each column. However, the same child may be reported in more than one column if he/she was involved in two or more incidents. In addition, the children reported in the final column (multiples sum to > 10 days) are a subset of the children reported in the third column (>10 days in school year).

- Data not available.

x Data suppressed.

Table 5-1j. Children and students with autism served under IDEA, Part B, unilaterally removed or suspended/expelled more than 10 days, by type of removal and state: 2005–06

	Number of Children			
	Removed to an IAES[a]		Suspension/expulsion[b]	
	By school personnel for drugs/weapons	By hearing officer for likely injury	> 10 days in school year	Multiples sum to > 10 days
State				
Alabama	x	x	x	x
Alaska	x	x	x	x
Arizona	x	x	6	5
Arkansas	x	x	x	x
California	x	x	x	x
Colorado	x	x	x	x
Connecticut	x	x	x	x
Delaware	x	x	x	x
District of Columbia	-	-	-	-
Florida	x	x	x	x
Georgia	x	x	x	x
Hawaii	x	x	x	x
Idaho	x	x	x	x
Illinois	7	x	x	x
Indiana	8	x	27	23
Iowa	x	x	6	6
Kansas	x	x	x	x
Kentucky	x	x	x	x
Louisiana	x	x	x	x
Maine	x	x	x	x
Maryland	x	x	11	9
Massachusetts	x	x	x	x
Michigan	x	6	27	19
Minnesota	x	x	x	x
Mississippi	x	x	x	x
Missouri	x	x	14	13
Montana	x	x	x	x
Nebraska	x	x	x	x
Nevada	x	x	x	x
New Hampshire	x	x	x	x
New Jersey	x	x	x	x
New Mexico	x	x	x	x
New York	-	x	8	6
North Carolina	x	x	15	12
North Dakota	x	x	x	x
Ohio	12	x	x	x
Oklahoma	x	x	x	x
Oregon	x	x	9	x
Pennsylvania	6	x	x	x
Rhode Island	x	x	x	x
South Carolina	x	x	x	x
South Dakota	x	x	x	x
Tennessee	x	x	x	x
Texas	x	x	15	13
Utah	x	x	8	6
Vermont	x	x	x	x
Virginia	x	x	13	13
Washington	x	x	13	x
West Virginia	x	x	x	x
Wisconsin	x	x	6	x
Wyoming	x	x	x	x

BIE schools	x	x	x	x
50 states and D.C. (including BIE schools)	53	12	233	180
American Samoa	x	x	x	x
Guam	x	x	x	x
Northern Marianas	x	x	x	x
Puerto Rico	x	x	x	x
Virgin Islands	x	x	x	x
U.S. and outlying areas	53	12	233	180

Source: U.S. Department of Education, Office of Special Education Programs, Data Analysis System (DANS), OMB #1820-0621:
Children with Disabilities Unilaterally Removed or Suspended/Expelled for More Than 10 Days, 2005-06. Data updated as of July 15, 2007.

Note: Please see the Part B Discipline Data Notes in appendix B for information the state submitted to clarify its data submission.

[a] IAES is an interim alternative educational setting.

[b] Children are reported only once within each column. However, the same child may be reported in more than one column if he/she was involved in two or more incidents. In addition, the children reported in the final column (multiples sum to > 10 days) are a subset of the children reported in the third column (>10 days in school year).

- Data not available.

x Data suppressed.

Table 5-1k. Children and students with deaf-blindness served under IDEA, Part B, unilaterally removed or suspended/expelled more than 10 days, by type of removal and state: 2005–06

	Number of Children			
	Removed to an IAES[a]		Suspension/expulsion[b]	
State	By school personnel for drugs/weapons	By hearing officer for likely injury	> 10 days in school year	Multiples sum to > 10 days
Alabama	x	x	x	x
Alaska	x	x	x	x
Arizona	x	x	x	x
Arkansas	x	x	x	x
California	x	x	x	x
Colorado	x	x	x	x
Connecticut	x	x	x	x
Delaware	x	x	x	x
District of Columbia	-	-	-	-
Florida	x	x	x	x
Georgia	x	x	x	x
Hawaii	x	x	x	x
Idaho	x	x	x	x
Illinois	x	x	21	21
Indiana	x	x	x	x
Iowa	x	x	x	x
Kansas	x	x	x	x
Kentucky	x	x	x	x
Louisiana	x	x	x	x
Maine	x	x	x	x
Maryland	x	x	x	x
Massachusetts	x	x	x	x
Michigan	x	x	x	x
Minnesota	x	x	27	27
Mississippi	x	x	x	x
Missouri	x	x	x	x
Montana	x	x	x	x
Nebraska	x	x	x	x
Nevada	x	x	x	x
New Hampshire	x	x	x	x
New Jersey	x	x	x	x
New Mexico	x	x	x	x
New York	-	x	x	x
North Carolina	x	x	x	x
North Dakota	x	x	x	x
Ohio	x	x	x	x
Oklahoma	x	x	x	x
Oregon	x	x	x	x
Pennsylvania	x	x	x	x
Rhode Island	x	x	x	x
South Carolina	x	x	20	20
South Dakota	x	x	x	x
Tennessee	x	x	x	x
Texas	x	x	x	x
Utah	x	x	x	x
Vermont	x	x	x	x
Virginia	x	x	x	x
Washington	x	x	x	x
West Virginia	x	x	x	x
Wisconsin	x	x	x	x
Wyoming	x	x	x	x

BIE schools	x	x	x	x
50 states and D.C. (including BIE schools)	4	0	71	71
American Samoa	x	x	x	x
Guam	x	x	x	x
Northern Marianas	x	x	x	x
Puerto Rico	x	x	x	x
Virgin Islands	x	x	x	x
U.S. and outlying areas	4	0	71	71

Source: U.S. Department of Education, Office of Special Education Programs, Data Analysis System (DANS), OMB #1820-0621:
Children with Disabilities Unilaterally Removed or Suspended/Expelled for More Than 10 Days, 2005-06. Data updated as of July 15, 2007.

Note: Please see the Part B Discipline Data Notes in appendix B for information the state submitted to clarify its data submission.

[a] IAES is an interim alternative educational setting.

[b] Children are reported only once within each column. However, the same child may be reported in more than one column if he/she was involved in two or more incidents. In addition, the children reported in the final column (multiples sum to > 10 days) are a subset of the children reported in the third column (>10 days in school year).

- Data not available.

x Data suppressed.

Table 5-1l. Children and students with traumatic brain injury served under IDEA, Part B, unilaterally removed or suspended/expelled more than 10 days, by type of removal and state: 2005–06

| | Number of Children | | | |
| | Removed to an IAES[a] | | Suspension/expulsion[b] | |
State	By school personnel for drugs/weapons	By hearing officer for likely injury	> 10 days in school year	Multiples sum to > 10 days
Alabama	x	x	x	x
Alaska	x	x	x	x
Arizona	x	x	x	x
Arkansas	x	x	x	x
California	x	x	x	x
Colorado	x	x	x	x
Connecticut	x	x	x	x
Delaware	x	x	x	x
District of Columbia	-	-	-	-
Florida	x	x	19	19
Georgia	x	x	x	x
Hawaii	x	x	x	x
Idaho	x	x	x	x
Illinois	x	x	x	x
Indiana	x	x	10	6
Iowa	x	x	x	x
Kansas	x	x	x	x
Kentucky	x	x	x	x
Louisiana	x	x	x	x
Maine	x	x	x	x
Maryland	x	x	x	x
Massachusetts	x	x	20	16
Michigan	x	x	7	x
Minnesota	x	x	5	5
Mississippi	x	x	x	x
Missouri	x	x	8	7
Montana	x	x	x	x
Nebraska	x	x	x	x
Nevada	x	x	5	x
New Hampshire	x	x	x	x
New Jersey	x	x	5	5
New Mexico	x	x	x	x
New York	-	x	18	15
North Carolina	x	x	13	11
North Dakota	x	x	x	x
Ohio	9	x	6	5
Oklahoma	x	x	x	x
Oregon	x	x	x	x
Pennsylvania	x	x	x	x
Rhode Island	x	x	x	x
South Carolina	x	x	x	x
South Dakota	x	x	x	x
Tennessee	x	x	x	x
Texas	10	x	14	14
Utah	5	x	x	x
Vermont	x	x	x	x
Virginia	x	x	10	8
Washington	x	x	9	x
West Virginia	x	x	10	10
Wisconsin	x	x	x	x
Wyoming	x	x	x	x

BIE schools	x	x	x	x
50 states and D.C. (including BIE schools)	43	3	211	169
American Samoa	x	x	x	x
Guam	x	x	x	x
Northern Marianas	x	x	x	x
Puerto Rico	x	x	x	x
Virgin Islands	x	x	x	x
U.S. and outlying areas	43	3	211	169

Source: U.S. Department of Education, Office of Special Education Programs, Data Analysis System (DANS), OMB #1820-0621:
Children with Disabilities Unilaterally Removed or Suspended/Expelled for More Than 10 Days, 2005-06. Data updated as of July 15, 2007.

Note: Please see the Part B Discipline Data Notes in appendix B for information the state submitted to clarify its data submission.

[a] IAES is an interim alternative educational setting.

[b] Children are reported only once within each column. However, the same child may be reported in more than one column if he/she was involved in two or more incidents. In addition, the children reported in the final column (multiples sum to > 10 days) are a subset of the children reported in the third column (>10 days in school year).

- Data not available.

x Data suppressed.

Table 5-1m. Children and students with developmental delay[a] served under IDEA, Part B, unilaterally removed or suspended/expelled more than 10 days, by type of removal and state: 2005–06

| | Number of Children | | | |
| | Removed to an IAES[b] | | Suspension/expulsion[c] | |
State	By school personnel for drugs/weapons	By hearing officer for likely injury	> 10 days in school year	Multiples sum to > 10 days
Alabama	x	x	x	x
Alaska	x	x	x	x
Arizona	x	x	x	x
Arkansas	x	x	x	x
California	x	x	x	x
Colorado	x	x	x	x
Connecticut	x	x	5	5
Delaware	x	x	x	x
District of Columbia	-	-	-	-
Florida	x	x	6	6
Georgia	x	x	x	x
Hawaii	x	x	x	x
Idaho	x	x	x	x
Illinois	x	x	x	x
Indiana	x	x	x	x
Iowa	x	x	x	x
Kansas	x	x	x	x
Kentucky	x	x	x	x
Louisiana	6	x	9	9
Maine	x	x	x	x
Maryland	x	x	6	6
Massachusetts	x	x	x	x
Michigan	x	x	x	x
Minnesota	x	x	x	x
Mississippi	x	x	x	x
Missouri	x	x	x	x
Montana	x	x	x	x
Nebraska	x	x	x	x
Nevada	x	x	x	x
New Hampshire	x	x	x	x
New Jersey	x	x	x	x
New Mexico	6	x	9	9
New York	-	x	x	x
North Carolina	x	x	20	19
North Dakota	x	x	x	x
Ohio	x	x	x	x
Oklahoma	x	x	8	5
Oregon	x	x	x	x
Pennsylvania	x	x	7	6
Rhode Island	x	x	x	x
South Carolina	x	x	x	x
South Dakota	x	x	x	x
Tennessee	x	x	7	5
Texas	x	x	x	x
Utah	x	x	x	x
Vermont	x	x	x	x
Virginia	x	x	38	34
Washington	x	x	x	x
West Virginia	x	x	x	x
Wisconsin	x	x	x	x
Wyoming	x	x	x	x

BIE schools	x	x	x	x
50 states and D.C. (including BIE schools)	17	1	148	130
American Samoa	x	x	x	x
Guam	x	x	x	x
Northern Marianas	x	x	x	x
Puerto Rico	x	x	x	x
Virgin Islands	x	x	x	x
U.S. and outlying areas	17	1	148	130

Source: U.S. Department of Education, Office of Special Education Programs, Data Analysis System (DANS), OMB #1820-0621:
Children with Disabilities Unilaterally Removed or Suspended/Expelled for More Than 10 Days, 2005-06. Data updated as of July 15, 2007.

Note: Please see the Part B Discipline Data Notes in appendix B for information the state submitted to clarify its data submission.

[a] Developmental delay is applicable only to children ages 3 through 9.

[b] IAES is an interim alternative educational setting.

[c] Children are reported only once within each column. However, the same child may be reported in more than one column if he/she was involved in two or more incidents. In addition, the children reported in the final column (multiples sum to > 10 days) are a subset of the children reported in the third column (>10 days in school year).

- Data not available.

x Data suppressed.

Index